Maine

AN EXPLORER'S GUIDE

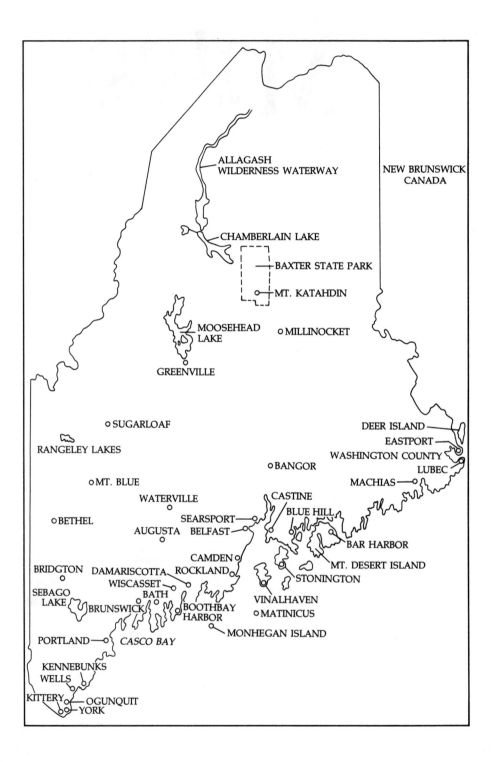

ALLAGASH
WILDERNESS WATERWAY

NEW BRUNSWICK
CANADA

CHAMBERLAIN LAKE

BAXTER STATE PARK

MT. KATAHDIN

MOOSEHEAD
LAKE

○ MILLINOCKET

GREENVILLE

○ SUGARLOAF

DEER ISLAND

EASTPORT

RANGELEY LAKES

WASHINGTON COUNTY

○ BANGOR

LUBEC

○ MT. BLUE

MACHIAS

WATERVILLE

CASTINE

BLUE HILL

SEARSPORT

○ BETHEL

AUGUSTA   BELFAST

BAR HARBOR

MT. DESERT ISLAND

CAMDEN

STONINGTON

BRIDGTON   DAMARISCOTTA   ROCKLAND

WISCASSET

SEBAGO
LAKE

BATH

VINALHAVEN

BRUNSWICK

BOOTHBAY
HARBOR

○ MATINICUS

PORTLAND   CASCO BAY

MONHEGAN ISLAND

KENNEBUNKS
WELLS

KITTERY   OGUNQUIT

YORK

Maine
AN EXPLORER'S GUIDE

Fifth Edition

CHRISTINA TREE
MIMI STEADMAN

The Countryman Press
Woodstock, Vermont 05091

The Countryman Press, Inc.
P.O. Box 175
Woodstock, Vermont 05091

Fifth Edition

Library of Congress Cataloging-in-Publications Data

Tree, Christina
    Maine : an explorer's guide / Christina Tree, Mimi Steadman. —
5th ed.
        p. cm.
    Includes index
    ISBN 0-88150-199-9 :
    1. Maine — Description and travel—1981 — Guide-books.
I. Steadman, Mimi. II. Title
F17.3.T73   1991
917.4104'43—dc20

                                                        91-8209
                                                        CIP

Printed in the United States of America

10 9 8 7 6 5 4 3 2 1

Cover design by Virginia L. Scott

Series design by Frank Lieberman

Maps by Helen Ryan and Alex Wallach

Cover photograph of York Harbor, Maine, by Craig Blouin

For Bill
—C.T.

For Rick
—M.S.

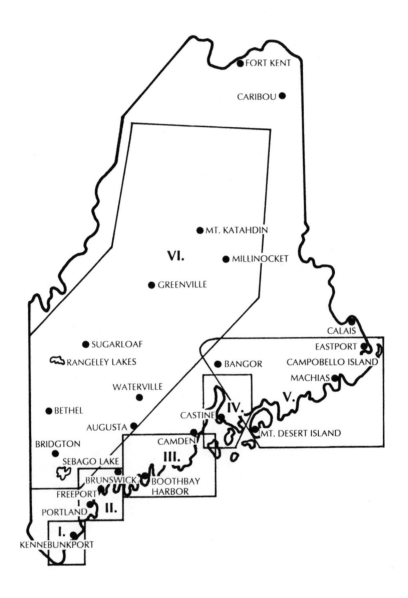

FORT KENT

CARIBOU

MT. KATAHDIN

VI.

MILLINOCKET

GREENVILLE

SUGARLOAF

RANGELEY LAKES

CALAIS

EASTPORT

CAMPOBELLO ISLAND

BANGOR

MACHIAS

WATERVILLE

BETHEL

CASTINE

IV.

V.

AUGUSTA

CAMDEN

MT. DESERT ISLAND

BRIDGTON

III.

SEBAGO LAKE

BRUNSWICK

BOOTHBAY
HARBOR

FREEPORT

I.

II.

PORTLAND

KENNEBUNKPORT

Contents

Introduction

Maine is almost as big as the other five New England states combined, but her residents add up to fewer than half the population of Greater Boston. That means there is plenty of room for all her visitors—first-timers just discovering her boundless beauty and old-timers who regularly come here for renewal.

Within the covers of this book we suggest the many faces of Maine's landscape and the amazing variety of things to do and see here. We describe more than 600 places to stay—in all corners of the state and in all price ranges, from elegant to economical. We have personally spent the night at or at least poked around 90 percent of these places (the remainder have come highly recommended to us). We also checked out many hundreds of places to dine and to eat (we make a distinction between dining and eating); and, since shopping is an important part of everyone's travels, we include exceptional stores we've discovered while browsing along the coast and inland, all the way to the top of Maine's ski mountains. We have opinions about everything we've found, and we don't hesitate to share them. In every category, we record exactly what we see because we charge no one to be included in the book.

Chris is an out-of-stater addicted to many Maines. As a toddler she learned to swim in the Ogunquit River and later watched her three sons do the same in Monhegan's icy waters—and then learn to sail at summer camp in Raymond and paddle canoes on the Saco River and down the St. John's. Before beginning this book, she thought she "knew" Maine, having already spent a dozen years exploring it for the *Boston Globe*, describing the charm of coastal villages and the quiet strength of inland mountains and lakes. For the *Globe* she continues to write about a variety of things to do, from skiing at Sugarloaf and Sunday River, and llama trekking in Bethel, to windjamming on Penobscot Bay. But after nine years, some 40,000 miles, and five editions of the book, Chris no longer claims to "know" Maine. What she does know are the state's lodging places, restaurants, and shops, from Kittery to Calais and Matinicus to Kokadjo and Grand Lake Stream. She also knows about some unexpectedly beautiful, peaceful, and reasonably priced pockets of Maine—not all of which are tucked away in unorganized townships or in Washington County.

Mimi, a native Virginian, recalls being intrigued in college by a girl who lived across the hall—she hailed from the faraway state of Maine and had even had a summer job as a sardine packer. It all seemed quite foreign to a young Southern girl. Fate and circumstances, however, were to conspire a few years later to bring Mimi to Maine, via Boston. Soon after she moved here, she found herself exploring nearly every hill and dale—traveling more than 3,000 miles without once crossing the state border—to research her first book, *One Hundred Country Inns in Maine*. Subsequently, she served as Assistant Editor of *Down East* Magazine, becoming thoroughly indoctrinated into the state of mind that is Maine. She admits that she was a very willing subject. Mimi is currently the Maine editor for *New England Living's Travel Guide*, and her curiosity about her adopted state has also stood her in good stead while hosting talk shows on Maine public television. Some two decades after moving here, she is still struck by Maine's grandeur, inspired by the flinty character of its natives, and smitten with its natural grace.

Maine continues to fascinate both of us. We are intrigued by the way in which she bears the marks of her unique history—by the traces of pre-pilgrim settlements on Manana Island and at Pemaquid Beach, of colorful seventeenth-century heroes like Baron de St. Castin (scion of a noble French family who married a Penobscot Indian princess), and by the state's legendary seafaring history, well told in both the Maine Maritime Museum (in Bath, where a total of 5,000 vessels have been launched over the years) and at the Penobscot Marine Museum (in Searsport, a small village that once boasted of being home to a full ten percent of all American sea captains). And of course there is the heady saga of the lumbering era (dramatized in the Lumberman's Museum in Patten), which finally insured Maine's admission to the Union in 1820—but not until Massachusetts had sold off all unsettled land, the privately owned "Unorganized Townships" which still add up to nearly half of inland Maine.

We are fascinated by the way in which long-vanished trains and steamboats still determine where you stay in Maine. With the exception of Sugarloaf/USA (one of Maine's largest ski resorts), all resort villages date from the time when visitors from Boston, New York, and Philadelphia were ferried directly to the tips of peninsulas and coastal islands or deposited at inland train depots, frequently to board boats bound for lakeside hotels.

Cars have altered this picture only to a degree, narrowing the number of towns geared to accommodating any volume of visitors. Ninenteenth-century resorts like Stonington, Castine, Pemaquid Point, and Christmas Cove—all of them too far off Route 1 to attract much traffic today—contentedly cater to yachtsmen and inn lovers. And of all the inland villages which once welcomed summer "rusticators," only Bridgton, Bethel, Rangeley, and the Moosehead area still serve non-cottage owners in any number.

Gilded Era summer people donated the core of Acadia National Park, now a big enough lure to draw more than three and a half million visitors per year all the way to Bar Harbor, the downeast terminus of the most popular tourist route, which also includes Camden and Boothbay Harbor. Otherwise, most summer visitors cluster in the beach towns spaced like stepping stones between Kittery and Portland.

Beyond the state line, however, it appears that Maine may still be something of a mystery to many. A friend recently told of calling out-of-state to order some merchandise. When he gave Maine as his address, the woman on the other end of the line inquired, "Is that in the United States?" Sometimes even *we* wonder whether it is.

This book's introductory section, "What's Where in Maine," is a quick-reference directory to a vast variety of activities available within the state. The remainder of the book is devoted to areas treated one by one.

Not only are the state's most popular resort areas described but also its lesser-known and forgotten beauty spots. The basic criterion for including an area is the availability of lodging there, be it in inns, guesthouses, rental cottages, or campgrounds.

We ask that you regard the lodging prices we've included as benchmarks in the rising tide of inflation. They were accurate when we did our research in the summer, fall, and winter of 1990 and into the spring of 1991; but please don't hold your host to these exact rates, as there will undoubtedly have been changes since we went to press. "Off-season" prices are often substantially less than those in July and August. June, by the way, can be rainy and cold, but September is dependably sparkling and frequently warm. Early October in Maine is just as spectacular as it is in New Hampshire and Vermont—with the long curving seacoast a beautiful backdrop to the foliage.

We would like to extend our thanks to Gordon Pine and Jeanie Levitan of The Countryman Press for shepherding our manuscript through the many stages to publication of this, the fifth edition. Our thanks go also to our husbands (and Chris's boys) for their patience during our frequent absences from home and our subsequent long hours sequestered away in front of our computers, putting all our research into understandable form.

We welcome our readers' comments and appreciate all your thoughtful suggestions for future editions of *Maine: An Explorer's Guide*.

What's Where in Maine

AGRICULTURAL FAIRS The season opens with the small family-geared Pittston Fair in late June (Pig Scrambles all three days!) and culminates with the big, colorful Fryeburg Fair during the first week of October. Among the best traditional fairs: the Union Fair (late August) and the Blue Hill (Labor Day weekend). The Common Ground Fair (late September at the fairgrounds in Windsor) draws Maine's back-to-the-earth and organic gardeners from all corners of the state, and the Full Circle Summer Fair in Blue Hill (mid-July) is a smaller, even less "commercial" gathering. Request a pamphlet listing all the fairs from Maine Department of Agriculture (289-3491), State House Station 28, Augusta 04333.

AIRPORTS AND AIRLINES The following airports have scheduled passenger service: Augusta State (Northwest Airlink), Bangor International (Air Atlantic, Business Express, Continental Express, Delta, Northwest Airlink, United), Bar Harbor (Continental Express), Portland International (Air Atlantic, Business Express, Continental, Continental Express, Delta Airlines, Northwest Airlink, USAir, United), Presque Isle (Business Express, Continental Express, Northwest Airlink), and Rockland/Knox County at Owl's Head (Continental Express, Northwest Airlink).

AIRFIELDS These have no scheduled service: Belfast, Blue Hill, Livermore Falls, Norridgewock, Dover-Foxcroft, Bethel, Old Town, Fryeburg, Eastport, Greenville, Islesboro, Lincoln, Lubec, Machias, Harrison, Millinocket, Oxford, Rangeley, Phillips, Sanford, Dexter, Moose River, Stonington, The Carrabassett Valley (near Sugarloaf USA), Turner, Brownville,

Wiscasset, Houlton, South Paris, Pittsfield, Princeton, and Biddeford.

AIR SERVICES Also called Flying Services, these are useful links with wilderness camps and coastal islands. Greenville, prime jump-off point for the North Woods, claims to be New England's largest base for flying services. Folsom's Air Service (695-2821) is the oldest and largest outfit, adept at transporting canoes and renting camps. Currier's Flying Service (695-2278) in Greenville Junction is Folsom's big competitor, and Jack's Air Service (695-2278) also transports campers, fishermen, and canoeists into the Allagash and beyond. Millinocket Lake Flying Service (723-990-8733) and Scotty's Flying Service (528-2528) in Shin Pond transport and rent canoes and furnish supplies and camps on the eastern fringe of Baxter State Park. Other services include: Central Maine Flying Service, Old Town (827-5911); Bisson Flying Service in Jackman (668-3927); Steve's Air Service in Rangeley (864-3349); Maine Air Taxi in South Windham (892-6381); Penobscot Air Service (596-6211) in Owls Head; Downeast Flying Service in Wiscasset (882-6752); and Telford Aviation, Inc., in Waterville (872-5555).

AMUSEMENT PARKS Funtown in Saco, which includes a Cascade Water Park, is Maine's biggest, and Aquaboggan (pools and slides) is also on Route 1 in Saco. Palace Playland in Old Orchard Beach is a classic with a 1906 carousel, a ferris wheel, rides, and a 60-foot waterslide. Animal Forest & Amusement at York Beach, Mariners Playland in Wells, Funland in Caribou are small areas offering kiddy rides and arcades.

ANTIQUES A listing of more than 100

dealers, produced by the Maine Antiques Dealers' Association, Inc., is available from the Maine Publicity Bureau, 97 Winthrop Street, Hallowell 04347 (send a business-sized SASE). Searsport claims to be the antiques capital of Maine and publishes its own listing, available from the Chamber of Commerce, Searsport 04974. The Chamber of Commerce in Bridgton (04009) also publishes a list. Other concentrations are found in Wiscasset, Hallowell, and Kennebunkport.

ANTIQUARIAN BOOKS   Maine is well known among book buffs as a browsing mecca. Within this book we have noted antiquarian bookstores where they cluster—along Route 1 in Wells and in Portland. More than 75 are described in the Directory published by the Maine Antiquarian Booksellers, available in Maine Publicity Bureau information centers (see Information). The biggest is probably Big Chicken Barn Books, a former chicken house on Route 1 south of Ellsworth, now boasting 110,000 hardcover titles, magazines, and paperbacks.

APPLES   A list of producers who permit "picking your own" comes from the Maine Department of Agriculture, Station 28, Augusta 04333.

AQUARIUMS   The Maine Aquarium in Saco is open daily year-round, exhibiting seals, penguins, sharks, and tidepool animals. The Maine Department of Marine Resources maintains an aquarium in Boothbay. The Mount Desert Oceanarium in Southwest Harbor has 20 tanks exhibiting sea life, and the Bar Harbor Oceanarium features everything you ever wanted to know about lobsters.

AREA CODE   The area code for Maine is 207.

ART MUSEUMS AND GALLERIES   Portland Museum of Art (775-6148), 111 High Street,

Photo by Neal Parent

Portland, has an outstanding collection of American paintings, and the Payson Gallery of Art at Westbrook College in Portland is another real find. The Farnsworth Museum in Rockland and the Bowdoin College Museum of Art in Brunswick are both worth a trip for lovers of nineteenth- and twentieth-century Maine artists. Among seasonal galleries, the Ogunquit Museum and Barn Gallery, the Maine Art Gallery in Wiscasset (also open weekends in winter), and the Maine Coast Artists Gallery (closed in winter) in Rockport stand out. Almost two dozen small galleries welcome visitors both in Ogunquit and in the Kennebunks. A half-dozen quality galleries are just off coastal Route 1 on Brunswick's Maine Street and another cluster can be found in Northeast Harbor. Blue Hill, Deer Isle, and Eastport are also known for some exceptional galleries. A partial listing of "Maine Art Galleries/Museums" is available from the Maine Publicity Bureau (289-2423, 97 Winthrop Street, Hallowell 04347).

BALLOONING Rides are available from Balloon Sports (772-4401), 15 Beacon Street in Portland; Balloon Drifters, Inc. (622-1211) based at the Augusta State Airport; Damn Yankee Balloons (843-7249) based in the Bangor area; Hot Fun (761-1735) in Gorham, Fantasy Ballooning Co. (929-3200) in Hollis; Lovell Balloon Works (499-7575) in Kennebunk; Sales Aloft (549-7483, 549-5774) in North Whitefield; and Natural High Hot Air Ballooning Center (339-1565) in Lebanon.

BEACHES Just two percent of the Maine coast is public, and not all of that is beach. Given the summer temperature of the water (from 59 degrees in Ogunquit to 54 degrees at Bar Harbor), swimming isn't the primary reason you come to Maine. But Maine beaches can be splendid walking, sunning, and kite-flying places (see York, Ogunquit, Wells, the Kennebunks, Portland, Reid State Park, Popham, and Pemaquid). At Ogunquit and in Reid State Park there are also warmer backwater areas in which small children can paddle, but families tend to take advantage of the reasonably priced cottages available on lakes,

many of them just a few miles from the seashore (see Lakes, Coastal). Other outstanding beaches include 7-mile-long Old Orchard and, nearby, state-maintained Crescent Beach on Cape Elizabeth, Scarboro Beach in Scarborough, and Ferry Beach in Saco. The big state-maintained freshwater beaches are on Lake Damariscotta, St. George, Sebec, Rangeley, Sebago, and Moosehead; also on Pleasant Pond in Richmond. All state beach facilities include changing facilities, rest rooms, and showers; many have snack bars. The town of Bridgton has several fine little lakeside beaches. In '91 state beaches charge $1.50 per person entrance; $2 at Crescent Beach, Montpelier, Range Ponds, and Sebago Lake.

BED & BREAKFAST We visited hundreds of B&Bs in the course of researching this book and were impressed by what we saw. They range from elegant townhouses and country mansions to farms and a fisherman's home. Prices vary from $40 to $125 double and average $75 in high season on the coast. With few exceptions, they offer a friendly entrée to their communities. Hosts are delighted to advise guests on places to explore, dine, and shop. The "Maine Guide to Bed & Breakfast Places" (available from the Maine Publicity Bureau, 97 Winthrop Street, Hallowell 04347) includes more than 250 descriptive listings for '91. The largest statewide reservation service, Bed & Breakfast Down East Ltd., includes many homes that advertise no other way (a $3 Directory describing more than 100 homes is available from Box 547, Eastbrook 04634).

BICYCLING Biking is big on Mount Desert, which offers more than fifty miles of carriage paths. Routes are outlined in local handouts and rentals are available. A few Maine islands are best toured by bike: see Casco Bay Islands, Vinalhaven, Islesboro, and Swans Island. Bicycle and moped rentals are available in Bar Harbor, Biddeford, Calais, Camden, Kennebunkport, Old Orchard Beach, Pittsfield, Portland, Rumford, Waterville, and Woolwich. Weekend and five-day inn-to-inn tours are offered by Maine Coast Cyclers, based in Camden. American Youth Hostels maintains nominally priced, bicyclist-geared hostels in Carmel (near Bangor) and Bar Harbor; contact AYH, Greater Boston Council, 1020 Commonwealth Avenue, Boston 02215 (617-731-5430). Mountain bikers should check out Sunday River's Mountain Bike Park's high-altitude trails and bike school (see Bethel).

BIRDING   The Maine Audubon Society (781-2330), based at Gilsland Farm in Falmouth, maintains a number of birding sites and sponsors nature programs and field trips. Gilsland Farm itself (open year-round) has 70 acres with nature trails through woodlands, meadows, and marshes. At Scarborough Marsh Nature Center in Portland classes are offered in marsh life. The Mast Landing Sanctuary in South Freeport consists of 150 acres of varied habitat. Maine Audubon's field trips include cruises to Matinicus Rock and to Eagle Island. (For details about the National Audubon Ecology Camp on Hog Island, see Damariscotta Area.) The most popular coastal birding spots are the National Wildlife Sanctuaries between Kittery and Cape Elizabeth. Biddeford Pool, Scarborough Marsh, Merrymeeting Bay, and Mount Desert are the other top birding sites. Monhegan is the island to visit. The Moosehorn National Wildlife Refuge (454-3521) in Washington County represents the northeastern terminus of the East Coast chain of wildlife refuges and is particularly rich in birdlife. We recommend *A Birder's Guide to the Coast of Maine* by Elizabeth Cary Pierson and Jan Erik Pierson (Down East Books). Also see Puffin-Watching.

BLUEBERRYING   An average crop of twenty million pounds of wild (lowbush) blueberries is harvested annually in Maine from an estimated 25,000 acres (half the actual acreage reserved for growing wild blueberries in the state). Because of pruning practices, only half the acreage produces berries in a given year, and there are absolutely no man-planted wild blueberry fields. Lowbush blueberry plants spread naturally in the present commercial fields after the forests are cleared or by natural establishment in abandoned pastures. Unfortunately, very few berries are sold fresh (most are

quick frozen), and few growers allow U-pick—at least not until the commercial harvest is over. Then the public is invited to go "stumping," for leftovers. On the other hand, berrying along roads and hiking paths, under power lines and on hilltops, is a rite of summer for all who happen to be in southern Maine in late July or farther Down East in early August. For a look at the Blueberry Barrens—thousands of blue-berry-covered acres—you must drive up to Cherryfield, Deblois, Beddington, Centerville, and Columbia, in Washington County. You'll find more blueberries in the Kennebunks. For more about Maine's most famous fruit write: Wild Blueberry Association of North America, 142 Kelley Road, Orono 04473.

BOAT EXCURSIONS   You don't need to own your own yacht to enjoy the salt spray and views, and you really won't know what Maine is about until you stand off at sea a ways to appreciate the beauty of the cliffs and island-dotted bays. For the greatest concentrations of boat excursions, see Boothbay Harbor, Rockland, and Mount Desert—there are also excursions from Ogunquit, Kennebunkport, Camden, and Stonington. (Also see Ferries, Sailing, and Windjammers. See Western Lakes and Mid-Maine for lake excursions.) A partial list of "Maine Boat Cruises/Ferries" can be found in the Maine Publicity Bureau's annual free magazine, "Maine Invites You."

BOAT LAUNCH SITES   A town-by-town list is included in "Outdoors in Maine," the pamphlet guide to Maine's State Parks available from the Bureau of Parks and Recreation, Maine Department of Conservation, Augusta 04333. Public launch sites on paper company land are indicated on the sportsmen's maps available from the North Maine Woods (435-6213), Box 283, Ashland 04732 and from Scott Paper Company, Woodlands Office, Greenville Junction 04442. Other New England boat licenses, with the exception of New Hampshire's, are honored in Maine waters.

BOAT RENTALS   Readily available in the Belgrade Lakes, the Sebago Lake area,

in Rangeley, Jackman, Rockwood, and all other inland lake areas. (Also see Canoes and Sailing.)

BOATBUILDING WoodenBoat School in Brooklin offers (see the Blue Hill area) more than 75 warm-weather courses including more than 2 dozen on various aspects of boatbuilding. The Maine Maritime Museum in Bath offers an apprenticeship program; and Boatbuilding School in Ken-nebunk offers summer courses in building sailboats.

BOOKS Among the current guidebooks to Maine, the following have proven helpful to us: *The Coast of Maine—An Informal History* by Louise Dickinson Rich (Thomas Y. Crowell Company); *The Maine Coast—A Nature Lover's Guide* by Dorcas Miller (The East Woods Press); *The Maine Atlas and Gazetteer*, published by David DeLorme and Company, PO Box 298, Freeport 04032; and *Fifty Hikes in Maine* by John Gibson and *Fifty Hikes in Northern Maine* by Cloe Caputo (Backcountry Publications). Down East Books (available from PO Box 679, Camden,

04843) offers: *A Birder's Guide to the Coast of Maine* by Elizabeth Cary Pierson and Jan Erik Pierson, *Walking the Maine Coast* by John Gibson, and *Islands in Time: A Natural and Human History of the Islands of Maine* by Philip W. Conkling. Serious hikers should secure the AMC *Maine Mountain Guide,* and all lovers of the Maine woods should take a look at *The Wildest Country—A Guide to Thoreau's Maine* by J. Parker Huber; both books are available from the AMC Books Division, Dept. B, 5 Joy Street, Boston, MA 02108. We also enjoy the books by retired Portland Press Herald columnist Bill Caldwell: *Enjoying Maine, Maine Magic,* and *Islands of Maine,* all published by Guy Gannett Publishing Company of Portland. We also recommend two photography books on Maine: *My Maine Thing,* photos by Tony King, published by The Countryman Press; and *A Maine Deeper In,* photography and text by Martin Brown, published by Down East Books. *Island Hopping in New England* by Mary Maynard (a Yankee Magazine Guidebook), "Pocket Guide to the Maine Outdoors" by Eben Thomas

(Thorndike Press), and *Maine Forever, A Guide to Nature Conservancy Preserves in Maine* (available from the Maine Chapter of the Nature Conservancy, PO Box 338, 122 Main Street, Topsham 04086) are also recommended.

BUSES   Greyhound links New York and Boston with Portland. It is the only line linking Portland with Brunswick, stopping in Lewiston, Augusta, and Waterville, among others. From Bangor there is service to Ellsworth and Bar Harbor.

CAMPING   Almost half of Maine lies within "unorganized townships": wooded, privately owned lands (see North Woods), most of which are open to the public on condition that basic rules be observed. These rules vary with the owners. A consortium of 20 companies that control more than 2.5 million acres maintains more than 2,000 miles of roads and several hundred campsites; visitors are required to register and pay fees at the access points to this area, and campsites within it may be reserved (there is an additional camping fee). For details and a map of this area, contact North Maine Woods (435-6213; PO Box 382, Ashland 04732); send $1 for the woodlands map, another $1 for mailing. You can also contact the Paper Industry Information Office (622-3166; 133 State Street, Augusta 04330) requesting "sportsmen's maps" published by Great Northern, Scott (which owns most of the land around Moosehead Lake), and Georgia Pacific (covering the eastern corner of the state). Camping beyond designated sites in these areas is generally permitted, but on the condition that a fire permit be obtained.

For camping within Acadia National Park see Mount Desert. For the same within the White Mountain National Forest see Bethel.

For private campgrounds, the booklet "Maine Guide to Camping" lists most privately operated camping and tenting areas in the state and is available from the Maine Publicity Bureau, 97 Winthrop Street, Hallowell 04347.

See the North Woods section for details about camping in Baxter where reservations are now necessary. Reservations are also advised for the State's 13 parks that offer camping (see State Parks). We have attempted to describe the state parks in detail wherever they appear in this book (see Camden, Damariscotta, Mount Desert, Greenville, Rangeley, and Sebago). Note that while campsites can accommodate average-size campers and trailers, there are no trailer hookups. Primitive campsites along the Allagash Wilderness Waterway are also maintained by the state (see Canoeing the Allagash). Note that Warren Island off Lincoln offers organized camping and that primitive camping is permitted on a number of islands through the Island Institute (see Islands).

CAMPS, FOR CHILDREN   More than 200 summer camps are listed in the exceptional booklet published annually by the Maine Youth Camping Association, PO Box 10178, Portland 04101; also available from the Maine Publicity Bureau (289-2423), 97 Winthrop Street, Hallowell 04347.

CAMPS, FOR ADULTS   The Appalachian Mountain Club maintains a number of summer lodges and campsites for adults and families seeking a hiking and/or canoeing vacation. Intended primarily for members, they are technically open to all who reserve space, available only after April 1. The full-service camps in Maine (offering three daily meals, organized hikes, evening programs) are at Echo Lake and Cold River Camp in Evans Notch (near the New Hampshire border within the White Mountain National Forest). For details about all facilities and membership write the AMC, 5 Joy Street, Boston, MA 02108 (617-523-0636). Outward Bound (594-5548), PO Box 429, Rockland 04841 offers a variety of adult-geared outdoors adventures. Audubon Ecology Camp on Hog Island off Bremen offers a series of week-long courses; contact the Registrar (203-869-2017), Northeast Camp/Workshops, Audubon Center, 613 Riverside Road, Greenwich, CT 06830. The University of Maine at Machias (255-3313), 9 O'Brien Avenue, Machias 04654, is a summer center for ornithology workshops, summer field courses, and Elder Hostel. Maine Folk Dance Camp (647-3424), Box 100, Bridgton 04009, has been a center for international dance and customs since 1950.

Nine weekly sessions start the last week in June; before then phone 516-661-3866.

CAMPS, RENTAL   In Maine a "camp" is the word for a second home or cottage. Since we assume that many of our readers don't know this, we have listed that information under Cottage Rentals.

CANOE RENTALS   Rentals are under To See and Do within this book. A "Maine Canoe Rentals" leaflet guide is available from the Maine Publicity Bureau (see Information).

CANOEING, BOOKS ON   Maine offers the best choice of canoeing spots and services in the East—everything from a guided trip down a placid stream for a first-timer to a 10-day, fly-in expedition through wilderness. A leaflet brochure, available from the Maine Publicity Bureau (see Information) lists most other sources of information (AMC *River Guide I/Maine* covers the state's eight watersheds, with maps for each; query AMC Books Division, Department 40, 5 Joy Street, Boston, MA 02108). There are also three books by Thomas Eben: *Hot Blood and Wet Paddles*—"an illustrated guide to canoe racing on fourteen Maine and New Hampshire rivers," *No Horns Blowing*—"Canoeing ten great rivers in Maine," and *The Weekender*—"a guide to family canoeing, ten more great rivers in Maine," all published by Hallowell Printing. *The Maine Atlas and Gazetteer,* DeLorme Publishing Company, Freeport, also describes dozens of canoe trips and supplies the maps to go with them. Further good reading on the subject: John McPhee's *The Survival of the Bark Canoe* (Farrar, Straus, Giroux) and *The Woods and Lakes of Maine*—"a trip from Moosehead Lake to New Brunswick in a birchbark canoe, to which are added some Indian place names and their meanings," by Lucius Lee Hubbard, first published in 1883 and reprinted by the New Hampshire Publishing Company. *Maine Rivers* is an illustrated paperback on the history, topography, and recreational uses of 18 Maine waterways (Thorndike Press).

CANOEING, GUIDED TRIPS   Saco Bound, just over the New Hampshire line (Box 113, Center Conway, NH 03813; 603-447-2177), offers guided tours on the calm (great for beginners) Saco River. A number of "outfitters," specializing in Allagash Waterway and other wilderness trips, are listed in the "Outdoor Guide to Maine" published by the Maine Professional Guides Association and available from the Maine Publicity Bureau (see Information) which also publishes a leaflet listing of "Guided Whitewater Rafting & Canoe Trips." Sunrise County Canoe Expeditions (454-7708), Cathance Lake, Grove Post Office 04638, offers week-long tours on most northern Maine waterways. Maine Outdoors, based in Union, offers guided tours geared to every ability.

CANOEING THE ALLAGASH   The ultimate canoe trip in Maine (and on the entire East Coast for that matter) is the seven- to ten-day expedition up the Allagash Wilderness Waterway—a 92-mile ribbon of lakes, ponds, rivers, and streams through the heart of northern Maine's vast commercial forests. Since 1966 the land flanking the waterway has been owned (500 feet back from the waterway on either side) by the state of Maine. A map pinpointing the 65 authorized campsites within the zone (and supplying other crucial information) is available free from the Bureau of Parks and Recreation (289-3821), State House Station 22, Augusta 04333. A more detailed map, backed with historical and a variety of other handy information, is DeLorme's "Map and Guide to the Allagash and St. John." Anybody contemplating the trip should also be aware of black flies in June and the "no-seeums" when warm weather finally comes. For further information check Camping, Guide Services.

CHILDREN, ESPECIALLY FOR   The Maine Publicity Bureau (see Information) publishes a pamphlet guide listing child-geared sites across the state. Among our favorites are: the Cliff and River Walk (across the Wiggly Bridge) in York Village; the Marginal Way in Ogunquit; the Wells Auto Museum; the Seashore Trolley Museum in Kennebunkport; Funtown USA, the Aquaboggan Water Park, and the Cascade Water and Amusement Park in Saco; the Scarborough Marsh Nature Center; the

Children's Museum in Portland; the Desert of Maine in Freeport; the Maine Maritime Museum in Bath; the Owls Head Transportation Museum in Owls Head; the Children's Museum in Rockland. Fort Knox in Prospect; Kartland in Trenton; Acadia National Park; the State Fish Hatchery and Game Farm Visitor's Center in Dry Mills (Gray); Washburn-Norlands Living History Center, the Maine State Museum, and the Sandy River Railroad in Phillips. All of these have been fully researched by Chris's sons and are described in this book within their regions.

CLAMMING   Maine state law permits the harvesting of shellfish for personal use only, unless you have a commercial license. Individuals can take up to a half-bushel of shellfish, or three bushels of hen or surf clams (the big ones out in the flats), in one day, unless municipal ordinances further limit "the taking of shellfish." Be sure to check locally before you dig, and make sure there's no red tide. Some towns do prohibit clamming, and in certain places there is a temporary stay on harvesting while the beds are being seeded. In a few places clamming has been banned because of pollution.

COASTAL CRUISES   "Cruise" is a much used (and abused) term along the Maine Coast, used chiefly to mean a boat ride. "Maine Invites You" (see Information) runs a descriptive listing of 55 "Boat Cruises and Ferries," most of them described as they appear in each chapter of this book. We have also tried to list the charter sailing yachts that will take passengers on multi-day cruises and have described each of the Windjammers that sail for three and six days at a time (see Windjammers). The *M/V Pauline*, based in Rockland, is an 83-foot former Maine sardine carrier that has been rebuilt as a luxurious motor vessel and takes up to 12 guests at a time on multi-day and weekly cruises throughout the summer.

COTTAGE RENTALS   Cottage rentals are the only reasonably priced way to go for families who wish to stay in one Maine spot for more than one week (unless you go for camping). If you have no special preference about where you want to be, request the booklet "Maine, Guide to Camp & Cottage Rentals" from the Maine Publicity Bureau (see Information). The 1990 booklet's weekly rates for coastal cottages in July and August began at $180, and we can attest to the quality of the cottage in Brooklin that was going for that price. Each spring we browse through this book when it comes out and then shoot off postcards to a half dozen places. We always receive pleasant letters back, and if cottages are already filled for the time we request, their owners frequently refer us to others. If you have your heart set on one particular area and cannot get satisfaction through the booklet, we recommend obtaining a printout of the realtors just for that county, then sending notes off to agents in the precise area in which you are interested. The printouts are available for a small fee by writing to the Maine Department of Business Regulation, Central Licensing Division, State House Station 35, Augusta 04333 (289-2217).

COVERED BRIDGES   Of the 120 covered bridges that once spanned Maine rivers, just 8 survive. A booklet guide to these is periodically available from the Department of Commerce, State House, Augusta 04330. The most famous, and certainly as picturesque as a covered bridge can be, is the Artist's Covered Bridge (1872) over the Sunday River in Newry, northwest of Bethel. The others are: Porter Bridge (1876) over the Ossipee River, 1/2 mile south of Porter; Babb's Bridge, recently rebuilt, over the Presumpscot River between Gorham and Windham; Hemlock Bridge (1857), 3 miles northwest of East Fryeburg; Lovejoy Bridge (1868) in South Andover; Bennett Bridge over the Magalloway River, 1 1/2 miles south of the Wilson's Mills Post Office; Robyville Bridge in the town of Corinth; the Watson Settlement Bridge between Woodstock and Littleton. Carefully reconstructed Lowes Bridge across the Piscataquis River between Guilford and Sangerville was added in 1990.

CRAFTS   "Maine Cultural Guide," published by the Maine Crafts Association (Box 288, Deer Isle 04627), is a free 83-page pamphlet guide to hundreds of studios, galleries, and museums in Maine. "Directions," a leaflet guide "to the professional crafts-people of Maine," is available from Peter Weil, Box 22, Route 1, Steuben 04680.

A "Directory" of United Maine Crafts-men, the statewide craft society that stages an annual fair in early August at the Cumberland Fairgrounds (just north of Portland), should be available through the Maine Publicity Bureau. *Handcraft Centers of New England* ($7.95, Yankee Books) de-tails a number of Maine crafts events, shops, co-ops, and the like.

CRAFTS CENTERS Haystack Mountain School of Crafts, Deer Isle 04627, is a nation-ally respected summer school in a variety of crafts, offering three-week courses begin-ning mid-June and continuing through September 14. Applicants must be more than eighteen years old; enrollment is lim-ited to 65. Work by students is displayed in the visitors center which also serves as a forum for frequent evening presentations. The surrounding area (Blue Hill to Stonington) is known for the quality of its potters, and many other craftsmen have opened summer studios and shops.

DEEP-SEA FISHING A "Maine Deep Sea Fishing Charter & Head Boats," available from the Maine Publicity Bureau (see Infor-mation), describes boats based in Kittery, York Harbor, Ogunquit, Kennebunkport, Biddeford, Saco, Portland, South Freeport, South Harpswell, Harpswell, Bailey Island, Boothbay Harbor, Rockland, Camden, Bar Harbor, Northeast Harbor, Milbridge, Jonesport, Lubec, and Eastport. Within the text we have described boats within each chapter.

DIVE SHOPS The Maine Publicity Bureau keeps a statewide list (see Information).

DOG SLEDDING This is a new category because, while sled-dog racing is a long-established winter spectator sport, the chance to actually ride on a dogsled is recent. It's possible in two places: Tim Diehl at Sugarloaf/USA offers half-hour rides throughout the day during ski season (you ride behind a team of friendly, frisky Samoyeds), and in Newry, Polly Mahoney

and Kevin Slater (Mahoosuc Mountain Ad-ventures) offer multi-day treks with their huskies. See the Sugarloaf and Bethel chapters for details.

EVENTS We have listed outstanding an-nual events within each chapter of this book and leaflet events guides are published by the state four times a year. Check with the Maine Publicity Bureau (see Information).

FACTORY OUTLETS We describe them in Kittery and in Freeport.

FACTORY TOURS Tours range from Thom's of Maine (toothpaste) to fruit win-eries (Trenton and Gouldsboro) and include Rackliffe and Rowantrees Pottery-makers, (Blue Hill), Blueberry Processors & Grow-ers (Cherryfield), Maine Wild Blueberry Company (Machias), and Old Town Canoe (Old Town).

FALL FOLIAGE Autumn is extremely pleasant along the coast; days tend to be clear and the changing leaves against the blue sea can be spectacular. Many inns re-main open through foliage season, and the resort towns of Ogunquit, Kennebunkport, Boothbay Harbor, and Camden all offer excellent dining, shopping, and lodging through Columbus Day weekend. Off-season prices prevail, in contrast with the rest of New England at this time of year. Phone 800-533-9595 for periodic foliage bulletins during the season.

FARMS A free 141-page guidebook titled "Producer to Consumer" is published by the Maine Department of Agriculture (289-3471; State House Station #28, Augusta 04333). It's a good thing to keep in the car for a county-by-county listing of farmer's mar-kets, orchards, and a variety of farms and roadside stands.

FARM B&Bs In 1991, 17 farms are de-scribed in a brochure available from the Maine Department of Agriculture (see Farms). This relatively new idea is particu-larly appealing to families with children since these farms offer animals, informal comfort, space, and reasonable prices. The Country Farm in Saco, for instance, with property running down to the Saco River, charges $45 per couple with shared bath, $50 with private bath, and that includes a whopping big breakfast.

FARMER'S MARKETS   A leaflet describing seasonal markets in Bath, Belfast, Blue Hill, Brewer, Brunswick, Camden, Caribou, Damariscotta, Ellsworth, Farmington, Fort Kent, Houlton, Lewiston, Newport, Portland, Rangeley, Rumford, Saco, Skowhegan, South Paris, Waldoboro, and Westbrook is available from. the Maine Department of Agriculture (see Farms).

FERRIES, TO CANADA   Portland to Yarmouth, Nova Scotia: Prince of Fundy Cruises offers nightly sailings (departing 9:30 PM), late April through the Columbus Day weekend. The ferry itself is a car-carrying cruise ship with gambling, restaurants, and cabins aboard (800-482-0955 in Maine; 800-341-7540 in the eastern United States). The Canadian National Marine Line (800-341-7981 for the continental United States) also offers overnight car and passenger service year-round aboard its new *Bluenose* between Bar Harbor and Yarmouth, Nova Scotia. East Coast Ferries Ltd. (605-747-2159), a year-round Quebec Provincial car ferry connects Deer Island (which in turn has service to Campobello) with L'Été, New Brunswick. For service to Grand Manan see Cutler (Washington County).

FERRIES, IN MAINE   Maine State Ferry Service (594-5543), Rockland 04841, operates year-round service from Rockland to Vinalhaven and North Haven, from Lincolnville to Islesboro, and from Bass Harbor to Swan's Island and Long Island. For private ferry services to Monhegan see Port Clyde and Boothbay Harbor; for the Casco Bay Islands see Portland; for Matinicus see Rockland; and for Isle au Haut see Stonington. A Maine State Ferry Service schedule is available by phoning 800-521-3939 in Maine or 207-596-2202.

FIRE PERMITS   Maine law dictates that no person shall kindle or use outdoor fires without a permit, except at authorized campsites or picnic grounds. Fire permits in the organized towns are obtained from the local town warden; in the unorganized towns, from the nearest forest ranger. Portable stoves fueled by propane gas, gasoline, or sterno are exempt from the rule.

FISHING   "The Maine Guide to Hunting and Fishing," published by the Maine Publicity Bureau (see Information), is a handy overview of rules, license fees, and other matters of interest to fishermen. (Also see Deep-Sea Fishing.) Detailed descriptions of camps and rustic resorts catering to fishermen can be found in the Rangeley Lakes and North Woods chapters.

FLYING SCHOOLS   The Maine Publicity Bureau keeps a list (see Information).

FORTS   To be married to a fort freak is to realize that there are people in this world who will detour 50 miles to see an eighteenth-century earthworks. Maine's forts are actually a fascinating lot, monuments to the state's own unique and largely forgotten history. "Outdoors in Maine," a pamphlet available from the Maine Publicity Bureau (see Information), describes Fort William Henry at Pemaquid, Fort Edgcomb in Edgcomb, Fort George in Castine, Fort Kent, Fort Knox near Bucksport, Fort McClary in Kittery, Fort O'Brien near Machias, Fort Popham near Bath, and Fort Pownall at Stockton Springs.

GOLF   A pamphlet guide to Maine golf courses that welcome visitors is available from the Maine Publicity Bureau (see Information). Within the book we list golf courses for each area. The major resorts catering to golfers are the Samoset in Rockland, the Bethel Inn in Bethel, Sebasco Estates near Bath, the Country Club Inn in Rangeley, the Cliff House in Ogunquit, and Sugarloaf USA in the Carrabassett Valley.

GUEST HOUSES   Old-fashioned guest houses always seem to clump in certain towns. In Maine these are Bar Harbor, Boothbay Harbor, Ogunquit, and the Yorks. See our own listings and check with local chambers of commerce.

GUIDE SERVICES   There are more than 1,000 registered Maine guides—men and women who have passed the test to qualify. Finding the guide to suit your needs—be it fishing, hunting, or canoeing the Allagash Waterway—can be a confusing business. A list of guides is available from the Maine Professional Guides Association, Box 265, Medway 04460. The "Outdoor Guide to Maine," published by the Maine Publicity Bureau (see Information), also lists guides. Flying services and camps also furnish their own guides.

HIKING   For organized trips contact the Maine chapter of the Appalachian Mountain Club. The Boston office (617-523-0636; 5 Joy Street, Boston, MA) will furnish the names of current offices. In addition to the AMC *Maine Mountain Guide* and the AMC map guide to trails on Mount Desert, we recommend investing in *Hikes in Southern Maine* by John Gibson and *Fifty Hikes in Northern Maine* by Cloe Caputo (both from Backcountry Publications), which offer clear, inviting treks up hills of every size throughout the state. The *Maine Atlas and Gazetteer* (DeLorme Publishing Company) also outlines a number of rewarding hikes.

HISTORIC HOUSES   The Maine Publicity Bureau's outstanding booklet, "Maine Guide to Museums and Historic Houses" is worth requesting (see Information). Within this book dozens of historic houses open to the public are listed by town. A booklet guide to its properties throughout New England is available from the Society for the Preservation of New England Antiquities, 141 Cambridge Street, Boston, MA. The SPNEA sites are: the Nickels-Sortwell House, Wiscasset; the Parson Smith Homestead, South Windham; Marrett House, Standish; the Jewett Memorial and Hamilton houses, South Berwick; the Jonathan Sayward House, York Harbor.

HORSE RACING   Harness racing at Scarborough Downs: US 1, or Exit 6 off the Maine Turnpike, May through mid-September, closed Mondays, daily double, Terrace Dining Room (883-2020), Downs Club. At Lewiston Raceway there is a Spring Meet (early February through early May) and a Fall Meet (early October through early December; closed Mondays and Tuesdays). The Bangor Raceway is open late May through late July; closed Mondays and Tuesdays. The leaflet guide, "Maine Agri-cultural Events," also lists harness racing dates at all agricultural fairs of the current season and is available from the Maine Department of Agriculture (see Farms).

HORSEBACK RIDING   Pleasant River Pack Trips (see North Woods) and Fry Mountain Trail Rides (see Belfast/Searsport/Bucksport) both offer entire days in the saddle. For trail riding check the Old Orchard Area, Boothbay Harbor, the Rockland Area, Camden, the Bethel Area, the Upper Kennebec Valley, and the Moosehead Lake Region.

HUNTING   Hunters should obtain a summary of Maine hunting and trapping laws from the Maine Fish and Wildlife Department, 284 State Street, Augusta 04333. For leads on registered Maine guides who specialize in organized expeditions (complete with meals and lodging), contact the sources we list under Fishing, Guide Services, Canoeing, and Camping. You might also try the Moosehead Region Chamber of Commerce, Box 581, Greenville 04441. A handy "Maine Guide to Hunting and Fishing" booklet (published annually by the Maine Publicity Bureau) is filled with information and ads for hunting lodges, guides, and the like.

INFORMATION   The Maine Publicity Bureau (289-6070; 97 Winthrop Street, Hallowell 04347) publishes "Maine Invites You," "Exploring Maine," "Maine Guide to Hunting and Fishing," "Maine Guide to Winter," and a variety of other booklet and pamphlet guides noted here under specific headings. Write or phone the bureau's office if you have a special query, or stop by one of the MPB year-round information centers: on I-95 in Kittery (439-1319), just off coastal Route 1 and I-95 in Yarmouth (846-0833), both northbound and southbound on I-95 in Hampden (near Bangor: 862-6628/6638), in Calais (454-2211), and in Houlton (532-6346); it also maintains seasonal info centers in Bangor (Bass Park, 519 Main Street),

INNS   In this book we have made an attempt to list every pleasant inn and B&B that could pass our personal inspection. We realize that "inn books" tend to focus on the higher end of the price spectrum, and frequently there are more reasonably priced, equally appealing options in the same area. The exception, of course, is *Best Places To Stay in New England* by Christina Tree and Kimberly Grant (Houghton Mifflin). The booklet guide "Inns and Bed & Breakfast Places" is also useful and is free from the Maine Publicity Bureau (see Information).

ISLANDS   In all there are said to be 3,000 uninhabited islands ranging from oversized rocks to several thousand acres. The state owns some 1,500 of these islands totaling 800 acres (the average size is a half-acre), and 45 are open to the public; so are 15 privately owned islands. Access is through the Maine Island Trail Association, part of the Island Institute (549-9202 or 785-4079; 60 Ocean Street, Rockland 04841). For a modest annual membership fee you receive a map guide to the 60 islands, scattered over 325 miles, from Casco Bay to Machias Bay. For details about camping on state-owned islands contact the Bureau of Public Lands in Augusta (289-3061) and request the brochure "Your Islands on the Coast." The islands that offer overnight accommodations are: Chebeague and Peaks islands in Casco Bay (see Portland), Monhegan, Vinalhaven and Islesboro, North Haven, Isle au Haut, Islesford, Swans Island and Matinicus. *Islands Down East* by Charlotte Fardelmann (Down East Books) is a must book for island collectors.

LAKES   There are more than 5,000 lakes in Maine, and every natural body of water over 10 acres—which accounts for most of them—is, theoretically at least, available to the public for "fishing and fowling." Access is, of course, limited by the property owners around the lakes. Because so much acreage in Maine is owned by paper companies and other land-management concerns which permit public use—provided the public obeys their rules (see Camping)—there is ample opportunity to canoe or fish in unpeopled waters. Powerboat owners should note that most states have reciprocal license privileges with Maine; the big exception is New Hampshire. For more about the most popular resort lakes in the state see Bridgton, Rangeley, and Greenville, and the Belgrade Lakes in the Kennebec Valley.

The state parks on lakes are Aroostook (camping, fishing, swimming; Route 1 south of Presque Isle), Damariscotta Lake State Park (Rt. 32 in Jefferson), Lake St. George State Park (swimming, picnicking, fishing; Route 3 in Liberty), Lily Bay State Park (8 miles north of Greenville), Peacock Beach State Park (swimming, picnicking; Richmond), Peaks-Kenny State Park (Sebec Lake in Dover-Foxcroft), Rangeley Lake State Park (Rangeley), Range Ponds State Park (Poland), Sebago Lake State Park (near Bridgton), Mt. Blue Lake Park (Weld), and Swan Lake State Park (Swanville). Families with small children should be aware of the many coastal lakes surrounded by reasonably priced cottages (see Cottages, Rental).

LIGHTHOUSES   The most popular to visit are Portland Head Light (completed in 1790, automated in 1990, due to open a museum in 1991) on Cape Elizabeth; Cape Neddick Light in York; Marshall Point Light at Port Clyde; Fort Point Light at Stockton Springs; Pemaquid Point (the lighthouse keeper's house is now a museum, there's an art gallery, and the rocks below are peerless for scrambling); Owl's Head (built 1826); Bass Harbor Head Light at Bass Harbor; and West Quoddy Head, start of a beautiful shore path. On Monhegan the lighthouse keeper's house is a seasonal museum, and at Grindle Point on Islesboro there is also an adjacent seasonal museum. True lighthouse buffs also make the pilgrimage to Matinicus Rock, the setting for children's books. "Maine Invites You" (see Information) lists 62 lighthouses.

LITTER   Littering in Maine is punishable by a $100 fine; this applies to dumping from boats as well as other vehicles. Most cans and bottles are redeemable at stores.

LLAMA TREKKING   (824-2211) RFD #2, Box 2100, Sunday River Road, Bethel 04217. Llama trekking is an increasingly popular means of getting around in the outdoors. The principle is appealingly simple: the llama carries your gear; you carry you. Owner Steve Crone's herd of these shaggy, nimble, and amiable beasts has grown to a dozen. He accompanies the hikers and, along with helpers, prepares sumptuous evening meals. Day treks are available but

Photo by Ralph Preston, courtesy of Telemark Inn & Llama Treks

can also last two to three days; longer outings are planned and include canoeing on nearby lakes in Maine's Blue Mountains. Pleasant Bay Bed & Breakfast in Addison (483-4490) is a working llama farm; guests are encouraged to meander the property's trails with the llamas.

LOBSTER POUNDS   A lobster pound is usually a no-frills seaside restaurant that specializes in serving lobsters and clams steamed in seawater. The most basic and reasonably priced pounds are frequently fishermen's co-ops such as that in New Harbor. Expect good value but no china plates and salads at Chauncey Creek Lobster Pound in Kittery, Harraseeket in South Freeport, Beal's Lobster Pound in Southwest Harbor, and the Fisherman's Landing in Bar Harbor. The Ogunquit Lobster Pound in Ogunquit is more of a formal restaurant but still good value and outstanding; other lobster-eating landmarks include Nunan's Lobster Hut in Cape Porpoise, Eaton's on Deer Isle, Robinson's Wharf at Townsend Gut, the Lobster Shack on Cape Elizabeth, the Lobster Pound in Lincolnville Beach, the Lobster Shack in Searsport, Trenton

Bridge Lobster Pound on Route 3 at the entrance to Mount Desert, and Tidal Falls Lobster Pound in Hancock.

LOBSTERS TO GO   The Maine Publicity Bureau (see Information) keeps a list of firms that will ship lobsters anywhere in the world.

MAPLE SUGARING   Maine produces roughly 8,000 gallons of syrup a year and the Maine Department of Agriculture (see Farms) publishes a list of producers who welcome visitors on Maine Maple Sunday (also known as Sap Sunday) in late March.

MOOSE   These creatures have made a comeback from their near-extinct status in the 1930s and now number more than 18,000. Baxter State Park publishes pointers on where to see moose within its bounds. The shallows of lakes and ponds are likely spots for moose-watching. See the Moosehead Lake Region for moose-watching spots and guided expeditions.

MUSEUM VILLAGES   What variety! There is Willowbrook at Newfield, a nineteenth-century village center consisting of 31 buildings that have been restored by one man, open seasonally as a commercial attraction; there is the old village center of Searsport, restored as a fine maritime museum; there is the Sabbathday Lake Shaker Museum, still a functioning religious community; and there is York Village with its Old Gaol, school, tavern, church, and scattering of historic houses open to the public, adding up to a picture of late eighteenth-century life in coastal Maine.

Then there is Norlands, which belongs in a category of its own, and, for lack of a better name, calls itself a "Living History Center." A former estate, Norlands is a self-contained village (complete with a neo-Gothic library open in July and August) that invites you to come and live for a weekend or longer as you would have had you been alive in this particular place (Livermore) in the mid-nineteenth-century. You eat, sleep, learn, work, worship, and dance as was done in this rural backwater in 1870. Norlands is a nonprofit foundation staffed by dedicated scholars and local people (for details call 897-2236).

MUSEUMS   "Maine Guide to Museums and Historic Houses," available from the Maine Publicity Bureau, is an exceptional free guide to the state's museums—big and small, historical, art, whatever. Our own favorites are the Perry-Macmillan Arctic Museum at Bowdoin College in Brunswick, the Seashore Trolley Museum in Kennebunkport, the Maine State Museum in Augusta, the Portland Museum of Art, the Owl's Head Transportation Museum near Rockland, the Robert Abbe Museum in Acadia National Park (outstanding for its regional Indian artifacts), the Wilson Museum in Castine, the Patten Lumberman's Museum in Patten (which surprises you with the extent and quality of its exhibits), and the Colonial Pemaquid Restoration in Pemaquid (which presents fascinating archeological finds from the adjacent, early seventeenth-century settlement). The Maine Maritime Museum in Bath stands in a class by itself and should not be missed. The Maine State Museum in Augusta has outstanding exhibits on the varied Maine landscape and historical exhibits ranging from traces of the area's earliest people to rifles used by State of Mainers in Korea; you can also see exhibits on fishing, agriculture, lumbering, quarrying, and shipbuilding. (Also see Art Museums.)

MUSIC   Among the most famous summer concert series are: the Bar Harbor Festival (288-5744) and the Mount Desert Festival of Chamber Music (276-5039); the Sebago Long Lake Region Chamber Music Festival in North Bridgton (627-4939); the Bay Chamber Concerts presented in the Rockport Opera House (236-4731), which offers concerts year-round; and the Kneisel Hall chamber concerts and Bowdoin College Summer Concerts in Brunswick (725-8731, extension 321).

The summer music schools are: Bowdoin College Summer School (see above), Kneisel Hall in Blue Hill (see above but only after June 24; prior inquiries should be addressed to Kneisel Hall, Blue Hill 04614), the Pierre Monteux Memorial Domaine School in Hancock (442-6251), Salzedo Summer Harp Colony in Camden (236-2289), Machias Bay Chamber Concerts in Machias (255-8685), Kotzschmar Memorial Organ Summer Series in Portland (775-5451), New England Music Camp in Oakland (465-3025), Maine Summer Youth Music at the University of Maine, Orono (581-1960), and Maine Music Camp at the University of Maine, Farmington (778-3501). There is, of course, the Portland Symphony Orchestra (773-8191), which also has a summertime pops series, and the Bangor Symphony Orchestra (945-6408).

NATURE PRESERVES, COASTAL   Rachel Carson National Wildlife Refuge is a total of nine separate preserves salted between Kittery and Cape Elizabeth along the Atlantic Flyway. Request a leaflet guide from the Parker River National Wildlife Refuge, Newbury, MA 01950. Laudholm Farm in Wells near the Rachel Carson preserve offers guided walks and well-marked trails.

The Maine Audubon Society maintains a nature center at Scarborough Marsh and offers canoe tours, bird walks, and a variety of other summer programs (883-5100). There are also nature trails to follow at the Audubon Society headquarters at Gilsland

Farm in Falmouth. And the society also maintains self-guiding nature trails (cross-country ski trails in winter) and facilities for picnicking and tenting at the 150-acre Mast Landing Sanctuary in Freeport. Birdsacre, a 40-acre preserve in Ellsworth, harbors 109 species of birds in and around a network of nature trails, and a museum that honors pioneer ornithologist Cordelia Stanwood, open June 15 through October 15, and other times by appointment (667-8683). Acadia National Park, with its miles of hiking trails and extensive naturalist-led programs, is the state's busiest preserve (see Mount Desert). Some 30 miles east of Ellsworth is Petit Manan National Wildlife Refuge (1,999 acres), a peninsula offering two hiking trails. At the extreme eastern end of Maine the Moosehorn National Wildlife Refuge in Calais (454-3521) consists of two units, roughly 20 miles apart. The bigger (16,065 acres) is partially bounded by the St. Croix River, and the 6,600-acre Edmunds Unit overlooks Cobscook Bay; a visitors center is open May through September, and there are hiking trails. The largest private land-owner of preservation land in Maine is the Nature Conservancy, protecting 71 preserves adding up to more than 25,000 acres throughout the state. For details request *Maine Forever, A Guide to Nature Conservancy Preserves in Maine,* available through the Maine chapter of the Nature Conservancy, PO Box 338, 122 Main Street, Topsham 04086. (Also see Islands.)

NATURE PRESERVES, INLAND   Steve Powell Wildlife Management Area, described in a booklet available from the Maine Department of Inland Fisheries and Wildlife, 284 State Street, Augusta 04333 (289-3651), consists of two islands and several hundred acres of intervening tidal flats at the head of Merrymeeting Bay. Southeast of Fryeburg there are the Brownfield Bog Wildlife Management Areas (5,454 acres)— a mix of marshland, floodplain, and upland which invites exploration by canoe; a campsite at Walker's Falls is maintained by the Appalachian Mountain Club (see Hiking). In the Bridgton area there is the Hiram Nature Study Area maintained by the Central Maine Power Company (647-3391)— some 60 acres of woodland in Baldwin with

a trail along the Saco River and picnic facilities. Vaughan Woods, a 250-acre state park, offers a few fine miles of wooded hiking trails along the Salmon Falls River, good for cross-country skiing and birding as well as hiking and picnicking (from Kittery take Route 236 north more than 9 miles, then west on Route 91, left at the T). Free. The greatest inland preserve is Baxter State Park in Maine's North Woods. (Also see Camping, Fishing, Hiking, and Hunting, and the Nature Conservancy under Nature Preserves, Coastal.)

PARKS AND FORESTS, NATIONAL   Acadia National Park, which occupies roughly half of Mount Desert plus scattered areas on Isle au Haut, Little Cranberry Island, Baker Island, Little Moose Island, and Schoodic Point, adds up to a 44,000-acre preserve offering hiking, touring, swimming, horse-back riding, canoeing, and a variety of guided nature tours and programs as well as a scenic 56-mile driving tour. Note that an entry fee is now charged to the park and that camping is by reservation only. See the Bar Harbor/Acadia/Bangor Area chapter for details. The White Mountain National Forest encompasses 41,943 acres in Maine, including five campgrounds under the jurisdiction of the Evans Notch Ranger District, Bridge Street, Bethel 04217 (824-2134). For details see Bethel.

PARKS, STATE   The Bureau of Parks and Recreation (289-3821), State House, Augusta 04333, publishes "Outdoors in Maine," a map/guide to 30 state parks, which we have described within the text as they appear geographically.

In 1991 day-use fees are between $1.50 and $2 per person, and camping fees are $7.50 to $9 per site for residents, $10 to $12 for nonresidents. There is also a $2 per night reservation fee for camping. Phone for information about campground reservations.

PUFFIN-WATCHING   Atlantic puffins are smaller than you might expect. They lay just one egg a year and were heading for extinction around the turn of the century when the only surviving birds nested either on Matinicus Rock or Machias Seal Island. Since 1973 the Audubon Society has had nesting areas on Eastern Egg Rock in Muscongus Bay, six miles off Pemaquid Point. Since 1984 there has been a similar puffin restoration project on Seal Island in outer Penobscot Bay, six miles from Matinicus Rock. The best months for viewing puffins are June and July or the first few days of August. Viewing must be from the water and binoculars are needed (we found the birds to be much smaller than their popular image suggests). Tours are offered by Cap'n Fish Boat Trips in Boothbay Harbor, Maine Whalewatch in Northeast Harbor, the *Hardy III* out of New Harbor, and Capt. Barna Norton out of Jonesport.

RAILROAD RIDES & MUSEUMS   Boothbay Railway Village delights small children and offers railroad exhibits in its depot. For railfans there is another site to see: the Sandy River Railroad in Phillips, with a reconstructed narrow-gauge engine and authentic old coaches from the old Sandy River and Rangeley Lakes Railroad. It operates entirely with volunteer help on the first and third Sundays of summer months, and by appointment (639-3001). The Belfast & Moosehead Lake Railroad Company in Belfast offers daily excursion runs Memorial Day through Labor Day.

RATES   Please view any prices listed for Lodging, Dining Out, and Eating Out, as well as for museums and attractions, as benchmarks in the rising tide of inflation. Call ahead to confirm them. MAP stands for Modified American Plan: breakfast and dinner included in rate. AP stands for American Plan: three meals included in rate. EP stands for European Plan: breakfast included in rate. B&B stands for Bed and Breakfast: continental breakfast included in rate.

ROCK-HOUNDING   Perham's Maine Mineral Store at Trap Corner in West Paris, which claims to attract an annual 90,000 visitors, displays Maine minerals and offers access (for a small fee) to its five quarries. The store also offers information about other quarries and sells its own guidebook to gem hunting in Oxford County ("Maine's Treasure Chest"). Open year-round daily (just 1–5 on Sundays, closed Thanksgiving and Christmas). For other rockhounding meccas

check the Bethel Area chapter. Thanks to the high price of gold, prospectors are back-panning Maine streambeds; a list of likely spots is available from the Maine Geological Survey, Department of Conservation, State House Station 22, Augusta 04333 (289-2801). A helpful pamphlet guide, "Maine Mineral Collecting," lists annual gem shows and gem shops as well as quarries and is available from the Maine Publicity Bureau (see Information).

SAILING   Windjammers and yacht charter brokers aside, there are a limited number of places that will rent small sailing craft, fewer that will offer lessons to adults and children alike. Those of which we are aware are: Willey's Wharf, Camden; Chance Along Sailing Center, Belfast; Sailways, Deer Isle; the Mansell Boat Company, Southwest Harbor; and WoodenBoat School, Brooklin. Sailboat rentals and day-trips are listed under To See and Do throughout the book.

SEA-KAYAKING   Guided trips and clinics are available from Sunrise Canoe in Cathance Lake, Sea Touring Kayak Center in Camden, H2Outfitters on Orrs Island, Explorers at Sea in Stonington, and Coastal Kayaking Tours and Acadia Bike & Canoe in Bar Harbor. Freeport-based L.L. Bean sponsors an annual sea-kayaking symposium in Castine that is an excellent introduction to both the equipment and skills required by this fast-growing sport. *Sea Kayaking Along the New England Coast* by Tamsin Venn (Appalachian Mountain Club, 1991) includes detailed guidance to kayaking routes from Portland to Cobscook Bay; it also offers tips of local lodging and dining as well as an overall introduction to the sport.

SKIING   Sugarloaf/USA is Maine's largest ski area and the largest self-contained resort in New England. But Sunday River in the Bethel area now boasts the largest "uphill capacity" (ability to move skiers uphill on chair lifts) and the most extensive snowmaking in either Maine or New Hampshire. They also have expanded from one to three mountains in recent years. Saddleback Mountain (in the Rangeley area) is a big mountain with a small, enthusiastic following. Mount Abram (also in the Bethel area) is a true family area with a strong ski school and some fine runs. Shawnee Peak, previously known as Pleasant Mountain (in the Western Lakes area) and Moosehead Resort & Ski Area (alias Squaw Mountain) in Greenville are other medium-sized areas. Locally geared ski hills include Lost Valley in Auburn, Mt. Jefferson in Lee, Camden Snow Bowl in Camden, Titcomb Mountain in Farmington, and Eaton Mountain in Skowhegan. At this writing Maine offers toll-free ski reports: 800-533-9595 for out-of-state callers. The annual magazine, *Maine Guide to Winter*, profiling all ski areas, is available from the Maine Publicity Bureau (see Information).

SKIING, CROSS-COUNTRY Carrabassett Valley Touring Center at Sugarloaf is the largest commercial Nordic network in the state. Bethel, with two major trail networks (Sunday River Inn and the Bethel Inn), also offers varied terrain. The trails at Saddleback Mountain in Rangeley are the highest in Maine and may, in fact, be snow-covered when no place else is. The most adventurous touring is found in the Katahdin/Moosehead area in Maine's North Woods. The Birches in Rockwood and Little Lyford Camps near Brownville Junction offer guided wilderness tours. The "Maine Guide to Winter," published by Maine Publicity Bureau (see Information), lists most Nordic areas, and the Maine Nordic Ski Council (PO Box 645, Bethel 04217) publishes its own pamphlet guide. The state's toll-free number (800-533-9595) should list cross-country conditions, too.

SNOWMOBILING Maine has reciprocal agreements with nearly all states and provinces; for licensing and rules write to the Fish and Game Department. The Maine Snowmobile Association represents 268 clubs and maintains 6,000 miles of an ever-expanding cross-state trail network. For details write the MSA Office, Box 77, Augusta 04330 (622-6983). For maps and further information write to the Snowmobile Division, Bureau of Parks and Recreation, State House Station 19, Augusta 04333.

SPA Northern Pines in Raymond is the only fully developed spa program of which we are aware in Maine.

SUMMER STUDY See Camps, for Adults; Crafts Centers; and Workshops.

THEATER, SUMMER The Ogunquit Playhouse (646-5511) is among the oldest and most prestigious summer theaters in the country. The Theater at Monmouth, housed in the fine old Custom Hall (933-2952), and the Brunswick Music Theater on the Bowdoin Campus (725-8769) are also well established. There are the Hackmatack Playhouse in Berwick (698-1807), the Theater Project in Brunswick (729-8584), Waterville Summer Music Theatre in Winslow (873-1309), Maine Theatre in Portland (871-7101), Bad Little Falls Summer Playhouse in Machias (255-3313), Pioneer Playhouse in Presque Isle (764-0311, ext. 336 or 352), Theater Project in Brunswick (729-8584), and Thomas Inn and Playhouse in South Casco (655-3292). A descriptive listing is available from the Maine Publicity Bureau (see Information).

THEATER, YEAR-ROUND Acadia Repertory Theater in summer is at Somesville, Mount Desert Island 04660 (244-7260), and in winter at 183 Maine Street, Bangor 04401 (942-3333). Other companies are the Performing Arts Center in Bath (442-8455), the Camden Civic Theatre in Camden (236-4885), and the Kennebec Performing Arts Center in Gardiner (582-1325). Portland Performing Arts Center is at 25A Forest Avenue, Portland 04112 (774-0465). Also, the Portland Players (799-7337) present a winter season of productions, as does the Maine Acting Company (784-1616) in Lewiston.

WATERFALLS The following are all easily accessible to families with small children: Smalls Falls on the Sandy River, off Route 4 between Rangeley and Phillips, has a picnic spot with a trail beside the falls; Step Falls on Wight Brook in Newry off Route 26, and just a ways farther up the road in Grafton Notch State Park is Screw Auger Falls with its natural gorge. Another Screw Auger Falls can be approached via the Appalachian Trail: take the Katahdin Iron Works Road off Route 11 north of Brownville Junction. Kezar Falls, on the Kezar River, is best reached via Lovell Road from Route 35 at North Waterford. An extensive list of "scenic waterfalls" is detailed in *The Maine Atlas and Gazetteer* (DeLorme Publishing Company). Check out 90-foot Moxie Falls at the Forks.

WHALE-WATCHING   Each spring humpback, finback, and minke whales migrate to New England waters where they remain until early fall, cavorting—it sometimes seems—for the pleasure of excursion boats. One prime gathering spot is Jeffries Ledge, about 20 miles off Kennebunkport, and another is the Bay of Fundy. For listings of whale-watch cruises see the Kennebunks, Portland, Bar Harbor, and Eastport (Washington County).

WHITE-WATER RAFTING   White-water rafting has grown so quickly in the past few years that it is difficult to keep track of all the groups offering day trips and longer expeditions down Maine's foaming rivers. Ten years ago Northern Whitewater Expeditions was the only rafting company in the Forks, handy to the dependable timed release of water rushing through scenic Kennebec Gorge. There are now a dozen white-water rafting outfitters in and around the Forks (see detailed description under To See and Do in the Upper Kennebec Valley section of North Woods), many offering trips on the Penobscot and Dead rivers as well as the Kennebec. Eastern River Expeditions and Wilderness Expeditions (see To See and Do in the Moosehead Area section of North Woods) are positioned between the Kennebec and the Penobscot rivers and offer trips on those two rivers and the Dead River; also kayaking and white-water canoeing lessons and guided trips. A current list of white-water rafting companies is available from the Maine Publicity Bureau (see Information).

WINDJAMMERS   In 1935 a young artist named Frank Swift fitted a few former fishing and cargo schooners to carry passengers around the islands of Penobscot Bay. At the time there were plenty of these old vessels moored in every harbor and cove, casualties of progress. Swift called his business Maine Windjammer Cruises, and during the next two decades it grew to include more than a dozen vessels. Competitors also prospered through the '50s, but the entire Windjammer fleet almost faded away with the advent of rigorous Coast Guard licensing requirements in the '60s and the increased cost of building and rebuilding schooners. The '70s and '80s have, however, seen the rise of a new breed of windjammer captain. Almost every one of those now sailing has built or restored the vessel he or she commands. The current Maine Windjammer Fleet (if you stretch the definition to include all passenger-carrying sailing vessels that offer regularly scheduled overnight cruises) is 18 strong. In age they range from the Stephen Taber and the Lewis French, both originally launched in 1871, to the Heritage, launched in 1983. Most of the older vessels have, moreover, been completely rebuilt, some more than once, most by the men and women who are sailing them.

In her cookbook, *A Taste of the Taber*, Stephen Taber co-captain Ellen Barnes recalls her own joy of first discovering the windjammers as a passenger: "No museums had gobbled up these vessels; no cities had purchased them to sit at piers as public-relations gimmicks. These vessels were the real thing—plying their trade as they had in the past with one exception: the present-day cargo was people instead of pulpwood, bricks, coal, limestone and granite."

Windjammers offer a sense of what the Maine coast and islands are all about. Most sail with the tide on Monday mornings with no set itinerary—where they go depends on the wind and the tide. Clad in old jeans and sneakers, passengers help haul a line and then lounge around the decks, gradually succumbing to the luxury of steeping in life on the face of Penobscot Bay. As the wind and sun drop, the schooner eases into a harbor. Supper is hearty Yankee fare, maybe fish chowder and beef stew with plenty of fresh corn bread. Before or after supper passengers can board the vessel's yawl for a foray into the nearest village or onto the nearest road (most landlubbers feel the need to walk a bit each day). By Wednesday the days begin to blur. Cradled in a favorite corner of the deck you sun and find yourself seeing more: flocks of cormorants and an occasional seal or minke whale, eagles circling over island nests. The sky itself seems closer, and you are mesmerized by the ever-changing surface of the sea.

Choosing which vessel to sail on in retrospect turns out to be the most difficult part of a Windjammer vacation. All have ship-to-shore radios and sophisticated radar, and some offer more in the way of creature comforts (hot showers and lounges) than others; some are known for their food or a captain with great jokes or songs. Within the Camden and Rockland chapters we have described each vessel in the kind of detail we devote to individual inns. Windjammers accommodate between 22 and 44 passengers and the cost is $435–$585 per person for the six-day cruises, from $275 for three days. Excessive drinking is discouraged on all the vessels, and guests are invited to bring their musical instruments. Children under 14 are usually not permitted. Contact the Windjammer Association (800-MAINE-80, Box 317, Rockport 04856) for brochures on 11 vessels. For similar material on the Stephen Taber phone 800-999-7352, and for material on the Timberwind phone 800-624-6013.

WORKSHOPS Maine Photographic Workshops (236-8581), 2 Central Street, Rockport 04856, offers more than 100 summer workshops, geared to all abilities. Kodak has just opened the Center for Creative Imaging (236-2333), 51 Knowlton Stree, Camden 04843. Elderhostel Inc. (80 Boylston Street, Boston) offers week-long programs ranging from ecological to literary studies in coastal locales from the south coast to the Searsport area and on up into Washington County. They are rewarding and exceptionally reasonably priced but open only to those over 55 or accompanying someone over 55. Finally, Maine Coast Art Workshops in Port Clyde in the Rockland area offers five-day courses on the St. George peninsula.

I. South Coast

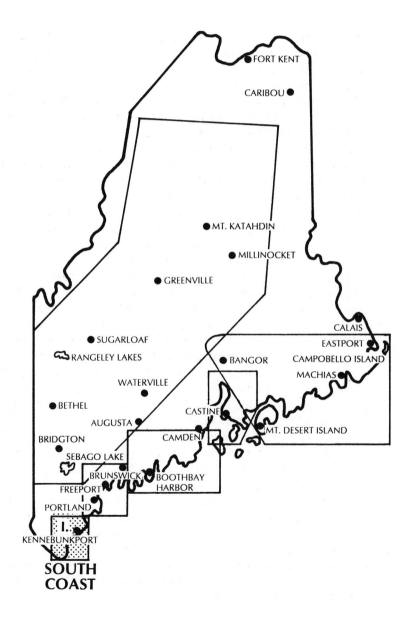

FORT KENT

CARIBOU ●

● MT. KATAHDIN

● MILLINOCKET

● GREENVILLE

CALAIS

● SUGARLOAF

EASTPORT

RANGELEY LAKES

CAMPOBELLO ISLAND

● BANGOR

MACHIAS

WATERVILLE

● BETHEL

CASTINE

AUGUSTA

MT. DESERT ISLAND

BRIDGTON

CAMDEN

SEBAGO LAKE

BRUNSWICK BOOTHBAY
HARBOR

FREEPORT

PORTLAND

I.

KENNEBUNKPORT

**SOUTH
COAST**

Kittery and the Yorks

The moment you cross the Piscataqua River you know you are in Maine. You have to go a long way Down East to find any deeper coves, finer lobster pounds, rockier ocean paths, or sandier beaches than those in Kittery and York.

Both towns claim to be Maine's oldest community. Technically Kittery wins, but York looks older . . . depending, of course, on which Kittery and which York you are talking about.

Kittery Point, an eighteenth-century settlement overlooking Portsmouth Harbor, boasts Maine's oldest church, some of the state's finest mansions, and "America's oldest family store," Frisbees. The village of Kittery itself, however, has been shattered by so many bridges and rotaries that it seems to exist only as a gateway, on one hand for workers at the Portsmouth Naval Shipyard and on the other for patrons of the mushrooming outlet malls on Route 1.

The Kittery Historical Naval Museum is well worth searching out as are the dining, strolling, and swimming spots along coastal Route 103.

In the late nineteenth century artists and literati gathered at Kittery Point. Novelist William Dean Howells, who summered just beyond the graveyard, became keenly interested in preserving the area's colonial-era buildings. Howells and his friend Sam Clemens (otherwise known as Mark Twain) were part of a group of wealthy summer people who began buying up splendid colonial-era buildings. They appreciated the fact that the old jail, the school, the church, the burial ground, and the abundance of 1740s homes in York comprised the oldest surviving village in Maine.

In 1900 Howells suggested turning the "old gaol" in York Village into a museum. At the time you could count the country's historic house museums on your fingers. In the Old Gaol of today, you learn about the village's bizarre history, including its origins as an American Indian settlement called Agamenticus, one of many settlements wiped out by a plague in 1616. In 1630 it was settled by colonists, and in 1642 it became Gorgeana, America's first chartered city. It was then demoted to the town of York, part of Massachusetts, in 1670. Fierce Indian raids followed, but by the middle of the eighteenth century the present colonial village was established, a crucial way station between Portsmouth and points east.

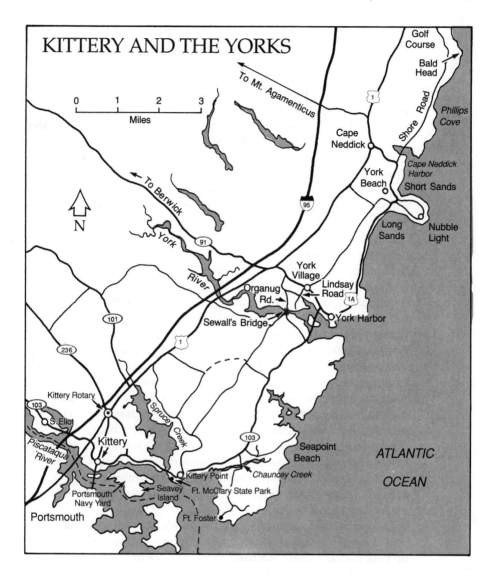

KITTERY AND THE YORKS

Golf Course
Bald Head
To Mt. Agamenticus
Phillips Cove
0   1   2   3
Miles
Cape Neddick
Cape Neddick Harbor
York Beach
Short Sands
To Berwick
95
N
York
River
91
Long Sands
Nubble Light
York Village
Lindsay Road
1A
Organug Rd.
Sewall's Bridge
York Harbor
101
1
236
Kittery Rotary
Spruce Creek
103
S. Eliot
Kittery
Piscataqua River
Seapoint Beach
ATLANTIC
OCEAN
Chauncey Creek
Kittery Point
Portsmouth Navy Yard
Seavey Island
Ft. McClary State Park
Portsmouth
Ft. Foster

York is divided into so many distinct villages that Clemens once observed, "It is difficult to throw a brick . . . in any one direction without danger of disabling a postmaster." Not counting Scotland and York Corners, York includes York Village, York Harbor, York Beach, and Cape Neddick—such varied communities that locals can't bring themselves to speak of them as one town; they refer instead to "the Yorks."

The rocky shore beyond York Village was Lower Town until the Marshall House was opened near the small grey sand beach in 1871 and changed its address to York Harbor. Soon the hotel had 300 rooms, and other mammoth frame hotels appeared at intervals along the shore.

They are all gone. All, that is, except the 162-room Cliff House which, although physically in York, has long since changed its address and phone to Ogunquit, better known now as a resort town.

Still York Harbor remains a delightful, low-key retreat. The Marshall House has been replaced by the modern Stage Neck Inn, and many of the dignified old summer "cottages" are now inns and B&Bs handy to York Harbor's Cliff Walk, a narrow mile-or-so path along the shore that was first traced by fishermen and later smoothed and graced with small touches such as the "Wiggly Bridge," a graceful little suspension bridge across the river and through Steadman Woods.

Landscaping and public spaces were among the consuming interests of the nineteenth-century summer residents, and around the turn of the century they also became interested in zoning. In *Trending into Maine* (1935) Kenneth Roberts notes York Harbor's "determination to be free of billboards, tourist camps, dance halls and other cheapening manifestations of the herd instinct and Vacationland civilization."

A York Harbor corporation was formed to impose its own taxes and keep out unwanted development. The corporation's biggest fight, writes Roberts, was against the Libby Camps, a tent-and-trailer campground on the eastern edge of York Harbor that "had spread with such fungus-like rapidity that York Harbor was in danger of being almost completely swamped by young ladies in shorts, young men in soiled undershirts, and fat ladies in knickerbockers."

Libby's Oceanside Camp still sits on Roaring Rock Point, its trailers neatly angled along the shore. Across from it is matching Camp Eaton, established in 1923. No other village boundary within a New England town remains more clearly defined than this one between York Harbor and York Beach.

Beyond the campgrounds stretches 3-mile Long Shores Beach, lined with a simpler breed of summer cottage than anything in York Village or York Harbor. There is a real charm to the strip and to the village of York Beach, with its Victorian-style shops, restaurants, and boardwalk amusements.

Whatever the day or weather, a group is sure to be standing spellbound in front of the Goldenrod's big plate-glass windows, watching taffy stirred, pulled, and neatly packaged into "Goldenrod kisses." It is still owned by the same family that opened it in 1896, about the time the electric streetcar put York Beach within reach of "the working class."

During this "Trolley Era" a half-dozen big hotels accommodated 3,000 summer visitors, and 2,000 more patronized boarding houses in York Beach. Today's lodgings are a mix of motels, cottages, and B&Bs. There are beaches (with free or metered parking), Fun-O-Rama games and bowling, and York's Zoo and Amusement Park with exotic animals and carnival rides.

York Beach, too, has now gained "historic" status, and the Old York Historical Society, keeper of the half-dozen colonial-era buildings open to the public in York Village, now sponsors York Beach walking tours.

GUIDANCE   Maine's biggest, busiest state-owned information center (439-1319) is located on I-95 northbound in Kittery and is a source of advice on local as well as statewide lodging, dining, and attractions. The **Kittery Information Center** is open daily except Christmas and Thanksgiving, 8–9 in summer months, otherwise 9–5 (bathrooms open 24 hours daily). We usually stop by the center for information and a weather update (press a button outside the men's room and you get a full report) and then exit through the rear of the complex to Route 1. Turn right for Kittery and the outlets, left for York.

York Chamber of Commerce (363-4422), PO Box 417, York 03909. A Route 1 information center just off the access to I-95 is open in summer, 10–5 (later on Fridays and Saturdays); shorter hours in May, October, and November. In winter, tourist information is still available from the same address and phone. You'll find the office at 3B Government Street.

The Kittery-Eliot Chamber of Commerce (439-7545), PO Box 526, Kittery 03904-0526, publishes a tourist's guide pamphlet describing lodging, dining, and sights.

GETTING THERE   **Trailways** and **Greyhound** serve Portsmouth, New Hampshire, some 12 miles south. Limousine service from Portland and Boston airports is available year-round from **George Munroe** (464-9067). **Little Brook Airport** in Eliot serves private and charter planes.

GETTING AROUND   From mid-June to Labor Day, 8:30 AM–9:30 PM, an open-sided trolley links York Village, Harbor, and Beach with Cape Neddick and Route 1. Narrated tours are offered every hour. For details check with the chambers of commerce.

MEDICAL EMERGENCY   **York Hospital 24-Hour Emergency Services** (363-4321), Lindsay Road, York Village.

TO SEE AND DO   *In Kittery:*   **Kittery Historical and Naval Museum** (439-3080), Route 1, just north of the Route 236 rotary. Open daily May through October, Monday to Saturday 1–4. $2 adults, $1 ages 7–15; family and group rates. A fine little museum filled with ship models, naval relics from the Portsmouth Naval Yard, and exhibits about the early history of this stretch of the South Coast. Displays include archaeological finds, ship models, early shipbuilding tools, navigational instruments, trade documents, and mariner's folk art, including samples of work by Kittery master ships' carver John Haley Bellamy (1836–1914).

Portsmouth Naval Shipyard (open by appointment: 438-1810), sited on Seavey Island at the mouth of the Piscataqua River. Also known as the Kittery Navy Yard, it is very visible from downtown Kittery. Established in 1806, it was the site of the treaty ending the Russo–Japanese War in 1905 and was responsible for building half of all American submarines during World War II. Today the navy yard remains an important submarine maintenance point. The PNS Command Museum has exhibits from the Yard's past.

Kittery Point. From Route 1, find your way to Route 103 and follow its twists and turns along the harbor until you come to a simple, old, white wooden church and small green across from a striking Georgian-style house. An old graveyard overlooking the harbor completes the scene. Park at the church (built in 1730, Maine's oldest), notice the parsonage (1729), and walk across to the old graveyard. The magnificent house was built in 1760 for the widow of Sir William Pepperrell, the French and Indian War hero who captured the fortress at Louisburg from the French. Knighted for his feat, Pepperrell went on to become the richest man in New England but lost all during the Revolution because he remained loyal to the king. Privately owned, the house is periodically open to the public; check with the chamber. Sir William's own handsome house still stands in Pepperrell Cove, but today everyone in the cove seems to be named Frisbee. Five generations of Frisbees have operated the store here; they also own Cap'n Simeons Gallery (see Dining Out) and the neighboring B&B.

Fort McClary, Route 103 (south of Pepperrell Cove). A state park open seasonally, grounds accessible year-round. A hexagonal 1846 blockhouse on a granite base, it was the site of fortifications in 1715, 1776, and 1808. The site was first fortified in the early eighteenth century to protect Massachusetts vessels from being taxed by the New Hampshire colony. There is a fine view of Portsmouth Harbor, but the formal picnicking area across the road has no view.

Fort Foster Park. Just beyond Pepperrell Cove look for Gerrish Island Lane and turn right at the "T" on Pocahontas Road which leads, eventually, to this 92-acre town park. It incorporates a World War I coastal defense site and fills the whole point of land at the entrance to Portsmouth (NH) Harbor. The fortifications are ugly, but there is a choice of small beaches with different exposures, one very popular with windsurfers. There are also walking trails and picnic facilities. The current entrance fee is $2 per car plus $1 per adult, $.50 per child under age 12.

In York: **Old York Historical Society** (363-4974), Box 312, York 03909. The society maintains an outstanding local historical research library in the waterside **George Marshall Store** (a former chandlery at which large schooners docked) on Lindsay Road. Open year-round, Tuesday through Saturday 10–4. In addition, all of the buildings described in the following paragraphs are open mid-June through September, Tuesday through Saturday 10–4; also Columbus Day weekend and for special events. $6 adults, $2.50 children ($16 maximum per family) includes admission to all buildings; admission to individual buildings also available. Purchase tickets at the Jefferds Tavern. The society also offers a full schedule of tours, crafts workshops, skits, walking tours, and other special events during July and August.

Jefferds Tavern, Route 1A, York Village. A 1759 building moved here from Wells in 1939 and furnished to reflect a coastal Maine country tavern in the late eighteenth century. Orientation to the town and other buildings is given by costumed guides. The **Old Schoolhouse** next door has been restored to illustrate local education during the same period.

Old Gaol, York Village center. Dating from 1719 and billed as the oldest remaining public building of the English colonies, it once served the whole province of Maine and continued to house York County prisoners until 1860. You may inspect the cells and jailer's quarters and learn about York's early miscreants.

Emerson-Wilcox House, Route 1A, York Village. Dating in part from 1742 and expanded over the years. Period rooms reflect its use as stage tavern and family dwelling; it has also been a general store and a tailor shop. People who know American textiles come just to see the earliest known complete set of bed hangings, embroidered by Mary Bulman in 1745.

Elizabeth Perkins House, Lindsay Road (at Sewall Bridge—a replica of the first pile bridge in America, built on this spot in 1761). Our favorite building, this is a 1730 farmhouse down by the York River. It is still filled with colonial-era antiques and the spirit of the real powerhouse behind York's original Historic Landmarks Society. It was "Bessie" Perkins who saved the Jefferds Tavern. She's buried under the simple plaque in a boulder at the edge of the lawn overlooking the river.

John Hancock Warehouse and Wharf, Lindsay Road. An eighteenth-century warehouse with exhibits of eighteenth-century life and industry on and around the York River.

Sayward-Wheeler House (363-2709), 79 Barrell Lane, York Harbor. Open June 15 to October 15, Wednesday through Sunday 12–5. $3. A fine, early eighteenth-century house built by Jonathan Sayward—merchant, ship owner, judge, and representative to the Massachusetts General Court—who retained the respect of the community despite his Tory leanings. It has Queen Anne and Chippendale furnishings, family portraits, and china brought back as booty from the expedition against the French at Louisburg in 1745. It overlooks the river and is accessible from York's Shore Path, near the Wiggly Bridge (see Walks).

First Parish Church, York Village. An outstanding mid-eighteenth-century meeting house with a fine old cemetery full of old stones with death's heads and Old English spelling.

Civil War Monument, York Village. Look closely at the monument

in the middle of the village. The soldier is wearing a rebel uniform. I'm
told that the statue commissioned for York stands in a South Carolina
town because the sculptor made a mistake. At the time, both towns
agreed that freight rates were too high to make the switch; and as time
went on, York became too attached to its soldier to consider swapping.
(Controversy continues to rage whether this story is true or not.)

In South Berwick: **Sarah Orne Jewett Birthplace** (384-5269), 5 Portland Street
(Route 236). Open June to October 15, Tuesday, Thursday, Saturday,
and Sunday 12–5. $3. A 1774 house preserved by the Society for the
Preservation of New England Antiquities (SPNEA) much as the
author left it. Some furnishings date from the eighteenth century.

Hamilton House (384-5269), Vaughan's Lane (turn off Route 236;
opposite junction with Route 91). Open the same time as Jewett
Birthplace, same price, same owners. The interior of the house was
recently refurbished to reflect its early twentieth-century appearance.
There's also an elaborate formal garden and garden house with
landscaped grounds sweeping down to the Salmon Falls River.

Counting House (742-4674), Route 4. Open July and August, Saturday 1–4 and by appointment. A Greek Revival commercial building
houses the Old Berwick Historical Society's collection of ship models,
navigational instruments, photos, and books of Sarah Orne Jewett and
Gladys Hasty Carroll. (Call the South Berwick Town Office at 384-
2263.)

TO SEE AND DO FOR FAMILIES **York's Wild Zoo & Amusement Park** (363-
4911 or 800-456-4911), York Beach. Rides open daily noon to 10 PM,
June through Labor Day weekend (weekends only in June); zoo is
open 10–5 weekends, May through Columbus Day. This is a combination amusement area and zoo with paddle boats, midway rides, and
over 500 animals including some real exotica. There are also miniature
golf and both pony and elephant rides (but the performing goats, long
a trademark, are gone). It's expensive: $8 per adult, $6.50 per child for
zoo admission only; $7 per adult, $6 per child for unlimited rides.

WALKS **Shore Path,** York Harbor. For more than a mile you can pick your
way along the town's most pleasant piece of shorefront. Begin at the
George Marshall Store (see To See and Do in York) and walk east until
you reach the Wiggly Bridge (a mini-suspension bridge), then continue
across Route 103, past the Sayward House, along the harbor, down
across the beach, and along the top of the rocks to East Point.

Nubble Light, York Beach. From Shore Road take Broadway out
through the Nubble (a cottage-covered peninsula) to the parking area,
which overlooks this 1879 lighthouse perched on a small island of its
own. It is one of the only ones in the county still manned. Park and
clamber around on the rocks.

Fort Foster Park, Gerrish Island, Kittery (marked from Route 103
just north of Pepperrell Cove). A 92-acre town park, incorporating a
World War I coastal defense site with trails for walking and cross-

Photo by Kim Grant

York Beach

country skiing as well as a beach, fishing pier, and picnicking pavilion. (See To See and Do in Kittery.)

Mount Agamenticus. The highest hill on the Atlantic seaboard between Florida and Mount Desert. A defunct ski area, it can be reached by an access road from Cat Mountain Road off Route 1.

Cape Neddick Park, River Road (off Route 1 at Pie in the Sky Bakery). This 100-acre preserve surrounding the Walt Kuhn Gallery is open Wednesday to Sunday 10–8. It includes a sculpture garden.

Vaughan Woods, South Berwick. A 250-acre preserve on the banks of the Salmon Falls River; picnic facilities and nature trails. The first cows in Maine are said to have been landed here at "Cow Cove" in 1634. From South Berwick take Route 236 for half a mile, turn right onto Vine Street and continue for 1 mile, turn right onto Old Fields Road, then follow signs.

The Old York Historical Society offers weekly guided tours of both York Village and York Beach.

BEACHES   **Long Sands** is a 3-mile expanse of coarse, grey sand stretching from York Harbor to the Nubble, backed by Route 1A and summer cottages.

Short Sands is a shorter stretch of coarse, grey sand with a parking lot (meters), toilets, and the Victorian-era village of York Beach just behind it.

York Harbor Beach is small and pebbly, but pleasant. Limited parking.

Cape Neddick Beach is smallest of all, at the river's mouth, sheltered, and a good choice for children.

Seapoint Beach, Kittery, is also very small and pebbly, with limited parking on Gerrish Island.

BICYCLING **Burger's Bike Shop** (363-4070), 243 Rok Street, York Village. Offers rentals.

BOAT EXCURSIONS **C. P. Charters, Ltd.** (363-3874, evenings), York Harbor. Takes up to six passengers on two-hour cruises to Nubble Light, Perkins Cove, and up the York River.

Isles of Shoals Steamship Co. (603-431-5000), PO Box 31, Portsmouth, NH 03803. Offers daily cruises in-season to the Isles of Shoals. (Also see Deep-Sea Fishing.)

DEEP-SEA FISHING *Blackback* (363-5675), York Harbor. Herb Pool sails his 38-foot Down-Easter in search of giant bluefin tuna, sharks, and mackerel; also available for sightseeing, whale-watching. Write to Seabury Charters, PO Box 218, York 03909.

E-Z (363-5634), York Harbor. Available for day-long fishing charters. Contact Lawrence Grant (he can also take you on an airplane ride).

Shearwater (363-5324), York Harbor. Also takes fishing parties.

The Judy-Marie (361-1969), York Harbor, is another deep-sea fishing option.

HOTEL **The Union Bluff Hotel** (363-1333), 8 Beach Street, York Beach 03910. Open year-round. The old hotel burned a few years ago, but the new one is almost an exact replica with 40 rooms. The view down the beach is great and you are right in the middle of things, but there's a price: $100–$135 per room in summer. Half that price off-season.

INNS **Dockside Guest Quarters** (363-2868), PO Box 205, Harris Island Road, York 03909. Open Memorial Day to Columbus Day; also weekends in May. The Lusty family—including longtime innkeepers Harriette and David Lusty, their son Eric, his wife, Carol, and son, Philip—imbue this fine little island hideaway with a warmth that few inns possess. The Dockside is a 7-acre compound with six buildings along the harbor: the gracious nineteenth-century Maine House, four newer multi-unit cottages, and the Dockside Dining Room. There are 22 guest rooms, including 7 apartment/suites with kitchenettes—all with water views. Breakfast is served buffet style in the Maine House. It's a nominally priced "Continental Plus" (fruit compote, baked goods, etc.), muffins-and-juice breakfast, laid out on the dining room table—a morning gathering place for guests who check the blackboard weather forecast and plan their day. Guests can rent a canoe or Boston whaler or take advantage of regularly scheduled harbor and river cruises. Special lodging and cruise packages are offered during June. Two-night minimum stay during July and August. May through early June and the last half of October: $65–$75 for double rooms, $90 for apartment/suites. High season: $75–$88 for rooms, $120 for apartment/suites (sleep four).

Stage Neck Inn (363-3850 or 800-222-3238), York Harbor 03911. Open year-round. An attractive 1970s complex of 58 rooms built on the site of the nineteenth-century Marshall House. Sited on its own peninsula, the inn offers water views (by request), a formal dining room, and cruise-ship luxury. Geared to groups and conferences; adjacent to York Harbor Beach. It has two clay tennis courts. $75–$170 double, depending on the view and season.

York Harbor Inn (363-5119 or 800-343-3869), PO Box 573, York Street, York Harbor 03911. Open year-round. The inn sits right on Route 1A across from the harbor. The beamed lobby, built in 1637, is said to have served as a fisherman's hut on the Isles of Shoals. By the nineteenth century the building was elegant enough to serve for a spell as an exclusive men's club, and it is now a popular dining spot. Its Cellar Lounge, which is graced with an elaborately carved bar, is a local gathering place. There are 24 rooms upstairs in the inn itself; request one with a fireplace or ocean view. Next door in the Yorkshire Building, eight more rooms have been fitted with private baths and furnished with antiques; a honeymoon suite features a Jacuzzi and a sitting area. $60–$110 double, off-season; $75–$125, in-season.

BED & BREAKFASTS AND GUEST HOUSES *In Kittery:* **Harbor Watch B&B** (439-3242), Follett Lane, RFD 1, Box 42, Kittery Point 03905. Perched right at the southernmost tip of Maine at the intersection of the Piscataqua River and Spruce Creek. The white 1750s clapboard house has been in Marian Craig's family since a seafaring ancestor bought it in 1797. The highboy actually came from England at that time as did the wallpaper in the master bedroom. All three guest rooms have water views, and the vista from the front lawn is mesmerizing. Students of American impressionists may actually recognize the house from a painting by Childe Hassam hanging in the Smithsonian's Freer Gallery. $60 double, breakfast included.

Whaleback Inn (439-9570), Box 162, Kittery Point 03905. Open Memorial Day to Columbus Day. Part of the Frisbee compound (see Introduction), this roadside house offers three upstairs bedrooms, all nicely but simply furnished with shared bath; also a parlor with TV and radio and an upstairs eat-in kitchen where breakfast is served. $55 double. Small pets and children over 12 years welcome. No smoking.

High Meadows Bed & Breakfast (439-0590), Route 101, Eliot 03903. Technically in Eliot, this pleasant retreat is really just a few miles off Route 1 in Kittery. Open May through October. A 1736 house with five nicely furnished rooms, three with private baths. Our favorite is the Wedgewood Room with its canopy bed and highboy. There's a great little den with a woodstove and a formal living room with a fireplace, also a wicker-furnished porch overlooking the beautifully landscaped grounds. No children under 14. $50–$60 double.

Gundalow Inn (439-4040), 6 Water Street, Kittery 03904. An attractive B&B in the village of Kittery that's actually within walking distance of downtown Portsmouth, NH (across Memorial Bridge). All rooms have private baths. $75–$95 double, including a full breakfast. No smoking.

In York: **Hutchins House** (363-3058), 209 Organug Road, York 03909. This is a spacious, gracious house overlooking the York River. Linda Hutchins has raised her six children here and now offers three pleasant rooms, all with private bath. Common rooms range from formal (there's a player grand piano in the parlor) to an inviting sun porch furnished in wicker. Breakfasts are full, maybe blueberry pancakes or eggs Benedict, and there's a canoe for use on the river. $85 double, in-season, $69 in spring/fall; includes continental breakfast.

Inn at Harmon Park (363-2031), PO Box 495, York Harbor 03911. Open year-round. A shingled Victorian home, attractive and airy, with four guest rooms right in the village of York Harbor; within walking distance of the beach and Shore Path. The Antal family are your hosts. $65 with private bath, $50 with shared; breakfast on the sun porch included.

Cape Neddick House (363-2500), Box 70, Route 1, Cape Neddick 03902. Open year-round. Although it is right on Route 1, this farmhouse (in the Goodwin family for more than 100 years) offers an away-from-it-all feel and genuine hospitality. There are six guest rooms, two with air-conditioning, each named for a New England state, all furnished with antiques. Breakfast is an event—maybe strawberry scones or ham with apple biscuits—served on the back deck (overlooking garden and woods), in the dining room, or in the homey kitchen. Fine dining and woodland trails are within walking distance. $55–$70 double, depending on season.

Edward's Harborside Inn (363-3037), PO Box 866, York Harbor 03911. Open year-round. Nicely sited across in York Harbor by the water, this is a solidly built summer mansion maintained by Jay Edwards as a bed & breakfast. $70 double with shared bath to $190 for a suite. $50–$140 off-season.

Canterbury House Bed & Breakfast (363-3505), Route 1A, York Harbor 03911. Open year-round. James Pappas and Jim Hager have refurbished a white clapboard home in the center of York Harbor, within walking distance of beach and paths. Candlelight dinners by request. There are eight rooms with shared baths. $55 double includes continental breakfast and afternoon tea; $69 with a full breakfast. No children under 12.

Scotland Bridge Inn (363-4432), PO Box 521, York 03909. Open year-round. A spacious nineteenth-century farmhouse on a quiet back road. Guest rooms (shared and private baths) are tastefully furnished with antiques, and the living room is unusually inviting. There's also an English herb garden and, in winter, cross-country ski trails. $65 for a double room, $85 for a two-room suite.

"A Summer Place" (363-5233), RD 1, Box 196, York 03909. Seasonal. Harriet and John Simonds have just one guest room, and lucky the guest who fills it. The grand old house is set in its own gardens amid 70 acres, overlooking the salt marshes and tidal York River. $50 includes a private bath and breakfast.

Wooden Goose Inn (363-5673), Route 1, Cape Neddick 03902. Open year-round except January. The eight guest rooms—and eight bathrooms—are fussily exquisite and the gardens beautiful. Hosts Tony and Jerry pride themselves on preparing breakfasts such as eggs Benedict or quiche Lorraine; tea is also served. $95 includes afternoon tea as well as breakfast. No children. No smoking.

The Bell Buoy B&B (363-7264), 570 York Street, Box 445, York Harbor 03911. Open year-round. A spacious nineteenth-century "summer cottage" recently renovated and converted to a B&B by Wes and Kathie Cook who've moved here from Iowa. $65 double includes a full breakfast; $10 less off-season.

Homestead Inn (363-8952), Box 15, Route 1A, York Beach 03908. Built as a summer boarding house in 1905 (and Dan and Danielle Duffy's family home since the 1960s), it is now a B&B with great ocean views. Four rooms share two baths, especially suited to small groups. It's within walking distance of Short Sands Beach and Nubble Lighthouse. This is a find for people without cars since the Duffys pick up from the bus stop in Portsmouth. No smoking and no children under 15, please. $59 double, in-season, $49 off-season; includes continental breakfast.

The Moorelowe (363-2526), York Harbor 03911. Open June to mid-August. A fading phenomenon: a genuine old-fashioned guest house, right in the middle of the village of York Harbor, within walking distance of the beach. Don't expect breakfast or fancy public rooms but the six guest rooms are fine; $45 with private bath. Proprietor F. Kenneth Day (aged 89) knows more about York Harbor history than anyone.

DINING OUT   Cape Neddick Inn and Gallery (363-2899), Route 1, Cape Neddick. Open year-round for dinner and Sunday brunch; closed Monday and Tuesday from Columbus Day to mid-June. When a fire damaged this dining landmark a few years back, the chef/owners rebuilt it beautifully, keeping the old facade and atmosphere but redesigning the dining area—the better to display quality artwork on loan from the nearby Walt Kuhn Gallery. Both the art and the menu change every six weeks, although roast duckling remains a year-round staple along with fish and pasta du jour. Lamb loin with Dijon mustard and Swiss chard sauce baked in phyllo and broiled haddock with sesame oyster hollandaise are examples. The desserts are spectacular. Reservations suggested. Entrées: $16–$23.

Cap'n Simeon's Galley (439-3655), Route 103, Pepperrell Cove. Open year-round for lunch and dinner; closed Tuesdays. A very special place with one of the best water views of any Maine restaurant. You enter through the original Frisbee Store (the building is said to date back to 1680; the store opened in 1828) to a spacious dining area with picture windows overlooking the cove and beyond to Portsmouth Harbor. Seafood is the specialty. Entrées run $5.95–$7.95.

The York Harbor Inn (363-5119), Route 1A, York Harbor. Open year-round for lunch and dinner; also Sunday brunch. Four pleasant dining rooms, most with views of water across the road. The menu is large. At lunch you might begin with a cup of seafood chowder (studded with shrimp, scallops, and crabmeat as well as haddock: $3.95) or try the shrimp and spinach salad ($4.95) or mussels Provençale ($4.95). The mussels are $5.50 as a dinner appetizer, and entrées run $13.50 (for vegetable strudel) to $22.95 for Yorkshire lobster supreme.

Dockside Dining Room (363-2628), Harris Island, York Harbor. Open late May through Columbus Day except Mondays; otherwise open for lunch and dinner. Docking facilities, glass-walled, overlooking York Harbor. Specializing in seafood (from $9.95 for broiled scrod to $15.95 for scallops and lobster pie) and roast stuffed duckling ($10.95); light lunches such as "Crabby English" (crab on English muffin) or lobster salad on a croissant.

Cape Neddick Lobster Pound (363-5471), Route 1A (Shore Road), Cape Neddick. Open April through December for dinner only. Situated at the mouth of a tidal river, it is a modern, shingled building with the look of always having been there. Besides lobster and clams there are tempters such as bouillabaisse or baked sole with Maine shrimp, crab, cheddar, and lemon stuffing or smoked trout with herb mayonnaise. Moderate to expensive.

Pipers Grill & Oyster Bar (363-8196), Route 1, York Corner. Open for lunch and dinner Monday through Saturday; also for Sunday brunch. Mesquite-grilled burgers and gourmet pizzas are the luncheon specialties, and the dinner menu is equally trendy—maybe soft-shell crabs with pesto and corn cakes. Entrées run $11–$13.

Stage Neck Inn (363-3850), Stage Neck Road, York Harbor. Open year-round for breakfast, lunch, and dinner. We find the crystal and the French provincial chairs with blue velvet seats a shade pretentious; but the view of rocks and sea is splendid, and we assume some people enjoy dining on baked stuffed lobster in this ambience. Reservations required. The top dinner entrée is $27.50.

Warren's Lobster House (439-1630), 1 Water Street, Kittery. Open year-round; lunch, dinner, and Sunday brunch; docking facilities. A low-ceilinged, knotty-pine dining room overlooking the Piscataqua

River and Portsmouth, NH, beyond. An old dining landmark with 1940s decor. The salad bar is famous, and the fish is fresh and fine, served both fried and broiled. Baked stuffed sole is $10.25 and scallops and shrimp Alfredo is $12.25; shore dinners vary with "market price."

The Lobster Barn (363-4721), Route 1, York. Open year-round for lunch and dinner. A pubby, informal dining room with wooden booths and a full menu with specialties such as scallop and shrimp pie earn this place top marks from locals. In summer lobster dinners (in the rough) are served under a tent out back. Moderate.

Bill Foster's Downeast Lobster and Clambake (363-3255), Route 1A between York Village and York Harbor. July through Labor Day regularly scheduled clambakes are staged in a weather-proofed pavilion. The clams and lobsters are cooked in seaweed, served with hot dogs, corn, and watermelon and folk music. By reservation only.

EATING OUT   **The Goldenrod** (363-2621), York Beach. Open Memorial Day to Labor Day. In business since 1896, one of the best family restaurants in New England; same menu all day 8–11, served up at time-polished wooden tables in a vast, old dining room with an old-style soda fountain. Famous saltwater taffy kisses cooked and pulled in the windows. Homemade ice cream and yogurt, good sandwiches (cream cheese and bacon is still just $2.35), generous hot plates; reasonable prices.

Chauncey Creek Lobster Pound (439-1030), Chauncey Creek Road, Kittery Point. Open during summer only, located off the beaten track (take the turnoff for Fort Foster Park just north of Pepperrell Cove), beloved by regulars, one of the better old-fashioned pounds left in Maine. Lobster in rolls and in the rough; steamed clams and mussels are the specialty. There is also a raw bar. Inexpensive to moderate.

Rick's All Season Restaurant (363-5584), 240 York Street (next to Cumberland Farms, middle of York Village). Open from early morning to 2:30 in the afternoon except Wednesday, Thursday when it's open for dinner. A find. Cheap, good, friendly. The breakfast special is $1.75, the chowder is homemade, the beer-batter haddock dinner is $5.95, the chili burger comes in a bowl (it's hot), and the cheesecake is delicious. There's also a pub side.

Bob's Clam Hut (439-4233), Route 1, Kittery. Open year-round. The best fried clams on the strip. Here since 1956 and now finally has indoor seating.

Surf 'n' Turf, Route 1A, York Beach. Seasonal. The appeal is the location: smack in the center of Long Sands beach with picnic tables outside, picture windows in. We had the worst tuna salad sandwich of our lives here, but the fried clams looked OK.

Pie in the Sky Bakery (363-2656), Route 1, Cape Neddick. Open Monday through Saturday except January; hours vary off-season. The purple house at the corner of River Road is filled with delicious smells and irresistible muffins, pies, tortes, and breads all baked here by John and Nancy Stern.

Weathervane (439-0330), Route 1, Kittery. One in a chain of sure-formula fish houses: pleasant atmosphere, fresh fish and seafood at reasonable prices, beer (including one on-tap). Try the fried smelt dinner, fried calamari, or broiled swordfish tips and haddock for a refreshing alternative to lobster. There are also landlubbers' specials and children's plates. Entrées run $2.99–$19.95. No credit cards.

ENTERTAINMENT   Hackmatack Playhouse (698-1807), in Berwick presents summer-stock performances most evenings; Thursday matinees.

York Beach Theater (363-2074), Beach Street. First-run movies.

SELECTIVE SHOPPING   Kittery Trading Post (439-2700), Route 1, Kittery. A local institution since 1926. T-shirts defiantly asking, "L.L. Who?"—once the store's most popular item—are no longer sold. You-know-who objected. But the sprawling store is always jammed with shoppers in search of sportswear, shoes, children's clothing, firearms, and fishing or camping gear. The summer-end sales are legendary, and many items are routinely discounted.

Williams Dry Goods Store, York Village (opposite firehouse). A good small-town shop for the basics you forgot to bring: socks, children's clothing, sweaters, and the like.

Art galleries: **Firehouse Gallery** (363-5452), Kittery. Open noon to 5 daily except Mondays and weekends in spring and fall.

York Art Association Gallery (363-4049 or 363-2918), Route 1A, York Harbor. Annual July art show, films, and workshops.

Walt Kuhn Gallery (363-4139). Open May to December, Wednesday to Sunday 10–4. A gallery created from the estate of artist Walt Kuhn, known for his paintings of solemn clowns and show-business portraits and also known as one of the organizers of the 1913 New York Armory show. Changing exhibits in addition to selected works by Kuhn and sculptures on the 100-acre grounds. (Also see Walks [Cape Neddick Park].)

Outlet malls: At this writing there are more than 100 discount stores within one and a quarter miles on Route 1 in Kittery. They represent a mix of clothing, household furnishings, gifts, and basics. All purport to offer savings of at least 20 percent on retail prices, many up to 70 percent. Note that the Kittery Trading Post (described above) is the original anchor store of this strip.

Maine Outlet Mall. Open daily 9:30–9:00 in summer (10–6 on Sundays), 9:30–6 (except Thursday through Saturday when it's still open until 9:30) in winter. Largest of the outlet malls with 24 shops, including Samuel Robert (tailored, top-drawer clothing for men and women), Timberland (men's and women's shoes and hiking boots), Rippoffs (name-brand casual menswear), Warnaco (sportswear and knitwear), and Mikaska (china, glassware, and gifts).

Tidewater Outlet Mall. Route 1 (north of the Maine Outlet Mall). Individual store hours vary slightly but generally conform with Maine Outlet Mall hours. This is a small but quality shopping center, worth the stop for Lenox china and crystal; also for North Country Leather (luggage, wallets, belts, and briefcases—quality stuff made nearby in East Rochester, New Hampshire).

Kittery Outlet Center, Route 1 (across from the Maine Outlet Mall). Roughly the same hours. Stores include Mighty-Mac (own-brand parkas, rain gear, and outerwear made in Gloucester, Massachusetts), Royal Doulton Shoppe (fine china and toby mugs), Totes (own-brand compressible raincoats, hats, boots, umbrellas, and luggage), Van Heusen (shirts for men and women), and Le Sportsac (own-brand lightweight luggage, totes, and accessories).

Dansk Square Outlet. Route 1 (south of the Maine Outlet Mall). Dansk is the anchor store here and a great place to shop for gifts: kitchenware, china, bowls, and plastic ware.

Maine Gate Outlets, Route 1. Corning is the big name here (Pyrex cookware, dinnerware). There are also the Kitchen Collection and the Leather Loft (stocking handbags, belts, and briefcases).

Kittery Factory Stores, Route 1. Bass Shoe is the anchor of a dozen stores here, including Hathaway (shirts and sportswear), Black & Decker (tools and gadgets), American Tourister (luggage), and a number of quality clothing stores.

Other outlets in the strip include Dexter Shoe (Maine-made footwear; note that Dexter has another shoe-box-shaped log cabin farther north on Route 1 in York), Dunham (also quality boots and shoes), Polo, Ralph Lauren, J. Crew, and Crate & Barrel.

SPECIAL EVENTS   June: **Strawberry Festival,** South Berwick.

July: **Independence Day celebrations,** York: parades, cannon salutes, militia encampment, crafts and food fair, picnic, and dinner. **Band concerts,** Wednesday evenings at Short Sands Pavillion, York Beach. **Old York Designers' Show House** sponsored by the Old York Historical Society. **York Days Celebration** (last days of month, see August): raffle, puppet shows, and skits.

August: **York Days Celebration** (beginning of the month): flower show, church supper, concerts, square dances, parade, and sand castle contest. **Seacoast Crafts Fair** (late in the month).

September: **House Tours. Eliot Festival Days** (late September).

October: **Harvest Fest,** York Village (last weekend): an oxen roast, ox-cart races, hay and horse rides, militia encampment, music, and live entertainment.

November: **Cooking Olympics.**

December: **Christmas Open House Tours. Kittery Christmas Parade and Tree Lighting** (first Saturday).

Ogunquit and Wells

Ogunquit and Wells are beach towns. Nowhere else in Maine will you find as much sand—more than seven scarcely interrupted miles from the entrance to Ogunquit Beach to the eastern end of Wells Beach and more sand beyond.

Named for the English cathedral town, Wells was incorporated in 1653. Ogunquit was technically part of Wells until 1980, but Ogunquit seceded in spirit long before that, establishing itself as a summer magnet for top artists and actors in the 1920s—the decade during which both the town's three-mile tongue of beach and dune, and the mile-long Marginal Way (an exceptional seaside path) were declared public. Ogunquit and Wells together continue to satisfy an amazing mix of visitors: white- and blue-collar, Canadians and New Yorkers, yuppies and families, retirees and gays.

Hotels in both towns began to appear in the 1880s. The first guests from New York and Philadelphia arrived by the Boston & Maine railroad, and residents of nearer cities began coming by the Atlantic Shore Line trolleys in 1907. Some very grand hotels and many splendid shingled cottages appeared along the shore in Ogunquit, and more modest cottages soon lined the beach-side streets in Wells.

"Motor Courts" mushroomed along Route 1 in the 1920s, and some of the best are still in the business of catering to families. Of course, they are lost among the many resort motels and condo complexes that now line the Route 1 Ogunquit/Wells "strip." Unlovely as it appears from the road, this lineup still holds great appeal for families. Thanks to the lay of the land, most of the lodgings on the water side of Route 1 actually have water views.

In the village of Ogunquit most of the old wooden hotels were razed during the 1960s and replaced by luxury motels. The 1980s brought condos, more motels, high-priced restaurants, many more art galleries and boutiques. Luckily it also brought the trolleys to solve the travel crunch at Perkins Cove and the beaches.

There are a dozen open-sided trolleys which circulate up and down Route 1—eight in Ogunquit connecting with four in Wells so patrons can access both town beaches. In summer they ferry as many as 12,000 people per day, shuttling constantly between the beaches, Perkins Cove, and lodging places to connect with the trolleys shuttling up and

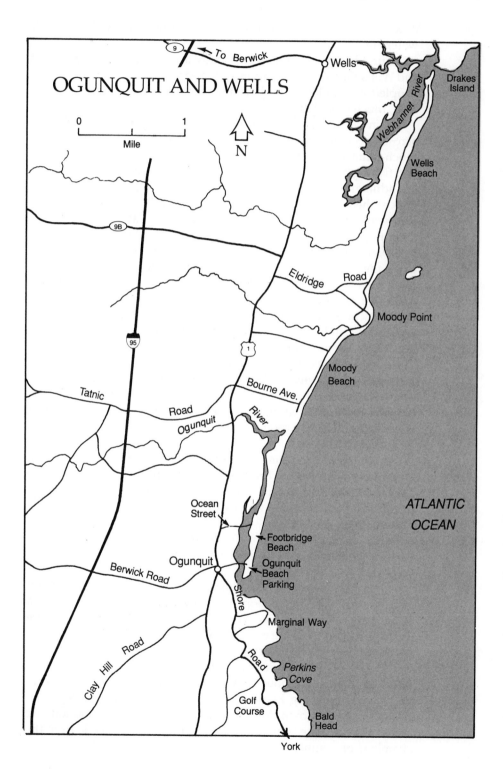

OGUNQUIT AND WELLS

To Berwick

Wells

Drakes Island

Webhannet River

Wells Beach

0   1
Mile

N

Eldridge   Road

Moody Point

Moody Beach

Tatnic

Bourne Ave.

Road

Ogunquit   River

ATLANTIC OCEAN

Ocean Street

Footbridge Beach

Ogunquit

Ogunquit Beach Parking

Berwick Road

Shore

Marginal Way

Road

Clay Hill Road

Perkins Cove

Golf Course

Bald Head

York

down between the Route 1 shops and restaurants and the Wells waterfront.

Natural beauty remains surprisingly accessible in both Ogunquit and Wells. Given the vast expanse of sand you can always find a little-peopled spot, and Wells harbors more than 4,000 acres of conservation land, much of it webbed with trails (see Walks).

Perkin's Cove, a man-made anchorage with a draw-footbridge across its center and a huddle of weathered fish shacks alongside, is a much-painted inlet and is the departure point for the area's excursion and fishing boats and sailboat cruises. It's right up there with the top of Cadillac Mountain for Maine's "must-see" places. Now visitors can park at their lodging place or in a public lot and come by trolley, and then walk back to the village via the Marginal Way.

Ogunquit Beach may just be the most beautiful in Maine. There is surf, soft sand, and space for kite flying, and there is a sheltered strip along the mouth of the Ogunquit River for toddlers. On weekends a tidal wave of day-tripping Bostonians spreads over the beach and eddies through Perkins Cove, but it recedes on Sunday evenings. Both Ogunquit and Wells are relatively peaceful midweek in summer and especially delightful in September and October.

GUIDANCE   Chamber of Commerce (646-2939), Box 2289, Ogunquit 03907. The information center (646-5533) on Route 1, just south of Ogunquit Village, is open Memorial Day through Labor Day, Monday to Saturday 9–5, Sunday 10–2; through Columbus Day, Friday to Sunday. It's the place to check for vacancies, menus, excursions, and events; it even has men's and ladies' rooms. During the off-season, phone the town office: 646-5139.

Wells Chamber of Commerce (646-2451), PO Box 356, Wells 04090. Open daily 9–5, until 9 on Fridays, June through fall foliage. Also open 10–5 the rest of the year, Tuesday through Saturday. Look for the information center on the water side of Route 1 in South Wells near Elmere Road.

GETTING THERE   By car: Coming north on I-95 take Exit 1 (York) and drive up Route 1 to the village of Ogunquit. Coming south on I-95 take Exit 2 (Wells).

By taxi: The nearest that **Greyhound** comes is Portsmouth, NH, but once you are here, you can hop the trolley to almost anywhere in town so it makes sense to take **Wells Taxi** (646-1126) or **Ledgemere Transportation** (limo service: 646-5502) from the bus stop in Portsmouth or the airport in Portland.

GETTING AROUND   During summer months eight open-sided trolleys make frequent stops throughout the village of Ogunquit, Perkins Cove, at the beach, and along Route 1. They connect with the trolleys that circulate up and down Route 1 and through the beach and lodging areas in Wells. Fare is nominal. Trolley maps are available from the chambers of commerce.

PARKING   Park and walk or take the trolley. In summer this is no place to drive. There are at least seven public lots; rates from $4–$6 per day. There is also free parking (two-hour limit) on Route 1 across from the Leavitt Theatre just north of Ogunquit Square or adjacent to Cumberland Farms. Parking at the main entrance to Ogunquit Beach itself is $2 per hour. (For more on beach parking see Beaches.) In Wells parking at the five public lots is $5 per day, and monthly permits are available from the town office.

MEDICAL EMERGENCY   Ambulance/Rescue Squad (646-5111), town of Ogunquit.

York Hospital (363-4321), 24-hour emergency, Lindsay Road, York Village.

In Wells the ambulance is 646-5521, and you may be nearer to **Webber Hospital** (283-3663), 1 Mountain Road, Biddeford.

TO SEE AND DO   See Beaches below.

Museum at Historic First Church (646-5325), Wells. Open July and August, Wednesdays 1–4. Opposite Wells Plaza; basic memorabilia.

Ogunquit's two most prominent art galleries qualify as museums. (For more galleries see Selective Shopping.)

Museum of Art of Ogunquit (646-4909), Shore Road, Ogunquit. Open late June through Labor Day, 10:30–5 daily; Sunday 1:30–5. Free. Built superbly of local stone and wood with enough glass to let in the beauty of the cove it faces, the museum displays the strong, bright oils of Henry Strater, other one-time locals such as Reginald Marsh; changing exhibits.

The Barn Gallery (646-5370), Shore Road and Bourne Lane, Ogunquit. Open June through Columbus Day weekend, Monday to Saturday 10–5 and Sunday 1–5. Showcases work by members of the Ogunquit Art Association; also stages frequent workshops, films, and concerts.

Perkins Cove. This is probably Maine's most painted fishing cove with some 40 restaurants and shops now housed in weathered fish shacks. It is departure point for the area's excursion and fishing boats, based beside the famous draw-footbridge. Forget trying to land one of the few parking places here in summer. Visitors can park at their lodging places or in a public lot and come by trolley or on foot via the Marginal Way (see Walks).

BEACHES   *In Ogunquit:*   Three-mile-long **Ogunquit Beach** can be approached three ways: (1) The most popular way is from the foot of Beach Street. There are boardwalk snacks, changing facilities, and toilets, and it is here that the beach forms a tongue between the ocean and the Ogunquit River (parking in the lot here is $2 per hour). (2) The **Footbridge Beach** access (take Ocean Street off Route 1 north of the village) offers rest rooms and is less crowded (parking is $6 per day). (3) The **Moody Beach** entrance is off Route 1 at Eldridge Street in Wells (parking is $6 per day). Be sure to park in the lot provided and to walk west onto Ogunquit Beach; Moody Beach is now private above the high-water mark.

In Wells: Parking is $5 per day, and monthly permits are available from the town office in the municipal building, Route 1.

Wells Beach. Limited free parking right in the middle of the village of Wells Beach. Wooden casino and boardwalk, clam shacks, clean public toilets, a cluster of motels, concrete benches—a gathering point for older people who sit enjoying the view of the wide, smooth beach.

Drakes Island. Take Drakes Island Road off Route 1. There are three small parking areas on this land spit lined with private cottages.

FOR CHILDREN   **Wells Auto Museum** (646-9064), Wells. Open daily mid-June to Labor Day, 10–5; weekends until mid-September. More than 80 cars ranging from 1900 to 1963 plus nickelodeons, toys, and bicycles. $3 adult, $2 child.

Wells Beach Mini-Golf, next to Big Daddy's Ice Cream, Route 1, Wells. Open daily in-season, 10–10.

Wonder Mountain, Route 1, Wells. A mini-golf mountain, complete with waterfalls, adjoins Outdoor World.

Sea-Vu Mini Golf is another Route 1 option in Wells.

GREEN SPACE   **Wells National Estuarine Research Reserve** (646-1555), Laudholm Road (marked from Route 1), Wells. This 1,600-acre tract offers 4 miles of coast line and an extensive system of nature trails. *Estuarine,* by the way, means whatever is formed by an estuary (the spot where ocean tides meet freshwater currents). Headquarters are at **Laudholm Farm,** a former estate, owned by the Lord family from 1881 until 1986 (George C. Lord was president of the Boston & Maine). It includes the old summer mansion and farm buildings, meadows, and two barrier beaches at the mouth of the Little River. The grounds are open year-round, and guided trail walks are offered daily in summer; also on spring and fall Sundays. Pamphlet guides to the trails are also available. The farm is marked from Route 1; it's east on Laudholm Farm Road; turn at the Tallwood Motor Court. Phone 646-4521 or 646-4522 or write for a brochure: PO Box 1007, Wells 04090.

The Reserve also includes a segment of the **Rachel Carson National Wildlife Refuge** (operated by United States Fish and Wildlife Service), off Route 9, subtly marked. There are 1,600 acres in Wells, but the nature trail is just a mile long—a loop through a white pine forest and along the Little River through a salt marsh area. Maps and guides are available from the resident manager's office near the entrance to the refuge along Route 9.

WALKS   **Wells Harbor.** A pleasant walk along a granite jetty and a good fishing spot.

Old Trolley Trail, an interesting nature walk and cross-country ski trail, begins on Pine Hill Road North, Ogonquit. There is also Mount Agamenticus, a defunct ski area and the highest hill on the Atlantic between Florida and Bar Harbor. Take the Big A access road off Agamenticus Road.

Marginal Way. In 1923 Josiah Chase gave Ogunquit this windy path along the ocean. A farmer from the town of York, just south, Chase had driven his cattle around rocky Israel's Head each summer to pasture on the marsh grass in Wells, just to the north. Over the years he bought land here and there until eventually he owned the whole promontory. He then sold off sea-view lots at a tidy profit and donated the actual ocean frontage to the town, thus preserving his own right-of-way. There is very limited parking at the mini-lighthouse on Israel's Head, midway.

Laudholm Farm, Laudholm Road (marked from Route 1), Wells. Offers frequent guided trail walks (see Wells National Estuarine Research Reserve under Green Space).

BOATING   **Wells Harbor Marina** (646-9087) rents sailboats and motorboats.

BOAT EXCURSIONS FROM PERKINS COVE   *Finestkind* (646-5227). Scenic cruises to Nubble Light, cocktail cruises, and "lobstering trips" (watch lobster traps hauled, hear about lobstering).

Ugly Ann '76 (646-7202). Half- and full-day deep-sea fishing trips with Captain Ken Young, Sr.

The Bunny Clark (646-5575). Half- and full-day deep-sea fishing trips with Captain Tim Tower.

BICYCLING   Bike rentals are available from **Movin' On** (646-2810), Route 1 in Ogunquit, and from **Wheels & Waves** (646-5774) in Wells.

FISHING   Tackle and bait can be rented at Wells Harbor. The obvious fishing spots are the municipal dock and harbor jetties. There is surf casting near the mouth of the Mousam River.

SAILING   *The Silverling* (361-1925), a 42-foot wooden Hinckley sloop, sails out of Perkins Cove on regularly scheduled two-hour cruises. $25, minimum six people; also available for half- and full-day charters.

TENNIS   Three public courts in Ogunquit. Inquire at **Dunaway Center** (646-9361).

Wells Recreation Area, Route 9A, Wells. Four courts.

Congdon's Tennis Courts, Route 1, Wells. Four lighted courts.

RESORT   **Cliff House** (361-1000), PO Box 2274, Ogunquit 03907. Open March to early December. The most dramatically sited hotel on the Maine coast, the Cliff House has made the most impressive comeback of any family-owned resort in New England. The tower-topped, mansard-roofed Cliffscape Building, opened in 1990, is now the centerpiece of the 162-room, 70-acre resort. The new building's multi-tiered lobby and dining rooms make the most of their oceanside roost, and the atmosphere is a rare blend of new amenities (including an indoor lap pool) and family antiques. It's all the work of Kathryn Weare, a great-granddaughter worthy of Elsie Jane Weare, the indomitable lady who opened the Cliff House in 1872.

No other hotel illustrates the ups and downs of New England's resort history quite as well as the Cliff House. It was the news that the Boston & Maine Railroad would be adding a spur line to York that prompted Elsie Jane to persuade her sea-captain husband to invest all their money in buying Bald Hill Cliff. Her brother built the hotel with wood from the family lots, milled in their own sawmill. The clean rooms, fine food (provided from the adjacent Weare Farm), fresh air, and dramatic location—all for $6 a week, including three meals a day—soon lured the Biddles of Philadelphia, the Havermeyers of New York, and the Cabots and Lodges of Boston.

The family-run resort continued to maintain its status throughout the Roaring Twenties and shaky 1930s, but World War II about did it in. The resort was literally drafted—as a radar station, keeping a 24-hour vigil for Nazi submarines. When the Weares were finally permitted back on their property, they found it in shambles. Discouraged, Charles Weare placed an ad in a 1946 edition of the Wall Street Journal: "For sale. 144 rooms. 90 acres, over 2,500' ocean frontage for just $50,000."

There were no takers. So Charles turned the property over to his son Maurice, who went with the times and shaved off the top two floors of the original inn, virtually transforming it into a "resort motel"—which is what it was until 1990. Rates range from $75 for a motel-like unit overlooking the ocean to $265 for a new suite; rooms with an ocean view in Cliffscape are $85–$160. These rates do not include meals, but a variety of packages are offered. Facilities include outdoor and indoor pools, a sauna and Jacuzzi, a game room, tennis courts, and a shuttle into the village and to the beach. Guests have privileges at the private 9-hole golf club across the road.

RESORT MOTELS   Our usual format places inns before motels, but some of Ogunquit's leading resorts have replaced their old hotel buildings with motel units.

Sparhawk (646-5562), Shore Road, Box 936, Ogunquit 03907. Open early April to late October. Billing itself as "Ogunquit's leading oceanfront resort since 1900," the Sparhawk is not the grand, brown-shingled hotel from which it is descended. A continental breakfast is served every morning in one-story Sparhawk Hall, a place where you may also play cards and games or arrange dinner and theater reservations. The large parking lot is now the centerpiece of the sprawling, low-profile complex. You can choose a motel unit with a view of the beach, a suite, or an apartment; 10 units are in the old inn, which was once the Barbara Dean. Facilities include a pool and a tennis court. One-week minimum stay, July 4 to August 23. Deluxe.

Aspinquid (646-7072), Box 2408, Beach Street, Ogunquit 03907. Open mid-March through October. A picture of the old Aspinquid hangs above the check-in counter of this condo-style complex just across the bridge from Ogunquit Beach. Built in 1971 by the owners of the old hotel, the two-story clusters still look spanking new and ultramodern. They are nicely designed and range in size from motel units to two-room apartments; all have two double beds, phones, and TVs; most have kitchenettes. Facilities include a pool, a lighted tennis court, a sauna, and a spa. Dining packages available with the Beachcrest Inn across the street, also owned by the Andrews family. $90–$110 for a regular room, $156–$185 in high season; $60–$65 for a room and $90–$105 for suites, off-season.

INNS AND BED & BREAKFASTS **Beachmere** (646-2021 or 800-336-3983), Box 2340, Ogunquit 03907. Open late March to early December. Sited on the Marginal Way with water views, this fine old mansion has a motel annex; there are also rooms in Mayfair and Bullfrog cottages, a half mile away on Israel's Head Road. Three of the rooms in the old mansion have working fireplaces, and most have decks and efficiency units. The spacious grounds overlook Ogunquit Beach, and smaller beaches are a few minutes' walk. One-week minimum stay during high season. Each unit is priced separately, from $595 per week for an efficiency accommodating two to $1,015 per week in high season; daily rates range from $55–$100 in shoulder season and from $40–$75 off-season.

Seafair Inn (646-2181), PO Box 1221, Ogunquit 03907. Open mid-April though October. A spacious 1890 home in the middle of the village with an elegant living room and 18 rooms, most with private baths (4 on the top floor share); efficiency units tucked away in back. A continental breakfast is served in the dining room or sun porch. $40 with shared bath off-season, $93 for efficiency units in-season; $80–$85 for a room with private bath in-season; continental breakfast included.

Marginal Way House and Motel (646-8801; 363-6566 in winter), Box 697, 8 Wharf Lane, Ogunquit 03907. Open late April through October. Ed and Brenda Blake have owned this delightful complex for more than 20 years. Just a short walk from the beach and really in the middle of the village, it is hidden down a back, water-side lane. There are old-fashioned bedrooms with private baths in the inn itself; also six standard motel rooms in a small, shingled water-side building and six efficiency apartments (one or two bedrooms). The landscaped grounds have an unbeatable ocean view. From $38 per room off-season in the motel; $64–$98 high season in the inn; $106 in the motel and $840–$1,015 per week for an apartment.

Morning Dove (646-3891), PO Box 1940, 30 Bourne Lane, Ogunquit 03907. On a quiet side street off Shore Road, within walking distance of everything, a carefully restored 1860s farmhouse with six unusually nice, antiques-furnished rooms. Breakfast is served on the porch, and there is wine upon arrival, chocolate on your pillow at bedtime. $55–$110 per room.

Rose Cottage (646-2261), PO Box 2092, 7 Bourne Lane, Ogunquit 03907. This charming house was once part of the Dunelawn estate (since condoed) by the Ogunquit River. It's now the other side of the village, within walking distance of the Marginal Way and Perkins Cove. It offers five rooms, ranging from $70 (for a single with shared bath) to $85.50 for a large double with private bath. Rates include breakfast. Innkeepers Larry and Marcia Smith also own Ogunquit's Camera Shop.

The Admiral's Inn (646-7093), PO Box 2241, 70 South Main Street, Ogunquit 03907. Open year-round. A big house on Route 1 just south of the village of Ogunquit (there's a trolley stop across the road). There are six old-fashioned guest rooms with shared baths ($32–$65 depending on room and season); also four motel-style units ($42–$75), four efficiencies ($48–$92), and one studio apartment ($52–$98). There's an outdoor pool in back. Breakfast is included in in-season rates, and children are welcome.

Blue Shutters Inn (646-2163 or 800-633-9550), PO Box 655, 6 Beachmere Place, Ogunquit 03907. Open April to Columbus Day weekend. Centrally located off Shore Road, a large, old house with five guest rooms, two with fireplaces; also six efficiencies in a two-story unit out back. Rooms are simple but comfortable.

Ye Olde Perkins Place (361-1119), Box 324, Shore Road (south of Perkins Cove), Ogunquit 03907. Open late June to Labor Day. Overlooking the ocean, a 1718 homestead with six rooms, three in an annex. This is a great spot, away from the village but within walking distance of a pebble beach. $55–$65 per room; coffee, juice, and muffins included. No credit cards.

Beachcrest Inn (646-2156), PO Box 673, Beach Street, Ogunquit 03907. Open year-round except January to mid-February. A small 1880s summer hotel with eight inviting rooms, all with small refrigerators, many with TVs, private baths, and water views. Within walking distance of both the beach and the village. $55–$90 per room, depending on room and season. Continental breakfast (delivered in a basket to your room in the morning) included.

Black Lantern Inn (646-4529), 89 Shore Road, Ogunquit 03907. A time-worn but comfortable old hotel with 22 guest rooms, patronized by actors at the Ogunquit Playhouse. Within walking distance of both Perkins Cove and the beach. Some shared, some private baths; all rooms have direct dial phones and color TV. Continental breakfast included. Moderate.

Yardarm Village Inn (646-7006), PO Box 773, 142 Shore Road, Ogunquit 03907. Open May through October, weather permitting. Comfortable rooms for two and suites for four in a rambling nineteenth-century house within walking distance of Perkins Cove. Amenities include cable TV, refrigerators, and air-conditioning. $59 (for two) to $89 (for four), coffee and blueberry muffins included.

Wells Harbor

The Haven (646-4194), RR 1, Box 2207, Church Street, Wells 04090. Open Memorial Day to Columbus Day. A former Catholic church in Wells Beach is now an attractive, informal bed & breakfast. There is plenty of common space for putting together puzzles and reading. All six guest rooms have private baths, skylights. Walls throughout are decorated with great graphics. Coffee and muffins served in the morning; 400 feet to the beach. $69 for a dougle room with private bath, $98 for a two-room suite in high-season; much less off-season.

MOTELS   **Riverside Motel** (646-2741), PO Box 2244, Shore Road, Ogunquit 03907. Open late April through late October. Overlooking Perkins Cove, a trim, friendly place with 41 units; rooms also in the 1874 house. The property has been in Harold Staples' family for more than 100 years. All rooms have color TV and a full bath, and all overlook the cove; continental breakfast is offered in the lobby. $50–$100, depending on season and location of room.

Norseman Motor Inn (646-7024), Box 896, Beach Street, Ogunquit 03907. Open late March through October. Unbeatable location right on the beach; 95 units. $50–$130, depending on room location and season.

Above Tide Inn (646-7454), Beach Street, Ogunquit 03907. Open May to Columbus Day weekend. A nine-unit, two-story motel right on the Ogunquit River at the beach. Moderate.

Forbes Wells Beach Resort (646-2831), PO Box 99, Wells Beach 04090. Open year-round. The Forbes family seem to own about all the commercial property there is to own in the middle of Wells Beach: eight separate buildings including a restaurant, the Driftwinds Motel, Wells Beach Motor Inn, Beach Front Lodge, and Ledgeview Inn, a total of 124 motel units. Rates change every few weeks throughout the summer: $75–$125 during the highest high-season compared to $35–$60 in winter. There's an indoor pool and jacuzzi as well as the expanse of beach across the street.

Seagull Motor Inn (646-5164), Route 1, Wells 04090. Open late June to mid-October. Twenty-four motel units, 24 cottages, a pool, a playground, and lawn games on 23 acres. Having spent four summer vacations here as a child (40 years ago), Chris Tree is happy to report that the place is still essentially the same solid value, with a loyal following. Rentals are per week, moderate.

Wonderview Motor Village and Housekeeping Cottages (646-2304), Route 1, Wells 04090 Open May through Columbus Day weekend. Twelve units (eight cottages and four motel units) are scattered on 2 acres; screened porches. Moderate.

COTTAGES   We have noted just a few among the dozens of cottage, condominium and motel complexes that line Route 1. The unusually helpful Wells Chamber of Commerce keeps track of vacancies in these and in many private cottages down along the ocean.

Dunes (646-2612), Box 917, Route 1, Ogunquit 03907. Open mid-

May to mid-October. Set way back from the highway, fronting on the Ogunquit River (offering direct access to Ogunquit Beach by rowboat at high tide and on foot at low tide). The 36 units include 19 that are old-style, Maine classics—cottages with white-and-green trim—scattered over 12 well-kept acres. Most have fireplaces. Cottages are $54–$76 off-season; $75–$110 in-season (June 22 to September 4). Two-week minimum stay in July and August. Rooms are $45–$65 double off-season, $64–$100 in-season.

Cottage in the Lane Motor Lodge (646-7903), Drakes Island Road, Wells 04090. There are 11 housekeeping cottages, built one at a time over the past 30 years, all facing landscaped grounds under the pines (an artistic play structure forms the centerpiece); salt marsh beyond. It's a three-quarter-mile walk or bike ride to the beach. Rentals are per week, moderate.

DINING OUT   Arrow's (646-7175), Berwick Road, Ogunquit. Dinner 6–10 late April through October. Considered one of the best—possibly THE best restaurant in Maine. It may just be the most expensive, too, but we've heard no one complain about the price. A 1765 farmhouse is the setting for nouvelle-inspired dishes such as bamboo-steamed Maine lobster with a vegetable role, sugar snap peas and red curry sauce or plank-roasted Atlantic salmon with fiddleheads, tarragon vinaigrette, and green beans. The chef/owners are Mark Gaier, former executive chef at Ogunquit's formerly famous (sadly defunct) Whistling Oyster in Perkins Cove, and Clark Frasier, a Californian who studied cooking in China. Entrées begin at $19.95.

Tavern at Clay Hill Farm (646-2272), Agamenticus Road (north of Ogunquit Village). Open year-round for dinner but closed Monday and Tuesday in winter. A gracious old farmhouse with specialties such as roast leg of lamb in sauce with fresh mint and poached salmon. Piano while dining, dancing late; appropriate dress requested. From $13 for eggplant Augusta to $20 for filet mignon.

Jonathan's (646-4777), 2 Bourne Lane, Ogunquit. Open for dinner nightly year-round, for breakfast daily in summer; otherwise just on weekends and for lunch Sunday through Friday. Now in its sixteenth season this inviting place—composed of a half-dozen different dining rooms—offers something for everyone, from vegetarian puffed pastry ($12.50) to charbroiled sirloin filet ($17.50). The chicken Dijon with Bermuda onion in a heavy cream sauce is $13.50.

Blue Water Inn (646-5559), Beach Street, Ogunquit. The water view is hard to beat, and the specialty is fish—Maho shark as well as mackerel and haddock. The haddock almondine is $12.50. Entrées run $9.95–$18.95.

Cliff House (646-5124), Bald Hill Cliff, Shore Road, Ogunquit. Open for breakfast and dinner most of the year, for lunch in July and August. The dining room is in the Cliffscape building with dramatic ocean views, and chef Matt Hinkle has been gathering awards for his chowder and imaginative entrées; the fare now represents some of the best around. Entrées run $11.95–$19.95.

Cove Garden (646-4497), Shore Road (overlooking Perkins Cove), Ogunquit. A pagoda-shaped building that has had many names and uses, currently open May Day through late September for dinner. The menu is northern Italian: fettucini, chicken Parmesan, and veal scaloppine. Entrées run $6.95–$12.95.

Ogunquit Lobster Pound (646-2516), Route 1 (north of the village). Open Mother's Day through Columbus Day weekend for lunch and dinner. More than 40 years of ownership by the Hancock family, one of the few pounds where you can still pick out your own lobster and watch as it's plunged into the big stone pit. Dine either in the rustic log building or outside on swinging, wood-canopied tables. Beer and wine are available along with cheeseburgers and steak, but lobsters and clams are what the place is about. Try the lobster stew and deep-dish blueberry pie. Unfortunately prices are what the market will bear: $9.50 per pound for lobster, slaw and baked potato extra.

Gypsy Sweethearts (646-7021), 18 Shore Road, Ogunquit Village. Open May to October. Breakfast all morning, dinner until 10. Fine dining in a charming old house. A great place for a leisurely breakfast on a rainy morning. The menu ranges through a variety of imaginative egg dishes and usually includes blueberry crêpes with sour cream. For dinner try fillet of sole à la meunière or chicken breast stuffed with spinach, mushrooms, and shallots in Boursin sauce. Upstairs bar, wine list. $12.95–$19.95.

Old Village Inn (646-7088), 30 Main Street (Route 1 north of Ogunquit Square). Open for dinner most of the year; also breakfast 7–12. Five Victorian-style dining rooms, an English pub-style bar; specialties include roast duckling ($14.95) and a range of pasta dishes like seafood primavera ($16.95) and linguini Florentine with smoked ham, spinach, and mushrooms ($14.95).

Hurricane Seafood Bar (772-8059), Perkins Cove. Year-round for lunch and dinner except Tuesday. An attractive, trendy place that maximizes its ocean view; raw shellfish bar, chowders; from bar burgers to lobster in parchment paper. Jazz on Sunday; hip, young crowd. Under same ownership as Portland's Horsefeathers. Entrées $10.95–$18.95.

Valerie's (646-2476), Route 1, Ogunquit Square. Open mid-May through mid-October for lunch and dinner. More than 40 years in the same family. Sandwiches and omelets for lunch; seafood such as crabmeat-stuffed sole for dinner but always some Greek specials like *spanakopita*. Moderate.

Charlie's Restaurant (646-2632), Ogunquit Beach. Seasonal, serving dinner. Easy to overlook, but there it is in the pavilion at the beach.

The decor is simple but pleasant. Steak and seafood are the specialties. Now in its 58th season. Moderately expensive.

Roberto's Italian Cuisine (646-8131), 82 Shore Road, Ogunquit. Ogunquit's chef-owned trattoria. Chef/owner Roberto specializes in no-nonsense southern Italian dishes like veal Parmigiana, chicken Marsala, and seafood lasagna. Veal scaloppine is $16.96, and linguini with mushroom sauce is $8.25.

Grey Gull Inn (646-7501), 321 Webhannet Drive, Moody Point (Wells). Open April to December for breakfast and dinner. There are five rooms upstairs, but this is primarily a restaurant. Dining rooms maximize the water view. Specialties include fillet of sole stuffed with spinach soufflé and baked in Mornay sauce ($16.95) and Maine shrimp pie. Pastas begin at $8.50.

Litchfield's (646-5711), Route 1, Wells. Open daily for lunch and dinner. This is a favorite spot among local officianados: reliable food and good value. Even the lobster is fairly priced, served baked and stuffed as well as straight. Specialties include Aztec Chicken and prime rib as well as seafood dishes. At lunch a wide variety of sandwiches are outstanding. Dinner entrees run $8.98–$17.95

EATING OUT   Einstein's Deli Restaurant (646-5262), 2 Shore Road, Ogunquit. Open year-round for breakfast, lunch, and dinner. On the corner in Ogunquit Square, an art-deco-style eatery, a real oasis with a curvy counter, booths, downstairs rest rooms, and Albert's Café, your friendly neighborhood bar. Open 4 PM to closing. The fish 'n' chips daily special hits the spot ($2.95).

Barnacle Billy's (646-5575), Perkins Cove. Open May through mid-October, 11–11 daily. Dining room with fireplaces and deck dining overlooking boats. Order lobster at the counter and wait for a number; beer and wine. Mobbed during summer. Dinners run $9–$18.

Lobster Shack (646-2941), end of Perkins Cove. Open May through Columbus Day weekend. A genuine old-style, serious lobster-eating place since the 1940s (when it was known as Maxwell and Perkins): oilcloth-covered tables, outstanding chowder, apple pie a la mode, wine and beer. Possibly the most reasonably priced and satisfying place in town to feast on lobster.

Oarweed Cove Restaurant (646-2316), at the entrance to the Marginal Way in Perkins Cove. Open daily late June through Labor Day for lunch and dinner, weekends in spring and fall. Less crowded than Barnacle Billy's. Water view; large, ordinary dining room with seafood menu.

The Cliff House, Shore Road, Ogunquit. Light fare is served in the dramatic new lobby with its ocean views. Lunch through the afternoon.

Wing Dynasty (646-112), Route 1, Ogunquit. A welcome addition to the Route 1 strip. A pleasant, moderately priced Chinese restaurant with a large, moderately priced menu. Moo Shu chicken is just $5.95, and crispy duck with hot sauce is $8.95.

Lord's Harborside Restaurant (646-2651), Wells Harbor. Open April to November for lunch and dinner, closed Tuesdays in spring and fall. A big, ungarnished dining room with an unbeatable harbor view and a reputation for fresh fish and seafood. Lobster (fried, boiled, and baked) is the big draw. Dine between 2 and 4 for a 15 percent savings. Moderate.

Billy's Chowder House (646-7588), Mile Road, Wells. Open daily year-round, closed for lunch on Thursdays in winter. A knotty-pine and shamrock atmosphere with views of salt marsh and water out the windows. Frequently a long line in-season for seafood like baked stuffed jumbo shrimp or grilled swordfish as well as lobsters and clams. Moderate.

Fisherman's Catch (646-8780), Lower Landing Road to Wells Harbor. Open May to October, 9–9. Smaller and less crowded than Billy's Chowder House. Informal, with views of marshes from a screened porch, red-checked tablecloths, children's menu, steamers, lobster, and fried clams. Inexpensive.

Jake's Seafood (646-6771), Route 1, Bourne Avenue, Moody. Open for all three meals year-round. Specializes in good American cooking, fresh seafood, homemade ice cream.

Bull 'n' Claw (646-8467), Route 1, Wells. Open daily 8–9 in summer, from 11 AM in winter. Bills itself as "the best family-style restaurant in Maine." A large dining room with a full menu: steaks, chicken, shrimp, all-you-can-eat salad boat, all-you-can-eat breakfast buffet, refills on soft drinks, wine, beer. Moderate.

Congdon's Donuts Family Restaurant, Route 1, Wells. Open from 6:30 AM year-round, seasonal, at Wells Beach. Fresh muffins, breads, pastries, and donuts; also ice cream made on premises. Inexpensive.

Maine Diner (656-4441), Route 1, Wells. Open year-round 7–8. Family restaurant with a large menu for all three meals; beer, wine, takeout.

SNACKS **Bread & Roses Bakery** (646-4227), 28A Main Street (up an alley), Ogunquit. A pleasant source of muffins, coffee, and delectable pastries.

Big Daddy's (646-5454), Route 1, just south of the Route 9 intersection, Wells. Open mid-March to late November, 11 to 11 in season. THE best ice cream around, made on the spot in delectable flavors like chocolate peanut butter chip. Steamed hot dogs, too.

ENTERTAINMENT   **Ogunquit Playhouse** (646-5511), Route 1 (just south of Ogunquit Village). Open late June through August. Billing itself as "America's Foremost Summer Theater," this grand old summer-stock theater (now air-conditioned) opened for its first season in 1933 and continues to feature top stars in productions staged every evening during the season except Sundays. Matinees are Wednesdays and Thursdays.

Leavitt Fine Arts Theatre (646-3123), Route 1 (in Ogunquit Village). Open early spring through fall. An old-time theater with new screen and sound; first-run films.

Ogunquit Square Theatre (646-5151), Shore Road (in Ogunquit Village). Another old-time theater with all the latest movies.

SELECTIVE SHOPPING *Galleries:* In addition to the **Museum of Art of Ogunquit** and the **Barn Gallery** (see To See and Do), there are more than a dozen galleries and studios in Ogunquit, among them:

Ogunquit's Art Center (646-5933), 9 Hoyt's Lane. Open seasonally, 10–5 daily. Housed in one of the town's oldest galleries, showing contemporary and traditional works in selected media.

The Ogunquit Photography School (646-7055), 28 Agamenticus Road. Seminars and workshops conducted by well-known photographers and photography teachers.

Hoyt's Lane Art Gallery (646-9964), Route 1 and Hoyt's Lane (just north of the village). Open Memorial Day through Columbus Day, 10–5. A wide variety of styles and media.

Main Street Art Gallery, Main Street at Berwick Road in the middle of the village. Exhibits work by 15 artists; receptions every Wednesday evening in-season.

June Weare Fine Arts (646-8200), Shore Road. Open mid-May to mid-December, 10–4. Original prints, paintings, and sculpture.

Thelin Studio/Gallery (646-2616), 190 Shore Road. Watercolor workshops. Antique and contemporary paintings. June to September, 10–6 daily.

George Carpenter Gallery (646-5106), Perkins Cove. Watercolors, oils, and pastel portraits by Virginia Carpenter.

Scully Gallery (646-2850), Perkins Cove (also studio/gallery on Route 1). Watercolors, original graphics, and acrylics.

Left Bank Gallery (646-3524), Perkins Cove. Oils, watercolors, and prints by Frances Borofsky.

Shore Road Gallery (646-5046), 106 Shore Road. Open Memorial Day through Columbus Day weekend, daily. Paintings, graphics, and sculpture by New England artists.

Bartok Studio/Gallery (646-7815), 104 Shore Road. Watercolors by John Bartok.

Jaslow Gallery (646-3555), Shore Road. Paintings, drawings, and graphics by Ted Jaslow.

PS Galleries (646-3254), Hoyt's Lane. Open June to September, daily. Works by nationally recognized artists from throughout the country.

Special shops: **Whistling Oyster Gallery** in Ogunquit Square is closed January to March. Stocks a range of quality gifts.

Ogunquit Camera (646-2251), at the corner of Shore Road and Wharf Lane in Ogunquit Village. Open year-round and features one-hour film developing. A great little shop that's been here since 1952. It's also a trove of toys, towels, windsocks, beach supplies, and sunglasses.

Chris Davis Stoneware Pottery, Perkins Cove. May through mid-December. A range of Maine-made stoneware and porcelain.

Harbor Candy Shop, 26 Main Street. Seasonal. Chocolates and specialty candies are made on the spot; also a selection of imported candies.

Antiques shops: Route 1 from York through Wells and the Kennebunks is studded with so many antiques shops that they publish their own "Antiques Shops on Coastal Route 1 in Southern Maine" flyer, available at the local chambers of commerce. MacDougall-Gionet (646-3531), open daily, is a particularly rich trouve of country furniture in a barn; 60 dealers are represented. The Wells Union Antique Center (646-6612) is a complex of nine individually owned shops representing 15 dealers. The Country Barn (646-5507) specializes in country oak and pine furniture. R. Jorgensen Antiques (646-9444) has nine rooms filled with antique furniture including fine formal pieces from a number of countries.

Factory outlets: Bass Shoe maintains an outlet, open daily, at Wells Plaza, Route 1. Quoddy Crafted Footwear is open daily in the Wells Corner Shopping Center, Route 1. Down East Company factory outlet in Moody is open year-round: blankets, pot holders, hearth mats, and vests. Hathaway Factory Outlet is open year-round and features brand-name sportswear.

Antiquarian books: Used bookstores cluster in Wells, great for browsing on non-beach days. They include: The Arringtons, the Book Barn, and Hardings Book Shop (4,500 square feet of old and rare books, maps, and prints) on Route 1, East Coast Books on Depot Street at Route 109.

SPECIAL EVENTS   April: Big Patriot's Day celebration at Ogunquit Beach.

June: Harbor Park Day in Wells (end of the month): a full day of events featuring launching of new boats built by the Arundel Boat School, a big chicken barbeque, sand sculpture contest.

July: Independence Day Fireworks at Ogunquit Beach. Sand building contest, middle of the month.

August: Sidewalk Art Show. Antique Show. Kite-Flying Contest. Great Inner Tube Race. Antique Show.

September: Open Homes Day sponsored by the Wells Historical Society. Nature Crafts Festival at Laudholm Farm (second weekend).

December: Christmas Parade in Wells; Christmas by the Sea in Ogunquit.

The Kennebunks/Old Orchard Beach Area

The Kennebunks have been around under one name or another since the 1620s. They began as a fishing stage near Cape Porpoise, which was repeatedly destroyed by Indian raids. In 1719 the present "port" was incorporated as Arundel, a name that stuck through its peak shipbuilding and seafaring years until 1821, when the name was changed to Kennebunkport. Later, when the novel *Arundel* by Kenneth Roberts (born in Kennebunk) had run through 32 printings, residents attempted to reclaim the old name and succeeded in doing so in 1957, at least for North Kennebunkport. Geographically, the Kennebunks are confusing. Kennebunk is a busy commercial center that straddles the strip of Route 1 between the Mousam and Kennebunk rivers. A 10-minute ride down Summer Street brings you to Kennebunkport. Then there is Kennebunk Beach, Cape Porpoise, Cape Arundel, and Kennebunk Lower Village. Luckily, free detailed maps are readily available, and all that most visitors care about is finding the summer White House, Walker Point.

President Bush's summer estate fills a private 11-acre peninsula off Ocean Drive (mansion row). Built by the president's grandfather George Herbert Walker in 1903, it's uncannily suited to its present use: moated on three sides by water yet clearly visible from the pull-out places along the drive, perfectly positioned for picture-taking.

In the 1870s this entire spectacular 5-mile stretch of coast—from Lord's Point at the western end of Kennebunk Beach all the way to Cape Porpoise on the east—was acquired by a Massachusetts group, the Boston and Kennebunkport Sea Shore Company.

No less than 30 grand hotels and dozens of summer mansions (including Walker Point) came with the easy train service that soon followed. The Kennebunks shared the 1940s-to-1960s decline suffered by all Maine coastal resorts, losing all but a sparse scattering of old hotels. Their comeback, visible during the 1970s, accelerated into a boom through the 1980s. Some of the surviving hotels were condoed, inns were rehabbed, and dozens of new B&Bs opened.

Unfortunately, the 1990s have brought a headache the 1890s boom didn't. Traffic. Back in the Golden Era you could come by train from

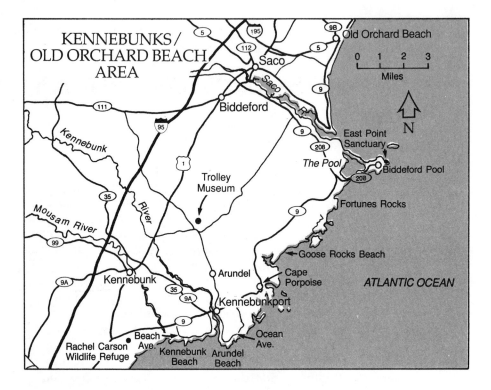

KENNEBUNKS/
OLD ORCHARD BEACH
AREA

Old Orchard Beach

Saco

Biddeford

East Point
Sanctuary

The Pool

Biddeford Pool

Fortunes Rocks

Goose Rocks Beach

Cape
Porpoise

ATLANTIC OCEAN

Arundel

Kennebunkport

Trolley
Museum

Kennebunk

Mousam River

Ocean
Ave.

Beach
Ave.

Rachel Carson
Wildlife Refuge

Kennebunk
Beach

Arundel
Beach

0 1 2 3
Miles

N

Boston to Dock Square or Kennebunk Beach. If you didn't mind
changing umpty-ump times, you could even get there by trolley.

The Kennebunks happen to be one of Maine's most convenient
resorts. Downtown Kennebunk is just off I-95 and a 10 minute ride
down Summer Street brings you to Kennebunkport or at least to the
back of the backup for the drawbridge. While the snarl is worse on
weekends, it is compounded on weekdays by tour buses that stop to
disgorge 40 passengers at a time. The point is that this is no place to day
trip. Like Nantucket and Newport, the Kennebunks are the kind of
place you should stay for at least two days, renting a bicycle or using
the trackless trolley to get around.

Try to stay within walking distance of Dock Square. Described in
Booth Tarkington's 1930 novel *Mirthful Haven* as "Cargo Square," this
is one of the liveliest summer spots on the New England coast.
Clustered around the classic monument "to our soldiers and sailors,"
the weathered, waterside buildings house an assortment of shops and
restaurants. It's a place to spend hours sipping, munching, and
browsing—eventually strolling down Ocean Avenue, along the river,
to the rocks and sea. You pass the dock where Tarkington used to
summer, writing on his schooner. The River Club across the way is a

very private gathering point for families who have been summering here in roomy "cottages" for generations.

Old inns still line Ocean Avenue, and a number of former captains' homes on neighboring streets also take in guests. The Kennebunks may just offer Maine's widest selection of accommodations. You can stay in an old-style resort hotel, a waterside cottage, or any number of bed & breakfasts and inns.

Although Cape Porpoise and Goose Rocks Beach shut down with Labor Day, many Kennebunkport inns and shops remain open for Christmas Prelude in early December.

GUIDANCE   **Kennebunk-Kennebunkport Chamber of Commerce** (967-0857), PO Box 740, Kennebunk 04043. Open year-round; information booth open May to Labor Day at Cooper's Corner, junction of Routes 9 and 35 in the Lower Village, 9:30–12:30, 1:30–4, 7–9. The chamber publishes a pamphlet guide and keeps track of vacancies.

The *Tourist News*, an unusually helpful tabloid, appears weekly in summer, biweekly in shoulder seasons. It describes dining, lodging, and sights in the Kennebunks, Wells, and Ogunquit and it's free, stacked everywhere around town.

Old Orchard Beach Chamber of Commerce (934-2500), PO Box 600 (First Street), Old Orchard Beach 04064, maintains a seasonal walk-in information center; offers help with reservations.

Biddeford–Saco Chamber of Commerce (282-1567), 170 Main Street, Biddeford 04005.

GETTING THERE   You can fly your own plane into **Sanford Airport;** otherwise, drive up I-95 to Exit 3. **Munroe's Limousine Service** (646-9067), **John's Coastal Taxi** (985-6291), and **Port Limo** (967-8885) serve Boston and Portland airports as well as most destinations.

GETTING AROUND   **Intown Trolley Co.** (967-3686) offers narrated sightseeing tours with tickets good for the day so you can also use them to shuttle between Dock Square and Kennebunk Beach. They leave Dock Square every half hour, daily late May through October.

PARKING   A **municipal parking lot** is hidden just off Dock Square beside the Congregational Church. In summer free **shuttle service** is offered from two outlying lots: one at St. Martha's Catholic Church on North Street, the other at the Consolidated School, Route 9. Another free lot adjoins the chamber of commerce office in the Lower Village (see Guidance).

MEDICAL EMERGENCY   **Southern Maine Medical Center** (283-3663), 1 Mountain Road, Biddeford.

TO SEE AND DO   **The Brick Store Museum** (985-4802), 117 Main Street. Open year-round, Tuesday through Friday 10–4:30; also Saturday (same hours), April 15 to December 15. Admission is $2 per adult, $1 per child. A block of early nineteenth-century commercial buildings, including William Lord's Brick Store (1825), a space used for changing exhibits of fine and decorative arts and marine collections. Architectural walking tours are offered of **Kennebunk's National Register District** in summer.

Taylor-Barry House, 24 Summer Street, Kennebunk. Operated by the Brick Store Museum. Guided tours are offered June through September, Tuesday through Friday 1–4, and by appointment; $2 per adult. A Federal-period sea captain's home with a stenciled hallway and period furnishings.

Seashore Trolley Museum (967-2800 or 967-2712), Log Cabin Road. It's located 3.2 miles up North Street from Kennebunkport or 1.7 miles off Route 1 at the blinker, 2.8 miles north of Kennebunk. Open daily late April to mid-October, 10–5 (phone to check on what's offered in spring and fall), usually for a slide-show, exhibits, and rides. Admission is $5.50 for adults; senior, children, and family rates. This non-profit museum displays more than 200 vehicles from the world over. In a depot-style visitors center, learn about how the Atlantic Shore Railway shaped the local resort scene in the days when you could come by trolley right from Boston to Dock Square. The 2-mile excursion circuit includes the old electric railroad right-of-way.

Kennebunkport Historical Society (967-2751). Based in the Old Town House School on North Street. Open year-round on Tuesdays 1–4; in July and August on Saturdays 10–12; also for special events. Displays local memorabilia; also maritime exhibits housed next door in the former office of the Clark Shipyard.

White Columns, also known as the **Nott House** (967-2513), Maine Street, Kennebunkport. Also maintained by the Kennebunkport Historical Society. Open June to Columbus Day, Tuesday, Friday, and Saturday 1–4. A Greek Revival house with a Doric colonnade; also with original wallpapers, carpets, and furnishings. $2 per adult. Inquire about walking tours.

Old Orchard Beach. The centerpiece is a 7-mile beach on Saco Bay. Camp meetings were held here in the nineteenth century, an era recalled in the Ocean Park section, but it's best known for the carnival-style atmosphere, centering around the Ocean Pier. The beach is backed by motels, condominiums, and apartments patronized primarily by French Canadians. There is no free parking in town; it's at least $3 even if you want to stop for just 10 minutes.

Cape Porpoise Pier. From Dock Square drive down Ocean Avenue and along the ocean into Cape Porpoise. The port's lobster and commercial fishing boats are based here.

St. Anthony Monastery and Shrine (967-2011). A Tudor-style mansion set on extensive grounds on Beach Road, now maintained by Lithuanian Franciscans as a shrine and retreat center. Visitors are welcome; gift shop. Inquire about lodging in the Guest House.

Wedding Cake House. Summer Street (Route 35), Kennebunk. Partially open as Ann Burnett's studio: artwork on furniture and clothing.

This 1826 house is laced up and down with white wooden latticework. The tale is that a local sea captain had to rush off to sea before a proper wedding cake could be baked, but he more than made up for it later.

South Congregational Church, Temple Street, Kennebunkport. Just off Dock Square, built in 1824 with a Christopher Wren–style cupola and belfry; Doric columns added in 1912.

Louis T. Graves Memorial Library (967-2778), Maine Street, Kennebunkport. Built in 1813 as a bank, which went bust, it later served as a customs house. It was subsequently donated to the library association by artist Abbott Graves, whose pictures alone make it worth a visit. You can still see the bank vault and the sign from the customs collector's office.

First Parish Unitarian Church, Main Street, Kennebunk. Built in 1772–1773 with an Asher Benjamin–style steeple added in 1803–1804, along with a Paul Revere bell. In 1838 the interior was divided into two levels, with the church proper elevated to the second floor.

Biddeford-Saco. No two Maine towns are more different or more closely linked. Saco is a classic Yankee town with white-clapboard mansions lining its main street, and Biddeford is a classic mill town with a strong French Canadian heritage and mammoth nineteenth-century brick textile mills that have stood idle since the 1950s. A few years back the largest mills were renamed Saco Island and slated for redevelopment as a combination hotel, office, shop, and condo complex. At present the project is on hold. Still Biddeford is worth visiting, especially for La Kremesse, the colorful Franco-American festival in late June.

It's also worth coming just to visit the **York Institute Museum** (282-3031), 371 Main Street, Saco. Open Tuesday through Friday 1–4, May to October; also Saturday (same hours) in July and August. November to April it's Tuesday and Wednesday 1–4, and year-round it's open Thursday 1–8. Admission is $2 per adult, $1 under 16 and over 60 (free under 6). Original paintings, furniture, decorative arts, and tools; also natural history specimens. Trace the history of southern Maine; inquire about frequent lectures, tours, and special exhibits. The Institute's **Dyer Library** next door has an outstanding Maine history collection.

FOR FAMILIES The Route 1 strip in Saco and nearby Orchard Beach add up to Maine's biggest concentration of kid-geared "attractions." Be prepared to pay.

Maine Aquarium (284-4511), Route 1, Saco. Open daily, year-round. Marine life exhibits include seals, penguins, sharks, tidepool animals. Located on 70 acres with a free petting zoo, nature trail, and picnic grounds. Handicapped accessible. $6 per adult, less for seniors and kids.

Funtown USA (284-5139), Route 1 just south of Route 195 in Saco. Open daily mid-June to Labor Day, weekends in spring and fall. A large amusement park: Cascade Water Park, bumper cars, log flume, kiddie rides, antique cars.

Aquaboggan Water Park (282-3112), Route 1, Saco. Open June through Labor Day. Water slides, swimming pool, bumper boats, mini-golf, arcade, shuffleboard. Expensive.

Pirate's Island (934-5086), 70 First Street, Old Orchard Beach. "Adventure Golf," 36 up-and-down miniature golf holes, waterfalls, ponds.

Palace Playland (934-2001), Old Orchard Street, Old Orchard Beach. Open late June through Labor Day. For more than 60 years fun-seekers have been wheeled, lifted, shaken, spun, and bumped in Palace Playland rides; there's also a 1906 carousel with hand-painted wooden horses and sleighs, a ferris wheel, and a 60-foot-high water slide. Charge is by the ride or $16 for an afternoon pass.

WALKS   **Henry Parsons Park,** Ocean Avenue, is a path along the rocks leading to Spouting Rock and Blowing Cave, both sights to see at mid-tide. **Biddeford Pool East Sanctuary,** Route 9 (north of Kennebunkport), is a place to observe shorebirds. **Rachel Carson National Wildlife Refuge** encompasses 1,600 acres with a 1-mile-long nature trail and is an excellent spot for birding (see Green Space under Wells). **Vaughns Island Preserve** offers nature trails on a wooded island separated from the mainland by two tidal creeks. Cellar holes of historic houses, accessible by foot, three hours before and three hours after high tide. (See also Laudholm Farm described in Green Space under Wells.)

BEACHES   The Kennebunks avoid the glut of weekend day-trippers by requiring a permit to park at its major beaches. Day and seasonal passes must be secured from either the Kennebunk or Kennebunkport town halls (open weekdays only), depending on which beach you want to use. Passes are, of course, also available from local lodging places. You can park in one of the town lots and walk, bike, or take a trolley to the beach.

In Kennebunk.   **Kennebunk and Gooch's beaches** are both long, wide strips of firm sand backed by Beach Avenue, divided by Oak's Neck. Beyond Gooch's Beach take Great Hill Road along the water to Strawberry Island, a great place to walk and examine tidal pools. Please don't picnic.

Parson's Beach, south of Kennebunk Beach on Route 9, requires no permit but in-season you will probably be able to stop only long enough to drop someone off; off-season you have a chance at one of the half-dozen parking spaces; you can always park along the road on the other side of Route 9 and walk down the grand avenue of sugar maples to the sand. It's a splendid place for an early morning or evening walk.

In Kennebunkport.   **Goose Rocks Beach,** a few miles north of Kennebunkport village on Route 9, is another wide, smooth stretch of sand backed by the road. You can also walk down Ocean Avenue to tiny **Arundel Beach** near the Colony Hotel at the mouth of the Kennebunk River. It offers nice rocks for climbing.

In Old Orchard. **Old Orchard Beach** extends a full 3 miles, accessible directly from I-95 via Route 195; $3 parking whether it's 10 minutes or a day.

In Saco. **Ferry Beach State Park,** marked from Route 9 between Old Orchard Beach and Camp Ellis. The 100-acre preserve includes 70 yards of sand; also a boardwalk through the dunes, nature trails, picnic area with grills, lifeguards, changing rooms. $1 per person, free under age 12.

Bay View Beach, at the end of Bay View road near Ferry Beach, is 200 yards of mostly sandy beach; lifeguards, free parking.

Camp Ellis Beach, Route 9. Some 2,000 feet of beach backed by cottages; also a long fishing pier. Commercial parking lots.

BIKING The lay of this land lends itself to exploration by bike, a far more satisfying way to go in summer than by car since you can stop and park where the view and urge hit you.

Rental bikes are available from **Cape-Able Bike Shop** (967-4382), Townhouse Corners (off Log Cabin Road), Kennebunkport, and at **Viking Enterprises** (934-5443), 84 West Grand Avenue in Old Orchard Beach.

BLUEBERRYING **The Nature Conservancy** (729-5181) maintains 1,500 acres of Blueberry Plains in West Kennebunk; take Route 99 towards Sanford.

BOATBUILDING SCHOOL **The Landing School of Boat Building and Design** (985-7976), River Road, Kennebunk, offers a September-to-June program in building sailing craft. Visitors welcome if you call ahead.

SCENIC BOAT EXCURSIONS Scenic Cruise: *Elizabeth II* (967-5595), May through October, offers one-and-one-half-hour narrated tours of the Kennebunk River and northeast along the Atlantic to Cape Porpoise Harbor. Departs Arundel Shipyard, Kennebunkport.

DEEP-SEA FISHING *Deepwater* (967-5595 or 967-4938). Captain Ben Emery offers daily trips (May to September) from Arundel Shipyard. "Bring your lunch and a warm jacket and leave the rest to us."

Sonnie W. (985-3893), a 73-foot party boat skippered by Captain Mike Olcott, sails mid-June to Labor Day on daily trips, weekends from May 1 to Columbus Day; food and drink aboard.

GOLF Cape Arundel Golf Club (967-3494), Kennebunkport, 18 holes. These are the local links President Bush frequents. Open to the public except from 11–2:30.

Webhannet Golf Club (967-2061), Kennebunk Beach, 18 holes. We've read that Edmund Muskie prefers this slightly more challenging course. Open to the public except from 11:30 to 1 PM.

Dutch Elm Golf Course (282-9850), Arundel, 18 holes; cart and club rental, lessons, pro shop, snack bar, putting greens.

HORSEBACK RIDING AND HAYRIDES **Bush Brook Stables** (284-7721 or

284-8311), 463 West Street, Biddeford. Hayrides and trail rides offered.

Long Horn Stables (934-9578), 93 Ross Road, Old Orchard Beach. Trail rides, hayrides, sleigh rides. A bridal path follows the Mousam River.

SAILING   *Discovery* (967-2921), billed as "Maine's littlest windjammer," offers four one-and-a-half hour trips daily in summer; reduced schedule in spring and fall. From the Nonantum.

Maine Sail School (967-5043). Ocean Avenue, Kennebunkport. Sailing lessons (private or in scheduled sessions), coastal cruises, sunset sails, half- and full-day charters.

Saco Bay Sailing (283-1624), 14 Beach Avenue, Camp Ellis Beach, Saco. Half- and full-day sails, sunset cruises; up to six passengers. (Also see Whale-Watching.)

WHALE-WATCHING   This is Maine's prime departure point for sighting the whales who feed on Jeffries Ledge, about 20 miles off-shore. If you have any tendencies to seasickness, be sure to choose a calm day. Chances are you will see more than a dozen whales. Frequently sighted species include finbacks, minkes, rights, and humpbacks.

Nautilus (967-5595), a 65-foot boat carrying up to 100 passengers, offers narrated trips daily from May to October. Departs Arundel Shipyard, Kennebunkport (behind the Mobil station next to the bridge on Route 9). Free parking.

Indian Whale Watch (967-5912 or 985-7857). July through October from the Arundel Wharf, Ocean Avenue. This is a 75-foot boat holding 72 passengers, and it's slower and takes longer to reach the whales but features narration by a mammalogist; sunset cruises.

CROSS-COUNTRY SKIING   **Harris Farm Stand** (499-2678), Buzzell Road, Dayton. A 500-acre dairy farm with more than 20 miles of trails. Equipment rentals available. Located 1 1/2 miles from the Route 5 and Route 35 intersection.

RESORT HOTELS   **The Colony** (967-3331), Ocean Avenue and Kings Road, Kennebunkport 04046. Open late June through Labor Day. A 133-room hotel, this is one of the last of New England's coastal resorts that's still maintained in the grand, three-meals-a-day and dress-code style. It's set on a rise, overlooking the point at which the Kennebunk River meets the Atlantic. It's been owned by the Boughton family since 1948, managed by John Banta; many guests have been coming for generations. Amenities include a saltwater pool, tennis, beach, social program, nightly entertainment, and dancing. A seven-night minimum for advance reservations mid-July through late August. $143–$244 double per day includes all three meals; $53 extra per child plus $17 for service. Worth it.

The Shawmut Inn (967-3931 or 800-876-3931), PO Box 431, Kennebunkport 04046. Open May through December. Away from the village on its 22 oceanfront acres, a complex that has had its ups and downs in recent years. The 96 units range from guest rooms in the

Main Inn and Seaview Lodge to cottages with efficiency units and standard motel rooms. The Main Inn contains a large, low-slung lobby and large dining room with ocean views; facilities include a beach, a pool, and lawn games. Per person double occupancy rates range from $34 for a back room off-season to $74 for an ocean-view room in high season; breakfast included.

INNS AND BED & BREAKFASTS   All inn listings are for **Kennebunkport 04046** unless otherwise indicated. (Note: Kennebunk is not Kennebunkport.) Lodging options are so varied that this is the one place in the book that we have divided them into price categories.

More expensive: **Captain Lord Mansion** (967-3141), PO Box 800. Open year-round at the corner of Pleasant and Green streets. One of the most splendid mansions in New England is now one of the most romantic inns around. The three-story, Federal-era home is topped with a widow's walk from which guests can contemplate the town and sea beyond. Other architectural features include a three-story suspended elliptical staircase and pine doors that have been painted *trompe l'oeil*-style to simulate inlaid mahogany. There are 16 rooms, 11 with working fireplaces and all meticulously decorated—some with high four-posters and canopy beds, all with antiques and private baths. The gathering room is also very elegant, but, surprise: breakfast (freshly baked muffins and sweet breads) is an informal affair, served in the large country kitchen. Hosts Bev Davis and Rick Litchfield try to make each guest feel special. Phoebe's Fantasy, a separate building, has four more rooms with fireplaces, and two more rooms in the Captain's Hideaway have both fireplaces and whirlpool tubs. $110–$195 per room in high season, breakfast and tea included; less off-season.

Old Fort Inn (967-5353), PO Box M. Open mid-April to mid-December. An unusual combination of things, but it works. The reception area is in the former barn, now a comfortable space in which guests find a morning buffet breakfast and are otherwise drawn to relax. Grounds and buildings represent the remnants of an 1880s resort, nicely converted to serve 1980s families. The sturdy stone and brick carriage house now offers 16 guest rooms with stenciled walls and antiques and fully equipped kitchen units or wet bars. Two suites available. Amenities include a pool, tennis court, and shuffleboard. A path leads down to the ocean. Unsuitable for children under 12. Three-night minimum during high season. $95–$195 in high season, breakfast included.

Bufflehead Cove (967-3879), Box 499, off Route 35. Open year-round except March. This is a hidden gem. Sequestered on 6 acres at the end of a dirt road but right on the Kennebunk River and less than a mile from the village of Kennebunkport. It's a Dutch Colonial-style home in which Harriet and Jim Gott have raised their children. Harriet is a native of nearby Cape Porpoise, and Jim is a commercial fisherman. There are four pleasant guest rooms and one suite (all with private bath), a living room with a hearth and deep window seats, an inviting veranda, and woods and orchard to explore. $75–$95 includes breakfast and afternoon wine and cheese.

Inn on South Street (967-5151 or 967-4639), South Street, PO Box 478A. A Greek Revival home on a quiet street preserves a sense of the era in which it was built. Innkeeper Jacques Downs is a college professor with a keen interest in the China Trade, and living room furnishings include the kind of Chinese furniture and furnishings a Kennebunkport sea captain might well have brought back. There are three guest rooms among which our favorite, named for "Mrs. Perkins," has a fireplace, a pine four-poster bed with a canopy and a Chinese spread. There's also a first-floor suite with its own sitting room, a four-poster bed and woodburning stove, a bath with Jacuzzi, a kitchen and porch. Eva Down's amazing breakfasts are delivered to this kitchen, also served upstairs in the dining room to other guests; afternoon tea is also served, included in rates which run $90–$95 for a double room, $155–$175 for a suite with fireplace. A fireplace room is $105, fall through spring; less off-season..

The Captain Jefferds Inn (967-2311), Pearl Street, Box 691. Open most of the year. This is a strikingly handsome Federal-era mansion, elegantly furnished (it has been featured as a *House Beautiful* cover story) and maintained by Warren Fitzsimmons. There are 12 rooms, all with private baths; also 3 efficiency units in the carriage house. A full breakfast (maybe eggs Benedict or blueberry crêpes) is served on china in the formal dining room, and afternoon tea is offered in cooler months. $75–$110 double for rooms, $110–$145 for suites in the Carriage House; rates include a full breakfast.

Cape Arundel Inn (967-2125), Ocean Avenue. Open April through October. Nicely sited overlooking the Atlantic between Spouting Rock and Blowing Cave. There are eight rooms (each with private bath) in the grand old "summer cottage," which offers guests a comfortable living room and porch with ocean view. The dining room is open to the public for breakfast on weekends and for dinner nightly. $80–$105 double in the house, $85–$115 in the adjacent motel units. Breakfast available but not included.

Kennebunkport Inn (967-2621), Dock Square. Open year-round; dining room closed November to March. Built as an 1890s mansion, an inn since 1926, just a skip from Dock Square but set back from the hubbub. There are 34 rooms, including 2 with fireplaces; 9 new rooms opened in 1987. All rooms have TVs and private baths; many have water views. The dining room is open to the public, but guests have their own living room and, in summer, a small pool on the terrace. Shoulder season packages include meals and a lobster cruise. High season rates run $79–$155 per room or $88–$114 per person MAP. Much cheaper off-season.

White Barn Inn (967-2321), Beach Street (mail: RR 3 Box 560C).

Finding crabs at the beach

Photo by Neal Parent

Open year-round. The barn is now a dining room (see Dining Out), attached to the old inn, built in 1865 as the Forest Hills Hotel. Guests choose from antiques-furnished rooms in the inn, deluxe suites in the annex, more rooms in the Gate House Cottage. The rooms in the recently refurbished May's Annex have fireplaces as well as sitting areas, phones, and TVs sequestered in armoires; four-posters and marble-floored baths with whirlpool tubs. Rooms in the main house do not have TVs or phones. Both are available in the elegant public rooms. From $95–$220 per couple, including a full breakfast, afternoon tea, and use of touring bikes. You can walk both to Dock Square and the beach. Cheaper off-season. Inquire about special packages. No children under age 12.

The Breakwater Inn (967-3118), Ocean Avenue. Inn and restaurant are open mid-May to mid-October; rooms in the annex are closed January to mid-February. Parts of two nineteenth-century river-side hotels merge to form this restored inn. The Breakwater itself, which also houses a popular public restaurant, holds eight pleasant rooms (private baths), and the adjacent Riverside holds a dozen rooms with either a porch or sliding door opening onto water views. Each has double beds, a small fridge, and bar sink as well as private bath and TV. $85–$125 includes a full breakfast; cheaper off-season.

Tides Inn By-the-Sea (967-3757), RR 2 Box 737, Goose Rocks Beach. Open May to October. Away from Kennebunkport village but right across from a great beach. Twenty-two rooms now all told. Those in the original inn are plain but bright, some with private bath; more rooms and apartments in Tides Too next door. The attractive, informal dining room and pub are open to the public, geared to singles and young couples. $75–$135 per room; efficiency apartment, $895 per week.

Kennebunk Inn (985-3358), 45 Main Street, Kennebunk 04043. Open year-round. A stage stop since 1799, a flophouse when Arthur and Angela Le Blanc bought it in 1978, now an inn with charm and a center-of-town feel. Thirty rooms, eight with private baths. The dining room and bar are popular local spots; also a gift shop and summer café. High season rates range from $65 for a room with shared bath to $125 for suites; double rooms with private baths are $80–$98, continental breakfast included.

The Ocean View (967-2750), 72 Beach Avenue, Kennebunk Beach 04043. Open spring through fall. All nine deftly decorated rooms have ocean views, and there is a fireplace in the living room. Breakfast includes your own heated carafe of tea or coffee, maybe a brioche with cheese, fruit, and jams, topped off with fresh strawberries and cream. High-season rates run $85–$135.

Welby Inn (967-4655), PO Box 774, Ocean Avenue. Open May to October. A fine, old gambrel-roofed home with a spacious living room with bright pillows, fresh flowers, oak furniture, wing chairs, and a piano. Through French doors, the breakfast room is the setting for morning egg dishes, fresh muffins, and fruit. There are seven rooms, all with private baths, old bedsteads decorated with handmade quilts. $77.50–$87.50.

Maine Stay Inn and Cottages (967-2117), Box 500A, Maine Street. Open April through mid-December; weekends the rest of the year. The 1860 house is big, white, and distinctive with a large cupola, offering 6 guest rooms, each with private bath; two suites, one with a working fireplace. There are also 11 cottages of varying sizes, 2 with fireplaces, all but 1 with efficiency kitchens. Full breakfast is included with inn rates (cottage guests have the option of breakfast delivered in a basket), and all guests can enjoy a full afternoon tea in the attractive living room or on the wraparound porch. $75–$150 per night.

The 1802 House (967-5632), PO Box 646-A, Locke Street. Open year-round. A carefully decorated old home with eight guest rooms, each with private bath, some with working fireplaces. The house is off and away from town with an out-in-the-country feel, shaded by two large pine trees; in winter you can step right off into the fields for cross-country skiing. There is a cozy breakfast room with a woodstove. From $70–$115 for a room with fireplace.

Chetwynd House Inn (967-2235), PO Box 130TN, Chestnut Street. Open year-round. This was Kennebunkport's first B&B, a gracious 1840s home just off Dock Square. There are five antiques-furnished guest rooms (two with private baths). Our favorite is the gable room with double beds. Extraordinary breakfasts, maybe crabmeat soufflé or oyster stew plus muffins, fresh fruit served family-style at the dining room table. High-season rates are $85–$125, including afternoon tea and a bottle of wine or champagne in the room; cheaper off-season.

The Inn at Harbor Head (967-5564), Pier Road, Cape Porpoise (mail: RR 2 Box 1180). Open year-round except November and April. Joan and Dave Sutter offer five rooms with private baths in their rambling, shingled home overlooking Cape Porpoise Harbor. The Summer Suite (available only in summer) has both a bath room and a spectacular water view. Guests have access to the inn's dock, terrace, and sitting room. Joan, who unabashedly claims to coddle lodgers, whips up fresh baked goods to top off her large breakfasts and prepares afternoon snacks (tea or wine and cheese, as tastes dictate). $85–$175 per room.

Sundial Inn (967-3850), 48 Beach Street, PO Box 1147, Kennebunk 04043. Open year-round; right on Kennebunk Beach. Built in 1891, virtually rebuilt and substantially enlarged several years ago, now has 34 rooms, most with ocean views. In high season from $98; from $133 with ocean views to $178 for a suite with Jacuzzi. Much less off-season.

Harbor Inn (967-2074), PO Box 538A, Ocean Avenue. Open mid-May through mid-December. This is a comfortable old summer home that offers nine bedrooms, two with canopy beds, each with an armoire because closets have been turned into bathrooms. The living room has built-in seats around the fireplace and plenty of books. A breakfast of muffins, breads, and cereal is served in the dining room. Rates begin at $85.

The Inn at Goose Rocks (967-5425), Dyke Road. Open year-round. Surrounded by 10 wooded acres near the saltwater marshes, also within walking distance of Goose Rocks Beach. A gracious old home with modern, traditionally decorated rooms (with phone, cable TV) added on. A total of 32 rooms with an upstairs lounge and rooftop deck, outdoor pool, dining room, and meeting space. $70–$95 per room in high season.

Nonantum Resort and Nonantum Portside (967-4050), PO Box 2626, Ocean Avenue. Open mid-April through October. This century-old landmark has been recently renovated and expanded to include the adjacent Portside condo-style units. Amenities include a full-service restaurant and outdoor pool. $135–$159 in-season; from $60 in spring and fall.

Less expensive: **The Green Heron** (967-3315), PO Box 2578, Ocean Avenue. Early April to December. Within walking distance of both village and shore, this old house has just 10 guest rooms which are simple, clean, and bright, filled with the spirit of a friendlier, simpler day. The famous breakfast is included in the guest rates; it's also available to the public by reservation. Ownership has recently changed, and the inn has been renovated; but it remains in the Reid family, retaining its special atmosphere. $60–$80 double in-season, $58–$76 off-season. Children are an extra $15 over 12, $10 under 12. This is one place that both children and pets are welcome.

Kylemere House (967-2780), Box 1333, South Street. Open May through December. A graceful Federal-era house with five bright, nicely furnished rooms—one with a fireplace, three with private baths. Shelves are well stocked with books, and the lawn is banked in flowers. $60–$90 includes a bountiful breakfast.

Old Parsonage Guest House (967-4352), School Street (Route 9). An 1850s former Baptist parsonage is now a pleasant B&B. Loretta Spita offers three rooms, two sharing a bath and one with private bath. We like the feel of this place and it's within walking distance of shops and restaurants. $55–$70 includes a very full breakfast.

Waldo Emerson Inn (985-7854), 108 Summer Street, Kennebunk 04043. A genuine eighteenth-century house built by a local merchant related to the poet Ralph Waldo Emerson (said to have summered here). It remains a pleasant family home with eight fireplaces, four guest rooms sharing two-and-a-half baths. The Wedding House is next door. Breakfast is included in $50–$65 double.

Flakeyard Farm (967-5965), RFD 3 Box 1616, South Main Street. Dating from 1737, this Georgian-style home has original paneling and fireplaces, a view of the Kennebunk River, private baths, and full breakfasts. $60 per room in-season.

The Lodge (284-7148), Biddeford Pool 04006. A summer cottage overlooking Saco Bay, within walking distance of a sandy beach. This house, built in 1949 by host John Oddy's father, offers two guest rooms with private baths and two guest rooms with shared baths; $65–$85 includes a full breakfast.

Country Farm (282-0208), 136 Louden Road, Box 330, Saco 04072. This working farm is a real B&B, more of a family home than most of the more commercial B&Bs in the Kennebunks. Just 8 miles from the coast, it is set in 150 acres of rolling farmland bordering the Saco River. Arlene and Norman Gonneville are warm hosts, and children feel unusually welcome. Animals include cows and goats. A full breakfast with freshly baked breads is included. $45 double.

MOTELS   All inn listings are for **Kennebunkport 04046** unless otherwise indicated.

Village Cove Inn (967-3993), Chick's Cove, Box 650. Open year-round. A resort motel with a dining room and meeting space, sited on a tidal cove with indoor and outdoor pools; 32 large, motel-style rooms with two double beds; color cable TVs and phones. There is a guest lounge with fireplace off the lobby. A housekeeping cottage sleeps six. Special weekend and midweek packages. $75–$115, in high season, includes continental breakfast; cottage rented by the week.

Rhumb Line (967-5457), RR 2 Box 1405. Open year-round. Off and away from the village. Near but not overlooking the ocean, this new motor inn offers 32 rooms, each with cable TV and phone. Amenities include indoor and outdoor heated pools, continental breakfast, lounge area.

Beachwood Motel (967-2483), Route 9. Emphatically geared to families: 92 units, most with kitchenettes, all with TVs. There is an adult pool and a kiddies pool, tennis court, shuffleboard, and restaurant. Handy to Goose Rocks. Moderate.

Idlease Guest Resort (985-4460), Route 9, PO Box 3086. Another family find. A traditional motel and cottage complex within walking distance of Parson's Beach (one of the most beautiful, least commercial beaches on the south coast). Motel and cottage rooms were $54 double in 1990; $59 for four people; housekeeping cottages ran $69–$85 (accommodating six), $435–$535 per week.

OTHER LODGING   **Franciscan Guest House** (967-2011), Beach Avenue, Kennebunkport 04046. The Franciscan monastery has extensive grounds and a modern facility with 70 air-conditioned rooms and suites, color cable TV, swimming pool, walk to beach, meals available. Moderate.

Coveside Cottages (967-5424), PO Box 631, South Main Street,

Kennebunkport 04046. Open mid-May through mid-October. Old-style, knotty pine-walled, brightly furnished cottages on 2 acres bordering a tidal cove. One- and two-bedroom units, all with new kitchen facilities. Within walking distance of both Dock Square and a sandy beach. $695–$895 per week.

Seaside Inn (967-4461 or 967-4282), PO Box 631, Gooch's Beach, Kennebunkport. Rooms in the inn are just July through Labor Day, cottages are May through October, motor inn is year-round. An attractive complex formed by a 1720s homestead, a 1756 inn, a modern, 22-room motor inn, and 10 housekeeping cottages—all on a private beach next to one of Maine's best public strands. This property has been in the Severance family for 13 generations. The old homestead is rented as a cottage, and there are still four guest rooms in the old inn. A light breakfast is included in the rates. Cottages are per month. One-week minimum in oceanfront rooms in high season. $140–$150 per night for motel rooms, $95–$125 for rooms in the 1756 house. Less off-season.

Schooners Wharf (967-5333 or 800-525-5599), PO Box 1121, Ocean Avenue, Kennebunkport. Open year-round. Billed as "a fleet of 17 luxurious rooms" (which is, in fact, what this is), it is not an inn in the usual sense. New, impersonal, and unquestionably posh, the rooms have water views and are reached by elevator; equipped with private bath, cable TV, some are with a raised sitting area with wet bar and Jacuzzi. $95–$225 per night in high season, substantially less off-season.

DINING OUT   Cape Arundel Inn (967-2125), Ocean Avenue, Kennebunkport. Open May to mid-October for breakfast, Sunday brunch, and dinner (the dining room closes Sunday at 1). The dining room windows overlook the ocean, and the dinner menu is continental. You might start with mussels steamed in white wine and then try poached sole and salmon with lime hollandaise or scallops in puff pastry with vermouth saffron cream. Breakfasts here also get rave reviews. Entrées: $15.25–$21.95.

Seascapes (967-8500), Pier Road, Cape Porpoise. Open for lunch and dinner daily in-season, varying days April through December. Seascapes combines a great location (on a working fishing pier) and well-known local management (Angela LeBlanc has put her Kennebunk Inn on the south coast dining map). Specialties include Maine bouillabaisse and lobster braised in Drambuie cream. Entrées are priced from $13.50–$22.95.

White Barn Inn (967-2321), Kennebunk Beach. Open for dinner year-round (closed Mondays in winter); also for Sunday brunch. One of New England's most luxurious barns, still attached to the nineteenth-century inn for which it was built but with its face now glassed; nicely decorated to create a warm, candlelit atmosphere. Specialty is steamed Maine lobster on fresh fettucine; tantalizing appetizers may include lobster-stuffed mushrooms or bacon-wrapped sea scallops in a maple mustard cream. Mixed reviews. Entrées: $19.95–$28.95.

Olde Grist Mill (967-4781), Mill Lane (off Route 9 just north of Dock Square), Kennebunkport. Open April through December for dinner; closed Mondays off-season. A genuine mid-eighteenth-century tidal gristmill, a restaurant since the Lombard family opened it in 1937. It's recently been renovated and expanded, and the traditional New England menu has been spiced with dishes like salmon en papillote and scallops with sherry sauce. The prices have also risen; entrées now run $14.50–$28.50, and a full lobster dinner is $32.50.

Kennebunkport Inn (967-2621), Dock Square, Kennebunkport. Open April through December. Breakfasts on weekends, 8–10:30, dinner nightly. Elegant dining in two lacy dining rooms. Specialties include mustard and ginger rack of lamb and bouillabaisse with lobster, shrimp, clams, and fish. Try the trout mousse appetizer. Entrées: $14.95–$24.95. Strong local following.

Cafe Topher (967-5009). Route 35 and 9, Lower Village, Kennebunk. Open for lunch and dinner (live entertainment) most of the year. We like the atmosphere and a varied menu here. Dinner entrées: $8–$12.50.

Windows on the Water (967-3313), Chase Hill, Kennebunkport. Open for lunch, dinner, and Sunday brunch. A sleek, new dining room with views of the port through arched windows, terrace dining, and live entertainment on Fridays and Saturdays. Seafood is the specialty. Lobster-stuffed potato is the lunch special. Reservations are a must for dinner. Dinner entrées: $14.50–$24.

Breakwater Restaurant and Inn (967-3118), Ocean Avenue, Kennebunkport. Open May through December for breakfast and dinner. Casual, attractive dining room. Menu selections range from Yankee pot roast to seafood scampi; specialties include broiled halibut with mustard butter and baked stuffed shrimp. Children's prices available. Dinner entrées: $9.95–$17.95.

Kennebunk Inn (985-3351), 15 Main Street, Kennebunk. Popular for lunch (outdoors in summer) as well as for dinner. Half of the menu is seafood, and the specialty is bouillabaisse. Expensive.

The Nonantum (967-4050), Ocean Avenue, Kennebunkport. Open May through October. A classic summer hotel dining room with linen tablecloths and bentwood chairs, serving all three meals. Dinner entrées: $8–$20.

Hennessey House Restaurant (967-4114), Route 9, Kennebunkport. Open daily for lunch and dinner. A genuine family restaurant, nicely decorated in light blue, white, and brass. A 50-item menu, which includes chicken, seafood, and prime rib. Entrées include "The Greenery": a buffet in itself with some 130 hot and cold items. Dinners average $10 and under.

Bartley's Dockside (967-4798), Kennebunkport (by the bridge).

Open 8–9 daily. There is candlelight dining by the fire and a water view. Known for its chowder. Dinner entrées start at $8.95.

Mabel's Lobster Claw (967-2562), Ocean Avenue, Kennebunkport. April to mid-October, open for lunch and dinner. A favorite with locals, including George Bush. The specialty is lobster pure or richly dressed with scallops, shrimp, and fresh mushrooms in a creamy Newburg sauce, topped with Parmesan cheese. The lunch special is a lobster roll with Russian dressing and lettuce in a buttery grilled hot dog roll. Entrées: $6.95–$27.

Cornforth House (284-2006), 893 Route One, Saco (near the junction with Route 98). Open for dinner except Monday, also for Sunday breakfast. A former brick farmstead is now an elegant dining oasis in the middle of Saco's Route 1 "strip." Specialties include veal dishes and pecan chicken. Chef/owner Lee Carleton makes the spectacular desserts.

Joseph's By the Sea, Old Orchard Beach. A very formal dining room with an ocean view in the midst of Old Orchard's amusement and snack bar strip. A long-established family place that's rated tops locally. The standout starter is escargots sautéed with wine and seaweed. The menu includes veal and steak dishes but the specialty is seafood, like shrimp moutarde. Entrées: $9.95–$16.95.

EATING OUT   Alisson's (967-4841), 5 Dock Square, Kennebunkport. Open from 6:30 for breakfast; also serves lunch and dinner. The Market Pub is the local hangout for various degrees of salts. Soups and sandwiches or you can dine on fried seafood. Given its atmosphere, convenience, and prices, this place is so popular in high season that you'd better plan on coming early or late. Entrées run $2.75–$16.95.

The Green Heron (967-3315), Ocean Avenue, Kennebunkport. THE place for breakfast, a long-standing tradition, served on a glassed-in, waterside porch. The menu is vast and varied.

Nunan's Lobster Hut (967-4362), Route 9, Cape Porpoise. Open for lunch and dinner May through October. This low, shed-like landmark packs them in and charges, too. This is the place for a classic lobster feed—there are sinks with paper towels to wipe off the melted butter. Lobster, clams, and pies are the fare. No credit cards.

Mei Le Wah Restaurant (985-4981), 60 Portland Road, Kennebunk. Open daily except Monday for lunch and dinner. Specialties include sautéed broccoli in oyster sauce and the seafood platter with crispy Chinese vegetables. Most dinner entrées are priced under $10.

1810 House Eatery (985-4290), 17 Main Street, Kennebunk. Open daily except Sunday, 11–8. An old house set back from the main drag with a deli takeout side and a delightful dining room. Under new ownership. Italian specialties, some special Italian family dining nights.

Tilly's Shanty (967-5015), Pier Road, Cape Porpoise. Open in-season, daily 10–8. At this writing there's some question about the future of this beloved landmark. THE place for fried seafood, even boiled lobster, weather permitting since the inside dining space is limited; "open-deck dining" overlooking Cape Porpoise Harbor.

The Lobster Pot, (967-4607), Route 9, Cape Porpoise. Open for lunch and dinner daily, May to December. A family restaurant with less atmosphere and less of a crowd than Nunan's. Same lobster, fine fried seafood. Dinner entrées: $8.50–$20.95.

Hattie's (282-3435), Biddeford Pool. The local gathering spot for breakfast and lunch. THE place (the only place) to eat in Biddeford Pool, and it's a find: shrimp and artichoke pie for $5.95. President Bush knows it well.

Wormwoods (282-9675), Camp Ellis Beach, Saco. Open year-round, daily for lunch and dinner. A large, friendly, old-fashioned place that you can count on for a good chowder and family-geared dining if you are exploring this quiet corner of the south coast.

Marnie's (282-0969), Main Street, Biddeford. Open for breakfast and lunch, pleasant atmosphere, good food, the local gathering spot.

Also see Litchfield's in Wells, the place Kennebunkers rate right up there with Alisson's.

SNACKS   **Chase Hill Bakery,** Chase Hill, Kennebunkport. Open year-round except on Mondays, Tuesdays, and all of January and February. Delectable cookies, brownies, and cakes such as "lemon cloud." Everything is made from scratch. A few tables and fresh-ground Green Mountain Coffee for those who like to linger.

SEAFOOD MARKETS   **Prebble Fish** (967-4620), Cape Porpoise, where the locals get their fish, and you can get steamed lobster to go.

Port Lobster (967-5411 or 967-2081), Ocean Avenue, Kennebunkport. Live or cooked lobsters packed to travel or ship, and both lobster and crab rolls to go (several obvious waterside picnic spots are within walking distance).

Shackford and Gooch, Inc. (967-3321), Kennebunkport (at the bridge). Clams, lobsters, and fresh fish. Look for their seasonal takeout stand at the bridge.

ENTERTAINMENT   **Hackmatack Playhouse** (698-1807), Route 9, Beaver Dam, Berwick. Local actors, rave reviews.

City Theater (282-0849), Main Street, Biddeford. A 660-seat, 1890s theater recently restored, now offering a series of live performances. (Also see Entertainment under Ogunquit.)

SELECTIVE SHOPPING   *Antiques:*   The Kennebunks are known as an antiques center with a half-dozen shops, representing a number of dealers, most on Route 1.

Oliver's (985-3600) at Plaza 1, Route 1, Kennebunk is a well-known auctioneer, holding monthly auctions. Open daily except Sunday.

Art galleries: More than 60 galleries, most of them seasonal, are now listed in the annual Art Guild of the Kennebunks map/guide.

Among the largest are the **Kennebunk Gallery** (967-2669), Route 35 in Lower Village, a converted church displaying works by some 30 artists; the **Priscilla Hartley Gallery** (967-3212), Wharf Lane off Ocean Avenue in Kennebunkport, billing itself as Maine's oldest group gallery; **Mast Cove Galleries** (967-3453), on Maine Street, the "largest group gallery in the area."

Special shops: **Kennebunk Book Port,** 10 Dock Square, Kennebunkport. Open year-round. The oldest commercial building in the port (1775) is one of the most pleasant bookstores in New England. Climb an outside staircase into this inviting mecca, which is dedicated to reading as well as to buying. Books about Maine and the sea are a specialty.

Lafayette Center, Storer and Main streets, Kennebunkport. Open daily year-round. A former shoe factory has been recycled as a complex of upscale shops.

Brick Store Exchange, 4 Dane Street, Kennebunk. Open year-round 10–4; closed Sundays, also Mondays in winter. A sweet-smelling, volunteer-run outlet for locally crafted gifts.

Port Canvas, Dock Square, Kennebunkport. Open April to December. Canvas totes, suitcases, and hats all made in Kennebunk; there is a branch store in Boston's Faneuil Hall Marketplace.

Carla's Dress Shop, Ocean Avenue, Kennebunkport. A long-established women's clothing boutique with a wide and enthusiastic following.

The Good Earth, Dock Square, Kennebunkport. Open daily May through October, varying hours except January to March. Stoneware in unusual designs—mugs, vases, and bowls. Great browsing in the loft showroom.

Amicus, Route 35 (at the light), Lower Village. Open seasonally, a cooperative gallery that exhibits a variety of crafts and art: cards, baskets, jewelry, woven textiles, watercolors, and glass.

SPECIAL EVENTS   May: **A Victorian Affair in the Kennebunks,** Kennebunkport.

Memorial Day to Columbus Day: Frequently scheduled **architectural and nature walks** (see To See and Do).

Late June: Annual **La Kermesse Franco-American Festival.** Parade, public suppers, dancing, entertainment.

July 3: Old-fashioned **picnic and band concert**.

August: **Art Show,** Kennebunk Artists Guild, Community House, Kennebunkport. **Merchants Seafood Festival.**

December: **Christmas Prelude** (first weekend). Dock Square is decked out for Yuletide, and there are church suppers, concerts, and carols.

II. Casco Bay

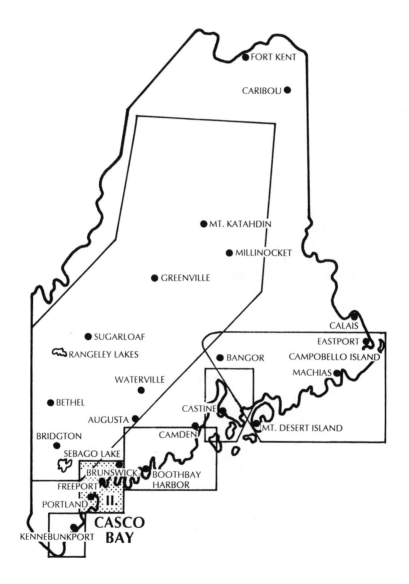

FORT KENT

CARIBOU

MT. KATAHDIN

MILLINOCKET

GREENVILLE

CALAIS

SUGARLOAF

EASTPORT

RANGELEY LAKES

CAMPOBELLO ISLAND

BANGOR

MACHIAS

WATERVILLE

CASTINE

BETHEL

AUGUSTA

MT. DESERT ISLAND

BRIDGTON

CAMDEN

SEBAGO LAKE

BRUNSWICK

BOOTHBAY

FREEPORT

HARBOR

II.

PORTLAND

KENNEBUNKPORT

CASCO BAY

Portland Area

Portland is a peninsula city where sea gulls perch atop downtown skyscrapers and where a smell and sense of the sea pervade. Northern New England's most sophisticated and one of its most important cities since the 1820s, it is blessed with distinguished buildings from every era. Portland is Maine's largest city, and it provides a showcase for resident painters, musicians, actors, dancers, and craftspeople.

Still, Portland has a small town feel. The total population still hovers around 66,000, and downtown is invitingly walkable. Hundreds of shops and galleries and dozens of restaurants are packed into ornate Victorian buildings in one five-block waterfront neighborhood. Known as the Old Port Exchange, this area was a canker at the city's heart until the 1970s, a skid row condemned for urban renewal.

Portland's motto, *resurgam* ("I shall rise again"), could not be more appropriate. First settled in 1632, Portland was wiped out twice by Indians, then once by the British. It was not until after the American Revolution that the community really began to prosper—as evidenced by the Federal-era mansions and commercial buildings, such as the granite and glass Mariner's Church built in 1820 to be the largest building in the capital of a brand new state.

This is the port that was loved by a small boy named Henry Wadsworth Longfellow, who later wrote:

> I remember the black wharves
and the ships
> And the sea-tides tossing free
> And the Spanish sailors with
bearded lips
> And the beauty and mystery of
the ships
> And the magic of the sea.

Portland continued to thrive as a lumbering port and railroad terminus through the Civil War, right up until the Independence Day at that war's end. Then it happened again. On July 4, 1866, a firecracker flamed up in a Commercial Street boatyard and quickly destroyed most of downtown Portland. When the city rebuilt this time, it did so with sturdy brick buildings replete with the kind of flourishes you

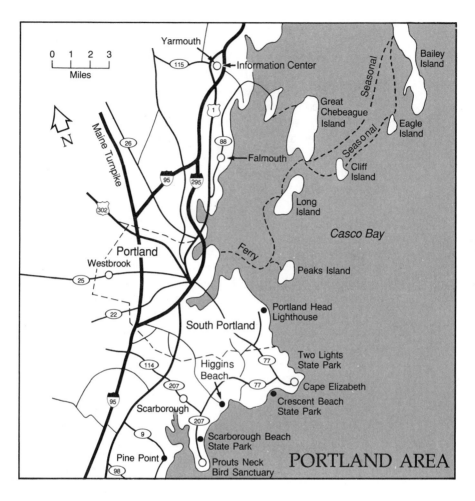

would expect of the Gilded Age, years during which these blocks were the core of northern New England's shipping, rail, and manufacturing businesses.

These were the very buildings that, a century later, were "going for peanuts," in the words of a realtor who began buying them up in the late 1960s. The city's prominence as a port had been eclipsed by the opening of the St. Lawrence Seaway in 1959, and its handsome Grand Trunk Station was torn down in 1966. Decent folk did their shopping at the department and chain stores up on Congress Street, itself threatened by the Maine Mall, which was burgeoning out by the interstate highway.

Down by the harbor, artists and craftspeople were renting shop fronts for $50 per month. They formed the Old Port Association, hoping to entice people to stroll through the no-man's-land that divided the shops up on Congress Street from the few famous fish restaurants and the ferry dock down on Commercial Street. That first winter they strung lights through upper floors to convey a sense of security, and they shoveled their own streets, a service that the city had long ceased to provide to that area. At the end of the winter they celebrated their survival by holding the first Old Port Festival, an exuberant street fair that continues to be staged in June.

Portland's Old Port Exchange continues to thrive, and on its fringes new semi-high-rise, red-brick buildings blend with the old and link Old Port with the Congress Street shops and offices.

Condominiums now line a wharf or two, but Portland remains a working port. It's also a departure point for the ferry to Yarmouth and Nova Scotia and for the flotilla of Casco Bay Liners which ply regularly between Casco Bay's Calendar Islands. These islands include Peaks Island, just 17 minutes off-shore with a frequent commuter ferry and a few B&Bs, and Cliff Island, more than an hour's ride, offering dirt roads, sandy roads, and the feel of islands usually found farther Down East. In summer these ferries bill their longer runs as "Casco Bay Cruises" and add "Music Cruises" and a lazy circuit to Bailey Island. Competing excursions offer jazz cruises, whale-watches, and service to Eagle Island, preserved as a memorial to arctic explorer Admiral Peary. The waterfront is also departure point for deep-sea fishing and day-sailing.

Art lovers can easily spend a day between Portland's museums and galleries. The size of the Portland Museum of Art quintupled in the 1980s, and it now exhibits American painters like John Singer Sargent, Winslow Homer, George Bellows, and Jamie Wyeth. The Joan Whitney Payson Gallery of Art at Westbrook College is also well worth finding: a small jewel-box of a building filled with an exquisite grouping of masterpieces that included Van Gogh's "Yellow Irises" until it was sold at auction several years ago for $49 million.

Portland also boasts more than 40 varied restaurants and some appealing bed & breakfasts as well as a few good downtown hotels. Cape Elizabeth, just south of Portland, offers some exceptional beaches and birding, and both Falmouth and Yarmouth, just east of the city, are also worth exploring.

GUIDANCE **The Convention and Visitors Bureau** (772-4994) publishes *Greater Portland Magazine*, a visitors guide listing restaurants, sights, museums, and accommodations. Its helpful walk-in information center is well stocked with menus and pamphlets, and courtesy phones connect with lodging places and services.

Intown Portland Exchange (772-6828), 477 Congress Street, is also a source of information.

The **Maine Publicity Bureau** (846-0833) staffs a major state information center on Route 1 in Yarmouth, just off I-95, Exit 17.

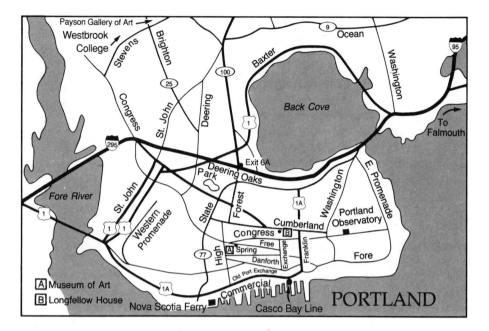

For details about guided walking tours of the city, contact **Greater Portland Landmarks** (774-5561), 165 State Street, Portland 04101. Be sure to request their self-guided walking tour leaflets (also available from the Visitors Bureau) that outline walking tours of Congress Street, the Old Port Exchange, State Street, and the Western Promenade. Each leaflet is $1.

GETTING THERE   By air: **Portland International Jetport** is served by Delta, Continental, United, USAir, Northwest Airlink, and Northeast Express, connecting with Boston, New York, and Quebec. It also offers direct flights to major cities such as Chicago, Newark, Philadelphia, and Washington. **Echo Helicopter** (775-5440) will take you almost anywhere.

By bus: **Greyhound** (772-6587) stops in Portland daily en route from Boston to points farther up the coast and to inland points north. But the terminal is dingy; inconvenient to Congress Street, the Old Port, or ferries; and closes early, forcing passengers to stand out in the cold and rain.

By ferry: Canadians may cruise to Portland aboard the **Prince of Fundy Company's** ferry, *Scotia Prince,* out of Yarmouth, Nova Scotia (775-5616 or, seasonally, 800-482-0955 in Maine; 800-341-7540 outside Maine). Overnight cruises are offered mid-May through October. Prices vary, depending on the season, cabin, or a variety of special packages. Restaurants, shops, and a casino are available on board. Departure time at this writing is 9 PM, arriving Yarmouth, Nova

Scotia, at 9 AM. The luxury cruise vessel accommodates 1,500 passengers in 800 cabins plus 250 cars.

PARKING   The **Fore Street Garage** (439 Fore Street) puts you at one end of the Old Port and the **Custom House Square Garage** (25 Pearl Street) at the other. The **Casco Bay Garage** (Maine State Pier) and **Free Street Parking** (130 Free Street, just up from the art museum) are also handy.

GETTING AROUND   The **Metro** (774-0351) bus transfer system serves Greater Portland.

The Metro City buses connect airport and city.

Maine Tour and Transit (775-4994) offers service to points up and down the coast and inland. Avis, Budget, and Dollar Rent- A- Car are also here. **Town Taxi** (773-1711) offers 24-hour service.

MEDICAL EMERGENCY   **Portland Ambulance Service** (Dial 911).

Maine Medical Center, 22 Bramhall Street, Portland (871-0111).

TO SEE AND DO   **Portland Museum of Art** (775-6148 or, for a weekly schedule of events and information, 773-ARTS), 7 Congress Square, Portland 04101. Open year-round, Memorial Day to October 1, Tuesday through Saturday 10–5, Thursday until 9 (when it's free), and Sunday noon–5; closed New Year's Day, July 4th, Thanksgiving, and Christmas. $3.50 per adult, $2.50 per student or senior citizen, and $1 per child 16 or under. With the completion of the Charles Shipman Payson wing, the museum quintupled in size. Its extensive collection of American artists features Maine-based masters such as Winslow Homer, Edward Hopper, and Andrew Wyeth. The adjoining museum buildings include the splendid Federal-style McLellan-Sweat mansion, built for Portland's biggest shipowner in 1800. The museum itself was founded in 1882.

Wadsworth-Longfellow House, maintained by the Maine Historical Society (774-1822), which offers its own exhibits and an extensive research library at the rear of Portland's first brick house (487 Congress Street). Open June 1 to Columbus Day weekend, Tuesday through Saturday; July and August 10–4; June and September 1–4; Sunday 1–4 throughout the season (closed July 4th and Labor Day). $3 per adult, $1 per child under 18. Allow 45 minutes for a guided tour. Built by the poet's grandfather, this was the home of an important Portland family. Peleg Wadsworth was a Revolutionary War hero, and the entire clan of Wadsworths and Longfellows was prominent in the city. The house, in which Henry spent his childhood, is a good example of how such families lived in the nineteenth century. The garden behind the house has been adapted from gardens of the era, and most furnishings are original. At Christmastime, the Wadsworth-Longfellow House has a popular open house, with decorations and festivities of the season.

Payson Gallery of Art (797-9546), 716 Stevens Avenue at Westbrook College. Open Tuesday through Friday 10–4, and weekends 1–5; but call first because they close while changing exhibits. Free. Special exhibits alternate with displays of their permanent collection, which includes works by Van Gogh, Renoir, Degas, Prendergast, Picasso, Homer, and Wyeth. This collection is a gem, housed in a building that resembles a jewel box, not to be missed; easy to find (see Portland map).

Portland Observatory (774-5561), 138 Congress Street. Open Friday to Sunday in June; Wednesday to Sunday in July and August; and weekends in September, October, or "when the flag is flying." Hours are 1–5 except on Saturdays when it's 10–5. $1.50 admission. This is the last surviving nineteenth-century signal tower on the Atlantic—an octagonal, shingled landmark that you can climb up 102 steps for a surprisingly rewarding view at the top and a sense of what it must have been like to scan the horizon for returning ships in the 1800s.

Morse-Libby House, the "Victoria Mansion" (772-4841), 109 Danforth Street (at the corner of Park Street). Open June 1 through Columbus Day, Tuesday through Saturday 10–4; during September, Tuesday through Saturday 10–1, Sunday 1–4; closed July 4th and Labor Day. $3 per adult, $1 per child under 12. About as Victorian as a mansion can be, this brownstone Italianate home was built in 1859 for a Maine native who had made his fortune in the New Orleans hotel business. The interior is extremely ornate: frescoed walls and ceilings, a flying staircase with 377 handcarved balusters of Santo Domingo mahogany, giant gold-leaf mirrors, marble mantels, ornate chandeliers, stained glass, and much more. The Victoria Mansion reopens during the Christmas season for special programs.

First Parish Church, 425 Congress Street. Open June to August, Tuesdays 11:30–1. Free. If you happen to be walking down Congress Street on a summer Tuesday afternoon, step into the vintage 1826 meetinghouse in which the pews are tipped forward—so that dozing parishioners would fall onto the floor.

Neal Dow Memorial (773-7773), 714 Congress Street. Open year-round, Tuesday through Friday 9–5 and Thursday until 9. A handsome Greek Revival house built in 1829 by the man responsible for an 1851 law that made Maine the first state to prohibit the manufacture and sale of alcoholic beverages. Currently the headquarters of the Maine Women's Christian Temperance Union, the mansion is a memorial to Neal Dow.

Portland Fire Museum, 157 Spring Street. Open mid-June to mid-September, Saturday 2–5 and Monday 7–9. Donations requested. Given Portland's unusual fire-fighting history, this collection of artifacts and photos is something to see. Housed in a granite Greek Revival firehouse.

George Tate House (774-9781), 1270 Westbrook Street (follow Congress Street west across the Fore River to Westbrook). Open July 1 to

September 15, Tuesday through Saturday 10–4, Sunday 1:30–4. $3 per adult, $1 per child. George Tate, mast agent for the Royal Navy, built this house in 1775 to reflect his important position. Both inside and outside are unusual, noted for its windows, gambrel roof, fine paneling, and elegant furniture.

Baxter Gallery of Portland School of Art (775-5152), 619 Congress Street. Art lovers shouldn't miss the photo and primary gallery in this beautiful, old building, just south up Congress Street from the Portland Museum of Art.

FOR FAMILIES   **Children's Museum of Maine** (797-5483), 746 Stevens Avenue (off the beaten downtown track—take Forest Avenue from Congress Street, then turn left on Stevens Avenue). Open Monday through Sunday 9:30–4:30. Admission charged. A delightful hands-on collection of exhibits; special programs for youngsters. (Also see the Kennebunks/Old Orchard Beach area.)

Lightship Nantucket (755-1181), Portland waterfront. Billed as the "World's largest lightship," this sturdy little vessel served major Eastern ports for 40 years, from 1936 until 1975. It's now open to the public, worth exploring to see how 20-man crews lived aboard for 30 days at a time.

GREEN SPACE   **Eastern Cemetery,** Congress Street and Washington Avenue (near the Portland Observatory on Munjoy Hill). More than 4,000 souls are interred in these 9 acres, and the headstones, dating back to the mid-seventeenth century, are embellished with angels' and death's heads. Despite its derelict state, this is an utterly fascinating place.

Fort Allen Park dates from 1814 and is on a blustery point on Casco Bay, a sure bet for a fresh breeze on the hottest day, as is the adjacent 68-acre **Eastern Promenade,** part of the turn-of-the-century park system that the famous Boston-based Olmstead Brothers designed. (The Olmstead Brothers were also designers of Boston's Emerald Necklace and New York's Central Park.) The Western Promenade, first laid out in 1836, is another part of this grand plan. Sited on the edge of a 175-foot-high plateau, it commands a long view to the west (theoretically you can see Mt. Washington on a clear day) and serves as the front porch for Portland's poshest and most architecturally interesting residential neighborhood. You might want to pick up a copy of the Portland Landmarks leaflet "Guide to the Western Promenade" ($1) from the Visitors Bureau (see Guidance).

Deering Oaks, a 51-acre city park also designed by Frederick Law Olmstead, has a pond, swans, fountains, a playground, and a fine grove of oak trees. A **farmer's market** is held here every Saturday morning throughout the summer and into November.

Portland Head Light is the oldest lighthouse in Maine. It was first illuminated in 1791 per order of George Washington. Grounds are open year-round, 8–7. It has recently been automated, and the former keeper's house is due to open as a museum sometime the summer of

'91. It's easy to find: take Route 77 south from Commercial Street for 4 miles. The lighthouse adjoins **Fort Williams Park.**

Two Lights State Park is open April 15 through November. No swimming, but 40 acres of shore for picnicking and fishing. $1.50 per person.

Gilsland Farm Sanctuary (781-2330), 118 Route 1, Falmouth Foreside (3 miles east of Portland). The headquarters of the **Maine Audubon Society** are located here. The sanctuary is open sunrise to sunset, year-round. The nature-oriented shop is open Monday through Saturday 9–5, Sunday 2–5. Sixty acres of trails, rolling fields, river frontage, and salt marsh. There is also a solar-heated education center with exhibits; special programs and field trips are year-round.

Scarborough Marsh Nature Center (883-5100, seasonal), Pine Point Road (10 miles south of Portland). Open daily mid-June to Labor Day, 9:30–5:30. The largest salt marsh (3,000 acres) in Maine. This Maine Audubon Nature Center offers canoe rentals, exhibits, a nature store, guided walking tours, and canoe tours throughout the summer.

BEACHES   **East End Beach** below the Eastern Promenade is a real city beach but, nevertheless, safe and clean, and it is the most convenient dunking spot.

Willard Beach in South Portland fringes a residential neighborhood (take Route 77 from Portland to Cottage Road; bear left at yellow blinking light to Willard Square; take the first right, Franklin Terrace).

Crescent Beach State Park (8 miles from Portland on Route 77) is a mile of sand complete with changing facilities, playground, picnic tables, and snack bar. $2 per person.

Higgins Beach, further down Route 77 in Scarborough, is an extensive strand within walking distance of lodging but no parking.

Scarborough Beach State Park (Route 207, 3 miles south of Route 1 on Prouts Neck) is a superb beach on which only a 65-foot stretch is technically public, but—thanks to limited parking—the crowd is rarely excessive. Take Route 207 from Route 1. $1.50 per person.

Scarborough Town Beach, farther down Route 207 and overlooking Pine Point, usually has parking space because the entrance fee is $8. Great for off-season walking. $1.

Pine Point, Route 9, the easternmost stretch of Old Orchard, usually offers space and parking.

BOAT EXCURSIONS   **Casco Bay Lines** (774-7871), Casco Bay Ferry Terminal, 56 Commercial Street at Franklin. Founded in 1845, it was said to be the oldest, continuously operating ferry company in the country when it went bankrupt in 1980. The present quasi-municipal Casco Bay Island Transit District looks and functions much the way the old line did. Its brightly painted ferries are still lifelines to six islands, carrying groceries and lumber as well as mail.

No one seems sure how many islands there are in Casco Bay. Printed descriptions range from 136 to 222, and seventeenth-century explorer

John Smith dubbed them the "Calendar Islands," saying there was one for every day of the year.

Of the six accessible via Casco Bay Lines, three invite exploring. There's a state-owned beach on Long Island (also a general store and restaurant) and a classic summer hotel on Great Chebeague. On Peak's Island, just a 17-minute ferry ride from Portland, you can spend the night, rent a bike and tour the rocky promontories of the undeveloped Back Shore. On Cliff, a full one-and-a-quarter-hour ferry ride from the rest of the city (it's technically a part of Portland), you can walk the dirt road to sandy beaches. Each island retains its own rarefied world of nineteenth-century summer cottages and fishermen's homes, of wildflowers and quiet inlets.

Casco Bay excursions include the year-round, daily mail boat run (2 hours, 45 minutes), putting into all the islands in the morning and again in the afternoon ($8.50 per adult, $4 per child), a year-round, 50-minute "Harbor Views" cruise ($4 per adult, $2 per child). Mid-June to Labor Day there is also a five and three-quarter-hour Bailey Island Cruise ($12.75 per adult, $11.50 per senior) (see Brunswick and The Harpswells), and a Diamond Pass run and Sunday night music cruises (5–8 PM). Also year-round, frequent, daily car-ferry service to Peaks.

Longfellow Cruise Lines (774-3578), No. 1 Long Wharf, Portland. Captain Rodney Ross offers year-round weekend tours of the harbor aboard his steamer replica *Longfellow II*; a wide variety of tours, April to November, include narrated harbor cruises and jazz, sunset, and dancing cruises.

Buccaneer Line (799-8188), Box 592, Portland. Mid-June to mid-October. Stops at House Island, where there is a Civil War fort and some sandy beaches, and at Cushing Island. One-hour cruises: $8 per adult, half-price for children under 12.

Eagle Tours, Inc. (774-6498 or 799-2201), Long Wharf, Portland. Late June through Labor Day, some trips through September. The *Kristy K* runs you out to Eagle Island, the former home of Admiral Peary, now maintained by the state as a historic site and nature preserve (see Brunswick/Freeport); the 49-passenger *Fish Hawk* is used for a harbor and lobstering cruise, and seal-watching. $15 per adult, $12 per senior, $9 per child for Eagle Island.

Bay View Cruises (761-0496), Fisherman's Wharf, Portland. June to September, narrated island and harbor cruises aboard the *Bay View Lady*, $8 adults, $7 seniors; charters.

SAILING   *Palawan III* (773-2163), Custom House Wharf. May through September, three-hour and full-day sails through Casco Bay; also two-hour evening sails, from $15.

Atlantic-Antigua Charters (443-3837). *Huntress* , a classic Hinckley Pilot sloop, available for one- to seven-day cruises or captained charters.

Sebago Sailing Charters (772-7966), 20 Custom House Wharf. Cruises of Casco Bay.

Odyssey (642-3270), Long Wharf, offers whale-watch cruises mid-April to Columbus Day; also cruises to Boothbay Harbor and around Casco Bay. Full service galley.

(See also Prince of Fundy Company's ferry under Getting There.)

BOAT RENTALS (See Brunswick/Freeport.)

CANOEING (See Scarborough Marsh Nature Center under Green Space.)

DEEP-SEA FISHING There are several options. Check with the Visitors Bureau (see Guidance).

GOLF AND TENNIS Riverside Municipal Golf Course (797-3524/5588), 1158 Riverside Street, Portland; 18- and 9-hole courses.

South Portland Municipal Golf Course (775-0005), Route 9, South Portland. Carts, club rentals, pro shop, snack bar, and tennis.

Willowdale Golf Club (883-9351), Scarborough, 18 holes.

HELICOPTER RIDES Echo (775-5440), based at Portland Jetport, offers sightseeing and whale-watching tours as well as shuttle service. From $30 per person. Will drop you on a harbor island ($50) or shuttle you to Monhegan for a half-day ($150).

HORSE RACING Scarborough Downs (883-4331), off I-95, Exit 6 in Scarborough. The largest harness racing facility in New England; Post Time: Tuesday through Saturday 7:30, Sunday 1:30. Downs Club Restaurant open for dinner and Sunday brunch.

HOT AIR BALLOONING Hot Fun (761-1735), Box 2825, South Portland. Hot air balloons carry up to six passengers.

LODGING There are 2,000 hotel and motel rooms in and around Portland. Right downtown, within walking distance of the Portland Museum of Art and the Old Port, you can choose from:

HOTELS Sonesta Portland Hotel (775-5411 or 800-777-6242), 157 High Street 04101. A 12-story landmark, built in 1927 as the Eastland Hotel, recently refurbished. There are 184 rooms, many with harbor views, and two restaurants, across the street from the Portland Museum of Art. Geared to business travelers but a distinct cut above most small city hotels with attractive rooms, unusually friendly service (including elevator operators), a rooftop lounge, coffee shop and dining room, and van service to Freeport shops. $75–$125 double depending on season; includes breakfast. Ask about weekend packages.

Portland Regency (774-4200 or 800-727-3436), 20 Mile Street, Portland 04101. The 95-room hotel, housed in a century-old armory, offers rooms decorated with reproduction antiques, equipped with amenities such as TV, two phones, and an honor bar. A formal dining room fills the atrium-like center of the hotel, and there is an informal pub, an attractive lounge, and a full health spa. $110–$150 in high season, otherwise $95–$130; no meals included.

Holiday Inn by the Bay (775-2311 or 800-HOLIDAY), 88 Spring

Street, Portland 04101. It is a high-rise, 216-room hotel. $83–$87, slightly more in high season, less the rest of the year.

Hotel Everett (773-7882), 51A Oak Street, Portland 04101. Describing itself as an "informal European-style hotel with a home-like atmosphere," this is an inexpensive place to stay that's a step up from the Y. There's a browsing library next to the front desk, and many of the patrons are young job hunters. From $35–$48.

Note: The major chains are here but sited out near I-95 or in South Portland. These include: **Howard Johnson's** (774-5861), **Sheraton Inn** (775-6161), **Ramada Inn** (774-5611), and the new, six-story, 227-room **Marriott** (871-8000) in South Portland (amenities include an indoor pool and health club and two tennis courts; an 18-hole golf course is planned), and **Quality Suites** (800-228-5151) at the airport.

BED & BREAKFASTS   **Pomegranate Inn** (772-1006 or 800-356-0408), 49 Neal Street, Portland 04102. This is an extraordinary place to stay. Isabel and Alan Smiles have turned an 1880s Western Promenade house into a work of art. Nothing stiff, just one surprise for the eye after another. An interior designer and former antiques dealer, Isabel has created six amazing rooms furnished in a mix of antiques and "objets," most with handpainted walls (not wallpapered) in bold, original designs. Downstairs the walls of the wide entryway are a hand-mottled tangerine, and the mantel and four columns in the living room are marbelized. Guest rooms have phones, discrete TVs, and private baths, and the living room is well stocked with art books. Breakfast is exquisite. Frankly, we're glad we stayed here before its fame spread because what has since been described as the Pomegranate's "high style" came as a complete surprise. (Note: our picture on the back cover was taken in the garden here.) Still, we can't imagine anyone being disappointed. $95 per room includes breakfast.

The Inn at Park Spring (774-1059), 135 Spring Street, Portland 04101. An 1835 three-story townhouse very near the Portland Museum of Art and Congress Street shops and restaurants. Innkeeper Judi Riley welcomes guests to one of seven elegant guest rooms, some with fireplaces and decks or terraces. Breakfast is brought to your room or served in the kitchen, living room, or courtyard. $80–$90, includes tea and brandy as well as breakfast.

46 Carleton Street (775-1910), Portland 04102. An attractive townhouse in the Western Promenade area offers seven rooms equipped with marble-topped sinks and furnished with Victorian-era antiques. We like the feel of this place. Proprietor (and professional bookbinder) Susan Holland makes guests feel welcome, and they tend to form a congenial group around the breakfast table. No smoking. From $40 for a single with shared bath to $89 for a double with private bath.

West End Inn B&B (772-1377), 146 Pine Street, Portland 04102. An 1871 townhouse in the Western Promenade area. Hilary and Rom

Jacobs have restored the house, carefully creating four guest rooms, each with private bath. A full, hot breakfast is included in $90 per room; cheaper off-season.

ON PEAKS ISLAND   Peaks Island is accessible by frequent ferry service (17 minutes) from the Casco Bay Line terminal. You can bring your car, but it's cheaper and simpler to park it at the adjacent Maine State Pier garage. The view of the Portland waterfront is an obvious plus here, along with a genuine Maine Island feel. It's just 1 mile square (5 miles around)—a great place to bring or rent a bicycle.

Moonshell Inn (766-2331), Island Avenue, Peaks Island 04108. Open late April to Columbus Day. This bed & breakfast is actually more convenient to the Old Port than most of the chain hotels and motels. Elinor (Bunny) Clark offers four guest rooms, some with water views, sharing three full baths. A breakfast of fresh fruit and homemade breads, juice, and coffee is served in the bright dining room with a deck overlooking Portland. Next door Ruth Sargent (a writer of books and short stories) offers two more rooms. Both hosts are delighted to tune guests in to the beauty of their island. $60 double, weekends in summer; $39–$50, midweek; $40 off-season.

Keller's (766-2441), Box 8, Peaks Island 04108. Open mid-May through mid-October. Just up from the ferry landing, Art and Elizabeth Keller have turned a former general store and restaurant into a home with four lower-level guest rooms, all with water views and full baths. $55 double, includes a breakfast featuring homemade sweet rolls, fruit, and coffee.

BEYOND PORTLAND   **Inn by the Sea** (799-3134), Route 77, Cape Elizabeth 04107. Just a 10-minute drive from downtown Portland (Cape Elizabeth is a residential neighborhood of the city), this luxurious, new resort is sited on a rise above Crescent Beach State Park. The marble lobby is hung with Audubon prints, and accommodations include one- and two-bedroom garden and loft suites, cottages, and a beach house. Furnishings include reproduction antiques, down comforters, TVs, VCRs; the kitchens are stocked with gourmet foods. The landscaping is superb, and there is a boardwalk to the beach. Amenities include an outdoor pool, indoor whirlpool, tennis courts, and croquet. A shuttle takes guests to the airport and Old Port. The dining room, open only to guests, specializes in seafood. July and August, $195–$210 per night; May and June, $160–$185. No meals included.

Homewood Inn (846-3351) in Yarmouth 04096. Open mid-June to mid-October. The Maine House, built in 1742, has four rooms furnished with antiques. There are 23 attractive rooms and suites in all, scattered in five houses, plus a number of cottages with fireplaces. The Lodge houses the dining room, cocktail lounge, and a lobby and gift shop. In all there are 40 rooms, many with water views. Minimum stay of one week for a cottage in high season. Expensive.

Black Point Inn Resort (883-4126), Prouts Neck 04074. Open early

May to late October. Easily one of the most elegant inns in the state, a vintage 1878 summer hotel that is such a part of its exclusive community that guests are permitted to use the Prouts Neck Country Club's 18-hole golf course and 14 tennis courts. Guests may also rent boats or moor their own at the local Yacht Club. Facilities include two sandy beaches, indoor and outdoor pools, two Jacuzzis, and a sauna. There are 80 rooms, poolside buffets with a pianist, afternoon tea (July and August only), evening cocktails, and dancing. No children under age 8. $230–$320 double per night plus 25 percent gratuity; all meals included.

Higgins Beach Inn (883-6684), 34 Ocean Avenue, Scarborough 04074 (7 miles south of Portland). Open Memorial Day to Columbus Day. A 1920s, three-story, wooden summer hotel near sandy Higgins Beach. The pleasant dining room, open July and August, features homecooking prepared with Gram's secret "receipts." There is also a cocktail lounge, homey TV room, and a sun porch. Upstairs, the 24 guest rooms are basic but clean and airy, 10 with private bath. Continental breakfast is available after Labor Day. $57–$70 double per day or $329–$630 per room in-season; an even better bargain at $539–$630 double MAP. Cheaper in shoulder months.

The Chebeague Inn By-the-Sea (864-9634; October to April call: 774-5753), Chebeague Island 04017. Open Memorial Day through September. A three-story, flat-roofed summer hotel set high on a knoll. What we like about this place is the large, open-beamed living room with its massive stone fireplace, brightly upholstered chairs, and rainy day board games. The 21 guest rooms (15 with private bath) have a nice sea-washed feel and are decorated simply but with taste. All three meals are served. On sunny days you can play golf (the 9-hole public course is just below the hotel), swim at Hamilton Beach, or explore the island by bike or moped (the hotel rents both), and on rainy days you can take the 15-minute water taxi ride to Cousins Island. From there a school bus transports you to your car, parked a short walk away at the Cumberland Elementary School, and drive to Maine's Fifth Avenue (see Selective Shopping in Freeport). Casco Bay Line service to Portland leaves from the other end of the island (shuttle service is available from the hotel). $82–$90 double in high season; less in May and June.

McKinley Estates (797-6241 or 800-292-1933), PO Box 3572, Portland 04104. On Great Diamond Island, served by regular Casco Bay Line service from Portland. Nineteenth-century Fort McKinley on Great Diamond Island has been turned into a townhouse complex with beaches, a restaurant, and tennis courts. In-season there's a three-night minimum of $270 per person, based on double occupancy; "residences" run $1,950–$2,800 per week.

COTTAGES BEYOND PORTLAND   South of Portland cottages in the Higgins Beach and Pine Point areas can be found through the Scarborough

Chamber of Commerce (772-2811), 142 Free Street, Portland 04101. Seasonal rentals are also listed in the *Maine Sunday Telegram*. For listings on summer cottages in the Casco Bay Islands, contact Casco Bay Development Association, Peaks Island 04108.

Also check the "Maine Guide to Camp & Cottage Rentals" available from the Maine Publicity Bureau (289-2423), 97 Winthrop Street, Hallowell 04347.

RESTAURANTS The claim is that Portland has more restaurants per capita than any other city in America. Take a look at the following incomplete list, and you will begin to believe it. The quality of the dining is as exceptional as the quantity. People from all over Maine look forward to a reason for dining in Portland. Enjoy!

DINING OUT **Cafe Always** (774-9399), 47 Middle Street. A small, strikingly decorated (in yellow and black), Old Port standout. The menu changes daily. It might be black-and-white ravioli filled with salmon mousse or roast pork tenderloin stuffed with sun-dried tomatoes and spinach in a red wine sauce. $12.95–$18.95.

Back Bay Grill (772-8833), 65 Portland Street. Open for dinner year-round, closed Sundays. The 20-foot mural of Portland is by Steve Quattruci, a professional artist and former maitre d' at Boston's Ritz Café. The menu changes daily but consistently includes some memorable soups, grilled pizza appetizers, pastas, and grilled (yes, grilled) lobster. Entrées: $12.75–$21.75.

Raphael's (773-4500), 36 Market Street. Open for lunch and dinner weekdays, dinner year-round. The fare is Northern Italian, the specialty "Veal Raphael" ($17.95), the dining space is dimly lit, deftly decorated. Entrées: $4.95–$19.95.

The Seamen's Club (772-7311), 375 Fore Street. Recently renovated, this charming, old club for seamen offers atmosphere appropriate to the Old Port and an engaging menu with an emphasis on fresh seafood. Try to get a table upstairs in the Library—if you are lucky enough to get a table by the window, you can watch shoppers hustling along the brick sidewalks below. Very pleasant service and atmosphere. Candlelight and small rooms make this an intimate setting. $1.95–$13.95.

Baker's Table (775-0303), 434 Fore Street. Upstairs there is a bakery, where this business got its start. Downstairs the lunchtime atmosphere suggests a European bistro; soups made from fresh ingredients are the specialty. At dinner, it is full-service dining with candlelight. Diverse European dishes include a marvelous bouillabaisse and creative treatment of veal, fresh seafoods, and tournedos. Breads, beautiful baked desserts. $2.95–$16.95.

Westside (773-8223), 58 Pine Street. Serving breakfast, lunch, and dinner; brunch Sundays. A find. A delightful café near the Western Promenade with an informal, friendly atmosphere featuring rotating paintings by local artists. The night we dined here the menu included beef tenderloin with pepper and ginger sauce ($14.95) and sole with hazelnut butter ($12.50). Pasta and tofu dishes were $9.95, and the lamb pattie was $5.95. Patio dining in the warmer months.

Street & Company (775-0887), 33 Wharf Street, Portland. Open for lunch and dinner year-round. A small, informal place serving seafood, only seafood. Seafood grilled, broiled, pan-blackened, and steamed, most of it served right in the pan it's been cooked in. A sample menu includes calamari in white sauce on linguini and salmon en paillote with fresh herbs. This newcomer outdoes the city's standby seafood places. Try it. Entrées: $8.95–$14.95.

Madd Apple Café (774-9698), 23 Forest Street. Open for lunch Tuesday through Friday and dinner Wednesday through Saturday. Adjacent to the Portland Performing Arts Center. The accent is southern here, and the menu includes Caribbean and Creole dishes and reliables like barbecued lamb ribs, pan-fired trout, and red beans and rice. Dinner entrées: $8.95–$15.95.

The Oyster Club Raw Bar & Grill (773-3760), 164 Middle Street. Open for lunch, dinner, and Sunday brunch. A lot of atmosphere for the price. The decor is a mix of nautical (a fake pilothouse and gleaming brass) and gentleman's club (wing chairs, dog and pony prints) all in a soothing dark green (no windows). It's a great place to meet to launch a book, the way we did this one. The lunch menu is vast and reasonably priced, good for salads and fried fish. Dinner features seafood and prime rib. Entrées run $6.95–$14.95.

DiMillo's Floating Restaurant (772-2216), Long Wharf. Open for lunch and dinner. Maine's only floating restaurant, this is a converted car ferry that now serves seafood, steaks, and Italian cuisine to customers who come as much for the old nautical atmosphere and the views of the waterfront as they do for the food. Touristy but a good bet for lunch. Entrées run $9.95–$14.95.

Channel Crossing (799-5552), 231 Front Street, South Portland. Open for lunch and dinner daily; standard but the view of Portland harbor makes this worth seeking out. $9.95–$17.95.

The Afghan Restaurant (773-3431), Exchange Street. Authentic Afghan food at very low prices. This storefront restaurant is hung with scenes of Afghanistan painted by the owner. Bring your own wine. Entrée and dessert are less than $10.

Beyond Portland: **The Galley Restaurant** (781-4262), 215 Foreside Road, Falmouth. Lunch and dinner daily. One of Maine's dining landmarks, overlooking a working marina. Specialties include seafood supreme in white sauce with wine and haddock cooked twelve different ways. Entrées: $12.95–$19.95.

The Cannery Restaurant at Lower Falls Landing (846-1226), Yarmouth. Open daily for lunch and dinner, Sunday brunch. Built in 1913 as a herring factory, then a sardine-packing plant from the 1920s right up until 1980. The building, now part of a complex that includes

Photo by Kim Grant

Downtown Portland

a marina and some interesting shops, makes an attractive restaurant space with a waterside terrace where you can lunch on sandwiches like "Bruschetta" (fresh sourdough bread brushed with olive oil, garlic, and basil topped with provolone cheese and tomatoes: $4.50) or Cannery Crabcakes ($10.95). Dinner is surprisingly reasonable, from $6.95 for spicy chicken stew to $13.95 for bouillabaisse.

Moose Crossing Restaurant (781-4771), Route 1, Falmouth. Open for dinner 4–10. The atmosphere is "Maine cabin" with tongue-and-groove paneling, old camping gear, antlers, and old photos of the Moosehead Lake Region. Specialties are mesquite-grilled fish and poultry. There is a wide selection of fish specials nightly. Entrées: $9.75–$12.95.

EATING OUT Thai Garden (772-1118), One City Center. Open for lunch and dinner weekdays, dinner on weekends. The atmosphere is basic, but the food is extraordinary and reasonably priced. Take care in ordering to counter spicy with bland dishes. Specialties include Pad Thai (sautéed rice noodles), honey ribs, fried shells filled with ground pork, corn and spices, crispy fish, and stuffed chicken wings.

May's Place (775-7141), 29 Wharf Street. A new addition to the Portland Thai food scene with a little more atmosphere and even more reasonable prices than Thai Garden.

Village Café (772-5320), 112 Newbury Street. Open for lunch and dinner except Sundays. This is an old family favorite that pre-dates the Old Port renaissance. A large, often crowded space with pasta specialties but standard American fare, too. Entrées run $5.50–$11.95.

Alberta's (774-5408), 21 Pleasant Street. Open for lunch Monday through Friday, dinner nightly. Specializing in California favorites like mesquite-grilled meat and seafood, pasta dishes; also some Tex-Mex and Cajun entrées. The atmosphere shows a pleasant sense of humor. There are only about 15 tables in this small, artsy, pink-walled restaurant. The value is good, for large servings. Daily specials; beer and wine.

Boone's Restaurant (774-5725), 6 Custom House Wharf. Open for lunch and dinner year-round. Still going strong since it opened in 1896, serving lobster and seafood specialties at competitive prices. A real slice of the waterfront's long history. $4.95–$12.95.

Dock Fore (772-8619), 336 Fore Street. Open for lunch and dinner. A sunny, casual pub serving hearty fare and homelike specialties. Large portions at good prices.

Horsefeathers (773-3501), 193 Middle Street. An entertaining atmosphere reminiscent of the gay nineties. Moderately priced soups, steaks, chili, and quiche; great big wedges of french fries.

F. Parker Reidy's (773-4731), 83 Exchange Street. Open for lunch, dinner, late supper, and Sunday brunch. One of the first restaurants to open when the Old Port was coming back to life. This is the traditional place to go after a Mariner's hockey game at the nearby Cumberland County Civic Center (see Entertainment). Victorian atmosphere, very cheery bar. Steaks, seafood, and fashionable fare. The restaurant is housed in the former Portland Savings Bank.

Tortilla Flat (797-8729), 1871 Forest Avenue. Serving lunch and dinner daily. A casual Mexican eatery with the standard tacos, enchiladas, nachos, burritos, and so forth. Screened porch and outdoor patio for summer dining.

Raoul's Roadside Attraction (773-6886), 865 Forest Avenue. Serves lunch and dinner year-round. The boast is "New American eclectic cuisine," which means whatever is stylish in California and New York right now. The food is good, and the prices are reasonable. Vegetarian specials. Varied entertainment.

The Great Lost Bear (772-0300), 540 Forest Avenue. Open Monday through Saturday for lunch and dinner. Portions are generous. There are big burgers, big "bear fries," big entrées.

Ruby's Choice (773-9099), 116 Free Street. Burgers, burgers, and more burgers. But very fancy burgers, with toppings such as hummus, cilantro salsa, garlic dressing, pickled vegetables, lettuce, onions, and tomatoes that you put on yourself at a toppings bar. Other specialties include burritos and deep-fried scrod on a bun. The burgers come in two sizes: half pounders and one-third pounders. A great place to entertain the kids while you get a good meal into them; also handy to the Museum of Art.

Good Egg Café and Pizzeria (773-0801), 705 Congress Street. Open for breakfast and dinner. No smoking. The breakfast choices run to eggs with chili and salsa, cheddar-scallion omelets, and multi-grain pancakes. Dinner, a relatively recent add-on, features a deep-dish pizza with some amazing variations on the theme.

Carbur's (772-7794), 123 Middle Street. Serves lunch and dinner daily. Be prepared to choose the first menu item on which your eye falls or to study the 20-page menu carefully to make sure you select the one thing that appeals to you the very most. This is a fun place where all of the sandwiches (their specialty) are big enough for a meal, and all come with outrageous names.

Victory Deli and Bake Shop (772-7299), 18 Monument Square. Breakfast, lunch, and dinner with the taste of a real deli plus fresh-baked breads and other goods available for takeout.

Porthole on Custom House Wharf. Open early for breakfast but closed after lunch. Great chowder; breakfast dishes at unbeatable prices. Clean; cheerful service at both counter and tables.

Beyond Portland: **The Lobster Shack** (799-1677), Cape Elizabeth (off Route 77 at the tip of the Cape, near Two Lights State Park). A local landmark since the 1920s, set below the lighthouse and next to the fog horn. Dine inside or out; known for chowder and lobster stew, fried Maine shrimp, scallops and clams, lobster and crabmeat rolls.

Spurwink (799-0006), 150 Spurwink Road (off Route 207 near Scarborough Beach), Scarborough. Open early spring to late October, from 11:30 to 2:30 for lunch only. Part of its beauty is that it's here at all, right where you don't expect to find someplace to eat. Then you discover it's a special place, looking much the same and serving much the same food as when Hope Sargent opened in 1955. Specials vary with the day and include soup, potato, vegetable or rolls, tea or coffee. Tuesday is homemade meat loaf or grilled liver and onion, Wednesday is homemade chicken pie ($6.75) or baked macaroni and cheese ($4.95). We happened to hit Friday for sautéed shrimp (fabulous: $6.75). On Sunday you can choose from roast turkey breast, roast pork, and roast lamb (all $8.95).

SNACKS   **Green Mountain Coffee Roasters** (773-4475), 15 Temple Street. A shop that sells all sorts of coffee beans and teas as well as elaborate equipment for preparing the perfect cup of either at home. More than half of the floor space has been given over to small tables and a counter where you can get all sorts of made-to-order sandwiches on good breads or croissants, fresh pastries, and, of course, excellent coffees and teas, plus real fruit drinks and so forth. A great place for a quick meal before an event at the nearby Cumberland County Civic Center (see Entertainment).

Lola's Kitchen (879-7000), 2 Free Street. Gourmet-to-go and find a place in the sun by the water.

ENTERTAINMENT   Cumberland County Civic Center (775-3481; hotline: 775-3825), 1 Civic Center Square. A modern 9,000-seat arena, the site of a year-round calendar full of concerts, special presentations, ice-skating spectaculars, winter hockey games, and other events. Pick up a free monthly calendar of events.

Theater: **Portland Performing Arts Center,** 25A Forest Avenue (just off Congress Street). The city's old Odd Fellows Hall now houses an elegant, intimate 290-seat theater that serves as home base for the **Portland Stage Company** (774-0465 for tickets), which performs September to April, and for the **Ram Island Dance Company** (773-2562), which stages weekend performances year-round.

Portland Players (799-7337), Thaxter Theater, 420 Cottage Road, South Portland also stages productions September to June.

The Mad Horse Theater Company (797-3338), 950 Forest Avenue, is another local group to watch for.

Portland Lyric Theater (799-1421), Cedric Thomas Playhouse, 176 Sawyer Street, South Portland. This community theater presents three musicals each winter.

"Mystery Cafe" (883-1035) is a who-done-it staged every Friday and Saturday in summer, every Saturday in winter in the Bakers Table Banquet Room (see Dining Out).

Music and dance: **Portland Symphony Orchestra** (773-8191), City Hall Auditorium, 389 Congress Street. The winter series runs October to April, Tuesday nights at 7:45 PM. In the summertime the symphony delights audiences throughout the state at outdoor pops concerts in some of the most beautiful settings, such as overlooking Casco Bay or by Camden Harbor.

Portland String Quartet (773-0544). This distinguished chamber group grows in stature every year; performances in a variety of Portland locations as well as around the state.

Portland Chamber Music Society (797-7261), at Westbrook College, 716 Stevens Avenue. Call for a copy of the winter schedule.

SELECTIVE SHOPPING   The Old Port Exchange and Congress Street complement each other, the latter offering solid department and chain store basics, the former filled with handicrafts, imported clothing, art, home furnishings, jewelry, books, and much, much more. Most Old Port shops are owner-operated and have been restored individually. We have returned home from Portland laden with purchases ranging from an egg separator to a dining room table. Even when you are not shopping, it is always pleasant to stroll along the Old Port's brick sidewalks, pausing at a bench beneath a gas lamp to watch the shoppers. At Christmastime, with all of the decorations and fairy lights, it resembles an old English town.

Congress Street shops include **Mitchel and Braun,** a full-service department store and **Owen Moore.**

In the Old Port, there are a half-dozen noteworthy galleries. Other favorite stores include the **Whip & Spoon,** a fascinating Commercial Street emporium that sells every imaginable piece of cookware plus gourmet foods and wines, and **Maine Potters Market,** a 14-member crafts cooperative in the Mariner's Church, Fore Street. **Nancy Margolis Gallery** (367 Fore Street) reserves half its space for special museum-quality shows, the remainder for selling unusual crafts pieces. **Abacus/Handcrafters Gallery** (44 Exchange Street) offers two floors full of crafted items, from jewelry to furniture. **The Stein Glass Gallery** (20 Milk Street) displays stunning pieces by 40 artists. The clothiers in the Old Port are **A. H. Benoit,** an old Portland institution moved from Congress to Exchange Street, and **Joseph's** (410 Fore Street), featuring well-tailored clothing for both men and women. Also, **The Bottle Shop** (428 Fore Street), over which Sam Kaman has been presiding for the past 56 years. The list could go on and on.

There are stores dedicated to selling records, posters, ballet outfits, tobacco, woodstoves, canvas bags, cheese, woodenware, paper products, art materials, stencil equipment, games, potting supplies, herbs, and more, more, more.

Bookstores: In the past couple of years Portland has become a mecca for book lovers. **Books Etc.** (38 Exchange), a very inviting store. **Bookland's** new in-town store at One Monument Way stocks a full range and has a great children's section and bargain table. **Anastasia's Books** (136 Commercial Street) specializes in psychology, women's studies, and fine arts. **Raffle's Cafe Bookstore** (55 Congress Street) caters to browsers and serves breakfast, lunch, and dinner. **Yes Books** (20 Danforth Street) is a trove of old paperbacks and art books, and **Allen Scott Books** (88 Exchange Street) also has bargain-priced art books. **Harbour Books** (846-6306), at Lower Falls Landing, Yarmouth. Part of the same rehabbed sardine cannery complex that includes The Cannery Restaurant, this is a very special independent bookstore, the kind booklovers will feel completely comfortable in and probably walk out with something they never intended to buy. Soft music, views of the harbor, and bargain tables. Open daily 9–6, Friday until 8 PM, Sunday 12–5. Visible from I-95; take Exit 17.

Beyond Portland Proper is the **Maine Mall** (Exit 7 off I-95), whose immediate complex of more than 100 stores is supplemented by large shopping centers and chain stores that ring it for several miles.

SPECIAL EVENTS June (first Sunday): **Old Port Festival:** special sales and a special performance in the streets that make up the Old Port.

Mid-July: **Deering Park Family Festival:** something for every age at the park in the middle of town. Also the **Yarmouth Clam Festival** in downtown Yarmouth.

August: **Cumberland Crafts Fair,** Cumberland Fair Grounds. **Sidewalk Art Festival,** Congress Street.

December 31: **Portland New Year's Celebration:** modeled after the First Night begun in Boston, with performances throughout the city all afternoon up to midnight.

Freeport

Freeport's shopping strip is now a priority stop for most Maine visitors. Each year as many as 15,000 cars per day squeeze up and down the mile of Main Street (Route 1) that is lined on both sides with upscale, off-price shops. L.L. Bean, ranked not only as Maine's number-one emporium but also as its number one man-made attraction, has been a shopping landmark for over 75 years. The more than 100 surrounding stores, on the other hand, have opened within the past decade.

Although the shops are the major reason most travelers come to Freeport, many visitors also come to stroll wooded paths in Wolfe's Neck Woods State Park and the Maine Audubon's Mast Landing Sanctuary or to enjoy the quiet countryside and waterside retreats away from the crowds.

Freeport itself has a long history, having celebrated its bicentennial in 1989. It is particularly proud that the papers designating Maine as a separate state from Massachusetts were signed here in 1820.

GUIDANCE The **Freeport Merchants Association** (865-1212), PO Box 452, Freeport 04032, does not have a visitors center, but they gladly respond to telephone and mail requests for information. Among the materials they send out is their free visitor's guide containing maps and a list of all the stores, restaurants, accommodations, and other services. The Maine Publicity Bureau's welcome center in Kittery stocks some Freeport brochures, and there is a state information center on Route 1 just south of Freeport, in Yarmouth, at Exit 17 of I-95. In Freeport itself, you'll find a limited selection of brochures at L.L. Bean's information desk and in a small building on Depot Street which also houses public restrooms.

GETTING THERE Bus service to Freeport from Boston and Portland via **Greyhound**. A number of **bus-tour companies** also offer shopping trips to Freeport from Boston and beyond. Most people drive, which means there's almost always a shortage of parking spaces. The best solution to this problem is to stay at an inn or B&B within walking distance and leave your car there.

MEDICAL EMERGENCY **Parkview Memorial Hospital** (729-1641), Brunswick.

TO SEE AND DO **Desert of Maine** (865-6962), Desert Road, Freeport (3 miles from L.L. Bean). Open daily, mid-May to mid-October, 9 AM to dusk. Narrated coach tours ($4.50 adults, $2.50 children, $3.50 senior citizens) and self-guided walks through a 35-acre patch of sand that was once the Tuttle Farm. Heavily farmed, then extensively logged to feed the railroad, the topsoil eventually gave way to sand, which spread . .. and spread until entire trees sank below the surface. It is an unusual sand, rich in mineral deposits that make it unsuited for commercial use but interesting to rock hounds. Children love it. There's also a sand museum and a 1783 barn museum here plus gift and souvenir shops. Two and a half miles from downtown Freeport. Overnight camping available.

Hot Air Balloon Rides (865-1712), Bob Scheurer, RR 4, Box 4392, Freeport. Year-round flights, weather permitting, just after sunrise and a few hours before sunset, when windspeed is usually below the maximum of 8 miles per hour. Most trips last a little over an hour and cover from 5 to 12 miles; there's always a champagne toast after touchdown. Rates start at $125 per person (the balloon accommodates up to three plus pilot). Reservation with deposit required.

Winslow Memorial Park (865-4198), Staples Point Road, South Freeport. Open Memorial Day through September. Day-use fee is $.75 per adult, free for children. A 90-acre municipal park with a sandy beach and large, grassy picnicking area. Facilities include rest rooms with showers.

GREEN SPACE   **Wolfe's Neck Woods State Park** (865-4465), Wolfe's Neck Road (take Bow Street, across from L.L. Bean), Freeport. Open Memorial Day weekend to Labor Day. $1 per person, free for children under age 12. A 244-acre park with shoreline hiking along Casco Bay, the Harraseeket River, and salt marshes. Guided nature walks are available; picnic tables and grills are spotted around.

Mast Landing Sanctuary, Upper Mast Landing Road (take Bow Street south), Freeport. Maintained by the Maine Audubon Society, this 100-acre sanctuary offers trails through apple orchards, woods, and meadows and along a mill stream. Several paths radiate from a 1-mile loop trail.

Bradbury Mountain State Park (688-4712), Route 9, Hallowell Road, Pownall (just 6 miles from Freeport: from I-95 take Exit 20 and follow signs). Open May 15 through October 15. $1 per person, free for children under age 12; overnight camping is $8 per night for nonresidents and $6.50 per night for Maine residents. The summit, accessible by an easy hike, yields a splendid view of Casco Bay and New Hampshire's White Mountains. Facilities in the 297-acre park include a playground, a softball field, hiking trails, toilets, and a small camping area.

Pettingill Farm (phone the Freeport Historical Society at 865-3170), Freeport. Open for periodic guided tours. A saltwater farm with 90 acres of open fields and woodland that overlook the Harraseeket Estuary with a totally unmodernized vintage 1810 saltbox house.

BOAT EXCURSIONS   *Anjin-San* (772-7168), near town landing, South Freeport. A 34-foot sportfishing boat custom-built for Captain Greg Walts. Day trips for mackerel, bluefish, and shark. Also charters diving and sightseeing trips.

Atlantic Seal (865-6112), Town Wharf, South Freeport. Trips aboard this 40-footer out into Casco Bay include three-hour cruises to Eagle Island, former summer home of Admiral Robert E. Peary, the first man to reach the North Pole; cruises to Chebeague Island for cocktails and dinner at the turn-of-the-century Chebeague Inn by-the-sea (fare does not include price of meal); seal- and osprey-sighting trips; and fall foliage cruises after Labor Day. Lobstering demonstrations are usually included, except late Saturday and all day Sunday, when Maine law prohibits lobstering.

CANOEING   The **Harraseeket River** in Freeport lends itself to canoeing. It is recommended to start at Mast Landing, the northeastern end of the waterway; there are also launching sites at Winslow Memorial Park on Staples Point Road and at South Freeport Harbor. Phone the **Maine Audubon Society** in Falmouth (781-2330) for details about periodic, scheduled guided trips through the area. Nearby lake canoeing can be found at **Run Around Pond** in North Pownal (the parking lot is off Lawrence Road, 1 mile north of the intersection with Fickett Road).

GOLF   **Freeport Country Club** (865-4922), Old Country Road, Freeport. Nine holes.

CROSS-COUNTRY SKIING   The areas listed under Green Space lend themselves to cross-country skiing; rent or purchase equipment from L.L. Bean, which also offers classes in cross-country skiing. (See Other Recreation.)

OTHER RECREATION   **L.L. Bean Workshops** (865-3111), Route 1, Freeport. An interesting series of lectures and lessons that cover everything from cross-country ski lessons (on weekends beginning in January) and golf to evening lectures on topics ranging from survival in the Maine woods to making soap, tanning hides, paddling sea kayaks, building fly rods, cooking small game, and fishing for Atlantic salmon. Write to L.L. Bean Clinic Coordinator, Freeport 04032.

INNS   **Harraseeket Inn** (865-9377 or 800-342-6423), 162 Main Street, Freeport. Just two blocks north of L.L. Bean, this luxury hotel has 54 rooms and 6 suites—the largest accommodation choice in the village. It has maintained the quietly elegant atmosphere of the 1850 Greek Revival house next door, where this operation first began as a five-room B&B. Although hosts Nancy and Paul Gray are native Mainers, their family also owns the Inn at Mystic, Connecticut, and they have a sure sense of how to make the most of their location. Twenty-three of the rooms at the Harraseeket Inn are thoughtfully decorated with antiques and reproductions and feature canopy beds and Jacuzzis or steambaths; 20 have fireplaces. The inn has two restaurants: the formal dining rooms featuring elegant table-side service and the casual Broad Arrow Tavern downstairs (see Dining). Other public rooms include a drawing room, library, and ballroom. Rates in season are $110–$165 for a room and $190–$225 for a suite; full breakfast and afternoon tea are included.

BED & BREAKFASTS   The **Freeport Area Bed & Breakfast Association** lists about a dozen members, all of which must meet certain standards established by the association. You can get a copy of their brochure by writing to PO Box 267, Freeport 04032. Below, we have put a ◊ next to member establishments. The majority of Freeport's B&Bs have opened in the past three or four years in the handsome old white-clapboard Capes and federal-style houses that stand side-by-side flanking Main Street just north of the shopping district.

◊ **The Isaac Randall House** (865-9295), 5 Independence Drive, Freeport. On a short road leading off and running parallel to lower Main Street, this handsome small inn has eight air-conditioned rooms furnished in antiques, oriental rugs, and lovely old quilts. A historic farmhouse still surrounded by 5 acres of woods, it's just a short walk or drive from the bustling outlets. A full breakfast is served in the beam-ceilinged country kitchen; and just down the street is Fiddlehead Farm, another lovely home that's now an exceptional restaurant serving delicious lunches and dinners (see Dining). Guests are also welcome to use an upstairs kitchen to prepare snacks or to cook a steak on the outdoor barbecue. Doubles are $60–$100, breakfast included, in season.

◊ **One-Eighty-One Main Street** (865-1226), 181 Main Street, Freeport. Featured in the June 1990 issue of *Country Home* magazine, this 1840s grey Cape with white trim and black shutters has seven guest rooms, all with private baths. Outside there is a garden and swimming pool. Inside are American primitive antiques from David Cates and Ed Hassett's collections, quilts made by David's mother, and oriental rugs. Full breakfast, served at the dining room's seven small tables, is included in the $90 room rate.

◊ **White Cedar Inn** (865-9099),178 Main Street, Freeport. This restored white-clapboard Victorian house was once the home of Arctic explorer Donald B. MacMillan, who went to the North Pole with Admiral Peary. It offers six welcoming bedrooms, four with private baths. Three of the rooms have a single bed in addition to a double or queen. Our favorite room, up under the eaves, has its own stairway and offers the most privacy. Full breakfast, included, is served at small tables in the sun room, adjacent to the country kitchen. Innkeepers Carla and Phil Kerber live in the remodeled ell which extends from the back of the inn. Double with private bath, $85; with shared bath, $70.

Captain Josiah A. Mitchell House (865-3289), 188 Main Street, Freeport. Original owner Captain Mitchell was commander of the clipper ship *Hornet*, which caught fire and sank en route from New York to San Francisco. The crew and passengers survived for a month and a half in three open boats; it is still the longest recorded survival at sea in an open boat. This attractive house, built in 1789, is set off by a white picket fence and café-au-lait shutters. Inside, it's high Victoriana with brocades, satins, velvets, a crystal chandelier, canopy beds, and old wicker. There is also a Jacuzzi. All rooms have private full or half baths. Rates begin at about $70.

Country at Heart (865-0512), 37 Bow Street, Freeport. This circa 1870 house is brimming with country collectibles and cute accents. Each of the three guest rooms, decorated with reproduction and antique furnishings, has a theme: Shaker, Quilt, and Teddy Bear, with appropriate collections on display. The Dubays' little Lhasa apso, Precious, enjoys welcoming guests. In season, double with private bath is $75; with shared bath, $65; extensive continental breakfast included. A gift shop, featuring counted cross-stitch, is off the dining room. Open year-round except Thanksgiving and Christmas.

◊ **Holbrook Inn** (865-6693), 7 Holbrook Street, Freeport. Just a block from Main Street and all its shops (turn off at the Mikasa store), this very pleasant, century-old Victorian is operated by welcoming Freeporters who have lived here all their lives. The rooms all have queen-size beds, private baths, color TV, air-conditioning, and antique furnishings. Double rooms are $65 including full breakfast.

Maple Hill B&B (865-3730), 18 Maple Avenue, Freeport. A short drive off Main Street just north of the shopping district, this hilltop farmhouse offers three guest rooms, a fireplaced sitting room, and a Steinway in the parlor.

◊ **Porter's Landing B&B** (865-4488), 70 South Street, Freeport. Spacious guest accommodations are in the post-and-beam carriage house next to an elegant house in the Historic District. Quiet country setting.

◊ **Harborside B&B** (865-3281), 14 Main Street, South Freeport 04078. A small, quiet inn just across from the harbor in the charming village of South Freeport.

Atlantic Seal B&B (865-6112), Main Street, Box 146, South Freeport 04078. Just five minutes away from downtown Freeport but eons away from the bustle, this 1850 Cape boasts views of South Freeport harbor from each of its three guest rooms. Owned and operated by the owners of the *Atlantic Seal* tour boat, it is furnished with antiques and nautical collections. Bathrooms are shared unless arrangements are made in advance for a private bath. Rates, including "hearty sailor's breakfast," range from $55–$125; guests also receive a discount on *Atlantic Seal* morning cruises. Van service from the Portland airport can be prearranged.

◊ **The Bagley House Bed and Breakfast** (865-6566), RR 3, Box 269C, Freeport. Ten minutes from downtown Freeport, this appealing B&B is operated by Sigurd A. Knudsen, Jr., who returned home to Freeport following a 24-year career in social services that included 10 years living with the Eskimos. Sig is a good cook and an avid sailor who used to own a 28-foot Friendship sloop. The house itself is one of the area's oldest, built in 1772; it showcases stencilled rugs, quilts, and other folk art by Sig's sister, Karen Parent. There are five guest rooms, mostly furnished in antiques, some with doubles and a single, two with queen-size beds. All have private baths. Two-night minimum stay required on holiday weekends and major Bowdoin and Bates college weekends. No smoking. $95 double in season, including full breakfast.

MOTELS   **The Village Inn** (865-3236), 186 Main Street, Freeport. Eight motel-style units to the rear of an old house, with color cable TV and air-conditioning. Walking distance to all the shops. Owned and operated by Freeport natives.

On Route 1, south of Freeport near the Yarmouth town line, there are a number of modern motels. Among these is the **Freeport Inn** (865-3106), Route 1, Freeport. Set on 25 acres of lawns and nature trails, the 110 units have wall-to-wall carpeting, cable TV, air-conditioning, and in-room phones. There's also a swimming pool and a pond where you can ice-skate in winter. Canoes are also available for paddling on the Harraseeket River. The inn's café and bakery serves breakfast and lunch, and just down the road is the Muddy Rudder restaurant (see Eating Out), under the same operation.

Other recommended motels along this strip are the **Super 8** (800-848-8888) and the **Coastline Inn** (865-3777), the latter with 109 rooms.

CAMPING   **Sandy Cedar Haven Campground** (865-6254), Baker Road, Freeport. Forty-five mostly wooded sites, each with fireplace and picnic table. Water and electricity hookups. Five tent sites. Store with wood, ice, and groceries. Two miles from Route 1 and downtown Freeport.

Desert of Maine Campgrounds (865-6962), Desert Road, Freeport. Wooded and open sites adjacent to this natural "beach" (see To See and Do). Hookups, hot showers, laundry, convenience store, nature trails.

DINING OUT   **Fiddlehead Farm** (865-0466), Independence Drive and Lower Main Street, Freeport. Formerly Sebastian's, this exceptional restaurant in a restored Greek Revival farmhouse continues to please diners with attentive but unpretentious service and a short but imaginative menu. Highlights include scaloppine done several ways, plus lamb chops, unusual pasta combinations, and lovely fresh seafood with simple but special sauces. Entrées are all under $20. Add $6 to the price of several selected entrées, and you can have starter, salad, and dessert, too. At lunch, there's a choice of delicious salads, sandwiches, and soups, all under $10. The two dining rooms' spare decor—wide pine floors, flowered wallpaper, simply swagged curtains—is warmed by fireplaces.

Harraseeket Inn (865-9377), 162 Main Street, Freeport. Continental cuisine and elegant service in three formally appointed dining rooms. Specialties include rack of lamb, roast chicken for two (carved at your table), shaslik of lamb, and such fresh seafood dishes as salmon steak au poivre. Main courses average about $20. Dessert lovers will not be disappointed here: try the baked Alaska, chocolate fondue with fruit, or crêpes suzette. In addition to dinner, the inn serves brunch, lunch, high tea, and a breakfast buffet. Proper attire required; reservations suggested.

EATING OUT   **The Broad Arrow Tavern** (865-9377), Harraseeket Inn, 162 Main Street, Freeport. Downstairs in this elegant inn, the atmosphere is relaxed and pubby. The menu is appropriate to the setting.

Horsefeathers (865-4005), Lower Main Street, Freeport. "Live lobster, fresh people, and you . . ." reads the banner on the side of this popular restaurant. The modern, upbeat atmosphere is enhanced by pink walls, high ceilings, and blond-wood tables, some with high stools. The chatty, self-consciously clever menu features such items as nachos, burgers, salads, stir-fries, trendy sandwiches, and steaks and seafood; most dishes are under $10.

Jameson Tavern (865-4195), 115 Main Street, Freeport. The informal tavern to the rear of the building serves inexpensive snacks and sandwiches until late in the evening.

Blue Onion (865-9396), Main Street, Freeport. Open for lunch and dinner except Mondays. A charming dining room in an old, blue roadside house located south of Freeport's downtown traffic squeeze. Soups, salads, and delectables such as sautéed shrimp scampi for lunch; baked and broiled fish, veal scaloppine marsala, lobster pie (meat of a one-and-a-half-pound lobster in a casserole with light cream and unsalted butter and served in a fine herb shell) and other fish, veal, and chicken dishes for supper. No liquor. Moderate.

Muddy Rudder (865-3106), Route 1, Freeport. Operated by the nearby Freeport Inn, this popular restaurant serves a wide selection of seafood dishes plus steaks, sandwiches, and salads; you can also have a full clambake on the deck. The atmosphere is relaxed, with piano music in the evening. Overlooking the water.

Harraseeket Lunch and Lobster Company (865-4888), South Freeport (turn off Route 1 at the giant wooden Indian outside Levinsky's, then turn right at a stop sign a few miles down). Open May through October. In the middle of the Harraseeket boat yard, this is a dockside pound where you order lobsters and clams on one side, fried food on the other, and eat at picnic tables (of which there are never enough at peak hours) overlooking a boat-filled harbor. There is also a small inside dining room. Freeport shoppers will do well to seek this place out.

Ocean Farms Market Restaurant (865-3101), 23 Main Street, Freeport. Breakfast, lunch, and dinner. Offering moderately priced seafood dishes, homemade chowder, and live boiled lobsters. Lobsters also packed to travel.

The Corsican (865-9421), 9 Mechanic Street, Freeport. Seafood, chowder, pizzas, calzones, sandwiches. Take-out menu, too.

The Lobster Cooker (865-4349), 39 Main Street, Freeport. Steamed lobster, sandwiches, chowders. Beer and wine.

FAST FOOD McDonald's (865-9566), 155 Main Street, Freeport. Open daily. Unobtrusively tacked onto Gore House, a stately Greek Revival home. Decorated with colonial reproductions and photos of Freeport past.

Arby's (865-1100), 123 Main Street. In the handsome Porter House, Arby's, like McDonald's, is cloaked in nineteenth-century white clapboard.

SELECTIVE SHOPPING—FREEPORT FACTORY OUTLETS As noted in the chapter introduction, Freeport's 100-plus factory outlets constitute Maine's mightiest new tourist magnet. *Boston Globe* writer Nathan Cobb describes it well: "a shoppers' theme park spread out at the foot of L.L. Bean, the high church of country chic." Cobb quotes a local landlord: "The great American pastime now is shopping, not hiking."

Of course it was hiking and hunting that put L.L. Bean on the tourist map in the first place. But times have unquestionably changed, and L.L. Bean has kept step by selling fashionable, sporty clothing and an incredible range of sporting equipment, books, gourmet and gift stuff as well as its golden boot (see below).

L.L. Bean says that it attracts at least 2.5 million customers annually—roughly twice the population of Maine. About a decade ago, neighboring property owners began to cash in on a share of this traffic, and they have done it with style. Instead of relegating the outlets to malls (see Kittery), they have deftly draped them in brick and clapboard, actually improving on the town's old looks (although longtime shopkeepers who were forced to move because of skyrocketing real estate prices might well disagree). Parking lots are sequestered behind the Main Street facade. In summer there is a real carnival atmosphere, with hot dog and ice-cream vendors on key corners. But it is the quality of the shops that ensures a year-round crowd. Think of just about any well-known line of clothing, accessories, or home furnishings, and chances are you'll find an outlet here. The following list is our personal pick of the lot. All stores except for L.L. Bean (and Bean's does have a separate discount store here, too) claim discount prices of 20 to 70 percent off suggested retail.

L.L. Bean (800-221-4221, orders; 800-341-4341, customer service), 95 Main Street Open 24 hours a day, 365 days a year. More than a store—

Photo by Fredrick D. Bodin

L.L. Bean

for millions it is the gateway to Maine. Most shoppers arrive having already studied the mail order catalog (which accounts for 85 percent of sales) and are buying purposefully. The store has been expanded several times in recent years to the point where it's impossible to find the old boot factory, built by Leon Leonwood Bean, that is at its heart. What with its outdoor waterfall, indoor trout pond, and thousands of square feet of retail space, the building now resembles a fancy shopping mall more than it does a single store. It was back in 1912 that Mr. Bean developed his boot, a unique combination of rubber bottom and leather top. He originally sold it by mail order but gradually began catering to the hunters and fishermen who tended to pass through his town in the middle of the night. L.L. Bean himself died in 1967, but grandson Leon Gorman continues to sell nearly a quarter of a million pairs of the family boots each year. Gorman's leadership, coupled with a staff of very savvy MBA marketing types, has seen Bean's grow by leaps and bounds in the last two decades. Current stock ranges from canoes to weatherproof cameras to climbing gear. There is a wide variety of clothing as well as every conceivable gadget designed to keep you warm. On the other hand, it is the anchor store for all of the outlets in town.

   L.L. Bean Factory Store (800-341-4341), Depot Street (in the middle of the parking lot across Main Street from the retail store). Seconds, samples, and irregular merchandise are offered here. You never know what you'll find, but it's always worth a look. Unlike the main store, the outlet is not open 24 hours a day.

Dansk Factory Outlet (865-6125), 92 Main Street (across from Bean's). Scandinavian-design tableware, cookware, and gifts.

Laura Ashley (865-3300), 58–60 Main Street. The Britain-based store with chic shops throughout the Western world chose Freeport for its first discount outlet. Dresses priced elsewhere at $100 plus are as low as $45.

Bass Shore Factory Outlet (865-4652), 102 Main Street. Classic footwear.

Benetton Factory Store (865-6369), 56 Main Street. Chic and colorful Italian sportswear for men, women, and children.

Perfumania (865-3399), 58–60 Main Street (upstairs). Wide selection of cosmetics and fragrances from such manufacturers as Calvin Klein, Dior, Anne Klein, Ricci, etc.

Cole-Haan Company Store (865-6321), 66 Main Street. Classic footwear at substantial savings but still far from inexpensive; also leather accessories, clothing, and gifts.

Corning-Revere Factory Store (865-3546), 22 Bow Street, lower level. Corning and Pyrex cookware, dinnerware, and housewares; Revere cookware.

Polo-Ralph Lauren Factory Store (865-4176), 76 Main Street. Designer clothing, home furnishings, and accessories.

European Collections/Oleg Cassini (865-3650), 58 Main Street. Daytime and special evening dressing from designers Oleg Cassini and Bill Blass.

Cuddledown of Maine Factory Store (865-1713), 6 Mill Street. Comforters, pillows, gift items all filled with goose down. "Only European down filling room in the country that we know of."

Dexter Shoe Factory Outlet (865-6625), Lower Main Street (Route 1 at Desert Road). American-made men's and women's shoes.

The Gap and Gap For Kids, Main Street. Casual sweaters, pants, jackets, and other separates for men, women, and children. The clothing downstairs is regular retail price; the bargains are upstairs.

Maine Wreath and Flower Factory Outlet (865-3019),13 Bow Street. Quality Maine dried flowers and wreaths at discount prices.

The Ribbon Outlet (865-4150), 22 Main Street. Ribbons and trims of every imaginable description. Some are as inexpensive as six yards for a dollar.

Buttons and Things Factory Outlet (865-4480), 24 Main Street (next to the Ribbon Outlet). A warren of rooms chockablock full of buttons and more buttons.

Mainely Bags (865-3734), 32 Main Street. Finely crafted leather bags.

Mikasa Factory Store (865-9441), 31 Main Street. Dinnerware, bone china, crystal, linens, and gifts. Three floors offering a large inventory.

Totes Factory Store (865-9405), 42 Main Street. Men's and women's raingear, umbrellas, hats, and luggage.

Van Heusen (865-3030), 140 Main Street. Men's and women's dress and casual wear.

Dooney and Bourke (865-1366), 52 Main Street (in back). Stylish pocketbooks, shoulder bags, belts, wallets, and portfolios in water-repellent, coarse-grained leather.

The Coach Factory Store (865-1772), 48 West Street (set back off Main Street next to Hickey-Freeman). Slightly imperfect and discontinued styles of fine leather bags.

Hickey-Freeman Factory Store (865-4002), 48B West Street (off Main Street). Men's suits, sportswear, sportcoats, and slacks.

Anne Klein Outlet (865-9555), 2 Depot Street, Fashion Outlet Mall. Designer sportswear and accessories.

Samuel Robert Direct/Joan & David Factory Outlet (865-3424), 2 Depot Street, Fashion Outlet Mall. Tailored clothing from fine fabrics, including beautiful shades of ultrasuede, and suedes. Joan & David shoes.

Harve Benard (865-1233), 2 Depot Street, Fashion Outlet Mall. Handsome dress and casual clothing for men and women.

Fila Factory Outlet (865-0462), 2 Depot Street, Fashion Outlet Mall. Italian sportswear, including swimsuits and tennis, golf, and ski gear.

Freeport Crossing, 200 Lower Main Street (Route 1 south of the center of town). A complex housing outlets for Calvin Klein (865-1051), Polly Flinders (865-6223), Leslie Fay (865-1052), Reebok/Rockport (865-1228), and others. A major expansion that will triple this complex is underway as we go to press.

London Fog Factory Store (865-1022), 48 Main Street and (865-9662) Freeport Outlet, Route 1 (south of town). Outerwear: raincoats, coats, leathers.

Carter's Childrenswear (865-3904), Freeport Outlet, Route 1 (south of town). Underwear and clothing for infants, toddlers, boys, and girls.

Carroll Reed Outlet (865-1348), 223 Route 1 (next to the Freeport Outlet, south of town). Classic women's fashions and skiwear for men and women.

SPECIAL SHOPS   **Harrington House Gallery Store** (865-0477), 45 Main Street, Freeport. This charming house, right in the middle of all the outlet shops, is owned by the Freeport Historical Society. Faced with escalating property taxes, the preservationists came up with a unique way to hold onto their house and "go with the flow" at the same time. Every room is furnished in 1830-to-1900-era reproductions, all of which are for sale. Pieces, all documented, range from handsome furniture and weavings to artwork, crafts, Shaker baskets, kitchen utensils, and toys.

Praxis—Fine Crafts (865-6201), 136 Main Street, Freeport. Distinctive signed works in pottery, weaving, leather, glass, jewelry, and wood by craftsmen from throughout Maine.

Brown Goldsmiths (865-4126),1 Mechanic Street, Freeport. Open Monday through Saturday. Original designs in rings, earrings, and bracelets.

DeLorme's Map Store (865-4171), Route 1 (south of downtown Freeport). The publishing company's own maps, atlases, and pamphlets; also guidebooks and maps of the United States and the world.

Bridgham & Cook, Ltd. (865-1040), 8A Bow Street (behind Polo-Ralph Lauren). Packaged British foods, toiletries, gifts—a must for the Anglophile.

SPECIAL EVENTS   Weekend before Christmas: **All-night Christmas shopping**. Not just L.L. Bean, but all the shops stay open throughout the night to accommodate late shoppers. Adding to the atmosphere are costumed carolers and hot refreshments.

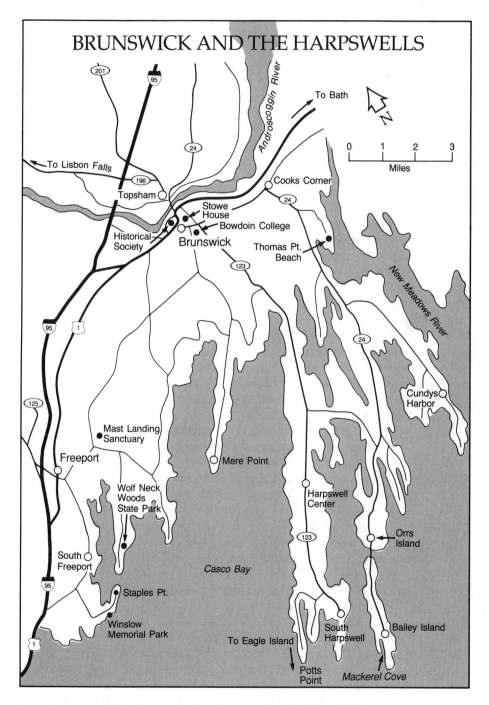

BRUNSWICK AND THE HARPSWELLS

Brunswick and The Harpswells

Brunswick, Maine's oldest college town, is the natural centerpiece for this area. Bowdoin College was founded in 1794, and its campus still rivals any in New England. Brunswick offers summer music and theater and some interesting shops, restaurants, and galleries.

Its Maine Street is a full 12 rods wide—just as it was laid out in 1717 as an early commercial site near the junction of the Androscoggin and Kennebec rivers, which generated power for nineteenth-century mills. Be sure to turn off Route 1 and drive down Maine Street with its shops and long, wide mall, complete with bandstand and frequent festivities.

Three narrow land fingers and several bridge-linked islands stretch seaward from Brunswick, defining the eastern rim of Casco Bay. Collectively they form the town of Harpswell, better known as "The Harpswells" because it includes so many coves, points, and islands (notably Orrs and Bailey). Widely known for its seafood restaurants, Bailey Island is on the tourist path. But, otherwise, these peninsulas are surprisingly sleepy, salted with crafts, galleries, and some great places to stay. They are Maine's most convenient peninsulas, yet they seem much farther Down East.

GUIDANCE   **Brunswick Area Chamber of Commerce** (725-8797), 59 Pleasant Street, Brunswick. Open Monday through Saturday, June through September; otherwise weekdays. Staff members keep tabs on vacancies and send out lodging and dining information. The walk-in information center displays area menus and stocks a wide range of brochures. From Route 1 north follow Brunswick business district signs (these will take you down Pleasant Street).

GETTING THERE   Bus service to Brunswick and Freeport from Boston and Portland via **Greyhound.**

MEDICAL EMERGENCY   **Parkview Memorial Hospital** (729-1641), Brunswick.

TO SEE AND DO   **Bowdoin College** (725-3000), Brunswick. Tours of the 110-acre, 40-building campus begin at Moulton Union. Phone for current hours. The college was named for a Massachusetts governor because Maine was still part of that state in 1794. Nathaniel Hawthorne and Henry Wadsworth Longfellow were classmates here in 1825; other notable graduates include Franklin Pierce and Robert Edwin Peary.

Founded as a men's college, the school now welcomes women students as well. Bowdoin ranks among the nation's top colleges both in price and in status. It isn't necessary to take a tour to see the sights.

Bowdoin College Museum of Art (725-5275), Walker Art Building. Open daily except Mondays, year-round, Tuesday through Saturday 10–5, Sunday 1–5; closed holidays. One of New England's outstanding art collections housed in a building designed by McKim, Mead, and White. Colonial- and Federal-era portraits by Gilbert Charles Stuart, Robert Feke, and John Singleton Copley; also a number of paintings by Winslow Homer and other American landscape artists plus sizable special exhibits.

Peary-MacMillan Arctic Museum (725-3416). Open same hours as the Museum of Art. A well-displayed collection of clothing, trophies, and other mementos from expeditions to the North Pole by two Bowdoin alumni. Robert Edwin Peary (class of 1877) was the first man to reach the North Pole, and Donald Baxter MacMillan (class of 1888), who was Peary's chief assistant, went on to dedicate his life to exploring Arctic waters and terrain.

Pejepscot Museum (729-6606), 159 Park Row, Brunswick. Open weekdays 10–3 and the first Saturday of the month 1–4. Free. Pejepscot (said to mean "crooked like a snake") is the Indian name for the local river. The museum houses exhibits reflecting various facets of local history. The Pejepscot Historical Society also maintains the **Skolfield-Whittier House,** 161 Park Row, a mid-nineteenth-century, Italianate brick double house preserved with original furnishings. Open via guided tours from 10–3 on summer weekdays offered by the Pejepscot Museum. Tours are $4 per adult, $2 per child.

Joshua L. Chamberlain Civil War Museum, 226 Maine Street, Brunswick. Open year-round by appointment; $2 per adult, $1 per child. A collection of Civil War artifacts and memorabilia of General Chamberlain, hero of Gettysburg, who also served as governor of Maine and as president of Bowdoin College.

Fishway Viewing Room (725-5521), Brunswick–Topsham Hydro Station, Maine Street, Brunswick. Memorial Day through mid-July is the best time to view migrating fish; a fish ladder leads to a holding tank beside the viewing room.

SCENIC DRIVE—A TOUR OF THE HARPSWELLS, INCLUDING ORRS AND BAILEY ISLANDS Allow a day for this rewarding peninsula prowl. From Brunswick follow Route 24 south past Bowdoin College and watch for the right turn onto Route 123, then 8 miles to the picturesque village of Harpswell Center. The white-clapboarded Elijah Kellog Church faces the matching Harpswell Town Meeting House built in 1757. The church is named for a former minister who was a prominent nineteenth-century children's book author. Continue south through West Harpswell to Pott's Point, where multi-colored nineteenth-century summer cottages cluster on the rocks like a flock of exotic birds that have wandered in among the gulls. You might want to stop by the first crafts studio you see here and pick up a map/guide to other studios.

Retrace your way back up Route 123—2 miles north of the church turn right onto Mountain Road. This brings you to busier Route 24 on Great (also known as Sebascodegan) Island. Drive south along the narrow spine of Orrs Island to and across one of only two cribstone bridges in the world. (Its granite blocks are laid in honeycomb fashion without cement to allow tidal flows.) This bridge brings you to Bailey Island. Continue past restaurants and lodging places, past picturesque Mackeral Cove to the rocky Land's End (there's a small beach and parking lot). Return up Route 24.

BEACHES AND SWIMMING HOLES   **White's Beach** (729-0415), Durham Road, Brunswick. Open Memorial Day to Labor Day. A pond in a former gravel pit (water no deeper than 9 feet). Facilities include a cement pier in the middle of the pond and a small slide for children. Sandy bottom, sandy beach, lifeguards, picnic tables, grills, and snack bar.

Thomas Point Beach (725-6009), Route 24, Cook's Corner. Open Memorial Day to Labor Day, 9 to sunset. Fee. This beach is on tidal water overlooking the New Meadows River with 42 acres of lawns and groves for picnicking (more than 500 picnic tables plus snack bar, playground, and arcade).

Coffin Pond (729-0114), River Road, Brunswick. Phone for current hours and fees. A strip of sandy beach surrounding a circular pool. Facilities include a 55-foot-long water slide, a playground, and changing rooms maintained by the town.

GREEN SPACE   **Eagle Island** (in Casco Bay). Located off Harpswell but accessible via Eagle Tours (774-6498), Long Wharf, Portland, or from South Freeport with Atlantic Seal Cruises (865-6112). A classic one-man's island, just 17 acres, it takes 20 minutes to walk around. But you can easily spend that much time in Admiral Peary's shingled summer home where, on September 6, 1909, his wife received the news that her husband had become the first man to reach the North Pole. Peary positioned his house to face northeast on a rocky bluff that resembles the prow of a ship. He designed the three-sided living room hearth, which was made from island stones and Arctic quartz crystals, and stuffed many of the birds that occupy the mantel. The upstairs bedrooms look as though someone has just stepped out for a walk, and the dining room is strewn with photos of men and dogs against ice and snow. There is a small beach and a nature path that circles the island and takes you past the pine trees filled with sea gulls on the ocean side.

GOLF   **Brunswick Golf Club** (725-8224), River Road, Brunswick. Incorporated in 1888, an 18-hole course known for beauty and toughness. Snack bar, lounge, and cart rentals.

The harbor at Harpswell

Photo by J. Norton, courtesy of Maine Dept. of Commerce & Industry

SEA KAYAKING H2Outfitters (833-5257), PO Box 72, Orr's Island 04066. Two-hour clinics include use of equipment; guided day trips and overnight excursions are also offered.

TENNIS   Brunswick Recreation Department (729-0114) maintains five lighted courts at Stanwood and McKeen streets.

CROSS-COUNTRY SKIING   The areas listed under Green Space lend themselves to cross-country skiing; rent or purchase equipment from L.L. Bean (see Freeport).

INNS   Driftwood Inn and Cottages (833-5461), Bailey Island 04003. Open June through mid-October; dining room (which is open to the public) is open late June through Labor Day. Sited on a rocky point within earshot of a foghorn, three grey-shingled traditional Maine summer houses contain a total of 16 doubles and 9 singles (7 with shared baths); there are also 4 housekeeping cottages. Everyone dines in the pine-walled lodge dining room (so request a room away from the lodge). Almost all views are of the sea, and there is a small swimming pool set in the rocks and plenty of room, both inside and out, to lounge. $50 per person, MAP; $69 double, without meals. Housekeeping cottages, available by the week, are moderate. This kind of atmosphere and value is possible only under longtime (50 years) ownership/management. Mr. and Mrs. Charles L. Conrad are very much your hosts.

Stowe House (725-8797), 63 Federal Street, Brunswick 04011. A Federal-era house in which Henry Wadsworth Longfellow once lodged. It is best known as the home of Harriet Beecher Stowe, where she lived for two years while she wrote *Uncle Tom's Cabin* (her husband was teaching religion at Bowdoin College). Overnight guests stay in the 54 motel units out back. There are also a large and busy restaurant, two lounges, and a gift store. Geared to bus groups but still pleasant. $69 double.

Captain Daniel Stone Inn (725-9898), 10 Water Street, Brunswick 04011. Fancy new accommodations in a handsome old Federal-style home that has been expanded to offer 25 rooms and suites, many with whirlpool baths. All have such modern amenities as color TV, telephone, VCR, alarm clock/cassette player. There are also two large function rooms and ample parking. Breakfast, lunch, dinner, and Sunday brunch are served in the Narcissa Stone Restaurant. Continental breakfast, included in the room rate, is set out in the breakfast room all morning. $89–$180 per room.

BED & BREAKFASTS   *In Brunswick/Topsham:*   **Brunswick Bed & Breakfast** (729-4914), 165 Park Row, Brunswick 04011. Open year-round. A beautifully restored mid-1800s Greek Revival home with floor-to-ceiling windows on the town's mall; within walking distance of the Bowdoin College campus. Travis and Nancy Keltner have created six outstanding guest rooms: four with double beds and one with twins (one room has a private bath, and the others share three baths). A full breakfast is included. Moderate. Smoking is permitted downstairs only. $55–$70 double.

Walker-Wilson House (729-0715), 2 Melcher Place, Topsham 04086. A handsome 1803 home, rambling back into its barn, set just off the main drag in Topsham (still just 1/2 mile from Bowdoin College). All 4 guest rooms have fireplaces; the 2 1/2 baths are shared. Unquestionably elegant, with original moldings and a delightful living room, Anne and Skip O'Rourke's home is also welcoming. $60–$70 includes a full breakfast.

Middaugh Bed & Breakfast (725-2562), 36 Elm Street, Topsham 04086. Off Route 1 and I-95 in Topsham's historic district, this Greek Revival house has two very attractive, comfortable second-floor rooms, each with private bath. $50 includes a full breakfast. Children in residence.

The Samuel Newman House (729-6959), 7 South Street, Brunswick 04011. Open year-round. The 1820s home of a Bowdoin Professor (Samuel Newman) in the very shadow of the Bowdoin campus. Five rooms in winter, seven in summer; all shared baths. From $35 single, $45–$55 double, and $65 triple.

The Tourist Inn (729-5790), 42 Pleasant Street, Brunswick 04011. A middle-of-town Victorian house with 10 guest rooms sharing 4 baths; also kitchen privileges, fresh-baked nibbles available 24 hours. $40–$60 double includes a full continental breakfast.

In The Harpswells: **Bethel Point Bed and Breakfast** (725-1115), Bethel Point Road 2387, Brunswick 04011. The mailing address is Brunswick, and it's just a short drive from Bowdoin but in a very different place. The house stands facing Hen Cove near the end of a narrow point not far from Cundy's Harbor. This is a find, an 1830 house with an attractive living room and three guest rooms, all sea-bright and furnished appropriately. The front room has a fireplace. Peter and Betsy Packard were hosting a Dartmouth College reunion the day we stopped by, but most days this must be a singularly peaceful place. $70 double per night includes a "continental plus" breakfast.

Vicarage East (833-5480), Route 123, West Harpswell 04079. Open year-round. Built in the 1980s right on Curtis Cove, this cozy Cape-style house is home for Joan Peterson-Moulton, a warm hostess who offers two or three rooms, one with a private bath and queen-size bed. All the rooms have ocean views, and the rocks that are uncovered at low tide are great for walking and beachcombing. This is a perfect place for dog lovers: the innkeeper's Irish wolfhound is the honorary hostess, and she's joined by other friendly canines. $55–$75 includes a full breakfast.

The Lady and the Loon (833-6871), PO Box 98, Bailey Island 04003. Gail Sprague has four antiques- and art-filled rooms with private bath. The house is situated on a bluff overlooking Ragged Island within walking distance of a private beach. $55–$70 includes breakfast. Gail is a gifted potter (the house also includes her shop) and attuned to the local arts scene.

Senter Bed & Breakfast (833-2874), Route 123, South Harpswell 04079. Owner of Brunswick's leading department store, Alfred Senter also owns an exceptional contemporary home by the ocean with landscaped gardens. Three bedrooms, two facing the ocean and one facing the rose garden. Full breakfast is included. Pets and children are welcome. $50 double.

The Johnson Bed & Breakfast (207-833-6053/6694), RFD 1, Box 308, Bailey Island 04003. Around the turn of the century, when guests arrived at Bailey Island by ferry, the Johnson was a four-story hotel. Later reduced to two stories, it became the Johnson family home—which it remains. George and Norma Johnson offer four comfortable guest rooms with ocean views, sharing two baths. $50 double includes breakfast. The Johnsons also rent five cottages by the week, all with access to a private beach.

MOTELS   **Little Island Motel** (833-2392), RD 1, Box 15, Orrs Island 04066. Open early May through October. One of the most attractive motels we know of. Just eight units, each with a small fridge and color TV; part of a complex that also includes a gift shop (the Gull's Nest) and reception area where coffee, fresh blueberry muffins, and fruit are served each morning. The complex is set on its own mini-island with its own beach, connected to land by a narrow neck. $99–$102 includes breakfast and use of boats, bicycles, and the outdoor picnic area.

Bailey Island Motel (833-2886), Route 24, Bailey Island 04003. Open May through October. A small, attractive motel near the cribstone bridge. $70–$80 includes continental breakfast. Light housekeeping units are available.

Note: If you are reading this section because you are headed north and just need a convenient bed for a night, we recommend the **Star Light Motel** (729-9195) in the lineup on Route 1 in Brunswick ($45–$55 in-season). If it happens to be a peak travel weekend and you are desperate for a bed, turn north on Route 24 into Topsham, then head up Route 196 toward Lisbon Falls. This is a truck route lined with inexpensive motels that never seem to fill.

COTTAGES   The Brunswick Area Chamber of Commerce (see Guidance) lists a number of weekly cottage rentals, most on Orrs or Bailey islands.

DINING OUT   *In Brunswick:*   **22 Lincoln** (725-5893), 22 Lincoln Street, Brunswick. Open for dinner except on Mondays. Among Maine's best-rated gourmet restaurants. The menu changes daily and could be either a la carte or prix fixe (three courses for $16–$19 or seven courses for $43–$49). The menu might include gratin of crayfish tails with truffles and saddle of veal with morels and calvados. The dining rooms are small and appropriately decorated for this Victorian house. Lighter, less expensive suppers are served from 5:30 PM in the less formal rooms of the Side Door Lounge, where there's frequently live jazz or folk music. From $8.94.

Bowdoin Steak House (725-2855), 115 Maine Street, Brunswick. Open weekdays for lunch and dinner, weekends for dinner. A downtown dining landmark with pub atmosphere; choices range from chicken and shrimp jambalaya to filet mignon. Specialties include barbecued shrimp (an appetizer), steaks, and homemade desserts. Live entertainment on weekends. Entrées: $3.95–$16.95.

Stowe House (725-5543), 63 Federal Street, Brunswick. Open daily for lunch and dinner. A large but delightful wood-paneled dining room. Specialties include sautéed shrimp and scallops in creole sauce over linguini and sliced loin of lamb sautéed with artichoke hearts. Harriet's Place is an inviting Victorian-style saloon. Dinner entrées: $12.95–$17.95.

Narcissa Stone Restaurant (725-9898), 10 Water Street, Brunswick. At the Captain Daniel Stone Inn. Open every day for breakfast, lunch, and dinner. Fresh seafoods prepared with a European influence are a specialty. Canned music and decor but pleasant. Entrées: $3.95–$19.

In The Harpswells: **Richard's** (729-9673), Route 123, South Harpswell. Open for lunch, dinner, and Sunday brunch. Offering continental fare like filet mignon and lobster thermidor ($10.95–$15.95), but also featuring more reasonably priced and very satisfying dishes like German farmer soup, Gemischter salat, Wienerschnitzel, and Schlachtplatte. The beer list is impressive.

J. Hathaway's Restaurant and Tavern (833-5305), Route 123, Harpswell Center. Open daily in summer for dinner; hours vary off-season. The Hathaways labor hard to create a casual country atmosphere and delectable dishes that range from vegetable lasagna to Swiss apple chicken to sirloin steak. Specialties include stuffed sole with broccoli and cheddar and rack of spare ribs. Entrées: $7.95–$12.95.

Jack Baker's Log Cabin Restaurant (833-5546), Route 24, Bailey Island. Open mid-March to mid-October, daily for lunch and dinner. A genuine log lodge built as an enormous summer cottage; nice atmosphere with an extensive menu and children's menu. Specialties include grilled and blackened seafood. Entrées: $4.95–$12.95.

Cook's Lobster House (833-6641), Bailey Island. Open Memorial Day to Labor Day for all three meals. A barn of a place, right on the water, adjacent to a working fishing pier. Save your leftover french fries and muffin crumbs to feed the sea gulls on the dock out back. In July and August try to get there before the Casco Bay Liner arrives with its load of day-trippers from Portland. Entrées: $2.50–$23.95.

Estes Lobster House (833-6340), Route 123, South Harpswell. Open mid-April through mid-October for lunch and dinner. Another barn of a place on a causeway with waterside picnic tables across the road. Entrées: $2.95–$21.95.

EATING OUT   *In Brunswick:*   **Omelette Shop** (729-1319), 111 Maine Street, Brunswick. Open daily for breakfast and lunch, year-round. This small, friendly storefront shop frequently jams on weekend mornings, spilling over onto the sidewalk tables. Dozens of omelets, which range from three kinds of cheese to strawberry-banana; also the delectable "Nova Scotia" with salmon fillets, capers, and cream cheese. The same menu holds all day and includes steaks and bulky burgers. Entrées: $3.95–$7.95.

The Great Impasta (729-5858), 42 Maine Street, Brunswick. Open daily for lunch and dinner. A storefront at the Route 1 end of Maine Street; a find if you go for creative Northern Italian fare like spinach noodle lasagna with fresh vegetables or shrimp baked with garlic, green peppers, prosciutto, and black olives. Entrées include antipasto salad and homemade bread. Entrées: $2.50–$11.95.

Giuseppe's Show Time Pizzaria and Cafe (721-0100), Fort Andross, Brunswick. The big, brick mill building visible from Route 1 has been rehabbed as Fort Andross with office space and this welcome addition to the local dining scene; great pizzas, river views, and live music.

In The Harpswells: **Holbrook's Lobster Wharf & Snack Bar** (725-5697), Cundy's Harbor (4 1/2 miles off Route 24). Open in-season for lunch and dinner. Lobsters and clams are steamed outdoors. Takeout and dining on picnic tables on the wharf; weekend clambakes; clams, crab rolls, fish 'n' chips, and homemade salads and desserts like Barbara's chocolate bread pudding with ice cream. The window boxes are filled with petunias, and you sit at picnic tables overlooking buoys and lobster boats. You can get beer and wine in the store next door.

Dolphin Marina and Restaurant (833-6000), South Harpswell (marked from Route 123; also accessible by water). Open year-round, 8–8 daily. The nicest kind of small Maine restaurant—family-owned and run with a combo chandlery/coffee shop partitioned by a model of a ketch from the more formal restaurant side—all overlooking a small but busy harbor. In the morning, fishermen gather on the six stools along the counter; the dining room fills for lunch and dinner. Chowder, lobster stew, and homemade desserts are specialties, but there is a full dinner menu. Inexpensive.

Mackerel Cove Restaurant (833-6656), Bailey Island. Open April through mid-October; coffee shop goes longer. This complex includes a marina, a coffee shop (6 AM–9 PM) that caters to fishermen, and a more formal restaurant (in the pine-paneled seafood barn tradition) that also serves breakfast, lunch, and dinner and that specializes in seafood at inexpensive prices (although the dinner menu runs to moderate for a shore dinner).

Block & Tackle, Cundy's Harbor Road. Open mid-May to mid-October, 6:30 AM to 8 PM. A family-run and -geared restaurant, a real find. Create your own omelet for breakfast; try shrimp stew or a real crabmeat roll for lunch, homemade clam cakes or seafood pie for dinner. The fried lobster platter ($9.25) is top of the menu.

ENTERTAINMENT   **Maine State Music Theater** (725-8769), Packard Theater, Bowdoin College, Brunswick. Performances at 8 every evening except Mondays, June through August. Musicals are the specialty here.

Theater Project of Brunswick (729-8584), 14 School Street, Brunswick. Serious drama presented late June through August, Tuesday through Sunday.

Brunswick Summer Music Festival. Performances are given June through early August. Concerts by music school students, internationally known artists, and music school faculty. The Aeolian Chamber Players are featured. Performances are at First Parish Church and Bowdoin College Kresge Auditorium.

SELECTIVE SHOPPING   **Senter's,** 124 Maine Street, Brunswick. Open Monday through Saturday. A great little department store with a surprising selection of clothing; also a sizable restaurant, the **Greenery,** tucked away on the top floor.

The Lady and the Loon, Route 24, Bailey Island. Gail Sprague's shop is the kind of place that local residents go for a special gift. Birds and other wildlife are depicted in paintings and on porcelain.

Ma Culley's (833-6455), Potts Point, South Harpswell. A bearded, one-legged fisherman was leaning against the small shingled shop the day we found it. He was stuffed. So were all the incredibly imaginative characters crowded into every corner of the shop. Colleen Moser introduces them one by one and says she doesn't like to sell to stores because she likes to meet the people who buy these lifelike soft sculptures. We came away with an amazing mask ($10). Ask for the pamphlet guide to other members of the Harpswell Craft Guild. It describes eight local studios.

Art and craft galleries: The north end of Brunswick's Maine Street has spawned some first-rate galleries in the past few years.

Elements Gallery (729-1108), 58 Maine Street, shows contemporary crafts and sculpture.

Hobe Sound Galleries North (725-4191), 58 Maine Street, specializes in vintage and contemporary art.

Icon Contemporary Art (725-8257), 19 Mason Street, sages changing exhibits of contemporary art.

Indrani's (729-6448), 1 Mason Street, stocks outstanding crafts.

O'Farrell Gallery (729-8228), 46 Maine Street. Changing exhibits of consistently fine art.

Bookstores: It's Academic, 134 Maine Street. This shop boasts "perhaps Maine's best selection" and invites browsers; worthy of a college town.

Gulf of Maine Books, Maine Street. A laid-back, off-beat store that specializes in Maine and poetry: "books that fall through the holes in bigger stores."

Beginnings, Etc., Maine Street. Geared to self-help and health.

Little Professor Bookstore, Topsham Fair Mall, also has a wide stock.

Bookland, Cook's Corner Shopping Center, Brunswick. One in a chain of Maine discount bookstores.

SPECIAL EVENTS   Throughout the summer: Farmer's Market (every Friday, May through October), on the downtown Brunswick Mall (the town common). Beanhole Suppers are staged during summer months by the Harpswell Neck Fire Department. (See Entertainment for summer theater, music.)

July: Annual Lobster Luncheon, Orrs Island United Methodist Church. Bailey Island Fishing Tournament, Mackerel Cove (to register phone Mackerel Cove Marina at 833-6645).

August: Topsham Fair (first week), a traditional agricultural fair complete with oxen pulls, crafts and food competitions, carnival, and livestock; held at Topsham Fairgrounds, Route 24, Topsham. Maine Arts Festival, the State's most colorful summer cultural happening.

Thomas Point Beach. **A weekend in Harpswell** (late in the month), annual art show, garden club festival in historic homes, and beanhole supper. **Annual Bluegrass Festival,** Thomas Point Beach (off Route 24 near Cook's Corner). **Maine Highland Games,** Thomas Point Beach, a weekend-long celebration of Scottish heritage, with piping, country dancing, border collie herding demonstrations, caber tossing, and Highland fling competitions.

III. Mid-Coast

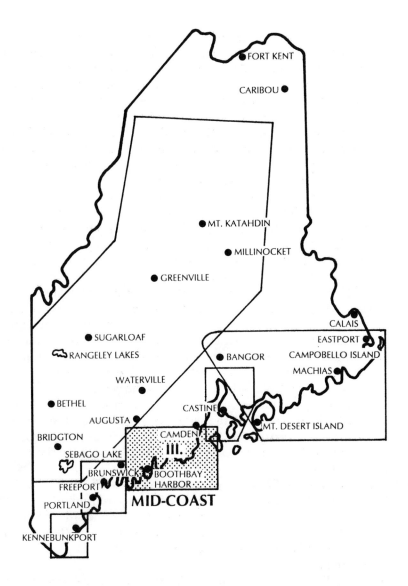

FORT KENT

CARIBOU

MT. KATAHDIN

MILLINOCKET

GREENVILLE

CALAIS

EASTPORT

SUGARLOAF

RANGELEY LAKES

BANGOR

CAMPOBELLO ISLAND

MACHIAS

WATERVILLE

BETHEL

CASTINE

AUGUSTA

MT. DESERT ISLAND

BRIDGTON

CAMDEN

III.

SEBAGO LAKE

BRUNSWICK

BOOTHBAY
HARBOR

FREEPORT

MID-COAST

PORTLAND

KENNEBUNKPORT

Bath Area

American shipbuilding began down the Kennebec River from Bath when the 30-ton pinnace *Virginia* was launched at the Popham colony in 1607. It continues today with tankers and naval ships up on the ways at Bath Iron Works. With about 9,000 workers, Bath Iron Works employs more people than worked in the 16 shipyards that stood here in the 1850s. Above the gates of the iron works, a sign proclaims: "Through these gates pass the world's best shipbuilders." This is no idle boast; many current employees have inherited their skills from a long line of forebears who did their part in the launching of more than 5,000 ships from this stretch of the river.

Obviously this is the place for a museum about ships and shipbuilding. The well-respected Maine Maritime Museum has one of the country's foremost collections of ship models, journals, logs, photographs, and other seafaring memorabilia. The museum complex encompasses a preserved nineteenth-century shipyard where small craft are still built and restored.

Allow a full day for Bath. Over the past decade the old red-brick city has undergone a renaissance, and it is an engaging place to stay, shop, and dine. Close to a dozen handsome sea captain's homes, most of them in the Historic District, have been converted to gracious bed & breakfasts and now offer overnight accommodations right in town. There are also some charming inns and bed & breakfasts in the surrounding countryside and down by the water.

There are a number of nature preserves nearby, all of them well worth visiting, and the Bath area boasts the only sandy beaches in mid-coast Maine. Also on the Phippsburg peninsula are engaging, pocket-sized fishing communities where the real flavor of the coast has not been diminished.

GUIDANCE **Bath Area Chamber of Commerce** (443-9751), 45 Front Street, Bath 04530. Open year-round. In addition, from mid-June to mid-October, an information center on the northbound side of Route 1, at Witch Spring Hill, is one of the state's busiest. It marks the gateway to Maine's mid-coast. There are also picnic tables and rest rooms (modern and old-style).

GETTING THERE Route 1 passes above the city (and the Kennebec River) via the Carlton Bridge, providing easy access to downtown. **Jet Limo** runs

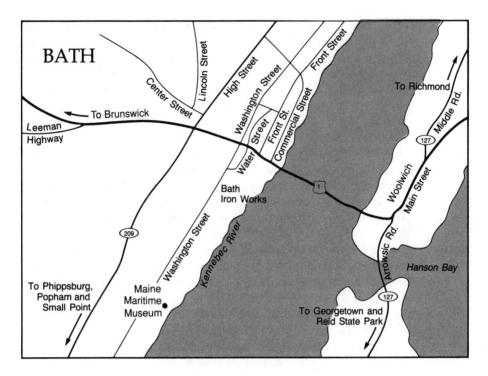

to and from the Portland Jetport (800-834-5500 within Maine or 800-992-1401 outside Maine).

GETTING AROUND   **Bath Shuttle Bus** (443-6258), a van which provides frequent service along this stretch of Route 1, picks up at the Maine National Bank about every half hour, follows a route through town, and stops at the Bath Shopping Center at the southern end of town. You can also flag them down. Although the service operates year-round, you really do need a car here.

MEDICAL EMERGENCY   **Bath Memorial Hospital** (442-8120), 1356 Washington Street, Bath. There is also an addiction resource center here.

TO SEE AND DO   **Maine Maritime Museum** (443-1316), 243 Washington Street, Bath 04530. Open 9:30 AM to 5 PM daily, year-round; closed Thanksgiving, Christmas, and New Year's Day. Admission is $5 per adult and $2.50 per child ages 6–15. The complex encompasses a large exhibition hall and the historic *Percy and Small Shipyard and Apprenticeshop* next to it.

Inside the grandly arched doorway of the striking red-brick *exhibition hall* is an extensive collection of marine art, ship models, half models, navigational instruments, and exhibits on several prominent local shipbuilding and seafaring families. A special hands-on children's exhibit invites youngsters to steer a ship's wheel, clang the bell, and climb the rigging. One entire wing of the museum is devoted to the history of Bath Iron Works and the famous yachts and naval vessels built there. At the Lobstering and the Maine Coast exhibit, you will see a replica lobster cannery and fisherman's shack, walk the indoor lobster wharf past historic boats in the "harbor," and sit in the stern of a replica lobsterboat to watch a film about a Maine lobsterman's day. In the adjacent 10-acre *Percy and Small Shipyard* were built more than 40 of the country's largest wooden sailing ships between 1896 and 1920; it is the only surviving shipyard of its kind. In the several restored buildings you will see exhibits and tools that describe how three-, four-, and five-masted schooners were built plus evidence of Maine's leading role in commercial shipping. At the *Apprenticeshop* a new generation of boatbuilders restores old vessels and builds reproductions of classic designs. The apprentices neither receive pay nor pay tuition for the experience. There is also an extensive collection of classic boats here. Go aboard the 142-foot Grand Banks schooner *Sherman Zwicker* (when she is in port) to learn how the crew fished for cod when she sailed the North Atlantic from 1942 to 1968. During the summer months a sightseeing boat usually makes regular runs along the Kennebec from the museum's dock.

Bath Iron Works, 700 Washington Street. Not open to the public (except for very occasional open houses), but you can't miss it beside the Carlton Bridge. The company's 400-foot-high crane—the largest on the East Coast—looms over the city. The largest civilian employer in Maine, the company is descended from a firm founded in 1884 and has been filling orders for the United States Navy since 1891. During World War II it actually produced more destroyers than did all of Japan, and it continues to do Navy jobs, always keeping to its pledge to deliver ships ahead of schedule and under budget. There is an extensive exhibit on BIW at the Maine Maritime Museum (see above).

Historic District. In the eighteenth and nineteenth centuries, Bath's successful shipbuilding and seafaring families built impressive mansions on and around upper Washington Street. The entire neighborhood, as well as all of Bath's downtown business section, has been entered on the National Register of Historic Places. Stroll the residential streets past white picket fences and white-clapboard houses and let your imagination take you back to Bath's heyday a hundred and more years ago. On Front Street handsome nineteenth-century commercial facades complemented by brick sidewalks and old-fashioned street lamps enhance the pleasure of shopping in Bath. Sagadahoc Preservation, Inc., offers walking tours; ask for a schedule at the Chamber of Commerce (see Guidance). The historical society also produces an excellent folder, "Architectural Tours—Walking and Driving in the Bath Area," available from the Chamber of Commerce.

Photo by Bonnie Scott

Bath Maritime Museum

1910 Farmhouse Tours, Woolwich Historical Museum, Route 1 (just north of Bath). Open late June to Labor Day, weekends during September.

GREEN SPACE   Fort Baldwin Memorial Park, Phippsburg. An undeveloped area with a six-story tower to climb for a beautiful view up the Kennebec and, downriver, out to sea. There are also remnants of World War I and II fortifications. At the bottom of the hill is the site where the Popham Colony tried to weather the winter of 1607 to 1608 but decided to go on to Virginia, where they were originally headed. They built the pinnace *Virginia* and sailed away.

Fort Popham Memorial Park (389-1335 in season) is located at one tip of Popham Beach. Open Memorial Day to Labor Day. Picnic sites are scattered around the ruins of the 1861 fort, which overlooks the beach.

BEACHES   If you are traveling with a dog, it is important to know that they are only allowed in picnic areas, not on the beaches. Also, be sure to abide by the mandate to take all your trash out with you.

Popham Beach State Park (389-1335), via Route 209 south from Bath to Phippsburg and beyond. An immense expanse of sand at the mouth of the Kennebec River. Also a sandbar, tidal pools, and smooth rocks. Never overcrowded, but it can be windy. The day-use fee of $1 per person (under 12 free) is charged from mid-April until mid-October.

Reid State Park (371-2303), Route 127, Georgetown (14 miles south of Bath and Route 1). Open year-round, seven days per week, but the entrance fee of $1 per person (under 12 free) is charged only between mid-April and mid-October. A bathhouse and snack bar plus 1.5 miles of sand in three distinct beaches that seldom become overcrowded although the limited parking area does fill by noon on summer weekends. You can choose between surf and slightly warmer sheltered backwater, especially good for children.

GOLF   Bath Golf Club (442-8411), Whiskeag Road, Bath. Pro shop, nine holes.

Sebasco Lodge (389-1161), Sebasco Estates. Nine-hole course and putting green. For hotel guests; open to the public by reservation.

SWIMMING   (Also see Beaches.)

Charles Pond, Route 27, Georgetown (about a half mile past the turnoff for Reid State Park; 15 miles from Carlton Bridge). Often considered the best all-around swimming hole in the area, this long and narrow pond has clear water and is surrounded by tall pines.

Pleasant Pond, Peacock Beach State Park, Richmond. Sand and gravel beach; lifeguards on duty. Water depth drops off gradually to about 10 feet in a 30-by-50-foot swimming area enclosed by colored buoys, removed from boating. Picnic tables and barbecue grills. Admission is $1 per person (under 12 free).

BICYCLING   Rentals available at **Bath Cycle and Ski** (442-7002), Route 1, Woolwich. As their name implies, they also have cross-country skis.

BALLOONING   Rides are offered by **Over the Rainbow Ballooning** (737-8232), RR 1, Box 1480, Dresden.

TENNIS   **Congress Avenue,** Bath. Open until 9:30 PM. Four lighted outdoor courts. First come, first served.

Sebasco Lodge (389-1161), Sebasco Estates (see Lodging).

SPECIAL PROGRAM   **Shelter Institute** (442-7938), 38 Center Street, Bath 04530. A year-round resource center for people who want to build or retrofit their own energy-efficient home. Three-week daytime courses are offered in the summer; night classes are given during the winter. Tuition varies according to course taken.

RESORT   **Sebasco Lodge** (389-1161), Sebasco Estates 04565. Open late June to early September. A traditional New England summer resort, this 650-acre, self-contained complex includes a saltwater pool and a nine-hole golf course plus putting green. Other amenities include swimming at a private beach, hiking, boating, lobster cookouts, and special evening programs. Choose a cabin, cottage, or lodge room (98 rooms in all). Rates are MAP: $75–$182 per person per night.

INNS   **Rock Gardens Inn** (389-1339), Sebasco Estates 04565. Open mid-June to September. Next door to the Sebasco Estates Lodge, Rock Gardens Inn offers the happy combination of an intimate inn and the facilities of the adjacent resort. Many guests return year after year, and the friendly feeling is pervasive. Longtimers are so much at home here that they sometimes even pitch in to tend some of the many flower beds. The inn is perched right at water's edge, and some of the rooms are so close to the rippling blue that your awakening view may make you feel as though you are on board a ship. Four rooms in the inn; ten cottages. No wonder Rock Gardens is such a perennial favorite: the lodging rates include breakfast, lunch, and dinner. No liquor is served, but you may brown bag it.

Fairhaven Inn (443-4391), North Bath Road, Bath 04530. Open year-round. Hidden away on the Kennebec River as it meanders down from Merrymeeting Bay, this 1790s house has six pleasant guest rooms, four with private bath and two sharing a bath. Everything is very neat; there are antique furnishings, and guests awaken to the aroma of unusual gourmet breakfasts. The inn's 27 acres of meadow are ideal for walking in summer and cross-country skiing in winter (the 10-acre golf course nearby makes for even more skiing). Two-night minimum stay weekends in July and August. In season rates, including a full breakfast, are $50 single; $60 double with shared bath; $70–$80 double with private bath.

The Grey Havens (371-2616), Georgetown 04548. Open mid-June to Labor Day. The same Mr. Reid who donated the neighboring state park built this turreted, grey-shingled summer hotel with a wide porch and Maine's first picture window—a big one commanding a sweeping view of Sheepscot Bay and its many islands. Opened in 1901 as the Seguinland Hotel, this gracefully aging old lady has a huge rock fireplace, an old-style dining room, and 24 upstairs rooms ranging from small doubles to large, rounded turret rooms—the latter have traditionally been honeymoon rooms. You may find the inn a shade stiff for children, with rules posted in too many places. Swimming is just up the road at Reid State Park. Moderate to expensive.

Squire Tarbox Inn (882-7693), Westport Island (write RD 2, Box 620, Wiscasset 04578). This charming inn on an island is reached by a road off Route 1 north of Bath and south of Wiscasset. (See complete description in Wiscasset chapter.)

BED & BREAKFASTS   **Packard House** (443-6069), 45 Pearl Street, Bath 04530. Open year-round. A gracious 1790 Georgian home in the heart of the historic district, one block from the Kennebec. Owned by Benjamin F. Packard, partner in one of the world's most successful shipbuilding companies (the captain's quarters of the clipper *Benjamin F. Packard* are displayed at Mystic Seaport in Connecticut). Three elegant guest rooms with period furnishings. No smoking; no children or pets. Rates include a full New England breakfast. $60 double with shared bath; $75 for a suite with private bath and sitting room. Minimum two-night stay weekends in season.

The Inn at Bath (443-4294), 969 Washington Street, Bath 04530. Open year-round. In the historic district, this rambling, recently restored 1830 home has twin parlors with marble fireplaces. There are four guest rooms with a choice of single or double beds; all have private baths. There's also a suite with a sitting room and "pocket bedroom" for two additional guests. You may choose a full breakfast or a continental one. $65 and $95 in season; suite higher.

1024 Washington Street (443-5202), 1024 Washington Street, Bath 04530. Open year-round. A handsome Victorian mansion in the historic district whose distinctive architecture has put it on the Preservation Society's walking tour. Six guest rooms are filled with chintz and period furnishings plus small color televisions; some have working fireplaces. You'll love the six-foot-long footed tubs and the European shower. Double with private bath $75; with semi-private bath $65; with shared bath $55–$65.

The Bath Bed & Breakfast (443-4477), 944 Middle Street, Bath 04530. Billed as offering "English hospitality in mid-coast Maine," this appealing B&B is operated by Mike Fear—a young British fellow who grew up near Bath, England—and his wife Betsy. Mike has worked as a steeplechase jockey, sheepshearer, folksinger, and riverboater; Betsy is a graphic designer and illustrator. Together, they operate a small publishing business as well as the B&B with its handsome staircase, several fireplaces, and antique furnishings which add to the atmosphere. Four guest rooms have double and queen-size beds; they share two bathrooms (a third is planned). In the evening, Mike sometimes plays his concertina and sings sea chanteys for guests. $60–

$80 double rates include a full breakfast that might feature sourdough pancakes, buttermilk waffles, a quiche, or an omelet.

Elizabeth's Bed & Breakfast (443-1146), 360 Front Street, Bath 04530. A welcoming old home overlooking the Kennebec River. Convenient in-town historic district location, near shopping. Two of the five guest rooms have river views; all are furnished with country antiques. Two-and-a-half shared baths. There is a guest living room with a TV and a resident cat. The continental breakfast is generous. Smoking downstairs only. $40–$60 per room.

Glad II (443-1191), 60 Pearl Street, Bath 04530. Open year-round. A Victorian home built in 1851, within an easy walk of the Maine Maritime Museum and the center of town. Cozy and comfortable. One room with twin beds, one room with a double bed; shared bath. Generous continental breakfast included. $45 double. Nonsmokers only.

The Front Porch B&B (443-5790), 324 Washington Street, Bath 04530. A turn-of-the-century home whose atmosphere is a blend of Victorian and country. In addition to rooms in the house, there is an efficiency apartment with private bath in the carriage house. Rooms are $50; the carriage house is $75; continental breakfast included.

Flower Cottage B&B (443-6182), 1207 Washington Street, Bath 04530. A circa 1860 cottage built by a paymaster for a shipbuilding company. Cozy, informal atmosphere in an intriguing old house with horsehair wall plaster, ship-lapped clapboards, and pumpkin-pine floors. Double rate of $45 includes a "continental-plus" breakfast featuring apple pie.

Levitt Family Bed & Breakfast (443-6442), 50 Pearl Street, Bath 04530. A Victorian-era in-town home with family atmosphere. Walking distance to shops and restaurants. Two spacious guest rooms are comfortably furnished with double beds and color TV; shared bath. $40–$55, including a continental breakfast featuring fresh-baked muffins. Children welcome.

Sebastian & Friends (443-4787), 2 Raymond Court, Bath 04530. Open year-round. In-town location with an antiques shop on premises. Two rooms, shared bath. Continental breakfast. Nonsmokers. Cat in residence. $45 double.

Captain Drummond House (389-1394), Parker Head Road, PO Box 72, Phippsburg 04562. Open year-round. A historic circa 1770 home (restored in 1977) halfway between Bath and the beaches. On a 125-foot-high bluff above the Kennebec, it offers exceptional views: woods, coves, peninsulas, a lighthouse. Built as a tavern, this quiet retreat has five fireplaces, antiques, and handsome architectural details. There are a private suite with whirlpool bath (available only in summer) and four guest rooms, one with a private second-floor balcony and others with private entrances. Smoking is permitted outdoors only. Leisurely breakfasts. Private baths. $65–$90 double. Innkeepers Donna

Dillman and Ken Brigham have recently purchased a 37-foot sloop on which they hope to take their guests for short sails.

Spinney's Guest House and Cottages (389-2052), RFD 3, Phippsburg 04562. Open May to October. Right on Popham Beach, 20 minutes from Bath. Six guest rooms share two baths. Coffee and donuts are served in the morning. Inexpensive.

Edgewater Farm Bed & Breakfast (389-1322), Route 216, Small Point 04567. Open mid-May through October. Five miles from Popham and a stone's throw to Morse's Mountain, where there is an easy 3-mile hike to a panorama of Seawall Beach, Popham, and Small Point. Also, 2 miles from a golf course, 2.5 from sandy Head Beach, and 13 miles from Bath. This early 1800s home has two cozy living rooms and five sunny bedrooms with shared baths. Three of the guest rooms are located in the main part of the house; the two others are in the wing and have a separate entrance. A full breakfast is served from 7 to 10 AM in the country kitchen or, on warm mornings, in the screened summer house.

Riverview (389-1124), Box 29E Church Lane, Phippsburg 04562. Open May through October. A secluded private home with a view of the Kennebec. Three rooms; possible handicap entrance. Next door to the old 1802 church in the center of Phippsburg. $25 single; $45 double; including continental breakfast.

MOTELS   **New Meadows Inn** (443-3921), Bath Road, West Bath 04530. Open year-round, with the exception of the cottages (open late May to mid-October). A good family place, with rooms for two, cottages for more, including a log cabin. Dining room with shore dinners, traditional family fare, snacks, salad bar, and luncheon buffets. Private docking and marina facilities. $26–$60 depending on season and accommodations.

Holiday Inn of Bath (443-9741), Western Avenue, Bath 04530.

COTTAGES   Listings are available at the Bath Area Chamber of Commerce (see Guidance) and in the Maine Publicity Bureau's *Maine Guide to Camp and Cottage Rentals.* (Also see Cottage Rentals under What's Where in Maine.)

DINING OUT   **The Osprey** (371-2530), at Robinhood Marina, Robinhood (just off Route 127, near Reid State Park). Open during the summer only; closed on Tuesdays. An unusual setting upstairs overlooking a boatyard and all of the activities along the dock—and, yes, there is an osprey nest on the day marker that you can see from the window, too. There is no atmosphere here—the room is brightly lighted, often loud and crowded, and you enter through a laundromat—but the cuisine is elegant, with prices to match. The menu changes frequently but might include appetizers such as baked brie in phyllo pastry with pistachio nut butter and shrimp ravigote; and entrées such as salmon en papillote with julienne of leeks, carrots, fresh herbs, and enoki mushrooms, or grilled breast of chicken marinated in olive oil, thyme, and savory and served with white-wine roasted potatoes. Moderate to deluxe.

J. R. Maxwell's (443-4461), 122 Front Street, Bath. Open year-round in a renovated 1840s hotel in the middle of the shopping district. At lunch there are burgers, salads, crêpes, and seafood sandwiches. At dinner there are steaks, chicken, and Maine seafood. Also Sunday brunch and a children's menu. Exposed old brick walls, hanging plants. Downstairs is the Boat Builder's Pub, with live bands on weekends. Moderate.

EATING OUT   Kristina's (442-8577), corner of High and Center streets, Bath. Open year-round, Tuesday through Saturday 7 AM–9 PM, Sunday 9 AM–2 PM, and Monday 7 AM–2 PM. Outdoor dining in summer. What began as a simple room with booths and a display case of scrumptious bakery treats and was known for its wonderful quiche and cheesecake has now grown to a full restaurant and cocktail lounge. You will still find the same great quiche, cheesecake, and other pastries plus things such as spanakopita, tortellini, honey mustard chicken, and steaks. There's a great breakfast menu, and brunch here is a real treat. Lunch choices include cashew chicken with vegetables, Kristina's changing specials, and burgers.

Truffles Cafe (442-8474), 21 Elm Street, Bath. Open Monday through Saturday 11–4. Luncheon served in a charming little room filled with tiny tables. Specialties include spicy chicken salad, unusual soups, and delicious desserts. No smoking.

Taste of Maine (443-4554), Route 1, Woolwich. Open daily mid-February to mid-December for lunch and dinner. Specializes in lobster, Maine seafood, steak, and chicken. Lots of nautical memorabilia here, with fishing nets draped about. Inexpensive to moderate.

Front Street Deli and Club (443-9815), 128 Front Street, Bath. Open year-round for breakfast, lunch, and dinner. Eggs, omelets, deli sandwiches (hot and cold), soup of the day. Downstairs is the Club, a cocktail lounge with live folk music on weekends. Inexpensive.

Harbor Lights Cafe (443-9883), 166 Front Street, Bath. Open year-round, seven days per week for lunch and dinner. Mexican fare: tacos, burritos, enchiladas, flautas, nachos, and so forth. Three evenings each week there is live entertainment: amateur band on Tuesdays, a professional band on Saturdays, and a DJ spinning golden oldies on Sundays (all begin at 9:30, when the kitchen closes). Inexpensive.

Donnelli's (443-6801), Route 1, Woolwich. Open year-round for lunch and dinner daily. Italian family favorites, such as lasagna, chicken cacciatore, and veal, chicken, or eggplant Parmesan. For strictly American tastes, steak and fried chicken. At lunch you can have a hamburger, one of several sandwiches, or smaller portions of the dinner entrées. Inexpensive.

Montsweag Restaurant (443-6563), Route 1, Woolwich. (See Wiscasset.)

New Meadows Inn (442-8562), 393 Bath Road, West Bath. (See Motels.) Inexpensive to moderate.

Spinney's Restaurant and Guest House (389-1122), at the end of Route 209, Popham Beach. Open weekends in April and daily May to October for breakfast, lunch, dinner. Our kind of beach restaurant: counter and tables, pleasant atmosphere with basic chowder and a sandwich menu plus reasonably priced hot plates. Beer, wine, and cocktails. Inexpensive to moderate.

Lobster House (389-1596), Small Point (follow Route 1 to Route 126). Open for the summer season. Mrs. Pye's place is a classic lobster pound specializing in seafood dinners and homemade pastry; beer and wine are served. Prices are inexpensive to moderate.

The Water's Edge (389-2756), Sebasco Estates. Open daily 10–8, mid-May through mid-September. Steamed lobster and clams, fried or broiled fish, steak, surf and turf, and lobster, crab, and tuna served as salad plates or sandwich rolls. Right at a commercial fishing wharf (the owner's father is the fisherman), this is a great place to enjoy the fruits of Casco Bay (you may even see the lobstermen hauling the catch as you munch).

SNACKS   **The Cabin** (443-6224), 552 Washington Street, Bath. Claims to serve "the only real pizza in Maine" plus sandwiches, pasta.

Bath House of Pizza (443-6631), 737 Washington Street, Bath. Open daily, year-round. Freshly made pizzas, seafood, and pasta dishes.

ENTERTAINMENT   **Center for the Arts at the Chocolate Church** (442-8455), 804 Washington Street, Bath 04530. Year-round presentations include plays, concerts, and a wide variety of guest artists. The handsome church has been completely restored inside. There is also a very nice gallery at the Chocolate Church (so-called because of the chocolate color of this Greek Revival building).

SELECTIVE SHOPPING   *Outlets:* **Factory Outlet Center,** Route 1, Woolwich (north of Bath). A collection of outlets representing several manufacturers of men's, women's, and children's clothing plus Bass Shoes.

Antiques: **C. N. Flood, Unlimited** (443-4573 or 389-1009), 619 High Street, Bath. Open in-season Wednesday through Saturday 10–5 and Sunday 12–5. This company has been in the antiques business almost 50 years and does appraisals as well as offering antiques for sale. The shop is in a former ship captain's home that is on the National Register of Historic Places.

Artisans: **Arrowsic Pottery** (443-6048), Route 127, Arrowsic (1/2 mile from the Carlton Bridge). Open daily June to August and weekdays the rest of the year, 9–5. An attractive studio designed by architect Jozef Tara for his potter wife, Nan Kilbourn-Tara. Features a full line of functional pottery, including mugs, bowls, lanterns, and casseroles, all rendered in colors that reflect Maine's flowers and fields. Also larger pieces made on commission: birdbaths, stoneware sinks.

Special shops: **Front Street,** which runs parallel to the Kennebec a block from the riverbank, is graced with an impressive row of nineteenth-century, red-brick commercial buildings that rose during the city's heyday. They are now completely restored and have been enhanced by landscaping, brick sidewalks, park benches, tasteful signs, and old-fashioned lamps. Along the several blocks you will happen upon specialty shops offering everything from clothing to Maine-made crafts. Among the latter, be sure to stop at **Mason Street Mercantile**, 50 Front Street, and **Yankee Artisan,** 178 Front Street. A waterfront park with a public landing is a short block away from the shopping district.

Flea market: **Montsweag Flea Market** (443-2809), Route 1, Woolwich. A field filled with tables weighted down by every sort of collectible and curiosity you could imagine. It is a beehive of activity every day during the summer and on weekends spring and fall. Antiques, rather than flea-market finds, are featured on Wednesdays.

SPECIAL EVENTS Three days surrounding the Fourth of July: **Bath Heritage Days,** a grand celebration with an old-time parade of antique cars, marching bands, clowns, guided tours of the historic district, craft sales, art shows, musical entertainment in two parks, a triathlon, and Firemen's Follies featuring bed races, bucket relays, and demonstrations of equipment and firefighting techniques. Fireworks over the Kennebec.

July and August: Wednesday evening concerts by the **Bath Municipal Band,** Library Park.

December: **Winter Solstice Celebration**. Bath calls itself the "Christmas City on the Kennebec" and sponsors a community sing-along at the Chocolate Church, a Christmas parade, and a Festival of Trees. Call or write the chamber of commerce for a Christmas events calendar (see Guidance).

Wiscasset

Wiscasset is Maine's gift to motorists toiling up Route 1. For pilgrims who have endured hours of interstate and commercial clutter—not to mention the inevitable tie-ups around the Bath bridge—here, finally, right before you, is what Maine is supposed to look like: a charming village of sea captains' mansions and a Main Street lined with picturesque brick buildings that house appealing shops which march down to the bank of the Sheepscot River. Traffic slows here as it curves into town so you can get a look at things even if you aren't planning to stop (but it's well worth taking time for a tour of the side streets). As you cross the bridge, be sure to look to your right to see the moldering wrecks of two schooners, the *Hesper* and the *Luther Little,* a delight for camera clickers.

Still shire town of Lincoln County, Wiscasset is only half as populous as it was in its shipping heyday 150 years ago. As the abundance of clapboard mansions attests, this was a thriving port between the time of the American Revolution and the War of 1812. Many fine old buildings are open to the public, and many more house antiques shops. There are a handful of B&Bs right in town, or you may choose to stay nearby and make a day's visit to Wiscasset. Taxi service runs between Wiscasset and the Boothbays.

GUIDANCE   Wiscasset does not have its own chamber of commerce, but the Bath, Boothbay Harbor, and Damariscotta chambers include Wiscasset information among the materials they distribute (see Bath and Environs, Damariscotta Area, and Boothbay Harbor Region [Guidance]).

GETTING THERE   From Portland's Jetport there is **limousine service** (800-834-5500 in Maine; 800-992-1401 outside). Air charters are available through **Downeast Flying Service** (882-6752), which also offers sightseeing and fall foliage flights ($39 for up to three passengers in a four-seater).

GETTING AROUND   Come by **car or taxi** from Boothbay Harbor. Once in Wiscasset, you will enjoy strolling around the narrow streets past picket-fenced gardens and beautifully kept homes. (For a walking-tour map, write to PO Box 226, Wiscasset 04578.)

MEDICAL EMERGENCY   **Bath Memorial Hospital** (443-5524), 1356 Washington Street, Bath.

TO SEE AND DO   **Old Lincoln County Jail and Museum,** Federal Street (882-6817 or 677-2826). Open July and August, Tuesday through Sunday

11–4:30 (last tour at 4), and by appointment through mid-December. Admission is $2 per adult and $1 per child. The museum comprises a chilling 1811 jail with damp, thick granite walls (in use until 1913) and the jailer's house (in use until 1953) with displays of tools and changing exhibits, including an antiques show in August.

Maine Art Gallery (633-5055), Warren Street (in the old 1807 academy). Open late June to Labor Day, Monday through Saturday 10–4. Free. Exhibits by Maine artists; special programs are offered year-round.

Nickels-Sortwell House, corner of Main and Federal streets. Open June 1 to September 30, Wednesday through Sunday 12–5. $2 admission fee. A classic Federal-era mansion in the middle of town that served as a hotel for many years. Some furnishings date from the early twentieth century when it was owned by a Cambridge, Massachusetts, mayor. The elliptical staircase is outstanding. Today the mansion is one of the properties administered by the Society for the Preservation of New England Antiquities.

Musical Wonder House (882-7163), 18 High Street. Open daily June to mid-October, 10–5, for guided tours (fewer tours after Labor Day). An intriguing collection of music boxes, reed organs, pump organs, Victrolas, and other musical machines displayed in a fine 1852 sea captain's mansion. Visitors are taken on tours of the house during which the various machines are played and demonstrated. Tours of just the ground floor are $7.50; tours of the entire house take about two hours and are $20 per person (or two for $35). There may also be evening candlelight concerts during July and August. Lasting about three hours, these old-fashioned soirées include elegant refreshments like champagne and shrimp (call for more information). The gift shop at the Musical Wonder House is open daily, 10 to 6, from Memorial Day until Thanksgiving (no admission charge for shop).

Castle Tucker (882-7364). Open during July and August, Tuesday through Saturday 11–4, and September through mid October by appointment. Adults $2, ages 6–12 $.50. An extremely unusual, privately owned mansion overlooking the harbor. It was built in 1807 by Judge Silas Lee, who overextended his resources to present his wife with this romantic house. After his death it fell into the hands of his neighbors, to whom it had been heavily mortgaged, and passed through several owners until it was acquired in 1858 by Captain Richard Holbrook Tucker. Captain Tucker, whose descendants still own the house, added the elegant portico. Castle Tucker is said to be named after a grand house in Scotland. Highlights include a freestanding elliptical staircase, Victorian furnishings, and original wallpapers.

Lincoln County Courthouse. Open during business hours throughout the year. Built in 1824, this handsome red-brick building

Lobster house

overlooking the town common is the oldest functioning courthouse in New England.

Maine Yankee Atomic Power Plant (882-6321 or 1-800-458-0066 in Maine), Route 144 (off Route 1 south of Wiscasset). Open every day, year-round, except Thanksgiving, Christmas, and New Year's Day. Monday through Saturday 10–5, and Sunday 12–5, in June, July, and August. Daily 12–4,September through May. Free. Maine's only nuclear generating station welcomes visitors for a one-and-a-quarter-hour tour that includes a video presentation, displays, a short tour of the grounds, and a visit to a simulated control room.

World's Smallest Church, Route 218. There is barely room for two worshippers in this tiny chapel, maintained as a memorial to a former Boston Baptist minister.

Pownalborough Court House (882-6817), Route 128, off Route 27, Dresden (8 miles north of Wiscasset). Open during July and August, Wednesday through Saturday 10–4 and Sunday 12–4. Worth the drive. The only surviving pre-Revolutionary courthouse in Maine, it is maintained as a museum by the Lincoln County Historical Association. The large building, which includes living quarters for the judge upstairs, gives a sense of this countryside along the Kennebec in 1761 when it was built to serve as an outpost tavern as well as a courtroom. It is a dramatic, three-story building, still isolated, with fascinating exhibits. Also on the grounds are a Revolutionary War-era cemetery and nature trails along the river. Special events and activities include cider pressing in October.

Fort Edgecomb State Memorial, Edgecomb (off Route 1; the turnoff is just across the Sheepscot River's Davey Bridge from Wiscasset, next to Muddy Rudder restaurant). The fort is open May 30 to Labor Day, daily 9–6. Free admission. This octagonal block house (built in 1809) overlooks a narrow passage of the Sheepscot River. For the same reasons that it was an ideal site for a fort, it is today an ideal picnic site. Tables are provided on the grassy grounds.

INNS   **Squire Tarbox Inn** (882-7693), RD 2, Box 620, Wiscasset 04578 (turn off Route 1 south of the village). Open mid-May to late October. The inn is located on Westport Island, 8.5 miles south of Route 1. A charming, quiet retreat in a Colonial farmhouse: 11 guest rooms, 7 of them in the barn. Very clean and attractive, with a big reputation for owner Karen Mitman's homemade goat cheeses, which are featured every evening. She and husband, Bill, welcome the public as well as guests to join them for dinner, by reservation only. Cocktail hour, accompanied by the inn's cheese, begins at 6 PM, followed by a five-course dinner at 7 PM. The cost per person for the set menu is about $25. Doubles are $110–$180 in season, including breakfast and dinner; $60–$130 or bed & breakfast.

Cod Cove Inn (882-9586), junction of Routes 1 and 27, PO Box 36, Edgecomb 04556. Open year-round. An imposing, attractively designed building on a hillside above the Sheepscot River with 28 deluxe motel rooms. Each has its own terrace or balcony with a view of the river and the village of Wiscasset beyond. All rooms are furnished with two queen-size beds and have convenient small refrigerators. Owned and operated by a very hospitable couple with long ties to the area, the inn has a nice feeling of personalized friendliness not usually found in an establishment of this size. Doubles are $80–$90 in season, including fresh muffins and coffee served each morning in the reception area.

Edgecomb Inn (882-6343), Box 11, North Edgecomb 04556 (off Route 1, across the bridge from Wiscasset). Open all year. Sprawling on the river's bank with a fine view of Wiscasset and the schooner hulks, it offers a variety of lodging choices including efficiency suites with separate outside entrances and efficiency cottages. Rates depend on your choice of services and accommodations (there are a total of 40 rooms). Next door, the Muddy Rudder serves breakfast, lunch, and dinner daily (see Eating Out). Doubles $69–$99.

BED & BREAKFASTS   **The Stacked Arms** (882-5436), c/o Dee and Sean Maguire, RFD 2, Box 146, Birch Point Road, Wiscasset 04578. Open all year except during January. A redecorated and expanded home with views of Wiscasset harbor, it offers five guest rooms with orthopedic beds and shared baths. Lodging includes a complete country breakfast served in the sunny dining room. There are fridges in the guest rooms, and picnic lunches can be arranged. $65–$75 double; $45–$50 single; lower winter rates.

Marston House (882-6010), Main Street, PO Box 517, Wiscasset 04578. The front of the house is a shop in which American antiques are engagingly displayed. Behind, in the carriage house, are two rooms, each with private entrance, fireplace, and private bath. Breakfast, which is served in your room, features fresh fruit and yogurt, home-baked muffins, and fresh orange juice; it is included in the rate. $75 double.

Sheepscot Framing & Gallery Bed and Breakfast (882-6024), Main and Pleasant streets, PO Box 701, Wiscasset 04578. The resident golden retriever greets you at the door of this eighteenth-century home. The works of noted artists and limited-edition prints are sold in the attached gallery. $65 double with private bath; $55 double with shared bath; full breakfast included.

The Captain Dodge House (882-6119 or 882-7561), Route 1, Wiscasset 04578. Despite this establishment's name and its attractive sign at the foot of the driveway, this is not a country inn. Its six motel-like units (all private baths) are very ordinary. Doubles are about $50.

DINING OUT   **Le Garage** (882-5409), Water Street. Open year-round, except

January, for lunch and dinner. A 1920s-era garage that still has a concrete floor has been converted into a very atmospheric restaurant with a glassed-in porch overlooking the schooner hulks (when you make reservations—a good idea—request a table on the porch). The one drawback is the very noisy kitchen; the cement floor seems to heighten the clinking and clanking of dishes and pots and pans. At dinner many large wrought-iron candelabra provide the illumination. An extensive menu, all fresh, features local seafood, lamb, and steaks. The food is good, and so is the value.

EATING OUT   **Muddy Rudder** (882-7748), Route 1, North Edgecomb (across the bridge from Wiscasset). Open year-round for breakfast, lunch, and dinner daily. Your basic good seafood and steak menu served in a nice riverside setting with an outdoor deck. Inexpensive to moderate.

Montsweag Restaurant (443-6563), Route 1, Woolwich (south of Wiscasset). Open year-round, 11:30–8 Sunday through Thursday; Fridays and Saturdays until 9 (8:30 off-season). A longtime landmark in these parts, it is known even by people who have never stopped. Filled with nautical memorabilia, this is the real thing: a Down East eatery that is just as popular with the locals as it is with visitors. The menu hasn't changed much over the years; comments on it reflect the wry humor of the family management. Exceptional value in steaks and seafood. Inexpensive.

The Coffee Shop, Main Street. Open for breakfast and lunch. Pleasant café atmosphere with blue-and-white tablecloths on white tables.

Village Deli (882-9727), Main Street. Summers only. Baked goods and deli foods.

Sarah's Pizza and Cafe (882-7504), Main Street. A cozy little restaurant with good pizza, soups, and such.

McLellan's Seafood (882-6000), Route 1, North Edgecomb. Seasonal. Reasonably priced lobster, fried seafood, chowders, and sandwiches. Picnic tables for summertime dining.

SELECTIVE SHOPPING   Wiscasset is known for its many fine **antiques shops,** both in town and just south of town on Route 1; many specialize in nautical pieces. (A word to the wise: The fancier the shop, the fancier the price tags.) Along Main Street, you'll find a clutch of interesting shops such as **Sheepscot River Pottery** (pastel, floral designs), **Area's Unique Gifts** (jewelry and gift items), **Sirius Graphics** (screen-printed clothing and Maine crafts), and **Richard Hasenfus'** art gallery. An irresistible stop is **Treats,** with its great selection of cheeses and gourmet foods, plus exceptional wines at very fair prices. **The Shops at Port Wiscasset,** on Water Street (to your right just before you head north across the bridge), include **Annie's Book Stop** (new and used books), **The Porringer** (selling antiques and needlework), and a menswear shop called the **Haberdashery.** Farther down the street, across from Le Garage (see Dining Out), is **New Cargoes,** with a carefully chosen selection of gifts, toys, and cookery needs housed in the first floor of the handsome, old, brick customhouse. Wiscasset is also home to a particularly curious shop called **The Butterstamp Workshop** (882-7825). Tucked away in a small courtyard behind a clapboard house on Middle Street, it is filled with three-dimensional, painted "hydrastone" castings made from the proprietors' collection of antique buttermolds (once used to stamp designs on hand-churned butter). Each symbol—pineapple, sheaf of wheat, shell, anchor, duck, cow, rooster, and so forth—has a special meaning. The castings are designed for use as wall decorations, magnets, and curtain tie-backs. Just north of Wiscasset, across the bridge in Edgecomb, is the studio where **Sheepscot River Pottery** is made. Attached to it is a large, extremely attractive showroom with displays on two floors and in a riverside garden. You'll find a wide selection of the delicately painted pottery plus all sorts of other top-quality items, including the work of several jewelry makers, teak garden furniture, baskets, blown and stained glass, clocks, wrought iron, and silk flowers.

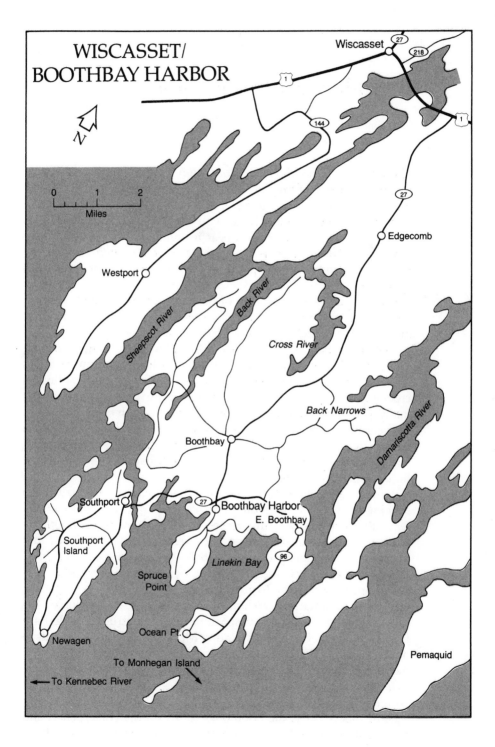

WISCASSET/
BOOTHBAY HARBOR

N

Wiscasset

27

218

1

144

1

0   1   2
Miles

27

Edgecomb

Westport

Sheepscot River

Back River

Cross River

Back Narrows

Damariscotta River

Boothbay

Southport

27   Boothbay Harbor
E. Boothbay

Southport
Island

96

Linekin Bay

Spruce
Point

Newagen

Ocean Pt.

To Monhegan Island

To Kennebec River

Pemaquid

Boothbay Harbor Region

The water in the Boothbay Harbor region is more than a view. It is an integral part of the raggedy peninsulas and islands carved by the glaciers into the ocean. You explore the water aboard a choice of more than two dozen excursion boats; you test it gingerly with your toes along quiet inlets and on pebbly beaches; and you enjoy its restorative powers in hidden, warm-water ponds. You can even walk across water—via footbridge—to get from one side of Boothbay Harbor to the other.

The Boothbays are made up of Boothbay Harbor, East Boothbay, and just plain Boothbay, together with Southport Island and a clutter of other islands tucked in between the peninsulas.

The undisputed focus of the area is Boothbay Harbor, an old fishing village that has been transformed by generations of summer visitors into one of Maine's liveliest coastal resorts. Enticing shops line its crooked streets; there are plenty of places to sup on local seafood; and many an inn, motel, and bed & breakfast (although never enough at the season's height) invite you to come rest your sightseeing-worn body. There is even a good measure of nightlife here, with musical entertainment in several of the restaurant/clubs and theaters offering light summertime fare.

But boats are what all three of the Boothbays have traditionally been best known for. They are built, repaired, and sold here, and you will feast your eyes on beautiful vessels in all of the harbors. Boothbay Harbor itself—with due respect to Newport, Rhode Island, and Marblehead, Massachusetts—calls itself the "Boating Capital of New England." Certainly it offers the region's greatest number and variety of opportunities for you to go out boating.

Excursions range from an hour-long sail out into the harbor to a 41-mile cruise up the Kennebec to see ships under construction at the Bath Iron Works. You can also ride out to Monhegan Island, an exquisite haven for fishermen and artists where public footpaths wind through the woods and along cliffs. And if you want to pursue giant tuna, stripers, and blues, there are several deep-sea fishing boats complete with electronic fish-finders.

Until this century, the Boothbays relied on the construction and operation of sailing vessels for both livelihood and transport. Even today, the harbor looks most complete during Windjammer Days, three days in mid-July when the masts of a dozen passenger-carrying sailing ships crowd among hundreds of smaller craft.

It is obvious from the very lay of the village that people here have always walked around town, and gone by boat to other destinations. The village of Boothbay Harbor packs most of its lodging and dining places into an amazingly small piece of waterfront, and regular-sized American cars seem mammoth on the narrow streets. The area's remaining undeveloped, extremely convoluted coastline takes a day to explore by car, and, unless one is willing to get out and hike, little more than glimpses of the water can be caught through the pine trees. That's because the self-contained resorts are all sequestered on head-lands and points, and the smaller inns and cottages also naturally hug the ocean.

Good public beaches are, unfortunately, something that the Boothbays lack entirely; but the resorts and many of the more expensive motels have pools and private beaches. Better yet are the warm-water lakes and ponds accessible from dozens of rental cottages, a few cottage colonies, and motels.

In the middle of the summer, Boothbay Harbor has somewhat of a carnival atmosphere—crowds mill along the wharf eating ice-cream cones, fudge, and taffy; shop for clever T-shirts and other souvenirs; and line up at the excursion boats. But you will also find some very nice craft shops, old-fashioned restaurants unchanged by trends, and delightful accommodations. So varied and numerous are the lodgings, not to mention the dining places and shops geared to visitors, that the Boothbays' chamber of commerce remains open year-round to keep tabs on what is available. Most of the establishments themselves, however, close during the winter months.

GUIDANCE   Boothbay Harbor Region Chamber of Commerce (633-2353), Box 356, Boothbay Harbor 04538. Open year-round, 9–6 Monday through Saturday in-season (May to October 31); 9–5 Monday through Friday off-season. A small information center on Route 27 in Boothbay is open seven days a week June to mid-October, 9–9 through Labor Day, and 9–6 after Labor Day (633-4743).

GETTING THERE   Jet Limo service from Portland Jetport (800-834-5500 in Maine; 800-992-1401 outside Maine).

GETTING AROUND   A free trolley on wheels circulates daily in-season between the Rocktide Motor Inn on the east side of the harbor and shops on the west side, also up to the Meadow Shopping Center on Route 27 at the entrance to town. The trolley runs every 30 minutes between 7 AM and 11 AM, seven days a week during July and August (check schedule for early and late season). Trolley route and walking maps are available at the Chamber's information centers and at inns and motels.

PARKING   There is a large parking lot on Route 27 as you enter town, near where the trolley stops at the Meadow Shopping Center. Try to walk or use the trolley as much as possible. Parking is also available on the street and in several municipal lots right downtown, but these spaces fill quickly.

MEDICAL EMERGENCY   St. Andrew's Hospital (633-2121), Hospital Point, Mill Cove, Route 27 south, Boothbay Harbor. A well-respected shoreside hospital, St. Andrew's serves the community by land and by water. Those who come **by water,** perhaps from an island offshore, may tie up at the hospital's own pier.

TO SEE AND DO   Marine Aquarium (633-5572), McKown Point, West Boothbay Harbor (turn left off Route 27 south). Open daily Memorial Day through Columbus Day, 8–5 weekdays and 9–5 weekends; by appointment off-season. A small but first-rate aquarium with local fish and lobsters inside, harbor seals penned in outside saltwater pools. A great spot for a picnic, with shoreside benches provided. Free admission.

   Boothbay Railway Village (633-4727), Route 27 (1 mile north of Boothbay Harbor). Open daily 10–5, mid-June through Columbus Day weekend. Maine's only 2-foot narrow gauge railway wends its way through a re-created miniature, turn-of-the-century village made up of 24 buildings. The ride is $5 per adult and $2 per child. Special events include a large antique auto meet (more than 250 cars) the third weekend in July.

   Boothbay Region Historical Society Museum (633-3666), 70 Oak Street, Boothbay Harbor. Open during July and August, Wednesday, Friday, and Saturday 10–4; off-season, Saturdays 10–2 or by appointment.

   Boothbay Region Art Gallery (633-2703), Boothbay Harbor (downtown, next to the post office). Open late June to mid-September, 11–5 weekdays and Saturdays, 12–5 on Sundays. Three juried shows are held each season in the 1807 Old Brick House. Displayed are works selected from submissions by more than 100 artists of the Boothbay region and Monhegan Island. Admission $.25.

   Monhegan Island. A day-long excursion aboard *Balmy Days II* (633-2284) to Monhegan gives you just time to explore briefly this unique island, where only footpaths link one side of the island to the other and residents still depend largely on kerosene lights. Most year-round families are involved in lobstering; many artists migrate here every summer. If you go for a day trip, take a picnic lunch to eat overlooking the ocean-side cliffs or dine at the Island Inn or one of the other lunch spots on the island. (See The Islands under Rockland for full information.)

BOAT EXCURSIONS   Do it. To find out what the Boothbays are all about, you really should board one of the dozens of boats sailing out of the harbor.

Photo by Charles Carey

Monhegan Island

Don't wait until the last day of your visit to do it—make it one of the first things you do to get your bearings and understand the geography and industry of the area. The boats leave from several piers in the center of Boothbay Harbor—anyone can direct you to them. (Because the boats' captains can so easily alter both which dock they use and the kinds of trips they offer, the following information is subject to frequent change. Please check ahead to avoid disappointment.)

Islander Cruises (633-5090 or 633-7166), Pier 6, Fisherman's Wharf. Operates May 20 to October 20. Aboard *The Islander* and *Linekin II*, eight daily trips in-season, ranging from the basic one-and-a-half-hour cruise that circles Southport Island to cruises up the Kennebec to Bath or north to Pemaquid Point. In July and August there are also supper sails. Rates for cruises range from $6 ($3 kids) for one and half hours to $13 for a supper sail. Also ask about the cruise that ends with a lobster feast ($23.50).

Balmy Days II (633-2284). 9:30 AM departures from Pier 8 to Monhegan Island, Memorial Day through Columbus Day (daily early June to late September; weekends only otherwise). This is the daytripper's boat to one of Maine's most beautiful offshore islands; also a good way to reach the island for an extended stay (the other choice is the *Laura B* from Port Clyde). The trip takes one and a half hours each way, and there are 4 hours on the island to spend walking the paths, picnicking, and visiting artists' studios. *Balmy Days II* also offers harbor tours. $25 per person, round-trip.

Maranbo II (633-2284). Departs from Pier 8 daily, rain or shine, May to October. Captain Campbell offers one-hour tours of the harbor: $6 per adult, $3.50 per child. Also a 9:30 AM Sunday church boat to All Saints by the Sea on Southport Island, and nightlights cruises four evenings each week.

Cap'n Fish Boat Trips (633-3244 or 633-2626), Pier 1 (red-ticket booth). Operates mid-May to mid-October, seven days per week. One-, two-, and three-hour excursions on the *Goodtime, Goodtimes Too,* and *Pink Lady.* Trips to see seals, puffins, whales, lobstering, lighthouses, etc; also cocktail cruises, sunset cruises, and fall foliage cruises. Monday is senior citizens' day. Unadvertised "noon specials" during July and August. Fares $5–$10 adults; children under 12 half price.

DEEP-SEA FISHING   Captain Bob Fish (633-3244 or 633-2626), Pier 1. In addition to sightseeing excursions, Captain Fish also operates fishing trips aboard the *Yellowbird, Buccaneer,* and *Mystery.*

Breakaway (633-4414), Ocean Point, East Boothbay, and Fisherman's Wharf, Boothbay Harbor. Half- and full-day fishing trips with Captain Peter Ripley.

Bingo Cruises (882-9309 or 633-5090), Pier 6, Fisherman's Wharf. Deep-sea fishing aboard *Bingo,* "Maine's fastest deep-sea party boat." 7:30–3:30. $26 adult, $16 under 12.

Charter fishing boats. Most charter fishing boats, including *Shark III* (Captain Barry Gibson: 633-3416 evenings),depart from Brown's Wharf; call them at 633-5440 for current information. Most take up to six people and provide all tackle and bait. Make reservations early. Skippers often require an advance deposit on a charter boat; your money will be refunded if weather cancels the trip. Before you board, ask your skipper who is entitled to the catch (in most cases, you can keep what you catch, but rules may vary). Also ask whether food will be provided on board, and pack lunch and snacks if necessary. Most boats do not allow hard liquor but may permit beer. Wear soft-soled shoes, long pants, a warm shirt, and bring a sweater and windbreaker (you can always take shorts and a T-shirt if it gets warm enough for them). Don't forget sunscreen, sunglasses, and a hat. Eat a light breakfast and consider taking a seasickness remedy if you are prone to *mal de mer.* Your mate or deckhand should be tipped at the end of the day if you feel he or she deserves it. A cheerful, helpful mate should be rewarded for efforts regardless of the catch, which the mate has no control over. If a mate has filleted fish for you, tip about $5. A tip for the captain is optional.

SAILING   Several traditional sailing yachts offer to take passengers out for an hour or two, a half- day, or a day. Some are also available for captained charters of a week or longer.

Appledore (633-6598; off-season 633-6599), Pier 6, Fisherman's Wharf. Cruises on a large windjammer that has sailed around the world. Two-and-a-half-hour trips to harbor's outer islands and seal rocks morning and afternoon. $16 per person (under 10, $8).

Friendship sloops include the following: *Eastward* (633-4780) takes up to six passengers on full- and half-day sails at $20 per person for a half day ($40 minimum). If a party wishes to charter the boat exclusively, the cost is $120 for a half day, $200 for all day. Captain Roger Duncan is a lecturer on local history and author of the New England sailor's bible, *A Cruising Guide to the New England Coast*, plus several other sailing reference works. *Bay Lady* (633-3244 or 633-6486), Pier 1, is a 31-foot Friendship sloop that offers one-and-three-quarter-hour sails in the outer harbor. $10 adults.

Holladay Marine (633-4767), Route 27, West Boothbay Harbor 04575. Half- and full-day charters, with or without a captain, aboard a variety of Tartan sloops. Also available for weekly charters.

Powerboats are rented by **Midcoast Yacht Sales and Rentals** (882-6445), Pier 8, Boothbay Harbor (or write PO Box 221, Wiscasset 04578).

GOLF   **Boothbay Region Country Club** (633-6085), Country Club Road (off Route 27), Boothbay. Open spring through late autumn. Nine holes, snack bar, carts, clubs for rent. Greens fee.

HORSEBACK RIDING   **Ledgewood Riding Stables** (882-6346), Route 27 and Old County Road, Edgecomb 04556.

SWIMMING   The beaches are all private, but visitors are permitted in a number of spots. Here are four: (1) Follow Route 27 toward Southport, across the Townsend Gut Bridge, to a circle (white church on the left, monument in the center, general store on the right), turn right and follow Beach Road to the beach, which offers roadside parking and calm, shallow water. (2) Right across from the Boothbay Harbor Yacht Club (Route 27 south), just beyond the post office, at the far end of the parking lot. This property is owned by the yacht club, which puts out a float by July; there are ropes to swing from on the far side of the inlet, a grassy area in which to sun, and a small sandy area beside the water, but the water is too deep for small children. (3) Barretts Park, Lobster Cove (turn at the Catholic church, east side of harbor), a place to picnic and get wet. (4) Grimes Cove, a little beach with rocks to climb at the very tip of Ocean Point, East Boothbay.

TENNIS   **Boothbay Region YMCA** (633-2855), Route 27 (on your left as you come down the stretch that leads to town). An exceptional facility open to nonmembers (use fee charged) in July and August, with special swimming and other programs for children. Well worth checking out if you will be in the area for a week or more. A wide variety of programs for all ages: tennis, racquetball, gymnastics, aerobics, soccer, swimming, and more.

Public tennis courts are located across the road from the YMCA, next to the Boothbay Region High School, Route 27 on the way into Boothbay Harbor.

LODGING   The chamber of commerce lists about 50 cottages and cabins and another 50 hotels, motels, inns, bed & breakfasts, and resorts. And of course there are even more. Lodging facilities are salted along the shore, around hidden ponds, up dirt roads, and deep in coves. Others ring the water in Boothbay Harbor. The most famous inns and motels are expensive in-season, but there is an unusually wide range of prices in this region. That the chamber of commerce is open year-round facilitates finding a cottage for July in March. Cottagers can also take advantage of the first-rate self-service laundry and large supermarket just outside the village, and there are plenty of places to buy lobsters to take back to the cottage to cook for dinner.

RESORTS   **Spruce Point Inn and Lodges** (633-4152; 800-553-0289 from outside Maine), Boothbay Harbor 04538. Open mid-June to mid-September. Sited on its own 100-acre peninsula at the eastern end of the harbor at the tip of Spruce Point. There are 50 double rooms, 14 suites, and 6 condominiums. Most rooms are scattered in cottages and larger "lodges" all set on the landscaped grounds in a manner reminiscent of a town common. Just 12 guest rooms are in the main inn, which also houses the dining room. There are two pools, tennis courts, a putting green, and lawn games. Sightseeing boats dock here to pick up passengers from the inn. $100–$135 per person including breakfast and dinner in rooms in season; condominiums (no meals) run $300–$425 per night. Breakfast only (no dinner included) in June and September.

Linekin Bay Resort (633-2494), Boothbay Harbor 04538. Open mid-June to Labor Day. Actually in East Boothbay, this is a marvelous "summer camp" for adults. With the largest resort fleet of sailboats in New England, Linekin Bay puts the emphasis squarely on sailing, including lessons and frequent for-the-fun-of-it races, but there are also a heated saltwater pool, clay and all-weather tennis courts, canoeing, fishing, and waterskiing. The sightseeing boat *Linekin* picks up passengers here, too (see Boat Excursions). There are a dozen rooms in 5 lodges, plus 33 cabins, some with Franklin stoves or fireplaces. Weekly rates include all meals and use of sailboats. Deluxe.

Newagen Seaside Inn (633-5242), Box 86, Newagen 04552. Open June to September. A landmark for nearly a century, this informal, authentic inn lies at the seaward tip of Southport Island, 6 miles "out to sea" from Boothbay Harbor. Secluded among the pines, the inn's lawn sweeps down to a mile of bold coastline. There are 22 rooms in the main inn, all with private baths. Heated freshwater pool, large saltwater pool, two tennis courts, many lawn games, rowboats. Full breakfast is included; lunch and dinner are also available. Doubles $85–$150 per night, including breakfast buffet; weekly cottage rentals $600–$1200 for up to three bedrooms.

Ocean Point Inn (633-4200), PO Box 409, East Boothbay 04544. Open mid-May to mid-October. Fifteen minutes from Boothbay Harbor, at the tip of the Ocean Point peninsula, next to the East Boothbay Town Pier on Fisherman's Passage. The setting is very dramatic, overlooking the open ocean. Long established, the complex offers 61 varied rooms in the inn, motel, and cottages, with either colonial or modern decor. All rooms have color televisions and private baths. There's also a pleasant restaurant (see Dining Out) and a heated pool. Boat excursions and fishing trips leave from the pier. Doubles $70–$99 in season; if your stay includes a Saturday night, you must stay for more than one night.

West Harbor Resort (633-5381), Lakeview Road, PO Box 516, West Boothbay Harbor 04575. Open early April to mid-October. Overlooking the water, a 31-unit, two-story luxury motel with a private sand beach and boats to use on the lake. Also the very nice Greenhouse Restaurant and Lounge (see Dining Out). Quiet location a mile from the center of town.

Smuggler's Cove Motor Inn (633-2800), Route 96, East Boothbay 04544. Overlooking Linekin Bay, a 60-unit resort motel with its own beach, heated pool, moorings, restaurant, and lounge.

Ocean Gate Motor Inn (633-3321; 800-221-5924 from outside Maine), Route 27, Southport 04576. Open May to November. A 72-room resort motel with function rooms, café, and bar. The 85-acre property encompasses tennis courts, a dock, boats, pool, playground, volleyball, table tennis, basketball, and playground. Three efficiencies and two cottages as well.

INNS **Five Gables Inn** (633-4551), Murray Hill Road (off Route 27), PO Box 75, East Boothbay 04544. Open mid-May through mid-November. Built around 1865, this old summer boarding house (the only remaining summer hotel in the area) has recently been renovated into an unpretentious but luxurious B&B inn. All 15 thoughtfully furnished rooms have ocean views and private baths; most have queen-size beds, and 5 have working fireplaces. The rocking chairs on the wraparound verandah provide the ideal spot for surveying the stunning view of Linekin Bay and its islands. There's a welcoming fireplace in the common room; a great buffet breakfast is served here or on the verandah. Boothbay Harbor is a short drive away. $80–$120 double. Children over 12 welcome.

Albonegon Inn (633-2521), Capitol Island 04538 (follow Route 27 to

Route 238 in Southport; look for sign). Open June to mid-October. "Determinedly old-fashioned," and proud of it, this is a true haven from the twentieth century. Part of a gingerbread-style summer colony that has been here for years on Capitol Island, linked to the real world by a tiny bridge. Fifteen cheerful, sea-bright rooms; some with private bath. Two beaches, tennis, and fishing. Doubles $58–$68 with shared bath; $69–$80 with private bath; includes a breakfast of freshly baked goodies and coffee.

Sprucewold Lodge (633-3600), Boothbay Harbor 04538. Open to the public July and August (and for groups June through September). There are 29 rooms in the 1920s rustic lodge, all with private baths, plus two log cabins with small kitchens across the road. Additional log cabins—all part of the original summer colony of about 30—are privately owned by members of the Sprucewold Beach Club. The club also maintains a saltwater pool, shuffleboard courts, a putting green, and a cookout area, all of which are open to guests of the lodge. Ocean swimming from a protected, crescent-shaped sandy beach a short woods-walk away. Continental breakfast is included in the rate.

The Green Shutters Inn and Cottages (633-2646), Bay Street, Boothbay Harbor 04538. Open Memorial Day through September. This is a friendly, family-geared, old-fashioned Maine resort complex. There's an open-timbered lodge with a dining room and 15 guest rooms (all private baths) and 7 cottages (accommodating from 2 to 14 people) scattered through the pines. Request a water view. Rates are reasonable: $35 per person (double occupancy) includes breakfast and dinner; for children 12 and under the charge is $17.

Russell House Inn (633-6656; off-season 633-2271), PO Box 632, Route 27, Boothbay 04538. Open May through January. A handsome New England farmhouse with five guest rooms, two with queen-size beds; all have color TV and a private bath. "Breakfast in bed" is delivered to your door. The restaurant, noted for its elegant yet casual atmosphere, serves distinctively prepared cuisine (see Dining Out). $50–$75 double.

Thistle Inn (633-3541), 53 Oak Street, Boothbay Harbor 04538. Open year-round. Eight rooms with two shared baths, one with private bath. Pleasant and friendly atmosphere, comfortable furnishings. The Thistle's pub has long been a gathering place for locals, especially fishermen and lobstermen. It is a great place to hear real Down East accents and pick up some good Maine stories, and there's "mellow" live entertainment most weekends. It can sometimes be a bit loud, however, if you are planning to retire upstairs early. Dining room serves good Maine seafood (see Eating Out). Inexpensive.

Lawnmeer Inn (633-2544), Box 505, West Boothbay Harbor 04575. On Route 27 on Southport Island, 2 miles from downtown Boothbay Harbor. Open May to October. Thirteen newly decorated rooms in the inn, plus a wing with eighteen motel-like rooms with decks, and a romantic little cottage that was once a smokehouse. On Townsend Gut, with all its boating traffic. Restaurant overlooking water is open to the public (see Eating Out). $55–$99 double or single occupancy. If you stay on a Saturday night in high season, you must stay more than one night.

BED & BREAKFASTS   Kenniston Hill Inn B&B (633-2159), Route 27, Boothbay 04537. Open April 1 through November. A stately, 200-year-old pillared colonial (Boothbay's oldest home) set back from the road as it curves around to the Boothbay town green. Ten comfortably restored rooms with handmade quilts and fresh flowers; all have private baths; four have fireplaces. Country breakfast is prepared by hosts who have many years of experience in the restaurant business; specialties include peaches-and-cream French toast and zucchini or walnut pancakes. Innkeepers Paul and Ellen Morrissette also own the Five Gables Inn in East Boothbay (see Inns, above). Walk to the Boothbay Country Club for golf. $60–$80 double or single; breakfast included. Two-night minimum stay on holidays.

Coburn House (633-2120), Route 27, Boothbay 04537. Open year-round. Just 2 miles from the harbor, this 1880s house has four guest rooms, all with private baths. There's also a very pleasant restaurant composed of several intimate rooms (see Dining Out) and a separate bar. Full breakfast served to overnight guests; dinner to the public. $50–$75 double.

Sweet Woodruff Farm (633-6977), Route 27, Boothbay 04537. Open May through November. One of the oldest homes in Boothbay, this rambling 1767 Cape has two antiques-filled bedrooms that share a bath and a sitting area. Breakfast is served on a porch overlooking fields and grazing sheep. Also here is an antiques and herb shop that features herbs that are grown and dried on the premises. $55.

Hodgdon Island Inn (633-7474), Barter's Island Road, Boothbay (mail: Box 492, Trevett 04571). A restored sea captain's house by the sea offering six rooms with private bath. Swimming pool. Three and a half miles from Boothbay Harbor.

Welch House (633-3431), 36 McKown Street, Boothbay Harbor 04538. Open mid-April through mid-October. A grand view of the harbor and islands beyond. Sixteen individually decorated rooms (some canopy beds), all with private baths: eight in the 1850 sea captain's house and eight more in the newer Sail Loft. Exceptional views of harbor and islands from a third-floor observation deck, main deck, and glass-enclosed breakfast room. Most guest rooms also have a view. Breakfast, included, is described as "continental plus." $50–$85. Two-night minimum stay weekends between July 4 and Labor Day.

Westgate Guest House (633-3552), 18 West Street, Boothbay Harbor

04538. Open May through October. Six rooms with shared baths in a turn-of-the-century Victorian right in the middle of town, handy to shops and the waterfront. Full traditional breakfast features a variety of omelets, eggs, granola, fruits, homemade pastries, and oatmeal-walnut or sourdough bread. $60 double.

Hilltop House (633-2941), McKown Hill, Boothbay Harbor 04538. Open year-round. Three rooms with shared baths, also one double with bath, and family units with kitchenettes. Great view, like the other two McKown Hill guest houses. Muffins and coffee served in summer.

Seafarer Guest House (633-2116; off-season 617-924-9159), 38 Union Street, Boothbay Harbor 04538. A redecorated early 1800s sea captain's home with an unobstructed view of the harbor from the big front porch. Five guest rooms, two with private baths. "Hearty continental breakfast." Doubles $64–$85 (depending on view).

Oak Ledge (633-6640), 41 Oak Street, Boothbay Harbor 04538. Memorial Day to Columbus Day weekend. Convenient to all of the shops and restaurants of the village. Three guest rooms, shared bath. Continental breakfast. Daily and weekly rates.

Lion's Den (633-7367), 106 Townsend Avenue, Boothbay Harbor 04538. Open March through October. Informal, family atmosphere. A short walk to downtown. A full country breakfast featuring pancakes or omelets is served. Seven rooms, some with views of the harbor; private or shared bath. $40–$70 double in season; weekly rates available.

Jonathan's (633-3588), 15 Eastern Avenue, Boothbay Harbor 04538. Open year-round. Named for that famous sea gull, this 100-year-old Cape offers three bedrooms (all private baths) in a quiet neighborhood, a few minutes from downtown Boothbay Harbor. $65–$85.

Captain Sawyer's Place (633-2290), 87 Commercial Street, Boothbay Harbor 04538. Open May to October. A century-old sea captain's house topped with a cupola overlooking the busy harbor. Ten guest rooms decorated with Laura Ashley fabrics, all with private baths, sitting areas, and cable TV. Also the Captain's Quarters, with its own kitchen and private deck. Homemade treats for breakfast include granola, breads, and blueberry muffins. $65–$85; Captain's Quarters $100 per night.

The Sleepy Lobsterman (633-5565), 57 Oak Street, Boothbay Harbor 04538. An 1865 house with three bedrooms sharing a bath. Full breakfast in the dining room. Five-minute walk from harbor. $50 per room.

Anchor Watch (633-2284), 3 Eames Road, Boothbay Harbor 04538. Open year-round. Oceanfront sea captain's home overlooking islands, lobstermen hauling their catches, lighthouses. Private baths. Within walking distance of downtown. Continental breakfast.

Topside, the Inn on the Hill (633-5404), McKown Hill, Boothbay Harbor 04538. Open mid-May to late October. Rooms in the inn, built by Captain Cyrus McKown a century ago, have great views of the harbor and outer harbor (all private baths). The complex also includes a motel, four-person cottage with kitchen, and even a three-bedroom house to rent. $85–$95 double in the inn; $ 85–$95 motel rooms; $150 cottage; $175 per day for house (one-week minimum).

Atlantic Ark Inn (633-5690), 64 Atlantic Avenue, Boothbay Harbor 04538. Open May through October. Furnished with antiques and oriental rugs, this small B&B is a pleasant respite from the bustle of the harbor. Four rooms in the inn, plus a cottage, all with private baths. All beds are queen-size, and some are mahogany four-posters. Some rooms have harbor views; some have private balconies. Full breakfast includes special egg dishes and home-baked breads; sherry and/or wine is served in the afternoon. $65–$85. Minimum two-night stay on weekends.

Emma's Guest House and Cottages (633-5287), 110 Atlantic Avenue, Boothbay Harbor 04538. Open May to November. An old-fashioned guest house, plus efficiency cottages. Each room accommodates three or four people. Water views. Breakfast not included in rental of cottages.

Villa by the Sea B&B (633-2584), HC 65 #901, East Boothbay 04544. Open July to October. At Ocean Point, 6 miles from Boothbay Harbor, this 1875 home has five bedrooms with floor-to-ceiling windows overlooking Linekin Bay. Shared baths. Homemade continental breakfast included in $55–$60 double rate.

Treasure Island (633-3333), East Boothbay 04544. Open year-round. On a tiny island linked to the mainland by a bridge, this off-the-beaten-track B&B offers four rooms plus one efficiency, all with private baths. Just across the bridge are a rocky beach and woods. Breakfast of homemade muffins or popovers.

Linekin Village (633-3681; off-season 407-278-7624), Ocean Point Road, Route 96, East Boothbay 04544. Open May 1 to mid-October. A variety of accommodations set on 2 acres of lawns and gardens that reach to the water's edge, where a 165-foot-long pier looks out to several lighthouses. Three rooms with shared bath in an 1882 home. All rooms have color TVs and radios. Continental breakfast. Also motel units (some with handicap access) and efficiency cottages with knotty-pine interiors and screened porches (no breakfast). B&B double rate $45; motels and cottages $60–$75 daily, $360–$450 weekly.

MOTELS   **"Resort motels"**—the kind with color TV in every room, balconies, oversized beds, pools, and games—are the specialty of the town. Expensive to deluxe, no meals included. Since they are described in countless guides, and this book focuses on a different breed of lodging, we will simply list them: **Brown Brothers Wharf** (633-5440),

Fisherman's Wharf Inn (633-5090), **Rocktide Motor Inn** (633-4455), **Ocean Gate Motor Inn** (633-3321), **Tugboat Inn** (633-4434), **Cap'n Fish's Motel** (633-6605), **Smuggler's Cove** (633-2800), **Boothbay Harbor Inn** (633-6302), and **Flagship Motor Inn** (633-5094). Some remain open year-round, but Boothbay Harbor is more seasonal than most other towns along the mid-coast so check before you go.

Smaller, moderately priced motels include the following:

The Harborage (633-4640), 73 Townsend Avenue, Boothbay Harbor 04538. Open year-round. An overgrown house with ten units, some overlooking the water plus a waterfront efficiency. In the middle of town.

Howard House Motel (633-3933 or 633-6244), Route 27, Boothbay Harbor 04538. Open year-round. Attractive natural-wood buildings set amid pine trees. Fifteen rooms with balconies; double, queen-, and king-size beds. Full breakfast buffet included (except December through March). $60–$75 in season; low winter rates.

Harbour Towne Inn (633-4300), 71-B Townsend Avenue, Boothbay Harbor 04538. Open most of the year. Centrally located, on the water. Three Victorian homes with inn rooms with private baths, plus motel rooms, efficiencies, and a penthouse.

Mid-Town Motel (633-2751), Boothbay Harbor 04538. Open late May to late October. Centrally located and pleasant, with plenty of parking. Eleven units and one cottage.

The Pines (633-4555), Sunset Road, PO Box 693, Boothbay Harbor 04538. Open late April to late October. Set literally in the pines and secluded. Tennis court, heated swimming pool. All rooms have private decks. $68 double.

Seagate (633-3900; 800-633-1707 from outside Maine), 124 Townsend Avenue, Boothbay Harbor 04538. Open April to November. Handy to shops and the harbor. Twenty-five tastefully designed units flanking a central house; some efficiencies. Complimentary coffee. $65–$70; two-bedroom efficiency $80; double with shared bath in guest house $45.

COTTAGES **YMCA Family Camps** (633-2597), Trevett Road, Boothbay 04537. Seasonal. A former children's camp (and most recently called Highmeadows), **Camp Knickerbocker** offers comfortable, clean housekeeping cottages accommodating as many as five people each. Set on manicured grounds with lawn games and access to a freshwater pond, up the road from a picnicking site on a saltwater inlet. A day camp for youngsters age 3–13 operates Monday through Friday 9–4. Weekly rentals.

Knickerbocker Lake Cottages. During the off-season, these must be reserved by writing or calling the owner, M. A. Blycher, 5234 Inverchapel Road, Springfield, VA (703-321-7242). It is well worth the trouble to line them up in advance, for these are two-bedroom cottages on a lake complete with sandy beach and boats. Weekly rentals.

Harborfields (633-5082), West Boothbay Harbor 04575. Open June to October. Eight housekeeping cottages, plus rooms and a suite in an 1870 house, and rental of the original 1750 homestead. All accommodations have private baths, and most have water views. Cottages are in a variety of sizes, but all have complete kitchens, fireplaces, and all you need including flatware, cookware, wood for the fireplace, and linens. There are 10 acres of woods and fields, plus a half mile of shorefront. Cottages $445–$690 per week; 1750 homestead $690 per week; rooms and suite in house $55–$95 per night.

Harbor Motor Court (633-5450), Box 326, Boothbay Harbor. Motel units in an old-style complex of Maine cottages, set on 5.5 acres of neatly kept grounds with a large pool. Of the 22 units, 17 have kitchenettes. No pets are permitted.

Hillside Acres Motor Court (633-3411), Route 27 (Adams Pond Road), PO Box 300, Boothbay 04537. Open mid-May through mid-October. Seven newly renovated cabins, including four efficiency units, plus an apartment and two B&B rooms, all on a quiet hillside. Electric heat, showers, color and black-and-white TVs. Swimming pool. Complimentary muffins, coffee cakes, and coffee. $40–$64; weekly rates, too.

A host of other cottages in the Boothbay area are rented by the week for inexpensive to moderate rates, depending on amenities, location, and season (July and August are the most expensive months). Write to the chamber of commerce (see Guidance) for a full listing, and then make your reservations early. There are, however, always last-minute cancellations so it can't hurt to check with the chamber once the summer has begun—you may luck into a dream cottage even in August. When and if you do, you will probably join the legion families who reserve the same cottage year after year and make summer in Boothbay a tradition.

RESTAURANTS   You will never go hungry in Boothbay Harbor—restaurants are everywhere. Traditionally, the area's restaurants have all served about the same thing: lobsters, local seafood, steaks, lobsters, fried clams, and more lobsters. Times are happily changing now, however, and you will find more originality and creativity in Boothbay Harbor kitchens. There is even a Chinese–American restaurant here now. And, as always, if you don't think you could ever get your fill of boiled lobsters, you've come to the right town. A word of caution: Unlike most other resort towns along the coast, which increasingly have become year-round communities, Boothbay Harbor remains very much a summer place, and many of the restaurants listed here close or go on a limited schedule as the fall foliage fades. It is not unusual for restaurants to decide on a year-to-year basis when to close so it is always best to call ahead except during the tourist season.

DINING OUT   **Russell House** (633-6656), Route 27, Boothbay Harbor. Serving dinner late April or early May to mid-October and mid-November to January; Monday through Saturday in season, and Wednesday through Sunday in the wintertime. A large menu of about 30 entrées, changing frequently. No fried foods, no boiled lobster. Instead, creatively prepared fresh fish, shrimp, and lobster, much of it sautéed. Delicious pasta dishes are a specialty (try the Lobster Russell); the bouillabaisse is exceptional, too. Everything is cooked to order; homemade desserts. Distinctive, elegant yet casual atmosphere removed from bustle of downtown.

Christiana's at the Boothbay Harbor Inn (633-6302), 37 Atlantic Avenue, Boothbay Harbor (east side of Harbor). Overlooking harbor. Seafood entrées such as seafood scampi and shrimp and crab casserole. The menu changes daily. Nightly entertainment.

Newagen Seaside Inn (633-5242), Cape Newagen, Southport Island. Shellfish dishes, fish of the day, lobster, and steak. Specialties include chicken Newagen, Newagen shortcake, and house pies.

Rocktide (633-4455), east side of the harbor, Boothbay Harbor. Two dining rooms: the more formal Dockside (jackets required) and the Chart Room (casual attire). Lobster, swordfish, seafood dishes, steak, veal dishes, and chicken cooked with mushrooms, white wine, and Swiss cheese. Lunch is also served.

Coburn House (633-2120), Route 27, Boothbay 04537. A very pleasant restaurant with several intimate dining rooms; part of a bed-and-breakfast establishment. The menu features fresh local seafood (try the blackened swordfish) and meats.

Brown Brothers Wharf (633-5440), Atlantic Avenue, Boothbay Harbor. Dining room opens in mid-June. One of Maine's better known seafood restaurants, the largest in the area. Established in 1945. Seafood and steaks; a variety of lobster dishes. Breakfast and dinner.

Spruce Point Inn (633-4152), east side of outer harbor at Spruce Point. Open mid-June to mid-September; reservations advised. A gracious old-fashioned inn atmosphere. A sampling from the menu includes fish of the day, Maryland softshell crabs, duckling, and French lamb chops. Breakfast and lunch are also served; weekly lobster bake and gourmet buffet.

Ocean Point Restaurant (633-4200), East Boothbay. Open mid-May to mid-October. Seafood and other local specialties served in dining room with spectacular view of Linekin Bay.

EATING OUT   **Greenhouse Restaurant at West Harbor Resort** (633-5381), Lakeview Road, Boothbay Harbor. Several daily specials which might include raspberry-peach duck, salmon with chive beurre blanc, or lobster and asparagus linguini. There's a dinner club for regular patrons. Breakfast and dinners are served with a beautiful view.

Lawnmeer Inn (633-2544), Route 27, Southport Island (just across the bridge). Ambitious continental menu plus daily old-fashioned New England specials. A very pleasant dining room with large windows overlooking the water.

Gilchrist's East (633-5692), Boothbay Harbor (downtown). Casual atmosphere and views of the harbor. Beef, lobster, scallops, and haddock prepared a variety of ways. There is also the candlelight Louis XIX Dinner for two, with each of several courses accompanied by a glass of the appropriate wine.

Maxfield's Harbour High Café (633-3444), Boothbay Harbor (across the street from the post office). Open February through December. Indoor and deck dining. Fine family fare, including Swiss cheese pie, seven-layer salad, and a variety of seafood and meat entrées, including surf and turf. Lunch served as well as dinner.

China by the Sea (633-4449), 73 Commercial Street, Boothbay Harbor. Lunch and dinner served. Features standard Chinese–American dishes such as Moo Goo Gai Pan. Very reasonable prices.

Ebb Tide (633-5692), Commercial Street, Boothbay Harbor. Open year-round. Great breakfasts are served all day plus good things such as lobster rolls, club sandwiches, and fisherman's platters; wonderful homemade desserts. An old-fashioned place that has long been a landmark here. Very inexpensive.

Thistle Inn (633-3541), 53 Oak Street, Boothbay Harbor. Open year-round. Real pub atmosphere that is popular with locals. Hearty dishes and moderate prices. Seafood, meats, and poultry. Fireside dining in winter.

Fisherman's Wharf (633-5090), Boothbay Harbor (on the water). Three meals are served daily. This is a big place, geared to groups and bus tours. Nicely prepared seafood, boiled lobster, and other standard fare.

Smuggler's Cove (632-2800), East Boothbay. An 1820 house with a very pleasant atmosphere. Broiled fish, chicken, and steak. Moderate prices, children's menu.

Andrew's Harborside Restaurant (633-4074), Boothbay Harbor (downtown, next to the municipal parking lot and footbridge). Open seven days a week, May to October. In what was for years the Blue Ship, this new restaurant is a bit more up-market than its predecessor, but it's still famous for the cinnamon rolls. The owner/chef specializes in creative seafood dishes. Three meals served daily. Round Top Ice Cream is still dished up at a window down below at the parking lot level.

Chowder House Restaurant, Granary Way, Boothbay Harbor (beside the municipal parking lot and footbridge). Serves lunch and dinner in a restored old building that also houses several small shops. Seating is around an open kitchen and outside on a waterside deck. Chowders, obviously, plus lobster stew, salads, homemade breads, seafood, and full dinners. Serves lunch from 11 AM to 5 PM, when the dinner menu is offered.

The Black Orchid (633-6659), Boothbay Harbor (downtown, on the byway). Seafood and oyster raw bar, plus lunch and light suppers, served in the Bocce Club Cafe, upstairs deck. The dining room downstairs serves an appealing selection of classic Italian dishes featuring local seafoods, meats, and pastas, prepared by the chef/owner. Sunday brunch is also served.

Jordan's Upstairs Downstairs (633-2600), Commercial Street, Boothbay Harbor. Serves lunch and dinner. Two-for-one lobster specials, salad bar, chowders, and seafood platters.

Tugboat Inn (633-4434), Boothbay Harbor (downtown, on the water). This is an actual old tugboat tied up to the dock, open for lunch and dinner year-round. A water view restaurant, lounge, piano bar, and outdoor cocktail deck. Seafood and steaks. Broiled haddock, sautéed lobster, and many seafood dinners.

McSeagull's (633-4041), Boothbay Harbor (on the water). Open all year. Good seafood dishes and exceptional desserts including strawberry crêpes, cheesecake, and such. Live music after 9 PM.

Everybody's (633-6113), Route 27 (in the shopping center across from Shop 'n' Save). Open year-round for breakfast, lunch, and dinner. A casual, inexpensive place that's very popular with locals. All sorts of salad entrées plus light suppers and dinners. Sandwiches at lunchtime.

Broken Anchor (633-5771), Boothbay Harbor (at the parking lot off Townsend Avenue). Open year-round, 5 AM–9 PM, for breakfast, lunch, dinner. Very plain decor. Chowders, seafood, and homemade muffins and pies. Entertainment on Saturday nights in the summer. Bargains you thought you'd never see again, like ice cream or pudding for $.74.

J. H. Hawk Restaurant and Pub, Boothbay Harbor (right on the dock in the middle of town, upstairs in the building next to McSeagull's). Seafood, beef, veal, chicken dishes. On Sundays there's rock music spinning on the stereo.

LOBSTER IN THE ROUGH **Robinson's Wharf** (633-3830), Route 27, Southport Island (just across Townsend Gut from West Boothbay Harbor). Open mid-June through Labor Day; lunch and dinner daily. 11 AM–8:45 PM. Children's menu. Sit outside at picnic tables and watch the boats unload their catch. Pick out your lobster before it's cooked, or buy some live lobsters to cook at home. Seafood rolls, fried shrimp, clams, scallops, fish chowder, lobster stew, sandwiches, and homemade desserts.

Boothbay Region Lobstermen's Co-Op (633-4900), Atlantic Avenue (east side of the harbor). Open mid-May to mid-October, 8 AM to 8 PM. The basics: boiled lobsters and steamed clams to be eaten at wooden tables on an outside deck on the water or indoors.

Lobsterman's Wharf (633-3443), Route 96, East Boothbay (adjacent to a boatyard). Open April to October. Popular with locals. Boiled lobsters to eat at the outside tables over the water or inside. The menu also includes a wide variety of more complex entrées.

Seth's Old Fashioned Downeast Lobster Fest (633-4925 or 633-3321), at the Ocean Gate Motor Inn on Southport Island. Memorial Day through October. In July and August you can cruise the harbor to the bake aboard *M/V Linekin II*. Two lobsters for $16, boat fare additional.

SNACKS   **Crunchy Snail** (633-2933), 89 Townsend Avenue, Boothbay Harbor. Bakery and donut shop with tables.

Brud's Hotdogs, in the middle of the village and on the east side of the harbor. Keep an eye out for Brud's pushcart—he has been selling juicy dogs around town for almost 50 summers.

Downeast Ice Cream Factory (633-2816), Boothbay Harbor (on the byway). Homemade ice cream and make-your-own sundae buffet; all sorts of toppings including real hot fudge.

ENTERTAINMENT   **Carousel Music Theatre** (633-5297), Route 27, near Boothbay Harbor. Performances mid-May to late October. Doors open at 6:30 PM; show begins at 7 PM. Closed Sunday. Light meals (sandwich baskets and such) and cocktails are served by the cast before they hop onto the stage to sing Broadway tunes cabaret-style and then present a fully costumed and staged revue of a Broadway play. Admission $12, food extra.

Boothbay Summer Theatre (633-6186), half a block from the harbor. Seasonal. Box office open 9 AM–9 PM. Doors open at 6:45 PM. Dinner choices range from a deli sandwich to a full meal. Smaller than the Carousel Music Theatre. This 150-seat theater was originally used to house traveling vaudeville shows and circuses. After hors d'oeuvres, the evening begins with a 40-minute Broadway revue. The cast sings as they serve dinner, and the evening is topped off by a Broadway musical.

Boothbay Playhouse (633-7601), Route 27, Boothbay. Musicals, musical revues, comedies. Dinner and show, $20 per person. Dinner buffet starts at 7 PM. Tickets for show only are $10 per person. Open till late, after the show, for informal cabaret.

McSeagull's (633-4041), on the water in the middle of town. Open year-round. This waterside restaurant livens up around 9 PM when young singles congregate for the live music (no dancing), drinks, and desserts.

Jordan's Downstairs (633-2600), 49 Commercial Street. Live music nightly during the summer in a barlike setting with a small dance floor. An older crowd than at McSeagull's.

Marina Deck (633-4434), Boothbay Harbor (at the Tugboat Inn). Open June through Columbus Day. A marvelous view of the harbor's lights and a good spot for a nightcap. Piano bar nightly. Specialty drinks emphasize low-alcohol choices. Light meals include salads of lobster, shrimp, or crab; steamers, burgers, and lobster rolls.

SELECTIVE SHOPPING The village of Boothbay Harbor is a browser's delight with crafts shops, gift shops, and souvenir shops lining the narrow streets. You can watch taffy and fudge being made and glass ornaments being shaped. And you can buy everything from a rubber lobster or a T-shirt bearing a clever saying to an original painting by a recognized artist or an exquisitely fashioned piece by a local artisan.

Galleries: **Pinchpenny Gallery,** Commercial Street, Boothbay Harbor. Long-established and claiming to have the most diverse collection of fine art in the state. Everything from $22 prints of Maine seascapes and landscapes to original Norman Rockwells with four-figure price tags.

Bridge House Studio–Gallery. In a little house smack in the middle of the footbridge linking the two sides of the harbor. Original water-colors by Captain Marion Dash. Local scenes, birds.

Artisans: **Andersen Studio,** East Boothbay. Acclaimed stoneware animal sculptures of museum quality.

Nathaniel S. Wilson, East Boothbay. A sailmaker who also fashions distinctive tote bags from canvas.

Hasenfus Glass Shop, Commercial Street, Boothbay Harbor. It's called glass-blowing, but it's really the heating and bending of glass tubes into all sorts of imaginative ornaments, from fully rigged sailing ships to tiny animals.

A Silver Lining, Boothbay Harbor. Working metalsmiths. Original sculpture and jewelry in brass, sterling, and gold.

Palabra, across from Hasenfus Glass. A warren of rooms offering everything from kitschy souvenirs to valuable antiques. Upstairs (open by request) is a Poland Spring Museum with an impressive collection of the Moses Bottles this natural spring water used to come in, plus other memorabilia from the heyday of the resort at Poland Spring.

Edgecomb Potter's Gallery, Route 27, Edgecomb. Lovely pottery lamps, bowls, cookware, and jewelry.

Abacus Gallery, Boothbay Harbor. An appealing shop showcasing the very best of contemporary crafts. Many pieces show the artists' wonderful sense of humor. Even if you are not buying, be sure to go browsing here.

The Gold Smith, Boothbay Harbor. In a white-clapboard house across the street from Abacus. Unusual selection of jewelry in both gold and silver.

Mung Bean, Townsend Avenue, Boothbay Harbor. Maine-made crafts. Across the street is **Lupine Court,** and in the center of town is **Centric,** all run by the same couple and offering very attractive and unusual crafts ranging from jewelry to sculpture and wall hangings.

Special shops: **Boothbay Country Store,** Boothbay Harbor (east side). A charmingly crowded shop with all sorts of country collectibles.

The Smiling Cow and Gimbel's Country Store, Boothbay Harbor. All sorts of souvenirs and collectibles. Their annual half-price sale in November, before they close, is a good opportunity to get started on Christmas shopping.

Village Shop, Townsend Avenue, Boothbay Harbor. Very nice home furnishings, gifts, and gourmet foods.

House of Logan, Townsend Avenue, Boothbay Harbor. Beautiful quality clothing for men and women.

Cavoli's (633-6131), 15 McKown Street, Boothbay Harbor. Sandwiches, salads, quiches, gourmet foods and sweets by the pound, smoked seafoods, French bread baked right here.

Basket Barn, Route 27, Boothbay. Baskets from all over the world.

SPECIAL EVENTS   Late April: **Fishermen's Festival:** contests for fishermen and lobstermen, cabaret ball, crowning of the Shrimp Princess, and blessing of the fleet.

Late June: **Windjammer Days** parade of windjammers into the harbor, fireworks, band concert, church suppers, parade of floats, bands, and beauty queens up Main Street. The big event of the summer.

Late July: **Friendship Sloop Days,** parade and race of traditional fishing sloops built nearby in Friendship. **Antique Auto Shows,** Boothbay Railway Village, Route 27.

Early August: **Tuna Tournament,** with prizes for the biggest catch.

Early October: **Fall Foliage Festival:** boat trips to view foliage, church suppers, and craft sales. Annual **Fall Fair** at Boothbay Railway Village.

Early December: **Harbor Lights Festival:** parade, crafts, holiday shopping.

Damariscotta Area

The Damariscotta area, which encompasses the surrounding communities of Newcastle, Bristol, Pemaquid, New Harbor, Round Pond, and Waldoboro, typifies the best of coastal Maine. There is something here for everybody—and not too many bodies to get in the way of enjoying it.

Damariscotta's musical name means "meeting place of the alewives," and in spring there are indeed spawning alewives to be seen by the waterfall at Damariscotta Mills, not far from a spot where ancient American Indians heaped oyster shells from their summer feasts. The Indians also had a name for the peninsula jutting 10 miles seaward from this spot: Pemaquid, meaning "long finger."

Pemaquid loomed large on sixteenth- and seventeenth-century maps because during that time its protected inner harbor was the nearest mainland haven to Monhegan, a busy fishing stage for European fishermen. It was from these fishermen that the Pemaquid Indian Samoset learned the English with which he welcomed the Pilgrims at Plymouth in 1621. The following winter the Pemaquid settlement provided the Plymouth settlement with supplies enough to see it through to spring. Pemaquid, however, lacked a Governor William Bradford to write down its history and plant it firmly in every child's history text. Although it is occasionally referred to as this country's first permanent settlement, Pemaquid's status remains murky.

The site of Maine's "Lost City" is a delightful mini-peninsula bordered by the Pemaquid River and Johns Bay (named for Captain John Smith, who explored here in 1614), where lobsterboats and sailing craft pass by. At one tip stands a round stone fort. In recent years more than 40,000 artifacts have been unearthed in the adjacent meadow, many of them now displayed at the fine state-run museum that is part of the Colonial Pemaquid Restoration. An old cemetery full of crooked slate headstones completes the scene.

Since the late nineteenth century, when steamboats put into New Harbor and other ports in the area, this has been a region of summer resorts. It is blessed with beaches, both freshwater and saltwater, and with fascinating coastal rocks. This is true especially at Pemaquid Point, where the fine old lighthouse—one of the most visited and most photographed in Maine—towers above rugged granite outcroppings

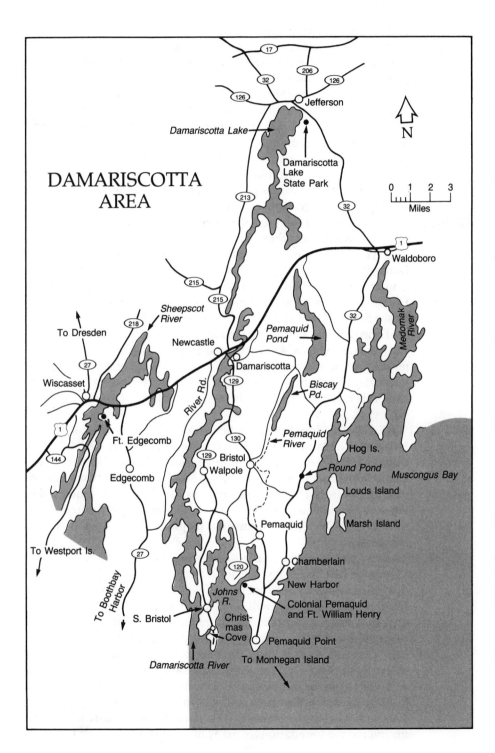

DAMARISCOTTA
AREA

Damariscotta Lake

Damariscotta
Lake
State Park

Jefferson

N

0 1 2 3
Miles

Waldoboro

Sheepscot
River

To Dresden

Wiscasset

Newcastle

Damariscotta

Pemaquid
Pond

Medomak
River

Biscay
Pd.

River Rd.

Ft. Edgecomb

Pemaquid
River

Hog Is.

Edgecomb

Bristol

Walpole

Round Pond

Muscongus Bay

Louds Island

To Westport Is.

Pemaquid

Marsh Island

To Boothbay Harbor

Chamberlain

New Harbor

S. Bristol

Johns
R.

Christ-
mas
Cove

Colonial Pemaquid
and Ft. William Henry

Damariscotta River

Pemaquid Point

To Monhegan Island

that splinter the dramatic waves as they roll ashore.

Clusters of rental cottages are scattered throughout the area, and there are some exceptional bed & breakfasts and inns. Motels may also be found along Route 1.

The twin villages of Newcastle and Damariscotta form the commercial center of the region. The main street is flanked by fine examples of nineteenth-century brick storefronts, many of them now restored. You will find engaging shops tucked inside and down side alleyways, but this is not a tourist town in the sense that Boothbay Harbor is. Alongside the more frivolous shops are a fishmonger's shop, a drug store, and a hardware shop—the kind of businesses that have been serving residents for generations.

GUIDANCE   **Damariscotta Region Information Bureau,** Damariscotta 04543, operates two offices where you will find personal assistance in planning your visit: one on Route 1 in Newcastle just south of the Damariscotta exit, and another on Business Route 1, in town, at Church Street (563-3175) at the top of the hill near Chapman-Hall House (563-3176). Both are open mid-June through September, 10–6, closed Sundays, but can be reached year-round by mail. There is also the **Damariscotta Region Chamber of Commerce** (563-8340), PO Box 13, Damariscotta 04543, with an office just off Main Street in the middle of town. Enter the side door of the building housing the Salt Bay Café. The chamber is open 9–1 Monday, Wednesday, Thursday, and Friday; and 1–5 Tuesday. Both organizations will help you to plan your visit.

GETTING THERE   **Jet Limo** transportation (800-834-5500 in Maine; 800-992-1401 outside Maine) to and from the Portland Jetport (Delta, United, Continental, USAir, Eastern Express, and Presidential airlines) is available to several points in the area. Most inns on the peninsula will pick up guests in Damariscotta, but basically this is the kind of place where you will want to have a car—or a boat—to get around.

MEDICAL EMERGENCY   **Miles Memorial Hospital** (563-1234), Bristol Road, Damariscotta.

TO SEE AND DO   **Colonial Pemaquid Restoration,** Pemaquid (off Route 130). Maintained by the State Bureau of Parks and Recreation and open daily Memorial Day to Labor Day, 9:30–5. $1 per person; under 12 free. (Tickets purchased here will also admit you to Fort William Henry—see below.) In the early nineteenth century, local farmers filled in the cellar holes of the seventeenth-century settlement that once stood here. Excavations in recent years have been made through the efforts of Rutgers University Professor Helen Camp, who noticed clay pipes and other artifacts in a newly plowed field. She submitted her initial findings to the Smithsonian Institute, which verified their importance. The state has since purchased this neck of land. Excavations have uncovered the foundations of many homes built in the first half of the

1600s as well as that of the Customs House, where clearance was once required of all ships traveling between the Kennebec and St. Croix rivers, and those of a tavern and the jail. Inside the museum—one of very few in-the-field archaeological museums open to the public anywhere—you view dioramas of the original 1620s settlement and artifacts such as a sixteenth-century German wine jug and slightly later tools and pottery, Spanish oil jars, and wampum—all found in the cellar holes just outside. Nearby is the old burial ground dating from 1695.

Fort William Henry, off Route 130, next to the archaeological museum. Open daily May 30 to Labor Day, 9:30–5. $1 per person; under 12 free (ticket also admits you to the museum—see above). This is a replica (built in 1907) of the third in a series of three English forts and one fortified warehouse built on this one site to fend off pirates and the French. In 1630 a stockade was built, but it was sacked and burned by pirate Dixie Bull (Captain Kidd is said to have buried treasure in a cave called Devil's Oven near New Harbor). In 1677 Governor Andros built a wooden redoubt manned by 50 men, but this was captured by Baron Castine and his Indians in 1689 (see Castine). The original of this particular fort, built in 1698, was to be "the most expensive and strongest fortification that has ever been built on American Soil," but it was destroyed by the French a year later. Fort Frederick, built in 1729, was never attacked, but during the American Revolution locals tore it down lest it fall into the hands of the British. There are exhibits on early explorations of Maine inside the fort and a panoramic view from the ramparts. The 1790 sea captain's house adjacent to the fort is not open to the public; it serves as the lab for the ongoing research work. There are picnic tables on the grounds with great views of the surrounding water.

Pemaquid Point Lighthouse, Fishermen's Museum, and Pemaquid Art Gallery (677-2494 or 677-2726), Route 130 (at the end), Pemaquid Point. The point is owned by the town, which charges a $1 per person entrance fee during the summer (over 55 $.50; under 12 free). The lighthouse, built in 1824 and automated in 1934, is a beauty, looking even more impressive from the rocks below than from up in the parking lot. These rocks offer a wonderfully varied example of geological upheaval, with titled strata and igneous intrusions. They are filled with tidal pools which can occupy children and adults alike for an entire day—but take care not to get too close to the water as the waves can be dangerous, catching people off balance and pulling them into the water. The rocks stretch for half a mile to Kresge Point. The **Fishermen's Museum,** housed in the former lighthouse keeper's home, is open Memorial Day to Columbus Day, Monday through Saturday 10–5, and Sundays 11–5. It contains fine photographs and ship models as well as other artifacts related to the Maine fishing industry and a description of the coast's lighthouses. Voluntary donations are requested of visitors to the lighthouse and museum. The complex also includes the **Pemaquid Art Gallery,** where works by local artists are exhibited from the end of June through mid-September. Donations requested here go towards an art scholarship for a local high school student. There are picnic tables and public toilets on the grounds. Next door to the lighthouse is the Seagull Shop and Restaurant, with a long, narrow dining room (you enter through the gift shop), whose window-side tables offer a beautiful view of the rocks and sea that more than overshadows the lackluster menu.

Thompson's Ice House, Route 129, South Bristol. Open daily year-round for outside viewing. One of the few surviving commercial ice houses in New England, this 150-year-old family business uses traditional tools for cutting ice from an adjacent pond.

Old Rock Schoolhouse, Bristol (follow signs from Route 130 to Route 132). Open during summer months, Tuesdays and Fridays 2–4. Dank and haunting, this 1827 rural stone schoolhouse stands at a long-overgrown crossroads in the woods.

Chapman-Hall House, corner of Main and Church streets, Damariscotta (in the village, diagonally across from Damariscotta National Bank). Open mid-June to mid-September daily, except Mondays, 1–5. Admission $1. Built in 1754, this is the oldest homestead in the region. The house has been restored with its original kitchen. There is also an herb garden with eighteenth-century rosebushes.

Shell Heaps. These ancient heaps of oyster shells, left by generations of American Indians at their summer encampments in what are now Newcastle and Damariscotta, have become incorporated into hillsides along the riverbank. A look at the soil, however, reveals the presence of the shells. The heaps—or middens, as they are called—are on private land. Inquire at the Damariscotta Region Information Bureau (see Guidance) regarding their whereabouts and permission to see them.

Samoset Memorial, New Harbor. Built of locally quarried stone, this is a monument in memory of Chief Samoset, who sold land to John Brown of New Harbor, creating the first deed executed in New England. Loud's Island, off Round Pond, was Samoset's home.

Rachel Carson Memorial Salt Pond, right at the side of Route 32, just north of Round Pond. There's a beautiful view of the open ocean from here, and at low tide the tidal pools are filled with a wondrous array of tiny sea creatures.

CHURCHES This particular part of the Maine coast possesses an unusual number of fine old meeting houses and churches, all of which are open to the public.

St. Patrick's Catholic Church, Academy Road, Newcastle (follow signs from the village). Open year-round, daily to sunset. This is the oldest surviving Catholic church (1808) in New England. It is an unusual building: brick construction, very narrow, and graced with a Paul Revere bell. The pews and stained glass date from 1896; and there is an old graveyard out back with forests all around.

St. Andrew's Episcopal Church, Glidden Street, Newcastle. A charming, half-timbered building on the bank of the Damariscotta River. Set among gardens and trees, it was the first assignment in this country for Henry Vaughan, the English architect who also designed the National Cathedral in Washington, D.C.

Old Walpole Meeting House (563-5660), Route 129, South Bristol. Open during July and August, Sundays for 3 PM services, and by appointment. A fine 1772 meeting house restored to its original shape; it has box pews and a pulpit with a sounding board.

Harrington Meeting House, Route 130, Pemaquid. Open during July and August, Mondays, Wednesdays, Fridays, and Saturdays 2–4:30 PM. Donations expected. The 1772 building has been restored and serves as a museum of "Old Bristol." A nondenominational service is held here once a year, usually on the third Sunday in August.

A bit farther east along the coast is the **Old German Church** (832-5100), Waldoboro. Open daily during July and August, 1–4. Built in 1772, this fascinating piece of history has a cemetery with the inscription, "This town was settled in 1748 by Germans who immigrated to this place with the promise and expectation of finding a prosperous city, instead of which they found nothing but wilderness." Bostonian Samuel Waldo—owner of a large tract of land in this area—obviously had not been straight with the 40 German families he brought to settle it. This was the first Lutheran church in Maine, long since gone native (Congregational).

BOAT EXCURSIONS/RENTALS   **Hardy Boat** (Captain Vern Lewis: 677-2026 days or 882-7909 evenings), Shaw's Wharf, New Harbor. Monhegan Island daily, plus sightseeing trips to watch lobster hauling, see puffins (with an Audubon narrator on board) and seals, and a sunset cruise to Pemaquid Point. Fares range from $5 to $20 (for the Monhegan trip), depending on length of cruise. On Wednesdays and Saturdays in July, August, and September, there's an optional clambake following the trip to Monhegan (cost is $35). There is a sign-up desk in season just off Main Street in Damariscotta.

Pemaquid River Canoe Rentals (563-5721), PO Box 46, Route 130 (across from Bristol Dam), Bristol 04539. Open May to mid-October. Canoes rented by the hour, day, or week, to be used on the Pemaquid River, which links Bristol Dam with Biscay Pond and Pemaquid Lake—a quiet chain of secluded spots just right for paddling along and spotting wildlife.

Lake Pemaquid (563-5202), Damariscotta. Sailboats, canoes, paddleboats, and outboards for rent. Snack bar, showers, and bait and tackle for sale.

GOLF   **Wawenock Country Club** (563-3938), Route 129 (7 miles south of

Damariscotta). Open May to November. Nine holes; visitors are welcome.

PICNICKING   There are two nice picnic areas on Route 130 in Bristol, one at **Lighthouse Park** and another at **Pemaquid Beach Park.** There are also picnic tables at Damariscotta Lake State Park (see Swimming).

SWIMMING   **Pemaquid Beach Park,** Route 130, Pemaquid. A town-owned area open Memorial Day to Labor Day, 9–7. Admission is $1 per adult, under 12 free. Bathhouse, rest rooms, refreshment stand, and picnic tables. Pleasant, but it can be windy, in which case try the more pebbly but more sheltered (and free) beach down the road.

On the peninsula there is also public swimming at **Biscay Pond,** off Route 32, and at **Bristol Dam** on Route 130, 5 miles south of Damariscotta.

Damariscotta Lake State Park, Route 32, Jefferson. A fine sandy beach with changing facilities, picnic tables, and grills at the northern end of the lake.

SPECIAL PROGRAMS   **National Audubon Ecology Camp,** Hogg Island (a quarter mile offshore at the head of Muscongus Bay). Established a half-century ago, these one- and two-week sessions study the wildlife on the island, including ospreys, black guillemots, moose, deer, porcupines, harbor seals, eider ducks, loons, warblers, and, from a boat, the puffins that were reintroduced to nearby Eastern Egg Rock by the Audubon-related Puffin Project. There are 5 miles of spruce trails, wildflower and herb gardens, mud flats, and rustic accommodations in a cluster of bungalows and a dining room in a restored nineteenth-century farmhouse. Famed instructors have included Roger Tory Peterson and Olin Sewall Pettingill. About 50 adult campers are accepted each session. For more information and dates, call 203-869-2017 or write National Audubon Society Ecology Camps and Workshops, 613 Riverside Road, Greenwich, CT 06831.

People to People Dance Company (563-1619), Damariscotta. Year-round. Classes in a wide variety of dance styles, including modern jazz, ballet, and modern dance.

INNS   **The Newcastle Inn** (563-5685), River Road, Newcastle 04553. Open year-round. Located just outside of the village center, this is one of the longest-operating inns in the region. Ted and Chris Sprague bought it in 1987 and have gussied it up considerably. All rooms now have private baths, and the beds in many of the rooms are four-poster or have crocheted canopies. The atmosphere downstairs is still comfortable and homelike, with a welcoming living room and a glassed-in room highlighted by a stenciled floor and a view down the lawn to the Damariscotta River. Chris's artful needlework and crewel tapestries grace many of the walls. In the intimate dining room, an elegant five-course dinner and generous breakfast are served (dinner to public with reservation; see Dining Out). Our favorite rooms upstairs are number 1, with a loveseat and a canopy bed; number 8, with an inviting sitting area; and number 9, with a huge bathroom. Guests may choose B&B rates (Expensive) or MAP rates (Deluxe). No smoking.

Gosnold Arms (677-3727), Route 32, New Harbor 04554. Open mid-May through November (restaurant opens Memorial Day weekend). New Harbor itself is a picture-perfect clutter of lobster boats and pleasure craft. The inn, just across the road from the water and the working waterfront, has been welcoming summer guests since 1925. Nothing fancy, it is a rambling white-clapboard complex set on a grassy lawn: a comfortable old farmhouse with a long, welcoming porch, an attached barn, and scattered cottages. Sixteen guest rooms have been fitted into the barn around a pleasant gathering room with a huge fireplace; the balance of the accommodations are in the cottages: everything from a one-person former tugboat pilothouse to the town's original steamboat freight office. Guests breakfast and sup on the enclosed porch overlooking the water; the dining room is also open to the public and has a reputation for fresh, local, simply prepared food. Entrées include baked haddock, baked stuffed shrimp, seafood casserole, seafood kabob, boiled lobster, prime rib, and grilled ham steak. The inn is named for Batholomew Gosnold, the commander of the British ship *Concord*, which sailed into the harbor in 1602. All rates include breakfast. $92–$125 double; less off-season.

Bradley Inn (677-2105), Pemaquid Point Road, New Harbor 04554. Open mid-May to the end of October. A restored turn-of-the-century Maine summer inn with Victorian atmosphere in the dining room and living room downstairs and in the 12 guest rooms upstairs. A pleasant walk to the lighthouse in one direction, to Kresge Point in the other. Specialties in the dining room include fresh seafood dishes and veal prepared several ways. Room rates include a large continental breakfast buffet. $45–$90 double.

Coveside Inn (644-8282), Christmas Cove, South Bristol 04568. Open early June to mid-September. Holly red, with a mansard roof, this Victorian inn is extremely popular. There are 5 old-fashioned guest rooms in the inn (all have private baths, though some baths are across the hall from corresponding rooms) plus 10 modern shorefront units across the road. The motel has recently been completely redone, with new pine paneling and cathedral ceilings with skylights. This building and the dining room are built right out over the water. The Dory Bar and Shore Restaurant (see Dining Out) are popular with the yachting set, many of whom sail into Christmas Cove and row ashore for dinner. Three meals are served every day. (Christmas Cove is said to have been christened by Captain John Smith, who first arrived here one Christmas morning.) Inn rooms $65, motel rooms $80; double.

Hotel Pemaquid (677-2312), Pemaquid 04554. Open mid-May to Columbus Day. A century-old classic just outside the gate to Pemaquid

Lighthouse, this rambling hotel was completely renovated in 1987. It's now an ideal spot for recapturing the traditional feeling of summering in Maine. Everything is as neat and tidy as can be, and the cozy decor is embellished with charming little "still lifes" reminiscent of days gone by—an arrangement of vintage magazines, for example, and an old steamer trunk accompanied by a pair of high-button boots. There's a stone fireplace in the living room to ward off the chill of foggy days and a long porch with wicker chairs for sunny afternoons. There are 24 rooms here, including some very nice motel units with private decks. The hotel does not have a restaurant, but guests enjoy strolling 150 yards to the restaurant at the lighthouse for breakfast. There are about a half-dozen nearby restaurants for dinner. Rooms have either shared baths or private baths. Credit cards are not accepted.

Snow Turtle Inn (832-4423), Route 32 and Old Route 1, Waldoboro 04572. Open year-round. There's a sizable restaurant downstairs (see Dining Out) and, upstairs, four or five bedrooms with stenciled walls and homey furnishings. The most unusual is the Christmas Room, complete with stockings hung above the fireplace (which may be used) and a fully decorated artificial tree at the head of the bed. Innkeeper Aileen Allen says guests love this room because it makes them feel cool in summer and cozy in winter. Shared baths; $60 double, including a full country breakfast.

Broad Bay Inn & Gallery (832-6668), PO Box 607, Main Street, Waldoboro 04572. Open year-round, except January. Within walking distance of the village and its restaurants, shops, and performances at the restored Waldo Theatre. Tennis courts, the Medomak River, Damariscotta Lake, and an Audubon sanctuary are also close at hand. This is a very pleasant, restored 1830 classic colonial home with Victorian furnishings and canopy beds. The five guest rooms share three baths. Afternoon tea and sherry are served on the sun deck in summer and by the fire in winter. The inn's art gallery exhibits the works of well-known Maine artists and sells limited-edition prints, crafts, and gifts. Libby Hopkins (who runs the bed & breakfast with her husband, Jim) also offers art workshops here. Rates include a full gourmet breakfast; on Saturday evenings, candlelight dinners may be arranged in advance (for guests and the public). Two-night minimum stay on weekends in July and August. Special rates are available for Thanksgiving, Christmas, and extended stays. On New Year's Eve, guests are treated to sleigh rides. $40–$60 double.

BED & BREAKFASTS   Brannon-Bunker Inn (563-5941), HCR 64, Box 045V, Route 129, Damariscotta 04543. Open year-round. A café-au-lait 1820 home with eight artfully furnished rooms plus a three-room suite in an adjacent coach house. An antiques shop is in the barn. There's a handy lake for swimming, and golf is down the road at the Wawenock Country Club (see Golf). Breakfast is served (and included in rates), and the kitchen is available for guests' use at other times of the day. Private and shared baths; $40–$55 double; $60–$100 for suites.

Glidden House (563-1859), RR 1, Box 740, Glidden Street, Newcastle 04553. A Victorian house overlooking the Damariscotta River on a street lined with elegant old homes. A convenient walk to the shops of both Newcastle and Damariscotta. Most guest rooms have private baths. There is also a three-room apartment. Exceptional breakfasts, included in the lodging, are served in the dining room or in the garden. A double with private bath is $55.

Hearthside Inn (563-8885), 20 River Road, Newcastle 04553. Set on a rise across from the Damariscotta River, it offers three spacious guest rooms with shared bath, two with queen-sized beds. Piano and TV in the living room. Full cooked breakfast is included. $55 double.

Markert House (563-1309), PO Box 224, Glidden Street, Newcastle 04553. Another elegant Victorian overlooking the Damariscotta River. Newly decorated guest rooms. Within walking distance of downtown Newcastle and Damariscotta. Doubles, with a full breakfast, are $45–$55, shared bath.

Captain's House (563-1482), Box 19, River Road, Newcastle 04553. Open year-round. Next door to Hearthside Inn (see above), with the same pleasant view of the Damariscotta River. Five guest rooms with shared bath. A full country breakfast is included. $45–$60 double.

The Crown 'n' Anchor Inn (563-8954), PO Box 17, Newcastle 04553. Also across the road from the Damariscotta River, this 1850s Greek Revival house was built by a ship's carpenter as an addition to an earlier Cape cottage. It offers three rooms with a shared bath and a two-room suite that includes a Victorian sitting area. Children 12 and over are welcome. $40–$55 double; $65 suite.

Mill Pond Inn (563-8014), Route 215, Damariscotta Mills (mailing address: RFD 1, Box 245, Newcastle 04553). Open year-round. A quiet spot a bit off the beaten track, perfect for nature-watchers. There are 46 different species of wildlife on the mill pond and Damariscotta Lake, and there is even a resident bald eagle. There's a two-person hammock under the willow trees and a beach at the freshwater swimming hole across the way. The 1780 grey-clapboard house with a red door offers six double rooms, one of which has an adjoining smaller room with twin beds. All have private baths. The "tummy-filling" breakfast might be pancakes with fresh blueberries or omelets with crabmeat and vegetables from the inn's garden. It is served in the fireplaced dining room with a picture window overlooking the lake. In winter pack a picnic lunch and skate across the lake to a miniature island. In summer ask for a ride in the 16-foot motorboat on the 14-mile-long Damariscotta River or go for a paddle in the canoe. $55–$65.

The Bristol Inn (563-1125), PO Box 130, Upper Round Pond Road, Bristol Mills 04539. Rooms with private baths, $55–$65.

Barnswallow B&B (563-8568), Routes 129 and 130, HC 61, Box 135, Damariscotta 04543. A pristine, warmly decorated 1830s Cape with fireplaces in the dining room, living room (with TV), and reading parlor. Hospitality includes munchies and setups at cocktail time as well as a generous continental breakfast in the morning. Children over 12 are welcome. All private baths; doubles $55 (private bath across hall) to $70.

Little River Inn (677-2845), Route 130, HC 62, Box 178, Pemaquid 04558. Open year-round. An 1840 Cape farm offering rustic accommodations in the attached converted barn. Dinners, served to guests by reservation, reflect Kristina's Hungarian heritage. $50–$60.

Windward Farm (845-2830), Washington 04574. Open all year. A short drive inland from Nobleboro, this 1880s farmhouse overlooks Crystal Lake, where you can enjoy swimming, sailing, and canoeing. Cross-country skiing and ice-skating in winter. Breakfast, included in the rates, features fresh fruits, whole-grain breads, muffins, and homemade jams. Moderate.

Storer Pond Farm (832-5143), RFD 2, Box 166A, Waldoboro 04572. This circa 1790 home caters to one family or group at a time, offering dormitory-style accommodations for up to 12 in a spacious, renovated attic with exposed beams and cathedral ceiling. Private dining is available for guests. Open year-round, the farm encourages guests to make use of the 239 acres and the 87-acre farm pond—cross-country skiing and skating in winter; swimming and hiking in summer. High chair and crib are available. If you're interested, call or write for their videotape. Rates include full family-style breakfast and dinner. $65 per person; $25 ages 2–12; under 2 free. For multiple-night stays it's $50 per adult.

The Roaring Lion (832-4038), PO Box 756, 75 Main Street, Waldoboro 04572. Open year-round. Comfortable accommodations in a 1905 home with tin ceilings, fireplaces, and a big screened porch. Coffee, tea, and hot chocolate are available in the upstairs hallway early each morning; then a full breakfast is served downstairs until 9 AM. Late risers may have a continental breakfast. The kitchen will also cater to special, vegetarian, and macrobiotic diets. One room with private bath; three with shared bath. $50–$60 double; $10 less for single occupancy.

Le Vatout B&B (832-4552), RR 1, Box 375, Waldoboro 04572. Open year-round. This is the pleasant 1830s home of Don Slagel, a retired actor/singer, composer/conductor, teacher, and inveterate collector. The guest rooms are furnished with antiques and oriental rugs and named after distinguished Mainers in literature, art, and the performing arts. Don's green thumb has manifested itself in beautifully laid out herb and flower gardens named in honor of composer Walter Piston. $45–$75; private and shared baths.

Photo by Bonnie Scott

Check newspapers for local auctions

COTTAGES   These and other cottages and cabins in the Damariscotta–Pemaquid region fill up long before summer's arrival, though you may always luck into a cancellation. The best advice is to start looking soon after New Year's Day—after all, some cabins are booked by repeat visitors a full year in advance.

Damariscotta Lake Farm (549-7953), Jefferson 04348. Open Memorial Day to the end of September. Sited at the junction of routes 32, 126, and 312 at the head of Damariscotta Lake, these lined-up, one-, two-, and three-bedroom efficiency cottages have screened porches. Private sandy beach, boat rentals. There's a small pitching golf course in summer, plus a marina. Weekly rates. Inexpensive.

Harborside Cottages (677-2701), Route 32, New Harbor 04554. Open May through the end of October. Six cottages with two bedrooms and Franklin stoves, four cottages with one bedroom. Weekly rates in summer are $350 for a two-bedroom cottage, $250 for a one-bedroom cottage. Book far in advance, especially if you are hoping for July or August.

Thompson House and Cottages (677-2317), New Harbor 04554. Two apartments, one and two bedrooms, in an annex to the main house. Also more than 20 cottages scattered along the harbor and back cove (less expensive) and along the ocean. Cottages accommodating up to five are $540–$700 per week in season.

Ye Olde Forte Cabins (677-2261), Pemaquid Beach 04554. (Off-season, write to Mrs. Mike Dodge, 33 Partridge Lane, Belmont, MA

02178.) Open early June to end of September. A parade of snug cabins up and down the grassy knoll beside Fort William Henry, all sharing a central "cook house" and a separate shower building. Four double and five single cabins with heat and half baths. There is one housekeeping cottage with a living room, bedroom, kitchen, and full bath. $42–$66.50 per night depending on accommodations and number of people; $260–$430 (for housekeeping cottage) per week.

MOTELS   Route 1 from Edgecomb to Waldoboro has its share of modern motels offering the usual: color TV, two double beds, private bath, often a swimming pool. There are also numerous crescents of miniature cottages, the more old-fashioned motor-court style. Just north of the center of Damariscotta, on Business Route 1, you will find some smaller motels and motor courts with bargain rates.

DINING OUT   **The Newcastle Inn** (563-5685), River Road, Newcastle 04553. This is the state's first inn to receive the *Maine Sunday Telegram*'s highest ratings for atmosphere, food, and service, and the honor is well-deserved. From spring through fall foliage season, the Spragues serve dinner to their guests and to the public, by reservation, six nights a week (closed Mondays). In the off-season, dinner is served Friday and Saturday nights. There is a prix fixe of about $35 for the five-course dinner (no choices), which is served at 7 PM. A cocktail hour, with complimentary hors d'oeuvres, begins at 6 PM. Innkeeper Chris Sprague is the chef, with her husband, Ted, serving as bartender. Chris's specialties include such starters as risotto primavera; fettucine with tomatoes, basil, and garlic; and scallops in puff pastry. For entrées, she often serves rack of lamb with green peppercorn sauce; salmon in orange madeira sauce; or breast of duck stuffed with apples and sausages. There is also a soup course, perhaps featuring cold blueberry soup or red and yellow pepper bisque; a salad; and homemade cream biscuits. For dessert, the choice may be a frozen white chocolate mousse, a peach crisp with white chocolate and brandy sauce, or chocolate hazelnut terrine with caramel sauce. For die-hard lobster lovers, it's available by prior arrangement. The inn has a full bar and a small but carefully selected, moderately priced wine list.

Schooner Landing (563-3380), next to the town landing in Damariscotta. A new venture in a location where several restaurants have come and gone, this is a pleasant spot overlooking the water (dining on the deck is especially enjoyable in nice weather—if the mosquitoes aren't hungry). The menu is big on seafood dishes, some of them very good. The live music—tending towards jazz and folk—adds to the atmosphere, unless the amps have been turned up too high. Dinner for two, with wine, is about $40–$50.

Coveside Inn Shore Restaurant and Dory Bar (644-8540), Christmas Cove. Open June through mid-September. Out of the way, but a nice excuse to drive down to the tip of Route 129 where you will actually be on an island connected to South Bristol by one of the world's smallest drawbridges. The cove was supposedly named by explorer Captain John Smith when he arrived on December 25, 1614. The restaurant, part of the inn complex (see Inns), serves three meals daily and is a beloved standby—especially with yachtsmen who make a point to stop here while cruising the coast. Dinner specialties include mussels baked with spinach and cheese, sautéed scallops, fish and pasta of the day, and lobsters boiled or baked and stuffed. For lunch, try the lobster or crab roll, or the seafood chowder, which can be ordered with a salad and a delicious "sunshine" muffin that tastes like carrot cake. There are also burgers and seafood salad plates. Moderate.

Bradley Inn (677-2105), Pemaquid Point Road, New Harbor. A full-service restaurant and inn (see Inns), serving fresh seafood and veal specialties on white linen. Good wine list. Moderate.

Gosnold Arms (677-3727), New Harbor. Open Memorial Day weekend until Thanksgiving weekend. An old-fashioned summer hostelry (see Inns) with a public dining room that seats 80. The kitchen specializes in the freshest local seafood in straightforward preparations such as baked haddock, baked stuffed shrimp, seafood casserole, prime rib, fried chicken, and boiled lobster. Dinner is served on the enclosed porch with a view of the harbor.

Pine Cone Public House (832-6337), Friendship Street, Waldoboro. Open 11–11, seven days a week from Memorial Day to Labor Day, and Friday through Sunday the rest of the year (earlier closing off-season); Sunday brunch. Overlooking the Medomak River, with a publike downstairs room, and an upstairs water-view dining room with outdoor deck. (There's sometimes live piano music which, unfortunately, can overpower conversations at nearby tables.) Seafood and vegetarian specialties with an international flavor, including shrimp Vera Cruz, lobster pie, salmon steak, oriental stir-fry, vegetarian quiche, and crêpes. There's also a daily pasta special. Salads feature unusual, locally grown greens and homemade dressings. Dinners are served all day, but less expensive sandwiches are also available. Sunday brunch features egg dishes and pastries and desserts prepared on the premises. Inexpensive to moderate.

Snow Turtle Inn (832-4423), Route 32 and Old Route 1, Waldoboro. Serving dinner Tuesday through Saturday, 5 PM to 9 PM; Sunday brunch and dinner 11:30 AM to 8 PM; year-round. The painting of Windsor Castle has hung above the mantel in the dining room ever since this house was built by a successful sea merchant in 1803. Its deep greens have determined the color the wood trim is painted; the pink tablecloths and candles provide an eye-pleasing complement. Serving up to 45 in the two dining rooms, and an additional 25 on the sun porch in summer, the Snow Turtle offers such entrées as steak, veal marsala, baked haddock, sautéed Cajun scallops, roast duckling, and raspberry chicken, all in the $12 range. Aileen Allen, who with her husband, Larry, runs the inn, is the chef; her daily specials feature such fresh fish as salmon, blackened red snapper, and lemon-pepper catfish.

EATING OUT   **Backstreet Landing** (563-5666), Elm Street Plaza, Damariscotta. Open year-round, daily. Just behind Main Street, overlooking the upper Damariscotta River, this very pleasant, low-key restaurant and gathering place has good, dependable food. Three meals are served each day, plus Sunday brunch. Seafood entrées, homemade soups and chowders, quiches, lunch specials, and light late-evening snacks. This is a popular place with locals who meet here year-round.

   Salt Bay Café (563-1666), Main Street, Damariscotta. Open year-round for breakfast, lunch, and dinner. A pleasant greenhouse-like entrance; conventional booths and tables. Serving simple favorites such as fried clams, french-fried vegetables, burgers, sandwiches, and soups.

   Pine Grove Family Restaurant (563-3765), Route 1, just north of Damariscotta. Open year-round. Open early for breakfast but closes somewhat early, too. A comfortable dining room with moderate prices and the motto, "Where friendliness adds flavor to your food." Fried seafoods and old-fashioned good food. Service can be a bit slow, but there is a takeout window for those in a hurry. Inexpensive.

   Szechuan House (563-3998 or 563-3992), Coastal Marketplace, Damariscotta. A typical family-run, no-atmosphere Chinese restaurant offering the standard Chinese–American menu. But if you've a yearning for sweet-and-sour or moo-goo-gai-pan, this is the place. Takeout available. Inexpensive.

   Anchor Inn (529-5584), Round Pond. Open for lunch and dinner, Memorial Day through Columbus Day. An unassuming place right in the middle of the small fishing village of Round Pond, overlooking the harbor. In addition to the regular fried seafood, chowder, seafood salad rolls, and charbroiled steaks and seafood, the menu also lists more creative dishes like brie and mushroom bake, crab in puff pastry, and scampi. Inexpensive.

   Pemaquid Chart House (677-3315), at the Pemaquid Restoration. Open Memorial Day through Labor Day. A casual dining spot offering lunch, afternoon snacks, dinner, and late snacks. Choose the takeout section adjacent to the pier (you can come by boat) or the inside dining room with views of the harbor. Menu selections range from seafood salads, burgers, and an appealing variety of sandwiches for lunch (most around $6) to fried, sautéed, and broiled seafood and steaks for dinner (most around $12).

   Moody's Diner (832-7468), Route 1, Waldoboro. Open 24 hours (except midnight to 5 AM on Friday and Saturday nights). A longtime landmark well-known for its cream pies and family-style food. Unbeatable breakfasts such as corned beef hash and eggs. Very digestible prices in a clean and warm, old classic of a diner, run by several generations of the Moody family along with other employees who have been there so long they have become part of the family, too. To re-create Moody's menu at home, take home a copy of their cookbook. Inexpensive.

LOBSTER IN THE ROUGH   Shaw's (677-2200), New Harbor (next to the New Harbor Co-Op). Open late May to mid-October, daily for lunch and supper. At this very popular dockside spot, you stand in line at the counter to order your lobster and then wait for your name to be called when it's ready. In addition to lobster and steamed clams, the menu includes a variety of basic foods like meat loaf, fish cakes, stews, shrimp, roast turkey, scallops, and sandwiches. Liquor is also served. Choose to sit at a picnic table either out on the dock over the water or in the inside dining room. Inexpensive to moderate.

Samoset Restaurant (677-2142), New Harbor. Open summers for breakfast, lunch, and dinner daily. Lobsters, clams, and a few additional selections. Cocktails are served. Inexpensive to moderate.

Captain's Catch Seafood (677-2396), Pemaquid Beach Road, New Harbor. Open throughout summer season, 11–8 daily. Indoor and outdoor picnic-style dining. Lobsters, clams (steamed or fried), seafood baskets, and dinners; fish fry every Friday; homemade desserts. Inexpensive to moderate.

SNACKS   Sun Café, Main Street, Damariscotta. A pleasant little room with miniature tables offering continental breakfasts, delicious lunches, and mouthwatering home-baked goods to go. The day we were there the lunch menu included two soups, salads with ruby-red garden tomatoes, fusili with pesto, a Mexicale sandwich, bagel pizza, quiche, and a pita pocket filled with herbed cream cheese and veggies. Most choices are about $4. Espresso, cappuccino, and mochaccino are also available.

Round Top Ice Cream (563-5993), Business Route 1, Damariscotta. Open Memorial Day to Columbus Day. This is the original Round Top, on the grounds of the farm where it all used to happen, beginning in 1924 (an expanded creamery is now just over the hill). The creamy ice cream comes in 36 flavors, including raspberry, Almond Joy, and fresh blueberry. This is the granddaddy of all ice-cream stands in the area, and we don't think the interior has changed since 1924. Hot dogs, burgers, sandwiches, and fried-seafood dinners are sold at an adjacent stand. There are umbrella-topped tables outside, stools inside. Also on the grounds is the Round Top Center for the Arts, offering concerts, classes, exhibitions, and festivals.

Zecchino's Submarines, Damariscotta, near the town landing (in back of Gilliam's fish market). A variety of submarine sandwiches, plus chili, soups, and salads.

The Bread Basket, Damariscotta, near the Courtyard Shops. Run by local ladies, this delightful little café with just a few small tables sells delectable bakery goods and coffee.

The Ice Cream Deck, Damariscotta. Next to Schooner Landing restaurant. Summer only. Have a cone and watch the rapids rush under the bridge.

River View Takeout, Damariscotta. A little stand in the parking lot behind the Maine Coast Bookshop (see Selective Shopping). Hamburgers, hot dogs, and the like at old-fashioned prices.

Newcastle Farms, Main Street, Newcastle. A convenience store/gas station that also sells pizzas, fried chicken, and stuffed potatoes.

The Wright Store, center of Newcastle Village. A small grocery store that looks more like a house, which it was originally. The pizzas, made to order, aren't half bad.

Subway, Upper Main Street, Damariscotta. One of a chain offering submarine sandwiches and similar fare.

SELECTIVE SHOPPING   Damariscotta and Newcastle—twin villages separated only by a short bridge across the Damariscotta River—together make up one of the better spots along the coast to look for antiques. You will also find a variety of pleasing gift shops, clothing stores, and specialty shops in the nineteenth-century brick buildings along Damariscotta's Main Street.

Antiques: **Partridge Antiques,** Route 1, Newcastle. Fine eighteenth-century furniture and accessories in a huge yellow barn.

Robert L. Foster, Route 1, Newcastle. A conglomeration of individual dealers' stalls, flea market tables outside, and an auction hall where Mr. Foster is the auctioneer. The auctions, scheduled throughout the summer, offer terrific free entertainment as well as all sorts of bargains in country furniture and a wide variety of other odds and ends.

Kaja Veilleux Antiques (563-1002), Newcastle Square, Newcastle. Fine antiques and free verbal appraisals on Thursdays.

Cooper's Red Barn, Business Route 1, Damariscotta. Old pine and oak furniture, rough or refinished. Gifts, crafts, old books, china, and glass.

Galleries: **Art for America Gallery** (563-1009), Newcastle Square, Newcastle. Changing exhibits of work by outstanding Maine artists.

Schooner Galleries (563-8031), Route 1, Edgecomb, and Main Street, Damariscotta. Specializing in eighteenth- and nineteenth-century marine paintings by artists such as Thomas Bush Hardy, Frank Mason, and W. H. Drake, plus works by local artists.

Artisans: **Ax Wood Products,** Route 129, Walpole (10 minutes from Damariscotta). Open year-round. This cluster of appealing buildings where Barnaby Porter makes his rustic wooden objects, both functional and decorative, is an engaging place to stop. Browse through his sales area, or watch him working on a current project. Specialties include imaginative wind vanes in such shapes as a Friendship sloop, mackerel, and Wind Maiden; and marvelous miniature houses built inside hollow tree stumps. Special orders are welcomed.

Gil Whitman Gallery (882-7705), Route 1, Edgecomb. Open weekdays, 9–5, and by appointment. Metal sculptures with "the Maine ingredient," which is usually just a touch of humor. Commissions are welcomed.

Damariscotta Pottery, just off Main Street, Damariscotta. Walk down a narrow alleyway and duck into this treasure trove of water-colored pottery. Reminiscent of Mallorcan ware, it is decorated in primitive floral and animal designs. You can watch this charming pottery being made and painted right in the shop.

David and Susan Margonelli, furniture makers (633-3326), River Road, Edgecomb. About 4 miles down a lovely tree-shaded road from the villages of Newcastle and Damariscotta. Showroom is open in season Monday through Saturday 10–5; and by appointment. Exquisite, completely handmade fine furniture with a classic influence. David and Susan make it all themselves.

Pemaquid Floorcloths (529-5633), Route 32, Pemaquid. Hand-stenciled canvas floor coverings in the traditional country style. Open by chance and by appointment.

Special shops: **Maine Coast Bookshop** (563-3207), Main Street, Damariscotta. A truly exceptional bookstore with engaging, knowledgeable staff members who delight in making suggestions and helping customers shop for others. This is certainly one of the state's best bookstores.

Victorian Stable, Water Street, Damariscotta. Seasonal. An old stable whose box stalls are now filled with the outstanding work of more than 100 Maine craftspeople.

Weatherbird Trading Co., Northey Square, Damariscotta. A complex of shops selling fine women's clothing and accessories, home furnishings, and gourmet foods, wines, and cheeses.

S. Fernald Country Store, Main Street, Damariscotta. Penny candy, cheeses and other deli items, magazines, and a nostalgic soda fountain, all meant to re-create the atmosphere of an old-time country store.

Ingrid, Ltd., Route 130, Damariscotta (a block or two off Main Street). A charming shop brimming with Scandinavian accessories for the home, fresh-baked goodies, some Scandinavian tinned foods, cards, and cooking gadgets. There's a small Christmas shop in the back.

The Maine Sale, River Road, Newcastle. A charming collection of country furnishings and accessories for the home.

Come Again Shop, Main Street, Damariscotta. A pleasant, old-fashioned gift and card shop.

Courtyard Shops, off Main Street, Damariscotta. **Bluebunnie,** selling children's clothes; **Loon's Landing Antiques,** selling primitives and kitchen things; and others.

Mostly Needlepoint and Yarns, Main Street, Damariscotta. In the handsome Nathaniel Austin House. Yarns, kits, and help on needle projects.

Alewives Fabrics, Route 215, Damariscotta Mills. An elegant selection of fabrics, both domestic and imported. The building is an old general store.

Granite Hall Store, Round Pond. A wonderful old building filled with Irish woolens and other handmade clothing from the British Isles, Eskimo sculptures, a good selection of greeting cards, a few antiques, toys, penny candy, hot peanuts, fudge, and, at an outdoor window, ice cream.

SPECIAL EVENTS   2nd weekend in July: **Damariscotta River Oyster Festival,** Damariscotta. A celebration of the oyster aquaculture conducted in the river. Oysters fixed every way (especially au naturel), music, crafts, and a canoe race through the rapids of the Damariscotta River.

Early August: **Olde Bristol Days,** Old Fort Grounds, Pemaquid Beach. Parade, fish fry, chicken barbecue, bands, bagpipers, concerts, pancake breakfast, road race, boat race, firemen's muster, crafts, and the annual **Bristol Footlighters Show** (which has been going on for almost 40 years).

Rockland Area and the Islands

Rockland is the unchallenged center of commerce for the region. This small city's Main Street, just a block inland from the harbor, hasn't changed much over the decades (many of its buildings are handsome examples of nineteenth-century commercial architecture), but there are a number of intriguing shops worth a visit. Rockland is also the location of the William A. Farnsworth Library and Art Museum, a real gem filled with watercolors and oils by some of the best eighteenth-, nineteenth-, and twentieth-century artists who have painted the Maine coast (the museum is renowned for its collection of works by all three Wyeths). Blessed with a wide, deep harbor, Rockland is home base for ferries to the islands of Vinalhaven, North Haven, and Matinicus; in addition, it lays claim to being the "Windjammer Capital of the World," with almost a dozen of these classic passenger-carrying schooners ported here. This is also the world's largest distribution center for lobster, and its active fishing fleet keeps the sardine factories and frozen-fish plants busy. (You may see the boats off-loading their catch at Tillson Avenue.)

Southwest of Rockland, two peninsulas divide Muscongus Bay from Penobscot Bay. One is the fat arm of land on which the villages of Friendship and Cushing doze. Friendship is best known as the birthplace of the classic Friendship sloop, originally used by local lobstermen to haul their traps; originals and reproductions of this sturdy little vessel hold races here every summer. The other arm of land is the skinnier St. George Peninsula. Port Clyde, at its tip, is the departure point for the year-round mailboat to Monhegan. It is a village with decent, simple places to eat and sleep before boarding the boat to the island. Tenants Harbor and Spruce Head, both a short distance up Route 131 from Port Clyde, also have a few well-estab-lished inns. The peninsulas are divided by the 10-mile-long tidal St. George River, at the head of which sits Thomaston. This beautiful old town has produced its share of wooden ships, and its handsome Main Street mansions stand today in white-clapboard testimony to the shipbuilders' success. Thomaston is today a quiet community with a few bed & breakfasts and eating places.

GUIDANCE   **Rockland-Thomaston Chamber of Commerce** (596-0376), Pub-lic Landing, Rockland (write PO Box 508, Rockland 04841). Open weekdays, 9–5 in summer and 8–4 in winter. The chamber serves as an information source for the entire Rockland area, which includes the islands. They also have cottage listings for North Haven, Vinalhaven, and the area from Owls Head to Cushing.

GETTING THERE   **Knox County Airport** (594-4131), at Owls Head, just south of Rockland, schedules daily service to Boston and New York on Continental Express. Keep in mind, however, that the airport is on a peninsula that is particularly susceptible to fog, and the absence of an instrument-landing system here means planes cannot land in low visibility—so flights may be diverted to Bangor or Augusta if conditions are poor (there is some talk of upgrading the airport's equipment by 1992). For charter flights to and from Portland and other points, check with **Penobscot Air Service, Ltd.** (800-777-6211 or 596-6211). For taxi service contact **R&H Taxi** (594-5525).

MEDICAL EMERGENCY   **Penobscot Bay Medical Center** (594-9511), Route 1, Glen Cove, Rockland.

TO SEE AND DO   **William A. Farnsworth Library and Art Museum** (596-6457), 19 Elm Street, Rockland. Open year-round, daily June through September (10–5, except Sundays 1–5), otherwise closed on Mondays; closed legal holidays. (See Farnsworth Homestead for admission information.) Lucy Farnsworth was a spinster who lived frugally in just three rooms of her family mansion. When she died in 1935, neighbors were amazed to find that she had left $1,300,000 to establish the present museum. It is a handsome building, but the big lures are paintings such as *Christina's World* and *Her Room* by Andrew Wyeth, posters and book illustrations by his father, N. C. Wyeth, and oils by Andrew's son Jamie. Winslow Homer is also well represented as is native Rockland sculptor Louise Nevelson. There are changing exhibits, a program of lectures and concerts, and an outstanding museum store. Admission to the Museum and the Homestead (see below) is $3 adults, $2 senior citizens and high school students, under 12 free.

Farnsworth Homestead (596-6457), Elm Street, Rockland. Open June to mid-September only; Monday through Saturday 10–4:30 and Sunday 1–4. The Farnsworth Homestead was built in 1840 and is maintained as it was in Miss Lucy's day—according to a stipulation in her will—with lavish, colorful Victorian furnishings (all original).

Montpelier (354-8062), Thomaston. Open May 30 to Labor Day, Wednesday through Sunday from 9 AM until 4:45 PM when the last tour begins. Admission is $1.50 for adults, children under 12 and senior citizens free. This is not the original, but it is a splendid reproduction of the grand mansion built on this spot in 1794 by General Henry Knox, the portly (5-foot 6-inch, 300-pound) Boston bookseller who became a revolutionary war hero, then our first secretary of war. He married a granddaughter of Samuel Waldo, the Boston developer who owned all of this area (and for whom the

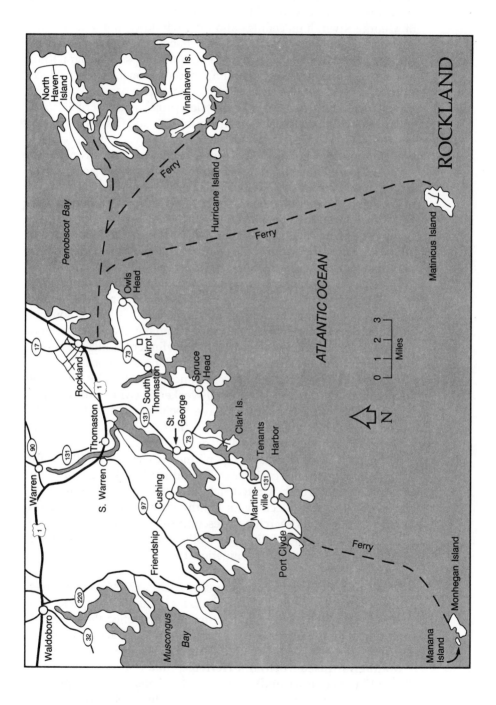

county is named), and built himself as elaborate a mansion here as any to be found in the new republic. It has an oval dining room facing the St. George River, high ceilings and long windows, not to mention a semi-flying staircase. Montpelier and its collection of Colonial and Federal period furnishings provide a unique glimpse of General Knox and his family by showing their impact on national, state, and local history. By 1871, however, it had fallen into disrepair and was torn down, then rebuilt as a Great Depression project at a cost of $300,000 (financed by Philadelphia magazine publisher and Camden summer resident Cyrus Curtis). General Knox, by the way, came to a sad end when his gluttony got the best of him—he choked to death on a bone.

Owls Head Transportation Museum (594-4418), adjacent to the Knox County Airport off Route 73, Box 277H, Owls Head (just south of Rockland). Open year-round. Daily, May through October, 10 AM–5 PM weekdays; November through April 10 AM–4 PM, and Sundays 11 AM–4 PM. $4.00 adult, $2.50 under 12, free under 5. Founded in 1974, this has become one of the country's outstanding collections of antique planes and automobiles, unique because everything works. On weekends there are special demonstrations (and sometimes rides) in such magnificent machines as a 1901 Oldsmobile or a 1918 "Jenny" airplane put through its paces. You can take a 100-year journey through the evolution of transportation, from horse-drawn carriages to World War I fighter planes; from a 16-cylinder Cadillac to a Rolls Royce; from the Red Baron's Fokker Triplane to a Ford Trimotor. There are also wagons, motorcycles, and bikes. Inquire about the frequent spring-through-fall special weekends (when admission is sometimes higher). All vehicles have been donated or lent to the museum, which is largely a volunteer effort.

Shore Village Museum (594-4950 or 236-3206, curator's residence), 104 Limerock Street, Rockland. Open June 1 to October 15, 10–4 daily; by appointment the rest of the year. Free admission. A large collection of historic artifacts of the United States Coast Guard, including one of the most extensive collections in lighthouse materials (working fog horns, flashing lights, search-and-rescue gear, buoys, bells, and boats), plus Civil War memorabilia and a collection of 34 dolls dressed in period costumes up to the gay nineties. There is also a small museum shop.

Mid-Coast Children's Museum (596-KIDS), 121 Maverick Street, PO Box 1285, Rockland. Call for hours and schedule of special programs. In a pink house with hands-on exhibits that reflect the museum's adoption of the old proverb, "I hear and I forget. I see and I remember. I do and I understand." Also at the museum is a resource center.

Matthews Museum of Maine Heritage, Union Fairgrounds (just off Route 17 west of Rockland). Open July 1 to Labor Day, except Mondays, 12–5. Adult $2.00, senior citizen $1.00, child $.50. A collection of more than 5,000 artifacts showing the ingenuity and craftsmanship of the area's settlers in the 1800s.

Friendship Museum, Friendship. Open July to Labor Day, Monday through Saturday 12–4; Sunday 2–4. Free. This former schoolhouse contains local memorabilia including an exhibit on Friendship sloops.

BEACHES   Johnson Memorial Park, Chickawaukee Lake, Route 17 (toward Augusta); **Birch Point Park,** Owls Head; and **Ayer Park,** Union.

PICNICKING   Route 1 **picnic area** overlooking Glen Cove, between the towns of Rockland and Camden; **Johnson Memorial Park,** Chickawaukee Lake, Route 17; **Sandy Beach Park,** Atlantic Street, Rockland.

LIGHTHOUSES   Maine has more lighthouses than any other coastal state, and Penobscot Bay boasts the largest number of lighthouses of all. Two in the Rockland area are accessible by land. One is the **Rockland Light,** perched at the end of the almost-mile-long granite breakwater (turn off Route 1 onto Waldo Avenue just north of Rockland, then follow Samoset Road to the end). Parking is free, and you can walk all of the way out on the breakwater to the light. Locals bring their lunches here on pretty days. The other lighthouse is the **Owls Head Light** (go north from the Owls Head Transportation Museum to a rough dirt road that diverges from the main route and leads to a good parking area complete with toilets). The 1825 lighthouse is impressive, set atop sheer cliffs, but with safe trails down one side to the rocks below— good for scrambling and picnicking. Lighthouse buffs should also be sure to visit the **Shore Village Museum** (see To See and Do).

DAILY BOAT EXCURSIONS   *Lively Lady* (594-4063 or 863-4461), a classic ex-lobsterboat, departs from the Black Pearl Restaurant (594-2250) on the public landing, taking about 24 passengers on one- and two-hour cruises of the bay.

The Bitter End (594-9040 or 354-8928), Public Landing, PO Box 1230, Rockland. This 65-foot vessel carries up to 90 passengers and offers narrated seal-sighting, lobstering, sunset, and fall foliage cruises ($9 adults; $5 children), plus an all-day cruise to North Haven Island for a lobsterbake ($38). There is a refreshment bar on board, plus indoor and outdoor seating.

The Friendship sloop *Grace O'Malley* (594-0661) takes passengers on two-hour cruises from the public landing thrice daily. The 65-foot gaff-rigged schooner *Memory* (763-4109, PO Box 621, Hope 04847) sails from the Black Pearl dock, offering half-day trips for $30 per person and, their specialty, an all-day lobster-and-champagne cruise for $80 per person. A pinky schooner named *Annie McGee* (594-9049, RFD 279, Rockland 04841) also offers day-sails for up to six passengers from Rockland Harbor. The choice of trips ranges from a sunset cruise ($18) to a half-day trip ($30) to a luncheon trip ($20) to a full-day trip ($50); food is extra.

Another Friendship sloop, *Surprise* (372-6366) offers three cruises daily from the East Wind Inn in Tenants Harbor ($25–$30).

The classic 67-foot schooner *Wendameen* (236-3472) offers overnight cruises from Rockland ($125 per person including dinner and breakfast). Built in 1912, the *Wendameen*'s atmosphere recaptures the Victorian era.

The 32-foot sloop *Dirigo* (354-6520) is also available, by appointment only, for day-sails and overnight cruises.

DEEP-SEA FISHING   Charter *Henrietta* (Captain John Earl: 594-5411), which departs daily at 7:30 AM and returns by 4:30 PM; or *Fishbusters* (596-6705 or call Sun Yacht Charters: 236-9611). The latter, a 45-foot Hatteras based at Journey's End Marina on Tillson Avenue, is available for half-day ($390), full-day ($650), and overnight fishing or sight-seeing trips in Penobscot Bay and beyond (accommodations for up to eight).

WINDJAMMERS   With more windjammers now homeported in Rockland than anywhere else, the harbor proudly calls itself the Windjammer Capital of the World. For about $550–$600, you can spend a week between May and October gunkholing around Penobscot Bay on one of these tall-masted schooners—choose a new reproduction or an authentic old coasting schooner. Go where the winds and the captain decide, help haul the sails or not as you wish, and get elbow-deep in lobsters and clams at a bake on a deserted island. These are not luxury cruises; you will have a small cabin with sink, shared heads, and a shower that may be no more than a hand-held sprayer under which you can wash your hair while wearing your bathing suit. But the experience is incomparable, and many passengers return year after year. All of the following vessels are inspected and certificated each year by the Coast Guard.

American Eagle (800-648-4544), PO Box 482, Rockland is 92 feet long and accommodates 28 guests in 14 double cabins; there is a hot freshwater shower. She was originally built as a fishing vessel in 1930 and fished out of Gloucester until 1983 when Captain John Foss brought her to Rockland's North End Shipyard—where he spent the next two years restoring and refitting her. The *Eagle* was built with an engine (so she still has one) as well as sails, and she offers some comfortable below-deck spaces. The *Eagle* frequently sails farther Downeast than most of the other Windjammers.

Isaac H. Evans (800-648-4544), PO Box 482, Rockland is 65 feet long with 11 double cabins for 22 passengers. She is just over a hundred years old, having been built in New Jersey in 1886 as an oyster-fishing schooner. She has been completely rebuilt in recent years. Hot freshwater shower on board. Captain Ed Glaser is a veteran seaman who plays the guitar and concertina.

Lewis R. French (800-648-4544), PO Box 482, Rockland was launched on the Damariscotta River in 1871. Before becoming a passenger vessel, she carried cargo along the coast. She was completely rebuilt between 1973 and 1976. Sixty-four feet long, she accommodates 23 passengers. Hot freshwater shower on board. Native Maine Captain Dan Pease met his wife, Kathy, when she came aboard for a vacation. Now their young son, Joe, comes aboard every chance he gets.

Heritage (800-648-4544 or 800-542-5030), PO Box 482, Rockland is the one of the newest schooners, designed along the lines of a nine-teenth-century coaster and built by her captain in the early 1980s. Captain Doug Lee is a marine historian who, with his wife and co-captain, Linda, designed and built the *Heritage* in Rockland's North Shore Shipyard. Their two daughters, Clara and Rachel, were raised aboard ship and sail as crew all summer long.She is 95 feet long and accommodates 33 passengers. There are showers in the deckhouse.

J&E Riggin was built in New Jersey in 1927 for the oyster-dredging trade. A speedy 89-footer, she was extensively rebuilt in the 1970s before joining the windjammer trade. Facilities include hot showers. Captain Dave Allen is a second generation Windjammer captain and his family has been sailing vessels out of Brooklin (where the *Riggin* frequently drops anchor) since the War of 1812—so he comes by his Maine humor rightfully. His wife, Sue, is also a Maine native and an excellent cook. The couple rebuilt the vessel themselves.

Stephen Taber (800-999-7352), at Windjammer Wharf, Box 1050, Rockland, launched in 1871, is the oldest documented United States sailing vessel in continuous use. She is 68 feet long and accommodates 22 passengers. She has a hand-held hot-water shower on deck. Ken and Ellen Barnes, both licensed captains, bought, restored, and con-tinue to sail the *Taber* after careers as (among other things) drama professors. Their enthusiastic following will attest that they approach each cruise as a new production, throwing their (considerable) all into each sailing.

Victory Chimes (594-0755), PO Box 1401, Rockland, named *Domino Effect* in recent years, is the only original three-masted schooner in the windjammer trade and, at 170 feet, the largest. In 1991 the vessel celebrates its return to the Maine Windjammer fleet in which she served for 35 years before an interlude on the Great Lakes under ownership by Domino's Pizza. She carries 44 passengers on three- and six-day cruises. Her present co-owner and captain, Kip Files, has sailed on the *Victory Chimes* for many years.

Nathaniel Bowditch comes by her speed honestly: she was built in East Boothbay as a racing yacht in 1922. Eighty-two feet long, she took special honors in the 1923 Bermuda Race and served in the Coast Guard during WW II. She was rebuilt in the early 1970s. A Maine guide from Rangeley, Captain Gib Philbrick came to the coast to sail aboard a Windjammer in 1966 and has been at it ever since. He and his wife, Terry, met aboard the *Bowditch* (she was a passenger).They re-main a great team.

Summertime (800-562-8290 outside Maine; 800-924-1747), 115 South Street, Rockland, is a 53-foot Pinky Schooner offering three- and six-day cruises for up to six passengers.

Most of these vessels are members of the Maine Windjammer Association, which distributes information on them all: 1-800-624-6380, PO Box 317, Rockport 04856. The Rockland Chamber of Commerce (see Guidance) also has all their brochures. (Also see Windjammers under What's Where in Maine.)

Rockland is site of the annual **Schooner Days** (the weekend following July 4), whose highlight is the **Great Schooner Race,** which finishes at the Rockland Breakwater. You can plan to be aboard one of the schooners the week of the race (passage is usually a bit higher than other weeks as it is the week the schooners participate in Boothbay Harbor's Windjammer Days in late June), or join the crowds of spectators at the breakwater and on the golf course of the Samoset Resort.

COASTAL CRUISE The *M/V Pauline* (800-999-7352), at Windjammer Wharf, Box 1050, Rockland, a graceful 83-foot motor vessel owned by the owners of the windjammer *Stephen Taber,* also offers weekly cruises of the Maine coast. A former sardine carrier, she has been converted to a handsome passenger motorboat, accommodating 12 guests. Able to cruise at up to 9 knots, the *Pauline* offers a wider range than the sailing windjammers. One day she may motor to Monhegan to attend an arts festival; the next, it could be off to Roque Island way Down East. Amenities and services on board are also a bit more luxurious than on a windjammer. The weekly per-person fare is under $1000, including all meals.

BOAT CHARTERS   **Jim Fitz-Patrick** (549-3196), PO Box 825, Gardiner 04345, has a fleet of Montego 25 sailing sloops for bareboat charter June through September for three ($350) to seven days ($700). The **Rockland Yacht Club** (contact through the chamber of commerce at 596-0376) can arrange charters of their members' boats. **Maine Coast Custom Yacht Charters** (354-8928), 16 Green Street, Thomaston 04861, can arrange specialized half- and full-day charters on any of 50 sailing and power yachts. **Sun Yacht Charters** (236-9611), based in Camden, operates from the dock at Journey's End Marina.

HORSEBACK RIDING   **Mt. Pleasant Farm** (785-4628), Union 04862. A 200-acre farm with 15 miles of trails through a mountain range offers hourly riding ($10–$25 per hour), lessons for ages four and up ($10–20 per hour depending on group or private), pony rides, hayrides, and a day camp designed for youngsters seven years old and up to learn about horses and ponies (by the day or by the week; $20 per day). The farm also welcomes visitors who just want to see and pet the animals, which also include sheep, Angora rabbits, Angora goats, and assorted other critters.

ROLLER SKATING   Rockland Skate Center (594-1023), 299 Park Street, Rockland.

OUTDOOR PROGRAMS   Maine Outdoors (785-4496), RR 1, Box 3770, Union 04862. Wilderness canoe trips for every level of ability led by a registered Maine Guide and naturalist. All gear is provided, including life jackets. Half day $30; full day $55 (includes lunch); sunrise or sunset trip $30 (includes light meal). Registered Maine Guides **Don Kleiner and Argy Nestor** (785-4873) lead canoe trips for all ages and abilities on the St. George River.

SPECIAL LEARNING PROGRAMS   Hurricane Island Outward Bound School (594-5548), Mechanic Street, Rockland. Courses lasting 5 to 26 days are offered on Hurricane Island in Penobscot Bay, May to October. There are courses tailored to every age and both sexes; they focus on sailing, rock-climbing, and outdoor problem-solving. An international program begun in Wales, Outward Bound challenges participants to do things they never thought they could and then push themselves just a little further. For details, write Box 429, Rockland 04841.

The Penobscot School (594-1084), Gay Street, PO Box 7, Rockland. This is a remarkable school, offering classes in Arabic, Japanese, Spanish, French, Italian, and German, plus informal cultural seminars (a recent series was taught by visiting professors from China).

The Island Institute (594-9209), 60 Ocean Street, Rockland. An organization dedicated to the preservation of Maine's beautiful islands; its activities include the development of an "island trail," for kayakers as well as courses.

Maine Coast Art Workshops, PO Box 236, Port Clyde 04855. Throughout the summer five-day workshops with recognized artists are held here on the St. George peninsula, taking advantage of the surrounding natural setting. Fourteen workshops to choose from; tuition is about $200.

INNS   East Wind Inn (372-6366 or 372-6367), PO Box 149, Tenants Harbor 04860. Open year-round. Originally a sea captain's house and sail loft, this building is now winterized and restored to its original simple country charm. The downstairs parlor has a piano that guests are welcome to play. The inn is very much a part of its surroundings: a salty village centering on the wharf where lobster traps are piled and lobsterboats tie up. The village has a good little library, and beyond there are beaches, rock cliffs, tidal pools, old cemeteries, and the kind of countryside described by Sarah Orne Jewett in *Country of the Pointed Firs.* Jewett lived just a few bends down Route 131 in Martinville while she wrote the book. The inn is very clean and well run; its 16 pleasant harbor-view rooms are filled with antiques. There's a black labrador retriever in residence here so no other pets are allowed. There are 10 additional guest rooms in the adjacent Meeting House. Rates vary according to size of room, ocean view, and bath accommodations;

doubles $64–$82, suite $95 in-season; lower off-season. The dining room, open to the public, serves three meals each day; it features Yankee cooking with a continental flair (see Dining Out).

Craignair Inn (594-7644), Clark Island, Spruce Head 04859. Open year-round. Sited on a granite ledge by the shore, this unusual building was originally erected to house workers at a nearby granite quarry. The simple but quaint bedrooms are furnished with antiques, and both shared and private baths are available. In the downstairs common rooms you'll find more antiques. The dining room, open to the public for dinner, is especially charming with its blue trim, tablecloths, and china. Wildflowers placed on the tables echo the simple goodness of the dinner menu: homemade breads, vegetables from the garden, and such family-pleasers as roast beef and potatoes, lasagna, and shrimp scampi, the latter an example of the continental touch that distinguishes some of the entrées. A shore dinner is offered every evening. (The dining room is closed Sundays.) Walking is the thing to do here, down the miles of paths meandering from the inn and on Clark Island. There's also good bird-watching and swimming in the old quarry hole. Lodging includes a full breakfast. Double with shared bath $62; with private bath $77; less off-season. Weekly rates are available.

Ocean House (372-6691), Port Clyde 04855. Open May 1 to November 1. The logical place to spend the night before boarding the morning ferry to Monhegan. You'll be amused by the salty sign on the front door: "Street girls bringing sailors into hotel must pay for rooms in advance." The small dining room is very attractive and serves breakfast to guests and the public, 7–11; dinner, for overnight guests only, is served at 6:30 PM (but not every night—inquire). Ten rooms. Rooms are $37.50–$56.

The Seaside Inn (372-6691) Port Clyde 04855. Also operated by the Ocean House but open year-round. Rates are the same as at the Ocean House.

BED & BREAKFASTS **Mill Pond House** (372-6209), Tenants Harbor 04860. Open year-round. No children or pets are permitted. This 200-year-old house offers three rooms with private or shared bath and a sitting room with television. Rates include continental breakfast. Double with shared bath $45; with private bath $55.

Cap'n Frost's (354-8217), 241 W. Main Street, Thomaston 04861. A pleasant, antiques-filled old Cape on Route 1 just southwest of Thomaston village. Bicycles, croquet, grill, and picnic tables provided for guests. "Arlene's Closet" antiques shop on premises. Rates are $40 and up.

The Captain's Rest (354-2000), 25 Gleason Street, Thomaston 04861. Open year-round. One of Thomaston's handsome mansions built by nineteenth-century sea captains, this one is Victoriana right up to its stained glass and turret.

Photo by Gordon C. Pine

Port Clyde

Weskeag Inn (596-6676), Route 73, PO Box 213, South Thomaston 04858. Open year-round (weekends only, in winter). Convenient to Owl's Head Transportation Museum, this early 1800s shipbuilder's home on the bank of the Weskeag River offers eight rooms ranging from singles with shared bath to doubles with private bath. Breakfast is included. A one-bedroom apartment with sofa bed in the living room (accommodations for four) is also available by the night or week. Its sliding glass doors open onto a deck overlooking the river. Rooms are $40–$75.

Cap'n Am's (832-5144), Flood's Cove, Friendship 04547. A pleasant sea captain's home right on the water, this early 1800s home welcomes guests from mid-June until the end of August. There is a large living room with fireplace, plus two ocean-view bedrooms accommodating three or four people each and a third guest room for two. All share baths. Swimming; tennis ($5 per day). Full breakfast. Off-season, write: Cap'n Am's, c/o Mary Flood Thompson, 105 East Boundry Road, Mequon, WI 53092 (414-241-8645).

Harbor Hill (832-6646), Town Landing Road, PO Box 35, Friendship 04547. Open year-round. An 1800s farmhouse, this comfortable B&B sits above the fishing village of Friendship, offering views of the islands in Muscongus Bay. Full breakfast, plus lunch and candlelight dinners with prior arrangements. Shared and private baths. Doubles $75 (shared bath) to $85 (private bath); suite for four people $150.

The Outsiders' Inn (832-5197), corner of Routes 97 and 220, Box 521A, Friendship 04547. Comfortable atmosphere in an 1830 house that was formerly the village doctor's home. Doubles with shared bath $45; with private bath $55. Also offered are sailing seminars on the Friendship sloop *Gladiator;* inquire of the inn or contact Captain Bill Zuber at 354-8036.

COTTAGES AND EFFICIENCIES   A tempting list of cottages, primarily in the Owls Head and Spruce Head areas, is available from the Rockland Area Chamber of Commerce (see Guidance).

The Off-Island Store & Motel (594-7475 daytime, 596-6088 evenings), Spruce Head 04859. If you want to sample a slice of life in a real Maine fishing village, book one of the four studio apartments above this traditional general store (separate outside entrance for each unit). Meet the locals and savor the gossip of small-town doings. The ocean is just 500 feet away. Each pine-paneled, carpeted unit has an efficiency kitchen, bathroom with shower, living-dining area, and sleeping loft; all linens and dishes are provided. You can also eat downstairs in the store or at one of the restaurants in the area. $38 per night, $245 per week for two; $50 per night, $295 per week for four.

Island View Oceanfront Cottages (594-7527), Patten Point Road, Spruce Head 04859. Open year-round. Two- and three-bedroom cottages with fireplaces and oceanfront decks set among spruce trees at the edge of the water. Furnished and equipped with everything (except linens and blankets) including washer/dryers and dishwashers. 14-foot, 6-horsepower outboard boats for rent.

The Mermaid (594;-0616), 256 Main Street, Rockland. Open year-round. This is one of Rockland's oldest center-chimney colonial homes, across from the public landing. No breakfast. Guest apartment and efficiency. Overnight and long-term rates.

MOTELS   There are a number of motels in the Rockland area, including the **Trade Winds** (596-6661), which has a large restaurant and a complete health club; the **Navigator** (594-2131), also with a dining room and conveniently located directly across from the ferry terminal; and the **Rockland Motel** (594-5471), on Route 1 in scenic Glen Cove.

DINING OUT   **Jessica's** (596-0770), 2 South Main Street (Route 73), Rockland. Open every day except Tuesday. Reservations are recommended. A "European bistro" in a restored Victorian home serving dinner and Sunday brunch. Nicely prepared cuisine in an inviting atmosphere.

The East Wind Inn (372-6366), Tenants Harbor. A very attractive dining room with white tablecloths and pink napkins; a wall of windows overlooks the working harbor. On warm summer evenings it's especially enjoyable to have a cocktail on the wraparound porch before dinner. The menu features fresh ingredients, including local seafood, prepared with a continental flair.

A Touch of Class (594-4516), 410 Main Street, Rockland. Right in the center of town, this is a casual gathering place for breakfast and lunch, and a more formal spot in the evening.

EATING OUT **Black Pearl** (594-2250), Rockland Public Landing (just off Main Street at the southern end of town). Open every day 11:30–10, mid-May to mid-October. Built over the water; features local seafood. Inexpensive to moderate.

The Brown Bag (596-6372), 606 Main Street, Rockland. Open Monday through Wednesday 6:30 AM to 4 PM, Thursday through Saturday till 9 PM. At the northern end of town, this recently expanded storefront restaurant has an inviting country atmosphere that complements the homemade goodies served. It's a favorite gathering spot for breakfast and lunch. The menu is extensive, creative, homemade, and delicious. You make your selection at the counter and carry it to your table when it's ready. Catering can also be arranged.

Harbor View Tavern (354-8173), Thomaston. Open year-round except during April. Tucked right down on the harbor on Snow's Pier (turn right off Main Street if you are coming from the south), this is a little jewelbox of a restaurant whose decor requires as much attention as the menu. All sorts of photographs and memorabilia ornament the walls, and some very contented-looking goldfish swim about in the water tank of a huge, old coffee maker. Try the seafood stew or the peel-your-own Maine shrimp or scallop sautée.

Dave's Restaurant (594-5425), Route 1, Thomaston. Seafood dinners and the area's only smorgasbord with old-fashioned classics, such as macaroni and cheese, beans and franks, etc. Breakfast and lunch buffets, too, plus a large salad bar. Breakfast is served all day.

Black Harpoon (372-6304), corner of Drift Inn and Marshall Point Road, Port Clyde. From July 1 through Labor Day, open for lunch 12–3, dinner 5–9, and later on Fridays and Saturdays. Spring and fall, dinner only, Wednesday through Sunday. This engaging little seafood restaurant in the seaside village of Port Clyde (just off Route 131, around the corner from the harbor) serves the local catch. Try the lazy lobster, fried combo plate, or prime rib. There is also a raw bar.

Chuck Wagon (594-8593), 275 Main Street, Rockland. Open year-round, 7 AM to 10 PM daily, until 11 PM on weekends. A longtime family favorite offering seafood and charbroiled meats, homemade soups and pies, and a salad bar. Noontime specials and children's menu.

Dip Net Coffee Shop, Port Clyde. Seasonal 8–4. Counter with only 15 stools. The idea is to park your car and buy your ticket for the 10 AM boat to Monhegan—then unwind over a breakfast of homemade coffee cake, muffins, or, better yet, fresh strawberry pie! The lunch menu runs to chowder, quiche, lobster stew, and a tantalizing lineup of desserts.

FOREIGN FOOD For tacos, tostados, and other Mexican fare, go to **El Taco**

Tico (594-7568), 294 Main Street, Rockland. Oriental–American menus are offered at **Mai Kai** (594-4626), 9 Park Street, Rockland, and **China Harbor,** Harbor Marketplace, Route 1 north of Rockland. **Mama Maria's** (596-6114), 63 Park Street, Rockland, serves traditional Italian dishes.

SEAFOOD IN THE ROUGH   **Miller's Lobster Company** (594-7406), Spruce Head. Open 10–7, seasonal. A family-owned and -operated business offering lobsters and clams cooked in seawater (much better than when cooked in freshwater, as too many places do); plus both packed to travel. Watch the lobsterboats at work as you dig into your shore dinner.

Cod End (372-6782), Tenant's Harbor. Open mid-June to mid-September every day 8–7:30; spring and fall 8–6. Lobster and clam picnics on their deck plus lobster rolls, chowders, and ice cream. Seafood packed for travel, live or cooked.

Waterman's Beach Lobsters (594-2489), off Route 73, South Thomaston. Open daily 11 AM to 7 PM in the summertime. Ocean-front feasting on the deck: lobster and clam dinners, seafood rolls, homemade pies.

FAST FOOD   **Wasses Wagon** (in the parking lot next to The Brown Bag, northern end of Main Street, Rockland) is a local institution for hot dogs. Chain restaurants include **Domino's Pizza** (594-9494), 212 Park Street and **Dunkin' Donuts** (594-7756), 632 Main Street, Rockland. **McDonald's** and **Burger King** are on Route 1 at the northern end of Rockland; **Dairy Queen** is on Route 1 at the southern end of town. Deli sandwiches and subs can be found at **Anita's Deli** (side door of Jordan's Fish Market, northern end of Main Street, Rockland), the **Rockland Deli** (596-0012), 421 Main Street; and **The Subway,** just around the corner from McDonald's.

SELECTIVE SHOPPING   Rockland's Main Street, a relatively well-preserved example of nineteenth-century commercial architecture, has been recorded in the National Register of Historic Places. Along its dozen or so blocks you will find local department stores, hardware stores, furniture stores, and the kind of old-fashioned atmosphere that has been chased away elsewhere by today's shopping malls. A few places well worth stopping at are **The Store,** with a wide selection of cooking supplies, cards, cheeses, and other food delicacies; **Mr. Bearymore,** an inviting toy shop brimming with wonderful bears, an international selection of dolls for collectors as well as children, and many other toys; and **Coffin's,** an exceptionally nice family clothing store. For boat shoes and foul-weather gear, try **Goldsmith's Sporting Goods.** **Jewell's,** in a house at the northern end of the street, has unusual women's clothing. Rockland is blessed with three bookstores: **New Leaf Books, The Reading Corner,** and **Shore Village Bookshop.** At the southern end of Main Street you will find a small **Sears** (mostly appliances and catalog orders) and, beyond it, **Doug Corson's Country Woodworks,** with pine furniture very reasonably priced. At the northern end of town is a shopping center with a **J. C. Penney,** and farther up Route 1 you will find **Ames.**

On Route 90, Warren, you might want to stop at the **Sheepskin Shop** in a lovely red farmhouse nestled against meadows filled with grazing sheep. Everything from car seats to coats and vests made out of sheepskin. There are even a donkey and a peacock to gawk at. The shop is open every day 7–7, April through Christmas Eve; by appointment the rest of the year.

In Thomaston, The Maine State Prison is famous for its **Prison Shop,** right on Main Street (Route 1) at the southern end of town. It has a variety of wooden furniture—coffee tables, stools, lamps, and trays—and a choice of small souvenirs, all carved by inmates. Prices are reasonable and profits go to the craftsmen. A dozen antiques shops can also be found along Route 1 between Thomaston and Rockland.

On Route 1 just south of Thomaston is **Newavom** (354-6995), an unusual workshop and showroom featuring custom-knitted textiles, hand-loomed rugs and throws, needlework packets, Portuguese and South American rugs and wall hangings, jewelry, sculpture, and hand-painted furniture. The store is open Monday through Saturday 10 AM to 4 PM; closed in winter.

A bit farther down Route 1 is the **Schoolhouse Farm** vegetable stand, with baskets of produce just harvested from the surrounding fields, jams and jellies, wheels of cheese, and fresh-baked muffins and breads. A highlight is the primitive paintings by owner Debbie Beckwith, whose work has also appeared on the cover of *Down East* magazine.

Galleries: **Gallery One at Houston Tuttle** (596-0059), 429 Main Street, Rockland, exhibits the works of distinguished Maine artists. On Route 73 in St. George, the **Open Air Gallery** (372-8037) exhibits the work of Robert "Dan" Daniels, a retired construction welder and radiator repairman whose whimsical metal sculptures of birds, animals, and people have caught the imagination of passers-by and turned them into collectors of these original works.

SPECIAL EVENTS   June: **Warren Day. A** pancake breakfast, parade, art and quilt shows, chicken barbecue, and auction.

July: **Fourth-of-July** celebrations in most towns, with parades. Thomaston's parade is especially well known and has been featured on NBC's *Today* show. **Schooner Days** (Friday, Saturday, and Sunday following July 4). See the wonderful windjammers vie for first place in a spectacular race that recalls bygone days. The best vantage point is the Rockland Breakwater next to the Samoset Resort.

August: **Maine Lobster Festival** (first weekend in the month plus the preceding Wednesday and Thursday). This is probably the world's biggest lobster feed, prepared in the world's largest lobster boiler. Patrons queue up on the public landing to heap their plates with lobsters, clams, corn, and all the fixings. King Neptune and the Maine Sea Goddess reign over the event, which includes a parade down Main Street, concerts, an art exhibit, and contests such as clam shucking and sardine packing, and a race across a string of lobster crates floating in the harbor. **Union Fair and Blueberry Festival** (late in the month). A real agricultural fair with tractor- and oxen-pulling contests, livestock and food shows, a midway, the crowning of the Blueberry Queen, and, on one day during the week, free mini-blueberry pies for all comers.

THE ISLANDS

MONHEGAN   Though barely a mile square, this storied island—among Penobscot Bay's smallest—boasts 600 species of wildflowers, more than 400 years of intriguing history, and unequaled beauty. Two-thirds of Monhegan is, moreover, wild land laced with footpaths which run along dramatic cliffs pounded by surf that might have come all the way from Spain, through meadows, and among tall stands of pine where the sounds of birds and crunching needles blend with the clanging of bell buoys down off the island's edge.

"Beached like a whale," one mariner in 1590 described it: the 150-foot-high headlands sloping down to coves, low and quiet at its tail. Miraculously, the beauty survives today. Prospect Hill, the only attempted development, foundered around 1900. It was Theodore Edison, son of the inventor, who amassed property enough to erase the first traces of Prospect Hill and to keep the island's 125 cottages bunched along the sheltered Eastern Harbor. In 1954 Edison helped to organize Monhegan Associates, a nonprofit corporation dedicated to preserving the "natural, wild beauty" of the island. Ironically, considering Edison's descent, this is one of the country's few communities to shun electricity—besides a few private generators, light is supplied by kerosene lamps. There are just a few trucks to haul lobstering gear and summer visitors' luggage to and from the dock; you may not bring your car with you. The island has three inns and a sprinkling of bed & breakfasts and summer cottages, all of which are booked months before the summer season begins.

The Indians named the island *Monahigan,* meaning "the island of the sea," and today, as always, it belongs to the sea, removed by at least 12 miles of ocean from the nearest point on the mainland, Port Clyde. Few places in this part of the world offer a pace so slow. The 50 or so residents, who for generations have reaped their livelihood from the sea, are joined in summer by visitors seeking time and space to appreciate nature and quiet, breathe the fresh salt air, and perhaps do a bit of painting, writing, or merely reflecting on things.

Artists, musicians, photographers, and writers find subject and sustenance here. Those who are not content to shed the conventions of twentieth-century living, however, may be unhappy on Monhegan. During a *New York Times* strike, for example, a sign in the Island Spa read, "If you cannot live without your newspaper, ferries depart daily for the mainland."

But if you can live—and indeed thrive—without the accoutrements of modern life, you will love Monhegan. Wander through the woods where "fairy houses" are said to be hidden on the moss-covered floor of Cathedral Woods; attend informal concerts and exhibits at the schoolhouse; stop in amazement as a young deer browses without fear just off your path.

Day-trippers and visitors come on the *Balmy Days* II (see Boothbay Harbor [Boat Excursions]) or the *Hardy III* (see Damariscotta [Boat Excursions]). Longer-term visitors tend to prefer the *Laura B* mailboat from Port Clyde (reservations are necessary: PO Box 238, Port Clyde 04855; or call Captain Jim Barstow: 372-8848) because they can park their car at Port Clyde (about $3 per day); the ticket for the one-hour mailboat trip is $20 round trip. The boat travels to Monhegan year-round, twice daily in-season. When you make a reservation, request a copy of the booklet *An Introduction to Monhegan Island* by Dr. Alta Ashley (the island's retired physician and naturalist in-residence). Dr. Ashley advises all visitors to arrive properly shod for the precipitous paths and equipped with sweaters and windbreakers; she also cautions against wading or swimming from any of the tempting coves on the back side of the island. Because of kerosene lighting and dark footpaths, anyone staying overnight should be sure to bring a flashlight. Heavy rubber boots are also a good idea.

The **Lighthouse,** built in 1824 and automated in 1959, offers a good view from its perch on the crest of a hill. The former keeper's cottage is now the **Monhegan Museum** (open daily in summer; free admission), displaying flora, fauna, and something of the geology, lobstering, and an artistic history of the island, including documents dating back to the sixteenth century.

Cathedral Woods of spruce and balsam fir is carpeted with needles and mossy rocks. The way the sunshine glints through the heavy leaf cover lends a distinctly fairy-tale quality to this area.

Headlands. Pick up a good trail map at one of the island's three stores and carefully follow the paths along the dramatic cliffs on the back side of the island. (Day-trippers should take the Burnt Head Trail out and loop back by the village by way of Lobster Cove, rather than try a longer circuit, because the boat just might return to the mainland without them.) **Manana Island** (across the harbor from Monhegan) is the site of a famous rune stone with inscriptions purported to be Norse or Phoenician. At Middle Beach on Monhegan you may be able to find someone willing to take you over in a skiff.

Lobster Cove, at the tail of the island, is a good spot for bird-watching (600 species recorded spring and fall). **Pebble Beach** at the northern end of the island is a good spot for picnicking and for watching seals and birds.

For rainy days, there is an exceptional library; the **Island Spa** (a general store with some antiques for sale in the loft upstairs); and artists' studios (a listing available on the island informs you which studios are open which days). Works by local artists are also hung in the **Plantation Gallery** across from the **Periwinkle Coffee Shop** (which offers three daily meals in-season).

Lodging: **Island Inn** (596-0371), Monhegan Island 04852. The largest inn on the island also offers the most amenities, including electricity from its generator. All of the rooms have views, either of the ocean (and sunset) or of the meadows (and sunrise). Six doubles have private baths; the rest, both singles and doubles, share baths. Rooms are small, clean, and plain. Downstairs are two small living rooms, part of the original pre-1850 house that is the nucleus of this 1900 inn, and a dining room that serves three meals a day to the public as well as to overnight guests. Lodging includes breakfast and dinner.

The Trailing Yew (596-0440), Monhegan Island 04852. Open mid-May through early October. This is the favorite place to stay of artists who come year after year. In all, more than 40 very basic rooms are scattered among the main house, adjacent buildings, and cottages on the grounds and even a bit up the road. Expect shared baths, kerosene lamps, and good food. Before meals, guests gather around the flagpole outside the main building to pitch horseshoes and compare notes; family-style dining at shared tables features lots and lots of good, homecooked food. The dining room is also open to the public. Lodging includes breakfast and dinner, tax, and tips. About $44 per person per day, including breakfast and dinner and all taxes and tips; ages 5 to 10, $15–$25.

Tribler Cottage (594-2445), Monhegan Island 04852-0007, has been in the same family for over three generations. Proprietors Martha Yandle and Richard Farrell offer four one-bedroom apartments with fully equipped kitchens, sheets, towels, and all utilities; each accommodates two to three people, from May to October. Their Apple Tree apartment is available year-round for people who wish to visit off-season or watch spring and fall bird migrations along the Atlantic Flyway. Summer rates are $65–$85 per day for two; $385–$525 per week for two.

Shining Sails (596-0041), Box 344, Monhegan Island 04852 (across from the library). Open year-round. Bill Baker and Amy Melenbacker have four efficiency apartments and one room, all with views. No meals are served. Cottage rentals and sales also offered.

Hitchcock House (594-8137), Horn's Hill, Monhegan Island 04852. On top of Horn's Hill, Barbara Hitchcock offers several rooms and efficiencies. Year-round. Rooms are $45 per night, $290 per week; efficiencies are $65 per night, $390 per week.

Monhegan House (594-7983). Open Memorial Day to mid-October. A large, picturesque old place with 32 rooms. Three meals are served daily (not included in lodging).

A list of **rental cottages** is available from the post office. There are also a few rooms to be found in private homes. Inquire around.

Snacks: If you are looking for a light lunch, check out the **Sea Hag,** run by a young fisherman and his wife (their boat is named the *Sea Hag,* too) and offering take-out seafood; and **North End Pizza,** also run by a young fisherman and his wife.

VINALHAVEN   In contrast to Monhegan, a small, hilly island that catches lobsters all winter and tourists all summer, Vinalhaven is a large (8-mile long) island with a year-round fishing fleet, some limited quarrying, and summer residents who tend to be from families who have been coming here for years.

In 1880, when granite was being cut on Vinalhaven to build Boston's Museum of Fine Arts and New York's Court House, there were 3,380 people living on Vinalhaven, a number now reduced to about 1,200—a mix of descendants of eighteenth-century settlers and the stonecutters who came here from Sweden, Norway, Finland, and Scotland. The summer people here and on nearby North Haven are an unusually well-heeled but old-shoe group. The roads are paved, and for bicyclists this makes a fine day trip. There are ample spots to swim (both pebbly saltwater beaches and former quarries) and nature conservancy areas in which to pick berries, watch birds, and generally unwind—for weeks on end if you are lucky. The **Vinalhaven Historical Society Museum,** in the old town hall, displays photos and mementos from the island's granite and fishing industries. The car-carrying ferry *Governor Curtis* from Rockland to Vinalhaven takes one and a half hours; inquire for a current schedule with the **State Ferry Service** in Rockland (596-2202). The fare is $3.50 per person round trip, $2 children ($15 for car and driver). If you choose to leave your car on the mainland, you can rent mopeds on the island.

Lodging: **The Morning Glory** (863-2051), Pleasant Street, PO Box 580, Vinalhaven 04863. Open April through December. Four guest rooms sharing two baths. The unusual decor features folk art collected by host Gloria Strazar while working and traveling in Asia, Africa, Europe, and the Americas. Rainy-day entertainments include games, puzzles, books, and a VCR. Children welcome. $35 to $70.

Libby House (863-4696; winter: 516-765-3756), Water Street, Vinalhaven 04853. Open June to September. A nineteenth-century home offering a suite, two doubles with shared bath, and a three-room apartment. A short walk from **Lane's Island Preserve,** with its meadows, wildflowers, beach, coves, and rocky coast. Breakfast included. $47–$90.

Fox Island Inn (863-2122), PO Box 421, Carver Street, Vinalhaven 04863. A restored, century-old townhouse just a 10-minute walk from the ferry landing, through the village and up the hill. Doubles about $50 and up; there's also a three-room suite.

Tidewater Inn (863-4618), Vinalhaven 04863. Open year-round. An outstanding little motel featuring waterfront units with private sun decks and kitchen units, located on the water a short walk from the heart of the village. All accommodations have private baths. Rates depend on whether your room is on the water and whether you want a kitchen unit. $52 doubles; $68–$79 for waterfront unit with kitchen. Lower rates in the winter.

Dining out: **The Haven** (863-4969), Main Street, Vinalhaven. A very special restaurant where you get the feeling that everything is done as a labor of love rather than for profit. As we go to press, the owners are debating whether to continue so be sure to call ahead. Open in summer for dinner only; seatings at 6 and 8. Everything is homemade here. You might begin with a seasonal treat such as cantaloupe soup with mint or smoked chicken with jicama and mango. Entrées have included lobster with tarragon and tomatoes on fettuccine, poached Norwegian salmon with black olive and basil butters, and panfried strip steak. The dining room overlooks the water. You are welcome to bring your own alcoholic beverages (this is an island-wide policy as liquor is not sold on Vinalhaven).

The Nighthawk is a good bet for muffins and sweet rolls in the morning and chowders and sandwiches later. It's popular with the islanders.

There are other restaurants in town, but day-trippers may prefer to bring a picnic to eat at **Round Pond** or **Grimes Park.**

NORTH HAVEN   A low-key, private sort of resort (more so than Vinalhaven) just across the Fox Island Thoroughfare from Vinalhaven. The car-carrying ferry *North Haven* (596-2202) departs from the **Maine State Ferry Terminal,** Rockland, and takes 1 hour, 10 minutes. The summertime round-trip fare is $5.75 ($23.50 extra to bring your car). For an additional $2.50, you can book one of the three reserved car spaces by calling a maximum of thirty days in advance—a good investment at the height of the season. There are grocery, clothing, and antiques shops, a small museum, an art gallery, and a library. The **North Island Yarn Shop** sells yarn, sweaters, and special sweater kits made from wool sheared from local sheep and spun on the island.

Lodging and dining out: **Pulpit Harbor Inn** (867-2219), North Haven Island 04853. A small, very special country inn and restaurant offering six guest rooms. The restaurant, closed Mondays, serves dinner by reservation. Bikes are available for overnight guests. For those who arrive by boat and walk the two miles or so from Pulpit Harbor to the inn, showers and laundry are available. Breakfast is included with overnight lodging. $55–$92.50.

MATINICUS   Home to about 35 hardy souls in winter, most of whom make their living lobstering, Matinicus' population grows to about 200 in summer. A very quiet, unspoiled spot in Penobscot Bay, the island has a small village made up of the **Offshore Store,** the powerhouse, and a lunch wagon. There are also two beautiful **sand beaches,** one at each end of the island. On nearby **Matinicus Rock** there is a protected nesting site for puffins.

Getting There: Dick Moody, who owns the store, runs the 40-foot *Mary and Donna* between Matinicus and Rockland on Mondays, Fridays, Saturdays, and Sundays in summer (and specially chartered trips at other times). The regular round trip is $30, and reservations are a must (366-3700). The *Mary and Donna* also makes day-trips to Matinicus Rock to see the puffins on weekends ($10 extra if you aren't taking the boat to or from Rockland that day). The Maine State Ferry *William Silsby* serves the island about once a month (596-2202); fare is $25 round trip; $35 if you bring your car. And you can charter a plane from **Penobscot Air Service Ltd.,** Owls Head (596-6211).

Lodging: The largest B&B on the island is the **Tuckanuck Lodge** (366-3830; off-season 207-766-3372 evenings and weekends), with four rooms and shared bath (it is currently expanding). Rates are moderate. The lodge also rents bikes to guests. Donna Rogers (366-3011) rents a double room in her home and serves breakfast to guests (three meals a day off-season). Her rates are modest. For information on **cottage rentals,** write to the Matinicus Chamber of Commerce, Box 212, Matinicus 04851.

Rockport/Camden/Lincolnville

> All I could see from where I stood
> Was three long mountains and a wood;
> I turned and looked another way,
> And saw three islands in a bay.
> —Edna St. Vincent Millay

These opening lines from "Renascence" describe exactly what Millay saw from the top of Camden's Mt. Battie. And anyone can climb—by foot or by car—to the peak and share it even today. From a monument to the poet fittingly placed here, you look down on Camden, laid neatly on a curving shelf between the long hills and Penobscot Bay. And there in the bay you will count the same islands that Vincent (as her friends called her) counted as a young girl. Down in the center of Camden there is a statue, in the harbor park, of Millay gazing wistfully out to sea.

Camden is right on Route 1, midway between Portland and Bar Harbor. The traffic moves slowly here (especially because of a stop sign and flashing light at the south end of the village that require Route 1 traffic to give right-of-way to cars entering from the side street). So even if you aren't planning to stay, you might as well take a break from your trip to at least stroll the town dock area. Chances are you will be lured into staying just a bit longer than planned. Camden is an unusually picturesque harbor filled with sailing craft, from traditional windjammers to sleek racing rigs, plus a 100-foot gold-plated motoryacht or two from time to time. Along the town's crooked streets you will discover a veritable treasure trove of shops, restaurants, boutiques, and galleries—some of the best anywhere in Maine. It is difficult to spend even an hour in Camden without realizing that this is indeed a special place.

Camden's early business was building and sailing ships. The town's first schooner was launched in 1769, and the world's first six-masted vessel, the *George C. Wells*, went down the ways of Holly Bean's yard in 1900. Now part of Wayfarer Marine Corporation, which takes up most of the harbor across from downtown, the land where the earlier shipbuilding concern stood is still referred to by oldtimers as the Bean Yard.

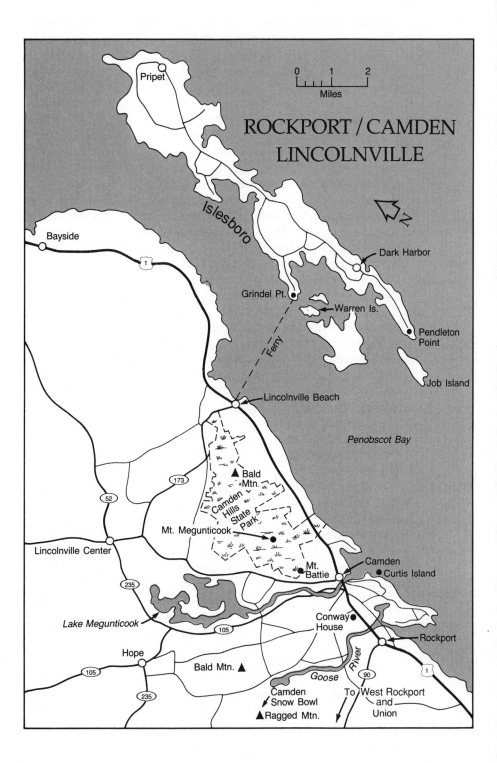

ROCKPORT / CAMDEN
LINCOLNVILLE

0   1   2
Miles

Pripet

Islesboro

Bayside

1

Dark Harbor

Grindel Pt.

Warren Is.

Ferry

Pendleton
Point

Job Island

Lincolnville Beach

Penobscot Bay

173

52

▲ Bald
Mtn.

Camden
Hills
State
Park

Mt. Megunticook

Lincolnville Center

Mt.
Battie

Camden
Curtis Island

235

Lake Megunticook

105

Conway
House

Rockport

Hope

Bald Mtn. ▲

River

90

1

105

Goose

To West Rockport
and
Union

235

Camden
Snow Bowl
▲ Ragged Mtn.

Then came the woolen mills; at least four of them lined up along the river from the early 1900s through World War II. The part of town where most of the workers lived continues to be called Millville.

It was the steamboat, however, that shaped the Camden that has drawn so many visitors and sightseers. As a stop on the Boston-Bangor line, its fame grew during the first half of this century. Soon the town "where the mountains meet the sea" had attracted a wealthy, cultured group of summer residents, primarily from Philadelphia and Boston. They built their summer mansions along the shore here and in the neighboring town of Rockport, a far sleepier charmer of a village just to the south, on the sea side of Route 1.

Fostered by longtime summer residents and a fast-growing, year-round population, Camden and Rockport offer a quantity and quality of music, art, and theatrical productions that are surprising for communities their size. There are also programs for photography and dance as well as the long-acclaimed summertime Salzedo Harp Colony.

Shopping here is a major pastime for visitors. There are crafts stores, fine clothing shops, souvenir shops that rise above kitsch to clever, and galleries filled with the work of contemporary Maine artists.

But Camden is probably best known as the birthplace of the Maine windjammer vacation. The three harbors of Camden, Rockport, and Rockland today shelter the country's largest concentration of traditionally rigged, passenger-carrying sailing ships. Visitors have been going down to the sea in them since the 1930s. For very reasonable fees, they offer three-day, week-long, and two-week trips along the Maine coast and in and around the many islands of Penobscot Bay.

There are a good number of fine medium-sized and small inns in Camden, Rockport, and Lincolnville, as well as at least a baker's dozen bed & breakfasts and numerous good motels.

GUIDANCE   Rockport–Camden–Lincolnville Chamber of Commerce (236-4404), PO Box 919, Public Landing, Camden 04843. Open year-round, Monday through Friday 9–5 and Saturday 10–5; open Sundays 12–4, mid-May through mid-October. You will find all sorts of helpful brochures here, plus maps of Camden, Rockport, Lincolnville, and Islesboro, and knowledgeable people to send you in the right direction. The chamber keeps tabs on available vacancies during the high season, also on what is open off-season and what cottages are for rent (a list is ready for requests each year by January). Be sure to secure their excellent 80-page booklet (write for it in advance if you can) as well as the brochure produced by the Camden–Rockport Historical Society that outlines biking, driving, and walking tours.

GETTING THERE   Knox County Airport, at Owls Head, is about 10 miles from Camden (just the other side of Rockland). There are daily flights between there and Boston, New York, and other New England cities.

PARKING   It is a problem here, unfortunately. Available space just can't seem to keep up with the numbers of people coming. In-town parking has a two-hour limit (just 15 minutes in a few spots so be sure to read the signs), stringently enforced by a strolling policeman, and fines have recently been raised. There are a few lots on the outskirts of town (try the Camden Marketplace and a lot on Mechanic Street); the best advice is to park and walk.

MEDICAL EMERGENCY Penobscot Bay Medical Center (594-9511), Route 1, Rockport.

TO SEE AND DO Old Conway House Complex (236-2257), Conway Road (off Route 1 just south of Camden). Open during July and August, Tuesday through Friday 10–4; admission $1.50. Administered by the Camden–Rockport Historical Society, this restored early-eighteenth-century farmhouse has been furnished to represent several periods. The barn holds collections of carriages, sleighs, and early farm tools, and there is a Victorian privy and a blacksmith shop. The **Cramer Museum** houses memorabilia from the area, including costumes, glassware, ship models, and Maine paintings.

Maine Coast Artists Gallery (236-2875), Russell Avenue, Rockport. Open June through late September; seven days a week 10–5. Free admission, but contributions encouraged. An engaging late-nine-teenth-century landmark, this building was originally a livery stable, then a firehouse, then the town hall. In 1968 it took on its current function. Dedicated to showcasing the best of contemporary Maine art, the gallery sponsors several shows each season, an art auction, gallery talks, a fine evening lecture series, and other educational programs. Among the nationally acclaimed Maine artists who have exhibited here are Rackstraw Downes, Robert Indiana, Alex Katz, Alan Magee, Louise Nevelson, Fairfield Porter, Neil Welliver, Jamie Wyeth, and Yvonne Jacquette.

Ducktrap River Fish Farms, Inc. (763-3960), Pitcher Pond, Lincolnville. This company produces more than 25 varieties of smoked seafood which they sell nationwide to restaurants, gourmet food stores, and individuals. Among their products are smoked trout, shrimp, and mussels, and a selection of smoked pâtés. Visitors may view the processes involved and purchase the products. It's best to call first.

GREEN SPACE Camden Hills State Park (236-3109), Belfast Road, Camden 04843. In addition to Mt. Battie, this 6,500-acre park includes Mt. Megunticook, one of the highest points on the Atlantic seaboard, and a shoreside picnic site. From Megunticook Street in Camden you can climb a footpath to the summit of Mt. Battie, or you can drive up the road that starts at the park entrance, just north of town. Admission through the gate is $1 per person. At the entrance, pick up a "Hiking at Camden Hills State Park" map. Other trails in the 25-mile network take you to the summits of Mt. Megunticook, Bald Rock, and Ragged

Mountain as well as up the more daunting, sheer face of Maiden Cliff (from which there's a gorgeous view of Megunticook Lake). In winter many of the trails are suitable for cross-country skiing, given snow. There are 112 campsites here.

Also administered by Camden Hills State Park is **Warren Island State Park,** just a stone's throw off Islesboro. There are picnic tables, trails, and tent sites here. Accessibility is the problem: You can arrange to have a private boat carry you over from the mainland, or you can take the ferry to Islesboro and perhaps arrange to have a lobsterman take you over from there. (Details and camping permits at the town office and Durkee's Corner Store.) You might want to rent your own boat in Camden (or a sea kayak if you are skilled [see Boat Rentals, below]).

Marine Park, Rockport. A nicely landscaped waterside area with sheltered picnic tables. Restored lime kilns and a train caboose are reminders of the era when the town's chief industry was processing and exporting lime. You read here that in 1816 some 300 casks of lime were shipped to Washington, D.C., to help construct the Capitol building. Another feature of the park is a granite sculpture of André the Seal, the longtime mascot of Rockport Harbor. André drew thousands of fans every summer to watch his performances until his death in the summer of 1986.

Vesper Hill Children's Chapel, Rockport. The site of an old summer hotel, this delightful spot has an outdoor chapel with wooden benches facing the sea (popular as a warm-weather wedding site so be considerate if a ceremony is in progress). The grounds were landscaped by a local legend, the late Stubby Wheeler, who spent his life landscaping the grounds of some of the area's foremost mansions. The gardens are maintained by volunteers.

Merryspring (236-4885), Camden. A 66-acre preserve with walking trails, an herb garden, a lily garden, a rose garden, raised beds, a demonstration garden, and an arboretum. The preserve is bisected by the Goose River and is accessible by way of Conway Road from Route 1 in Camden. Weekly talks in the summertime. The organization is dedicated to planting and preserving flowers, shrubs, and trees in this natural setting and to interpreting them through workshops and special events. Donations are encouraged.

Camden Amphitheatre, Atlantic Avenue, Camden. A magical setting for summertime plays and concerts and a good place to sit, think, and read anytime. Tucked behind the library and across the street from the harbor park—a gentle, manicured slope down to the water.

Curtis Island, in the outer harbor. A small island with a lighthouse that marks the entrance to Camden. It is a public picnic spot if you can get yourself out there (if you are a sailor, you might hire a small sailboat at Willey Wharf [see Boat Rentals] and tack out to it).

BOATING   Windjammer Cruises, offered mid-June to mid-October. A half-dozen schooners and a ketch sail from Camden and Rockport every week, carrying experienced sailors and landlubbers alike along the Maine coast to deserted islands, quaint fishing villages, and seaside resort towns. It is a vacation like none other. Highlights can include lessons in navigation and sailing for those who want them, plenty of time to read and think, and the ever-changing scenery of beautiful mid-coast Maine. Meals on board are hearty, honest cooking prepared on a woodstove (even the bread); a highlight of most cruises is a clambake and lobster feed on some out-of-the-way shore. Accommodations are small and Spartan—a simple, efficient cabin with berths and a sink, a shared head down the hall or on deck, and, in most cases, limited bathing facilities (several windjammers have real showers, but some just have a hand-held sprayer on deck under which you can wash your hair and rinse off in your swimsuit). But shipboard camaraderie abounds, and you will be telling your friends about the experience for years to come; many passengers get so hooked on windjamming that they return year after year. Some of the ships are authentic nineteenth- and early twentieth-century coastal cargo schooners; others have been built in recent years according to traditional design (these tend to have slightly more modern accommodations). Windjammer trips cost about $550 to $600 per week per person; rates reflect the time of the season, whether the vessel will be participating in a special event like the Great Schooner Race or Windjammer Days while you're on board, and whether you choose one of the special art or music cruises on some of the vessels. Some of the boats also offer three-day and two-week cruises. In most cases, 16 is the minimum age for windjammer passengers. While all of the vessels listed below give you the classic windjammer experience, each differs a bit in personality and history as well as size and accommodations.

The rugged *Angelique* (236-8873), PO Box 736, Camden, is a 95-foot ketch that was built expressly for the windjammer trade in 1980. Patterned after nineteenth-century English fishing vessels, she offers a pleasant deck-level saloon and below-decks showers.

The *Grace Bailey* (236-2938), Maine Windjammer Cruises, PO Box 617, Camden, for years known as the *Mattie*, has taken back her original name following a recent thorough restoration. Built in 1882 in New York, she once carried cargo along the Atlantic coast and to the West Indies. She has below-decks showers.

The 114-foot *Roseway* (236-4449 or 800-255-4449), Yankee Schooner Cruises, PO Box 696, Camden, was built in 1925 as a fishing schooner and later spent 32 years as a pilot vessel, escorting ships in and out of Boston Harbor. She has been sailing out of Camden since 1975. There are enclosed hot freshwater showers on deck.

The *Mercantile* (236-2938), Maine Windjammer Cruises, PO Box 617, Camden, was built in Maine in 1916 as a shallow-draft coasting schooner. Seventy-eight feet long, she has been in the windjammer trade since its beginning, in 1942. Each cabin has its own private head (toilet and sink), and there are below-decks showers nearby.

The graceful, 90-foot *Mary Day* (236-2750 or 800-922-2218), PO Box 798, Camden, built in 1962, was the first schooner built specifically for carrying passengers. There's a hand-held shower on deck.

The *Timberwind* (236-6095 or 800-624-6013), PO Box 247, Rockport 04856 was built in Portland in 1931 as a pilot schooner. This pretty, 70-foot vessel was converted to a passenger vessel in 1969 and has been operated by the same family ever since. She has an enclosed hand-held shower on deck. The *Timberwind* is the only windjammer sailing out of Rockport Harbor, next door to Camden.

The *Mistress* (236-2938), Maine Windjammer Cruises, PO Box 617, Camden, at 40 feet the smallest of the fleet, carries just six passengers. A topsail schooner built along the lines of the old coasting schooners, she is also available for private charter. All three cabins have private heads, but there is no shower on board.

You may also contact the Rockport-Camden-Lincolnville Chamber of Commerce (see Guidance) or the Maine Windjammers Association (374-5400 or 800-624-6380), PO Box 317P, Rockport 04856 for brochures and sailing schedules. (Also see Windjammers under the What's Where in Maine and Rockland, home of nine more Windjammers.)

Yacht Charters, offered spring to autumn along the Maine coast. For a more luxurious and personalized cruise, you may choose to charter your own yacht. Experienced sailors can opt for a bareboat charter (no crew provided) while both the experienced and the novice may indulge in a crewed charter. Most charters run for a week, although sometimes it is possible to charter a boat just for a long weekend. On crewed boats you will find yourself pampered by professionals who prepare meals according to your preferences and plan the itinerary with your input. For more information, contact **Windward Mark Yacht Charters,** (236-4300; 800-633-7900 outside Maine), Bayview Street, PO Box 307, Camden or **Sun Yacht Charters,** (236-9611; 800-772-3500 outside Maine), Mechanic Street, PO Box 737, Camden. The former handles only crewed charters, while the latter, using the dock at Journey's End Marina in Rockland, handles bareboat charters, too. Another company, **Bay Island Yacht Charters** (236-2776), 21 Elm Street, PO Box 639, Camden, acts as a clearinghouse for yachts available for bareboat charter the length of Maine's coast. All three companies also arrange charters in the Caribbean.

DAILY BOAT EXCURSIONS   Offered spring to autumn. For an hour's tour of nearby waters or a day's sail, the Camden fleet of excursion vessels presents many choices. There are the *Appledore* (236-8353), an 86-foot schooner (the largest of the day-sailing fleet), which has sailed around the world and now offers several trips daily, including sunset cruises; the *Olad* (236-2323), a lovely 47-foot schooner; and the *Surprise* (236-4687), a traditional, historic 57-foot schooner that also sails thrice daily. Per-person rates for all three range from about $20–$30, depending on the length of the cruise. Weather is, of course, always a factor in whether the boats go out; and for full-day cruises, it is wise to make arrangements in advance. The motor launch *Betselma* (236-2101) provides hourly sightseeing trips from the public landing 10:30 AM–7:30 PM. And the traditional lobsterboat *Lively Lady* (236-6672) takes passengers on one-and-a-half-hour cruises that include seeing lobster traps being hauled ($10 adults, $5 children). Passengers may even buy the lobsters as they're caught.

BOAT RENTALS   Willey Wharf (236-3256) rents three Bullseye fiberglass sloops ($75 full day; $50 half day). Kayaks, canoes, and sailboards may be rented at **Maine Sport** on Route 1 just south of town. Maine Sport also offers courses in kayaking and canoeing and guided excursions around Camden Harbor and out into Penobscot Bay. Contact them for their catalog of activities. Kayaks may be rented at **Indian Island Kayak Center** (236-4088), Rockport. They also offer guided kayak tours of two hours' to two days' duration.

From its Camden office, **Viking River Expeditions** (763-3094 or 800-244-8799), Box 1, Camden books upcountry whitewater rafting trips on the Kennebec and Dead rivers. The day-long adventure includes a barbecued steak lunch and costs just under $100 per person.

LEARN-TO-SAIL PROGRAMS   **Camden Yacht Club Sailing Program** (236-3014), Bayview Street, provides sailing classes for children and adults, boat owners and non-boat owners, during July and August; among them is an excellent week-long course just for women. There is also a lecture series open to the public. The **Rockport Boat Club Sailing Program** sponsors month-long classes for children and adults.

DEEP-SEA FISHING   You will find fishing vessels for hire at **Lincolnville Beach,** just north of Camden on Route 1.

GOLF   **Goose River Golf Club** (236-8488), Simonton Road, Camden. Nine holes, but you can play through twice using different tees. Cart rentals.

Samoset Golf Course (594-2511 or 800-341-1650), Rockport, has 18 holes on a course that has been described as the "Pebble Beach of the East." Many of the fairways skirt the water, and the views are lovely. Carts are available.

SWIMMING   Saltwater swimming from Camden's **Laite Memorial Park and Beach,** upper Bayview Street; at **Lincolnville Beach,** Route 1 north of Camden; and in Rockport at **Walker Park.** Freshwater swimming at Megunticook Lake (**Barret Cove Memorial Park and Beach;** turn left off Route 52 northwest of Camden), where you will also find picnic grounds and a parking area; **Shirttail Beach** on Route 105; and at the **Willis Hodson Park** on the Megunticook River (Molyneaux Road). At the **Camden YMCA** (236-3375), Chestnut Street, visitors can pay a day-use fee of $5 which entitles them to swim in the Olympic-size pool (check hours for family swimming, lap swimming, etc.), use the weight rooms, and play basketball in the gym.

TENNIS   Samoset Resort (594-2511), Rockport, has indoor and outdoor courts. In addition, there are two public tennis courts at the **Camden Snow Bowl** on Hosmer's Pond Road.

SKIING   There's alpine skiing in winter at the **Camden Snow Bowl** (236-3438), Hosmer's Pond Road, Camden. With a 950-foot vertical drop, nine runs for beginner through expert, and night skiing, this is a comfortably sized area where everyone seems to know everyone. Lift tickets are $10 weekdays and $20 weekends—a bargain in this day of $30-plus prices. Facilities include a base lodge, a rental and repair shop, and a cafeteria.

Guests at the **Samoset Resort** (see Resort Hotel) are welcome to cross-country ski on their almost-100-acre golf course. There is also cross-country skiing on the trails at **Camden Hills State Park;** they lead to the ski hut on Mt. Battie.

SPECIAL PROGRAMS   **Center for Creative Imaging** (236-2333), 51 Mechanic Street, PO Box 1348, Camden 04843. Eastman Kodak operates a state-of-the-art facility offering week-long workshops in the use of Macintosh computers in magazine and book publishing; special emphasis is placed on digital manipulation of photographic images. Courses scheduled most of the year.

Maine Photographic Workshop (236-8581), Rockport 04856. A nationally respected year-round school offers programs that vary in length from one week to three months for every level of skill in photography, cinematography, television production, and related fields. Teachers are established, recognized professionals who come from across the country as do the students. There is also a gallery with changing exhibitions open to the public, and below it is a very good photographic supply shop called the Maine Photo ReSource. The school provides housing for most of its students and helps to arrange accommodations for others.

Rockport Apprenticeshop (236-6071), Box 539, Rockport 04856. Open to visitors year-round, 10–5 Monday through Saturday (and sometimes on Sundays if you call ahead). Perpetuating the art of wooden boat-building, this school offers two-year apprenticeships, six-week internships, and six-week volunteer stints. A wide variety of boats have been built here, reflecting the maritime heritage of the Atlantic from Newfoundland to the Bahamas. The Visitors' Gallery overlooks the boat-building in progress on the main floor below. There are also exhibits of models, boats, photographs, and marine art.

RESORT HOTEL   **Samoset Resort** (594-2511 or 800-341-1650), at the Rockland Breakwater, Rockport 04856. Open year-round, this is the only property of its magnitude in the region. A full-service resort, with 150 rooms, many enjoying ocean views, all with balconies, private baths, color TVs, and climate-controlled air-conditioning and heat. Amenities include an 18-hole golf course, indoor and outdoor tennis courts, a Nautilus-equipped fitness club, tanning beds, a glass-enclosed swimming pool, and an outdoor pool. Facilities are available for banquets and small conventions. The dining room, Marcel's, and the adjacent lounge with a large fireplace and floor-to-ceiling windows overlooking the water are extremely pleasant, although service tends to be slow. $175–$190 in summer; $85–$99 in winter. Packages are also available.

INNS   (All listings are Camden 04843 unless otherwise indicated.)

Lord Camden Inn (236-4325), 24 Main Street. In a restored 1893 brick commercial building, the inn occupies several floors above a row of Main Street shops. Restored antique furnishings, including some canopy beds, blend with modern amenities: color TVs, private baths, in-room telephones, and elevator service. Most rooms have two double beds and balconies overlooking the town and harbor or the river and hills beyond. Rates include continental breakfast. $118–158, depending on the view, in summer; $68–$118 in winter.

Whitehall Inn (236-3391), 52 High Street (Route 1). Open Memorial Day to Columbus Day weekend. A longtime favorite with summer visitors, this historic colonial inn is where Edna St. Vincent Millay was discovered when, as a young chambermaid, she recited some of her poetry for the guests. Listed on the National Register of Historic Places, the inn's main building rambles off the original 1834 sea captain's house, and the 40 guest rooms are furnished with antiques. There are five additional rooms each in two houses across the road: Wicker House and Maine House. The public rooms of the inn are comfortably proper but not stiff; there is a jigsaw puzzle on the table and a library of inviting books. The inn's tennis court is across the street, and it's just a short walk to the Salzedo Harp Colony (summer concerts) and a "sneaker" beach (which means you have to wear shoes because of the rocks) on Camden's outer harbor. In the evening, there's sometimes a performance by a musician, humorist, or magician. Dinner and breakfast are served in the notable dining room (see Dining Out). Doubles are $100–$150, including breakfast and dinner for two. (There are a few less expensive rooms with shared baths.) Dinner credits are given if you choose to dine in town. When making reservations for July and August or foliage season, you must book for more than one night. However, should you arrive during these peak times looking for a room for just one night, if there's one available, you may have it.

Hartstone Inn (236-4259), 41 Elm Street (Route 1). Open year-round (may be closed in March). An 1835 Victorian at the southern end of the village, within walking distance of just about everything. Downstairs there's a comfortable parlor with fireplace and a library with many books on sailing and Maine plus a cable TV. The seven guest rooms are bright and airy, and two have fireplaces; all have private baths. In addition, the restored carriage house has two housekeeping suites with dining/kitchen areas. Sherry and coffee liqueur are offered in the parlor, and rates include a full breakfast in the dining room or a continental breakfast in bed. Dinner, served only to inn guests, is moderately priced and features a multicourse meal (guests may also request lobster in advance). $70–$90 double (less off- season). Special offerings include a Picnic Sail (June to September) on the schooner *Surprise* ($50–$70 for two depending on menu) and a Fireside Special (November to April) that features two nights and a dinner for two served in front of the dining room fireplace ($160 per couple).

Camden Harbour Inn (236-4200), 83 Bayview Street. Open year-round. A landmark inn perched on a hilltop above the town, overlooking the harbor, with views inland to the Camden Hills, too. A few years ago new owners added a good deal to the size of the inn without adding any rooms, thereby making the existing 22 rooms considerably larger. All have private baths, and many have balconies, patios, or fireplaces. The dining room, called the Thirsty Whale, serves breakfast and dinner to the public as well as the inn's guests (see Dining Out). On warm summer evenings dinner is served on a large outdoor porch as well as inside in the dining room solarium. Doubles $145–$185 in high season; lower in "mid-season" and off-season. Between April 29 and December 1, rates include a full breakfast, but a charge of 20% of the breakfast check is added to your lodging bill to cover service and tax; from December 2 to April 28, a complimentary continental breakfast is offered. Minimum two-night stay between June 10 and October 13 and on all holiday weekends.

BED & BREAKFASTS   (All listings are Camden 04843 unless otherwise indicated. All rates are high summer rates; most have off-season rates as well.)

Bed & Breakfast Society of Camden, PO Box 1103, counts among its members numerous very pleasant bed & breakfasts, most of them located right in the village, and most open year-round. All are professionally run by hosts who seem genuinely delighted to welcome you and help you get to know Camden. All serve breakfast; some do not permit smoking. The society will be glad to send you a copy of their extremely attractive booklet, which gives complete details on each member B&B.

The Belmont (236-8053), 6 Belmont Avenue (formerly the Aubergine). Open mid-May through New Year's Eve. An 1890s house with a wraparound veranda, this bed & breakfast has six guest rooms and suites, each furnished with nice touches such as matching bedspreads and wallpaper. All have private baths. In the living room, accented by oriental rugs on shining wood floors, guests are invited to relax in comfortable wing chairs and chat about the day's adventures or enjoy a cocktail from the bar. The chef (one of the owners) offers imaginative "New American" fare (see Dining Out) in an inviting dining room. A full country breakfast—egg dishes or perhaps blueberry pancakes—is included in lodging. $95–$125, single or double occupancy, in-season; less off- season. Two-night minimum stay on weekends July through mid-October.

The Maine Stay (236-9636), 22 High Street (Route 1), Camden. At the northeastern end of town. Open year-round. One of the oldest homes in Camden's High Street Historic District—and also listed on the National Register of Historic Places—this old colonial home has eight attractive bedrooms furnished in period decor. There are two cozy fireplaced parlors plus a TV den and a country dining room. The hosts (Captain Peter Smith, USN Ret, his wife, Donny, and her twin sister, Diana Robson) obviously enjoy extending a warm welcome—they'll even serenade you in three-part harmony. A full hot breakfast and afternoon tea are included in the $65–$86 double room rate (off-season lower).

Hawthorn Inn (236-8842), 9 High Street (Route 1), Camden. On your right soon after Route 1 curves around to the right and heads north out of Camden. A handsome 1894 turreted Victorian, now on the National Register, the Hawthorn offers elegant accommodations ranging from five rooms upstairs off the three-story staircase to garden rooms downstairs to a variety of choices in the adjacent carriage house. These latter have harbor views and include studio rooms and suites with whirlpools in the bathrooms. Afternoon tea (served by the English innkeeper) and full buffet breakfast are included (breakfast not served to accommodations with their own kitchens). Doubles $85–$135.

Windward House (236-9656), 6 High Street (Route 1), Camden. A handsome clapboard Greek Revival home surrounded by a lovely lawn and garden, the Windward House is almost directly across from the Hawthorn. It offers five welcoming guest rooms, all with private baths. Full "gourmet" breakfast included, served in the sunny dining room. Doubles $85–$111.

Mansard Manor (236-3291), 5 High Street (Route 1), Camden. Just around the corner from the center of town. Open year- round. Named for its distinctive mansard roof, this small mansion built in 1881 is now on the National Historic Register. The guest rooms are individually decorated with country antiques and folk art and have queen-size beds and private baths. Full breakfast, served outside on the deck in the summertime, includes home-baked breads, egg dishes, and fresh fruit. $95 double.

A Little Dream (236-8742), 66 High Street, Camden. Open year-round. This is a charming little white farmhouse with wraparound porch topped by a diminutive turret. In keeping with its late 1800s vintage, the decor here is ruffled Victorian with a touch of English country. Guests may take a continental breakfast to their rooms or join other guests for a full breakfast in the dining room, where specialties include smoked salmon omelet and blueberry or banana pancakes; dinner is occasionally served guests as well. Featured in *Country Inn* magazine. Doubles $89–$139 for a large room with VCR and private sun deck.

Edgecombe-Coles House (236-2336), 64 High Street (Route 1), HCR 60, Box 3010, Camden. Open year-round. This inviting B&B set on a hilltop looking out to Penobscot Bay was once a gracious summer home. It's a 1-mile drive north of the center of Camden and also a mile from Camden Hills State Park's ocean shores and Mt. Battie. The country decor is enhanced by the owners' special collections of whimsical animals and other antiques displayed throughout. The rooms offer a choice of garden/forest view or ocean view, and double, queen, or king-size bed. All have private baths, and one bedroom has a working fireplace. There are also fireplaces in the living room, dining room, and den. A full breakfast is served in the dining room; continental breakfast is delivered to guests' rooms if they prefer. $100–$145 for two. Two-night minimum stay in July and August and on holiday weekends.

The Blackberry Inn (236-6060), 82 Elm Street, Camden. Open year-round. Painted the color of blackberry ice cream, this 1860 Italianate Victorian is hard to miss as you approach Camden from the south. The decor—including marble mantels, tin ceilings, oriental rugs, and Bar Harbor wicker—captures an elegant bygone era, but the atmosphere is casual and comfortable. Full breakfast in the dining room, or a continental breakfast brought to your room, is included. $75–$90 double in summer.

The Elms (236-6250), 84 Elm Street, Camden. Open year-round. Next door to the Blackberry Inn, this is a restored 1806 clapboard colonial with accommodations in the house and in the adjacent carriage house. Rates include a full breakfast served in the formal dining room. $65–$85 double in-season.

The Blue Harbor House (236-3196 or 800-248-3196), 67 Elm Street (Route 1), Camden. Open year-round. This is a Cape-style house built in 1835, on your left as you approach Camden from the south. An intimate B&B, its ten rooms are cozy and pleasantly decorated in the country style; most have private baths. Doubles $75–$140 for a suite with a whirlpool bath.

Norumbega (236-4646), 61 High Street (Route 1), Camden. Open year-round. With one of the most imposing facades of any B&B anywhere, this turreted stone "castle" has long been a landmark just

View of Camden Harbor

Photo by Neal Parent

north of Camden. Inside, the ornate staircase with fireplace and loveseat on the landing, formal parlor, and dining room capture all the opulence of the Victorian era. Its nine guest rooms, some with fireplaces and all with king-size beds and private baths, are located both upstairs and downstairs, the latter with private terrace entrances. Doubles $175–$195, including full breakfast and afternoon wine and cheese; penthouse $350.

Hosmer House (236-4012), 4 Pleasant Street, Camden. A block off Route 1. Open year-round. In the Hosmer family from the time it was built in the early 1800s until 1985, this historic house stands in the center of an attractive, quiet neighborhood a block from the center of town and all the shops and restaurants. The pleasant rooms are simply furnished and have private baths. Continental breakfast included. $85–$110 double.

Swan House (236-8275), 49 Mountain Street (Route 52), Camden.. Open during the summer and fall only. At the foot of Mt. Battie, yet only four blocks to the harbor. Six guest rooms, all with private baths, are furnished with antiques. Located both in the house and in the Cygnet Annex, each is named for a different type of swan. Some have sitting rooms, decks, or private entrances. We like the little gazebo, just right for afternoon reading or daydreaming. The hosts like to describe the atmosphere as "country elegance." Full breakfast included. Doubles $75 to $100.

Sign of the Unicorn (236-4042), Box 99, 191 Beauchamp Avenue, Rockport 04856. Open year-round. A delightful place overlooking Rockport Harbor. Full gourmet breakfasts include treats such as tipsy French toast or stone-ground three-grain pancakes, both served dripping with maple syrup or, on the Fourth of July, piled high with strawberries, blueberries, and ice cream. You may also opt for eggs with onions, cheese, wine, and herbs, or homemade granola and homemade coffee cakes and fruit cobbler. Coffees are flavored with cinnamon or chocolate-almond. Guests have kitchen privileges. Choose among the White Room, which has its own grand piano and velvet Victorian loveseats, a room measuring 17-feet square with a sleeping loft, or an upstairs room with its own balcony. Rates depend on the room you choose and whether you have a private bath.

Twin Gables (236-4717), Spear and Beauchamp streets, PO Box 189, Rockport 04856. Open mid-June through mid-October. In a quiet neighborhood near the harbor and the meadow where the black-and-white Belted Galloway cows graze, this small B&B offers two accommodation choices: a double room with a "sometimes shared" bath and a suite with sitting room and private bath. Breakfast included. $65–$100.

Mary Helen Amsbury House (236-4653), 25 Amsbury Street, PO Box 777, Rockport 04856. Open year-round. The Amsburys of Rockport were a family of sea captains. One of them built this attractive home for his wife in 1856 on what is now Amsbury Hill, high above the harbor. Two guest rooms, both with water views and private baths. Rates include a full breakfast, served in the dining room or on the porch, depending on the season. Doubles $85–$100.

Bed & Breakfast at The Red House (236-4621), Lincolnville Beach 04849. Open year-round. Overlooking Penobscot Bay near the ferry landing, antiques shops, and lobster restaurants. This is one of the area's few B&Bs that welcome children. Full breakfast served to house guests. Doubles $50 in-season; $35 October 15 to May 15. There's also a fully furnished cottage accommodating four that's available for $300 per week during the summer season (discount for longer rentals).

Longville Inn (236-3785), The Other Road, PO Box 75, Lincolnville Beach 04849 (4 miles north of town on Route 1). Open year-round. This restored Victorian has five guest rooms with private baths. There's a pleasant country atmosphere with spacious grounds. A full breakfast is included, and special weekend packages include a Saturday lobster bake. Depending on accommodations, rates range from $55–$80 double in-season. Discounts on multiple-night stays; special honeymoon rates; lower rates between mid-October and mid-May.

The Spouter Inn (789-5171), Route 1, PO Box 176, Lincolnville 04849. Open year-round. Just across the road from Lincolnville Beach and the ferry to Islesboro, this early 1800s home invites guests to enjoy the view from a rocker on the front porch or relax by the fire in the library and parlor. The four rooms, all pleasantly decorated, are named for naval ranks: first mate, captain, admiral, and commodore, and increase in luxury accordingly. Doubles $70–$85; $135 for the commodore's quarters, which includes a living room, bedroom, kitchen, bath, and private sun deck and accommodates up to four.

Sign of the Owl (338-4669), Route 1, RR 2 Box 85, Lincolnville Beach 04849. Open May through December. Nine miles north of Camden. Three double rooms with shared bath. Well-behaved pets welcome. Also on the premises is a gift and antiques shop specializing in Victorian pieces and oriental paintings, scrolls, porcelains, and note papers. Doubles $40–$50 per night; $240–$280 per week.

Littlegrove (236-3867), Route 1, HCR 60, Box 3285, Camden. A good bet for families and other travelers looking for comfort without elegance. Great views of the bay from spacious, sunny rooms. Fluffy Newfoundland dog and Maine coon cat in residence. $40 per night; $200 per week.

MOTELS   North and south of Camden, Route 1 is lined with motels, most of them offering exceptionally nice accommodations. There are also numerous cottage colonies: identical miniature houses, sometimes log cabins, dotting a parklike setting or arranged in a semicircle around a central green space. Many of the latter have fireplaces. For a complete listing, contact the Rockport–Camden–Lincolnville Chamber of Commerce (see Guidance).

High Tide Inn (236-3724), Route 1, Camden. Open May to October. A fine selection of accommodations for every taste, including 5 inn rooms, 17 motel units, a duplex, and 4 cottages. Most have exceptional water views. All are set on 7 quiet acres—formerly a private estate— of landscaped grounds and meadow that slope to the water. There's over 250 feet of private beach during high tide. Home-baked continental breakfast, included in lodging, is served during the summer on the glass-enclosed porch; the living room also has ample windows to afford views of the bay. Rates for two, depending on accommodations, range from $55–$115 in-season; less before July and after early September. There are plans to open the dining room to the public.

The Owl and Turtle Harbor View Guest Rooms (236-9014 or 236-8759), PO Box 1265, 8 Bayview Street, Camden. Open year-round. Conveniently located right in the midst of all the shops, yet perched high enough to offer the best view of the inner harbor of any lodging in town. There are only three rooms, and repeat business is heavy so book early for the summer months. Each room has air-conditioning, TV, telephone, and private bath, and two face directly over the water. Private parking is provided. Downstairs is one of the state's best bookshops, no longer owned by the family that operates the guest rooms. No smoking; no pets. Rates include continental breakfast brought to the room. $70–$75 double in-season; less off-season.

DINING OUT   Camden is a mecca for dining in Maine, as it has one of the largest concentrations of exceptional restaurants anywhere outside of Portland. You will find good, old-fashioned family restaurants; lobster served simply and succulently; a collection of upscale restaurants serving what might be called "current" food; and a few dining establishments that strive for the higher levels of culinary art.

The Belmont (236-8053), 6 Belmont Avenue, Camden (formerly Aubergine). Open early May through New Year's Eve. There is a lot of creativity in the kitchen here, and the menu reflects the great care that goes into every dish. The chef/owner characterizes his cuisine as "New American," with such specialties as sautéed salmon in champagne beurre blanc topped with thinly shredded leeks; medallions of veal with sweetbreads in a heavily reduced veal essence; and a trio of duck, featuring a crisp-roasted leg, a breast cooked only to rare, and a thigh in confit with zinfandel and oyster mushrooms.

Whitehall Inn (236-3391), High Street (Route 1), Camden. Open late June to mid-October. Reservations are required. A historic inn (see Inns) serving dinner and breakfast in a gracious yet unstuffy atmosphere. The dining room enjoys an exceptional reputation for its traditional and creative American cuisine, including entrées such as fresh salmon with herbs and boneless duck breast. Proper dress is requested.

The Waterfront (236-3747), Bayview Street, Camden. Open daily year-round (closes for a short while in the dead of winter). In an unbeatable location right down on the harbor, with lots of windows and an outside deck with an awning. An appetite-whetting menu of creative luncheon dishes such as Suzette's Sin, a grilled sandwich of chicken, ham, bacon, tomato, avocado, Swiss cheese, and mustard sauce; and Mediterranean Melt, a combination of linguica sausage, tomatoes, basil, onion, garlic, and smoked mozzarella baked in French bread. Lighter eaters choose among delicious locally smoked salmon with a bagel and fresh fruit, huge salads such as Greek, Caesar, and unusual cold pasta and vegetable combinations. At dinner, entrées include chicken breast glazed with rum-laced apricot sauce; sesame shrimp and chicken brochette; Mediterranean seafood stew; and a seafood sampler consisting of char-grilled halibut and crumb-fried shrimp and sole, all with an herb butter. There are also the old faithfuls of steamers and lobster plus delicious garlic-scented steamed clams and a good selection from the raw bar. Pleasant atmosphere, good food, and good value.

The Sail Loft (236-2330), Rockport. Open year-round for lunch and dinner daily and Sunday brunch. A longtime favorite of residents and visitors to the area, the Sail Loft overlooks Rockport Harbor and the activities of the boatyard below (owned by the same family). At lunch, the avocado stuffed with crabmeat is one of the most popular items on the menu; other choices include chicken salad, creative omelets, and mussels steamed in garlic and wine. At dinner, entrées feature native seafood (including lobster) and prime beef, all prepared deftly. The daily specials usually highlight the freshest of local fish. An added treat: small melt-in-your-mouth blueberry muffins come with every meal.

Marcel's (594-2511), Rockport (at the Samoset Resort). Open every day year-round for breakfast, lunch, and dinner. Specializing in New England and continental cuisine, the dining room offers many dishes prepared tableside, and a pastry cart is wheeled by at the end of the meal. Good choices include fettuccine with lobster, shrimp, and scallops; rack of lamb for two; filet mignon; and stir-fried dishes. Lunch is also served on the patio in summer. Piano music at dinner plus nightly entertainment in the adjacent Breakwater Lounge.

Camden Harbour Inn (236-4200), Bayview Street, Camden. A nineteenth-century inn (see Inns) with dining overlooking all of Camden Harbor and Camden Hills. Open year-round. Fresh Maine seafood, lobster, and steaks are featured. Moderate.

Peter Ott's (236-4032), Bayview Street, Camden. Open spring, summer, and fall for dinner only. Known as a steak house, this pleasant restaurant also serves fresh local seafood (including lobsters, scallops, clams, and swordfish) prepared in imaginative ways and a very good chicken teriyaki. Good desserts, too, and potent liqueur-laced coffees.

Cassoulet (236-6304), 27 Elm Street, Camden. Open for dinner only. A seasonally changing menu featuring country continental cooking served by candlelight. As you might expect, the cassoulet, a peasant casserole, is the specialty; its ingredients change from night to night. This is an intimate spot, seating only 24, so reservations are recommended. Good wine list.

EATING OUT   Cappy's Chowder House (236-2254), Main Street, Camden. Open year-round for lunch and dinner and for breakfast, spring through fall (7:30 AM to midnight). An extremely popular pub—they claim that "sooner or later, everyone shows up at Cappy's," and it's true. Good food with reasonable price tags: eggs, granola, treats from the on-premises Vie de France bakery for breakfast; croissant sandwiches, burgers, full meals for lunch; seafood entrées, special pasta dishes, meat dishes for dinner. The clam chowder has been written up in *Gourmet.* Upstairs in the Crow's Nest (open in the summertime only), you will find a quieter setting, a raw bar, a harbor view, and the same menu as downstairs. Cappy's is an especially good choice for families as there are a lot of special touches for kids: their own menu with selections served in a souvenir carrying box, a placemat with puzzles, crayons for coloring, and even balloons.

O'Neil's (236-3272), Bayview Street, Camden. Open for lunch and dinner daily, almost year-round. Salads, soups, sandwiches, nachos, burgers, deep-fried veggies, enchiladas, and steaks. Full bar. You'll love the big Ma and Pa soft-sculpture dolls overseeing things from their perch above the stairway.

Chez Michel (789-5600), Lincolnville Beach (across the road from the beach). Serving lunch and dinner. Short on atmosphere, this unpretentious restaurant serves exceptional food with a French flair. Moderately priced entrées include bouillabaisse ($12.95), scallops Provençale, fried and poached seafood, pork chops with mustard sauce ($9.95), vegetable pasta with pesto, and vegetable couscous. A well-kept secret among Camdenites who have become loyal regulars.

Village Restaurant (236-3232), Main Street, Camden. Open year-round. Long a favorite with locals, this traditional restaurant serves lots of fried local seafood and fish chowder. The dining room overlooks Camden Harbor.

Gilbert's Public House (236-4320), Bayview Street, Camden. Tucked underneath the shops along Bayview Street (you enter through a side door just off the street), this is a good place for a beer and a sandwich, snacks or light meals for the kids, or a simple supper before the evening's activities. There's an international flavor to the "pub food" offered: Mediterranean shrimp salad, wurst platter, egg rolls, veggie stir-fry, and nachos are among the favorites. There's also a frozen drink machine here, so frothy and colorful daiquiris, Margaritas, and the like are popular. Live music for dancing in the evening.

The Helm (236-4337), Route 1, Rockport (1.5 miles south of Camden).

Open for lunch and dinner April to late October; closed Mondays. There's a French accent to the menu, with such dishes as Coquilles St. Jacques, bouillabaisse—plus Maine shore dinners. The menu includes about 50 entrées, all homemade. Salad bar. There are three dining rooms, including a glass room overlooking the Goose River. Children's menu, too. There is a takeout window—probably the only one in New England from which you can order real onion soup, fresh rabbit pâté, and the like plus delicious crabmeat rolls and other sandwiches on real French bread. At the ice-cream window, you can choose chocolate or vanilla ice milk if you are counting calories.

Spinnaker (596-6804), Route 1, Rockport. Open year-round for lunch and dinner. Salad bar, daily soup and sandwich specials, steaks, fresh seafood, and a variety of lobster dishes.

Mama and Leenie's (236-6300), Elm Street, Camden. Open year-round for breakfast pastries, lunch, tea, and dinner. A warm, mothering atmosphere where fresh meat pies, chocolate chip cookies, and other wonderful-smelling bakery treats come out of the oven the whole time you are there. Hearty home cooking includes soups, sandwiches, salads, cheesecake, and pineapple upside-down cake. No liquor. This is a small place with only a handful of tables.

Fitzpatrick's Deli Café (236-2041), Sharp's Wharf, Bayview Street, Camden. Open March through early January for breakfast, lunch, and dinner. More than 100 different sandwiches and salads plus quiche of the day and special soup-salad-sandwich plates. Informal atmosphere: you order at the counter, and they call you by name when it is time to pick up your food. Popular with regulars. Outside patio for summertime dining.

Camden Deli (236-8343), Main Street, Camden. Choose among about 35 sandwiches combining all of the regular deli meats and cheeses; the Possible Dream is whatever you can come up with, and the New Deli Special changes daily. For kids they have PB&Js plus they gladly make half sandwiches (the whole ones are hefty). At the window opening onto Main Street, you can stop for an ice-cream cone. At the back of the deli is a small room with chairs and tables where you can take your food and dine overlooking the harbor.

Rockport Corner Shop (236-8361), Rockport (right in the middle of the village, across from the Rockport Photo Workshop so there are a lot of students). Open year-round for breakfast and lunch. Regulars greet each other warmly, but newcomers are made to feel welcome, too. Help yourself to coffee. An exceptional find with almost no decor but plenty of atmosphere. Fresh coffee cakes are baked each morning; all salads are made with garden-grown vegetables. Omelets, chowders, and lentil burgers are specialties. There is a vegetarian bent, but choices do include fish and meat dishes. No liquor. Very reasonable prices.

LOBSTER IN THE ROUGH   Lobster Pound Restaurant (789-5550), Route 1,

Lincolnville Beach. Open every day for lunch and dinner, the first Sunday in May through Columbus Day. Also serving breakfast between July 4th and Labor Day. This is a mecca for lobster lovers—some people plan their trips around a meal here. Featuring lobster, steamed or baked, also clams, other fresh seafoods, roast turkey, ham, steaks, and chicken. This is a family-style restaurant that seats 260 inside and has picnic tables near a sandy beach and takeout window. Always popular (always crowded).

Captain Andy's (236-2312), Upper Washington Street, Route 105, Camden. Call and order your lobsters with all the fixings, and they'll be delivered right to you at the harbor park or town landing for a delicious picnic.

SNACKS *Pizza:* **Guido's** (236-2050), Route 90, West Rockport, and **Lady Millville** (236-6570), upper Washington Street, Camden. Both offer a variety of other takeout foods as well (if you're a garlic lover, try Guido's garlic and cheese pizza). Call ahead to have your order ready; Guido's has tables and chairs.

Takeout: **The Market Basket** (236-4371), Routes 1 and 90, Rockport. A terrific place to pick up everything you'll need for a gourmet picnic. The daily menu includes a selection of two or more unusual soups plus generously portioned Greek and garden salads. This is a specialty food store so you can buy French bread (the best we've had anywhere), cheeses, pâtés, slices of cheesecake, and a good bottle of wine or imported beer to top things off.

Camden Coffee Company (236-9660), Public Landing, Camden. Open in summer only. As the name implies, this takeout cafe specializes in good coffee, including espresso and cappuccino. You can also buy the Fairwinds beans by the pound. Also offered are quiche, soups, sandwiches, luscious-looking cakes by the slice, and ice cream. There are a few tables inside and a few more outside in warm weather.

Scott's Place (236-8751), Elm Street, Camden. A tiny building in the parking lot of a small shopping center serving hundreds of toasted crabmeat and lobster rolls, marinated chicken sandwiches, burgers, hot dogs, and chips. Prices are among the best around: under $1 for a hot dog, under $5 for a lobster roll. This is one of several small takeout buildings here and there around town, but it is the only one open year-round.

Ayer's Fish Market (236-3509), Main Street, Camden. A great little fish store with live lobsters, too. But the *pièce de résistance* is what has to be the best lunch bargain in town: a large serving of steamy fish chowder for just $1.50. What goes into it varies from day to day, and it is sometimes chunkier than at other times; but it is always delicious.

ICE CREAM Pick up a cone as you stroll around the harbor at either **The Pine Cone**, Bayview Street (next to the Pine Tree Shop), the **Camden Deli** on Main Street, or **Down East Trading Company**, next to the town landing. **The Blue Lobster** gift shop sells frozen yogurt.

Miss Plum's, Route 1, Rockport. Open most of the year, except for the dead of winter. Its entire exterior painted a deep plum color, this is a real, old-fashioned ice-cream parlor. All of the great-tasting flavors are made right on the premises. There are homemade cones and edible dishes and nostalgic treats such as egg creams and extra-thick frappes. Miss Plum's also serves breakfast in summer and lunch year-round. The menu lists hot dogs, nachos, soups (including cold summer soups), and a variety of sandwiches.

The Helm, Route 1, Rockport. Open spring through fall; closed Mondays. Ice cream and ice milk at the takeout window.

ENTERTAINMENT   Bay Chamber Concerts (236-2823), Rockport Opera House, Rockport 04856. Thursday and Friday evening concerts are given during July and August (also monthly winter concerts from October through May). Outstanding chamber music presented every year for more than 30 years. Summer concerts are preceded by free lectures. Tickets are $13 to $15 in summer, $10 in winter; students less.

Camden Civic Theatre (John Ferraiolo 594-5161), Camden Opera House, PO Box 362, Main Street, Camden 04843. A variety of theatrical performances is presented from April through December. Tickets are $8 reserved seats, $7 general admission, and $6 students under 16 and senior citizens.

Camden Shakespeare Company. Sadly, this commendable organization has had its financial difficulties in recent years and no longer produces Shakespearean plays during the summer. However, they do sponsor four children's plays presented on Saturday afternoons in July and August. The setting is the verdant Camden Amphitheatre, a magical place.

The Camerata Singers (236-8704). A 14-member, a capella singing group presenting concerts in Camden and surrounding towns throughout the year.

Bay View Street Cinema (236-8722), Bayview Street, Camden. Showings daily. A mixed bag of old favorites, foreign and art films, and some current movies.

SELECTIVE SHOPPING   The Camden area has always had a few pleasant, top-quality shops, but in recent years the number has mushroomed, making this attractive harbor village a real shopping destination. You'll find an engaging mix of crafts shops, boutiques, clothing stores, book shops, and art galleries here, most of them lining Main Street and Bayview Street. Several additional clusters lead from Bayview Street down to the harbor.

Antiques: **Suffolk Gallery,** Bayview Street. A charming little maroon clapboard house filled with English antiques, including silver and china. When the shop is closed in winter, the English owners return to England to search for new treasures.

Boxwood Farms, 165 Russell Avenue, Rockport. Open June to September. Antique prints, including such subjects as hand-colored botanicals, maps, fashions and costumes, birds, and historical views.

Galleries: **Maine's Massachusetts House Galleries** (789-5705), Route 1 (2 miles north of Lincolnville Beach). The gallery is open May to Christmas; the gift shop is open year-round. Hours are Monday through Saturday 9–5 (and Sunday 12–5 during summer and fall). A charming setting for outstanding exhibits of works by well-known Maine artists and craftspeople. A landmark since 1949, just across the road from the 1718 homestead for which it is named. The gift shop also has gourmet foods.

Artisans: Camden and its surrounding villages draw artisans in all crafts, including pottery, metalwork, textiles, glass, and hand-illustrated notepapers. The following are among them:

Anne Kilham Designs, 142 Russell Avenue, Rockport. Charming scenes of the Maine countryside rendered in bold colors on postcards, notecards, and prints. Also an unusual selection of Advent calendars that have become a Christmas tradition in many families. Anne's fame has spread, and her mail-order business reaches across the country. Call before going to the studio because Anne is not always there. Her stationery line is also sold in several other area shops.

Windsor Chairmakers, Route 1, Lincolnville Beach. Filling two floors of an old farmhouse, the inviting display encompasses not only Windsor chairs but also tables, highboys, and four-poster beds, all offered in a selection of finishes including "distressed," i.e., instant antique. The owner welcomes commissions—he's always ready to make a few sketches as you describe your ideas—and enjoys chatting with visitors and showing them around the workshop.

Exotica Woodworks, intersection of routes 90 and 17, West Rockport. Beautiful, multihued exotic woods laminated together into handsome cutting boards, boxes, and other pieces. Exotica's work is also sold in Camden at **Once a Tree** on Bayview Street.

Camden–Rockport Brass Foundry, Park Street, West Rockport (diagonally across from Exotica Woodworks). Custom metal castings in bronze and aluminum. Also hand-blown glass vases, bowls, and goblets.

James Lea (236-3632), 9 West Street, Rockport. Showroom is open by appointment Monday through Friday. Jim Lea is a third-generation craftsman fashioning museum-quality furniture reproductions using antique tools as well as more modern devices; all work is done on commission.

Special shops (open year-round unless otherwise indicated): **The Grasshopper Shop,** Bayview Street. A perennial favorite with all ages. Stylish and fun clothing, mostly for women (some men's items), moderately priced. Downstairs, the counters are brimming with home furnishings, crockery, linens, baskets, and bath accessories. Also a great selection of greeting cards, novelties, stickers, gifts, etc.

The Owl and the Turtle Bookshop, Bayview Street. Six rooms full of books, including special ones devoted to arts and crafts, boats, sports, and young adults and children. Special orders and searches for out-of-print books. Great for browsing.

Unique 1, Bayview Street. Woolen items made from Maine wool, designed and handloomed locally. Also some pottery.

The Market Basket, corner of routes 1 and 90, Rockport. An exceptional gourmet store with a limited selection of wines plus a small produce section featuring the best locally produced and exotic fruits and vegetables. Good selection of ingredients for international cooking.

The Smiling Cow, Main Street. Open during the summer only. Three generations ago a mother and five children converted this stable into a classic gift shop, one with unusual warmth and scope. Customers may help themselves to coffee on a back porch overlooking a waterfall and the harbor.

Pine Tree Shop and Bay View Gallery, Bayview Street. One of the largest galleries in the mid-coast area. Original paintings and sculptures by contemporary Maine artists plus several thousand posters and prints. Expert custom framing, too.

51 Bayview Street. An exceptional collection of decorative pieces for the home, including vases, sculptures, silk flowers, glassware, and lamps. The building itself, artfully remodeled, is worth a look.

Made the Maine Way, Washington Street, Camden. A carefully selected presentation of Maine's finest crafts, including artworks, pottery, canvas bags, even locally produced musical tapes that capture the sounds of loons, sea gulls, and other fauna.

Ducktrap Bay Trading Company, Bayview Street. Stunning decoys and wildlife art. Many of these really special pieces have earned awards for their creators. There are also some less expensive carvings plus jewelry.

Heather Harland, Bayview Street. Cookware, cookbooks, and coffees.

Etienne, Main Street. Gallery of designer jewelry in 14- and 18-carat gold; very contemporary and unusual pieces made on the premises.

Good Hands, Bayview Street. One-of-a-kind designs, many created here in the studio, in gold and silver. Jewelry, sculptures, and decorative pieces.

Once a Tree, Bayview Street. Poetically named shop, brimming with appealing objects made from wood. The success of this store has led to the opening of five additional stores throughout northern New England.

Stitchery Square, Bayview Street. Everything for needlework, including unusual, hand-colored needlepoint kits of Maine scenes. For those of us who don't do needlework, there are lovely already-finished pieces plus other handmade items.

The Right Stuff, Main Street. Country collectibles, antiques, and reproductions.

Bayview Artisans, Bayview Street. Jewelry, weaving, blown glass, handmade hats, stained glass, pottery, knitted wear, and handmade clothing.

Camden boasts a number of fine women's clothing stores, among them **House of Logan,** Main Street (Route 1); **Harborside Shop,** Bayview Street (sportswear for men and women); and the **Admiral's Buttons,** Bayview Street (fine menswear as well). Also, be sure to stroll along **Sharp's and Willey's wharves,** each with its jumble of intriguing antiques, clothing, and gift shops. Another collection of shops worth checking out tumbles down the street leading to the town landing.

In both Rockport village and Lincolnville Beach you will find a number of antiques shops, many of them in private houses. Their hours tend to be erratic off-season, but during the summer you will find them open and ready to welcome you.

SPECIAL EVENTS   July: **Fourth of July.** A full weekend of special events culminating in fireworks over the harbor. **Great Schooner Race** (see Rockland Area).

Early July: **Rockport Folk Festival,** Rockport Opera House.

Late July: **Annual Open House and Garden Day,** sponsored by the Camden Garden Club. Very popular tour of homes and gardens in Camden and Rockport held every year for four decades.

Third Saturday and Sunday in July: **Arts and Crafts Show,** Camden Amphitheatre.

Mid-August: **Downeast Jazz Festival,** Camden Opera House.

Late August: **Union Fair and Blueberry Festival,** Union Fairgrounds (see Rockland Area).

Early October: **Camden Fall Festival.** Crafts and harvest market, chicken barbecue, street dancing, lobster-eating contest.

Early December: **Christmas by the Sea.** Tree-lighting, Santa's arrival, caroling, holiday house tour, refreshments in shops, Christmas Tree Jubilee at the Samoset Resort.

ISLESBORO

Islesboro is a 10-mile-long, stringbean-shaped island just 3 miles off Lincolnville Beach. The ferry ride takes about 25 minutes and round-trip fares in summer are $6.25 for car and driver, $1.75 per additional adult, and $1 per child. Bikes are $1 each. (Call 789-5611 or 734-6935 for schedule and possible price increases being discussed as we go to press.) Leave your car on the mainland if you like, for this is a terrific biking island. There are several lovely sand beaches, too. Dark Harbor, at the southwestern end of the island, has long been an extremely exclusive resort. In the best-seller *Master of the Game,* author Sidney Sheldon called it the "jealously guarded colony of the super-rich." The expansive summer "cottages" are tucked down on the water at the end of long drives so you can see more from the water than you do from land. But you might spot a white-uniformed nanny pushing a ruffled pram or an obviously professional chef buying the evening's victuals at the local grocer.

At the opposite end of Islesboro is Pripet, a thriving year-round neighborhood of boat-builders and fishermen. The ferry lands mid-island, at Grindle Point, next to the old lighthouse. The keeper's cottage is now an engaging museum of local history and memorabilia called the **Sailors' Memorial Museum** (open in the summer, Tuesday through Sunday 9:30–4:30). It is a great place to poke about while you wait for the returning ferry. (The zip code for Islesboro is 04848.)

GUIDANCE   Islesboro Town Office (734-2253), Whitemarsh Building, Dark Harbor.

TO SEE AND DO   Chamber Music Concerts at the Free Will Baptist Church, summers. Donations requested.

Up Island Church. More a historical landmark than a church now, this lovely structure houses some beautiful wall stencils (check with town office for hours the church is open). The adjacent graveyard— please step carefully to preserve its unspoiled nature—has some fascinating old headstones.

Flying Fish (734-6984 or 734-6714). Earl and Bonnie MacKenzie take passengers on their 45-foot gaff-rigged schooner for day and evening sails and dinner cruises. Their vessel was built in 1936 for artist Frank Vining Smith.

LODGING   Dark Harbor House (734-6669), Box 185, Main Road, Dark Harbor 04848. Open mid-May to mid-October. Built on a hilltop at the turn of the century as a summer cottage for the president of the First National Bank of Philadelphia, this imposing yellow-clapboard inn offers elegance from a past era. There are a summery living room with glass doors opening onto a porch and a cozier library with a fireplace just right for crisp autumn afternoons. Fine antiques are found throughout the Dark Harbor House and its seven bedrooms. All have private baths, and some feature balconies. There's also a two-room suite with a wet bar and a fold-out sofa bed in its living room. The inn serves cocktails and hors d'oeuvres every evening except Tuesday, and the public as well as dinner guests are invited to gather. In the oval dining room, a prix fixe multicourse dinner, served to guests and to the public by reservation, features specialties of the house with a Jamaican accent. Entrées might be swordfish or quail with grapes, curried shrimp, or ginger-lime pork; popular desserts include baked banana and mango-rum meringue. It's not unusual for dinner guests to request that the cook come in for a round of applause at the end of the meal. The inn also serves traditional afternoon tea, accompanied by scones and finger sandwiches (by reservation to the public). Doubles are $98–$165, including a full, four-course breakfast. Dinner is $35; afternoon tea is $12.

The Annex (734-6470), Sabbathday Harbor, Islesboro 04848 (winter address: Mr. and Mrs. Frank Ryder, Box 29, Batesville, VA 22924). Quiet and privacy make this waterside B&B an ideal honeymoon spot. The Victorian house offers one double room with a fireplace, bath, refrigerator and antiques ($70 per couple includes breakfast). The Boat House ($475 per week) has a kitchen, spectacular views and a deck overhanging the beach.

SHOPPING   The Dark Harbor Shop, Main Road, Dark Harbor. Tucked in among the predictable souvenirs are such surprises as dhurrie rugs, Italian pottery, and other lovely gifts. There's also a **luncheonette** running along one wall where locals and visitors gather for sandwiches and gossip.

DINING OUT   The Blue Heron (734-6611), Dark Harbor (just off the Main Road beyond the Dark Harbor Shop). Open in-season for dinner, Thursday through Sunday 6–10 (and Tuesday and Wednesday at the height of the season); Sunday brunch 12–2. Reservations appreciated. Rated by local fans as "as good as anything you'll find anywhere in Maine," the Blue Heron's menu reflects the skills and creativity of the young couple who own it and do all the cooking. Highlights of the menu include stuffed filet of sole with crabmeat, baked salmon with dill, shrimp with a garlicky Bordelaise sauce, rack of lamb with anise and sweet roasted garlic, veal marsala with prosciutto and mushrooms, and New York steak with mushrooms. "Sinful" desserts include cheesecake with strawberry or blueberry sauce, fresh fruit tarts, carrot cake, and chocolate cake.

IV. East Penobscot Bay Region

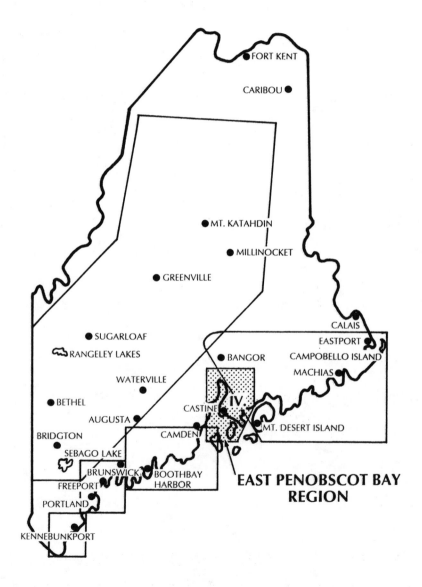

FORT KENT

CARIBOU

MT. KATAHDIN

MILLINOCKET

GREENVILLE

CALAIS

SUGARLOAF

EASTPORT

RANGELEY LAKES

CAMPOBELLO ISLAND

BANGOR

MACHIAS

WATERVILLE

BETHEL

CASTINE

IV

AUGUSTA

MT. DESERT ISLAND

BRIDGTON

CAMDEN

SEBAGO LAKE

BRUNSWICK

BOOTHBAY
HARBOR

FREEPORT

EAST PENOBSCOT BAY
REGION

PORTLAND

KENNEBUNKPORT

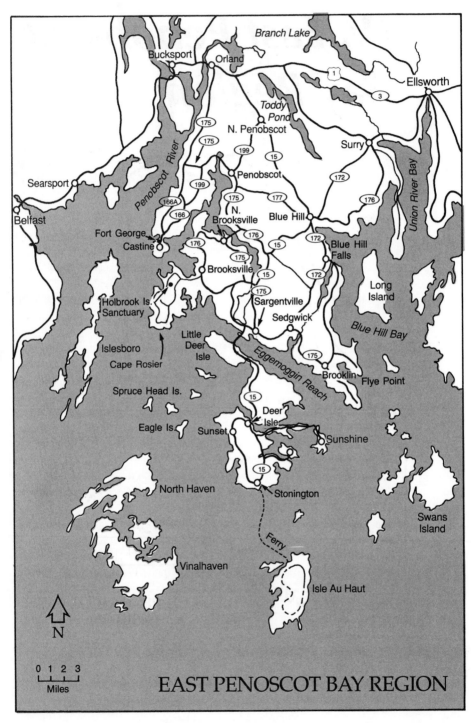

EAST PENOSCOT BAY REGION

Belfast/Searsport/Bucksport

Penobscot Bay narrows at its head so that following Route 1 east from Belfast you have the sense of following a mighty river. With its sheltered harbors this was once prime ship-building country. In 1845 Searsport alone managed to launch eight brigs and six schooners. In Searsport's Penobscot Marine Museum you learn that more than 3,000 different vessels have been built in and around Penobscot Bay since 1770. Searsport also once boasted more sea captains than any town its size, explaining why dozens of nineteenth-century mansions still line the Searsport stretch of Route 1; many are now B&Bs.

Neighboring Belfast has had a history of unusual diversification, including a highly successful sarsaparilla company, a rum distillery, and a city-owned railroad, not to mention poultry and shoes. In the past few years a number of its fine old houses have become bed & breakfasts, and its Victorian brick downtown has become a genuinely interesting place to shop.

Bucksport, north of Searsport at the mouth of the Penobscot River, overlooks New England's biggest fort, a memorial to its smallest war.

Pleasant lodging places are scattered along the bay between Belfast and Bucksport, making this a logical hub from which to explore the entire region, from Camden to Bar Harbor.

GUIDANCE **Belfast Chamber of Commerce** (338-2896) maintains a seasonal information booth on the waterfront. Information can be obtained year-round by writing PO Box 58, Belfast 04915.

Searsport Chamber of Commerce (548-6510), PO Box 139, Searsport 04974, maintains a seasonal information booth on Route 1 and is the source of a guide that includes information about antiques stores.

GETTING THERE By air: **Ace Aviation** (338-2970) in Belfast offers charter service to all points.

By car: The most direct route to this region from points south and west is via I-95 (the Maine Turnpike), either exiting in Augusta and taking Route 3 to Belfast or continuing to Bangor.

MEDICAL EMERGENCY **Waldo County General Hospital** (338-2500), Northport Avenue, Belfast.

TO SEE AND DO **Penobscot Marine Museum** (548-2529), Route 1, Searsport. Open Memorial Day to mid-October, Monday through Saturday 9:30–5 (Sundays 1–5). Adults $4; ages 7–15 $1.50. Housed in a cluster of public and private buildings that formed the town's original core. Displays in the 1845 town hall trace the evolution of sailing vessels from seventeenth-century mast ships to the Down-Easters of the 1870s and 1880s—graceful, square-rigged vessels that were both fast and sturdy cargo carriers. In other buildings there are fine paintings, scrimshaw, a variety of lacquerware, Chinese imports, and more. You learn that Searsport didn't just build ships; townspeople owned the ships they built and sailed off in them to the far reaches of the compass, taking their families along. In 1889 Searsport boasted 77 deep-sea captains, 33 of whom manned full-rigged Cape Horners. There are pictures of Searsport families meeting in far-off ports, and, of course, there is the exotica they brought home—much of which is still being sold in local antiques shops. The museum sponsors lecture, film, and concert series.

Fort Knox State Park (469-7719), Route 174 (off Route 1), Prospect (just across the Penobscot from Bucksport). Open daily May 1 to November 1, 9 AM to sunset. $1 per adult. Built in 1844 of granite cut from nearby Mount Waldo, it includes barracks, storehouses, a labyrinth of passageways, and even a granite spiral staircase. There are also picnic facilities. The fort was to be a defense against Canada during the boundary dispute with New Brunswick called the Aroostook War. The dispute was ignored in Washington, and so in 1839 the new, lumber-rich state took matters into its own hands by arming its northern forts. Daniel Webster represented Maine in the 1842 treaty that formally ended the war, but Maine built this fort two years later, just in case. It was never entirely completed.

Bucksport Historical Society Museum (469-2591), Main Street, Bucksport. Open July and August, Wednesday through Friday 1–4, and by appointment. $.50. Housed in the former Maine Central Railroad Station; local memorabilia.

Searsport Historical Society (548-6663), Route 1, Searsport. Open July through September, Wednesday to Sunday 1–5. A collection of local artifacts, photos, maps, clothing, and town records.

Belfast Museum (338-2078 or 338-1875), 6 Market Street, Belfast. Open Sundays, June through September, 1–4, and by appointment year-round. Local area artifacts, paintings, scrapbooks, and other displays.

Craig Brook National Fish Hatchery (469-2803), East Orland (turn off Route 1 in Orland, just east of Bucksport). Open daily 8–4:30. Opened in 1871, this is the country's oldest salmon hatchery. Situated on the shore of a lake, it offers a visitors center with aquariums, also a nature trail, picnic tables, and a nineteenth-century ice house.

Perry's Tropical Nut House (338-1630), Route 1, east of Belfast. Open spring through fall until 9:30 in high season. A nutty store in every way, this landmark began in the 1920s when the South produced more pecans than it could sell, a situation that inspired a Belfast man who had investments in southern groves to sell pecans to the new tourist traffic coming up Route 1 in Maine. Irving Perry was soon doing so well that he moved his shop to the old cigar factory that it still occupies, along with the original shop building tacked on. He traveled throughout South America collecting nuts (the display includes every nut species known to man) as well as alligators, monkeys, ostriches, peacocks, gorillas, and other dusty stuffed animals now on display. It is all a bit fusty now and Perry himself is long gone, but everyone still has to stop and pose next to the various exotica and outsized carved elephants.

GREEN SPACE   (Also see Swimming.)

Moose Point State Park, Route 1, south of Searsport. Open May 30 to October 15. A good spot for picnicking; cookout facilities are in an evergreen grove and open field overlooking Penobscot Bay.

Fort Pownall and **Fort Point State Park,** Stockton Springs (marked from Route 1; accessible via a 3.5-mile access road). This is the site of a 1759 earthwork fort built to defend the British claim to Maine (the Kennebec River was the actual boundary between the English and French territories). It was burned twice to prevent its being taken; only earthwork remains. The adjacent park, on the tip of a peninsula jutting into Penobscot Bay, is a fine fishing and picnic spot. A pier accommodates visitors who arrive by boat. The lighthouse is another great spot. Views from the point are back down to the Camden Hills.

CEMETERIES   The **Bowditch Cemetery** on Route 1 in Searsport has an unusual number of memorials to mariners lost at sea or buried on foreign shores. It is named for the famous Nathaniel Bowditch of Salem, Massachusetts, author of the navigational guide by which most seamen of his era sailed, the idea being that if he helped them to navigate in this world's water, he could do so in the next as well.

In the **Bucksport Cemetery,** near the Verona Bridge, a granite obelisk marks the grave of Colonel Jonathan Buck, who was founder of Bucksport and the judge who condemned a mentally retarded resident to death for killing a woman whose body had been found minus one leg. The man proclaimed his innocence; and when in time the judge died and was buried beneath this obelisk, the outline of a leg soon appeared in the stone and reappeared whenever erased. It is still there.

BOAT EXCURSIONS   **Penobscot Bay Cruises** (338-5191 or 594-9191), Belfast. The 385-passenger excursion boat *Katahdin,* based in Belfast, offers a variety of seasonal cruises through Penobscot Bay on a daily basis; September cruises range from Bangor to Boothbay Harbor.

TRAIN EXCURSION   **Belfast and Moosehead Lake R. R. Co.** (338-2330) operates a daily excursion train from Belfast to Brooks and back (one hour, fifteen minutes); $9 per adult, $5 children ages 5–12.

Coastal cross-country skiing

AIR RIDE   Ace Aviation Inc. (338-2970) offers scenic flights from Belfast Municipal Airport; two-person minimum; $8 per person for 15 minutes.

HORSEBACK RIDING   Frye Mountain Trail Rides (342-5500), RR 1, Box 520, Morrill 04952. Twelve miles northwest of Belfast, daily trail rides offered beginning at 9 AM, returning at 4 PM.

GOLF   Northport Golf Club (338-2270), bayside south of Belfast. Offers nine holes and power carts.

    Bucksport Country Club (469-7612), Duckscove Road (Route 46), Bucksport.

SAILING   Chance Along Sailing Center (338-4785), Belfast. Sailboat rentals, day sails, and sailing lessons.

SWIMMING   Lake St. George State Park (589-4255), Route 3, Liberty. Open May 15 to October 15. A great way stop for travelers going to or from Down East. A deep, clear lake with a small beach, lifeguard, bathhouse, parking facilities, 31 campsites, and boat launch.

    Swan Lake State Park, Route 141, Swanville (north of town; follow signs). This beach has picnicking facilities on Swan Lake.

    Belfast City Park, Route 1, Belfast (south of town). Swimming pool, tennis courts, picnicking facilities, and a gravel beach.

    Sandy Point Beach, off Route 1 north of Stockton Springs (it's posted "Hersey Retreat": turn toward the water directly across from the Rocky Ridge Motel). No facilities but a great spot to cool off if you're headed up or down Route 1; particularly popular with windsurfers.

    Mosman Beach Park, Searsport. Town dock, boat ramp, swimming, fishing.

INNS, BED & BREAKFASTS   Homeport Inn (548-2259), Route 1, Searsport 04974. Open year-round. An 1861 captain's mansion complete with widow's walk that overlooks the bay. Dr. and Mrs. George Johnson were the first Searsport B&B hosts, and they now offer 10 elegantly decorated guest rooms; also a two-bedroom cottage on the water. Rooms in the front of the house are old-fashioned with shared baths, but those in the back have private baths and bay views. A full breakfast is included in the rates which range from $30 (single with shared bath) to $75 (double with private bath), lower November through April; the cottage is $450 per week.

    Captain Green Pendleton Inn (548-6523), Route 1, Searsport 04974. Open year-round. Another fine old captain's home set well back from Route 1 in its own 80 acres. The house has been restored with gleaming wood floors and spacious, comfortable common rooms. The three tastefully decorated guest rooms (one down, two up) have fireplaces. A path circles the meadow, a cross-country ski trail goes through the woods, and there's a large, spring-fed trout pond; $45 per night includes tax as well as a full breakfast.

    The Hichborn Inn (567-4183), Church Street, PO Box 115, Stockton

Springs 04981. Open year-round except Christmas. It's a stately Victorian Italianate mansion complete with widow's walk, up a side street in an old shipbuilding village that's now bypassed by Route 1. Built by a prolific shipbuilder (N. G. Hichborn launched 42 vessels) and prominent politician, it remained in the family, preserved by his daughters (there's a story!) until 1939. For Nancy and Bruce Suppes, restoring this house has meant deep involvement in its story—and its friendly ghosts. Bruce, an engineer on super tankers, has done much of the exceptional restoration work himself. There's a comfortable "gent's parlor" and a music room, also an elegant library. Elaborate breakfasts are served either in the carefully restored dining room or on the sun porch. Rooms vary. We recommend the "Harriet Room" with its deftly created bath and glimpse of water. Books, magazines, and water are by all the beds, and Nancy brings hot coffee with your wake-up call. $40–$80 per night, less off-season.

Hiram Alden Inn (338-2151), 19 Church Street, Belfast 04915. A handsome 1840s home in downtown Belfast offers eight guest rooms (five are available year-round), most with marble-top sinks, shared baths. Nicely furnished with iron bedsteads and antique quilts. There is an upstairs sitting room as well as a gracious downstairs living room. The price includes a full breakfast such as blueberry-nut pancakes or ham on French toast. During July and August "inn helpers" Jennifer, Jon, and Jeffrey pick raspberries for the table. $45–$50.

Frost House (338-4159), 6 Northport Avenue, Belfast 04159. Open year-round except Christmas and Thanksgiving. A gracious, turn-of-the-century house with five guest rooms, some water views. $60–$80 including a full breakfast served promptly at 8 AM.

Thurston House B&B Inn (548-2213), 8 Elm Street, Searsport 04974. An 1830s village house with four guest rooms, two upstairs in the front of the house and two back in the rear wing, good for a family of five. A full breakfast is included in the moderate rates.

The Capt. Butman Homestead (548-2506), Route 1, Searsport 04974. A classic 1830s farmhouse on five and a half acres. It's open summers only because hosts Lee and Wilson Flyte teach school in Massachusetts. This was home for two generations of Searsport deepwater captains, and there's a view of the water from one upstairs window and a right-of-way down to Penobscot Bay. The four guest rooms share two baths. A continental breakfast is included in $42–$45 double. If you have high school age children, you might want to ask about the Downeast Outdoor Education School, a two-week program which the Flytes have just launched; it includes ample time sailing and exploring Acadia National Park.

Daniel Faunce House (338-4205), 15 Church Street, Belfast 04915. Open year-round. An 1850s house with an extraordinary front staircase, a comfortable living room, and an upstairs sitting room with TV.

Three guest rooms share two baths. Lorraine Therriault's breakfasts include homemade granola, maybe an egg casserole with ham. $40–$45.

Summerwood Inn (548-2259), Route 1, Searsport. A 1790s farmhouse that's better known as a restaurant (see Dining Out), but with four guest rooms and a sitting room. $40–$65 includes a continental breakfast.

Carriage House Inn (548-2289), Route 1, Searsport 04974. Open year-round, a Victorian sea captain's home with matching carriage house. Owners Brad and Cathy Bradbury offer five guest rooms, three with private baths, two with shared baths. Continental breakfast is included; $55–$65 per room.

Horatio Johnson House (338-5153), 36 Church Street, Belfast 04915. A handsome 1840s Belfast home with three guest rooms, all private baths. Rates include a full breakfast such as Belgian waffles and bacon, depending on the chef's mood. $40–$45.

The Jeweled Turret Inn (338-2304), 16 Pearl Street, Belfast 04915. A gabled and turreted house built richly inside and out in the 1890s, furnished mostly with antiques, plenty of knickknacks, private baths, full breakfast and tea included in the rate. $45–$75.

Londonderry Inn (338-3988), Star Route 80, Route 3, Belfast 04915. Open June through mid-October. Off Route 1 and 1 mile from downtown Belfast, this is a vintage 1803 farmhouse with four antiques-furnished guest rooms sharing two baths. Guests can relax in the inn's library, sun porch, or parlor. A full breakfast is served in the large country kitchen. $45–$50 per couple.

Whistlestop Bed & Breakfast (567-3726), RFD 1, Box 639, Maple Street, Stockton Springs 04981. Open year-round. A comfortable, nicely sited house at the end of a quiet street within walking distance of a rocky beach. Both guest rooms (which share a bath) have ocean views. $50 double includes a muffin and fruit breakfast.

Jed Prouty Tavern (469-1271), 52–4 Main Street, Bucksport 04416. Open year-round. The 1798 building, billed as "the fifth oldest continuously run hostelry in America," was totally renovated and re-opened in November of 1989. The 14 upstairs rooms now all have private baths and phones, canopy beds, reproduction antiques, and matching curtains, wallpaper, and coverlets ($75–$125 depending on room and time of year). Forty additional rooms in a four-story, motel-style building are built into the bluff across the street, overlooking the Penobscot River and Fort Knox ($65–$85).

DINING OUT   **Nickerson Tavern** (548-2220), Route 1, Searsport. Open Tuesday through Saturday and 12–9 on Sunday. Patrons drive from Bar Harbor and Bangor to this handsome 1860s sea captain's house on Route 1. Thomas and Linda Weiner are rated among the state's top chefs; they are meticulous about quality and imaginative about the combination of ingredients. Entrées include veal browned in butter with apples and cider and finished in a brandy cream sauce, chicken with a light coating of crushed hazelnuts in raspberry sauce, and shrimp simmered in wine and served with a creamy garlic and mushroom sauce and artichoke hearts. All entrées come with a delectable bread basket and fresh vegetables with dip, but the appetizers are also outstanding, and the dessert tray is irresistible. Reservations are a must. Entrées are $11–$17.

Summerwood Inn (548-2259), Route 1, Searsport. Open year-round. Ken and Caroline Estes have created a fine little restaurant, less formal and slightly less expensive than their famous neighbor (see above) but ambitious, with a menu that changes every few months. The last menu we saw included salmon en croute and "Lamb Moroccan." Entrées run $9.95–$17.50.

McCloeds (496-3963), Main Street, Bucksport. Open weekdays 11–9, weekends 5–9. A pubby bar with booths, informal atmosphere, dependable dining. Appetizers like tomato cognac bisque; entrées like scallops supreme ($11.95) or lobster and broccoli on linguini ($14.95).

Jed Prouty Restaurant and Tavern (496-3113), 52 Main Street, Bucksport. Open for lunch and dinner. The dining room has been recently redecorated with pink flowery wallpaper and lacy curtains, and the menu is large and traditional: seafood (fried, pan-fried, or broiled) and the usual choice of steaks. Dinner entrées from $11.95–$17.95.

Penobscot Meadows Inn (338-5320), Route 1, Belfast. Open daily for dinner. A renovated turn-of-the-century inn with a dining room overlooking Penobscot Bay and a menu specializing in "creative country cooking." Specialties include lobster puff. Entrées are $13–$18.

L'Ermitage (469-3361), 219 Main Street, Bucksport. Open Tuesday through Sunday for dinner. Dine on traditional French fare in the dining rooms of this small B&B. It may be the only place in Maine you will find blueberry trifle. Entrées begin at $12.

EATING OUT   **Darby's Restaurant and Pub** (338-2339), 105 High Street, Belfast. Open for lunch and dinner. A friendly, storefront café with salads, burgers, and upscale lunch sandwiches. A reasonably priced dinner find: entrées range from black bean enchilada ($6.50) and fish 'n' chips ($8.50) to spicy grilled Indonesian shrimp ($12.25). Wine and beer.

Young's Lobster Pound (338-1160), Mitchell Avenue (posted from Route 1 just across the bridge from Belfast), East Belfast. Open in-season 7–6:30. A classic pound with tanks holding as many as 30,000 lobsters. Order and enjoy the view of Belfast across the Passagassawakeag River while you wait.

Belfast Cafe (338-2949), corner of High and Main streets, Belfast. Open for lunch (from 11 AM) and dinner daily. Pocket sandwiches, salad, and coffeehouse atmosphere with Victorian-era photos; sidewalk dining in-season.

Weathervane (338-1774), City Landing, Belfast. One in a Northern New England chain. Same menu for lunch and dinner, daily. "Appetizers & satisfiers" can include calamari, smelts, or crabmeat stew. Fried seafood dinners are a specialty. You can also have lobster or steak, a burger or crabmeat roll, a sloe gin fizz or wine by the glass.

Light's Diner (548-2405), Route 1, Searsport. Open daily for all meals. A local favorite for fried seafood or lobster sautée. $9.95 for a one-and-a-quarter-pound lobster complete with salad bar.

Seafarer's Tavern (548-2465), Route 1, Searsport. Open for lunch and dinner except Sundays. Right in the middle of the village, good for sandwiches and pizza, also homemade desserts, chicken Parmesan, or ribs.

Jordan's Restaurant (548-2555), Route 1, Searsport. Open for breakfast, lunch, and dinner. Large menu, eat-in and takeout; specials ranging from seafood to beef; also a children's menu.

Lobster Shack (548-2448), Trunday Road, Searsport (off Route 1 south of the village). Open 8–8 in summer, varying hours in spring and fall. Reasonably priced lobsters. Also a seafood market; lobsters packed to travel.

TEA **Homeport Inn** (548-2259), Route 1, Searsport. Serves an elegant English tea on summer weekend afternoons; the dining area here is a nicely decorated sun porch, just the right place for tea and cake.

ENTERTAINMENT **Penobscot Theater Company** (942-3333), Main and Union streets, Bangor. October through February series; inquire about summer performance sites.

Myth Weaver Theater (338-3848). Performances at various locations, including Belfast Opera House.

The Chamber Theater of Maine (525-0927). Based in Brooks but plays staged throughout Waldo County.

The Belfast Maskers (338-4240). A year-round community theater that's making waves. Check local listings.

SELECTIVE SHOPPING *Antiques shops:* A dozen dealers can be found in Searsport, which claims to be "the Antique Capital of Maine." A directory is available from the chamber of commerce (see Guidance).

The **Searsport Flea Market,** weekends in-season, is big.

Art galleries: **Artfellows Gallery** (338-5100), 24 Main Street, Belfast (access through Rockport Blueprint). Open Monday through Saturday 9–5. A cooperative gallery that represents the work of 40 artists working in a variety of media. Changing exhibits; annual **Invitational Painters Show.**

Gallery 68 (338-1558), 68 Main Street, Belfast. Open daily 10–5. Features prints by well-known artists and printmakers.

Frick Gallery (338-3671), 139 High Street, Belfast. Features "contemporary and applied art."

MH Jacobs Art Gallery (338-3324), 44 Main Street, Belfast. Original paintings.

Books: **Fertile Mind Bookshop** (338-2498), 13 Main Street, Belfast. An outstanding browsing and buying place featuring Maine and regional books and guides, maps, records, and cards.

Canterbury Tales (338-1171), 52 Main Street, Belfast. A full-service bookstore.

Special shops: **Cyote Moon** (338-5659), 54 Main Street, Belfast. A nifty, reasonably priced women's clothing and gift store.

Waldo County Arts and Crafts, Route 1, Searsport Harbor. Open June to October, daily 9–5. A showcase for the local extension service. Dolls, needlework, wooden crafts, quilts, pillows, jams, and ceramics—and lots of them.

Northport Landing (338-5555), Route 1 between Lincolnville and Belfast. Open mid-May to mid-October, 10–6. A barn filled with crafted gifts, antiques, and art.

Silkweeds (548-6501), Route 1, Searsport. Specializes in "country gifts": tinware, cotton afghans, rugs, wreaths.

SPECIAL EVENT July: **Belfast Bay Festival,** mid-month week of events; giant chicken barbecue, midway, races, and parade.

Castine

Castine is one of Maine's most photogenic coastal villages, the kind writers describe as "perfectly preserved." Even the trees that arch high above Main Street's clapboard homes and shops have managed to escape the blight that has felled elms elsewhere.

Situated on a peninsula at the confluence of the Penobscot and Bagaduce rivers, the town still looms larger on nautical charts than on road maps. Yacht clubs from Portland to New York visit annually.

Castine has always had a sense of its own importance. According to the historical markers that pepper its tranquil streets, Castine has been claimed by four different countries since its early seventeenth-century founding as Fort Pentagoet. It was an early trading post for the Pilgrims but soon fell into the hands of Baron de Saint Castine, a young French nobleman who married a Penobscot Indian princess and reigned as a combination feudal lord and Indian chief over Maine's eastern coast for many decades.

Since no two accounts agree, we won't attempt to describe the outpost's constantly shifting fortunes—even the Dutch owned it briefly. Nobody denies that in 1779 residents (mostly Tories, who fled here from Boston and Portland) welcomed the invading British. The Commonwealth of Massachusetts retaliated by mounting a fleet of 18 armed vessels and 24 transports with 1,000 troops and 400 marines aboard. This small navy disgraced itself absurdly when it sailed into town on July 5, 1779. The British Fort George was barely in the making, manned by 750 soldiers with the backup of two sloops, but the American privateers refused to attack and hung around in the bay long enough for several British men-of-war to come along and destroy them. The surviving patriots had to walk back to Boston, and many of their officers, Paul Revere included, were court-martialed for their part in the disgrace.

Perhaps it was to spur young men on to avenge this affair that Castine was picked as the home of the Maine Maritime Academy, which occupies the actual site of the British barracks and keeps a training ship anchored at the town dock, incongruously huge beside the graceful white-clapboard buildings bred of a very different maritime era.

Castine saw its shipbuilding days in the mid-nineteenth century when it claimed to be the second wealthiest town per capita in the United States. Its genteel qualities were recognized by summer visitors who later came by steamboat to stay in the eight hotels. Many built their own seasonal mansions.

Only two of the hotels survive, and just two of the mansions take in guests. But the town dock is an unusually welcoming one, complete with picnic tables, parking, and rest rooms. It remains the heart of this walking town where you can amble uphill past shops or along Perkins Street to the Wilson Museum.

Some natives complain that Castine is in danger of becoming a museum. They complain that the inns, shops, and restaurants are all owned by relative newcomers, many of whom want to keep it exclusive. Like many of New England's most beautiful villages, Castine's real danger seems to lie in the perfect preservation of its beauty, a shell unconnected to the lives that built it. Few visitors complain, however. Castine is exquisite.

GUIDANCE   Town Office (326-4502). The town clerk is helpful. Inquire about the pamphlet guide to Castine's inns, shops, and restaurants, usually available.

GETTING THERE   By air: See Bar Harbor/Bangor Area and Portland for air service.

By car: The quickest route is the Maine Turnpike to Augusta and Route 3 to Belfast, then Route 1 to Orland and Route 175; follow signs.

MEDICAL EMERGENCY   Blue Hill Memorial Hospital (374-2836), the largest facility in the area, has a 24-hour emergency room.

TO SEE AND DO   Fort George. The sorry tale of its capture by the British during the American Revolution (see above) and again during the War of 1812, when redcoats occupied the town for eight months, is told on panels at the fort—an earthworks complex of grassy walls (great to roll down) and a flat interior where you frequently find Maine Maritime Academy cadets being put through their paces.

Wilson Museum, Perkins Street. Open May 27 to October 1, Tuesday through Sunday 2–5. Housed in a fine waterside building donated by anthropologist J. Howard Wilson, a summer resident who amassed many of the displayed American Indian artifacts as well as ancient ones from around the world. There are also changing art exhibits; collections of minerals, old tools, and farm equipment; an 1805 kitchen; a Victorian parlor; and Hearse House (a blacksmith shop open Wednesday and Sunday afternoons in July and August, 2–5).

John Perkins House, Perkins Street. Open during July and August, Wednesday and Sunday 2–5. $2 admission. A pre-Revolution home, restored and furnished in period style. Guided tours and crafts and fireside cooking demonstrations.

State of Maine (326-4311). Open daily July and August from 9–12 and 1–4. Free. Visitors are welcome to come aboard and tour the ship, a former troopship that dates from 1952 and still takes Maine Maritime Academy cadets on an annual cruise. Midshipmen serve as guides.

BOAT RENTALS Sailboats and powerboats are available from **Dennett's Wharf** (326-4861) and from **Eaton's Boatyard** (326-8579).

FISHING We are told that you can catch flounder off the town dock and mackerel at Dyce's Head, below the lighthouse.

GOLF AND TENNIS **Castine Golf Club** (326-4311), Battle Avenue. Offers nine holes and four clay courts.

SWIMMING **English Canal,** Backshore Road. During the War of 1812 the British dug a canal across the narrow neck of land above town, thus turning Castine into an island. Much of the canal is still visible, and at its western terminus there is a fine swimming hole.

Maine Maritime Academy (326-4311) offers, for a nominal fee, gymnasium facilities to local inn guests. This includes the pool, weight room, and squash and racquetball courts.

WALKS **Witherle Woods** is an extensive wooded area webbed with paths at the western end of town. The ledges below **Dyce's Head Light,** also at the western end of town, are great for clambering. **Castine Conservation Commission** sponsors weekly walks in July and August, departs from Town Hall. Check local bulletin boards.

LODGING (All listings are for Castine 04421).

Castine Inn (326-4365), PO Box 41, Main Street. Open mid-April through mid-November. A cheerful 1898 summer hotel that offers 20 light and airy guest rooms, all with private baths and many with a harbor view. Guests enter a wide, welcoming hallway and find a pleasant sitting room and a pub, both with frequently lit fireplaces and interesting, original art. Innkeeper Margaret Hodesh, an artist herself, has painted a mural of Castine on all four walls of the dining room— a delightful room with French doors leading out to a broad veranda overlooking the inn's terraced, formal gardens. Children over eight welcome. Hosts Mark and Margaret Hodesh take some trouble to orient guests to the region, annually updating their own guide to sights and shops. $70–$95 includes a full breakfast.

Pentagoet Inn (326-8616), PO Box 4, Main Street. Open April to November. The main inn is a very Victorian summer hotel with a turret and gables. Rooms in the inn itself are rather small but unusually shaped and cozy, and the room in neighboring Ten Perkins Street (a 200-year-old home) has a working fireplace. In all there are 17 guest rooms, each with private bath. There are two sitting rooms and a pink-walled dining room that opens onto the garden. $120–$135 single, $149–$190 MAP. Children over age 12 are welcome.

The Manor (326-4861), Box 276, Battle Avenue. Open year-round. A majestic summer home built in 1895 by the commodore of the New York Yacht Club. It is set in 5 acres of lawn and offers spacious, nicely decorated guest rooms, some with fireplaces, and opulent public

A soft scoop at The Breeze in Castine

Photo by Christina Tree

rooms. The long marble oyster bar off the library is open year-round. Moderate to deluxe rates include continental breakfast. Children and "well-behaved pets" are welcome both here and at **The Holiday House** (326-4335) on Perkins Street, another nicely restored mansion, this one on the water; also owned by Paul and Sarah Brouillard. Together the two houses offer a total of 30 rooms. Prices at The Manor are $75–$135 per night plus 15 percent service charge; and a housekeeping cottage is $850 per week. Rates at The Holiday House are $95–$115 per night plus 15 percent service charge.

DINING OUT   Castine Inn (326-4365), Main Street. Open daily for breakfast and dinner. The ambience, quality, and value of this dining room is well known locally, filling it most nights. Crabmeat cakes in mustard sauce are a specialty, available either as an appetizer ($4.50) or main course ($13). Poached salmon with asparagus, egg sauce, and salmon caviar ($17) is a real treat but it's no hardship to settle for the chicken and leek pot pie ($12.50) or fettucini with mussels, sun-dried tomatoes, basil, and garlic ($12.50). The menu changes frequently but always features local seafood and produce. A mural of Castine by innkeeper/artist Margaret Parker Hodesh, wraps around all four walls of the room, punctuated by windows and French doors, overlooking the inn's spectacular garden.

Pentagoet Inn (326-8616), Main Street. Open April to January, dinner by reservation. Lindsey and Virginia Miller have expanded and brightened the dining room. Chowder and lobsters are staples of the frequently changing dinner menu. There is an extensive wine list. Dinner at 7 PM. $35 prix fixe.

EATING OUT   Dennett's Wharf (326-4861), Sea Street (off the town dock). Open daily spring through fall for lunch and dinner. Boasts "Maine's largest seafood selection" and "the world's largest oyster bar." An open-framed, waterside building said to have been built as a bowling alley after the Civil War. Exotic and raw seafood are the specialties (sea urchins, periwinkles, cockles, soft-shelled clams, four types of oysters, and horseshoe crabs); also smoked fish and seafood pasta salads, a seafood market, and outdoor dining.

Gilley's (326-4001), Water Street. Open for lunch and dinner. A cozy, low-beamed dining room with fish tanks and wooden booths. Homemade soups such as scallop stew and baked onion; fresh seafood and steak dinners.

Village Pizza (326-4047), Water Street. Open daily, all day. Loved locally: calzones and fresh dough pizzas are the specialty; beer, wine, and natural juices. A good spot for breakfast.

The Breeze (326-9034), town dock. Seasonal. When the summer sun shines, this is the best place in town to eat: fried clams, hot dogs, onion rings, and soft ice cream. The public facilities are next door and, with luck, you can dine at the picnic tables on the dock.

ENTERTAINMENT   Cold Comfort Productions (326-9041), PO Box 259. A resident company performs a series of popular productions from early July through late August. Performances are either in Emerson Hall on Court Street or at the Maine Maritime Dock Area.

SELECTIVE SHOPPING   Water Witch (326-4884), Main Street. Jean de Raat sells original designs made from Dutch Java batiks, English paisley prints, and Maine-made woolens.

Four Flags Ship Chandlery (326-8526). Nautical gear and fancy perfumes, soaps, and cards. Overlooks the harbor; a pleasant place to browse through maritime books. An eclectic selection of gifts.

Compass Rose (326-9366), Main Street. A fully stocked bookstore with a large selection of children's titles; specializing in summer reading, regional titles, and Penguin classics.

McGrath Dunham Gallery (326-4798), Main Street. Features a variety of New England artists.

Oakum Bay Ltd. (326-8786), Main Street. This gallery specializes in contemporary crafts: quilts, pewter, decoys, and paintings.

French Creek Decoy Shop (326-9033), Main Street. Accomplished decoy artist Chris Murray maintains a shop behind his house. He sells the highly detailed birds for which he is known (and the books and tools necessary for making them) and conducts classes in carving.

The Blue Hill Area

In Maine "Blue Hill" refers to a specific hill, a village, a town, a peninsula—and also to an unusual gathering of artists, musicians, and craftspeople.

The high, rounded hill overlooks Blue Hill Bay. The white wooden village is graced with no fewer than 75 buildings on the National Historic Register: old mansions, an 1840s academy, a fine town hall, a busy music hall, two gourmet restaurants, some lively cafés, a half-dozen galleries, and two potteries.

Blue Hill is a shade off the beaten path, one peninsula west of Mount Desert and nowhere near a beach. But it always has had its own following—especially among craftspeople, artists, musicians, and writers.

Most tourists whiz on by up Route 1 to Mount Desert and few stray as far off the beaten track as the village of Blue Hill, let alone ever explore Deer Isle, attached to the southern tip of the Deer Isle Peninsula by Maine's most amazing bridge. The peninsula itself wanders off in all directions and a number of its villages, although technically linked to the mainland by causeways and villages, retain the atmosphere of islands.

Follow narrow roads through the countless land fingers around Blue Hill, searching out the studios of local craftspeople and artists. What you remember afterwards is the beauty of clouds over fields of bachelor's buttons; quiet coves; the beauty of things woven, painted, and blown; and conversations with the people who made them.

GUIDANCE A map/guide is available from PO Box 520, Blue Hill 04614 or by calling the Liros Gallery: 374-5370.

GETTING THERE Follow directions to Castine (see Getting There in Castine chapter), but turn off Route 1 onto Route 15 south instead of Route 175 (it's between Orland and East Orland).

MEDICAL EMERGENCY **Blue Hill Memorial Hospital** (374-2836), the largest facility in the area, has a 24-hour emergency room.

TO SEE AND DO (Also see Kneisel Hall Chamber Music Festival and Bagaduce Linding Library under Entertainment.)

Jonathan Fisher Memorial (374-2459), Route 15. Open Tuesdays and Fridays 2–5; Saturdays 10–12. A house built in 1814 by Blue Hill's first pastor, a Harvard graduate who augmented his meager salary with a varied line of crafts and by teaching (he founded Blue Hill Academy), farming, and writing. His furniture, paintings, books, journals, and woodcuts are exhibited.

Holt House, Water Street. Open during July and August, Tuesdays and Fridays 1–4. The Blue Hill Historical Society collection is housed in this restored Federal-era mansion noted for its stenciled walls. The annual quilt show is held here.

Blue Hill Library (374-5515), Main Street. Open daily except Sundays. A handsome WPA project building with periodicals and ample reading space; changing art shows in summer.

Merrill House, Route 172, Sedgwick (1 mile north of the village, opposite Sedgwick Town House). Open July and August, 2–4. A 1795 house displaying one-man shows, prints, paintings, books, and artifacts. (Also see Selective Shopping [Galleries].)

BOATBUILDING **Wooden Boat School** (259-4651), PO Box 78, Brooklin 04616. A spinoff from *Wooden Boat Magazine,* a seafaring institute in its own right offering 77 summer courses, ranging from navigation to boatbuilding to sailing. Some 700 students enroll during Maine's 18 warmest weeks.

CANOEING   **Reversing falls** at South Blue Hill and the area between Snow Cove and the Bagaduce Estuary in Brooksville are popular with canoeists and kayakers. A 15-mile flatwater run is possible between Walker Pond in Brooksville and Castine. Sea kayaks can be rented from **Explorers at Sea** (367-2356), Stonington.

SAILING   *Haraka* (326-8839), a 43-foot, teak-decked yacht, based in Bucks Harbor, is available for day and overnight sails, also longer cruises.

WALKS   **Holbrook Island Sanctuary** is a state wildlife sanctuary of more than 1,230 acres, accessible by car only from North or South Brooksville. No camping is permitted, but there is a lovely picnic area adjacent to a pebble beach as well as hiking trails.

INNS   *In Blue Hill:* **Blue Hill Inn** (374-2844), near the junction of Main Street and Route 177, Blue Hill 04614. Open year-round. A classic 1830s inn within walking distance of downtown shops but on a quiet, elm-lined street. There are 11 guest rooms, some with sitting rooms and/or working fireplaces, all with antiques and private baths. Public rooms are also furnished with antiques and oriental rugs. In good weather guests gather for cocktails in the garden. A number of Kneisel Hall concerts (see To See and Do) are performed here in the course of the summer. A full breakfast, six-course candlelight dinner, and hors d'oeuvres are included in $90–$125 single, $120–$160 double plus 15 percent service charge. Rental bikes are available.

John Peters Inn (374-2116), Peters Point, Blue Hill 04614. The main house is open May through October but rooms in the Carriage House are available year-round. An imposing mansion, a fantasy place with columns and airy, superbly furnished rooms (six with fireplaces) is set on 25 shorefront acres, a mile from the center of town. Guest rooms offer great views, private baths; some have outside decks, and two have kitchens. There's a glassed-in breakfast room, a pool, and lawns sloping down to the water. $80–$125 includes an ambitious breakfast and gratuity. No children under age 12.

Surry Inn (667-5091), PO Box 25, Route 172, Surry 04684. Open year-round. The main house, which dates from 1834, once served steamship passengers. There are 13 guest rooms, 11 with private baths, and 3 living rooms with fireplaces plus a 60-foot glassed-in porch. The grounds slope to a private beach on Contention Cove. Facilities include croquet, horseshoes, a canoe, and a rowboat. The dining room (see Dining Out) is open to the public. $48–$62 plus 12 percent service includes full breakfast.

Blue Hill Farm (374-5126), Box 437, Blue Hill 04614. Open year-round. An attractive old farmhouse on 48 acres with a trout pond. The barn is now a combination breakfast area and lounge with seven small guest rooms upstairs, each with a private bath. Seven more old-fashioned guest rooms in the house itself include one appealing single, and they share baths. There are also comfortable common rooms, one with a woodstove; $58–$68 double includes breakfast.

Elsewhere on the Blue Hill Peninsula: **The Lookout** (359-2188), Flye Point (2 miles off Route 175), North Brooklin 04661. This classic old summer hotel has a spectacular view of Herrick Bay on one side and the Acadia Range on Mount Desert beyond Blue Hill Bay on the other. It has been in the same family for 200 years and an inn since 1891 (when the farmhouse was enlarged). The restaurant is esteemed locally (see Dining Out). Rooms are upstairs; a few cottages are equipped with kitchenettes; available weekly and monthly. Rates are reasonable. Phone for information.

Buck's Harbor Inn (326-8660), Box 268, South Brooksville 04617. Open year-round. Technically in the town of South Brooksville but really smack in the middle of the delightful yachting center of Buck's Harbor. A mansard-roofed building with six bedrooms, two and a half baths, and pleasant common rooms. The dining room is open to the public November to April 1 on Saturday nights, and in summer the neighboring Landing Restaurant (see Dining Out) offers fine food and views. We like the feel of this place, from the sea-bright rooms to the glass-faced breakfast room; a full breakfast features fresh fruit. From $40 single, $50 double; $60 for the suite with an attached room, ideal for a family with one child.

Breezemere Farm (326-8628), Box 290, South Brooksville 04617. Open May through October. An 1850 farmhouse with six rooms and seven cottages, four with kitchens. On a clear day the view is of Orcutt Harbor, and there are 60 acres to roam. Extras include bikes, a beach, boats (including a Daysailer). Rooms are $70–$85 per night; cottages are $600–$800 per week.

Rockmeadow Farm (326-4124), Brooksville 04617. A nineteenth-century farm overlooking Walker's Pond. Four guest rooms, each with a private entrance and a fireplace; the bath is shared. $38–$75 depending on the seasons; $114–$155 for the whole house (sleeps 12).

RUSTIC RESORTS   Hiram Blake Camp (326-4951), Cape Rosier, Harborside PO 04642. Open mid-May to mid-October. Well off the beaten track and celebrating in 1991 its 75th season in the same family, this is the kind of place you come to stay put. All of the cottages are situated within 200 feet of the shore with views of Penobscot Bay. There are six one-bedroom cottages, five with two bedrooms, and three with three bedrooms; each has a living room with a woodburning stove; some have a fireplace as well. Each has a kitchen, a shower, and a porch. Guests with housekeeping cottages cook for themselves in the four shoulder months, but in July and August everyone dines in the dining room, which doubles as a library because thousands of books are ingeniously filed away by category in the ceiling. There are rowboats at the dock, a playground, and a recreation room with table tennis, and board games; also ample hiking trails (see Walks). The camp is run by the children, grandchildren, and great-grandchildren of Captain Hiram Blake, who founded it in 1916. $540 for a family of four in a two-bedroom cottage MAP; $100 per extra adult, $50 per extra child; $200–$500 for a three-bedroom cottage during "housekeeping months."

Oakland House (359-8521), Herricks, Sargentville 04673. Open May to late October. A picturesque old place with a mansard roof, run by Jim and Sylvia Littlefield as it was by Jim's forebears back to 1889. His family has been living on this choice piece of property by Eggemoggin Reach since 1776. Meals are served in the delightful old dining room, but there are no longer any guest rooms upstairs. Instead there are 16 cottages (each different, all with water views, and many with living rooms and fireplaces) scattered over the property, each accommodating four to six people. There is also a 10-room guest house. The resort caters to families with children. There is swimming at a private lake beach, also sailing, deep-sea fishing, badminton, croquet, and a choice of hiking trails. Dinner is served between 6 and 7 (liquor is not allowed in the dining room), and the fixed entrée varies with the night: roast beef on Saturday, turkey on Sunday, and always a lobster picnic on Thursday. All three meals are large. Three-fourths of the guests here are repeaters. $378–$609 per adult per week depending on the accommodation and season; children's prices vary from free to two-thirds, depending on age. Housekeeping cottages in the four shoulder months (when the dining room is closed) are $225–$475; the 10-room house is $950.

DINING OUT   Firepond (374-2135), Main Street. Open Memorial Day through December, dinner nightly 5–9:30. This village restaurant is exceedingly popular, with reason, and reservations are a must. Try for a table on the porch, within earshot of an old mill stream (and don't forget a sweater). The specialties are delicately flavored veal, lamb, and sea-food dishes, also roast duckling with mangoes and ginger, and tournedos with roquefort and lingonberries. $12–$19.

Jonathan's (374-5226), Main Street. Open daily for lunch and dinner. Two pleasant dining rooms. The menu is large and features seafood, local produce, and products made in imaginative ways. The specialty of the house is shrimp flavored with ouzo and feta cheese on linguini. The wine list is extensive. Dinner entrées come with soup, vegetable, and French bread. $11.50–$16.50.

Surry Inn (667-5091), Route 172, Contention Cove, Surry. Open nightly for dinner. The dining room overlooks the cove, and the often-changing menu includes a choice of interesting soups—maybe Hungarian mushroom or sweet and sour cabbage. A choice of veal, chicken, pork, seafood, and fish. On a given night you might choose between veal marsala, mako shark, or scallops Nicoise. Desserts include chocolate Grand Marnier mousse and Creole applesauce-rum cake. $12–$17.

The Blue Hill Inn (374-2844), Union Street, Blue Hill. Dinner to non-guests is by reservation only but the candlelit dining room is large enough and the fare ambitious enough to encourage dinner patrons. The set $35 prix fixe menu changes nightly. It might be hazelnut and morel soup, then crabmeat garnished with lemon and capers, followed by a Cointreau sorbet. The entrée might be rack of lamb or sea scallops, then strawberries Romanoff.

The Landing Restaurant (326-9445), Buck's Harbor, South Brooksville. Open May to October, Tuesday through Saturday from 3 PM. Chef/owner Fred Channell has established a reputation for pleasant dining. The restaurant overlooks the area's most scenic yachting harbor (you can sail in) and features local fish and produce, breads and desserts made daily, vegetarian and children's menu. Moderately priced.

The Lookout (359-2188), Flye Point (2 miles off Route 175), North Brooklin. Seasonal. Open for dinner 6–9; Sunday brunch. Great views, fresh fish and seafood, traditional American fare, great desserts. Moderate.

EATING OUT   The Left Bank (374-2201), Route 172, Blue Hill. Open daily 7 AM–10 PM. Arnold Greenberg presides over an array of tantalizing things he's baked—from onion and peasant breads to delicate strudels. There are also full-bodied soups, freshly picked salads, and reasonably priced dinners like mushroom bean stroganoff or apricot chicken. Folk, jazz, blues, and chamber music are performed frequently.

Sarah's Shoppe, Main Street. Open 7–9 daily. A snug little restaurant that features blueberry pancakes for breakfast, homemade soup du jour and quiche for lunch, and broiled garlic shrimp and steamed crabmeat for dinner.

Pie in the Sky (374-5570), Mill Street, Blue Hill. Open daily for lunch and dinner: pizzas, calzones, and subs from $2.60 to $5.40. Four sizes of pizza—and it's good.

Phillips Gallery and Cafe (374-2711), Main Street. Open 9:30–4:30. Eat on the deck or in the gallery which features paintings, photographs, and handcrafted jewelry. The specialties are broccoli quiche ($4.95) and a selection of pies, cakes, and sweets.

Bagaduce Lunch, Route 176, North Brooksville (at the Reversing Falls). A great spot with picnic tables by the river and delicious fried clams. One of THE best snack bars Down East.

The Harbor View at The Landing, Buck's Harbor. Sandwiches, chowder, soups, ice cream; picnic tables overlooking the yachting harbor.

The Country View, Route 15, Sedgwick. Fried clams, crab rolls, picnic tables. Touristed and not much of a view but a handy way stop.

Benjamin's Pantry, Sedgwick, next to the post office. Open 6:30 AM to 1:30 PM. Breakfast specials include biscuits, blueberry pancakes or muffins, cinnamon rolls, and pie. Homemade soup, sandwiches, and specials such as meatloaf or sweet and sour pork for lunch; omelets and rootbeer floats all day.

Morning Moon Cafe (359-2373), Brooklin. An old-fashioned local place featuring traditional American fare. Open daily 7 AM–2 PM except Mondays and for dinner Thursday through Sunday from 5–8 PM.

ENTERTAINMENT *Music:* **Kneisel Hall Chamber Music Festival** (374-2811), PO Box 648, Blue Hill 04614. Faculty and students at this prominent old summer school for string and ensemble music present a series of Sunday afternoon and Friday evening concerts, early July through mid-August.

Bagaduce Lending Library (374-5454), Blue Hill. Open Tuesdays through Fridays 10–3; houses thousands of copies of printed music.

WERU, a non-profit community radio station based in Blue Hill Falls (89.9–FM), is known for jazz and reggae. It's based in the former hen house on Route 175, which is owned by Paul Stookey (of Peter, Paul and Mary fame). It also houses Northeast Historic Film, the region's only "moving image" archives, source of the silent Maine-made films which are staged periodically around town.

Theater: **New Surry Theater** (374-5057), a local repertory group, usually stages four plays during July and August in the Blue Hill Town Hall.

SELECTIVE SHOPPING *Craft shops and art galleries:* **Rowantrees Pottery** (374-5535), Union Street. Open year-round, daily in summer (weekdays 7–5, Saturdays from 8:30, and Sundays from 12) and on weekdays in winter (7–3:30). Find your way back behind the friendly white house into the large studio. It was a conversation with Mahatma

Rowantrees Pottery in Blue Hill

Gandhi in India that got Adelaide Pearson going on the idea of pottery in Blue Hill by using local craftsmen and glazes gathered from the town's abandoned copper mines, quarries, and bogs. Fifty years later Sheila Varnum continues to make the deeply colored glazes from local granite and feldspar. She invites visitors to watch tableware being hand-thrown and to browse through the upstairs showroom filled with plates, cups, vases, and jam pots.

Rackliffe Pottery (374-2297), Route 172. Open Monday through Saturday 9–5; also Sunday afternoons. Phyllis and Phil Rackliffe worked at Rowantrees for 22 years before establishing their own business. They also use local glazes and their emphasis is on individual small pieces rather than on sets. Visitors are welcome to watch.

Cole House Quilts (374-2175), 10 Union Street. Open June through September, Monday through Saturday 10–5. A gallery-like setting for art-quality quilts featuring Amish and Mennonite designs plus local crafts.

Leighton Gallery (374-5001), Parker Point Road. Open June to October. Exhibits in the two-floor gallery change every few weeks but there are some striking staples: Judith Leighton's own bright oils; the wonderful variety of sculpted shapes in the garden out back; and the unforgettable wooden animal carvings by local sculptor Eliot Sweet.

Handworks Gallery (374-5613), Main Street. Open Memorial Day to mid-October, Monday through Saturday 10–5 and Friday until 8. An upstairs, middle-of-town space filled with unusual handwoven clothing, jewelry, furniture, rugs, and blown glass.

Liros Gallery (374-5370), Main Street. A long-established gallery specializing in fine paintings, old prints, maps, Russian icons, and restoration.

Jud Hartman Gallery and Sculpture Studio (374-9917), Main Street. Changing exhibits complementing Jud Hartman's own realistic bronze sculptures of Northeastern Indians.

Other shops: **Blue Hill Tea & Tobacco Shop** (374-2161), Main Street. Open Monday through Saturday 10–5:30. An appealing shop dedicated to the perfect cup of tea or coffee, well-chosen wine, and the right blend of tobacco.

Blue Hill Yarn Shop (374-5631), Route 172 north. Open Monday through Saturday 10–4. A mecca for knitters in search of a wide variety of wools and needles. Lessons and original hand knits are sold.

Blue Hill Books (374-5632), 2 Pleasant Street (two doors up from the post office). A full-service, two-story bookstore that also sells greeting cards.

Galleries, studios, and crafts shops beyond Blue Hill: **David Larson Gallery,** Route 175, South Penobscot (upstairs over North Country Textiles). Open summer months, Monday through Saturday 10–5. The varied work of one man: sculpture, aquatints, paintings.

North Country Textiles (326-4131), Route 175, South Penobscot. Open summer months. A partnership of three designer/weavers: Sheila Denny-Brown, Carole Ann Larson, and Ron King. The shop displays jackets and tops, mohair throws, guest towels, and coasters, all in bright colors and irresistible textures.

Scott Goldberg Pottery, Route 176, Brooksville. Open daily May to October. Scott Goldberg and Jeff Oestreich display their own stoneware pottery as well as work by others.

Gail Disney (326-4649), Route 176 between South Brooksville and Brooksville Corners. Visitors are welcome year-round. Handwoven cotton and wool rag rugs, custom made.

Janet Redfield (326-4778), Harborside. One more reason to find the Cape Rosier Road (it's off Route 176 just north of South Brooksville). Exceptional stained glass: lampshades, planters, windows. Call to make sure someone's home.

Other shops beyond Bue Hill: **Golden Stairs** (326-4369), Buck's Harbor, South Brooksville. A combination Johnson Outboard dealer and gift shop with an unusually varied stock; nicely sited above a pebbly beach.

H.O.M.E. (469-7961), Route 1, Orland. Open daily in-season, 9–5. An organization dedicated to reclaiming exploited land and developing the skills of Maine's rural poor. Virtually a crafts village with weaving and pottery demonstrations on the premises and a big store that sells thousands of items made in Maine.

SPECIAL EVENTS Mid-July: **Full Circle Summer Fair**, sponsored by WERU-FM, the stress is on everything natural and on crafts.

Last weekend in July: **Blue Hill Days.** Arts and crafts fair, parade, farmers' market, antique car rally, shore dinner, boat races.

August: **St. Francis Annual Summer Fair.**

Labor Day weekend: **Blue Hill Fair,** at the fairgrounds. Harness racing, a midway, livestock competitions; one of the most colorful old-style fairs in New England.

December: a weekend of Christmas celebrations.

Deer Isle, Stonington, and Isle au Haut

The narrow, soaring suspension bridge across Eggemoggin Reach connects the Blue Hill Peninsula with a series of wandering land fingers linked by causeways and bridges. These are known collectively as "The Island" or "Deer Isle" and include the towns of Deer Isle and Stonington and the villages of Sunset and Sunshine, site of the nationally respected Haystack Mountain School of Crafts. A number of prominent craftspeople have come here to teach or study—and stayed. Galleries in the resort village of Deer Isle display outstanding work by dozens of artists and craftspeople who live, or at least summer, in town. Stonington, by contrast, remains a working fishing harbor, little changed since John Marin painted it in the '50s. Its buildings are perched around the harbor on the smooth, pink granite rocks for which the town is famous, and its many-colored houses are hedged with flowers. The whole town resembles a giant rock garden. The harbor is filled with lobster boats, not pleasure craft. But windjammers put in regularly now, and sea kayaks are increasing. By the same token the waterfront includes a weathered sardine-and-shrimp-packing plant, a boat yard, a lobster co-op, and some unexpectedly fine shopping.

The inns, studios, and natural sights salted through Deer Isle are excuses to explore its myriad beautiful coves and corners. Isle au Haut, accessible by mailboat from Stonington, is a glorious place to walk trails maintained by the National Park Service.

GUIDANCE **Deer Isle–Stonington Chamber of Commerce** (348-6124) maintains a seasonal information booth on Route 15 at Little Deer Isle, just this side of the bridge.

The *Annual Bay Community Register,* listing some useful touring information, is available from Penobscot Bay Press (367-2200), Box 36, Stonington 04681. The press also publishes *Island Advantages* and the *Weekly Packet*—sources of what's going on.

GETTING THERE Follow directions to Castine, but continue on Route 1 to Orland and take Route 15 on down through Blue Hill to Deer Isle.

MEDICAL EMERGENCY **Island Medical Center** (367-2311), Airport Road, Stonington. (Also see Blue Hill.)

TO SEE AND DO   **Haystack Mountain School of Crafts** (348-2306), Deer Isle (south of Deer Isle Village, turn left off Route 15 at the Gulf gas station; follow signs 7 miles). Mid-June through Labor Day three-week sessions are offered, attracting some of the country's top artisans in a variety of crafts. Phone to check when visitors are welcome to view craftsmen at work and to see their work displayed; also to attend evening concerts and lectures.

Salome Sellers House, Route 15A, Sunset. Open July to Labor Day, Wednesdays and Fridays 2–5. This is the home of the Deer Isle–Stonington Historical Society, an 1830 house displaying ships models, American Indian artifacts, and old photos; interesting and friendly.

BOAT EXCURSIONS   *The Miss Lizzie* (367-5193). Operates June to mid-September and departs from the Atlantic Avenue Hardware dock at 2:30; one-and-a-half-hour cruise among the islands of Penobscot Bay. $9 per adult, $4.50 per child under age 10.

Palmer Day IV (367-2207). Seasonal 2 PM sailings. Captain Reginald Greenlaw offers cruises of Penobscot Bay. $9 per adult, $5 per child under age 10. Longer excursions to Vinalhaven and North Haven are also offered.

Mail Boat to Isle au Haut (367-5193) departs Stonington at least twice daily except Sunday year-round. During summer months a ranger meets the boat at Duck Harbor to orient passengers to the seven hiking trails, the picnic area, and drinking water sources (otherwise a pamphlet guide serves this purpose).

Be sure to check the schedule, and in July and August come as early as possible for the first ferry. The boat tends to fill up and it's first-come, first-served; if you miss the first boat, you can at least make a later one.

The Eagle Island Mailboat (348-2817) leaves Sylvester's Cove in Sunset, daily in-season.

GOLF AND TENNIS   **Island Country Club** (348-2379) in Deer Isle welcomes guests mid-June to Labor Day; nine holes.

SAILING   **Sailways** (367-5909 or 348-2279), Fiefield Point Road (off Sandbeach Road), Deer Isle. Charter by half-day, day, or week, with or without crew; private lessons, children's lessons, nine sloops and a Laser.

SEA KAYAKING   **Explorers at Sea Incorporated** (367-2356), PO Box 51, Main Street, Stonington. May through September, half-day to nine-day "instructional adventures." A half-day geared to beginners is $50 and a full day is $75; multi-day trips include camping on islands. Stonington's isle-specked harbor is favored by kayakers and makes a great place to learn the sport. Gary Atkinson also sells kayaking equipment.

WALKS   **Ames Pond,** east of town on Indian Point Road, is a pond full of pink-and-white water lilies in bloom June to early September.

Holt Mill Pond Preserve. A walk through unspoiled woodland and marsh. The entrance is on Stonington Cross Road (Airport Road)—look for a sign several hundred feet beyond the medical center. Park on the shoulder and walk the dirt road to the beginning of the trail, then follow the yellow signs.

Isle au Haut. Isle au Haut (pronounced *eelaho*) is 6 miles long and 3 miles wide; all of it is private except for the 2,800 acres of national park that are wooded and webbed with hiking trails. More than half the island is preserved as part of Acadia National Park (see Bar Harbor). Camping is forbidden anywhere except in the five Adirondack-style shelters at Duck Harbor (each accommodating six people) that are available through reservations only. To secure one write on or as near to April 1 as possible to Acadia National Park, RFD 1, Box 1, Bar Harbor 04609; send $5, good for a stay of up to three days in summer, up to five days in spring or fall. For more about day-trips to the island see Boat Excursions.

Crockett Cove Woods (a Maine Nature Conservancy property) comprises 100 acres along the water with a nature trail. Take Route 15 to Deer Isle, then the Sunset Road; 2.5 miles beyond the post office bear right onto Whitman Road; a right turn at the end of the road brings you to the entrance, marked by a small sign and registration box.

Barred Island Preserve is a 2-acre island just off Stinson Point, accessible by a wide sandbar; request permission for access from Goose Cove Lodge (see Rustic Resort).

RUSTIC RESORT   Goose Cove Lodge (348-2508), Sunset 04683. Open mid-May to mid-October, but dinner is served mid-June to mid-September only. One-week minimum stay during July and August. Situated on a secluded cove, this lodge is popular with families, hikers, and bird-watchers. Guests sleep in cabins and in two annexes to the main lodge, all different but simply furnished, most with fridges. The dining room has a fine water view and a great central fireplace. There in no choice of dinner entrée, but complaints are rare. A hearty, freshly made soup is followed by a main course of roast beef, baked salmon, leg of lamb, or perhaps veal fricassee. Desserts are homemade. Children dine early while adults gather for hors d'oeuvres in the living room, and after dinner guests regroup for a movie, music, a lecture, or a slide-show, often staged by other guests. There is swimming at the private beach and hiking on Barred Island. Weekly rates, which include breakfast and dinner each day, are $410–$525 per person MAP; children's rates, off-season room and cottage rates; add 10 percent service charge.

INNS   Pilgrim's Inn (348-6615), Deer Isle 04627. Open mid-May through mid-October. Squire Ignatius Haskell built this house in 1793 for his wife, who came from Newburyport, Massachusetts, and demanded an elegant home. The story goes that he built the house in Newburyport and had it shipped up to Deer Isle, where it stands in the middle of the village overlooking Northwest Harbor and his mill pond. Of the 13 guest rooms just 8 have private baths, but all have water views and most have a fireplace. Downstairs there are four common rooms and a dining room in the old barn, known for its gourmet fare. Eighteenth-century colors predominate, and the inn is furnished throughout with carefully chosen curtains and rugs, antiques, and local art (much of it for sale). $65 single MAP plus 12 percent gratuity; the one-bedroom cottage up the street is $120 EP, $180 double MAP. Weekly rates are also available.

The Keeper's House (367-2261), PO Box 26, Isle au Haut 04645. Open May through October. Jeff and Judi Burke have turned the lighthouse keeper's home on this scenic island into a small inn with six guest rooms and a cottage. No electricity, no phones; shared baths or use of an outhouse; $225 double includes three meals.

OTHER LODGING   **The Inn at Ferry Landing** (348-7760), Old Ferry Road, RR 1, Box 163, Deer Isle 04627. Overlooking Eggemogin Reach, an 1850s seaside farmhouse with magnificent views, spacious rooms, patchwork quilts, a great common room with huge bay windows. There are seven guest rooms, $50–$75; $90 for the "queen suite" with great water views. A full breakfast included.

Captain's Quarters Inn and Motel (367-2420), Stonington 04681. Open year-round. A lineup of several waterfront buildings creatively renovated into 15 suites and housekeeping units, a coffee shop, a gift shop, and a gallery. You can buy lobsters at the co-op, boil them in your room, and eat them on the deck overlooking the harbor. The brochure includes floor plans and rates for each room. Both #10 and #11 have working fireplaces. Coffee and muffins are included in $36–$80 per unit in-season; $20–$50 in winter. The complex is accessible by water; both pets and children are welcome. Guests receive a 10 percent discount on meals at the Bay View Restaurant, under the same ownership (see Eating Out).

Ocean View House (367-5114), Main Street, Box 261, Stonington 04681. Open July and August only. A Victorian inn set on a knoll near the dock, built to board quarry workers employed on Crotch Island. Midwesterners Christine and Jack Custer have created bright, cheerful rooms; the three guest rooms share baths, but all have bay views. $50 per room; breakfast of homemade pastries.

Pres du Port (367-5007), Box 319, Stonington 04681. Open July and August only—a find. An unusually cheery, comfortable B&B with harbor views. Charlotte Casgrain is a warm, locally knowledgeable hostess who enjoys speaking French. Moderately priced.

Holden Homestead (348-6832), Route 15, Deer Isle. Open seasonally. Formerly a church parsonage. Host Cynthia Bancroft Melnikas is a fifth-generation Holden. The breakfast buffet features blueberry muffins along with gourmet coffees. $35 single, $40–$45 double, $60 for the suite.

Eggemoggin Inn (348-2540), Little Deer Isle 04650. Open spring through fall. Built as a summer estate in 1906 with a sweeping view of

Eggemoggin Reach. Sophie Broadhead has maintained it as an inn since 1964. The seven guest rooms are spread over the top two floors and vary in size. Our family of five has slept comfortably in the largest, which has a sun deck and view. Mid-June through late September rates are $45–$65 double; $10 per extra cot. Continental breakfast included.

Laphroaig B&B (348-6088), Deer Isle Village 04627. Open year-round. This 1850s house in the village of Deer Isle offers two two-room suites, one with a sitting room and the other with a study. $50 single, $60 double, includes a full breakfast featuring local seafood. Handicapped accessible; box lunch and dinner available; no smoking, no children, weekly rates.

King's Row Inn (348-7781), Box 426, Deer Isle Village 04627. A very Victorian sea captain's house set high on a hill overlooking the water. Kate Olson offers six guest rooms, all with water views and furnished with Victorian antiques, some private baths. From $75 double to $100 for the suite; continental breakfast is served in the conservatory. No smoking and no children.

MOTEL   **Beachcomber Motel** (348-6115), Little Deer Isle 04650. Open Memorial Day weekend through September. If you must stay at a motel, this one is beautifully sited—just beyond the unusual Deer Isle Bridge, overlooking Eggemoggin Reach. Nancy and Butch Soo Hoo pride themselves on the cleanliness of the 20 rooms; facilities include a small beach and a restaurant. $36–$48.

CAMPING   **Small's Trailer & Camp Sites** (367-2497), Sunset Road, Deer Isle 04627. Open May 30 to October 1. Although we do not usually include commercial campgrounds, this one is special. Just 15 sites, 7 with hookups, all with picnic tables and fireplaces, handy to Crockett's Cove.

DINING OUT   **Pilgrim's Inn** (348-6615), Main Street, Deer Isle Village 04627. Open mid-May to late October. Reservations only for single-seating dinner at 7, Friday through Wednesday. Fixed price of $25 for a five-course dinner, including hors d'oeuvres, served from 6 PM in the living room or on the deck. Meals begin with soup, then salad followed by an entrée that varies with the night, maybe halibut with artichokes and cream, poached salmon with beurre blanc, and paella. Produce is organically grown, and breads and desserts are baked daily. The dining room is a converted barn; tables are covered with checked tablecloths and lighted by candles.

Eaton's Lobster Pool Restaurant (348-2383). Seasonal. Monday through Saturday 5–9; Sunday 12–9. Be sure to order lobster à la carte and by the pound instead of the higher priced "lobster dinner." The restaurant is still in the family that settled the spot, and it is the area's premier lobster pound. It offers a full menu and a fine view. BYOB.

EATING OUT   **Fisherman's Friend Restaurant** (367-2442), School Street (just up the hill from the harbor). Open 11 AM to 9 PM. Simple decor but one of the best values in Maine: You can lunch on a superb chowder or crabmeat roll or dine handsomely on a mini-fisherman's platter for well under $10. Everything is fresh-caught and homemade.

Bayview Restaurant (367-2274), Sea Breeze Avenue (near the dock). Open mid-May to mid-October, daily 8 AM to 8 PM or later. A pleasant dining space with reasonably priced candlelight dinners featuring local seafood, broiled and baked as well as fried. BYOB.

Connie's Restaurant (367-2742), School Street. Open 7–7:30 daily. Upstaged by its competition but also good, serving fish and lobster caught by proprietor Barbara Bridge's husband and son; dine in or take out.

Rainbow's End (367-5806), Main Street, Stonington. Trendier than the other local eateries with lobster or crab croissants as well as a variety of subs and a dinner menu that includes lobster thermidor ($9.50). Our chowder wasn't the greatest, but the atmosphere was fine and we'd try again.

Austin Wood's Ice Cream, Main Street. Open May to December, 8 AM–9 PM. The ice cream is from Hancock County Creamery, and the view is of the harbor. Sandwiches are also available.

SELECTIVE SHOPPING   Pick up a current (free) copy of the "Maine Cultural Guide" published by the Maine Crafts Association. It covers all Maine but is produced locally and is helpful in tracking down the art galleries and crafts studios which are probably more plentiful here per capita than anywhere else in the state. It's available at most local galleries, also at its source: Ronald Pearson's studio (348-9943), 158 Old Ferry Road, Deer Isle.

Art galleries: **Deer Isle Artists Association,** Route 15, Deer Isle Village. Open mid-June to September. A series of four-person shows; members' exhibition every summer.

Turtle Gallery (348-2538), Deer Isle Village. Open June through September, Monday through Saturday (closed for lunch 12:30–2), and Sunday 2–4. One of Maine's top small galleries. A series of one-person shows: prints, paintings, sculpture, and photographs.

Joy Biddle Gallery (359-2114), High Street, Sedgwick. Open Wednesday through Sunday 10–5 in summer; by appointment year-round. Acrylic paintings of Maine and prints.

Crafts studios: **Eastern Bay Gallery** (367-5006), Main Street, Stonington. Open mid-May through Christmas, daily in summer and Tuesday in slow. This long-established and outstanding gallery sells works by more than 40 artists and craftsmen within a 50-mile radius. The space, filled with fine clothing, jewelry, pottery and such, overlooks the working harbor.

Pearson's Jewelry (348-2535), Old Ferry Road (off Route 15), Deer Isle. Ron Pearson has an international reputation for creative designs in gold and silver jewelry as well as delicately wrought table-top sculpture in other metals. From $22 for small silver earrings to $8,000 for a gold necklace. Wife Caroline Hecker handles sales and also serves as executive director of the Maine Craft Association. The shop also displays work by local blacksmith/sculptor Douglas Wilson.

The Weave Shop–Pottery (348-2883), Route 15, Deer Isle. Open 10–6. Ebba Hance weaves scarves, throws, and ponchos ($20–$100), also rugs; Charlie Hance makes earthtone pots, dinnerware, bowls, and household accessorie such as lamp bases, birdbaths, toothbrush holders, and flameproof earthenware cooking pots (safe on top of the stove; also freezer-to-oven).

Kathy Woell (348-6141), 156 Old Ferry Road, Deer Isle. Open Monday through Saturday 10–5. This home/studio is tucked away deep in the pines, filled with soft, vivid scarfs and hats, vests, jackets and coats—each one of a kind. "I put colors together. That's the gift I have," says Woell, a former painter who recently discovered weaving as her media at Haystack.

William Mor (348-2822), Reach Road, Deer Isle. Open mid-June through October. Hand-thrown pottery in interesting shapes, functional and handsome. Designs are based on Oriental folk pottery; the studio, kiln, and shop are in a garden setting.

The Blue Heron (348-6051), Route 15, Deer Isle (near the center of the village). An old barn is stocked with crafted gifts and clothing from around the world; also kitchen utensils, cookbooks, baskets, and boxes. A gallery, adjacent to the shop, features changing exhibits of crafted items.

Other shops: **Island Supply Co.** (367-5558), Main Street. Open daily June to September. Cotton sweaters from Greece, silk kimonos from Japan, and Indian skirts and tops. Natural fibers are the common denominator. Baskets, fabrics, and rugs are in the back room.

Gallery of the Purple Fish, Main Street, Stonington. Open when the windjammers are in port and otherwise by chance. Evelyn and Jan Kok maintain this weathered old waterside building (said to be a former fishermen's church) as a gallery, filled with paintings and wonderful clutter. Evelyn also hand inks bookmarks and cards.

Dockside, West Main Street. Seasonal. Elmer Webber's waterside bookstore has an exceptional selection of Maine and marine books; also gifts.

Dry Dock (367-5528), Main Street. Open Monday through Saturday in-season. Indian clothing, salt-glazed pottery, gourmet cooking utensils, children's books, and handmade toys.

Stonington Lobster Cooperative (367-2286), near the dock. Lobsters, shrimp, and scallops in-season; fishermen's supplies.

SPECIAL EVENTS   July: **Independence Day** parade and fireworks. **Lobster boat races** (mid-month).

August: **Stonington Fire Department auction.**

V. Down East

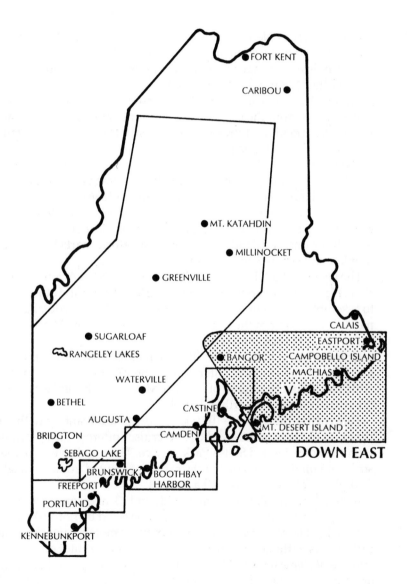

FORT KENT

CARIBOU

MT. KATAHDIN

MILLINOCKET

GREENVILLE

CALAIS

SUGARLOAF

EASTPORT

RANGELEY LAKES

CAMPOBELLO ISLAND

BANGOR

MACHIAS

WATERVILLE

V.

BETHEL

CASTINE

AUGUSTA

BRIDGTON

CAMDEN

MT. DESERT ISLAND

SEBAGO LAKE

DOWN EAST

BRUNSWICK

BOOTHBAY

FREEPORT

HARBOR

PORTLAND

KENNEBUNKPORT

Bar Harbor/Acadia Area

Mount Desert is New England's second-largest island, one conveniently linked to the mainland and laced with roads for touring by car plus 50 miles of carriage roads just for exploring by bike, horse, or skis, and another 120 miles of hiking paths.

Mount Desert's beauty cannot be overstated. Seventeen mountains rise abruptly from the sea, and the interior contains five large lakes, numberless ponds and streams, an unusual variety of flora and fauna, and more than 300 species of birds.

Named L'Isle de Monts Deserts by Samuel de Champlain in 1604 and settled in the eighteenth century, this remained a peaceful, out-of-the-way island even after a bridge was built in 1836 to connect it to the mainland. In the mid-nineteenth century, however, millionaires began arriving by steamboat. More than 200 grandiose summer cottages were built on the island by the time the stock market crashed. A number still survive, many as inns.

The legacy of Bar Harbor's wealthy "rusticators" is Acadia National Park. Harvard University president Charles W. Eliot and others began to assemble parcels of land that were donated to the federal government in 1916 to form the first national park east of the Mississippi. It is now a 35,000-acre preserve.

Unfortunately, most visitors limit their explorations to an introductory film in the visitors center and to the 27-mile Park Loop Road, which includes the summit of Cadillac Mountain, the highest point on the eastern seaboard north of Brazil.

Still, each summer some 100,000 visitors take advantage of the rich program of hikes, nature walks, and cruises offered during summer months by the United States Park Service. The number who actually strike out on their own (using the excellent printed guides available) find plenty of solitude as well as beauty.

Acadia National Park is 16 miles wide and 13 miles long, but it seems far larger, primarily because it is almost bisected by fjord-like Somes Sound. Bar Harbor is the big town: a jumble of motels, inns, shops, and restaurants within easy reach of the park visitors center on one hand and the *Bluenose* ferry to Nova Scotia on the other. The other villages are Northeast Harbor, Southwest Harbor, Seal Harbor, Somesville, and Bass Harbor, all small and sleepy by comparison with Bar Harbor

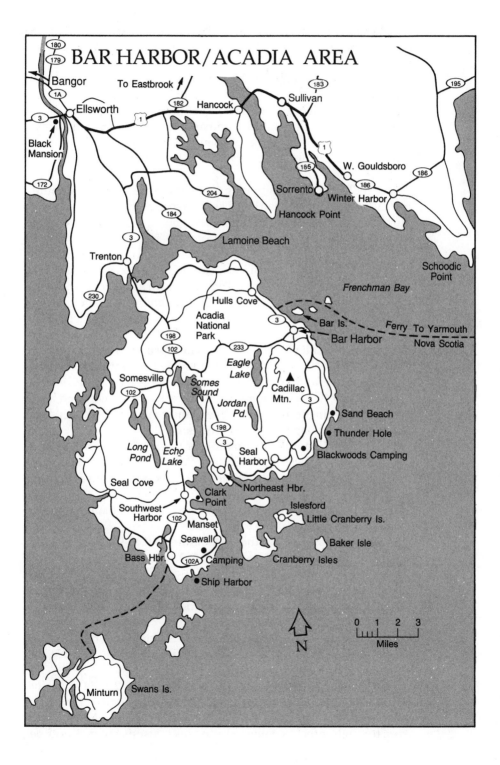

BAR HARBOR/ACADIA AREA

180
179
Bangor
1A
To Eastbrook
Ellsworth
182
Hancock
1
183
Sullivan
195
3
Black
Mansion
172
204
1
165
Sorrento
186
W. Gouldsboro
186
184
Hancock Point
Winter Harbor
Trenton
230
3
Lamoine Beach
Schoodic
Point
Hulls Cove
Frenchman Bay
Acadia
National
Park
198
3
Bar Is.
Ferry To Yarmouth
102
233
Bar Harbor
Nova Scotia
Eagle
Lake
Somesville
Somes
Sound
Cadillac
Mtn.
102
Jordan
Pd.
3
Long
Pond
Echo
Lake
198
3
Sand Beach
Thunder Hole
Seal
Harbor
Blackwoods Camping
Seal Cove
Clark
Point
Northeast Hbr.
Southwest
Harbor
102
Manset
Islesford
Little Cranberry Is.
Seawall
Baker Isle
Bass Hbr.
102A
Camping
Cranberry Isles
Ship Harbor

N
0 1 2 3
Miles

Minturn Swans Is.

but offering a far wider choice of places to stay, eat, and shop than just a few years ago. Northeast Harbor has become the region's showcase for art and fine crafts.

During July and August the island is expensive, crowded, and exquisite. Between Labor Day and Columbus Day it is cheaper, less crowded, and still beautiful. The rest of the year is off-season. If you take advantage of the solitude and bargains available in June (which tends to be rainy) or February (which can be spectacular if snow conditions permit cross-country skiing), be sure you have access to a fireplace.

East of Ellsworth, the shopping center for the eastern coast, Route 1 continues along Frenchman Bay. The most spectacular views of Cadillac Mountain and its pink-shouldered neighbors are actually enjoyed from the shore in Sullivan and from the Hancock and Schoodic peninsulas. Schoodic Point, with its own rewarding mountain to hike, is a part of Acadia National Park, and lodging places are scattered along the eastern rim of the bay. There are also a number of B&B hosts, who list with a local reservation service, and a number of rental cottages that are available at rates far below those commanded on Mount Desert.

GUIDANCE   (See also Acadia National Park.) **Thompson Island Information Center** (288-3411) is open daily May to late September (8–8 during high season) on Route 3, just after you cross the causeway. It is a walk-in center that offers rest rooms, national park information, and assistance with lodgings on all parts of the island. Staff members keep track of vacancies and help with reservations.

Bar Harbor Chamber of Commerce (year-round: 288-5103; seasonal: 288-3393), Box 158, 93 Cottage Street, Bar Harbor, maintains seasonal information booths. Write for the free booklet guide to sights and lodging.

Mount Desert Chamber of Commerce (276-5040) maintains a seasonal walk-in cottage at the town dock.

Southwest Harbor Chamber of Commerce (244-9264) maintains a seasonal information booth on Route 102.

Ellsworth Chamber of Commerce (667-5584 or 667-2617), 163 High Street, Ellsworth (in the Ellsworth Shopping Center; look for Burger King), also maintains a well-stocked, friendly information center.

GETTING THERE   By air: **Continental Express** (667-7171) services Hancock County Airport in Trenton (between Ellsworth and Bar Harbor). **Rental cars** are available at the airport. **Airport Taxi** (667-5995) also serves the island.

By boat: **Marine Atlantic *Bluenose* Ferry** (800-432-7344 in Maine; 800-341-7981 elsewhere in the continental United States) carries passengers and cars between Bar Harbor and Yarmouth, Nova Scotia, April through early December. The trip takes just six hours. $36.25 per adult, $18.15 per child aged 5–12 (in high season); cars, $67; cabins, extra. Service is daily, late June to late September, three times per week in the shoulder seasons and twice per week in winter.

By private boat: An amazing number of visitors arrive aboard their own yachts; contact the Mount Desert Chamber of Commerce (see Guidance) for details about moorings, or check with the Harbor Masters for Bar Harbor (288-5571), Northeast Harbor (276-5737), Seal Harbor (276-5823), Somesville (244-9282), or Southwest Harbor (244-5802). **Island Rent-A-Car** (276-3383) is based at Northeast Harbor.

Greyhound (667-8596) serves Bangor, and—with luck (some years it does and some it doesn't)—Bar Harbor.

By car: From Boston and New York there are two routes. One is via I-95 (the Maine Turnpike) to Bangor, then Route 1A to Ellsworth, and Route 3 to Mount Desert. The other takes you to Augusta on I-95, then Route 3 east to Bar Harbor. The latter has the edge on scenery and is our daytime preference (see Belfast to Bangor for details about a swim/break at Lake St. George State Park).

GETTING AROUND   Car rentals: Avis (667-5421), Hertz (667-5017), and U-Save Auto Rental (667-6130) are available at the airport.

Local ferries: **Beal and Bunker, Inc.** (244-3575), Northeast Harbor. Operates daily ferry service to the Cranberry Islands.

Swan's Island Ferry (244-3254), Bass Harbor. Daily ferry service to Swan's Island; service twice weekly to Frenchboro.

Water Taxi Service (244-5724) is available 24 hours to the Cranberry Islands, offered April to November by Capt. John Dwelley of Islesford.

Taxis: **Ralph Savage Taxi** (276-3249) offers local service.

National Park Tours (288-3327) offers narrated two-and-a-half-hour bus tours through Bar Harbor and along the Park Loop Road, daily in-season.

Oli's Trolley (288-9899). Narrated tours of Acadia National Park and Mount Desert Island.

MEDICAL EMERGENCY   **Mount Desert Island Hospital** (288-5081) provides 24-hour emergency care.

Southwest Harbor (244-5513).

Northeast Harbor (276-3331).

ACADIA NATIONAL PARK   The park maintains its own visitors center (288-5262 or 288-4932) at Hulls Cove, open early May to early November. From mid-June to August 31, hours are 8–6 daily; during shoulder seasons, hours are 8–4:30. The park headquarters at Eagle Lake (Route 233) is open daily throughout the winter from 8–4:30. For more information about the park, write to Superintendent, PO Box 177, Bar Harbor 04609. The glass and stone center, set atop 50 steps, shows its 15-minute **introductory film** every half hour. Books, guides, and postcards may be purchased here; an excellent AMC trail map/guide costs $5.95. This is also the place to pick up a free map and a copy of the current "Acadia's Beaver Log" (a listing of all naturalist activities) or to rent a cassette tape tour and to sign up for the various programs offered. **Special evening programs** are scheduled by the national park staff, nightly June through September, at the amphitheaters in Blackwoods and Seawall campgrounds.

Note that for the past few years an admission charge of $5 per car or $2 per hiker or biker has been levied at entrances to the 20-mile Park Loop Road, the prime tourist route within the park.

Sights within the park include the following:

Seiur de Monts Spring and the Robert Abbe Museum of Stone Age Antiquities (288-3519), open May to October, 9–5 daily during July and August, otherwise 10–4; posted from Route 3 and the Park Loop Road. Don't miss this exceptional collection of New England Indian artifacts: sweet grass baskets, moccasins, a birch bark canoe, dioramas of American Indian life during all seasons. You can walk in the **Wild Gardens of Acadia,** where more than 300 species of native plants are displayed and labeled. Museum admission, $1.25.

Sand Beach, Park Loop Road. The beach is really composed of minute shells. A great beach to walk—and to take a dip, if you don't mind 50-degree water; there are changing rooms and lifeguards. Take the time to walk the **Ocean Path** along the rocks.

Thunder Hole, Park Loop Road. The water rushes in and out of a small cave, which you can view from behind a railing. The adjacent rocks can keep small children scrambling for hours.

Cadillac Mountain, Park Loop Road. From the smooth summit you look out across Frenchman Bay dotted with islands that look like giant stepping-stones. This is a great spot for a picnic, so come prepared.

Ship Harbor, Route 102A (near Bass Harbor), offers a fine nature trail that winds along the shore and into the woods; it is also a great birding spot.

Cranberry Isles. Accessible by boat six times a day in-season; $6 per adult, $3 per child (round-trip). There are five islands of Northeast Harbor, accessible by regular mail launch, but most enjoyable when you come on naturalist-led trips to **Baker Island** or to the **Islesford Historical Museum** on **Little Cranberry Island** (open daily late June to late September, 9:45–4:30). The museum traces the area's history from 1604; there are some juicy smuggling stories told here about the War of 1812.

Schoodic Peninsula. More than an hour's drive from Bar Harbor, but the drive itself is rewarding because of spectacular views back across Frenchman Bay to Mount Desert. The tip of the Schoodic Peninsula is part of Acadia National Park; the one-way loop road begins beyond Winter Harbor. Look sharp (an unmarked left after the Frazier Point Picnic area) for the side road up to Schoodic Head. Park here and follow the short trail to the summit. The loop road leads to

Schoodic Point, where flocks of people feed bread to flocks of sea gulls. There are also flat, smooth rocks, ideal for clambering.

Isle au Haut. See Stonington, from which it is accessible on the mail boat. Roughly 6 by 2 miles, the island is heavily wooded with a 554-foot peak; half of the island is part of Acadia National Park. There are hiking trails and very limited camping by reservation only (see East Penobscot).

TO SEE AND DO **Asticou Azalea Gardens,** Route 3 (near the junction of Route 198), Northeast Harbor. A delightful place to stroll down windy paths and over ornamental bridges. Azaleas and Japanese-style plantings.

Jackson Laboratory (288-3371), Route 3, Otter Creek. Open to the public mid-June through August; phone ahead to check times for the audiovisual presentation about one of the world's largest mammalian genetics research facilities. Cancer, diabetes, and birth defects are among the problems researched.

Wendell Gilley Museum (244-7555), Route 102, Southwest Harbor. Open May through December 10–4 (10–5 July and August), daily except Mondays; Friday through Sunday only in May, November, and December. A collection of more than 200 bird carvings by the late woodcarver and painter Wendell Gilley. $3 per adult, $1 per child under age 12.

Bar Harbor Historical Society (288-3838), Jesup Memorial Library, Route 3, Bar Harbor. Open mid-June to October, Monday through Saturday 1–4. A fascinating collection of early photographs of local hotels, steamers, cottages, the cog railroad, and the big fire of 1947.

Colonel Black Mansion, West Main Street, Ellsworth. Open June to mid-October, Monday through Saturday 10–4:30. Off Mount Desert, but a place not to miss en route. An outstanding Georgian mansion built as a wedding present in 1862 by John Black, who had just married the daughter of the local agent for a Philadelphia land developer, owner of this region. It is said to have been built with bricks brought by sea from Philadelphia, and it took Boston workmen three years to complete it. There is a fine garden and a carriage house full of vehicles. $4 per adult, $2 per child.

Stanwood Homestead Museum, Route 3, Ellsworth. Open daily mid-June to mid-October, 10–4; sanctuary open year-round. Don't miss this exceptional place: a 100-acre nature preserve that is a memorial to Cordelia Stanwood (1865–1958), a pioneer ornithologist, nature photographer, and writer. The old homestead (1850) contains family furnishings and a collection of stuffed birds, eggs, and old photos. There are gardens, a picnic area, and a gift shop. $2.50 per adult and $.50 per child for the museum; no admission charge for the sanctuary.

Mount Desert Historical Society (244-7872), Route 102, Somesville. Open July and August, Wednesdays and Sundays 2–5, or by appointment. Two tidy little houses connected by a moon bridge. Collections include mill-town and marine-related items, furniture, books, and such.

Great Harbor Collection at the Old Firehouse Museum, Northeast Harbor. Open Memorial Day through Columbus Day, Monday through Saturday 10–5. A collection of historical artifacts representing life past on Mount Desert. Exhibits include an early fire engine, parlor room, kitchen, and workshop.

Natural History Museum, College of the Atlantic (288-5015), Route 3, Bar Harbor. Open mid-June to Labor Day, 9–5 daily; evening speaker series, 7:30 on Wednesdays. This is a nice little museum with stuffed birds and animals, skeletons of local species, and a "discovery corner," but it really isn't worth the charge: $2.50 per adult, $.50 per child.

Ellsworth Historical Society, State Street, Ellsworth. Open July and August, Tuesdays and Thursdays 10–4. A former brick 1880s jail and sheriff's office houses the local historical society.

(Also see Islesford Historical Museum under Acadia National Park.)

FOR FAMILIES   Mount Desert Oceanarium, Clark Point Road, Southwest Harbor. Open mid-May to mid-October, 9–5 daily except Sundays. A large, old waterside building filled with exhibits, including 20 tanks displaying sea life, whale songs, a "lobster room," and a touch tank. $3.75 per adult, $2.50 per child.

The Bar Harbor Oceanarium, Route 3 (at entrance to the island). Open weekdays 9–5. Everything you ever wanted to know about a lobster plus the Thomas Bay Marsh Walk. $4.75 per adult, $3.50 per child.

Seal Cove Auto Museum, Route 102, Seal Cove. Late June through Labor Day, 10–5 daily. A collection of more than 100 antique autos, including an 1899 DeDion Bouton and Clark Gable's 1934 Packard. $4 per adult, $1.50 per child.

AIR RIDES   Acadia Air (667-5534), Route 3 at Trenton Airport. Flight instruction, aircraft rentals, and sight-seeing and whale-sighting flights.

Island Soaring Glider Rides (667-SOAR). Also at the Airport; offered daily.

BIKING   Carriage Road tours are outlined in much of the free literature. **Acadia Bike & Canoe Company** (288-5483), 48 Cottage Street, rents child trailers and every kind of bike; **Bar Harbor Bicycle Shop** (288-3886), 141 Cottage Street, rents a wide variety and offers handy access to the park. **Northeast Harbor Bike Shop** (276-5480), Main Street, Northeast Harbor, also has rentals. **Southwest Cycle** (244-5856), Main Street, Southwest Harbor, rents mountain and ten-speed bicycles.

**BIRDING   For special programs led by park naturalists, consult "Acadia's Beaver Log," which is available at the park visitors center.

BOAT EXCURSIONS   Acadia Boat Tours & Charters, Inc. (288-9505), 60 West

Street, Bar Harbor. Lobster fishing on *Aunt Elsie;* one-and-a-half-hour trips; frequent departures in high season; free lobster and crab cooked on board.

Acadian Whale Watcher (288-9794 or 288-9766), Golden Anchor Pier, Bar Harbor. Two-and-a-half-hour whale-watching cruises; also eagle watches. Galley and heated cabin.

Bass Harbor Cruise (244-5365), Bass Harbor (next to Swan's Island ferry). Daily cruises except on Sundays.

Beal and Bunker Co. (244-3575). Operates daily. Islesford historical cruise, mail boat, and ferry service to Cranberry Isles.

Frenchman Bay Co. (288-3322), 1 West Street, Harbor Place, Bar Harbor. Operates over 20 different trips each day on six different boats, ranging from a windjammer to a lobster boat. Offers everything from whale-watching to deep-sea fishing.

Islesford Ferry Co. (244-3366), Northeast Harbor dock. Nature and sunset cruises; also naturalist-guided cruise to Baker Island.

Maine Whalewatch (276-5803), Northeast Harbor dock. All-day whale and sea bird cruises.

Sea Princess Naturalist Cruises (276-5352), Northeast Harbor. May through October. Trips to Islesford or around Somes Sound.

BOAT RENTALS **Harbor Boat Rentals** (288-3757), at the Pier, Bar Harbor. Powerboats and sailboats available. (Also see Sailing.)

CAMPING There are two campgrounds within Acadia National Park: **Blackwoods** (288-3274), open all year and handy to Bar Harbor; and **Seawall** (244-3600), open late May to late September. Check with the visitors center for the reservation policy.

Note: Although Blackwoods and Seawall frequently fill during July and August, waterside sites in nearby **Lamoine State Park** (667-4778), open mid-May to mid-October, are often empty. An attractive area on the grounds of a former estate, the park is just minutes from Route 3 on Route 184 in Lamoine. Facilities include picnicking and a boat launch. There is a general store across the street. The park is just up the road from **Lamoine Beach** (great for walking and skipping stones).

There are also more than a dozen commercial campgrounds in this area; request a copy of the "Maine Camping Guide" from the **Maine Publicity Bureau** (289-2423), 97 Winthrop Street, Hallowell 04347.

CANOEING AND KAYAKING Most ponds on Mount Desert offer easy access. Long Pond, the largest lake on the island, has three access points. Boats can be launched at Echo Lake from Ike's Point, just off Route 102. Seal Cove Pond is less used, accessible from fire roads north of Seal Cove. Bass Harbor Marsh is another possibility. Canoe rental sources offer suggestions and directions. Kayaking is a recent but booming sport, easier to master than saltwater canoeing.

Acadia Bike & Canoe Company (288-5483), 48 Cottage Street, Bar Harbor. Both canoe and kayak rentals; offers half-day and sunrise kayaking tours on Frenchman Bay and Blue Hill Bay.

National Park Canoe Rentals (244-5854), Route 102, 2 miles west of Somesville (at the north end of Long Pond). Open daily May through October. Half- and full-day rentals; rooftop carriers available.

Canoe Works (422-9095), Route 1, Sullivan. Guy Cyr is known nationally as a canoe-maker and mender; he also rents canoes by the day and half-day.

Life Sports (667-7819), 34 High Street, Ellsworth. Rents canoes, kayaks, and windsurfers; runs clinics in kayaking and windsurfing.

Coastal Kayaking Tours (288-9605 or 800-526-8615), Cottage Street, Bar Harbor. Offers half- and full-day tours in the area; also offers three- and five-day island camping tours (no previous paddling experience required).

FOR CHILDREN   Visitors aged 7–12 are eligible to join the park's **Junior Ranger Program;** inquire at the visitors center.

GOLF   **Kebo Valley Club** (288-3000 or 288-5000), Route 233, Bar Harbor. Open daily May through October. 18 holes; "oldest golf grounds in America," since 1892.

Bar Harbor Golf Course (667-7505), Route 3 and 204, Trenton. 18 holes.

Causeway Golf Club (244-3780). Nine-hole course, club and pull-carts, pro shop.

HIKING   Acadia National Park is a recognized mecca for rock climbers as well as hikers. Several detailed maps are sold at the visitors center, also the source of an information sheet that profiles two dozen trails within the park. These range in difficulty from the Jordan Pond Loop Trail (a 3.3 mile path around the pond) to the Precipice Trail (1.6 miles, very steep, with iron rungs as ladders). It is generally agreed that you haven't experienced the beauty of the park unless you have hiked a piece.

HORSEDRAWN TOURS   **Wildwood Stables** (276-3622), follow the Park Loop Road from the visitors center; turn left at the sign a half mile beyond Jordan Pond House. One-hour horsedrawn tours in multiple-seat carriages offered five times a day and one-and-a-half-hour sunset hayrides.

SAILING   *Day sails: Bay Lady* (288-9554), a windjammer operated by **Frenchman Bay Co.**

Blackjack (288-3056), Northeast Harbor. A 33-foot Friendship sloop offers five trips daily, May through October, Monday to Saturday.

Chamar, **Great Harbor Charters** (276-5352 or 276-3993), Northeast Harbor. Full- and half-day sails and private charters aboard a 30-foot sloop.

Golden Anchor Sloop (288-9505), Golden Anchor Pier, West Street, Bar Harbor. Cruises daily in-season aboard a classic Friendship sloop.

Gullhaven (244-9233), Southwest Harbor. Cruises daily.

Natalie Todd (288-4585), sails from the Bar Harbor Pier, late June through early October. Maine's only three-masted commercial schoo-

Windjammers in Somes Sound

ner, built in 1941 in Brooklyn as a two-masted schooner dragger. Capt. Steven Pagels found the vessel in Gloucester in 1986 and rebuilt her in Thomaston as a three-masted, gaff-rigged schooner. The two-hour cruises through Frenchman Bay are offered several times a day in high season, less frequently in slower summer weeks.

Whispering Sands (422-9992), Sand Dollar Maritime Enterprises, Box 164, Sorrento 04677. Half- and full-day sails; also dinner cruises, crewed charters.

Sailing lessons: **Mansell Boat Company** (244-5625), Route 102A, Manset (near Southwest Harbor).

Sailboat charters, rentals: **Classic Charters** (244-7159), Northeast Harbor.

Hinckley Yacht Charters (244-5008), Bass Harbor.

Libby's Sailboat Rental/Charter (288-3604 after 5 PM). For experienced sailors only, 26-foot Pearsons for charter by day or week.

Mansell Boat Rental (244-5625). See Sailing Lessons.

Morris Yachts (244-5509), Southwest Harbor.

WALKING   **Best of Bar Harbor Walking Tour** (288-4648), two-hour tours depart from the Village Green, mid-June through Columbus Day.

SWIMMING   Within Acadia there is supervised swimming at **Sand Beach,** 4 miles south of Bar Harbor, and at **Echo Lake,** 11 miles west. At **Seal Harbor** there is a small, free town beach with parking in a small lot across Route 3.

At **Lake Wood** near Hull's Cove there is a pleasant freshwater beach that is ideal for children. The trick is finding it: Turn off Route 3 at the

Cove Motel and take your first left up a dirt road (there is a small official sign), which leads to a parking area; there is a short walk down to the beach. No facilities or lifeguard but warm water.

TENNIS   **Atlantic Oaks by the Sea** (288-5218), Route 3, Bar Harbor, offers use of its courts as does **Maine Racquet and Fitness Club** (667-3341), Route 3 in Trenton. Also check with chambers in Northeast Harbor and Southwest Harbor.

CROSS-COUNTRY SKIING   More than 43 miles of carriage roads at Acadia National Park are maintained as ski-touring trails. An additional 41 miles of unpaved roads are available for skiers. Request a "Winter Activities" leaflet from the park headquarters (write to Superintendent, PO Box 177, Bar Harbor 04609).

SNOWMOBILING   The motor and unpaved (see above) roads are open for snowmobiles.

GRAND OLD RESORTS   **Claremont** (244-5036), Claremont Road, Southwest Harbor 04679. Open May to mid-October. Mount Desert's oldest hotel, substantially renovated. Sited with spectacular views of Cadillac Mountain across Somes Sound and the waterfront estates in Northeast Harbor. This is a classic, grand resort hotel with green wicker rockers on the veranda, spacious common rooms that include a game room lined with books, and a large dining room designed so that every table has a water view. Food is excellent with an emphasis on fresh fish. Jacket and tie are required for dinner, but the atmosphere is relaxed and friendly. Lunch is served at the Boat House, right on the water with splendid views of the mountains and Northeast Harbor. The 25 old-fashioned double rooms, 2 single rooms, and 3 suites are in the main hotel and in Phillips and Clark houses; there are also 12 cottages, each with living room and fireplace. Facilities include clay tennis courts, croquet, badminton, and water sports; rowboats and motorboats are available. The Croquet Classic in August is the social high of the season. A room in the hotel is $130–$155 double, MAP, in-season in the hotel; $110–$140, EP, in the cottages; $55–$75 double, EP, off-season in the hotel.

   Asticou Inn (276-3344), Route 3, Northeast Harbor 04662. Cranberry Lodge is open May to late December and the main house, mid-June to mid-September. The epitome of elegance, the Asticou Inn caters to a distinguished clientele, with superb food, simply furnished rooms with water views, luxurious public rooms with oriental rugs and wing chairs by the hearth, and a vast porch overlooking formal gardens. In all there are 51 rooms and suites, most with private baths, divided between the main house and smaller lodges, which include the former Cranberry Inn across the road (6 rooms here have fireplaces). Facilities include a cocktail lounge, tennis courts, and a swimming pool. $198–$234 double, MAP.

INNS AND BED & BREAKFASTS   *In Bar Harbor:*   According to the Bar Harbor

Chamber of Commerce there are some 3,000 beds in town. We cannot claim to have inspected every room, but we offer this partial listing of places that we have actually checked out.

Ledgelawn (288-4596), 66 Mount Desert Street, Bar Harbor 04609. Open year-round. Two turn-of-the-century "cottages" gilded to the hilt. Each room is different, but all are furnished with antiques, some with whirlpool tubs, saunas, and steam baths, working fireplaces, verandas, private entrances, and sitting areas. There are 21 rooms in the main building, 8 in the recycled coach house, 4 in Balanced Rock Cottage on the water. Facilities include a bar, pool, and Jacuzzi. Rates include afternoon tea, a buffet-style continental breakfast, and shuttle to the airport, ferry, or your yacht. $75–$175.

Bayview (288-5861), 111 Eden Street (Route 3),Bar Harbor 04609. Open year-round. This former estate, which overlooks Frenchman Bay, is now a complex of Hotel Chateau with 26 units (each with bath, water view, phone, and TV), the original mansion or inn with rooms, and a cluster of townhomes (each with 2 fireplaces, 2 $1/2$ baths, and 2 or 3 bedrooms). There is a restaurant and bar. It is very elegant, as it should be at $85–$200 for a room in the inn, $95–$195 in the hotel, and $375–$425 for a townhome. Per day, in-season, that is.

Thornhedge (288-5398), 47 Mount Desert Street, Bar Harbor 04609. Open April to mid-November. A cheerful yellow mansion, its porch garnished with geraniums, offering 23 guest rooms, all with baths and 5 with fireplaces. Thirteen rooms are in the mansion, which was built for the Boston publisher who persuaded Louisa May Alcott to write *Little Women*. The remaining rooms are in two other Victorian-style homes located just behind (both with their own public rooms). Continental breakfast served in the dining room; wine and cheese at 5 PM. $65–$125.

Nannau (288-5575), Box 710, Lower Main Street, Bar Harbor 04609. Open May through October. Too good to be true, almost. A vintage 1904 shingled "cottage" right on Compass Harbor, just a mile from downtown Bar Harbor and abutting the National Park, Nannau offers three rooms, ranging from a third-floor aerie ($65 double) with a shared bath to a bedroom with a large bay window on the ocean, fireplace, and private bath ($95); Vikki and Ron Evers serve a large breakfast, invite guests to make themselves at home in the parlor and living room where there are plenty of books and frequently a dog is napping on the hearth. No smoking.

Mira Monte Inn (288-4263; 800-553-5109 outside Maine), 69 Mount Desert Street, Bar Harbor 04609. Open May to mid-October. A gracious 1865 mansion with a welcoming porch and some rooms with private balconies overlooking the deep, peaceful lawn in back or formal gardens on the side. Marian Burns, a native of Bar Harbor, offers 11 rooms with private baths; 4 with fireplaces; and all with antiques and

TV. Guests may take advantage of the inviting library and sitting room with fireplaces. The per-night rate includes a continental breakfast and evening refreshments. $57–$135 per room, 10–20 percent discount in shoulder season and for longer stays.

Primrose Cottage Inn (288-4031), 73 Mount Desert Street, Bar Harbor 04609. Open year-round. A delightful "stick Gothic cottage" built in 1878 for the first Episcopal bishop of Maine, renovated in bright, tasteful colors. Some shared baths and balcony sitting areas and two working fireplaces. Continental breakfast and 5 PM wine and cheese are included; $75–$125 double.

Atlantean Inn (288-3270), 11 Atlantic Avenue, Bar Harbor 04609. Open June-October. A Tudor-style "cottage." When vacancies permit, you can stay here for a day or two, but the inn specializes in week-long (six nights, five days) "adventures": Guests arrive Sunday and follow a daily regimen of pre-breakfast exercise (hiking, kayaking, or sailing), then a day of rock climbing on Otter Cliffs, windsurfing, racquetball, or biking. $950 per person.

Bass Cottage in the Field (288-3705),The Field, Bar Harbor 04609. Open late May to mid-October. Anna Jean Turner is the gracious hostess of this grand old home, just off Main Street but in a quiet world of its own, set above the town pier and park. The porch is large and enclosed, stacked with magazines, furnished with wicker, and brimming with flowers. The stamped tin ceilings are high, and there is stained glass. The 10 rooms are traditionally furnished and airy; some with private baths. $45–$85 double, $35 single.

Cove Farm Inn (288-5355), RFD 1, Box 429, Crooked Road, Bar Harbor 04609. Open May to February. This is a great place for families. Located a short drive from downtown Bar Harbor, it is handy to Lake Wood (see Swimming). A friendly old farmhouse with nine guest rooms, some private baths, use of the fridge. Jerry and Barbara Keene are an energetic young couple, and Jerry, a native, enjoys advising guests on how to see the island. The moderate rates per room include freshly baked breads or muffins, honey butter, and fresh summer fruit. No smoking. Horseback riding, also winter skating and sleigh rides. $30–$75 double.

Manor House Inn (288-3759), West Street, Bar Harbor 04609. Open May through mid-November. This 1887 "cottage" is on the National Register of Historic Places. All 14 rooms have private baths, and most are furnished with Victorian pieces. Two have working fireplaces. Rare woodwork and nicely preserved details add comfort and beauty. The gardens are quite lovely, and guests have access to the clay tennis courts and pool at the Bar Harbor Club across the street. $50–$150 per room includes a generous continental breakfast.

Holbrook House (288-4970), 74 Mount Desert Street, Bar Harbor 04609. Open mid-May through mid-October. A restored 1876 "cottage." Thirteen rooms, all with private baths, furnished with antiques. A full buffet breakfast and afternoon refreshments served in the sun porch. $90–$105 double.

Inn at Canoe Point (288-9511), Box 216, Hulls Cove, Bar Harbor 04609. Open year-round. Two miles from Bar Harbor, right across from Acadia National Park. Divided from the busy road by its own small pine forest, overlooking the ocean. The five guest rooms all have water views and private baths; two have private decks overlooking the water. The Ocean Room with its 180-degree view and fieldstone fireplace is the focal point. The Garret Suite, which occupies the whole third floor, is great for families, and the Master Suite with its fireplace and deck is ideal for a romantic getaway. $65–$170 includes a full breakfast, served on the oceanside deck, weather permitting.

McKay Lodging (288-3531 or 800-TO-MCKAY), 243 Main Street, Bar Harbor 04609. Two Victorian houses, The Main House (open year-round) and The Summer House (open May through October; no smoking) offer a total of 26 rooms, each different but all with TV, direct-dial phones, some with refrigerators. $47–$105 includes breakfast.

Bay Ledge Inn & Spa (288-4204), 1385 Sand Point Road, Bar Harbor 04609. Open year-round. Perched on a cliff overlooking the ocean, surrounded by towering pines, you could hardly ask for a more Maine-like setting. The inn offers 10 guest rooms and spa amenities like a sauna, hot tub, heated pool, and exercise machines. The inn's own pebble beach leads to Cathedral Rock. November to June a full spa program is offered (maximum of six people), otherwise rates are $65–$185 plus 10 percent gratuity. No children under age 15.

Canterbury Cottage (288-2112), 12 Roberts Avenue, Bar Harbor 04609. Open May to mid-October. A small, centrally located B&B whose owners share a lifetime familiarity with the island. The Victorian house is architecturally interesting (its original owner was the B&M stationmaster, and its architect specialized in railroad stations), and rooms are comfortably, tastefully decorated. No children, pets, or smokers. $65–$85 double includes breakfast in the country kitchen.

Mount Desert Beyond Bar Harbor: **Harbourside Inn** (276-3272), Northeast Harbor 04662. Open mid-June to mid-September. An 1880s shingle-style inn set in 4 wooded acres, with 22 guest rooms on three floors, all with private baths, some kitchens. There are also working fireplaces in all the first- and second-floor rooms. All are large and bright with interesting antiques and fine rugs. Guests mingle over breakfast muffins served on one of the wicker-furnished sun porches. There is also a comfortable living room, but most guests spend their days in adjacent Acadia National Park (its wooded paths are within walking distance) or on boat excursions out of Northeast Harbor, also just down the road. Your hosts, the Sweet family, are longtime island residents.$90–$135 (for a suite).

Penury Hall (244-7102), Box 68, Main Street, Southwest Harbor

04679. Open year-round. An attractive village house with three guest rooms sharing two baths, all nicely decorated with interesting art and tempting reading material salted about. This was the first bed & breakfast on the island, and Toby Strong takes his job as host seriously (wife Gretchen is the town manager). Toby does the cooking and housekeeping and makes guests feel part of the family. Breakfast includes juice, fresh fruit, a choice of eggs Benedict, blueberry pancakes, or a "penurious omelet." A canoe, a 21-foot sloop, and a windsurfer are available, and you can relax in the sauna after hiking or cross-country skiing. $30–$55.

Kingsleigh Inn (244-5302), Box 1426, 100 Main Street, Southwest Harbor 04679. Open May through mid-November. A spacious colonial revival home in the middle of the village. The eight guest rooms all have private baths and some have water; the entire third floor is one suite. A full breakfast is included; $55–$145 (for the turret suite).

Harbour Cottage Inn (244-5738), PO Box 258, Southwest Harbor 04679. Open year-round. A mansard roofed house originally built in 1870 as an annex to Mount Desert's first (and long gone) summer hotel. Recently renovated, the five guest rooms now all have private baths, ranging from a claw foot tub to steam showers and whirlpools. No children under age 12; recommended as a great place to honeymoon off-season (by friends who did). $45–$85 double including breakfast and 5:30 nibblies.

Seal Cove Farm (244-7781), HCR62, Box 140, Mount Desert 04660. Open year-round. Overlooking a lake, the century-old farmhouse on Route 102 offers three spacious rooms, one with private bath. This is a great place for children; there are sheep, ducks, geese, chickens, turkeys, and a goat herd from which the Brooks family makes several varieties of cheese. A full country breakfast is included. Double $53.50–$64.20; $10.70 per extra person in room.

The Maison Suisse Inn (276-5223), PO Box 1090, Northeast Harbor 04662. Open May through October. This is a gem—just steps from Northeast Harbor's shops and galleries but set back from Main Street in landscaped grounds—an elaborate turn-of-the-century "cottage" with spacious common rooms and 10 guest rooms (4 are suites), all with private baths; a full breakfast is included. $85–$145 double; $10 for each child; $18 per additional guest over age 18, less in shoulder seasons.

Lindenwood Inn (244-5335), Box 1328, Southwest Harbor 04679. Open all year. A turn-of-the-century sea captain's home with seven guest rooms, many with harbor views, that share three baths, plus a guest cottage with living room and kitchen. A full breakfast is served in the paneled dining room (where the fire is lit most mornings). Swing on the porch, relax in the parlor, or play the harpsichord. $40–$115 double; $20 per extra person.

Island House (244-5180), Box 1006, Southwest Harbor 04679. Open May 1 through October. Right across from the harbor, a large 1850s house, part of the first summer hotel on the island. There are four double rooms with shared baths, also an efficiency apartment in the Carriage House. $40–$95 includes a full breakfast; no minimum stay required.

Pointy Head Inn and Antiques (244-7261), HC33, Box 2A, Bass Harbor 04653. Open mid-May to late fall. This rambling, old sea captain's home on Route 102A overlooks the ocean. Six guest rooms, some with water/mountain views. "Mature" children only. A favorite with artists and photographers; $35–$65 per room, shared baths; $15 per extra person.

Bass Harbor Inn (244-5157; in winter: 203-767-8106), Shore Road, PO Box 326, Bass Harbor 04653. Open June through October. A vintage 1832 house offers nine rooms, ranging from doubles with shared baths to a top floor suite with kitchenette. One room with a half-bath has a fireplace. $45–$90 includes great breakfast breads and pastries.

The Inn at Southwest (244-3835), PO Box 593, Southwest Harbor 04679. Open March to November. A high Victorian "cottage" right in the village with a wraparound porch and harbor views, nicely restored with waverly wallpapers and designer fabrics and antiques. All nine rooms have private baths; Double $45–$98 includes a full breakfast.

East of Mount Desert: More bed & breakfasts in Hancock County towns are listed with Bed & Breakfast Down East Ltd. (565-3517), Box 547, Eastbrook 04634. Send $3 to cover the cost of the directory.

Crocker House Country Inn (422-6806), Hancock Point 04640. Open late April to New Year's Eve. Just 30 minutes north of Bar Harbor, Hancock Point has a different feel entirely: quiet, with easy access to water, hiking trails, crafts shops, and concerts. The attractive old inn has 10 guest rooms, all with private baths (new and nicely done with natural woods). Furnishings are tasteful, and there are nice touches such as soap and shampoo in the baths, chocolates by the bed. Across the road sits one of the world's smallest post offices. The tennis courts next door, and the nearby dock are made available by the Hancock Improvement Association. Breakfast and dinner are served in the dining room, which is open to the public (see Dining Out). $50–$75 double includes breakfast.

Le Domaine (422-3395; 422-3916), Route 1, Hancock 04640. Best known for the French fare of its dining room (see Dining Out), but also an inn with attractive, carefully furnished rooms upstairs, which include private baths. Each of the seven rooms is named for a different herb. While the house is right on Route 1, a large garden offers a quiet haven. $80 single, MAP plus 15 percent gratuity.

Island View Inn (422-3031), Route 1, Sullivan Harbor 04664. This is a spacious, gracious turn-of-the-century summer "cottage" set well back from Route 1 with splendid views of Frenchman Bay and the dome-shaped mountains on Mount Desert. The eight guest rooms, some with private baths and water views, are nicely decorated, and there is ample and comfortable common space; a continental breakfast is included. $40–$68; no charge for children five years and younger, otherwise $10 per extra person in room.

Wildfire Run (422-3935), Sullivan 04664-0097. Open year-round. This is the place for quilt lovers. Peg McAloon makes, collects, and sells quilts—which decorate each guest room and bathroom. $40–$50 per room includes a full breakfast.

Sunset House (963-7156), Route 186, West Gouldsboro 04602. Open year-round. A large, late Victorian home with seven guest rooms and shared baths spread over three floors; four rooms have ocean views, and a fifth overlooks Jones Pond. A full country breakfast is included. $39–$65 double. No smoking. No children under age 12.

MOTELS **Atlantic Oakes by-the-Sea** (288-5801; 800-696-2463), Box 3, Eden Street (Route 3, next to the *Bluenose* ferry terminal), Bar Harbor 04609. Open year-round. This is a modern facility on the site of Sir Harry Oakes's 10-acre estate: 109 units, many with balconies, 12 with kitchens. Facilities include a pebble beach, heated pool, five tennis courts, and pier and float. $92–$118 in-season; $39–$59 off-season.

Bar Harbor Motor Inn (288-3351; 800-248-3351), Newport Drive, Bar Harbor 04609. Overlooking the water but centrally located in Bar Harbor, next to the municipal pier. The new 64-unit Oceanfront Lodge is open year-round. The original complex, which includes a turn-of-the-century house that once served as an elite men's club, and 54 guest rooms in an adjoining wing, is open late April to October. All rooms have private baths, phones, and color TV. There is an elegant dining room, a pool, and 7 acres of manicured lawns on the water. $59–$190.

Wonder View Motor Lodge (288-3358; 800-341-1553), Box 25, Eden Street, Bar Harbor 04609. Open mid-May to mid-October. Both pets and children are welcome in the 85-unit motel built on the site of an estate once owned by Mary Roberts Rinehart, author of popular mystery stories. Handy both to the *Bluenose* ferry and to downtown Bar Harbor, the motel overlooks Frenchman Bay and its extensive grounds are nicely landscaped. Includes a swimming pool and the Hilltop Dining Room, which serves breakfast and dinner. $44–$97.

Eden Village (288-4670), Box 1930 (10 minutes north of Bar Harbor on Route 3), Bar Harbor 04609. The housekeeping cottages are set on 25 acres, accommodate two to seven people, and are equipped with fireplaces and screened porches. $365–$390 per week; nightly and lower off-season rates.

Golden Anchor Inn (288-5033; 800-242-1231), Granite Point (off West Street), Bar Harbor 04609. Open year-round. Right on the water.

Eighty-eight rooms with balconies, dock, and pool. $85–$125, cheaper off-season; includes continental breakfast.

COTTAGES **Emery's Cottages on the Shore** (288-3432), Sandy Point Road, Bar Harbor 04609. Open May to mid-October. Twenty-two cottages, (fourteen with kitchens), electric heat, showers, TVs, and private pebble beach. $335–$550 per week; $52–$75 per day.

Hinckley's Dreamwood Motor Court, Route 3, Box 15, Bar Harbor 04609. Open May to mid-October. Sited under tall pines. Twenty-five cottages (nineteen with kitchens), three two-bedroom units (some with fireplaces), also a four-bed house and four-bedroom cottage that sleeps as many as eight. Three-night minimum stay. Facilities include a heated pool. Moderately priced.

Salisbury Cove Cottages (288-4571), PO Box 723, Bar Harbor 04609. Open late May to October. Classic Maine motor court cottages; pine paneled with tidy screened porches, kitchenettes, accommodating two to six people. $40–$50 double.

Edgewater Motel and Cottages (288-3491), Box 566, Bar Harbor 04609. Open April through October. Just eight units right on Frenchman Bay in Salisbury Cove; four units have Franklin stoves and complete kitchens, and all have balconies and TVs. $52–$80 per night, $335–$550 per week.

OTHER LODGING *In Bar Harbor:* **Mount Desert Island YWCA** (288-5008), 36 Mount Desert Street, Bar Harbor 04609. Open all year. Offers 26 rooms (singles and doubles) and a dorm room for eight women. Gym and tennis courts.

Mount Desert Island AYH Youth Hostel (288-5587), 41 Mount Desert Street (behind St. Savior's Episcopal Church), PO Box 32, Bar Harbor 04609. Open mid-June through August to AYH members. Twenty beds, kitchen facilities. $8 per person, reservations advised. For membership information contact AYH, Greater Boston Council, 1020 Commonwealth Avenue, Boston, MA 02215 (617-731-5430 or 617-731-6692).

Mount Desert Beyond Bar Harbor: **Appalachian Mountain Club's Echo Lake Camp** (244-3747), AMC/Echo Lake Camp, Mount Desert 04660. Open late June through August. Accommodations are platform tents; family-style meals are served in a central hall. There is a rustic library reading room and an indoor game room. The focus, however, is outdoors: There are boats for use on the lake, daily hikes, and evening activities. Reservations should be made on April 1. Rates for the minimum one-week stay (Saturday to Saturday) are inexpensive per person but add up for a family. All meals included. For a brochure write to Echo Lake Camp, AMC, 5 Joy Street, Boston, MA 02108.

Swan's Island Vacations (526-4350), Box 27, Minturn 04659. Open May through October. Maili Bailey coordinates rentals for cottages, houses, and apartments on Swan's Island, accessible from Bass Harbor. These range from $280 to $700 per week. A picturesque lobstering island with quarry swimming. There is also a guest house available at Burnt Cove Harbor.

East of Mount Desert: Given our large family, limited income, and dislike of crowds, we searched the annual "Maine Guide to Camp & Cottage Rentals," available free from the Maine Publicity Bureau (289-2423; 97 Winthrop Street, Hallowell 04347) for a cottage within comfortable striking distance of Mount Desert. We found an inexpensive, classic, two-story shingled cottage in Lamoine. It had a working fireplace and a wraparound porch and a lawn sloped down to Frenchman Bay.

   Edgewater Cabins (422-6414), Sullivan. Open late April to November. Emery and Lydia Dunbar have passed on management of their Route 1 store but still accommodate summer guests in seven old-style Maine cottages, all with splendid views across Frenchman Bay. Inexpensive.

GUEST HOUSE   **Daney Cottage** (288-3856), 18 Hancock Street, Bar Harbor 04609. Neat as a pin, this small house is handy to ocean and shops. Mrs. Vincent Daney offers inexpensive rooms, $10–$18 single.

DINING OUT   *In Bar Harbor:*   **George's Restaurant** (288-4505), 7 Stephen's Lane (just off Main Street behind the First National Bank). Open mid-June through October. Dinner from 5:30 to midnight. Creative, fresh, vaguely Greek cuisine in a summery house with organdy curtains. You might dine on seafood sausage, a Greek salad, and seafood strudel with a glass or two of Greek wine; entrées run $10–$19. Desserts include homemade ice creams.

   Jordan Pond House (276-3316), Park Loop Road. Open for lunch 11:30–2:30, for tea 2:30-5:30, and also for dinner 5:30–9. Seasonal. Best known for its popovers at tea, this landmark is also pleasant, and less crowded, for dinner (jackets suggested). Specialties include crabmeat au gratin, broiled halibut, and lobster pie. Children's dinner includes beverage and ice cream. The dining room overlooks the pond and mountains. The restaurant dates from the 1870s; it was tastefully rebuilt after a fire destroyed it in 1979. From $2.50 for peanut and jelly to $19.50 for lobster salad.

   Testa's at Bayside Landing (288-3327), 53 Main Street. Open 7 AM to midnight, June 15 through September when the family moves to Palm Beach where they run a second restaurant. Three daily meals (breakfast served from 7 AM) are served in the newly rebuilt dining rooms. Italian and seafood specialties include spaghetti Testa with diced chicken, peppers, and cheese. Blueberry and strawberry pies. In Bar Harbor since 1934; recently rebuilt.

   The Reading Room (288-3351), Bar Harbor Motor Inn, Newport Drive. A horseshoe-shaped formal dining room with a view of the harbor; frequent live entertainment at dinner. Open for all three meals, specializing in daily lobster bakes on the outdoor terrace. $12–$22.

Brick Oven (288-3708), 21 Cottage Street. Open May to mid-October, 5–10 PM only. Cozy dining room decorated with antiques, old tools, toys, posters, and gadgets. Specializes in broiled and fried seafood. Children's plates. Moderate.

Mary Jane Restaurant (288-3410), 119 Main Street. Open mid-June to October, 7 AM through dinner. One of Bar Harbor's oldest restaurants; street-side patio and dining room, seafood specials, steak pit, full bar. Moderate.

The Porcupine Grill (288-3884), 123 Cottage Street. Open May to October for dinner. Well-chosen antiques and fresh flowers complement imaginative dishes like homemade chicken and veal sausage and scallops with sweet peppers and leeks on homemade pasta. $12.50 to $18.

The Fin Back (288-4193), 78 West Street. No smoking. Dinner nightly and weekend brunch. A small, chef-owned restaurant featuring deliciously healthy entrées like chicken stuffed with pesto and goat cheese or a lobster and asparagus coquille. Entrées run $10–$16.

La Cadie (288-9668), 137 Cottage Street. Open May-October, dinner nightly. You will remember this small restaurant for tasty seafood and vegetarian dishes like seafood boursin. Entrées run $12–$17.

Elsewhere on Mount Desert: **Breakneck Hollow Cafe** (288-4113), Breakneck Road, Hulls Cove (turn off Route 3 at the Hulls Cove General Store and the Exxon station). Closed Tuesdays, otherwise open 5:30–10. Housed in a red farmhouse decorated with books and pictures, this delightful place serves gourmet vegetarian and seafood; beer and wine are available. Moderate.

Chart Room (288-5493), Route 3, Hulls Cove. Open for breakfast, lunch, and dinner. A waterside restaurant with seafood specialties. Moderate.

Asticou Inn (276-3344), Northeast Harbor. Open mid-June to mid-September for breakfast, lunch, and dinner. Thursday-night buffet and dance, $29 per person. Grand old hotel atmosphere with waterside formal dining room (window seats, however, are reserved for longtime guests). Specialties include veal medallions in Roquefort cream sauce and lobster prepared to order. Jacket, tie, and reservation required. Prix-fixe $25.

Claremont Hotel (288-5036), Clark Point Road, Southwest Harbor. Open late June through Labor Day; lunch at the Boathouse, mid-July through August.The formal dining room has been designed so that most tables have at least some water view, and both the food and service enjoy a fine local reputation. Our menu included grilled lamb tenderloin with mint pesto, grilled scallops prosciutto with pear puree, sautéed duck breast with roasted red pepper sauce, and brioche filled with sautéed crabmeat, lobster, and scallops. Entrées average $15. The Boathouse, down on the water below the hotel, is a great place for pre-dinner cocktails or for lunch; the view may just be the most spectacular on the island.

The Burning Tree (288-9331), Route 3, Otter Creek. Open 5–10:30. Dine inside or on a lattice-enclosed porch on entrées like Cajun lobster, saffron scallops, and four cheese pasta; moderately priced.

Clark Point Cafe (244-5816), Clark Point Road, in the village of Southwest Harbor. Pleasant, informal atmosphere with a varied menu, from pasta and seafood stew to veal and lobster dishes. Good service. $11–$16.

Seafood Ketch (244-7463), on Bass Harbor. Open May to November, from 7 AM–9 PM daily. Ed and Eileen, Lisa and Stuart Branch all do their part to make this a special place, known for homemade breads and desserts, also for fresh, fresh seafood. Dinner specialties include baked lobster-seafood casserole ($12.95) and baked halibut with lobster sauce ($12.95); luncheon fare includes burgers, BLTs, and crabmeat rolls.

Deck House Restaurant (244-5044), end of Swan's Island Ferry Road, Bass Harbor. A snug place featuring nightly cabaret theater and seafood. Entertainment cover. Full bar. Reservations are a must.

Drydock Cafe (244-3886), 108 Main Street, Southwest Harbor. Open May to October, 7 AM–10 PM. An informal dining find specializing in seafood and pasta dishes; entrées from $9–$17.

Seawall Dining Room (244-3020), Route 102A, Manset. Open for lunch and dinner. Entrées range from chicken fritters to baked stuffed lobster. Ocean view. Inexpensive to moderate.

Puddles (244-3177), Little Cranberry Island. Open for lunch, by reservation for dinner. Sited right on the fishing wharf with a view of Mount Desert Island. Moderately priced seafood specialties.

East of Mount Desert: **Le Domaine** (422-3395), Route 1, Hancock. Nicole Purslow, *propriétaire et chef*, prepares very French entrées, which generally receive rave reviews. The atmosphere is that of a French country inn, complete with a small European-style bar. Specialties include *brandade de morue* (an appetizer of codfish creamed with garlic and olive oil for $6.75) and *lapin au pruneaus* (rabbit in a dark sauce with brandied prunes for $17.50). Daily specials vary: On our most recent visit they included *poisson grille au fenouil* (native fish grilled with fennel and lemon for $17.50) and *ris de veau sauté a l' Anglaise* (lightly breaded veal sweetbreads with capers and lemon).

Crocker House Inn (422-6806), Hancock Point. A genuine country inn atmosphere and varied menu, which includes poached salmon Florentine, veal Oscar, coquille St. Jacques, and broiled halibut Dijon. Sunday brunch is big here as are desserts. Moderate to expensive.

EATING OUT *In Bar Harbor:* **Epi Sub & Pizza** (288-3507), 8 Cottage Street. Open 7 AM to 11 PM. Tops for food and value but zero atmosphere. Cafeteria-style salads, freshly baked calzone, pizza, quiche, pasta, and crabmeat rolls. Clean and friendly; game machines in back.

Bubba's (288-5871), 30 Cottage Street. Open 11:30 AM to 1:00 AM but serving food to 8:30 PM only. Steam-bent oak and mahogany in art-deco style creates comfortable atmosphere. Soup and sandwiches, full bar.

Island Chowder House (288-4905), 38 Cottage Street. Open 11–11. Bentwood chairs and bright decor; homemade soups, thick chowder, seafood pasta, and chicken. Lunch and dinner specials.

Jordan's Restaurant (288-3586), 80 Cottage Street. Open 5 AM to 2 PM all year, Jordan's boasts Bar Harbor's best blueberry muffins and pancakes.

Fisherman's Landing (288-4632), 47 West Street. Open in-season 11:30–8. Eat boiled lobster dinner on the dock, inside or out. Steamed clams, hamburgers, hot dogs, and fried foods; liquor license.

West Street Cafe (288-5242). Open for lunch and dinner. Features homemade soups and pies, fried and broiled seafood, and six different lobster dishes. Children's menu and early bird specials are available.

Elsewhere on Mount Desert: **Docksider** (276-3965), Sea Street, Northeast Harbor. Open 11:30–9. The lunch menu is available all day: chowder, salads, burgers, clam rolls, and shore dinner. Wine and beer.

Cottage Street Bakery & Deli (288-3010), Cottage Street, Bar Harbor. A wide variety of reasonably priced sandwiches; also box lunches.

Colonel's Restaurant (276-5147), Main Street, Northeast Harbor. Open in-season for breakfast, lunch, and dinner. Offers tables on the back deck. Deli sandwiches, pizza, and broiled haddock. Liquor license.

Beal's Lobster Pier (244-7178 or 244-3203), Clark Point Road, Southwest Harbor. Dock dining on picnic tables. Crabmeat rolls and lobster (packed and shipped air freight, too).

The Deacon Seat (244-9229), Clark Point Road, Southwest Harbor, open 5 AM–4:30 PM except Sunday. A great place for breakfast and the local gathering spot, near the middle of the village.

Off Mount Desert: **The Mex** (667-4494), 185 Main Street, Ellsworth. Open daily for lunch and dinner. Nice atmosphere: white stucco walls, beaded curtains, heavy wooden chairs and tables. The Mex serves great Mexican food—we always order too much. (The bean soup is a meal in itself.) Specialties include the Mex sampler: soup, enchilada, chimichanga, chili with rice and beans. Sangria and Mexican beer.

Maidee's (667-3640), Main Street, Ellsworth. A former diner with oriental and standard American fare.

Fisherman's Inn (963-5585), Winter Harbor. Open April to October, then weekends until Christmas, dinner only, 4:30–9 on weekdays and Saturdays, 12–9 on Sundays. A cozy restaurant near the entrance to the park. Specialties include Tony's famous baked stuffed shrimp ($10.95) and steamed local crabmeat in butter ($8.95).

Chase's Restaurant (963-7171), Winter Harbor. Open all day in-season. A convenient eatery at the entrance to the park. Fried lobsters and clams; will pack a picnic.

LOBSTER POUNDS   At the entrance to Mount Desert you can take your pick of pounds strung along the narrows on Route 3. Of these the standout is **Trenton Bridge Lobster Pound** (667-2977), which is open in-season 8:30–8. George Gascon's family mans this landmark pound with the brick steamers out front. On a clear day the view is great.

Oak Point Lobster Pound (667-8548), Route 230 (4 miles off Route 3), Trenton. Open in-season for lunch and dinner. Picnic tables and weatherproofed dining on Western Bay: lobster rolls, stews, and seafood dinners.

Tidal Falls Lobster Pound (422-6818), Hancock (a half mile off Route 1). Open 11–8 in-season. It is getting so that local summer people cannot find a table overlooking the reversing falls. This is the kind of place where you bring your own wine, salad, and dessert; drink in the view; and feast on steamed lobster, mussels, and crabs. A weatherproofed pavilion has a lobster weathervane.

SNACKS   **Jordan Pond House** (276-3316), Park Loop Road. Tea on the lawn at the Jordan Pond House (served 2:30–5:30 PM) has been *de rigueur* for island visitors since 1895. The tea comes with freshly baked popovers and homemade ice cream. Reservations suggested.

ENTERTAINMENT   *Theater:*   **Acadia Repertory Theatre** (244-7260), Route 102, Somesville. Performances during July and August, Tuesday through Sunday, 8:40 PM. A resident theater group based in the Somesville Masonic Hall (8 miles from Bar Harbor) performs a half-dozen popular plays in the course of the season.

Hancock County Auditorium (667-9500 or 800-462-7616). Live performances by singers, comedians, and theatrical groups. Check current listings.

Deck House Cabaret Theatre (244-5044), Swan's Island Ferry Road, Bass Harbor. July and August, dinner at 6:30, waiters and waitresses stage a cabaret show at 8:15. (See Dining Out.)

Music: **Bar Harbor Festival** (288-5744), YWCA Building, 36 Mount Desert Street, Bar Harbor. Mid-July to mid-August. For more than 25 years this annual series has brought top performers to the island. The 8:30 PM concerts are staged at various sites: the Congregational Church, the Maine Sea Coast Mission Verandah, the Bar Harbor Club, and the Blackwoods Campground Amphitheater. Music varies from piano, violin, and chamber to jazz and pop. There is also a folk program.

Mount Desert Festival of Chamber Music (276-5039), Neighborhood House, Main Street, Northeast Harbor. A series of six concerts presented for more than 25 seasons during mid-July through mid-August.

Arcady Music Festival (288-3151 or 244-7211). Late July through August. A relative newcomer (this is its ninth season) on the Mount

Desert music scene. A series of concerts featuring a resident orchestra and held at varying locations, including the Holy Redeemer and St. Saviours Episcopal Church in Bar Harbor and the Somesville Meeting House.

Pierre Monteux Memorial Concert Hall (442-6251), Hancock, is the setting for a series of summer concerts presented by faculty and students at the respected Domaine School for orchestra conducting.

Film: **Criterion Theater** (288-3441), Cottage Street, Bar Harbor. A vintage 1932 art deco theater that presents first-run and art films.

The Grand Auditorium of Hancock County (667-9500), Main Street, Ellsworth. A classic old theater. When not in use for live performances, first-run and art films are shown.

Ellsworth Cinemas (667-3251), Maine Coast Mall, Route 1A, Ellsworth. Two evening shows; matinees on weekends, holidays, and rainy days. First-run films.

SELECTIVE SHOPPING *Art and fine crafts galleries:* Worth the trip. The **Barter Family Gallery and Shop** (422-3190), North Sullivan. Open mid-May through December, Monday through Saturday 9–5 or by appointment. We put this first although it's way off the beaten track because it's our favorite in the entire region. You will find Philip Barter's paintings in the best Northeast Harbor and Blue Hill galleries (we first saw them in a Massachusetts museum). Mostly landscapes, they are primitive, bold, and evocative of Northern Maine. Barter's furniture creations and moderately priced pen and ink landscapes are also displayed. This is the Barter home, and the gallery and shop (featuring Maine and Scottish woolen products, local crafts, and Irish tweeds) is manned by the family. Phone for directions. It's less than 15 miles from Ellsworth.

On Main Street, Northeast Harbor. The quality as well as quantity of artwork showcased in this small yachting haven is amazing. **Islesford Artists** (276-3200). Artists from a variety of Maine islands are represented in this unusually friendly gallery; works range from realistic to abstract and the quality is high; note that a related Islesford Artists (244-3145), representing only works by residents of Great and Little Cranberry Islands, is in Islesford itself. **Smart Studio & Art Gallery** (276-5152). Changing exhibits of watercolors, oils, and serigraphs. **The Wingspread Gallery** (276-3910), an outstanding assemblage of unusual art; changing exhibits in the main gallery and a selection by well-established artists in the back room. **G. E. Redfield Gallery** (276-3609). The furniture (all made right here) is exquisite, and there are small, affordable pieces; also imaginative stone sculptures and impressionist paintings. **Shaw Contemporary Jewelry** (276-5000). The designs are bold and fun, executed in everything from baked enamel over bronze (four or five pins in a package for $19) to sterling and jeweled creations for up to $5850.

Birdnest Gallery, 12 Mount Desert Street, Bar Harbor. Works by more than 100 contemporary New England artists.

Island Artisans, 99 Main Street, Bar Harbor. A cooperative run by 24 area craftspeople. The quality and variety of work is outstanding.

Lone Moose, West Street, Bar Harbor. For more than 20 years a waterfront collection of pottery, textiles, baskets, furniture, jewelry, watercolors, and glass.

Caleb's Sunrise, 115 Main Street, Bar Harbor. Open May to October. Fine crafts: leather, wood, clay, fiber, metal, and graphics.

Jones Gallery, Main Street, Southwest Harbor. Contemporary works by New England artists.

West Side Gallery (244-4329), Main Street, Southwest Harbor. Old prints, etchings, lithos, and paintings.

The Pottery/Weaving Shop (565-2282), East Franklin on Route 200. Open daily, except Sunday, 9–4. Kitchenware, stoneware, custom-designed rugs and clothes.

Pine Tree Kiln, Route 1, West Sullivan. Ruth and Denis Vibert and Dorothea and Frank Stoke have made the shop behind an easy-to-miss clapboard home into an insider's landmark. Their own ovenproof stoneware is outstanding as is the selection of prints, jewelry, weaving, glass, and leather by other Maine craftspeople. Books and cards are also sold here.

Maine Kiln Works, Route 186, West Gouldsboro. Open year-round, Monday through Saturday 10–5. An amazing number of unusual items: dinnerware, ceramic sinks, soap dishes, and lamps are made on the spot; there are also unusual quilts and work by other local craftspeople.

Heirloom Weavers, Little Cranberry Island, Islesford. Kathleen Bowman spins, weaves, and designs the clothing on display in her handweaving gallery.

Wineries: **Bartlett Maine Estate Winery** (546-2408), Route 1, Gouldsboro. Open June to mid-October, Tuesday through Saturday 10–5; Sunday 12–5. Also mid-November to Christmas, Tuesday through Saturday 10–4, Sunday 12–4. Founded in 1983, Maine's first winery, specializing in blueberry, apple, and pear wines; also limited raspberry, strawberry, raspberry, and honey dessert wines; tasting room; and gift packs.

Downeast Country Wines (667-6965), Route 3, Trenton. Open in-season Monday through Saturday 9:30–6, Sunday 1–5. Winter hours, generally Tuesday through Saturday 10–4. Opened in '84 in Pembroke, moved to a former blacksmith's barn on the route to Bar Harbor in '87. Especially fine are a semi-sweet wild blueberry and a medium-dry wild blueberry wine. There's also a spiced apple and "Blue Blush," a dry blend of apples and wild blueberries. Complimentary tasting.

Bookstores: **Sherman's Bookstore and Stationery,** Main Street, Bar Harbor. A great browsing emporium; really a combination traditional five-and-dime, stationery store, gift shop, and well-stocked summer bookshop.

Mr. Paperback, Maine Mall, Route 1A, Ellsworth. A fully stocked bookstore with popular titles and magazines.

Curtis Books (667-7200), 100 Main Street, Ellsworth.

Memories of Maine, 4 West Street, Bar Harbor. A nice selection of regional books, cards, and gifts.

Other shops: **Willey's,** Route 1A, Ellsworth. A large, Maine-based clothing store specializing in name-brand sporting clothes plus a large selection of guns. Sidewalk sales and some discounted clothing.

Life Sports, 34 High Street (Route 1), Ellsworth. A large, trendy store that features camping and hiking, running, tennis, racquetball, fishing, and swim clothes. Life Sports also rents and sells canoes, kayaks, and windsurfers and even offers windsurf and kayak clinics.

Acadia Shops, 85 Main Street, Bar Harbor, with branches in the park at Jordan Pond House, Cadillac summit, and Thunder Hole. Maine-made clothing and gifts, souvenirs.

By Way of Maine (244-7027 or 800-423-0403), Main Street, Southwest Harbor. An outstanding selection of things made in Maine; also a mail-order catalog.

L.L. Bean Outlet, High Street, Ellsworth. Clothing, sporting equipment, a wide variety of discounted items from Maine's most famous store.

Big Chicken Barn (667-7308), Route 1 south of Ellsworth. Maine's largest used bookstore fills the vast innards of a former chicken house on Route 1. Annegret and Mike Cukierski have 80,000 books in stock: hardbacks, paperbacks, magazines, and comics; also used furniture and collectibles. The day we stopped by, a Florida restaurant owner was loading up an old dory with books and heading south. He had bought the dory (he planned to make it into a salad boat), the trailer to carry it, and the books here. Browsers are welcome.

SPECIAL EVENTS Throughout the summer: **Band concerts,** Bar Harbor Village Green (check current evenings).

June: **Antique Auto Rally, Lobster Races.**

July: **Independence Day** midnight square dance with breakfast for dancers followed by sunrise dance on top of Cadillac Mountain, street parade, and seafood festival. **Art Show,** Bar Harbor Village Green (later in the month). **Dulcimer and Harp Festival,** Bar Harbor. **Southwest Harbor Days:** craft show, parade, sidewalk sales. **Tour d'Arcadie,** largest amateur bicycle race in Maine (begins in Bar Harbor). **Ellsworth Craft Show** (end of month).

August: **Crafts Show** and **Art Show,** Bar Harbor. **Winter Harbor Lobster Festival,** Winter Harbor, includes road race, lobster feed, and lobster boat races.

September: Marathon road race, bicycle race.

October: Scottish performing arts concert and workshop on Columbus Day weekend.

Trenton Lobster Pound

Photo by Kim Grant

BANGOR AREA

It is no coincidence that 1820—when big-city merchants began buying timberland along the upper reaches of the Penobscot River—was also the year in which the Massachusetts District of Maine became a state and planted a white pine in the center of its official seal.

By the 1830s the Penobscot River was filled with pine logs, all of which were processed in the sawmills just above Bangor where they were loaded aboard ships. In Bangor the offices of land brokers shouldered saloons and houses dedicated to taking in "gentlemen's washing." In 1835 it was reported that two paupers who had escaped from Bangor's almshouse had each cleared $1,000 by speculating in timberland (the land offices worked around the clock) by the time they were caught the next morning. Bangor was the world's leading lumber port.

Today a modern paper mill stands at the confluence of the Penobscot River and Penobscot Bay, and the only Paul Bunyan you will find in Bangor is the 31-foot-high wooden statue in the park. The old rip-roaring Bangor has disappeared. What a 1911 fire did not claim has since been eaten by urban renewal. Still, Bangor is Maine's second largest city, and Bangor International Airport is departure point for craft (admittedly air instead of sailing) bound for faraway points of the globe.

GUIDANCE   **Bangor Area Chamber of Commerce** (947-0307), 519 Main Street (just off the I-95 exit, across from the Holiday Inn), maintains a seasonal Bangor Visitors Information Office (945-5717). This is a Paul Bunyan Park on lower Main Street (Route 1A).

The Maine Publicity Bureau maintains two rest area/information centers on I-95 in Hamden between exits 43 and 44: northbound (862-6628) and southbound (862-6638).

GETTING THERE   By air: **Bangor International Airport** (947-0384) is served by Delta Airlines, Continental Express, Northwest Airlink, and United Airlines. **Rental cars** are available at the airport.

By bus: **Greyhound**.

By car: The Maine Turnpike.

MEDICAL EMERGENCY   **Eastern Maine Medical Center** (947-3711), Bangor. **St. Joseph Hospital** (947-8311), Bangor.

TO SEE AND DO   In **Bangor** two neighborhoods have survived fire and renewal to tell of past grandeur. One is the West Market Square Historic District, a mid-nineteenth-century block of shops (it includes the Phenix Inn). The other is the Broadway area, studded with lumber barons' mansions and the turreted Victorian home of author Stephen King (look for the bat and cobweb fence). It's here that you find the **Bangor Historical Society Museum** (942-5766), 159 Union Street (at

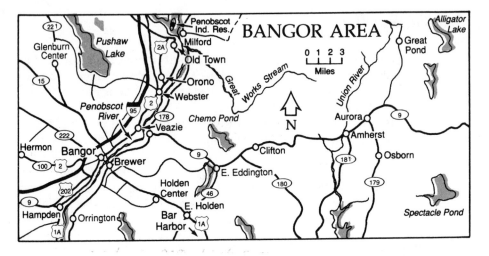

High Street), Bangor. Open February to mid-December, Tuesday through Friday and Sundays 12–4. Admission i s $1per adult, $.25 per student. A collection of city memorabilia is housed in the Greek Revival Thomas Hill House. Architecture buffs might also want to check out the neighboring **Isaac Farrar Mansion,** 166 Union Street, open weekdays 9–4, a carefully restored Greek Revival lumber baron's mansion with marble fireplaces, mahogany paneling, and stained glass windows.

Best of Bangor Bus Tours, sponsored by the Bangor Historical Society, are offered on Thursdays in July, August, and September, departing from the Bangor Visitors Information Building at 519 Main Street (see Guidance).

Galen Cole Family Land Transportation Museum, 405 Perry Road (junction I-95 and 395), Bangor. Open early May through October, daily 9–5 . $2 per adult; children free. A collection of nineteenth- and twentieth-century Maine vehicles: snow plows, wagons, trucks, sleds, rail equipment, and more.

Mount Hope Cemetery in Bangor is one of the nation's oldest garden cemeteries, designed by noted Maine architect Charles G. Bryant.

Indian Island. In 1786 the Penobscot Tribe deeded most of Maine to Massachusetts in exchange for 140 small islands in the Penobscot River; they continue to live on this one, connected by a one-lane bridge to Old Town. The 1970s discovery of an eighteenth-century agreement that details the land belonging to the tribe (much of it now valuable) has brought the island a new school and a large community center, which attracts crowds to play high-stakes Bingo (phone: 800-255-1293 for the schedule). A general store in the center sells locally made crafts as does the Moccasin Shop at Ernest Goslin's house on Bridge Street. A **Penobscot Nation Museum** (827-6545), 6 River Road, is theoretically open weekdays 1–4 ($1per adult, $.50 per child), but it was not open when we visited. There is also the **Sockalexis Memorial Ice Arena** (827-7776), open year-round, skate rentals available. The island is accessible from Route 2, marked from I-95, Exit 51.

University of Maine museums (581-1901), Orono. The **Hudson Museum** (open Tuesday through Friday 9–4, Saturday 9–3, Sunday 11–3) has an exceptional anthropological collection including a special section on Maine Indians and Maine history. **University of Maine Museum of Art,** 109 Carnegie Hall (open weekdays 8–4:30, Saturday 1–4) shows a fraction of its collection of 4,500 works; also it has changing exhibits. The campus is on Route 2A, 8 miles from Bangor.

Old Town Museum (827-7256), North Fourth Street Extension, Old Town. Open early June through mid-August, Wednesday to Sunday 1–5. A former waterworks building houses exhibits on the Penobscot Indians and local logging; early photos; an original birchbark canoe.

FISHING   **Bangor Salmon Pool.** A gathering spot for salmon traveling upstream to spawn, located 2 miles south of Bangor, Route 9 off North Main Street, Brewer.

GOLF   **Bangor Golf Course** (945-9226), Webster Avenue. Eighteen holes. **Penobscot Valley Country Club** (866-2423), Bangor Road, Orono. Eighteen holes.

SWIMMING   **Violette's Public Beach and Boat Landing** (843-6876), East Holden (between Ellsworth and Bangor). $1 admission. Swim float with slide, paddleboats, rental boats, jet skis, windsurfing classes, boat launch, and picnic tables.

CROSS-COUNTRY SKIING   **Ben-Loch Farm Ski Touring Center** (257-4768), North Road, Dixmont. Open daily in-season, 10 AM to dusk. Billed as "Maine's most complete ski touring center." More than 30 miles of groomed, double-tracked trails through orchards, meadows, and pine groves with mountain views. Rentals, lessons, moonlight tours, snacks. (Also see Lodging.)

LODGING   **Phenix Inn** (947-3850), 20 Broad Street, West Market Square, Bangor 04401. Open year-round. A gem of a downtown hotel in a restored 1873 building. All 36 rooms are furnished with mahogany reproduction antiques, and all are air-conditioned and equipped with telephone, TV, and private baths. Some rooms are handicapped accessible, and two are suites. The lobby is attractive and amenities include parking, a coffee shop, and a conference room. $44.50–$80 depending on room and time of year, breakfast included ($80 is for a suite and includes champagne).

Ben-Loch Inn (257-4768), North Road, Box 1020, Dixmont 04932. Five miles off I-95, Exit 42. Open all year. Three guest rooms feature antiques, Oriental rugs and handcrafted quilts, shared or private bath.

Dinner is served to the public on weekends. The house sits on 359 acres, webbed with trails used for cross-country skiing in winter. There's also a pond, good for both fishing and swimming. $50–$60.

The Lucerne Inn (843-5123), RFD 2, Box 540, Lucerne-in-Maine 04429. A nineteenth-century mansion on Route 1A, overlooking Phillips Lake in East Holden. Best known as a restaurant, it also has 25 rooms with private baths, working fireplaces, heated towel bars, whirlpool baths, phones, and TVs. $78–$140. No guests under age 21.

Hamstead Farm (848-3749), RFD 3, Box 703, Bangor 04401. Barns and outbuildings trail picturesquely behind a snug 1840s farmhouse. There are two pleasant guest rooms, shared bath. Resident animals include 70 turkeys, 40 cows, 15 breed sows, 100 feeder pigs, one black sheep, and any number of kittens. The farm is set on 150 acres; a path leads into the village of Hermon. $30–$40 includes a farm breakfast.

Lake Sebasticook Bed and Breakfast (368-5507), 8 Sebasticook Avenue, PO Box 502, Newport 04953. A Victorian home on a quiet street, a short walk from Lake Sebasticook. Bob and Trudy Zothner welcome guests to their comfortable home, 27 miles west of Bangor on I-95 (Exit 39); a good waystop if you are heading Down East or for the Moosehead Lake region. $45 double, $35 single (shared baths; full breakfast). No smoking, alcohol, or children.

American Youth Hostel (898-2262), Ring Hill, RFD 2, Box 235, Carmel 04419. Once the town "poor farm," the Ring Hill Home Hostel sits on 100 forested acres. Free pick-up at the airport is offered. There are just six beds, and family arrangements are accepted. $7 per night for AYH members, more for non-members.

DINING OUT   Lucerne Inn (843-5123), Route 1A, East Holden (11 miles out of Bangor, headed for Ellsworth). Open for lunch and dinner daily, Sunday brunch. A grand old mansion with a view of Phillips Lake. Specialties include beef Wellington. $11–$19.

Seguino's Italian Restaurant (942-1240), 735 Main Street, Bangor. A series of small dining rooms and terraces creates an intimate atmosphere in a big, old house. The menu is vast: a dozen varieties of antipasta; pastas; veal dishes; seafood and chicken choices. *Baccella Napolitano* (whitefish in basil, garlic, and wine on linguini) was especially nice. $10–$16.

Pilots Grill (942-6325), 1528 Hammond Street (Route 2, 1.5 miles west of Exit 45B off I-95), Bangor. Open daily 11:30–10. Most people will tell you this is the best place to eat in town: a large, long-established place with '50s decor and a huge all-American menu. $10–$14.

The Greenhouse (945-4040), 193 Broad Street. Lunch Tuesday through Friday, dinner Tuesday through Saturday. Tropical plants and an exotic menu are not what you'd expect to find in Bangor. We suggest coming for lunch on a warm summer day: there's a large riverside deck.

EATING OUT   **Bagel Shop** (947-1654), 1 Main Street, Bangor. Open Monday to Friday 6–6; Sunday 6–2. A big, genuine, reasonably priced kosher restaurant, delicatessen, and bakery that features egg dishes, bagels, and chocolate cheesecake.

Governor's Take Out and Eat In (947-7704), 643 Broadway, in Bangor and Stillwater Avenue in Stillwater (827-4277). Open from early breakfast to late dinner: big breakfast menu, hamburgers to steaks, specials like German potato soup, fresh strawberry pie.

Dysart's (942-4878), Coldbrook Road, Hermon (I-95, Exit 44). Open 24 hours. Billed as "the biggest truck stop in Maine"—one room for the general public and another for drivers. Known for great road food and reasonable prices.

House of Blarney (848-3618), Horseback Road, Carmel. Housed in an old farmhouse, a family restaurant specializing in chicken pie, homemade bread and desserts. No liquor license; no credit cards.

Weathervane Seafoods (989-4232), 710 Wilson Street, Brewer. Another in the New England chain. (See Eating Out under Belfast to Bangor.)

ENTERTAINMENT   **Maine Center for the Arts,** at the University of Maine campus in Orono, has become *the* cultural center for the area. It's now home for the Bangor Symphony Orchestra.

Maine Masque Theater (581-2000). Classic and contemporary plays presented October through May at the University of Maine, Orono.

Bass Park (942-9000), 100 Dutton Street, Bangor. Complex includes **Bangor Auditorium, Civic Center, State Fair,** and **Raceway** (featuring harness racing, Thursday through Sunday, May to July).

SELECTIVE SHOPPING   *Canoes:*   **Old Town Canoe Company** (827-5513), 58 Middle Street, Old Town. Displays Indian wood designs; varieties sold on premises include fiberglass, wood, Kevlar, Crosslink, and Royalex. Factory tours offered.

White Canoes, 82 North Brunswick Street, Old Town. In business since 1889 and claims to be "America's oldest canoe manufacturer"; also sells canoes.

Books: **Mr. Paperback.** Bangor is home base for this eastern Maine chain with stores here at: 1 Central Street (945-9038), Main Square (492-6494), and Airport Mall (942-9191). All are fully stocked stores with Maine sections.

BookMarc's (942-3206), 10 Harlow Street, Bangor. A great little full-service bookstore.

Special shops: **Winterport Boot Shop,** Twin City Plaza, Brewer. Largest selection of Redwing work boots in the Northeast. Proper fit for sizes 4–16, all widths.

The Briar Patch (941-0255), on West Market Square, Bangor. A large and exceptional children's book and toy store.

The Grasshopper Shop (945-3132), 1 West Market Square. Trendy women's clothing, toys, jewelry, gifts, housewares.

The Bangor Mall, Hogan Road (just west of the I-95 Exit 49 interchange). Boasts more than 80 stores and has spawned a number of satellite mini-malls. Since this is precisely the kind of strip most visitors come to Maine to escape, we won't elaborate. But it certainly has its uses.

SPECIAL EVENTS   January: **Paul Bunyan Snowmobile Derby,** Bangor (last weekend).

July: **Bangor State Fair,** Bass Park, agricultural fair with harness racing.

Washington County and Campobello

As Down East as you can get in this country, Washington County is a ruggedly beautiful and lonely land unto itself. Even along its coast, which harbors some of the most dramatic cliffs and deepest coves—certainly the highest tides on the eastern seaboard—you rarely see tourists. Harbors are filled with lobster boats and trawlers instead of pleasure craft. Lodging is limited.

This Sunrise County is larger than the states of Delaware or Rhode Island, and yet it is home for just 35,000 people widely scattered among fishing villages, canning towns, logging outposts, Indian reservations, and backcountry farms.

Many people (not just some) survive here by raking blueberries in August, making balsam wreaths in winter, and digging clams and sea worms the remainder of the year.

Remarkably few visitors find their way to Washington County. Cobscook State Park, which offers superb shoreside campsites, is rarely full in August. The only "groups" you meet are birders scouting for American bald eagles or osprey and naturalists searching for the whales in the Bay of Fundy and the puffins on Machias Seal Island. You may also see fishermen angling for Atlantic salmon in the tidal rivers or for landlocked salmon and smallmouth bass in the lakes.

For exploring purposes Washington County divides into three distinct regions: (1) the 60-mile stretch of Route 1 between Steuben and Lubec (this actually includes some 600 miles of rugged coast and the Roosevelt International Park on the Canadian island of Campobello), an area for which Machias is the shopping, dining, and information center; (2) Eastport and Cobscook Bay, the area of the highest tides and a sense of being at the end of the world; and (3) Calais and the St. Croix Valley, including the lake-splotched backwoods and the fishermen's havens at Grand Lake Stream.

Wherever you explore in Washington County—from the old sardine-canning towns of Eastport and Lubec to the coastal fishing villages of Jonesport and Cutler and the even smaller villages on immense inland lakes—you find a Maine that you thought had disappeared decades ago.

You are surprised by the beauty of old buildings such as the eighteenth-century Burnham Tavern in Machias and Ruggles Man-

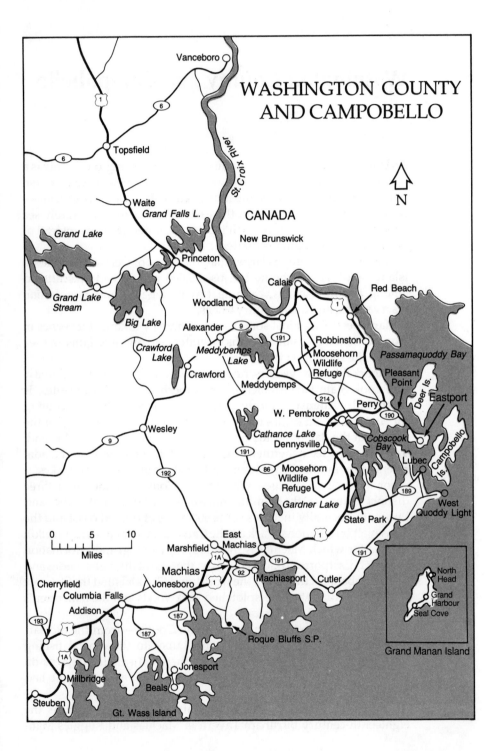

WASHINGTON COUNTY
AND CAMPOBELLO

sion in Columbia Falls. You learn that the first naval battle of the Revolution was won by Machias men; that some local eighteenth-century women were buried in rum casks (because they were shipped home that way from the Caribbean); and that Pirate Captain Richard Bellamy's loot is believed to be buried around Machias.

And if any proof were needed that this has always been one isolated piece of coast, there is Bailey's Mistake. Captain Bailey, it seems, wrecked his four-masted schooner one foggy night in a fine little bay 7 miles south of Lubec (which is where he should have been). Considering the beauty of the spot and how far he was from the Boston shipowner, Bailey and his crew unpacked their cargo of lumber and settled right down on the shore. That was in 1830, and many of their descendants have had the sense to stay put.

But what impresses you most about Washington County is its people. Just as glaciers have scoured the landscape, so the long winters and isolation have weathered a "state of Mainer," who is even more contrary and individualistic than his brothers to the west—also more interested in everything that grows or breathes, including that rare species of visitor who strays this far east.

GUIDANCE   The **Washington County Regional Planning Commission** (255-8686), 63 Main Street, Machias 04654, furnishes basic information.

The **Quoddy Loop Regional Tourism Office** (454-2597), Box 688, Calais 04619, publishes a useful map/guide and serves as an information source for the entire coastal area from Machias to Campobello Island and on around Cobscook and Passamaquoddy bays, including Deer Island, Grand Manan Island, and the resort town of St. Andrews, New Brunswick.

The **Calais Information Center** (454-2211), 7 Union Street, Calais. Open year-round and staffed by the Maine Publicity Bureau, it provides material on the entire county and state.

(Also see Guidance for each region of the county.)

GETTING THERE   By air: See Bangor and Bar Harbor for scheduled airline service. Charter service is available to the following airports: **Eastport Municipal** (853-2951), **Machias Valley** (255-8709), **Lubec Municipal** (733-5532), and **Princeton Municipal** (796-2744).

By bus: **Greyhound** serves Bangor.

By car: There are two equally slow ways **to reach coastal Route 1** from the rest of Maine and beyond: (1) I-95 to Augusta, then Route 3 to Belfast (stop at Lake St. George for a swim), then Route 1; or (2) I-95 to Bangor, then Route 1A to Ellsworth, then Route 1. You save a few miles by taking Route 182 from Ellsworth through Franklin to Cherryfield.

For eastern Washington County, take I-95 to Bangor, then the Airline Highway (Route 9) for 100 miles straight through the blueberry barrens and woods to Calais. The state maintains camping and picnic sites at intervals along this stretch, and there is food and lodging in Beddington, Wesley, Alexander, and Baring.

GETTING AROUND   For information about car ferry service from Eastport or Campobello to Deer Island contact **East Coast Ferries** (506-747-2159). A year-round **Provincial Ferry** (506-851-3600) connects Deer Island with L'Etete, New Brunswick. **Grand Manan Ferry Service** (506-662-8829) to Grand Manan, the isolated fishing island clearly visible from Quoddy Light State Park, is from Black's Harbor, New Brunswick, not far from L'Etete. **Bold Coast Charter Company** (259-4484), in Cutler makes the run out to Grand Manan in two hours. Captain Patterson will take you over for the day or drop you off and come back when you want. $60–$75 per person, minimum of four.

MEDICAL EMERGENCY   **Calais Regional Hospital** (454-7531).
    Downeast-Machias Hospital (255-3356).

THE COAST

GUIDANCE   **The Machias Bay Area Chamber of Commerce** (255-4402), PO Box 606, Machias 04654, maintains a seasonal information center in the former railroad station across from Helen's Restaurant on the northern fringe of town. **The Campobello Chamber of Commerce** (506-752-2396), Wilson's Beach, Campobello, New Brunswick EOG 3L, is a source of information for lodging on that island.

TO SEE AND DO   **Roosevelt Campobello International Park** (506-752-2922), Welshpool Campobello Island, New Brunswick, Canada (for a brochure write Box 97, Lubec 04652). Open daily Memorial Day weekend to mid-October from 9–5 Eastern daylight time (10–6 Atlantic daylight time). Although technically in New Brunswick, this manicured 2,600-acre park with a visitors center and shingled "cottages" is the number-one sight to see east of Bar Harbor. You turn down a side street in Lubec, and there is the bridge (built in 1962) and Canadian customs. The house in which Franklin Delano Roosevelt summered as a boy has disappeared but the airy "Roosevelt Cottage," a wedding gift to Franklin and Eleanor, is maintained just as the family left it, charged with the spirit of the dynamic man who succumbed to polio here on August 25, 1921. During his subsequent stints as governor of New York and then as president of the United States, F.D.R. rarely returned here. Excellent documentaries and newsreels conjure the Great Depression and war periods. Neighboring Hubbard Cottage, with its oval picture window, gives another slant on this turn-of-the-century resort. The grounds are banked with flower beds, and beyond stretch more than 8 miles of trails to the shore and inland through woods to lakes and ponds. There are also 15.4 miles of Park Drives, modified from the network of carriage drives that the wealthy "cottagers" maintained on the island. Beyond the park is East Quoddy Head Lighthouse, a popular whale-watching station. There is the picturesque fishing village of Head Harbor and the small car ferry to Deer Island that runs during July and August (see Getting Around).

West Quoddy Light State Park, South Lubec Road, Lubec. Open mid-April through October, sunrise to sunset. Marking the easternmost tip of the United States, the red-and-white-striped lighthouse dates back to 1858. The park, adjacent to the lighthouse, offers benches from which it is possible to be the first person in the United States to see the sunrise. There is also a fine view of Grand Manan Island, a pleasant picnic area, and a 2-mile hiking trail along the cliffs to Carrying Place Cove. Between the cove and the bay, roughly a mile back down the road from the light, is an unusual coastal raised-plateau bog with dense sphagnum moss and heath.

West Quoddy Marine Research Station (733-8895), PO Box 9, Lubec 04652 (down the road from the light). Open 10–6 in-season. A visitors center has exhibits about local whales, which include finbacks, humpbacks, and minkes; there are whale tapes, seminars, and nature walks.

Burnham Tavern (255-4432), Route 192 (just off Route 1), Machias. Open mid-June to Labor Day, Monday through Friday 10–5; otherwise by appointment. $1 per adult, $.25 per child. A gambrel-roofed tavern with period furnishings and mementos from the British man-of-war *Margaretta* captured on June 12, 1775, by townspeople in the small sloop *Unity*. This was the first naval battle of the American Revolution. Unfortunately, the British retaliated by burning Portland.

Machias itself is the county seat, an interesting old commercial center with falls running through the middle of town (*Machias* is said to be the Indian word for "bad little falls"). There are concerts on the tracker organ in the graceful 1836 Congregational church and plays at the **University of Maine at Machias;** there's also a park at Bad Little Falls with picnic tables and a suspension bridge. **O'Brien Cemetery,** on Elm Street overlooking the river, has many stones worth pondering. Machias is also a great place to eat, and it is the home of the **Maine Wild Blueberry Company,** a new plant in a former textile mill that processes a quarter of a million pounds of berries a day and ships them as far as Japan (tours offered).

Machiasport. This picturesque village includes the **Gates House** (open May through September, Monday through Friday 12:30–4:30), a Federal-style home with maritime exhibits and period rooms. **Fort O'Brien** is an earthwork mound used as an ammunitions magazine during the American Revolution and the War of 1812. We recommend that you continue on down Route 92 to the fishing village of Bucks Harbor (see Eating Out) and take one of the roads to **Jasper Beach,** so named for the wave-tumbled and polished pebbles of jasper and rhyolite that give it a distinctive color. The road ends with great views and a beach to walk in Starboard.

Cutler. A beautiful little fishing village with an inn, happily shielded from a view of the Cutler communications station, whose 26 antenna towers (ranging from 800- to 980-feet tall) light up red at night and can be seen from much of the county's coast (it is said to be the world's most powerful radio station). Cutler is the departure point for Captain Norton's excursions to see the puffins on Machias Seal Island (see Boat Excursions).

Jonesport and Beals Island. Jonesport and Beals are both lobstering and fishing villages. Beals, connected by a bridge (rumored to have been purposely built low enough to exclude sailing yachts) to Jonesport, is also connected by a shorter bridge to **Great Wass Island** (see Hiking). Jonesport is the kind of village that seems small the first time you drive through but grows in dimensions as you slow down. Look closely and you will find two restaurants, three grocery stores, two antiques shops, two bed & breakfasts, chandleries, a hardware/ clothing store, a realtor, and much more. Together the towns are home for eastern Maine's largest lobstering fleet, but the big buy at the co-op in Jonesport is crabmeat.

Milbridge. A Route 1 town with a wandering coastline, home of one of the oldest wild blueberry processors (Jasper Wyman and Sons) as well as one of the county's five surviving sardine canneries, a Christmas wreath factory, a commercial center with a fine crafts cooperative, a movie theater, and a choice of bed & breakfasts. **McLellan Park,** overlooking Narraguagus (pronounced *nair-a-gway-gus*) Bay, has picnic tables, fireplaces, rest rooms, and drinking water.

Cherryfield. A few miles up the Narraguagus River, Cherryfield boasts a fine Atlantic salmon pool. The **Cherryfield–Narraguagus Historical Society** (546-7979), Main Street (just off Route 1), is open during July and August, Wednesdays and Saturdays 1–4, and by appointment. Picnic tables in Stewart Park on Main Street and in Forest Mill Dam Park on River Road are on the banks of the river. Cherryfield (why isn't it called *Berryfield?*) bills itself "Blueberry Capital of Maine"; there are two processing plants in town.

Ruggles House, Columbia Falls. Open June to mid-October, Monday through Saturday 9:30–4:30; Sunday 11–4:30. Admission is $.50. This 1818 Federal-style mansion was built by wealthy lumber dealer Thomas Ruggles. It is a beauty, with a graceful flying staircase, a fine Palladian window, and superb woodwork. Legend has it that a woodcarver was imprisoned in the house for three years with a penknife. There is an unmistakably tragic feel to the place. Mr. Ruggles died soon after its completion, and his heirs petered out in the 1920s.

Lubec. Most visitors now pass through this "Easternmost town" quickly—on their way over the FDR Memorial Bridge to Campobello Island. Take a minute to find the old town landing where there's a public boat launch and a breakwater well known to fishermen. It's also a great spot for a picnic: Campobello is in the distance, and a distinctive little lighthouse is just offshore amid very fast-moving currents. Once there were 20 sardine-canning plants in Lubec; the wonder is that there are still two, along with the country's only smoked herring plant. Luckily Barney Rier has preserved much of the flavor of Lubec's heyday in **The Old Sardine Village Museum** (733-2822), Route 189, on your way into Lubec. Open late June through mid-October, Tuesday through Saturday 1–5; $3 per adult, $2 teens. A large warehouse-like structure is filled with displays depicting the growth of the food-canning industry from the first hand-formed can of the 1830s; a variety of old machines, photos, and blueberry cannery equipment is also on view.

BOAT EXCURSIONS **Captain Barna B. and his son John Norton** (497-5933; call between 7 and 9 PM), of Jonesport, take charter groups out to see the puffins on **Machias Seal Island,** May through August, departing Jonesport early morning. Although just 10 miles off Cutler, the island is disputed by Canada (Canadians man the lighthouse), and Captain Barna Norton is known for his views on the subject; he usually brings along an umbrella, which he opens once off the island to display an American flag on top. The 40-foot party boat *Chief* (built by this able father-and-son team) also offers fishing from late August to October and duck hunting in-season.

Bold Coast Charter Company (259-4484), Cutler. Captain Andrew Patterson offers two-hour sight-seeing trips along the rockbound coast around Cutler; also excursions to Machias Seal Island and to Grand Manan Island.

CANOEING The Machias River, fed by the five Machias lakes, drops through the backwoods with technically demanding rapids and takes three to six days to run. The Narraguagus and East Machias rivers are also good for trips of two to four days. For rentals, lessons, advice, and guided tours contact **Sunrise County Canoe Expeditions** (454-7708), Cathance Lake, Grove Post Office 04638.

FISHING Salmon fishing is the reason why many people come to this area (see Cherryfield under To See and Do); the Narraguagus and Machias rivers are the places to fish mid-May through early June. Six Mile Lake in Marshfield (6 miles north of Machias on Route 192), with picnic facilities, shelters, and a boat ramp, is known for trout. For information about licenses, guides, and fish, write to the regional headquarters of the **Inland Fisheries and Wildlife Department,** Machias 04654.

GOLF **Great Cove Golf Club** (434-2981), Jonesboro Road, Roque Bluffs, offers nine holes, water views, clubhouse, rental clubs, and carts.

Herring Cove Golf Course (506-752-2449), in the Herring Cove

Provincial Park (open mid-May to mid-November), has nine holes, a clubhouse restaurant, and rentals.

HIKING   (Also see West Quoddy Light State Park under To See and Do.)

Great Wass Island. A 1,540-acre tract at the southern tip of the Jonesport-Addison peninsula. The interior of the island supports one of Maine's largest jack pine stands and has coastal peatlands maintained by the Maine chapter of the Nature Conservancy. There is a choice of trails; we prefer the 2-mile trek along the shore to Little Cape Point where children can clamber on the smooth rocks for hours. Bring a picnic.

Great Heath, a vast peat bog that straddles Columbia Falls and Township 19MD, is a haunt for naturalists and biologists: 3,200 acres of heath supervised by the Bureau of Public Lands. The National Audubon Society offers periodic tours.

Petit Manan National Wildlife Refuge, Petit Manan Point, Steuben (6 miles off Route 1 on Pigeon Hill Road). A varied area with pine stands, cedar swamps, blueberry barrens, marshes, and great birding.

SWIMMING   **Roque Bluffs State Park,** Roque Bluffs (6 miles off Route 1). There is a pebble beach on the ocean, frequently too windy to use even in August. A sheltered sand beach on a freshwater pond is an ideal place for children. Facilities include tables, grills, changing areas with vault toilets, and a children's playground.

Gardner Lake, Chases Mills Road, East Machias, offers freshwater swimming, a picnic area, and a boat launch. **Six-Mile Lake,** Route 192, North Machias, is also good for a dip. On Beals Island, the **Backfield Area,** Alley's Bay, offers saltwater swimming.

WHALE-WATCHING   The unusually high tides in the Bay of Fundy seem to foster ideal feeding grounds for right, minke, and humpback whales and for porpoises and dolphins. East Quoddy Head on Campobello and West Quoddy Head in Lubec are favored viewing spots. Two father-and-son teams, the Nortons (see Boat Excursions) and the Harrises (see Deep-Sea Fishing under Eastport) offer whale-watching cruises.

INNS AND BED & BREAKFASTS   **Little River Lodge** (259-4437), Cutler 04626. Open May through October. Built in 1845 as a logging camp, converted to a hotel in 1870 when the Eastern Steamship ferries stopped here; nicely decorated. Carl and Nancy Sundberg offer seven bedrooms, some with fireplaces, sharing three baths. A dining room and modern sun porch overlook Cutler Harbor. Dinner is served by reservation. Double $40–$60, includes breakfast.

The Overview (733-2005), RD 2, Box 106, Lubec 04652. Sited on the road overlooking Bailey's Mistake (see the introduction to this chapter), this is a delightfully out-of-the-way old place (but just three-quarters of a mile from Quoddy Light) where Edith Heter welcomes guests with three rooms—two singles and a double. There is an organic garden out back, a sauna, and space for cross-country skiing. $25–$35 per room, full breakfast included.

Ricker House (546-2780), Cherryfield 04622. A classic Federal house with a double parlor, furnished comfortably with plenty of books and an inviting country kitchen. There are three guest rooms (two with river views) and one bath. A path leads to a picnic table by the river, and the tennis courts across the road are free. The Conways are delighted to help guests explore the area. $40–$45 per room ($10 per extra person) includes a full breakfast. No smoking.

Home Port Inn (733-2077), 45 Main Street, Lubec 04652. Open May 15 to November 15. Tim and Miyoko Carman offer seven antiques-furnished rooms (two on the ground floor, all with private baths) in a gracious old hilltop Lubec home, built in 1880. Breakfast and dinner are served. $50–$70 double.

Tootsie's Bed and Breakfast (497-5414), RFD 1, Box 252, Trynor Square, Jonesport 04649. This was the first bed & breakfast in Washington County, and it is still one of the nicest. Charlotte Beal ("Tootsie" is what her grandchildren call her) offers two rooms—nothing fancy but homey and spanking clean. The shipshape house sits in a cluster of lobstermen's homes on the fringe of this fishing village handy to Great Wass Island. $25–$40 includes a full breakfast.

Chandler River Lodge (434-2651), Jonesboro 04648. Open July and August only. For advance reservations contact the Kerr Family, 21 Bertrand Street, Old Bridge, NJ 08857. The Kerrs have been welcoming guests to their summer home for 24 years. Nicely sited on 30 riverfront acres, this old home has six guest rooms. $30–$38 ($10 per extra person) includes breakfast.

The Gutsy Gull (255-8633), PO Box 313, Route 92, Machiasport 04655. Alvin Bowker and Larry Payne have renovated a fine 1850s house overlooking a picturesque old sardine cannery and the Machias River. The five rooms are each carefully decorated; my favorite is the third-floor double tucked under the eaves. The new dining room, overlooking an inviting backyard is the setting for memorable breakfasts; the hot tub is icing on this cake.

Riverside Bed & Breakfast (255-4134), East Machias 04630. This Victorian house fronts on Route 1, but the back rooms and deck overlook the East Machias River. Tom and Carol Paul owned an antiques shop in Newport before creating this attractive waystop, which is pure 1890s—right down to the antique linens. Note the old train baggage rack over the clawfoot tub. The three rooms are moderately priced, breakfast included; lunch and dinner on request.

Clark Perry House (255-8458), 59 Court Street, Machias 04654. One of the handsomest homes in Machias, built in 1868 and newly renovated by Robin and David Rier who offer three guest rooms. The inexpensive rate includes full breakfast.

Pleasant Bay Bed & Breakfast (483-4490), PO Box 222, West Side Road, Addison 04606. A 110-acre llama farm on the shores of the Pleasant River and Pleasant Bay. Guests are invited to meander the trails accompanied by the llamas. $45–$50 per couple includes breakfast.

K. J. Tucker's (255-6256 or 483-4308), Machias 04654. A fine, old downtown house with a bakery on the side. $45–$65, breakfast included; lunch and dinner on request.

Harrington House (483-4044), PO Box 92, Harrington 04606. Open year-round. This is a modest but comfortable house beside the Village Green on the Harrington River in the center of the small village. Carol and Richard Weidenbacher offer six guest rooms, five baths. $35–$45 per night, breakfast included.

Starboard Cove (255-4426), HCR 70, Box 442, Bucks Harbor 04618. This is a snug Cape, with a large deck and garden, overlooking a working boatyard in the cove. Two bedrooms are available, one with a private half-bath and a dressing area or child's room. $30–$40 includes breakfast.

Peacock House (733-2403), 27 Summer Street, Lubec 04652. Open late May through October. An 1880s house on a quiet side street, home for four generations of the Peacock family (owners of the major local cannery). There are four guest rooms which, like the formal common rooms, are immaculate. $45-65 with a full breakfast if you're up at 7, otherwise continental.

The Milbridge Inn (546-7339), Main Street, Milbridge 04658. Ava Skinner's comfortable home with a pleasant, old-style guest house atmosphere. $32–$35.

For further leads on area bed & breakfasts, contact **Bed & Breakfast Down East Ltd.** (565-3517), Box 457, Eastbrook 04634.

MOTELS   **Blueberry Patch Inn** (434-5411), Jonesboro 04648. A small spic-and-span motel on Route 1 near the village of Jonesboro with some reconditioned cottages, fridge and coffee in each room, a few efficiencies, a pleasant office with announcements of local events and space to sit and read, a pool and sun deck surrounded by berries, and a short nature trail. Inexpensive. The neighboring White House restaurant offers all meals (see Eating Out).

Red Barn Motel (546-7721), Milbridge 04658. Open year-round. Thirty-four standard motel units behind a popular restaurant (see Eating Out) that serves all three meals. Facilities include an outdoor pool. $40–$58.

Maineland Motel (255-3334), Route 1, East Machias 04630. Open year-round. Thirty rooms with cable TV. $25–$55.

Machias Motor Inn (255-4861), East Maine Street, Machias 04654. A large, two-story motel adjoining Helen's Restaurant (see Eating Out); all have river views, some efficiencies. $49–$55.

COTTAGES **Micmac Farm Guest Cabins** (255-3008), Machiasport 04655. Open May to November. Best known for their restaurant (see Dining Out), Barbara and Daniel Dunn also offer several housekeeping cabins. Each has two double beds and a view of the Machias River through sliding glass doors. A real find at $45 per unit.

Additional rental cottages are listed in the booklet "Maine: Guide to Camp & Cottage Rentals" available from the **Maine Publicity Bureau,** 97 Winthrop Street, Hallowell 04347. Summer rentals in this area still begin at around $275 per week.

CAMPING **McClennan Park,** Milbridge. A town shoreside park with limited sites.

Mainayr Campground (546-2690), Steuben 04680. Open Memorial Day to mid-October. Thirty acres on a tidal cove. Special programs in drawing and crafts.

DINING OUT **Micmac Farm Restaurant** (255-3008), Machiasport. Open year-round (except for two weeks at Christmas), Tuesday through Saturday 6:30–8, by reservation. Set off down a bumpy dirt road off Route 92, you wouldn't think anyone could find it, but it tends to be full most summer evenings. Last season the Dunns had to turn away customers, but they don't want to enlarge and risk losing "some of the present ambience and charm." This is an exquisite riverside house built in 1776 by Tristam Thurlow Corbett. Just 25 diners can be seated in the low-beamed dining room, and meals are served by candlelight. There is usually a choice of five entrées. The price includes the entire dinner. BYOB, since the town is dry. Inexpensive to moderate.

The Homeport Inn (733-2077), 45 Main Street, Lubec. Open nightly June through late October, otherwise on weekends. The attractive dining room in the back of this inn contains just seven well-spaced tables. Innkeeper Tim Carman has brought extensive restaurant experience to this effort and provides a full menu featuring seafood dishes like shrimp scampi served over linguini and creamed haddock with artichoke hearts ($7.95).

The Red Barn (546-7721), Main Street (junction of routes 1 and 1A), Milbridge. Open daily year-round, 6:30 AM for coffee and muffins and full service 7 AM to 9 PM. Credit cards are not accepted. There is a counter in the back, an abundance of deep booths in the main pine-paneled dining room, and more seating in the overflow "banquet" room. The Red Barn is a landmark—not the kind that's geared to bus groups, just the obvious meeting place between Ellsworth and Machias; also handy to the movies (see Entertainment). The salad bar is really a buffet (soup and bread are included), a meal in itself. A seafood stew is thick with shrimp, scallops, haddock, and crabmeat. The menu is large: pastas, burgers, steak, seafood, and fried chicken. Children's menu, great cream pies. Inexpensive to moderate; no credit cards.

EATING OUT **The White House** (434-2792), Route 1, Jonesboro. Open 4:30

AM to 9 PM. A very white building with red-striped awnings, cheery blue booths, a counter, and friendly service. The fish chowder is outstanding as are the fried seafood platters and delectable pies. Just don't order the spaghetti.

Helen's Restaurant (255-6506), 32 Main Street, Machias (north of town on the water). Open 5 AM to 10 PM. The new Helen's is bigger, geared to bus groups en route from Campobello to Bar Harbor. It even has a gift shop. No liquor but the food is generous and good: a wide choice of seafood, meat entrées, salads, fish stews, and sandwiches. The special pie is strawberry, but there are also whipped pies and standbys like blueberry. The breakfast payoff is blueberry pancakes in-season.

Tall Barney, Jonesport. Open 7–7. It's easy to miss this cozy haven set back behind its parking lot almost across from the access to the big bridge. It is particularly welcoming for breakfast on a foggy morning. The papers are stacked on the counter, and the booths are filled with local people. Just don't sit at the long table down the middle of the front room the way we did. No one says anything but it's obvious, after a while, that it's reserved for the local lobstermen, who come drifting in one by one.

Milbridge House (546-2020), Main Street, Milbridge. Open early and late, a great family-owned restaurant that's bigger and more attractive than it looks from the road. Don't pass up the pies.

Seaview Restaurant (733-2234), Route 189, Lubec. Open mid-May to mid-October, noon to 9 PM except Mondays. New ownership has spiffed up this old place with mauve vinyl tablecloths, pictures of the Roosevelts, hanging plants, and bentwood chairs. There is a water view from booths along one wall.

Hillside Restaurant (733-4223), Route 189, Lubec. Open every day except Tuesdays in-season from 11 AM–9 PM. "We're not fancy, and we don't have a view, but we serve the kind of food that brings folks back" boasts the ads for this main drag eatery. The fish chowder is superb and the lobster salad sandwich is outstanding; get it from the takeout window and bring it down to the breakwater.

Graham's Restaurant (255-3351), Lower Main Street, Machias. Open year-round for all three meals. A combination diner atmosphere for breakfast and lunch; the more formal dining room (with banquet room) features live boiled lobster, seafood, salad bar, homemade pies, and cocktails.

MacKenzie's Yankee Grocer (255-3661), Machias (on the dike, Route 1 north of town). The lunch counter in this general store (geared to a camper's needs) is a source of breakfast and lunch specials: seafood, pizza, sandwiches, baked beans, and fresh coleslaw.

SNACKS   **Milbridge Theater Ice Cream Shop,** Main Street, Milbridge. Open in-season from noon. Delectable fudges and candy as well as ice cream, some old-fashioned ice-cream parlor tables, and an information center of sorts for the region.

The Islander (497-2000), Alleys Bay Road, Great Wass Island. Open in-season 3–9 PM. The back of a house fronts on the water and in summer becomes a great takeout place with a deck for consuming fried clams and soft ice cream—a different flavor every day of the week—with a variety of toppings. *The* place to stop after a 4-mile hike (see Hiking).

Sugar Scoop Bakery (546-7048), Main Street, Milbridge. Open Tuesday through Saturday 5 AM to 6 PM. Good for a cup of coffee and a freshly baked doughnut or turnover, even a chicken pie or baked beans and brown bread.

ENTERTAINMENT   Milbridge Theater (546-2038), Main Street, Milbridge. Open nightly May through November, 7:30 showtime; Saturday and Sunday matinees for children's films, all seats $2. A very special theater: a refurbished moviehouse featuring first-run and art movies and truly affordable prices. Fresh popcorn, ice-cream parlor.

University of Maine, Machias (255-3313, extension 284 or 216) offers both a winter and summer series of plays, musicals, and concerts. The plays are by the local resident company: the Bad Little Falls Players. Down River Productions (255-4465) stages plays in the Machias Valley Grange in Machias, June through mid-August.

Machias Bay Chamber Concerts (255-3889), Center Street Congregational Church, Machias. A series of eight chamber music concerts, July through early August, Tuesday at 8 PM. Top groups such as the Kneisel Hall Chamber Players and the Vermeer Quartet are featured.

SELECTIVE SHOPPING   Hands On (formerly the Eastern Maine Craft Co-op; 546-2682), Main Street, Milbridge. Open daily June to mid-September from 10 AM–5:30 PM. An outlet for work by 21 outstanding local craftspeople, including weavers, potters, quilters, a jeweler, a metal sculptor, and a woodworker. So special that they demand mention are contemporary quilts by Carol Schutt and Old World Pottery Mocha Ware by Roscoe Mann (the two have recently married) and metal sculptures by Peter Weil.

The Ferris Wheel Emporium (255-4649), Machias. Open May to December. This is a showcase for more than five dozen Washington County craftspeople and entrepreneurs who can't afford their own stores. The array of antiques, clothing, wooden toys, and pottery makes for good browsing.

Country Duckling (255-8063), 1 Water Street, Machias. Locally made handcrafted gifts.

Sea-Witch (546-7495), Milbridge. Describing itself as "the biggest little gift shop in Washington County," this is a trove of trinkets and treasures: collector dolls, spatterware, stuffed animals, local seafood, and berry products.

Crossroads Vegetables (497-2641), posted from Route 187 (off Route 1), Jonesport. Open daily, 9–5:30 in-season. Bonnie and Arnold Pearlman have built their house, windmill, sauna, and barn and have reclaimed acres of productive vegetable garden from the surrounding woods. In addition to their outstanding vegetables (salad lovers get their greens picked to order; Bonnie adds the edible parts of flowers like nasturtium), they also sell the hand-hollowed wooden bowls that Arnold carves all winter and the dried flower wreaths that Bonnie makes.

Sunrise Workshop (255-8596), 14 Bruce Street, Machias. Wooden boxes and picnic tables, many made by handicapped residents of Washington County, available by mail order; shipping is free within Maine. Also handwoven rugs, placemats, and tote bags.

Your Store (255-3726), 28 Main Street, Machias. Open year-round, Monday through Saturday. A "whole foods" cooperative store that also carries some crafts.

Downeast 5 & 10 Cents (255-8850), Water Street, Machias. Open Monday through Saturday 9–5 and until 8 on Fridays. A superb old-fashioned Ben Franklin store: two stories of crammed aisles.

Columbia Falls Pottery (483-4075), Main Street, Columbia Falls. Open June though mid-October. Striking, bright, sophisticated terra cotta creations by April Adams and Alan Burnham: mugs, platters, kitchenware, lamps, wind chimes, and more.

Christmas wreaths: Wreath-making is a major industry in this area. You can order in the fall and take delivery of a freshly made wreath right before Christmas. Prices quoted include delivery. Sources include: **Cape Split Wreaths** (483-2983), Box 447, Route 1, Addison 04606; **Simplicity Wreath** (483-2780), Sunset Point, Harrington 04643; **The Wreath Shoppe** (483-4598), Box 358, Oak Point Road, Harrington 04643 (wreaths decorated with cones, berries, and reindeer moss); and **Maine Coast Balsam** (255-3301), Box 458, Machias 04654 (decorations include cones, red berries, and bow).

SPECIAL EVENTS July: **Independence Day** celebrations in Jonesport/Beals (lobsterboat races, easily viewed from the bridge), Cherryfield (parade and fireworks), and Steuben (fireman's lobster picnic and parade). **Homecoming Celebration,** in Machiasport, sponsored by the historical society, features clam/lobster feed, tour of the Gates House, and church services.

August: **Milbridge annual homecoming. Blueberry Festival and Machias Craft Festival,** Machias (third weekend) is sponsored by Penobscot Valley Crafts and Center Street Congregational Church: concerts, food, major crafts fair, and live entertainment.

EASTPORT AND COBSCOOK BAY

There is a haunting, end-of-the world feel to Eastport with its nine-teenth-century storefronts along Water Street and its sole-surviving sardine factory. Eastport prides itself on being the birthplace of the sardine industry (the canning process was invented by Julius Wolfe in 1875, and, at one time, 18 canneries were all operating full tilt). It also has the distinction of having been occupied by the British for four years during the War of 1812 (a tale told in the Barracks Museum); one of the old cannons used to fend off the enemy still stands in front of the Peavey Library. A small town of 2,500 people (less than half its turn-of-the-century population), Eastport has many gaps in its old water-front, which has been walled with a pink granite seawall to form Overlook Park. Situated on Moose Island in Passamaquoddy Bay, Eastport has the highest tides in the country (ranging from 12 to 27 feet). The project of harnessing this flow to generate electricity began in the 1930s under Franklin Delano Roosevelt (see Roosevelt Campobello International Park in the previous section). At present the local waterpower company is owned by the Passamaquoddy Tribe; their 100-acre reservation is at Pleasant Point on the Route 190 approach to the city.

GUIDANCE   Eastport Chamber of Commerce (853-4644), Water Street, Eastport 04631. The chamber shares office space with the Eastport Port Authority (853-4614), open weekday office hours. It also maintains a seasonal, volunteer-run information booth on the highway.

TO SEE AND DO   **Reversing Salt Water Falls,** West Pembroke. From Route 1 take the local road out along Leighton Neck, which brings you to a 140-acre park with hiking trails and picnic sites with a view of the incoming tidal current as it passes between Mahar's Point and Falls Island. As the saltwater flows along at upwards of 25 knots, it strikes a series of rocks, resulting in rapids.

Barracks Museum, Washington Street, Eastport. Open seasonally weekdays. Originally part of Fort Sullivan, this house has been restored to its 1820s appearance as officers' quarters and displays old photos and authentic local memorabilia.

Quoddy Tides Foundation Marine Library, 123 Water Street, Eastport. Open Monday through Friday 10–4; Saturday 10–12. A small waterfront aquarium, library, and gift shop maintained by the county's largest newspaper.

Meddybemps is a little white wooden village with a church, general store, and pier on Meddybemps Lake; a good spot for a picnic and swim. **Reynolds Beach** by the town pier is open daily 9 AM to sunset.

AIR RIDES   **Eastern Maine Aviation** (853-4727) offers scenic rides, whale watching, and charters.

Eastport breakwater in wintertime

CAMPING   Cobscook Bay State Park (726-4412), Route 1, Dennysville. Open mid-May to mid-October. Offers 150 camping sites, most of them for tents and many with water views. There are even showers (unusual in Maine state campgrounds). The 864-acre park also offers a boat launch area, picnicking benches, and a hiking and cross-country ski trail. (*Cobscook* means "boiling tides.")

DEEP-SEA FISHING AND WHALE-WATCHING   Captain George Harris and his son Butch sail the *Quoddy Dam* (853-4303) from Harris Island, Eastport. A 50-foot, 35-passenger party boat.

FERRY   East Coast Ferries Ltd. (506-747-2159), based on Deer Island. Operates June to September. A small car ferry between Deer Island and Eastport, also between Deer Island and Campobello—with connecting ferries to the New Brunswick mainland at L'Été, near St. George. Check local papers for current schedules (once per hour). Deer Island boasts the world's largest lobster pound and some fine beaches.

INNS AND BED & BREAKFASTS   Lincoln House (726-3953), Dennysville 04628. A yellow, four-square mansion built in 1787 by Judge Theodore

Lincoln, reportedly an ancestor of President Lincoln. (Audubon stayed here while studying the region's birds.) There are six nicely furnished guest rooms sharing four baths; the two front rooms are the classics, with working fireplaces. The public rooms have wide pine floorboards, hooked rugs, and an abundance of antiques. There is fishing for Atlantic salmon just across the road in the Dennys River and hiking or cross-country skiing in the Moosehorn Wildlife Refuge. The dining room is open to the public (see Dining Out), and the Woodshed Pub is the classiest pub in the county. $75 per person MAP in summer; $45–$65 per room off-season, B&B.

Weston House (853-2907), 26 Boynton Street, Eastport 04631. Open year-round. A very elegant Federal-style house built in 1802 by a Harvard graduate who became a local politician. There are five large guest rooms, one with a working fireplace, views of the bay and gardens, antiques. You can have the Audubon Room (John James Audubon slept here on his way to Labrador in 1833) for $55 double, including a generous breakfast (heavenly pancakes with hot apricot syrup and fresh fruit) in the formal dining room. In the off-season it also includes afternoon tea (complete with scones) and sherry. Dinner and a picnic lunch are also available. The common rooms are furnished with oriental rugs and wing chairs, but if you want to put your feet up, there is a very comfortable back room with books and a TV. Jett and John Peterson decorate the house for holidays and enjoy guests on all occasions.

The Inn at Eastport (853-4307), 13 Washington Street, Eastport 04631. A nineteenth-century captain's house offers five guest rooms, furnished with antiques. Breakfasts are bountiful, and amenities include a hot tub with an ocean view, afternoon tea, sherry, and snacks. Picnic lunches and dinner are available on request. $50–$65 double.

Todd House (853-2328), Todd's Head, Eastport 04631. Open year-round. A restored 1775 Cape with great water views. Breakfast is served in the common room in front of the huge old fireplace. In 1801 men met here to charter a Masonic Order, and in 1861 the house became a temporary barracks when the Head was fortified. The house has changed little in a century. The four large double rooms—two with private bath, several with views of the bay, with working fireplaces and cable TV—range from $40–$50. There are also two efficiency suites ($65–$75), both with water views. Guests are welcome to use the deck and barbecue.

The Ship's Inn (853-4688), 34 Washington Street, PO Box 157, Eastport 04631. You do a double take inside the door of this gracious early eighteenth-century house because the front staircase is so ornate and obviously off a high Victorian steamship. It was salvaged from the *Winthrop,* which caught fire in Eastport in 1893. The doors on the three guest rooms, each with etched glass panels and cabin numbers, are also from the *Winthrop.* $32–$38 per day includes breakfast.

MOTEL   The Motel East (853-4747), 23a Water Street, Eastport 04631. This new two-story motel has just nine units, all with water views and balconies, direct-dial phones, cable TV, kitchenettes, and nice touches like fresh flowers. Handicapped accessible. $70 per night; $80 for a suite.

DINING OUT   Flag Officers' Mess (853-6043), 73 Water Street, Eastport. Open daily 11–9; closed Monday in winter. This waterfront building has been splendidly restored, and the second-floor dining room, with its brick walls and wide water view, is downright spectacular. Shepherd's pie ($9.95) or local salmon, broiled or blackened, ($12.95).

Rolando's Italian Harborview Restaurant (853-2334), 118 Water Street, Eastport. Open year-round except Mondays from 4–9 PM; closed Tuesdays, too, in winter. Claiming to be the closest Italian restaurant to Italy in the United States, a nineteenth-century captain's home with an attractive dining room. Specialties include chicken Alfredo and fettucini Rolando. You can also get pizza, sandwiches, fried clams, seafood, steak, and cocktails. Don't pass up the pie.

Lincoln House (726-3953), Dennysville. Dinner is by reservation at 7 with just one set entrée that changes nightly. It's a prix-fixe, multi-course meal, $17.50 plus tax and gratuity. Specialties include shrimp Provençale, veal Amelio, and roast tip loin of beef with béarnaise. There are two small dining rooms in this eighteenth-century house.

EATING OUT   Cap'n T's (853-2307), 75 Water Street. Open daily 10–10. Home-made chowders are the specialty along with baked haddock with lobster sauce and baked scallops. Downstairs in the same waterfront building which houses the Flag Officers' Mess (see Dining Out); great views. Standard choice of lunch sandwiches.

New Waco Diner, Water Street, Eastport. Open year-round, Monday to Saturday 6 AM to 9 PM. A friendly haven with booths and a long shiny counter with everything posted on the wall behind. You can get a full roast turkey dinner. There is also beer, pizza, and great squash pie.

SELECTIVE SHOPPING   Eastport Art Galleries. Eastport has become a genuine showcase for Downeast artists. Best known is the **Eastport Gallery** (853-4166), Water Street, a cooperative showcase for more than 20 local artists. Also check out **Studio 44** (44 Water Street), **Joan Monroe's Wildflower Shop** across the street, and the **Rhodes West Studio,** 43 Key Street.

Guilford Industries (853-4331), Quoddy Village, Eastport. Open Monday through Saturday 9–5. A true factory outlet for fabrics, blankets, and sewing notions.

Border Crafts, Water Street, Eastport. Open Monday through Saturday 10–4. Operated by the Border Historical Society: a large selection of local crafts, from paintings to ceramics, also souvenirs.

Mainely Quilts (853-2933), Route 1, Perry. At this writing Judy Tarbell plans to convert a former schoolhouse on Route 1, Perry, into an outlet for her locally famous quilts. Check.

Indian craftswork: For locally made baskets and other work by the Passamaquoddy Indians, check out **The Wigwam** and **The Trading Post,** both Route 1 in Perry.

Smoked salmon, available from Jim Blankman (853-4831), 37 Washington Street, makes a great present. Blankman will ship salmon or trout anywhere.

SPECIAL EVENTS   July: **Independence Day** is celebrated for a week in Eastport with parades, an air show, and fireworks. **Cannery Wharf Boat Race** (last weekend).

August: **Annual Indian Ceremonial Day,** Pleasant Point Reservation.

September: **Eastport Port Days:** barbecue and speakers. **Eastport Salmon Festival:** arts and crafts sale.

CALAIS AND THE ST. CROIX VALLEY

GUIDANCE   **Calais Information Center** (454-2211), 7 Union Street, Calais. Open year-round, daily 8–6 in spring and fall, 8–5 in winter. This is a state facility, operated by the Maine Publicity Bureau; also a source of a brochure on the area published by the Calais Area Chamber of Commerce, PO Box 368, Calais 04619.

Grand Lake Stream Chamber of Commerce, Box 76, Grand Lake 04619.

TO SEE AND DO   **Calais.** The largest city in Washington County (4,400 residents) is a busy border-crossing point and shopping center for all of eastern Washington County.

Moosehorn National Wildlife Refuge (454-3521), Box X, Calais 04619. Established in 1937, this is the northeast end of a chain of wildlife and migratory bird refuges extending from Florida to Maine and is managed by the United States Fish and Wildlife Service. The refuge comprises two units, some 20 miles apart. The larger 16,000-acre area is in Baring, 5 miles north of Calais on Route 1.

Grand Lake Stream. A remote but famous resort community on West Grand Lake with access to the Grand Lakes chain, Grand Lake Stream claims to have been the biggest tannery town in the world for some decades before 1874. Fishing is the big lure now: landlocked salmon, lake trout, smallmouth bass, also pickerel and white perch. Some of the state's outstanding fishing lodges and camps are clustered here.

St. Croix Island Overlook, Red Beach. The view is of the island on which Samuel de Champlain and Sieur de Monts established the first white settlement in North America north of Florida. That was in 1604. Using the island as a base, Champlain explored and mapped the coast of New England as far south as Cape Cod.

CANOEING   Sunrise Canoe Expeditions (454-7708), Cathance Lake, Grove Post Office 04638. Offers advice, canoe rentals, guided trips down the Grand Lake chain of lakes and the St. Croix River, which runs along the Maine–New Brunswick border and is good for a three- to six-day run spring through fall. We did this with Sunrise (putting in at Vanceboro) and highly recommend it.

Rental canoes and boats are also available from most of the lodges listed below.

CAMPING   Georgia Pacific (see To See and Do) dispenses a sportsman's map and information about camping on its extensive woodland holdings.

Duck Lake Preserve, accessible by County Lake Road west from Grand Lake Stream. Primitive campsites on Duck Lake and on the narrows between Middle and Lower Unknown lakes.

FISHING   Salmon is the big lure. Ranging from 8 to 20 pounds, Atlantic salmon are taken by fly fishermen in the Dennys and St. Croix rivers, mid-May through early July. **Smallmouth bass** is the other big catch, best in June. There is also **chain pickerel, lake trout, and brook trout.** Fishing licenses, available from three days to a season, are also necessary for **ice fishing.** For information on fishing guides, lodges, and rules, write to the **Regional Headquarters of the Inland Fisheries and Wildlife Department,** Machias 04653.

GOLF   St. Croix Golf Club, Calais. A tricky nine-hole course on the banks of the St. Croix River.

SWIMMING   Red Beach at Calais on the St. Croix River—named for the sand on these strands, which is deep red. There is also swimming in dozens of crystal clear lakes. Inquire about access at local lodges and general stores.

FISHING LODGES, INNS, AND CAMPS   Weatherby's (796-5558; 246-7391 in winter), Grand Lake Stream 04637 (in winter write Box 256, Stratton 04982). Open early May through September. A rambling white 1870s lodge with flowers along the porch, set in roses and birches by Grand Lake Stream, the small river that connects West Grand Lake with Big Lake. Ken and Charlene Sassi make you feel welcome. There is a big sitting room—with piano, TV, and hearth—in the lodge; also a homey dining room with better than down-home cooking and a tin ceiling. Each of the 15 cottages is unique, but most are log with screened porches, bath, and a Franklin stove or fireplace. Fishing is what this place is about, and it's a great place for children. $68 per person double occupancy, MAP; $40 per child. Motor boats are $34 per day and a guide, $120; family rates available; 15 percent gratuity added.

Leen's Lodge (795-5575), Grand Lake Stream 04637. At this writing this grand old rustic resort is for sale; it's worth phoning to check the outcome.

Colonial Sportsmen's Lodge (795-2655), Grand Lake Stream 04637. Another serious fisherman's lodge. Meals are served in the dining room of Steve and Pat Pattakach's clapboard home; the six cottages range from mini-Victorian houses to A-frames. Open May to mid-November; boats available. $65 per adult, $53 per child with all meals or $20 per adult, $17 per child per cottage; boat rentals, $15 per day, guides $100.

Grand Lake Lodge Camps (796-5584), Grand Lake Stream 04637. Open May through October. A string of six attractive log cabins accommodating from two to eight people. Each cabin has a woodstove and a large screened porch. Available by the day or week; well-maintained by Ken and Tina Smith. Boat rentals available. From $23 per cabin per night; $180–$300 per week.

Lakeside Inn and Cabins (796-2324), Princeton 04668. Open May through November. A handsome old inn with twin chimneys and seven guest rooms; also five basic housekeeping cabins on Lewy Lake (the outlet to Big Lake, also a source for the St. Croix River). Rooms in the inn are simple, nicely furnished with in-room sinks and, while baths are shared, there are plenty. Betty Field is a warm, grandmotherly host. $40 per person includes all meals; $35 double B&B in the inn; cabins from $45 per couple per day, no meals.

MOTELS   **Redclyffe Shore Hotel** (454-3270), Route 1, Robbinston 04671. Open May to October. A grand old mansion on a bluff above the St. Croix River with 14 motel rooms, one efficiency cottage, and a restaurant open 5–9. Request a room with a river view. $45–$65 double.

Heslin's Motel and Cottages (454-3762), Box 203, Calais 04619 (5 miles south of the village on Route 1). Open May through October. Fifteen motel units and ten cottages on 57 acres with woods, trails, heated pool, restaurant, and cocktail lounge. Moderate.

DINING OUT   **The Chandler House** (454-7922), 20 Chandler Street, Calais. Open 11–11 daily. Chef-owned for the past decade, specializing in seafood like blackened whitefish ($9.95). Try the crab cake appetizers.

Bernardini's, 89 Main Street, Calais. Open year-round for lunch and dinner except Sundays. Basic Italian, inexpensive to moderate.

Heslin's (454-3762), Route 1, Calais (south of the village). Open May through October, 5–9. A popular local dining room specializing in steak and seafood entrées and "French cooking." Moderate.

EATING OUT   **Wickachee** (454-3400), 282 Main Street, Calais. Open year-round, 6 AM to 10 PM. Steak and seafood with a big salad bar are the dinner specialties, but even dinner entrées start at $4.

SELECTIVE SHOPPING   **Pine Tree Store,** Grand Lake Stream. Open daily, year-round. A great general store that also carries many sportsmen's essentials.

Knock on Wood, Route 1, Baring. A gift shop in the wildlife motif; Santa's loft.

The Something Special Shop, Grand Lake Stream. Open Memorial Day to Labor Day. Joan Barton turned her garage into a gift shop 18 years ago, and it seems to get better every year. A nice selection of crafts and gifts.

SPECIAL EVENTS   July: **Indian Festival and Indian Township,** Princeton.

August: **North Country Festival,** Danforth. **International Festival,** Calais: a week of events including a parade, suppers, canoe and raft races.

VI. Inland

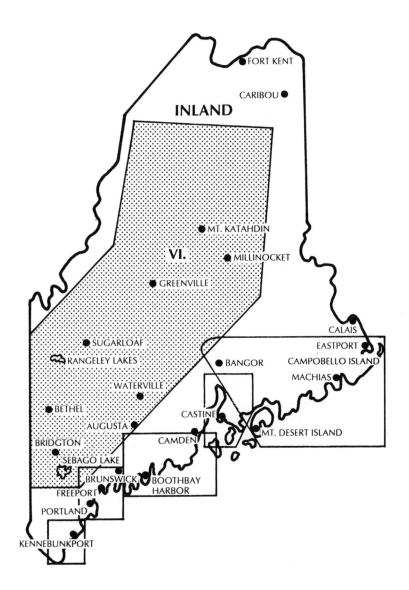

Western Lakes Region

From the summit of Pleasant Mountain it is possible to see 50 lakes, 10 of which are in the town of Bridgton.

Before the Civil War, Bridgton's pioneer tourists could actually come by boat all the way from Boston. From Portland they would ride 20 miles through 28 locks on the Cumberland and Oxford Canal, then across Sebago Lake, up the Songo River, Brandy Pond, and Long Lake to Bridgton.

Although summer travelers now arrive by car, the majority waste little time getting onto or into water. At the Naples Causeway you can rent aqua bicycles and sailboards as well as every form of boat, and you can board an excursion boat for the ride across Brandy Pond and through the only surviving lock from the 1830 canal. The fishing is good; Sebago, Maine's second largest lake, is known for its salmon. This is also Maine's most popular waterskiing area; both rentals and lessons are available.

Fryeburg, just west of the lakes, is headquarters for canoeing the Saco River. Sandy-bottomed and clear, the Saco meanders for more than 40 miles through woods and fields, rarely passing a house. Too shallow for powerboats, it is perfect for canoes. There is usually just enough current to nudge along the limpest paddler, and the ubiquitous sandbars serve as gentle bumpers. Tenting is permitted most places along the river, and there are six public campgrounds. Outfitters rent canoes and provide shuttle service.

Most summer visitors stay in lakeside cottages—of which there are hundreds. The few motels and long-established inns, also the mushrooming crop of bed & breakfasts, tend to be filled on many summer weekends by parents visiting their children at camps, of which there also seem to be hundreds.

This southwestern corner of the state actually offers enough to keep camp parents busy all week. Sights include the fine old Shaker community at Sabbathday Lake, an outstanding state game farm in Gray, and the reconstructed late-nineteenth-century village of Willowbrook at Newfield.

But most lakes region visitors don't go anywhere to look at anything. They swim and fish and fish and swim. On rainy days they browse through the area's antiques and crafts stores. In winter, come

WESTERN LAKES REGION

sun or snow, they ski—downhill at Shawnee Peak (alias Pleasant Mountain) or cross-country almost anywhere.

GUIDANCE   **Bridgton-Lakes Region Chamber of Commerce** (647-3472), Box 236, Bridgton 04009. The chamber maintains a seasonal walk-in information bureau on Route 302 (daily from mid-June to Labor Day; weekends from Memorial Day through October) . Request a copy of the chamber's "Lakes Region Vacation Directory." Year-round information is also available from the **town office** (647-8786).

Naples Business Association (693-3285; winter: 693-6365), PO Box 412, Naples 04055, publishes a map/guide to the Sebago–Long Lake Region just south of Bridgton; it also maintains a seasonal information bureau next to the town's historical society museum on Route 302.

Windham Chamber of Commerce (892-8265), PO Box 1015, North Windham 04062, maintains a seasonal information booth on Route

302 and publishes a booklet guide.

Oxford Hills Chamber of Commerce (743-2281), PO Box 167, Norway 04628, publishes a booklet directory to the area.

The Harrison Business and Professional Association (583-2978), PO Box 443, Harrison 04040, publishes a brochure describing local lodging and dining.

Fryeburg Information Center (935-3639), Route 302, Fryeburg. The Maine Publicity Bureau staffs this state-owned log cabin on the New Hampshire line. A source of pamphlets on the state in general, western Maine in particular.

GETTING THERE   By air: **Portland Jetport,** served by Continental, United, Delta, and USAir is a half-hour to an hour's drive from most points in this area. **Rental cars** are available at the airport.

By car: From New York and Boston, take I-95 to the Westbrook exit, then Route 302, the high road of the lakes region.

For the Sabbathday Lake/Poland Spring/Oxford area take I-95 to the Gray exit and Route 26 north.

MEDICAL EMERGENCY   **Northern Cumberland Memorial Hospital** (647-8841), South High Street, Bridgton.

Stephens Memorial Hospital (743-5933), Norway.

TO SEE AND DO   **Sabbathday Lake Shaker Community and Museum** (926-4597), Route 26, New Gloucester (8 miles north of Gray). Open Memorial Day to Columbus Day, except Sundays, 10–4:30. $3 per adult, $1.50 per child. Founded by an Englishwoman in 1775, Shakers by the Civil War numbered 6,000 Americans in 18 communities. Only six of these communities survive sufficiently to tell their story. With five Shaker Sisters and three Shaker Brothers, ranging in age from 22 to 88, this is the largest surviving village. These men and women still follow the injunction of founder Mother Ann Lee to "put your hands to work and your heart to God." There are still 17 white-clapboard buildings on the 1,900-acre property. Visitors can see the 1794 Meeting House, the 1839 Ministry Shop, the 1850s Boys' Shop, and the Shaker Store. Trained students serve as guides at Sabbathday Lake, and the Sisters run the gift shop, which sells Shaker wares and the haunting record of Shaker songs made by the Sisters here. Visitors are welcome at Sunday meetings, 10 AM.

Willowbrook at Newfield (793-2784 or 793-2210), Newfield (off Route 11). Open May 15 to September 30, daily 10–5. $5.50 per adult, $3 per student. Devastated by fire in 1947, the village was almost a ghost town when Donald King began buying buildings in the 1960s. The complex now includes more than 30 buildings displaying more than 10,000 items: horsedrawn vehicles, tools, toys, and many other artifacts of late nineteenth-century life. A restaurant for light lunches, a picnic area, and a Christmas gift shop open most of the year are located on premises.

State Fish Hatchery and Game Farm, Route 26/100 north, Gray. Open daily 10–4; $.50. A 1,300-acre farm, set up to breed ring-necked pheasant, has become a refuge for injured or threatened animals: moose, deer, raccoon, bear, bobcat, porcupine, mink, skunk, fisher, coyote, and a variety of birds and fish.

Jones Gallery of Glass and Ceramics (787-3370), Douglas Hill 04024. Open most of the year, Monday to Saturday 9:30–5, and Sunday 1–5. $2.50 per adult, $1.50 per student. More than 3,000 works in glass and china. Displays include ancient Egyptian glass, Chinese porcelains, Wedgwood teapots, and French paperweights. There are also gallery tours, frequent lecture/luncheon seminars, and identification days (visitors bring their own pieces to have identified).

Oxford Plains Speedway/Dragway (539-4401), Route 26, Oxford. Open April to September, Saturdays at 7:30 PM, Sundays at 2 PM, and for special events. The Oxford 250 draws competitors from throughout the world during July.

State of Maine Building from the 1893 Columbia Exposition in Chicago, Route 26, Poland Spring. Open July and August, Friday through Monday 9:30–3:30, Tuesday through Thursday 9:30–noon; June and September, weekends 9:30–3:30. $1 admission. A very Victorian building now maintained by the Poland Spring Preservation Society on the grounds of the former Poland Spring Resort (the water is now commercially bottled in an efficient, unromantic plant down the road).

Naples Historical Society, Village Green, Route 302, Naples. Open July and August, Tuesday through Friday 10–3 and Saturday 11–2:30. The old brick complex includes the former jail, some great memorabilia, and slide presentations on the Cumberland and Oxford Canal, the Sebago–Long Lake steamboats, and vanished hotels like the Chute Homestead.

Songo Locks, Naples (2.5 miles off Route 302). Dating from 1830, the last of the 27 hand-operated locks that once enabled people to come by boat from Portland to Harrison. It still enables you to travel some 40 watery miles. The boat traffic is constant in summer.

Daniel Marrett House, Standish. Open mid-June to Labor Day weekend, Tuesdays, Thursdays, Saturdays, and Sundays 1–5. $2 admission. Money from Portland banks was stored here for safekeeping during the War of 1812. This Georgian mansion remained in the same family from 1789 until 1944; architecture and furnishings reflect the changing styles over 150 years, and the formal gardens are in full bloom throughout the summer.

Hopalong Cassidy in the Fryeburg Public Library, 98 Main Street, Fryeburg. Open year-round; Tuesday through Thursday and Saturday 10–5; Friday 5–8. The library is housed in an 1832 stone schoolhouse. It is decorated with many paintings by local artists and also contains a collection of books, guns, and other memorabilia belonging to Clarence Mulford, creator of Hopalong Cassidy.

Bridgton Historical Society Museum (647-2873), Gibbs Avenue, Bridgton. Open June to August, except Sundays, 1–4; June and September by appointment. Housed in a 1902 former fire station, the collection includes slides on the old narrow-gauge railroad.

Hamlin Memorial Hall, Paris Hill. Open year-round; Tuesday through Friday 10–4, and Saturday 10–2; also Wednesday 7–9. The old stone Oxford County Jail now houses the public library and museum. Worth a stop for the American primitive art; also local minerals and displays about Hannibal Hamlin (who lived next door), the vice president during Abraham Lincoln's first term.

Peabody–Fitch Museum, Ingalls Road, South Bridgton. Open June 5 through Labor Day, Tuesday through Sunday 1–4. Admission fee. A Federal period home in an unspoiled rural setting, includes a blacksmith shop. House still under restoration.

Parson Smith House (892-5315), 89 River Road, South Windham. Open mid-June to Labor Day; Tuesdays, Thursdays, Saturdays, and Sundays 12–5. Admission is $2. A Georgian farmhouse with an exceptional stairway and hall; some original furnishings.

Nathaniel Hawthorne's Boyhood Home (655-3349), Hawthorne Road (off Route 302), South Casco. Open by appointment April to October. If you happen to be passing by, it is worth stopping to see the exterior and setting of this old house in which Hawthorne spent his early years; but it is furnished as a community hall and not worth a detour.

(Also see Norlands Living History Center under To See and Do in Central Maine.)

AIR RIDES   Naples Flying Service, Naples Causeway. Operates daily in-season, 9–7. Offers 25-mile scenic flights over the Sebago–Long Lake area.

Parasailing (693-6591), Songo Queen dock, Naples Causeway.

BOAT EXCURSIONS   *Songo River Queen II* (693-6861), Naples Causeway. Operates daily July through Labor Day; weekends during June and September. Offers a two-and-a-half-hour Songo River Ride ($8 per adult, $5 per child) and a one-hour Long Lake Cruise ($5 per adult, $4 per child). A 90-foot-long stern-wheeler built in 1982; snack bar and rest rooms. The ride is across Brandy Pond and through the only surviving lock from the 1830 canal. It is a pleasant ride to the mouth of Sebago Lake down the Songo River, which is about as winding as a river can be. The distance is just 1.5 miles as the crow flies, but 6 miles as the Songo twists and turns.

Mail Boat Rides (693-6861), Naples Causeway. Operates daily in-season (see above) except Sundays. This pontoon offers varied rides on Songo and Long lakes. No toilets on board.

Point Sebago Princess (655-7891 or 655-3821), Casco (1 mile off

Route 302). During summer months, a pontoon offers daily two-hour cruises on Sebago Lake.

BOAT RENTALS   **Naples Marina** (693-6254), Naples Causeway. Rents a variety of powerboats.

Long Lake Marina (693-3159). Rents powerboats, ski boats, and jet skis.

Mardon Marina (693-6264), Route 302, Naples. Rents boats for fishing, waterskiing, and sailing.

Sebago Lake Lodge (892-2698), White's Bridge Road (off Route 302), North Windham. Fishing boats, ski boats, canoes, and rowboats are available by the hour, half-day, day, or week; delivery is available for rentals of three days or more.

Sporthaus Paddle and Sail Center (647-5100), Route 302 (off Moose Pond Causeway), West Bridgton. Canoe, sunfish, sailboat, and sailboard rentals.

Rod's Marina (583-2226), Main Street, Harrison. Rents boats and jet skis.

Sunny Breeze Sports (693-3867), Route 302, Naples (on the causeway). A source of sailboard rentals and lessons.

Kettle Cove Marina (655-4775), Route 302, Casco. Rents canoes, motorboats.

CANOEING   The only hitch to canoeing the **Saco River** is its popularity. On Friday afternoons in August would-be canoeists are backed up bumper to bumper along the access roads at Swan's Falls and Canal Bridge in Fryeburg. The **Saco Recreational Advisory Council,** formed to study and regulate the use of the river, has published an excellent map/guide showing campsites, portages, and water descriptions for the river's length; available locally for $1.50. Their summer river runner patrols for flotsam and trash and reminds canoeists to carry out what they carry in. If possible, come mid-week during the high season.

CANOE RENTALS   **Saco River Canoe and Kayak** (935-2369), PO Box 111, Route 5, Fryeburg (across from the access to Swan's Falls). "For canoeing, the Saco is the number one river east of the Mississippi," enthuses Fred Westerberg. "Nowhere else can you canoe so far without having to portage. Nowhere else can you find this kind of wilderness camping experience without the danger of remoteness. Nowhere on the river are you far from help if you need it." Westerberg, a registered Maine guide, runs Saco River Canoe and Kayak with the help of his wife, Prudy, and daughters, Beth and Chris. They also offer shuttle service and canoe rentals, which come with a map and careful instructions geared to the day's river conditions.

Saco Bound (603-447-2177 or 603-447-3801), Route 302, Center Conway, NH (just over the New Hampshire line, south of Fryeburg). The largest canoe outfitter around. Offers rentals, guided day-trips during the summer (Tuesdays and Thursdays in July and August), white-water canoeing on the Androscoggin River, a campground at Canal Bridge in Fryeburg, and a shuttle service. Its base is a big, glass-faced store stocked with kayaks and canoes, trail food, and lip balm. Staff members are young and enthusiastic.

Canal Bridge Canoes (935-2605), Route 302, Fryeburg Village. Pat and Carl Anderton offer rentals and a shuttle service.

Woodland Acres (935-2529), Route 160, Brownfield. Full-facility camping, canoe rentals, and a shuttle service.

River Run Canoe (452-2500), Brownfield. Free primitive camping on their own wooded 130 acres with canoe rentals, shuttle service.

FISHING   See also Boat Rentals. **Fishing licenses** are available at town offices and other local outlets; check marinas for information. Salmon, lake trout, pickerel, and bass are plentiful.

G. F. Snell Outfitters (647-2666), 62 Main Street, Bridgton, sell licenses and rent fishing boats.

HIKING   **Douglas Mountain,** Sebago. A Nature Conservancy Preserve with great views of Sebago and the White Mountains.

The trail to the top is a 20-minute walk, and there's a three-quarters-mile nature trail at the summit; also a stone tower with an observation platform. Take Route 107 south from the town of Sebago and turn right on Douglas Mountain Road; go to the end of the road to find limited parking.

HORSEBACK RIDING   **Sunny Brook Stables** (787-2905), Sebago, offers trail rides pitched to beginners and intermediate riders. $10–$12 per hour.

GOLF AND TENNIS   **Bridgton Highlands Country Club** (647-3491), Bridgton, has a nine-hole course, snack bar, carts, and tennis courts. Other nine-hole courses include **Lake Kezar Country Club** (925-2462), Route 5, Lovell; **Naples Country Club** (693-6424), Route 114, Naples; and **Summit Golf Course** (998-4515), Poland Spring.

Tennis at Brandy Pond Camps (693-6333), old Route 114, Naples.

MINIATURE GOLF   **Steamboat Landing** (693-6429), Route 114, Naples. Open daily in-season, 10–10 (2–10 on Sundays). A delightful 18-hole course with a Maine theme in a wooded setting.

Maplewood Miniature Golf and Arcade (655-7586), Route 302 across from State Park Road, Casco. Eighteen holes and a full arcade with video games, pinball, snacks.

HAYRIDES AND SLEIGH RIDES   **Harrison Stagecoach Co.** (583-4677). Available year-round; "no party too large or small."

SWIMMING   **Sebago Lake State Park** (693-6613, June 20 to Labor Day; 693-6231, otherwise), off Route 302 (between Naples and South Casco). The day-use area includes beaches, tables, grills, a boat ramp, lifeguards, and bathhouses. There is a separate camping area (see Campgrounds) with its own beach, a program of summer-conducted hikes on nature trails, and presentations in the amphitheater. Songo Lock is nearby.

Lake swimming options abound

Photo by Neal Parent

The town of Bridgton maintains a tidy little beach on **Long Lake** just off Main Street, another on **Woods Lake** (Route 117), and another on **Highland Lake.** The town of Fryeburg maintains a beach, with float, on the **Saco River,** and **Casco** maintains a small, inviting beach in its picturesque village.

Range Pond State Park (998-4104) in Poland offers swimming and fishing.

In addition, most camps, cottages, and lodges have their own waterfront beaches and docks, and there are numerous local swimming holes.

ROCKHOUNDING   This area is particularly rich in minerals. Rock hounds should stop at **Perham's Maine Mineral Store** in West Paris, a landmark in its own right claiming 90,000 visitors per year. It displays samples of all minerals to be found in Maine, dispenses maps to its own quarries, and sells rough stones as well as ones that are polished and set.

CROSS-COUNTRY SKIING   **Carter's Farm Market** (539-4848), Route 26, Oxford. Extensive acreage used to grow summer vegetables is transformed into a ski center during the winter. Equipment rentals, lessons, 10 km of groomed trails, some lighted trails for night skiing, and food.

DOWNHILL SKIING   **Shawnee Peak at Pleasant Mountain** (647-8444), Route 302, Bridgton. An isolated, 1,900-foot hump, 1 mile west of the center of town. Maine's oldest ski area, it has a vertical drop of 1,300 feet, 31 trails, 95 percent snowmaking, and night skiing. Lifts include one triple chair, three double chairs, and a T-bar. Other facilities include ski school, rentals, and child care.

RUSTIC RESORTS   The western lakes area offers some unusual old resort complexes, each with cabin accommodations and dining and relaxing space in a central, distinctively Maine lodge. In contrast to similar complexes found farther north, these are all geared to families or those who vacation here for reasons other than hunting and fishing.

Migis Lodge (winter: 655-4524; spring: 892-5235), PO Box 8, South Casco 04077 (off Route 302). Open early June through Columbus Day weekend. There are 7 rooms in the two-story main lodge and 25 cottages scattered in the pines on 97 acres. All cottages have fireplaces, and guests enjoy use of the private beach, tennis, lawn games, waterskiing, sailboats, canoes, and boat excursions. Children under four are not permitted in the dining room during the high-season (July to Labor Day) so the resort provides a supervised dining and playtime 6:30–8:30; older children are also welcome to join in. $70–$120 includes three meals; children's rates.

Aimhi Lodge (892-6538), North Windham 04062. Open spring through fall. More than 70 years in the same family, this classic complex accommodates 75 guests. The lodge and 25 cabins are sited on Little Sebago Lake. The cabins have one to three rooms, Franklin stoves, and screened porches. Down-home cooking; turkey every summer Sunday since the 1930s, at least; the Holdtman/Hodgson family has been running the lodge since the 1920s. Facilities include game rooms, lawn games, a beach, sailboats, canoes, and rental boats. Rates include three meals.

Farrington's (925-2500), Lake Kezar, Center Lovell 04016. Open late June to Labor Day, serving all meals; open again for foliage season on a B&B basis. A great old summer resort on Lake Kezar. There are 16 guest rooms and 30 cottages with one to three bedrooms each. Meals are served in the pine-paneled dining room with white tablecloths and white bentwood chairs. Facilities include a sand beach, waterskiing, boats, movies, a recreation hall, and tennis. Moderate rates considering they include three meals.

Quisisana (925-3500), Lake Kezar, Center Lovell 04016. Open mid-June to Labor Day. A long-established resort featuring opera and concerts performed by staff recruited from top music schools. The 16 guest rooms are in two lodges, and there are 38 one- to three-room cottages (some with fireplaces) scattered through the woods. Sand beaches, waterskiing, boats, and fishing guides are all available. Lodge rooms $70–$92, cottages $80–$123 single, all three meals included.

Northern Pines (655-7624), PO Box 279, Route 85, Raymond 04071. Open May through October and January through March. A holistic health resort housed in a 1920s women's camp on the shores of Crescent Lake. A personal escape hatch! A few rooms are available in the main lodge, but others are scattered among a wide variety of cottages that range from rustic log cabins with fireplaces to a yurt. Evergreen Lodge has two large rooms with lake views, one handicapped-accessible. All are scattered in the pines and woods, some with screened porches overlooking the lake. In summer there are never more than 50 guests and in winter no more than 25. Some take part in supervised fasting, but most simply take advantage of the daily regimen, which begins at 6:30 AM with exercises, including aerobics and yoga; usually an evening program and optional lectures. Meals are vegetarian and delicious. Summer facilities include sailboats, canoes, paddleboats, and a lakeside hot tub; cross-country skiing and ice-skating January through March. The central lodge (open May to October) has a massive two-sided fireplace, and there is a large library. $120–$185 daily; $715–$1,100 weekly; 25 percent off in spring and fall, 50 percent off in winter.

Maine Folk Dance Camp (647-3424), Wood Pond, Bridgton 04009. For more than 30 years it has been a center for learning and performing folk dances from many countries.

INNS   Westways on Kezar Lake (928-2663), Center Lovell 04016. Open most of the year. Built as a summer retreat for the self-made Maine millionaire who founded the Diamond Match company, this lakeside home offers seven guest rooms (three with private bath) and nine cottages. The low-beamed living room has a massive fireplace and furnishings that range from plush to baronial. The game room, with a two-lane bowling alley, is in a neighboring library. The view is of Lake Kezar with its backdrop of mountains, and there is a dock for sunning and swimming. Guests can also play tennis, fish, or sail. Cross-country ski trails traverse the property, but downhill skiers need to drive 13 miles to Pleasant Mountain or 25 miles to Sunday River. $135–$195 double MAP; $105–$165 EP; $85–$145 off-season.

Oxford House Inn (935-3442), Fryeburg 04037. Open year-round, this spacious 1913 house in the middle of Fryeburg has a view across the Saco River to the White Mountains. The public restaurant is popular for dinner, but there is ample space for inn guests to relax. The five upstairs guest rooms are all large and nicely decorated, with private baths. Request one with a view. $65–$85 includes a full breakfast.

Lake House (583-4182), Routes 35 and 37, Waterford 04088. Open year-round. Our favorite in this area. A graceful, old stagecoach inn with vestiges of the old ballroom under the eaves. Suzanne and Michael Uhl-Myers have totally overhauled this landmark in the middle of picturesque Waterford Village. They now offer four spacious guest rooms, including a two-room suite, all with private baths. Downstairs there is a comfortable sitting room, off and away from the two small public dining rooms. Lake Keoka is just across the street. $69–$115.

Kedaburn Inn (583-6182), Route 35, Waterford 04088. London natives Margaret and Derek Gibson bring an English accent to this pleasant 1850s house. The inn offers seven guest rooms, including two with private baths, and one two-room suite with private bath. The dining room is open to the public for dinner and afternoon tea; breakfast and tea are included. $60–$75 double.

Bear Mountain Inn (583-4404), routes 35 and 37, South Waterford 04081. Open year-round. One of the area's original farmhouses to take in guests, still with an informal farmhouse feel. There are seven guest rooms, four full baths, and a two-room suite with bath. Read and Sheila Grover offer "healthy" vacations. The place is geared to groups (it accommodates 16 to 20 people), but everyone is welcome. The 40 acres include frontage on Bear Pond. Amenities include an exercise machine, table tennis, and hiking trails. $45 single, $55 double; includes a full breakfast.

Center Lovell Inn (925-1575), Route 5, Center Lovell 04016. Open May to late October. A striking, old inn with a widow's walk and a busy public dining room. There are 10 guest rooms, including one two-room suite; some in the 1835 Norton House. $42–$79 EP plus 15 percent gratuity. Open to the public for dinner.

The Cornish Inn (625-8501), Route 25, PO Box 266a, Cornish 04020. Open all year. A classic, old village inn with 17 rooms (some shared baths) replete with antique decor and hand-stenciled wall borders. Candlelit dinners served. $50–$75 includes breakfast.

BED & BREAKFASTS   **Tarry-a-While** (647-2522), Ridge Road, Bridgton 04009. Open mid-June to Labor Day. A delightful resort with 10 guest rooms upstairs in the old summer hotel, 16 in the four cottages; all private baths, some handicapped units. Swiss owners Hans and Barbara Jenni are known for their hospitality. There are 30 acres of lakeside grounds, and guests have access to two fine beaches, boats (canoes, row, motor, and sail), windsurfers, tennis, golf, and bicycles. $100–$120 double includes Swiss-style breakfast.

Sebago Lake Lodge (892-2698), PO Box 110, White's Bridge Road, North Windham 04062. Open year-round. A rambling, old white inn on a narrows between Jordan Bay and the Basin, seemingly surrounded by water. Debra and Chip Lougee, both Maine natives, have refurbished the rooms to create six units with their own kitchens, four two-room units that share a kitchen, and two standard rooms with kitchen privileges. A light buffet breakfast is set out in the gathering room, a pleasant space to read, play games, or watch TV. There are also nine moderately priced cottages. Facilities include an inviting beach, picnic tables and grills, boats with water skis and tow tubes, fishing boats and rowboats, and canoes. Fishing licenses are available on the spot. $48–$63 per room, $73–$95 per housekeeping unit; cheaper off-season.

Noble House (647-3733), Box 180, Bridgton 04009. Open year-round but October 15 to June 15 by prior reservation only. There is a formal feel to the public rooms with their grand piano, crystal, and oriental rugs. This was a senator's manor, and it looks it—set among stately oaks and pines with a view of mountains. The nine guest rooms vary from a single to large family suites; all are decorated with antiques. There are niceties such as Australian fleece mattress covers and sherry set out on the upstairs landing; also new rooms in a rear annex, three with whirlpool bath. In winter both downhill and cross-country skiing are nearby. There is a private beach (with a hammock, canoe, and dock) on Highland Lake across the road. $68–$110 double includes full breakfast and use of a canoe and pedal boats.

The Inn at Long Lake (693-6226), PO Box 806, Naples 04055. Built in 1911 as an annex to the (vanished) Lake House Resort, this four-story, clapboard building has been recently renovated to offer 16 large guest rooms, each with private bath, TV, and air-conditioner. Views are off across pastures to Long Lake. There's a Great Room with a magnificent fieldstone fireplace. $63–$80 per room. The energetic new owners are Irene and Maynard Hincks.

Augustus Bove House (693-6365), routes 302 and 114, Naples 04055. Open year-round. A welcoming 150-year-old brick mansion with seven guest rooms (four shared baths) furnished with comfortable antiques. Set back from the road yet handy to all of the water sports at nearby Naples Causeway and to Sebago Lake State Park. No smoking or alcohol. A hearty breakfast is included in the moderate rate.

Admiral Peary House (935-3365), 9 Elm Street, Fryeburg 04037. Once the residence of Maine's famed Arctic explorer. Four large guest rooms, each with antiques, private bath, and air-conditioning. Guests can relax in the living room, outdoor spa, or perennial gardens, and amenities include a clay tennis court. $87–$96 includes a full breakfast and high tea. No smoking.

Songo Bed & Breakfast House (693-3960), Box 554, Naples 04055. Open year-round. The entrance to this find is unpromising. You drive in past a small snack bar to a gaping garage area. But the house is delightful, overlooking the Songo Locks and its summer-long boat traffic. There are four guest rooms and some inviting common spaces: a sun deck, a living room with a fireplace, and a dining room with a long table in front of a big river-view window, set each morning with a full breakfast. Sebago Lake State Park is very near for winter cross-country skiing as well as summer beaching. Moderately priced.

Tolman House Inn (583-4445), PO Box 551, Tolman Road, Harrison 04040. Open year-round. A former carriage barn, artfully transformed into an unusually inviting inn. Nine guest rooms with private baths and antiques; a dining and lounging area overlooking lovely gardens. The inn is situated on 100 hillside acres sloping to the tip of Long Lake. There is a game room in a former icehouse. The moderate rate includes a full breakfast; weekly rates are available. Children under two stay free, but there are no cribs. $55 single, $75 double.

1859 Guest House (647-2508), 60 South High Street, Bridgton 04009. Open year-round. A handsome 1859 home within easy walking distance of the public beach on Highland Lake. Mary Zeller offers twin and double rooms. $40 double.

Snowbird Lodge (583-2544), Route 2, Harrison 04040. There's a large common room, paneled in knotty pine with a big stone fireplace, piano, TV, VCR, stereo, and some games. Some baths are private, but the rooms are very basic. The 100-acre property includes birch and pine woods and a pond complete with sandy beach. $45 double, includes a full breakfast.

Moose Crossing Farm (743-7656), RFD 1, Box 370, South Paris 04281. This is a nicely renovated eighteenth-century farmhouse set high on Christian Ridge with long views west to the White Mountains. Anne and Allen Gass raise black and brown sheep; offer woodland trails (good for cross-country skiing), comfortable guest rooms, a hearty breakfast. $55 per room, shared bath.

Victorian House (998-2169), PO Box 709, Pond Spring 04274. A Victorian farmhouse on Route 26. Rooms are furnished with antiques, and there's cable TV and air-conditioning; also a spring-fed pond and apple orchard. Includes breakfast.

COTTAGES   The "Lakes Region Cottage Directory," listing some two dozen cottages and cottage clusters, is available from the **Bridgton-Lakes Region Chamber of Commerce** (647-3472), Box 236, Bridgton 04009. Many area cottages are also listed in the "Maine Guide to Camp & Cottage Rentals," free from the **Maine Publicity Bureau** (289-2423), PO Box 2300, 97 Winthrop Street, Hallowell 04347-2300. Specific cottages that we recommend include the following:

Crescent Lake Cottages (655-3393), PO Box 354, Raymond 04071. Small but clean and nicely sited one- and two-bedroom cottages across the road from a beach on Crescent Lake. Lawn games, boat rentals, shuffleboard, and a recreation lodge; set on 12 acres. Inexpensive.

Hewnoaks (925-6051), Center Lovell 04016. Six unusually attractive, distinctive cottages scattered on a steep hillside overlooking Lake Kezar. Rates are moderate.

Lakeside at Pleasant Mountain (647-5091 or 647-8660). Harbingers of the future, these condominiums are two- and three-bedroom townhouses on Moose Pond at the base of the ski area; in summer there is access to a sandy beach, tennis courts, and a boat dock. Expensive.

CAMPGROUNDS   See Canoe Rentals for information about camping along the Saco River. In addition to those mentioned, the **Appalachian Mountain Club** maintains a campground at Swan's Falls.

The "Maine Camping Guide," available from the **Maine Campground Owners Association** (782-5872), 655 Main Street, Lewiston 04240, lists dozens of private campgrounds in the area.

Sebago Lake State Park (693-6613; 693-6611 before June 20 and after Labor Day), off Route 302 (between Naples and South Casco). Open through mid-October. On the northern shore of the lake, 1,300 thickly wooded acres with 250 campsites, many on the water; the camping area has its own beach, hot showers, a program of evening presentations, and nature hikes. Rates per site are $14 (nonresident) and $12 (resident). For information about reservations phone 800-332-1501 or 207-289-3824 from outside the state.

Point Sebago (655-3821), RR 1, Box 712, Casco 04015. Such a phenomenon that it demands mention: 500 campsites, most with trailer hookups, on a 300-acre lakeside site plus 130 rental trailers ranging from small trailers to large models of near-mobile home size. Campers have access to the beach, marina, dance pavilion, child day care, teen center, excursion boats, soccer and softball fields, horseshoe pitches, 10 tennis courts, video game arcade, general store, and combination restaurant/nightclub/gambling casino; full daily program beginning with 6 AM exercises and ending at 1 AM when the club closes.

DINING OUT   **Epicurian Inn** (693-3839), routes 302 and 35, Naples. Open for lunch, dinner, and Sunday brunch year-round. A mansard-roofed, French-style, brightly colored (somewhere between salmon and Pepto-Bismol pink) house specializing in "classical French and New American Cuisine served in an atmosphere of cozy elegance." The menu changes weekly. On a typical evening you can choose from scalloped veal, roast duckling, bouillabaisse (with lobster, clams, and mussels), or sole with a shrimp mousse and topped with butter sauce. Reservations sometimes needed days ahead of time. $15.95–$19.95 includes salad before and sorbet after entrées; also a selection of cheese and fruit.

Lake House (583-4182), routes 35 and 37, Waterford. Open from 5:30 PM daily; also for Sunday brunch. A picturesque old inn with two intimate dining rooms. Specialties include Atlantic salmon, with a light sauce of tequila and lime, and shelled lobster in fennel and cream. Brunch specialties include crêpes Mediterranean and mama's scrambled eggs. Homemade desserts include parfait pie and mocha mousse. No liquor license. $14.95–$19.95.

Center Lovell Inn (925-1575), Center Lovell. Open nightly. The northern Italian specialties include steamers, veal Marsala, and shrimp sautéed in olive oil and butter. Young children are accommodated between 5 and 6 PM. There are two pleasant dining rooms and a wrap-around porch in summer. Reservations required. $9.95–$17.95.

Kedarburn Inn (583-6182), Route 35, Waterford. Open for dinner year-round: three nights in winter, six in summer. Candlelight dining, featuring English "country dishes" like steak and mushroom pie, shepherd's pie, and beef Wellington ($10.00–$17.35); tea also served 3:00–4:30.

Westways on Kezar Lake (928-2663), Route 5, Center Lovell. Open nightly during summer; call to check off-season. Ask for a table on the dining porch with views over Kezar Lake and the mountains beyond. The dining room itself is formal, almost baronial. The menu changes daily but usually includes duck in cumberland sauce and at least two seafood dishes—frequently sea scallops sautéed with peppers and tomatoes and served with Havarti cream sauce. There's a full wine list. No smoking in the dining room. Reservations requested. $14.95–$21.95.

The Olde House (655-7841), just off Route 302 on Route 85, Raymond. Closed Mondays; otherwise open year-round for dinner and weekdays for lunch. Elegant candlelight dining in a 1790 home. The specialty is beef Wellington. Moderate to expensive.

Oxford House Inn (935-3442), 105 Main Street, Fryeburg. Open nightly in summer and fall, Wednesday through Sunday in winter, and for Sunday brunch. Entrées include salmon Pommery, veal Oxford, turkey Waldorf, and grilled pork tenderloin with black currant sauce. The setting is the former living room and dining room of a handsome 1913 house. $16–$19.

Maurice Restaurant Francaise (743-2532), 113 Main Street, South Paris. Open daily 5–9, to 9:30 Saturday, and for Sunday brunch. A very reasonably priced, classic French restaurant that has expanded under new ownership (there are now four dining rooms). The specialty is scampi a la Provençale. Reservations recommended. $7.50–$16.00.

Lobster Pound Restaurant (647-5226), Route 302, Bridgton. Open year-round for lunch and dinner. A classic 25-year-old seafood restaurant with fish tanks, fishnet decor, worn wooden tables, and a sink in the dining room to wash off the lobster and butter. You can get a hot dog or a cheeseburger, but the specialties are lobster dinners, lobster salad dinners, and fried clam dinners. Wine and liquor are served. Moderate.

EATING OUT   **Cracked Platter** (583-4708), Maine Street, Harrison. Open 6 AM to 1 AM daily, 7 AM to 1 AM on Sundays. This is a terrific place, worth holding out for if you are driving up and going out once you are here. The menu is large, and the cooking is down-home—a friendly, family atmosphere.

Enterprise Restaurant (625-4452), Route 25, Cornish. Open for lunch and dinner Wednesday through Sunday; closed in winter. A casual atmosphere with a great view of mountains and river. An Italian–American menu with specialties such as Yankee pot roast and roast leg of lamb and such staples as meat loaf and clam cakes. $5.50–$14.95.

Cole Farms (657-4714), Gray. Open 5 AM to 10:30 PM daily. Specialties include the fried fish plate and seafood Newburg. This is Maine cooking from family recipes. Everything from soups and chowders to ice cream and pastries made on the premises. No liquor.

Country Way Restaurant (743-2387), Route 26, South Paris. Open Tuesday to Sunday for lunch and dinner. An inviting family restaurant with good soups and a salad bar.

Maple Ridge Inn (583-4272), Maple Ridge Road, Harrison. Open year-round for breakfast, also for dinner Wednesday through Saturday evenings and for a Sunday "Breakfast Buffet" (8:00–11:30 AM). A large, informal dining room on a back road, known for large portions and value: chicken stuffed with scallops and lobster, homemade calzone, and full dinners (including soup, salad, homemade bread, calzone, entrée with potato and vegetable, dessert, and coffee).

SNACKS   **Chase's Ice Cream Parlor** (655-7765), Route 302, Raymond. Seasonal. A red A-frame that looms large in the daydreams of many hundreds of summer campers.

ENTERTAINMENT   *Movies:*   **Magic Lantern,** Main Street, Bridgton, presents film classics and first-run cartoons. **Windham Hill Mall** on Route 302 has a cinema that shows first-run movies.

Music: **Sebago–Long Lake Region Chamber Music Festival** (627-4939), Bridgton Academy Chapel, North Bridgton. A series of concerts held mid-July through mid-August.

Theater: **The Thomas Inn and Playhouse** (655-3292), Route 302, South Casco.

A small, 100-seat theater stages summer plays, live entertainment.

Celebration Barn Theatre (743-8452), South Paris. Summer season performances at 8 PM Fridays and Saturdays: mime, improvisations, storytelling, new vaudeville.

SELECTIVE SHOPPING   *Antiques:* Bridgton is the regional center for antiques.

Wales & Hamblen Antique Center (647-8344), 134 Main Street, Bridgton. A showcase for the wares of 30 dealers; the 1882 building itself has been restored with original woodwork and shelving.

Crafts: **Glassworks,** Route 114 (2.8 miles off Route 302), Naples. Open Memorial Day to Labor Day, 10–4. The showroom and studio of glassblower Glenn Ziemke and jeweler Kathe Ziemke. Glenn designs and hand-blows perfume bottles, paperweights, goblets, and vases in striking color combinations. Kathe makes porcelain earrings and porcelain bead necklaces.

Bridgton Arts and Crafts Society, Depot Street, Bridgton. Open during July and August, Tuesday through Saturday. Displays a variety of handicrafts by members.

Emphasis on Maine, 36 Main Street, Bridgton. Open daily. Displays work by more than 700 New England artists and craftspeople— superior stuff.

Books: **Annie's Book Stop** (892-9366), Cumberland Farms Plaza, Route 302, North Windham. Current best-sellers at major discounts, children's corner, out-of-print and used books.

Books 'n' Things (743-7197), Oxford Plaza, Route 26, Oxford. Billing itself as "Western Maine's Complete Bookstore," a fully stocked store with a full children's section.

Downtown Bookshop (743-7245), 200 Main Street, Norway. Closed Sundays. A source of general titles, stationery, cards, and magazines.

Other: **Sportshaus,** 61 Main Street, Bridgton. Open daily. Known for its original Maine T-shirts; also a selection of casual clothes, canvas bags, tennis rackets, downhill and cross-country skis, athletic footwear, swimwear, and golf accessories. All housed in a pillared eighteenth-century house.

Sheep Shop at Chardia Farm (583-2996), 1533 Maple Ridge Road, Harrison. A working farm selling wool and sheepskin products, handspun yarn, and shearling coats, vests, hats, and gloves.

United Society of Shakers (926-4597), Route 26, New Gloucester. Open Memorial Day to Columbus Day: sells Shaker herbs, teas, handcrafted items.

SPECIAL EVENTS   July: **Independence Day** is big both in Bridgton and Naples. Bridgton events include a lobster/clam bake at the town hall, a road race, a concert, and fireworks. In Naples the fireworks over the lake are spectacular. Also in early July the **Oxford 250 NASCAR Race** draws entrants from throughout the world to the Oxford Plains

Speedway. In late July a major **crafts fair** at the town hall is sponsored by the Bridgton Arts and Crafts Society; on the third weekend of the month antiques dealers gather from throughout New England for the three-day **Lake Region Antique Show** at the high school. Also in late July the **Bean Hole Bean Festival** in Oxford draws thousands.

August: **Gray and Windham Old Home Days,** both in the beginning of the month, include a parade, contests, and public feeds. In Lovell the **Annual Arts and Artisans Fair** (mid-month) is held on the library grounds: chicken barbecue, book and crafts sale.

September: **Oxford County Agricultural Fair** in West Paris is usually held during the second week.

October: **Fryeburg Fair,** held the first weekend, is an old-fashioned agricultural happening—one of the most colorful in the country.

December: **Christmas Open House and festivals** in Harrison and Paris Hill.

The Kennebec Valley

CENTRAL MAINE

Augusta, the capital of Maine, rises in tiers above the Kennebec River at its head of navigation. In 1625 the Pilgrims sailed to this spot and traded "seven hundred pounds of good beaver and some other furs" with the Abenakis for a "shallop's load of corn." They proceeded to procure a grant to the Kennebec, from Gardiner to a waterfall half-way between Augusta and Waterville with a strip of land 15 miles wide on either side of the bank. At the Indian village of Cushnoc (present-day Augusta), they built a storehouse and, with the proceeds of their beaver trade there, were soon able to pay off their London creditors.

Augusta was obviously a good-luck spot. Although settlers fled during the French and Indian War, they returned in 1754 when the British built Fort Western. The area was selected as the capital in 1827, and a state house, designed by Charles Bulfinch and built of granite from neighboring Hallowell, was completed in 1832. During the mid-nineteenth century this area boomed: some 500 boats were built along the river between Winslow and Gardiner, and river traffic between Augusta and Boston thrived. The era is still reflected by the quaint commercial buildings lining the river downstream in Hallowell (known for shopping and dining) and in Gardiner (recently restored; also a place to dine and browse).

Today Augusta remains worth a visit, if just to see one of the most interesting state museums in the country; exhibits vividly depict many aspects of landscape and industry. Not far downriver from the museum door are some enticing restaurants, and shops line Water Street in Hallowell and Gardiner.

The Kennebec Valley is rolling, open farmland, spotted with lakes. Just north of the city the Belgrade Lakes form an old resort area, blessed with cottage colonies that need not advertise, and east of the city the China Lakes form another low-profile haven. Good summer theater can be found in Waterville (upriver), Monmouth (another old resort area, west of town), and Skowhegan (also known for its art school). In the past few years attractive old homes throughout this

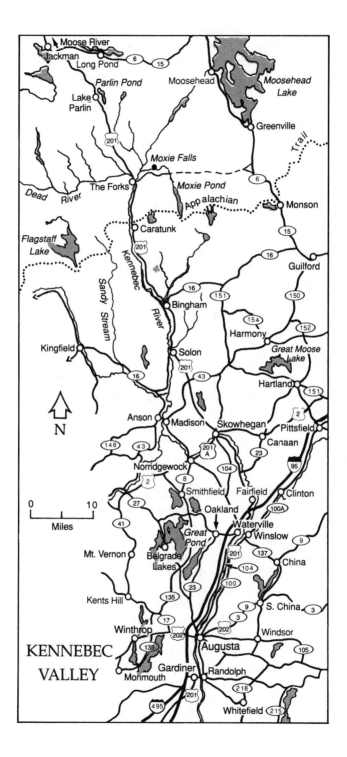

KENNEBEC
VALLEY

region have opened their doors to guests—who are discovering not only the beauty of the immediate area but also that central Maine is the only true hub in this sprawling state, handy to not just one but many parts of the coast, also to the western lakes and mountains and to the North Woods.

GUIDANCE   **Kennebec Valley Chamber of Commerce** (623-4559), PO Box E, University Drive, Augusta 04330. The office is off I-95 (the exit for Route 27) in the civic center complex. This is a year-round source of information, primarily on the area from Augusta to Gardiner.

Belgrade Lakes Region, Inc., PO Box 426, Belgrade 04917, maintains a seasonal (late June to September) information booth on Route 27 and also publishes a pamphlet guide to the area.

China Area Chamber of Commerce (445-2890), Box 317, South China 04358. Year-round.

Mid-Maine Chamber of Commerce (873-3315), PO Box 142, Waterville 04901. Open year-round.

Skowhegan Chamber of Commerce (474-3621), PO Box 326, Skowhegan 04976, maintains a seasonal information center in town on Route 201 north. This is actually the last information booth until Jackman and serves as a source of advice on lodging in the Upper Kennebec Valley as well as in the immediate area.

GETTING THERE   By air: **Northwest Airline** (622-3240) connects Augusta with Boston and Presque Isle.

By bus: **Greyhound** serves Augusta and Waterville.

By car: You don't have to take the Maine Turnpike to reach the Augusta area; from points south, I-95 is both quicker and cheaper (I-95 and the turnpike merge just south of Augusta).

MEDICAL EMERGENCY   **Kennebec Valley Medical Center** (626-1000), East Chestnut Street, Augusta.

Mid-Maine Medical Center (873-0621), North Street, Waterville.

Waterville Osteopathic Hospital (873-0731), Waterville, also offers emergency service.

Redington-Fairview General Hospital (emergency: 474-5085), Fairview Avenue, Skowhegan.

TO SEE AND DO   **Maine State Museum** (289-2301), Maine State House, State Street, Augusta. Open weekdays 9–5, Saturdays 10–4, and Sundays 1–4. Turn into the parking lot just south of the capitol building. This outstanding museum is poorly marked! You have to know that it is in the State Library in order to find it. Without question, the best state museum in New England! "This Land Called Maine" is a life-like re-creation of the variety of Maine's landscape. "Producing and Exchanging" depicts traditional industries: fishing, agriculture, granite-quarrying, ice-harvesting, shipbuilding, and lumbering. "Made in Maine" re-creates more than a dozen nineteenth-century industrial scenes: textile mills and shops producing shoes, guns, fishing rods, and more. The 1846 narrow-gauge locomotive "Lion" arrived from Machias in 1988. On the third floor are changing exhibits.

State House (289-2301), State Street, Augusta. Open year-round, Monday through Friday 8–5. Much modified since the original design by Charles Bulfinch, its size has actually doubled. A 180-foot dome has replaced the original cupola.

Blaine House (289-2301), State Street, Augusta. Open year-round, Monday through Friday 2–4, and by appointment. A 28-room mansion built in the 1830s by a Captain James Hall of Bath, later purchased by James Blaine, a speaker of the United States House of Representatives, United States senator, and twice secretary of state; known as the "plumed knight" when he ran for the presidency in 1884, battling "Rum, Romanism and Rebellion." His daughter gave the mansion to the state, and it has since served as home for Maine governors.

Fort Western Museum on the Kennebec (626-2385), City Center Plaza, 16 Cony Street, Augusta. Open weekdays year-round, 10–5; weekends, summer only, 1–5. Guided tours daily. Admission is $2.50 per adult, $1.50 per child over age six. The original 16-room garrison house has been restored to reflect its use as a fort, trading fort, and lodge from 1754 to 1810. The blockhouse and stockade are reproductions. A seventeenth-century Pilgrim trading post (Cushnoc) is nearby, and in the adjacent City Hall there is a "learning gallery."

Norlands Living History Center (897-2236 or 897-4918), Livermore Falls 04254. Open July and August, daily 10–4 for general tours of all buildings. $4.50 per adult, $2 per student. Also open by reservation for live-in weekends and week-long programs, year-round. A 450-acre living history complex re-creates life in the late nineteenth century. The working farm with barn and farmer's cottage, church, stone library, and Victorian mansions of the Washburn family, are open to visitors. This is the genuine 1870–1890 rural experience, right down to the corncobs in the outhouses. You'll never be the same person after one experience! Try it. Come for a special weekend like Heritage Days in June, the Autumn Celebration in late September, or Christmas early in December.

Monmouth Museum (933-4444), Monmouth (at the intersection of routes 132 and 135). Open Memorial Day to October 1, Tuesday through Sunday 1–4; year-round by appointment (933-2287 is the answering machine or call Annie Smith: 933-2752). $3 per adult, $1 per child. A collection of buildings: 1787 Blossom House, stencil shop (1849), blacksmith shop, freight shed, and carriage house.

Colby College (872-3000), Waterville 04901 (2 miles from Exit 33 off I-95; marked). Founded in 1813, Colby College enrolls 1,675 students from 45 states and 22 foreign countries. Its 900-acre campus includes a performing arts center and an art museum featuring Maine works by Winslow Homer, Andrew Wyeth, and John Marin (open daily).

Student-led tours are offered weekdays throughout the year.

Redington Museum and Apothecary (872-9439), 64 Silver Street, Waterville. Open mid-May to mid-September, Tuesday through Saturday 2–6, and by appointment. $3 admission. The local historical collection: furniture, Civil War and Indian relics, a children's room, period rooms, and a nineteenth-century apothecary.

Waterville-Winslow Two Cent Bridge, Front Street. Until recently the only known remaining toll footbridge in the country. Toll-taker's house on Waterville side. Free.

Fort Halifax, Route 201, Winslow (1 mile south of the Waterville–Winslow bridge at the junction of the Kennebec and Sebasticook rivers). Just a blockhouse remains but it is original, built in 1754; the oldest blockhouse in the United States.

In Skowhegan: **Skowhegan History House** (474-3140 or 474-6632), Norridgewock Avenue. Open June to September, Tuesday through Sunday 1–5. A Greek Revival brick house exhibiting nineteenth-century furnishings, artifacts, and local maps.

Margaret Chase Smith Library Center (474-7133). Open Monday through Friday 10–4. Set above the Kennebec, an expanded version of Senator Smith's home is a research and conference center housing records, scrapbooks, news releases, tape recordings, and memorabilia from 40 years in public life.

The Skowhegan Indian. Billed as "the world's largest sculptured wooden Indian," this 62-foot-high statue is dedicated to the memory of the Maine Indians. It's just off Route 201 near the Kennebec.

BALLOONING   Balloon Drifters (622-1211), Augusta State Airport. Offers free flights and tethered rides.

BOAT EXCURSIONS   Mailboat Rides on Golden Pond (495-2213), Belgrade Lakes Village. Operates daily 9:30–12:30 in-season.

FISHING   Belgrade Lakes are known as a source of smallmouth bass; **Day's Store** in Belgrade Lakes Village devotes an entire floor to fishing gear. Boat rentals are available.

McLeod's, Route 27, Belgrade Lakes, specializes in fly-fishing.

Charlie's Log Cabin, 22 Dunn Street, Oakland, supplies bait and guides.

GOLF AND TENNIS   Natanis Golf Club (622-3561), Webber Pond, Vassalboro. Eighteen holes; tennis courts.

Waterville Country Club (465-7773), Waterville (off I-95). Eighteen holes, clubhouse, carts, and caddies.

SWIMMING   Peacock Beach State Park, Richmond (just off Route 201, 10 miles south of Augusta). A small, beautiful sand beach on Pleasant Pond; lifeguards and picnic facilities. $1 per adult, free under age 12.

Public beaches include **Sunset Camps Beach** on North Pond, Smithfield; **Willow Beach** (968-2421), China. While public access is limited at the **Belgrade and China lakes,** every cottage cluster and most rental "camps" are on water.

The Kennebec Valley

Lake St. George State Park (589-4255), Route 3 in Liberty. A pleasant, clean, clear lake with a sandy beach and changing facilities, a perfect break if you are en route from Augusta and points south to the coast. $1.50 per adult and $.50 per child aged 5–11. There are also 38 campsites and a boat launch.

BED & BREAKFASTS   Maple Hill Farm (622-2708), RFD 1, Box 1145, Hallowell 04347. Little more than 4 miles from the turnpike and downtown Augusta, this pleasant old house sits on 85 acres. Rooms are large and comfortable; $45–$55 includes a full breakfast.

Home-Nest Farm (897-4125), Baldwin Hill Road, Box 2350, Kents Hill, 04349. This is really an old family estate, and there are three historic homes on the extensive property. The main house, built in 1784, offers a panoramic view of the White Mountains. Lilac Cottage (1800) and the Red Schoolhouse (1830) are available for rent as separate units. $40–$60 per room, $80–$95 for houses with one to three bedrooms; breakfast included.

The Inn at Silver Grove (873-7724), 184 Silver Street, Waterville 04901. Handy to I-95 (Exit 33) this elegantly furnished 1830s house offers tastefully decorated guest rooms, upstairs sitting rooms, and a living room with a seventeenth-century grand piano. There's also a cedar hot tub. Breakfast is included; $65 double.

Blueberry Hill Farm (549-3063), RFD 1, Box 1265, North Whitefield 04353. Open year-round. An extended 1860 farmhouse on 84 acres—including 25 acres of wild blueberries and frontage on Clary Lake in Jefferson. This is a working farm with sheep, donkeys, chickens, turkeys, and ducks. $40 double includes a very full farm breakfast.

CAMPS AND COTTAGES   **Bear Spring Camps** (397-2341), RFD 2, Box 1900, Oakland 04941. Open mid-May to October. A gem of a family resort with 75 percent repeat business. Serious fishermen come in early May for trout and salmon, and in July there is still bass. Each of the 32 cottages (niceties include open fireplaces and hammocks) is right on the water with its own dock and motorboat (sailboat rentals are available). Also available are a tennis court and a variety of lawn games, and the swimming is great (the bottom is sandy). Meals are served in the main house. $375 per week for two adults plus $70 for children under 8 and $25 for children under 3. Rates include all meals.

Castle Island Camps (495-3312), Belgrade Lakes 04918. Open May through mid-September. In winter contact Horatio Castle, 1800 Carambola Road, West Palm Beach, FL 33406 (407-641-8339). A dozen comfortable-looking cottages clustered on a small island (connected by bridges) in 12-Mile Long Pond. This is the second generation of Castles to maintain the camps geared to fishing (the pond is stocked; rental boats are available). Meals are served in the small central lodge; weekly and children's rates are available. Friday is always lobster night. $43–$44 per person per night; $194–$301 per week, including all three meals.

DINING OUT   **Dr. Sylvester's** (582-4810), 1 Church Street, Gardiner. Closed Sundays; serving lunch Monday through Friday and dinner Monday through Saturday. Reservations are suggested. Owner Michel Tessier is a genuine French chef, and the dining rooms are trendy Victorian. Specialties include salmon and filet mignon in a whisky cream sauce with peppercorns. Entrées run $9.25–$15.95 and include salad and fresh rolls.

Slate's (622-9575), 167 Water Street, Hallowell. Open from 7:30 for breakfast, lunch, and dinner weekdays (except Monday nights); for brunch and Saturday night dinner on weekends. Coffeehouse atmosphere in three adjoining storefronts with brick walls, tin ceilings, changing art, a great bar, and a patio in back. Live music: jazz, blues, and contemporary. The brunch menu is huge and hugely popular. The dinner menu changes daily but might include pan-grilled coho salmon with smoked shrimp and Jarlsberg cheese or cashew chicken. $8.95–$13.95.

Hazel Green's Restaurant (622-9903), 349 Water Street, Augusta. Open nightly for dinner, weekdays for lunch. A dark, pubby atmosphere. You wonder why no one has punched a window into the rear wall; it would be a river view. Prime rib is the specialty (according to the menu, "our reputation is at steak"); also, chicken supreme (stuffed with lobster and scallops). Buffet every Thursday. Moderate.

La Casa Ristorante (623-2938), 37 Water Street, Hallowell. Closed Sundays; otherwise open for lunch and dinner. A homey decor in an old building. Specialties include ravioli filled with three Italian cheeses, homemade sauce. Moderate.

Village Inn (495-3553), Route 27, Belgrade Lakes. Open late April through mid-November for dinner nightly and lunch on Sundays. A rambling old place with a lake view and early-bird specials. The specialty is duckling, roasted for up to 12 hours and served with a choice of sauces. Moderate.

Silver Street Tavern (873-2277), 2 Silver Street, Waterville. Open for lunch Tuesday through Friday, dinner Tuesday through Sunday, and Sunday brunch. Turn-of-the-century pub atmosphere (tin ceiling). Specialties include teriyaki sirloin and coquille St. Jacques. $7.50–$16.95.

John Sebastian B. (465-3223), 40 Fairfield Street, Oakland. Open Wednesday to Saturday for dinner in summer; Friday and Saturday the rest of the year. A Victorian house in the Belgrade Lakes area. Specialties include chicken cordon-bleu and sauerbraten; homemade European pastries and dessert drinks. $11.00–$21.50.

Feather Bed Inn (293-2020), Mount Vernon. Sundays 8–3, otherwise 5–9 by reservation. Continental fare served in pleasant dining rooms in a restored 1800s house overlooking Lake Minnehonk. The specialty is roast duck in orange allspice. Moderate.

Ashley's (582-3005), 151 Water Street, Gardiner. Open for lunch and dinner. Housed in the old Cobbossee National Bank building, the town's newest dining option.

River Café (622-2190), 119 Water Street, Hallowell. Open for lunch and dinner except Sunday. Mediterranean/American specialties include shish kebab and shish Tawook (marinated chicken tips). Reservations required for dinner. Moderate.

Senator Inn (622-0320), Western Avenue, Augusta. Open daily from 6:30 AM through dinner. A big, all-American dining room (buses are welcome) specializing in seafood; salad bar. Moderate to expensive.

The Village Candle Light (474-9724/2978), 1 Madison Avenue, Skowhegan. Open for dinner except Monday. The specialties are seafood, native vegetables, home baking. Moderate.

The Last Unicorn (873-6378), 8 Silver Street, Waterville. Open daily 11-10. This is a find for vegetarians. "Healthful" choices here include a few meat dishes but the focus is on vegetarian dagwoods, quiche, and spreads. Dinner entrées run $8.50–$9.50.

EATING OUT   **Bravo's** (582-4058), 61 Water Street, Gardiner. This is a comfortable, casual Mexican place open for lunch and dinner. Fajitas are the specialty, and there's a lounge.

Burnsie's Homestyle Sandwiches (622-6425), State Street, Augusta, next to the Capitol. This is the perfect place if you are visiting the Maine State Museum. Keep your car parked where it is and walk up past the Capitol to this out-of-place house, a source of famous lobster rolls, Reubens, and a variety of sandwiches, many named for local legislators.

Patricia's Restaurant (395-4150), South Road, Winthrop (turn at the Winthrop Gem & Mineral Shop on Route 202). Open May to October, Tuesday through Saturday 5 AM–9 PM, and Sunday 11:30–4. A country farmhouse specializing in homemade breads, soups, desserts, and full dinners from $5.95.

Old Mill Pub (474-6627), 41-R Water Street, Skowhegan. Open Monday through Saturday for lunch and dinner. A picturesque old mill building set back from the main drag, overlooking the Kennebec. A friendly bar and scattered tables; sandwiches (a good Reuben), quiche, and specials for lunch; spinach lasagna or stir-fry shrimp for dinner. $5.95–$10.95.

Giberson Diner (582-4804), Gardiner. Open daily from 5 AM. A classic diner with a river view.

My Cousin's Place (634-3016), Route 2 between Skowhegan and Norridgewock. Open for breakfast and lunch. Convenient and friendly with tables overlooking the river.

ENTERTAINMENT   Theater at Monmouth (933-2952), PO Box 385, Monmouth 04259. Performances during July and August, nightly except Mondays; Wednesday and Saturday matinees; children's shows. Housed in Custom Hall, a striking turn-of-the-century building designed as a combination theater, library, and town hall. A resident company presents classics (season included Shakespeare's *Merry Wives of Windsor* and Molière's *The Miser*).

Waterville Summer Music Theater (872-2707), in the Waterville Opera House. Performances during July and August, Tuesday through Saturday 8 PM; Wednesday and Sunday matinees.

Lakewood Theater at Skowhegan, the Cornville Players (474-7176), RFD 1, Box 1780, Skowhegan 04976. Mid-June through August, a community group performs in one of Maine's oldest summer theaters. Broadway plays and children's performances.

Park Street Players at Constitution Hall, Skowhegan State Fair Grounds, Route 201, Skowhegan. A regional theater staging summer plays and musicals. Curtain time is 8 PM.

SELECTIVE SHOPPING   *In Hallowell*: This picturesque riverside lineup of shops harbors fewer antiques dealers than it did a few years ago, but it is still a worthwhile browsing street: **Earthly Delights** (622-9801), 81 Water Street, carries handcrafts and gifts made in New England.

In Gardiner: The mid-nineteenth-century commercial buildings along Water Street have hatched some interesting shops.

In Belgrade Lakes Village: The heart of the Belgrade Lakes is **Day's Store** (495-2205). Open year-round, recently expanded to serve as general store; state liquor store; fishing license, gear, boot, and gift source; and rainy-day mecca. **Maine Made Shop,** open late May to Labor Day, stocks pottery, books, and Maine souvenirs.

OUTLETS   **Carleton Woolen Mills Factory Outlet** (582-6003), Griffin Street, Gardiner. Fabrics, woolens, and notions.

Cascade Fabrics, Oakland. Open Monday through Saturday, 8:30–4:30. A genuine mill store.

Dexter Shoe Factory Outlet (873-6739), Kennedy Memorial Drive, Waterville.

Russell's (872-6777), JFK Highway, Waterville. Ladies apparel.

Keenan Factory Outlet (474-8977), 142 Madison Avenue, Skowhegan (north of town on Route 201). Good for some famous name-brand bargains.

SPECIAL EVENTS   July: **The Great Kennebec River Whatever Week:** Ten days of activities ending with the Kennebec River Whatever Race, running downriver from Augusta to Gardiner. Beginning of the month. **China Connection:** public supper, pageant, road race, greased pig, and pie-eating contests in China. **Old Hallowell Days** (third week).

August: **Skowhegan State Fair:** harness racing, a midway, agricultural exhibits, big name-entertainment, and tractor and oxen pulls; week-long. **Annual Scottish Games & Gathering of the Scottish Clans** sponsored by the St. Andrew's Society of Maine, Thomas College, Waterville.

September: **Common Ground Fair,** Windsor: Maine's Celebration of Rural Living, a gathering of organic farmers and Maine craftspeople.

THE UPPER KENNEBEC VALLEY AND JACKMAN

Route 201, as it follows the Kennebec River north through Solon to Bingham, through the Forks, and on up to Jackman, traverses lonely but beautiful wilderness. The route is known as the Arnold Trail because it is the way Benedict Arnold came in 1775. Within the past decade the Forks have become a legendary center for white-water rafting companies, here to take advantage of the timed water release through Kennebec Gorge. The Dead River, which joins the Kennebec at the Forks, is another popular rafting site.

Commercial rafting on the Kennebec only began in 1976 when outfitter Wayne Hockmeyer shepherded some 400 people through the dramatic Kennebec Gorge. As many as 20 companies are now involved in the course of the season, and their patrons total more than 30,000; no more than 800 rafters are allowed on the Kennebec at a time.

In order to compete, rafting companies based in and around the Forks have added their own lodging in recent years, and some of these "base camps" now remain open year-round, an enticement to visit this unusually beautiful, previously little-touristed area.

The surrounding wilderness harbors many miles of wilderness hiking trails and sites (such as spectacular Moxie Falls), also some genuinely remote sportsmen's camps on fish-rich ponds.

GUIDANCE   Upper Kennebec Valley Chamber of Commerce (672-4100), PO Box 491, Bingham 04920 maintains a seasonal storefront, walk-in information booth on Route 201 in the middle of Bingham. Open daily. **Jackman-Moose River Chamber of Commerce** (668-4094) also maintains a seasonal log information on Route 201 in Jackman.

MEDICAL EMERGENCY   Bingham Area Health Center (672-4808); **Ambulance Service** (672-4410).

TO SEE AND DO   Moxie Falls (drop 90 feet) is said to be the highest falls in New England (see Hiking). **Caratunk Falls** is a 36-foot falls located near Solon. **Wyman Dam** (155 feet high) walls the Kennebec River between Moscow and Bingham. It was built in the 1930s by Central Maine Power. It raises the river 123 feet, creating the most popular rafting route in the Northeast. **Wyman Lake** stretches out for many miles behind it, and there is public boat access from Route 201.

AIRBOAT TRIP   Maine Whitewater (672-4814), Gadabout Gaddis Airport, Bingham 04920. Daily 14-mile scenic rides on the Kennebec between Solon and Bingham.

CANOEING   The Moose River Bow Trip is a Maine classic: a series of pristine ponds form a 42-mile meandering route which winds back to the point of origin, eliminating the need for a shuttle. The fishing is fine; remote campsites are scattered along the way, and the put-in place is accessible. One major portage is required. Canoe rentals are available from a variety of local sources (check with the two local chambers of commerce), and guided canoe trips can be arranged through some of the larger rafting companies (try Wilderness Expeditions for starters).

HIKING   Hiking possibilities abound in this area. *Take a Hike* by Susan Varney (available locally and from Voyager Whitewater) describes 20 hikes in the Upper Kennebec Valley Region. The standout is Moxie Falls, an 89-foot waterfall that is considered the highest in New England, set in a dramatic gorge. It's an easy .6-mile walk from the trailhead. Turn off Route 201 onto Moxie Road on the south side of the bridge across the Kennebec in the Forks. Park off the road at the trailhead sign on the left.

FISHING   Fishing is what the sporting camps are all about. The catch is landlocked salmon, trout, and togue. Rental boats and canoes are available (see Rustic Resorts).

GOLF   Moose River Golf Course (668-5331). Mid-May through October; club rental, putting green, nine holes.

MOOSE-WATCHING   Remember that the best time to see a moose is at dawn or dusk. Favorite local moose crossings include Moxie Road from the Forks to Moxie Pond; the Central Maine Power Co. road from Moxie Pond to Indian Pond; Route 201, the 25 miles north from the Forks to

Jackman; and Route 16, the 30 miles from Jackman to Rockwood. Drive these stretches carefully; residents all know someone who has died in a car/moose collision.

WHITE-WATER RAFTING   Driving up Route 201 around 4 PM on a bright summer day you may wonder what all of those people are doing sipping drinks in darkened lodge rooms. The scene resembles a series of dating bars, except that the young people are all watching videos of themselves rafting that morning through the Kennebec River Gorge and on down over the sheer 12-foot drop of Magic Falls. Rafting is the kind of thrill ride that people brag about back in the office and, for many customers, it is a first-time adventure in the big outdoors. The nature of the rafting companies varies; you may want to shop around. Some are based elsewhere but do a good job of transporting their patrons to the Forks to take advantage of the timed releases from Harris Station Dam. All charge $75–$100 per person (the exception is Voyagers' .$60 midweek no-frills) and run April through October. In the past few years most rafting companies have either bought and renovated existing camps or inns or built new lodges to house their patrons. An appealing alternative for budget-minded rafters is Mrs. G's in Bingham.

Northern Outdoors, Inc. (663-4466), PO Box 100, the Forks 04985. Wayne Hockmeyer was the first rafter on the Kennebec, and he is still the biggest, now also with a permanent base on the Penobscot near Ripogenus Dam. The Base Lodge at the Forks is very attractive: a new, open-timbered building with high ceilings, a huge hearth, comfortable seating, a cheerful dining room, a bar, and a hot tub. Accommodations vary from camping to cabins and lodge double rooms. Northern Outdoors offers Kennebec River day and overnight trips, Dead River runs, and canoe and kayak clinics. In winter the lodge caters to snowmobilers and cross-country skiers. $70 per person for a day trip on the Kennebec ($85 on weekends); $155 for an overnight camping trip.

Voyagers Whitewater (663-4423), the Forks 04985. This small company caters to fewer than 20 rafters at a time. Owner John Kokadjo is an experienced raftsman, and his wife, Susan Varney , was chef at the Winter's Inn in Kingfield before devoting herself to making rafters' fiddlehead quiche breakfasts and steak lunches (vegetarians are also accommodated) on the river. Two-day packages include a lobster dinner. At this writing there are just two pleasant upstairs guest rooms with private baths and views towards the Kennebec, but accommodations for a full trip of 20 people is promised by the summer of '91. $80 double.

Crab Apple White Water (663-2218), the Forks 04985. The Crab Apple Acres, an 1830s edifice with a fan light over the door and flowery wallpaper in the seven guest rooms, serves as the base camp,

Kennebec Gorge

Photo by Wayne Hockmeyer, courtesy of Northern Whitewater Expeditions

but the river experience is similar to the other outfitters. Rate includes lodging, breakfast, and a steak dinner.

New England Whitewater Center (663-4455; 800-766-7238), Box 15, West Forks 04985. Offers day and overnight rafting trips on the Kennebec and Penobscot rivers. This enterprising outfit can sleep 120 people between its properties; the Sterling Inn (17 rooms, $70 double with shared baths, includes breakfast) and the Marshall Hotel and Marshall Cabins (open year-round) at the Forks. They also operate a campground at the Dead River Campgrounds in the West Forks.

Maine Whitewater (672-4814; 800-345-MAIN), Gadabout Gaddis Airport, Bingham 04920. Offers Kennebec rafting trips (also see Airboat Trip) and a base complex with a restaurant, game room, spa, and camping area.

North Country Rivers (663-4476), PO Box 18, the Forks 04985. Daily rafting trips May to September.

Downeast Whitewater (663-2277), based at Northern Pines Cottages and Restaurant, the Forks. Serves as the local camp for New Hampshire-based Saco Bound.

Unicorn Rafting Expeditions (725-2255), PO Box T, Brunswick 04011. Offers trips on the Kennebec and the Penobscot; also kayaking workshops.

John Palmer's All Outdoors (663-2231), Lake Moxie Camps, Box 60, West Forks 04985. Classic old Maine Moxie Pond forms the base camp for this high-powered newcomer to the Forks scene. Rafting trips include a steak lunch, and you can stay on in the housekeeping cabins to canoe or hike. Facilities include a full-service dining room, hot tub, and campsites. Lake Moxie Camps are open year-round.

Wilderness Expeditions (534-2242; 800-825-WILD), PO Box 41, Rockwood 04478. Based an hour away at a great resort on Moosehead Lake (see Moosehead Lake Area [Rustic Resorts]), Wilderness maintains a base camp in the Forks offering horseback riding (trail rides and full-day pack trips) as well as rafting.

Eastern River Expeditions (695-2411/2248; 800-634-7238) offers a variety of rafting trips from its Greenville base and maintains an Indian Pond campsite near Kennebec Gorge.

RUSTIC RESORTS   (These are classic Sporting Camps geared to fishermen and hunters.)

Harrison's Pierce Pond Sporting Camps (243-2930; this is a radio phone so let it ring and try again if it doesn't work. December 15 to April 15 or when unable to get through, call 603-279-8424), Box 315, Bingham 04920. Open May through October. Sited on the Appalachian Trail, 15 miles of dirt road from Bingham. Fran and Tim Harrison are breathing new life into this classic, old log camp set on a hillside and overlooking a stream with a waterfall in the distance. Nine-mile-long Pierce Pond is a short walk across the stream and through the woods. Each of the nine log cabins has a bedroom and token bath; rates include three abundant meals per day. Word has gotten out about Fran's cooking, and some people actually drive the bumpy road for Sunday turkey or Friday lobster.

The Falcon Resorts on Spencer Pond (800-825-8234; good in Maine as well as outside), Falcon.Inc., PO Box 1899, Bangor 04401. Open year-round. Unquestionably the poshest, most expensive sporting camp in the East, the new log lodge at the southern end of remote Spencer Pond accommodates a dozen people. $25 per person per day (based on double occupancy with a three-day minimum) includes air transport here from Bangor International Airport; also "gourmet" food, liquor, guides, and all fishing equipment. Falcon has also acquired and rehabbed Hardscrabble Wilderness Cabins and Lodge at the northern end of Spencer Pond. The five log cabins now have full baths, woodstoves, and small fridges, but guests eat all meals in the classic, mansard-roofed log lodge; $125 a day per person (double occupancy, no minimum stay); rates include use of boats and all meals, but guests must arrive under their own steam. It's a 15-mile drive over gravel roads from Route 201, easier in winter by snowmobile. We flew in with Folsom's from Greenville (see Moosehead Lake Region [Getting Around]).

Cobb's Pierce Pond Camps (628-2819 in summer; 628-3612 in winter), North New Portland 04961. There are 11 guest cabins, accommodating from two to eight; each has a screened porch, woodstove, bathroom, and electricity. Home-cooked meals and between-meal snacks are served in the main lodge. The camp dates from 1902, and the Cobb family has been running it for almost 30 years. It is the kind of place that doesn't advertise. It has a loyal following among serious fishermen; also a sand beach. Weekend fly-fishing instruction and boats are available; guides. Rates include three meals.

Attean Lake Resort (668-3792; 668-3321 or 668-7726 in winter), Jackman 04945. Frankly, this is one of the few out-of-the-way places that we didn't get to for the revision of this book, and it was in flux when we last visited it. Sited on an island in Attean Lake, surrounded by mountains; 20 cabins, luxurious by sports-lodge standards, with open fireplaces and even a small oriental carpet, night-lights, and an attentive cabin boy. The resort also maintains three cabins along the Moose River Trip (see Canoeing). Fishing boats and canoes are available. The resort is easily accessible from Jackman; you phone from the shore, and a boat fetches you. Rates include three meals.

OTHER LODGING   **Mrs. G's Bed & Breakfast** (672-4034), Box 389, Meadow Street, Bingham 04920. A tidy house on a side street in the middle of town. The aroma of fresh baking may well greet you, and Frances Gibson (Mrs. G) delights in orienting guests to the full range of local hiking, biking, and cross-country skiing possibilities as well as rafting.

There are four cheerful guest rooms; also a delightful loft dorm room; shared baths. $22 single and $50 double includes a full breakfast and state tax; will pick up hikers on the Appalachian Trail.

Briarwood Mountain Lodge (668-7756), Route 201, Jackman 04945. This is a spiffy 20-room, three-story motel with indoor pool, cable TV, and restaurant and bar with weekend entertainment. $54 double.

Bingham Motor Inn (672-4135), PO Box 683, Route 201, Bingham 04920. Open year-round. A clean, standard 16-unit motel; some efficiencies. Amenities include phones, TV, a pool. $35–$50 double, from $30 single.

Sky Lodge (668-2171), Moose River 04945. A splendidly built lodge with two-story fieldstone hearths in the living room, presently geared to groups and closed to the public in June, July, and the first half of August. Individuals are welcome in other months but on the understanding they will be incorporated into larger groups. Seven rooms in the lodge have fireplaces. Meals are buffet-style. $55 single includes three meals.

EATING OUT   **Thompson's Restaurant** (672-3245), Main Street, Bingham. Open daily from 5:30 AM year-round. An unusually inviting eatery in business since 1939; its old-fashioned look—complete with red awning, deep booths, and the original moose head in the dining room—is preserved by Rodney and Carolyn Farrington. The menu includes homemade doughnuts, fresh fish, pea soup on Thursday, baked beans on Saturday, and (always) custard pie; pizza, wine, and beer also served.

Hog's Breath, Moose River. Open 11–9, more or less year-round. Great road food.

Loon's Look-Out Restaurant at Tuckaway Shores Cabins (668-3351), on Big Wood Lake, Jackman. Take Spruce Street off Route 201, bear right onto Forest Street, and it's at the end on the right-hand side. Open Friday through Sunday 5–9. A great little Italian place with specialties like chicken parmigiano and bistecca a la pazzarella (steak chunks sautéed with bell peppers, onions, mushrooms, and spices). Call ahead. From $8.95 for lasagna to $9.95 for steak.

Moose Point Tavern, Jackman. Open for lunch and dinner more or less year-round. Standard road food.

Maine's Western Mountains

BETHEL AREA

Bethel is a natural farming and trading site on the Androscoggin River. Its town common is the junction for routes west to the White Mountains, north to the Mahoosucs, east to the Oxford Hills, and south to the lakes.

When the train from Portland to Montreal began stopping here in 1851, Bethel also became an obvious summer retreat for city people. Nothing fancy. Families stayed the season in the big, white farmhouses, which still abound. They feasted on homegrown and homecooked food, then walked it off on nearby mountain trails.

Hiking remains a big lure for many visitors. The White Mountain National Forest comes within a few miles of town, and trails radiate from nearby Evans Notch, many of them used for llama treks. Just 12 miles northwest of Bethel, Grafton Notch State Park also offers some short hikes to spectacles such as Screw Auger Falls and a wealth of well-equipped picnic sites. Blueberrying and rockhounding are local pastimes, and the hills are also good pickings for history buffs. The hills were once far more peopled than they are today—entire villages have vanished.

Hastings, for example, now just the name of a National Forest campground, was once a thriving community complete with post office, stores, and a wood alcohol mill that shipped its product by rail to Portland, then to England.

The Bethel Inn, born of the railroad era, is still going strong. Opened in 1913 by millionaire William Bingham II and dedicated to a prominent neurologist (who had himself come to Bethel to recuperate from a breakdown), it originally featured a program of strenuous exercise—one admired by the locals (wealthy clients actually paid the doctor to chop down his trees) as well as by the medical profession. It is still recognized as a pioneer concept in physical therapy, and the inn still has an extensive exercise program (golf, tennis, swimming, boating, and cross-country skiing) and a sports center.

Bethel is also one of New England's liveliest ski towns. Sunday

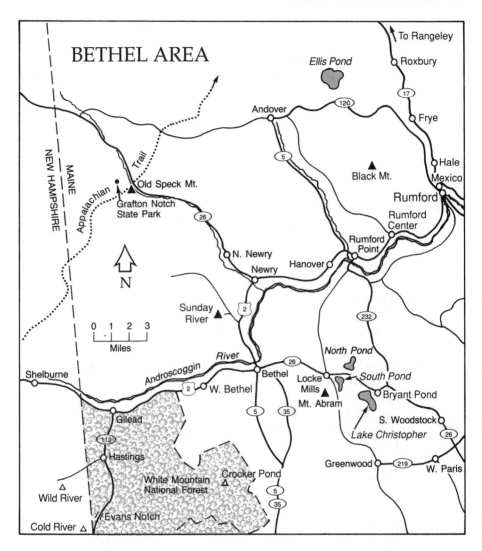

BETHEL AREA

Ellis Pond

To Rangeley

Roxbury

Andover

120

17

Frye

NEW HAMPSHIRE

MAINE

Appalachian

Trail

5

Hale

Black Mt.

Mexico

Old Speck Mt.

Rumford

Grafton Notch
State Park

Rumford
Center

26

Rumford
Point

N. Newry

Newry

Hanover

N

232

Sunday
River

2

0 1 2 3

Miles

River

26

North Pond

Shelburne

Androscoggin

Bethel

South Pond

Locke
Mills

2

W. Bethel

Bryant Pond

5

35

Mt. Abram

Gilead

S. Woodstock

113

Lake Christopher

26

Hastings

Crocker Pond

Greenwood

219

W. Paris

△
Wild River

White Mountain
National Forest

△

5

35

Cold River △

Evans Notch

River, 6 miles north of town, bills itself as the largest ski resort in Maine
and New Hampshire in uphill capacity. The ski area has expanded
quickly in recent years, gearing its lodging and prices to families—and
drawing them in droves from Portland and Boston. Mount Abram, a
few miles east of the village, remains one of Maine's friendliest, low-
key family areas. A wide choice of inns, bed & breakfasts, shops, and
restaurants complete the inviting scene.

For Bethel, however, tourism has been the icing rather than the cake.
Its lumber mills manufacture pine clapboards, furniture parts, and
most of this country's broom handles. Three dairy farms ship 7,000

gallons of milk per week, and a poultry farm packs 1,300 dozen eggs per day.

Bethel is also the home of Gould Academy, a co-ed prep school with a handsome campus which is summer home to the NTL Institute, an internationally respected management training program.

In Bethel, Brooks Brothers is the name of the hardware store, not a men's clothier; and, while Maine Street has more than its share of quality crafts shops, it also has Prim's. Carrying envelopes, diapers, liquor, ice cream, Timex watches, toys, and stationery, Prim's is proof that Bethel is one great old town that has not gone down the tourist tubes.

GUIDANCE **Bethel Area Chamber of Commerce** (824-2282), PO Box 121, Bethel 04217, publishes an excellent area guide and maintains a reservation service (824-3585).

Sunday River maintains its own toll-free reservation number (800-543-2SKI), good nationwide and in Canada; it's winter- and condo-geared but also serves local inns and B&Bs.

GETTING THERE By air: **Portland Jetport,** served by Continental, United, Delta, USAir, and Business Express, is 75 miles from Bethel. All major **car rentals** are available at the airport.

By car: Bethel is a convenient way stop between New Hampshire's White Mountains (via Route 2) and the Maine coast. From Boston take the Maine Turnpike to Gray, Exit 11; Bethel is 55 miles north on Route 26. There are restaurants en route in South Paris (see Dining Out and Eating Out).

MEDICAL EMERGENCY **Bethel Area Health Center** (824-2193) or Sheriff's Dept. (800-482-7433).

TO SEE AND DO **Moses Mason House** (824-2908), Broad Street, Bethel. Open July and August, 1–4 daily except Mondays, and by appointment the rest of the year; $1.50 per adult, $.75 per child. This exquisite Federal-style mansion is proof of the town's early prosperity. Maintained by the Bethel Historical Society, it has Rufus Porter murals in the front hall and fine furnishings, woodwork, special exhibits, and a Wednesday afternoon film series.

Bryant Pond Telephone Museum (336-9911), Rumford Avenue, Bryant Pond. This was the last town in the country to use an old-style crank phone (until 1983), and visitors are welcome to see an exhibit of the magneto telephone system. By appointment.

Woodstock Historical Society Museum (665-2450), Route 26, Bryant Pond. Open Memorial Day to Labor Day, Saturday 1-4 or by appointment. An old barn housing a collection of old furniture, glass, uniforms, books, wooden toys, pictures, and, of course, a crank phone.

Artist's Covered Bridge, Newry (across the Sunday River, 5 miles northwest of Bethel). A weathered town bridge built in 1872 and painted by numerous nineteenth-century landscape artists, notably

John Enneking. A great spot to sun and swim. Other swimming holes can be found at intervals along the road above the bridge.

GREEN SPACE   Evans Notch. Follow Route 2 west to Gilead and turn south on Route 113, following the Wild and then the Cold rivers south through one of the most spectacular mountain passes in northern New England. (Also see Camping and Hiking.)

Grafton Notch State Park. A beautiful drive even if you don't hike. (See Hiking.)

Patte Brook Multiple Use Management Demonstration Area. A 4-mile, self-guided tour with stops at 11 areas has been set up along Patte Brook near the National Forest's Crocker Pond campground in West Bethel. The tour begins on Forest Road No. 7 (Patte Brook Road), 5 miles south of Bethel on Route 5. A glacial bog, former orchards and homesites, an old dam and pond are among the clearly marked sites.

CAMPING   In the Evans Notch area of the **White Mountain National Forest** there are five campgrounds: Basin (21 sites), Cold River (12 sites), Crocker Pond (seven sites), Hastings (24 sites), and Wild River (11 sites). All cost $8 except Basin, which is $10, and three (Basin, Cold River, and Hastings) accept reservations during the May 15 to October 15 camping season. Phone: 800-283-2267, Monday through Friday 12-9 or Saturday and Sunday 1-6. For information phone the Evans Notch Ranger Station (824-2134), Bridge Street, Bethel.

CANOEING   Popular local routes include the **Ellis River** in Andover—13 easy miles from a covered bridge in East Andover to Rumford Point; the **Androscoggin River**—the reach from Gilead to West Bethel has many islands, splendid mountain views; the **Sunday River**—Newry to Bethel beginning at the covered bridge, great white water in spring; **South Pond and Round Pond** in Locke Mills are also easily accessible and rewarding.

Canoe rentals are available at **Bob's Corner Store & Texaco Station** (875-2419), Route 26 south, Locke Mills. Also from **Port Sports** (824-3733), in the Mountain View Mall on Lower Main Street, Bethel. **Mahoosuc Mountain Adventures** (see Dog Sledding) offers a variety of white-water and wilderness canoe trips in summer and fall.

DOG SLEDDING   **Mahoosuc Mountain Adventures** (824-2073), Bear River Road, Newry 04261. Polly Mahoney and Kevin Slater offer combination backcountry skiing, ice-climbing expeditions, and mushing trips in winter. You can be as involved with the dogs as desired. $255 per person fully outfitted for a three-day, two-night trip.

FISHING   Temporary nonresident licenses are available at the Bethel Town Office, Main Street, or at **Bob's Corner Store** (see Canoeing).

GOLF   **Bethel Inn and Country Club** (824-2175), Bethel. An 18-hole, championship-length course and driving range. Club and golf cart rentals are available.

HIKING   **White Mountain National Forest,** although primarily in New

Hampshire, includes 41,943 acres in Maine. A number of the trails in the Evans Notch area are spectacular. Trail maps for the Baldface Circle Trail, Basin Trail, Bickford Brook Trail, and Caribou Trail are available from the Evans Notch Ranger District (824-3124), Bridge Street, Bethel. Open Monday through Friday 8–4.

Grafton Notch State Park, Route 26, between Newry and Upton. From Bethel take Route 2 east to Route 26 north for 7.8 miles. Turn left at the Getty station (Newry Corner) and go toward New Hampshire for 8.7 miles. Screw Auger Falls is 1 mile farther. A spectacular area at the end of the Mahoosuc Range. Sights include **Screw Auger Falls, Mother Walker Falls, and Moose Cave,** a quarter-mile nature walk. The big hike is up **Old Speck,** the third highest mountain in the state; the loop trek up Old Speck Trail and back down the Firewarden's Trail is 5.5 miles.

Step Falls. Just before the entrance to Grafton Notch State Park (see directions above). From the Getty station go 7.9 miles. On the right will be a white farmhouse followed by a field just before a bridge. There is a road leading to the rear left of the field where you may park. The well-marked trail is just behind the trees at the back. Please respect the private property adjoining the trail and falls. This scenic area, maintained by the Nature Conservancy, has been enjoyed by local families for generations.

In Shelburne there are hiking trails on **Mount Crag, Mount Cabot, and Ingalls Mountain,** and there are more trails in **Evans Notch.** For details check the AMC *White Mountain Guide* and *Fifty Hikes in Southern Maine* by John Gibson, published by Backcountry Publications, Woodstock, Vermont 05091.

GUIDE SERVICE **Mahoosuc Mountain Adventures** (824-2073), Bear River Road, Newry 04261. Polly Mahoney and Kevin Slater offer dog sledding, backcountry skiing, ski touring, and ice climbing expeditions in winter and a variety of white-water and wilderness canoe trips the rest of the year. The couple are very qualified, geared to introducing their patrons to a variety of new skills, day trips as well as longer outings offered.

HORSEBACK RIDING **Philbrook Farm Stables** (603-466-2993), 18 miles west of Bethel, either via North Road (scenic but rough) or Route 2. At the Philbrook Farm Inn just over the New Hampshire line Nancy St. John offers trail rides; also lessons and pony rides. The hour-long rides on the inn's vast property are geared to all level riders and cost just $15. (See Inns.)

LLAMA TREKKING **Telemark Inn & Llama Farm** (836-2703), RFD 2, Box 800, Bethel 04217. Treks offered April through October. "Llamas are a natural for these mountains," enthuses owner Steve Crone. You lead a llama, and it carries your gear plus the tent and food supplied by Steve and his fellow guides, who prepare a feast on top of the mountain and set up camp. We went for a weekend and loved it; one-to six-day treks are offered. $70 per adult and $50 per child for a single day; also three-day camping/llama treks and week-long adventures which include three days of llama trekking and three days of canoeing, four days camping out and four days at the Telemark Inn; multiple-day packages with camping or lodging at Steve's Telemark Inn. These are proving popular with families.

MOUNTAIN BIKING   Sunday River's Mountain Bike Park (824-3000 or 800-543-2SKI), Sunday River Ski Area, Newry. Billed as "the only lift-serviced mountain bike park in the east." Lift and trail access passes are $15, sold at the White Cap Base Lodge. There are 13 trails; lodging, lift, and meal packages are available. Rental bikes are available from Port Sports (825-3733), Lower Main Street, Bethel.

SWIMMING   There are numerous lakes and river swimming holes in the area. It is best to ask the chamber (see Guidance) where access is currently possible. Never-fail spots include the following:

Artist's Covered Bridge. Follow Sunday River signs north from Bethel but continue on Sunday River Road instead of turning onto the ski area access. Look for the covered bridge on your left. Space for parking, bushes for changing.

Wild River in Evans Notch, Gilead, offers some obvious access spots off Route 113 as does the **Bear River,** which follows Route 26 through Grafton Notch.

ROCKHOUNDING   This corner of Oxford County is recognized as one of the world's richest sources of minerals and gems. More than a third of the world's mineral varieties are said to be found. Gems include amethyst, aquamarine, tourmaline, and topaz. Mining has gone on around here since tourmaline was discovered at Mount Mica in 1821. While Perham's of West Paris (see Rockhounding under What's Where in Maine) is the famous starting point for most rockhounders, Jim Mann's Mt. Mann shop on Main Street, Bethel, is a trove of information as well as the fine gemstone jewelry which he has mined himself, then cut and set (he also designs settings to order). Jim admits that he spends too much of his day talking with fellow rockhounders and plans to have a "How To/Where To" guide for rockhounders published within the year.

CROSS-COUNTRY SKIING   Sunday River Ski Touring Center (824-2410), Bethel (based at Sunday River Inn, near the ski area). A total of 25 miles of double-tracked trails looping through the woods, including a 5-mile loop to Artist's Covered Bridge. Thanks to the high elevation, careful trail prepping, and heavy-duty grooming equipment, snow tends to stick here when it's scarce in much of Maine. The center offers guided night skiing, rentals, instruction, and snacks.

Bethel Inn and Country Club (824-2175), Bethel. Trails meander out from the inn, over the golf course, and down through the pines to the Lake House at Songo Pond (10 km round-trip); off around the Gould Academy campus; and, in another direction, up around Grover Hill. In all, Sally Sawyer maintains 42 km of marked, groomed trails and provides telemark instruction, rentals, lessons, and guided moonlight tours.

Mount Abram (875-2601), Locke Mills. A 10-mile network of maintained cross-country trails; rentals are available.

Telemark Inn & Llama Farm (836-2703), West Bethel. While it's not a formal touring center, the inn maintains 9 miles of trails for its guests and invites the public to use them, too (for a fee). Because of their elevation (1,500 feet) and wooded nature, they hold snow when there's relatively little around.

Black Mountain of Maine (364-8977), 50 Congress Street, Rumford. A total of 55 km of groomed trails, ski school, child care (call ahead), cafeteria, and lounge.

DOWNHILL SKIING   **Mount Abram Ski Slopes** (875-2601), Locke Mills. This is the way ski areas used to be. It is still owned by the family who began buying up the mountain for its timber in the 1950s. Don Cross, one of the three brothers who helped cut the original trails, install the lifts, and build the lodge, still gets out and grooms the slopes at 3 AM. Instead of a cafeteria there is chief cook Anthony Rowe, serving freshly made soup and cookies. Instead of a toll-free reservations number there is Bill Riley sitting at a table with a "Lodging" sign propped up on it. But this is no small ski hill; the 22 trails and slopes, which include a 2.5-mile trail from the top, hold some pleasant surprises. The vertical drop is 1,000 feet.

Facilities include 80 percent snowmaking; two double chair lifts and three T-bars; a base lodge with lounge, snack shop, ski shop, nursery, and ski rentals; and 40 condominiums (a total of 400 beds at the mountain). Ski school is offered at a separate area—Duane's Retreat with ski lessons by the American Teaching Method and a "plus program" (a series of two-hour lessons with videotaping for experienced skiers who want to improve).

Lift tickets are $26 per adult and $18 per junior on weekends; $12 for everyone on weekdays. Morning as well as afternoon tickets are available; $30 buys an introductory lesson including lifts and ski rental.

Sunday River Ski Area (824-3000; resort reservations: 800-543-2SKI), Bethel 04217. Sunday River offers all of the amenities of a full-scale resort plus more snowmaking on more trails and greater lift capacity than any other ski area in Maine or New Hampshire. And the price is right, especially for families. It was begun by a local group in 1959 and acquired snowmaking and its first condominiums under ownership of the Sherburne Corporation (owners of Killington in Vermont, the largest ski resort in the East). It is now owned by youthful and aggressive Les Otten, who was manager during the Sherburne era (1972–1980).

There are 60 trails in all, including a 3-mile trail from the summit and "White Heat," billed as "the steepest, longest, wildest, lift-serviced expert trail in the East." The vertical drop is 1,854 feet. Four quad chair lifts, four triple chair lifts, two double chair lifts. Snowmaking on 390 acres (93 percent of the skiing terrain); top-to-bottom coverage for all skiing abilities. Other facilities include three base lodges, a ski shop, and three restaurants; 3,300 beds in condominium hotels with pools and Jacuzzis; and townhouses. The ski school offers Guaranteed Learn-to-Ski in One Day ($30 includes rentals, lifts), SKIwee for ages 4–6, Mogul Meisters for ages 7–12, Junior Racing Program, and the Maine Handicapped Skiing Program.

Lift tickets are $36 per adult and $20 per junior on weekends; $31 per adult and $16 per junior on weekdays.

ICE-SKATING   In winter a portion of Bethel's common is flooded, and ice skates can be rented from the cross-country center in the Bethel Inn.

SLEIGH RIDES   Steve Crone offers sleigh rides in winter (see Llama Trekking); so does Sunday River Ski Resort (see Downhill Skiing).

INNS   (Also see Lake House, Bear Mountain Inn, Kedarburn Inn, Westways, Farrington's, and Quisisana under Western Lakes Region.)

Bethel Inn and Country Club (824-2175; 800-654-0125; and in Maine: 800-367-8884), Bethel 04217. This rambling, yellow structure with mansion-like cottages dominates the town common. There are 65 guest rooms, all with phones and private baths. The common rooms downstairs are large and formal, but there is nothing starchy about the downstairs Mill Brook Tavern, where you can sup informally. The formal dining room is one of the loveliest around, with a fireplace and windows overlooking the mountains (see Dining Out). There are also 40 condominiums and a recreation center with an indoor-outdoor pool and hot tub, two saunas, exercise room, game room, and lounge. The pool is outdoors but hot enough to use in winter. Other amenities include an 18-hole golf course, tennis court, a boat house with canoes and sailfish, and a sandy beach on Songo Pond; winter facilities include a small sauna and an extensive cross-country ski network (see Golf and Cross-Country Skiing). $59–$123 single MAP in rooms; $98–$227 per condo unit (no meals). Many packages available, including bargain-priced theater weekends (plays performed on premises) in late fall and spring.

Philbrook Farm Inn (603-446-3831), Shelburne, NH 03581. Open May through October and December 26 through March. Although it is 2 miles into New Hampshire, this grand old inn is very much a part of the Bethel area, the last survivor among the dozens of local farms that began taking guests in the 1860s. A framed child's drawing in a hallway reads, "Only generations can come here. We are the fifth generation." Actually the fifth generation of Philbrooks run the place, but newcomers are welcome. The 19 guest rooms are furnished with the kind of hand-me-downs for which most innkeepers scour antiques stores and auctions. The five cottages (summer only) are very Victorian. There is a pine-paneled dining room, and the maze of public rooms includes spacious summer parlors. The rambling white building is secure in its own 1,000 acres, sited on a knoll above the floodplain of the Androscoggin River. In winter it caters to cross-country skiers, in summer to hikers. It is accessible from Route 2 in Shelburne and from Bethel by a dirt road. $65 single to $110 double, MAP (breakfast and dinner) plus 15 percent gratuity; $400 per week for a housekeeping cottage.

Telemark Inn (836-2703), RFD 2, Box 800, Bethel 04217. Set 2.5 miles up a country road, this unusual summer mansion is set among birch trees and its own private estate, surrounded in turn by National Forest. It's the perfect place for Steve Crone's herd of llamas. Steve was the first person in New England to offer llama treks, and they are the reason most people come to stay; but in winter there is also cross-country skiing and horse-drawn sleigh rides. The inn itself is beautifully built with rich wood-paneled walls and a mineral-rich fireplace; it's furnished with turn-of-the-century birch furniture. It accommodates 12–17 guests who dine on a huge, round dining table supported by slim tree trunks. Rooms share baths. $75–$80 per room with breakfast; also packages combined with llama treks.

Sunday River Inn (824-2410), RFD 2, Bethel 04217. Primarily a winter inn; open only to groups in summer and fall. A large fireplace, a selection of books and quiet games are in the living room, and an adjacent room can be used for small conferences. A game room and sauna are also available to guests. Sleeping arrangements range from dorms to private rooms in the inn or adjacent chalet. The inn maintains its own extensive cross-country trail system and is handy to Sunday River Ski Area (see Cross-Country Skiing and Downhill Skiing). $36–$68 single includes two meals; children's rates.

L'Auberge (824-2774), Mill Hill Road, Bethel 04217. A former barn (belonging to a long-vanished mansion), now a gracious inn with seven guest rooms including one with shared bath and one large loft suite. A grand piano stands in the large living room, which also has a hearth, plenty of books, and comfortable seating. Dinner is available by reservation to the public. You can ski cross-country out the door (the Bethel Inn trails adjoin) and walk to village shops and restaurants. $65–$80 double, breakfast included.

Sudbury Inn (824-2174), Bethel 04217. A nicely restored 1870s village inn with 15 guest rooms, all with private baths. The downstairs public rooms are attractive, and there are two public dining rooms and two pubs. $60–$90 double, includes a full "made-to-order" breakfast.

The Bethel Inn

BED & BREAKFASTS **Chapman Inn** (824-2657), Bethel 04217. A family find. A rambling white building on the common in the National Historic District. It offers six spacious rooms (nothing fancy but comfortable; shared baths) and four apartments with full kitchens. Breakfast is served in the dining room. Facilities include an inviting TV room, a game room with pool table and sauna, and a new bunk room. Handy to cross-country trails at the Bethel Inn, also to village shops, restaurants. $45–$55 per room, $65 for apartments, $25 for the dorm; all rates include a full breakfast.

Douglass Place (824-2229), Bethel 04217. A handsome 20-room home that once took in summer boarders. Dana and Barbara Douglass have raised four daughters here and now graciously welcome guests. There are four guest rooms with twin beds, a game room (with piano and pool table), a big homey kitchen, attractive living and dining rooms, grounds, a gazebo, and a large barn. $35–$45 includes a continental breakfast with homemade muffins and fresh fruit.

Four Seasons Inn (824-2755), PO Box 390, Bethel 04217. Sandy Mahon maintains this Victorian village mansion as an elegant bed & breakfast. Rooms are furnished with antiques and garnished with niceties such as fresh flowers, fruit baskets, and candies on your pillow. Afternoon tea with petits fours as well as breakfast included. $45–$90 double.

Hammons House (824-3170), Broad Street, Bethel 04217. Sally Rollinson has turned this exquisite 1859 home on the common into a bed & breakfast. There are four spacious double rooms, two to a bath. A rear sun porch has been converted into an unusual two-story conservatory where full breakfast is served. There are a number of pleasant, relaxing spaces and formal gardens in back. $40–$75 double. No smoking.

Glen Mountain House (665-2043), Bryant Pond 04219. A bed & breakfast with three large guest rooms, a spacious living room and family room with fireplace; handy to Mount Abram. A full breakfast is included. $50 double.

Holidae House (824-3400), PO Box 851, Bethel 04217. A gracious Bethel house built by a local lumber baron. Guest rooms are furnished in comfortable antiques and reproduction period furnishings; each has cable TV. The common rooms include a formal living room and a family room with a woodburning stove. $40–$80 double includes a very full breakfast.

The Norseman (824-2002), Route 2, Bethel 04217. A fine, old (parts date to 1799) farmstead that's changed hands twice in the past three years but seems back on an even keel with Dale and John Cheney. Rooms come both with and without private bath, and the living room has a superb fireplace made from local stones; also a player piano. $58–$85 includes breakfast.

Abbotts Mill Farm (364-2697), RFD 2, Box 3702, Bryant Pond 04219. Three rooms with shared bath in this friendly, comfortable farm just a few miles off the beaten track. No children under age 10 and no smoking, please. $25 single, $40 double.

The Farwell House (824-2446), Elm and Railroad streets, Bethel 04217. A large in-town house with two large bedrooms and adjoining bath. $45–$55 double includes a full breakfast.

Blueberry Mountain Inn (824-2004), RFD 2, Box 211, Bethel 04217. A 150-year-old farmhouse near the Artist's Covered Bridge. Some rooms with private, others with shared baths. $45 double includes a full breakfast with a view of the Mahoosuc Range.

SKI LODGES AND CONDOMINIUMS   Sunday River (824-2187; resort reservations: 800-543-2SKI), PO Box 450, Bethel 04217. Now offers a total of 3,300 "slopeside beds." There are six three-story condominium hotels. **Cascades** has 24 studio units and 48 one-bedroom, split-level units; **Sunrise,** 64 one-bedroom units; **Brookside,** 120 units; **North**

Pride, 108 units; **White Cap,** 64 units; and **Fall Line,** 128 units. Each complex has its own pool, Jacuzzi, sauna, laundry, recreation room, and game room; Cascades and Sunrise offer large common living rooms with fireplaces, and Fall Line has a restaurant. **Merrill Brook Village Condominiums** are one- and two-bedroom units above the village shops; each unit has a fireplace and a whirlpool steam bath. **South Ridge** has two- and three-bedroom townhouses, and **North Peak** is a three-story condominium complex. Our family of five has stayed in a Cascades unit and can vouch for the luxury of a slopeside pool and comfortable living quarters. From $112 for a studio to $240 for a two-bedroom unit; rates are lower off-season.

Pine-Sider Lodge (875-2636), RR 2, Box 4160, Bryant Pond 04219. Bill and Ernestine Riley have designed and built Pine-Sider for families and groups. Open year-round, it is divided into four efficiency units, each sleeping five to ten people. The lodge is just 5 minutes from Mount Abram, 15 minutes from Sunday River. $225–$275 per week for four people in summer; $140 per weekend in winter.

Mt. Abram Birch Road Country Homes (875-2636). 40 attractive condominiums sleep four to eight people. $210 for a one-bedroom, $275 for a two-bedroom per weekend; from $125 per night mid-week. A few of the area's old A-frames (no, they're not tacky) built here over the past 20 years are also for rent from $250–$300 (sleeps 10) per weekend.

Bethel Opera House (824-2312), Bethel 04217. The town's old opera house, right on the common, has been converted into 10 one-bedroom and studio loft condos, sleeping one to four. Very comfortable and tasteful. $69–$125; five-day packages.

The River View Inn (824-2808), HCR 61, Box 126, Bethel 04217. A recently rebuilt motel now offering 31 two-bedroom suites, each with a fully equipped kitchen, living room, dining area, and large new bath; each unit sleeps four comfortably and has cable TV, phone, air-conditioning, and daily maid service. The complex also offers a jacuzzi, sauna, game room and tennis court. $60–$65 double in summer, $12.50 for each additional child.

Cameron House (824-3219), Mason Street, Bethel 04217. Sited just off the common on a quiet side street, a large, renovated Victorian house with three bright one- and two-bedroom efficiencies. $55–$120 per night.

MOTELS   **Bethel Spa Motel** (824-2989), Main Street, Bethel 04217. The 10 units are upstairs in the middle of the village, over shops. Nothing fancy, just clean and comfortable with phone and color cable TV. $26 single, $34–$38 double.

Mollyockett Motel (674-2345), West Paris 04289 (20 minutes down Route 26 from Bethel). An 18-unit motel with highly rated rooms, three efficiencies, heated indoor pool, sauna, and whirlpool. $55–$75.

Rostay Motor Inn (824-3111), Bethel 04217. A 10-unit motel on the fringe of the village in the pines. Country breakfast is included in the very moderate rate.

Pleasant River Motel (836-3575), PO Box 27, West Bethel 04286. Sited in the woods. Ten units, all with TV and hot plates; also four efficiency apartments. $50–$60.

CAMPGROUNDS   Also see Camping.

Littlefield Beaches (875-3290), RFD 1, Box 1630, Bryant Pond 04219. Open mid-May to October. A clean, quiet family campground surrounded by three connecting lakes. Full hookups, laundry room, miniature golf, game rooms, swimming. Weekly and seasonal rates are available.

DINING OUT   **Bethel Inn** (824-2175), Bethel Common. An elegant formal dining room with a hearth and large windows overlooking the golf course and hills with a screened-in veranda in summer. All three meals are open to the public. Traditional New England fare; entrées from $10.95 for Yankee pot roast to $13.95 for prime rib of beef, including salad, potato or rice, and vegetable. Specialties include crabmeat casserole and sole amandine; don't pass up the desserts.

Mother's (824-2589), Main Street, Bethel. Open daily for lunch and dinner. A green-and-white gingerbread house with three dining rooms, eclectically furnished with books, old pictures and oddments, and stoves. Lunch specialties are homemade soups and sandwiches. At dinner the specialties are veal Marsala and lamb kebab. Try the pasta of the day or Mother's steak. Inexpensive to moderate.

Sudbury Inn (824-2174), Main Street, Bethel. Open for breakfast, lunch, and dinner. A pleasant dining room and a summer deck in a nineteenth-century village inn. The lunch menu includes pizza and salads, but at dinner you can choose between lemon scallops beurre blanc and beef Wellington. Moderate to expensive.

Restaurant Francais at the Four Seasons Inn (824-2755), Main Street, Bethel. Closed Monday and Tuesday in winter. Classic French fare and service. Onion soup, escargots, bouillabaisse, exquisitely served in three small, elegant dining rooms. Reserve.

Fall Line (824-3000), Sunday River Ski resort in the Fall Line condominium complex. Open during ski season nightly from 5 PM for dinner. Prime rib and seafood specialties. Moderately priced.

Michael's at l'Auberge (824-2774), Mill Hill Road, Bethel. A sampling of the menu in this pleasant inn's small dining room includes roast duck au frambois ($12.95), marinated steak tips ($9.95), and scallops Dijon ($11.95).

The Boiler Room Restaurant (665-2500), Bryant Pond Village, Route 26. Closed Monday and Tuesday. Housed in the former powerhouse of a clothes-pin factory, overlooking Lake Christopher. A huge 1880s steam engine (once the power source of the plant) sits in the middle of the lounge and tables are big wooden spools. Seafood, steaks, outdoor barbecue; Sunday breakfast buffet ($4.95); all-you-can-eat smorgasbord Wednesday and Thursday, $7.95.

Pleasant River Restaurant (836-3575), West Bethel. Open for breakfast, lunch, and dinner. The dinner specialties are prime rib and seafood, $9.50–$12.99.

(Also see Kedarburn Inn and The Lake House in Waterford and Westways on Kezar Lake in the Western Lakes Region.)

EATING OUT **Cisco & Poncho's** (824-2902), Mountain View Mall, Lower Main Street, Bethel. Closed Mondays. Outstanding Mexican cuisine but beware: hot means HOT.

Red Top Truck Stop, Bridge Street (Route 2), Bethel. Breakfast served from 5:30-11 AM Monday through Saturday; 7 to noon on Sunday. Lunch and dinner Monday through Friday 11–7; closing at 1:30 Saturday, noon on Sunday. The eggs and corned beef hash are hard to beat.

Rossetto's Ristorante (824-3000), White Cap Base Lodge at Sunday River. Open daily for lunch and dinner during ski season; closed Monday and Tuesday in summer. A family place featuring Italian dishes and steak.

The Backstage Restaurant and Lounge, Summer Street, Bethel. A great après ski place, good for anytime snacks (buffalo chicken wings, mozzarella sticks, chili); also pasta, burgers, ribs, and steak.

The Suds, downstairs at the Sudbury Inn. Entertainment on weekends in ski season, otherwise a friendly pub with a reasonably priced pub menu.

The Only Place (836-3663), Route 2, West Bethel (3.5 miles west of Bethel). An oasis with a strong local reputation for its pizza, subs, and hot sandwiches; specialties such as frittata (egg soufflé with onion, pepper, mushrooms, and Romano cheese). Draft beer; wine and soda by the carafe.

The Bread & Butter Bake Shop (824-2319), Main Street, Bethel. Open daily from 6:30 AM until early afternoon. Try the raspberry muffins and some coffee at one of the tables here. Pastries, cookies, and bread are also made daily.

Skidder's Deli (824-3696), top of Main Street, Bethel. Great deli meats plus baby back ribs, homemade pastries, box lunches.

SELECTIVE SHOPPING **Bonnema Potters** (824-2821), Lower Main Street, Bethel. Open daily 9–5. Distinctive stoneware, noteworthy for both design and color: lamps, garden furniture, dinnerware, and the like produced and sold in Bonnema's big barn. Seconds are available.

Bethel Craft Works, Main Street, Bethel. Open daily 9:30–5:30. A great showcase for local craftspeople as well as for things woven, potted, painted, and blown throughout New England: jewelry, sculptures, Arriba rugs, Paul Beaton's iron work, and baskets made by owners Don and Lind Best.

Groan and McGurn's Tourist Trap (836-3645), Route 2, West Bethel.

Begun as a greenhouse—to which the owners' own specially silk-screened T-shirts were added. Now there is so much that an ever-changing catalog is available.

Main Line Products (824-2522), Main Street, Bethel. Made-in-Maine products and souvenirs among which the standout is the Maine Woodsman's Weatherstick. We have one tacked to our back porch, and it's consistently one step ahead of the weatherman—pointing up to predict fair weather and down for foul ($4.95 or three for $12.00; available by mail but add $2 shipping).

Mt. Mann (824-3030), Main Street, Bethel. Jim Mann mines, cuts, and sets his own minerals and gems. (See Rockhounding.)

Prims Rexall Pharmacy (824-2820), Main Street, Bethel. Open daily from 8:30 until 10 (except Sunday in winter), until 11 in summer, until 9 on Sundays. A full-service pharmacy; also the Western Union agent, Agency Liquor Store, and local source of Ben & Jerry's ice cream.

Antiques: **Hammons House** and **Holidae House** in Bethel and the **Rumford Center Inn** in Rumford Center (Route 2), all maintain seasonal antiques shops. There is also **Bethel Depot Antiques.**

The Wood & Glass Gallery, top of Main Street, Bethel. A gallery featuring handmade wood and glass gifts.

Crafts: **Mountainside Country Crafts** (824-2518), Sunday River Road, Bethel. "Thousands" of crafted creations, many of them made locally.

Mainely Fibers, Main Street, Bethel. Knitting, spinning, and basket-weaving supplies. Specializing in handspun yarns.

Baker's Art Gallery & Frame Centre (824-2088), Sunday River Road. A framing and matting shop that sponsors summer workshops in watercolor, drawing, oils, color theory.

Eden Dorf (665-2506), Main Street, Bryant Pond. Open daily. Watch Fay Corrin make pottery; works by more than 70 other craftspeople are also displayed.

SPECIAL EVENTS   February: **Western Mountains Winter Wonderland Week.**
March: **Pole, Paddle and Paw Race:** a combination ski and canoe event at the end of ski season.

July: **Strawberry Festival,** Locke Mills Union Church (date depends on when strawberries are ready; announced in local papers). **Mollyockett Day** (mid-month weekend): road race, parade, bicycle obstacle course, fiddler contest, fireworks. Festivities honor an eighteenth-century medicine woman who helped the first settlers.

August: **World's Fair,** North Waterford (first weekend). **Sudbury Canada Days,** Bethel: children's parade, historical exhibits, old-time crafts demonstrations, bean supper, and variety show. **Blueberry Festival** at Locke Mills Church.

Autumn: **Blue Mountain Crafts Fair** at Sunday River Ski Resort.

RANGELEY LAKES REGION

Seven lakes—Aziscohos, Richardson, Cupsuptic, Mooselookmeguntic, Kennebago, Umbagog, and Rangeley—plus dozens of ponds are scattered among magnificently high, fir-covered mountains, all within a 20-mile radius of the village of Rangeley. The big summer lure is fishing (landlocked salmon and brook trout), and in winter there's snowmobiling and both alpine and cross-country skiing.

The Rangeley Lakes Region offers a sense of splendid isolation, thanks to 450 square miles of commercially forested land and genuine beauty; thanks to the mountains which hump up in every direction, inviting you to climb.

This has been a resort area since steamboat days as evidenced by the dozens of vintage rustic log lodges and cottages.

In summer the town's population jumps from 1,000 to 5,000. In winter loggers outnumber skiers in the IGA. The skiers are here for Saddleback Mountain—a 4,116-foot-high, 40-trail mountain that may just be New England's best-kept ski secret. On snowy weekends it generally attracts little more than 800 skiers—about the same number of snowmobilers here to take advantage of one of Maine's most extensive and best groomed trail networks.

Doc Grant's Restaurant proclaims that Rangeley is 3,107 miles from the North Pole and the same distance from the equator. It actually feels like a million miles from everywhere but with all of the amenities.

GUIDANCE   Rangeley Lakes Region Chamber of Commerce (864-5364), PO Box 317, Rangeley 04970. Open year-round, Monday through Saturday 9–5. The chamber maintains a walk-in information center in the village, publishes a handy "Accommodations and Services" guide and an indispensable map, and keeps track of vacancies and makes reservations.

GETTING THERE   By air: **Mountain Air Service** (864-5307) will pick you up at the **Portland Jetport;** also serves remote ponds and camps.

By car: From points south take the Maine Turnpike to Exit 12, then Route 4. From New Hampshire's White Mountains take Route 16 east. From the Bethel area take Route 17 north. Rangeley is two and a half hours from Portland.

MEDICAL EMERGENCY   Franklin Memorial Hospital (778-6031) in Farmington, is a good ride. **Dr. Anne Hunter** (864-3303) handles local emergencies.

Rangeley Ambulance (235-2222).

TO SEE AND DO   Wilhelm Reich Museum (864-3443), Route 4/16, Rangeley. Open July through September, Tuesday through Sunday 1–5. $4 per adult; children under 12 free. The 200-acre property, "Orgonon," is worth a visit for the view alone. Wilhelm Reich was a controversial pioneer psychiatrist and scientific thinker concerned with "objectifying the presence of a ubiquitous life force." He is buried on a promontory overlooking a sweep of lake and mountains next to one of his many inventions, a "cloudbuster." The museum occupies a stone observatory that Reich helped design; it contains biographical exhibits, scientific equipment, paintings, and a library and study that remain as Reich left them.

Sandy River–Rangeley Lakes Railroad (639-3001). Open May through November on the first and third Sundays of each month and by appointment. $2 per adult, $1 per child 6–12. From 1873 until 1935 this narrow-gauge line spawned resort and lumbering communities along its 115-mile length. Begun as seven distinct lines, it was eventually acquired by the Maine Central, which built shops and a large roundhouse in Phillips. Over the past decade volunteers have produced a replica of the old steam locomotive, and others have helped to lay a mile of track so that now you can rattle along in an 1884 car just far enough to get a sense of getting around Franklin County back when. A depot houses railroad memorabilia.

Rangeley Lakes Region Historical Society (864-3317), Main and Richardson streets, Rangeley. Open July and August, Monday through Saturday 10–noon. Photographs and local memorabilia, including Squire Rangeley's spittoon.

Phillips Historical Society (639-2088 or 639-2001). Open August, Fridays and Saturdays 2–4, and by appointment June through October. The library and historical society are both in an 1820 house in the middle of the village. The collection includes many pictures of the railroad (see above) and an attic full of clothes for children to try on.

Weld Historical Society (585-2586), Weld Village. Open July and August, Wednesday and Saturday 1–3, and by appointment. The 1842 Museum House is filled with period furniture and clothing; also photographs. The original Town House (1845) houses farming, logging, and ice-cutting tools. A Heritage Day Fair is held here the last Saturday in July, 1–3.

GREEN SPACE   Rangeley Lake State Park (864-3858) covers 691 acres, including more than a mile of shoreline on the southern rim of Rangeley Lake between routes 17 and 4. Open May 15 to early October. There are 40 scattered picnic sites, a pleasant swimming area, a boat launch, a children's play area; admission fee. Also see Camping.

Mount Blue State Park (585-2347), Weld (off Route 156). Open May 30 to October 15. The 6,000-acre park includes Mount Blue itself, towering 3,187 feet above the valley floor, and a beachside tenting area (136 sites) on Lake Webb, 3 miles wide and 6 miles long, good for catching black bass, white perch, pickerel, trout, and salmon. Boats may be rented from the ranger, and there is a recreation hall complete with fireplace. The view from the Center Hill area looks like the opening of a Paramount Picture. Despite its beauty and the outstanding hiking, this is one of the few state camping facilities that rarely fills up.

Small's Falls, Route 4 (12 miles south of Rangeley). The Sandy River drops abruptly through a small gorge, which you can climb behind railings. A popular picnic spot and a swimming hole for daring youths. You can follow the trail to the **Chandlers Mill Stream Falls,** equally spectacular.

Hunter Cove Wildlife Sanctuary, off Route 14/16 west of Rangeley Village. Offers color-coded trails, winding in and out of the trees along a cove.

Height O'Land. Route 17 south of Rangeley climbs the shoulder of a mountain to a point where lakes spread below you for a sight to remember. There are seven scenic turnout spots.

The Rangeley Lake Overlook, also on Route 17, provides spectacular views in the opposite direction.

BOAT RENTALS   **Citgo Lakeside Service** (864-5888), Main Street, Rangeley. Boats.

Clearwater Camps (864-5424), Bald Mt. Road, Oquossoc. Boats, canoes.

Cupsuptic Campground (864-5249), Route 16 West, Oquossoc. Canoes, shuttle service.

Grant's Kennebago Camps (864-3608), Kennebago Lake. Boats, canoes, sailboats.

Haines Landing Marina (864-2962), Oquossoc. Boats.

Mountain View Cottages (864-3416), Route 17, Oquossoc. Boats.

North Camps (864-2247), Mingo Loop Road, Rangeley. Boats, canoes.

Rangeley Region Sport Shop (864-5615), Main Street, Rangeley. Canoes.

Rangeley Watersports (864-3440), Rangeley. Sailboats.

South Arm Campground (784-3566), Andover. Canoes.

Sundown Lodge (864-3650), Bald Mt. Road, Oquossoc. Boats, canoes.

Town & Lake Motel (864-3755). Boats, canoes.

Wildwind Boat Rentals (864-5845), Bald Mt. Road, Oquossoc. Boats.

CAMPING   For information and reservations in both the state parks described below, phone 800-332-1501 from within Maine or 207-289-3824 from outside the state; phone only Monday through Friday 9–3. Reservations can be charged to Visa or MasterCard. Mailed reservations for the summer season are accepted after the first working day in January of that year. Mail a check or money order to: Bureau of Parks and Recreation, Attn. Reservation Clerk, State House Station #22, Augusta 04333. You will receive a confirmation receipt.

Rangeley Lake State Park (864-3858), between routes 17 and 4 at the southern rim of Rangeley Lake. Some 50 campsites are well spaced among fir and spruce trees; facilities include a beach and boat launch, picnic sites, and a children's play area. $11–$14 for nonresidents. There are also a number of **private campgrounds and wilderness sites** accessible only by boat; inquire at the chamber of commerce (see Guidance).

Mount Blue State Park (585-2347), Weld. Campsites cost $13 for out-of-staters, $10.50 for Mainers and tend to get filled up after those in better-known parks. (See Green Space.)

CANOEING **Rangeley** is departure point for an 8-mile paddle to Oquossoc. On **Lake Mooselookmeguntic** there is a 12-mile paddle to Upper Dam, then a carry around the dam and another 8 miles to Upper Richardson Lake through the Narrows to South Arm. Check with the chamber of commerce about campsites (see Guidance). (For canoe rentals see Boat Rentals.)

Registered Maine guide Rich Gacki (864-5136), in Oquossoc, offers guided canoe trips.

FISHING Brook trout are plentiful in local streams. In the lakes the big catch is landlocked salmon, for which the season is early spring through September. A number of **fishing camps** supply boats, equipment, and guides. Local **registered Maine guides** include Cy Eastlack (864-3416), Harold Blake (864-5608), and David Kreshpane (864-5428).

GOLD PANNING A program is offered mornings at Mount Blue State Park. (See Green Space.)

GOLF **Mingo Springs Golf Course** (864-5021), Proctor Road (off Route 4), Rangeley, offers 18 scenic holes; also carts and club rentals.

HIKING The regional map published by the chamber of commerce (see Guidance) outlines more than a dozen well-used hiking paths, including a portion of the Appalachian Trail that passes over **Saddleback Mountain.** The longest hike is up **Spotted Mountain** (4.25 miles to the top), and the most popular is the mile trail to the summit of **Bald Mountain;** both yield sweeping views of lakes, woods, and more mountains. Other favorites are Bemis Stream Trail up **Elephant Mountain** (6 hours round-trip), and the mile walk into **Angels Falls.**

In Weld the tried and true trails are **Bald Mountain** (3 miles round-trip), **Mount Blue** itself (3.25 miles), and **Tumbledown Mountain** (a particularly varied climb with a high altitude).

SWIMMING **Rangeley Lake State Park** offers a pleasant swimming area and scattered picnic sites. $1 per person day-use fee; free under age 12. There is also a town beach at **Lakeside Park** in the village of Rangeley, and almost all lodging places offer water access.

TENNIS **Public courts** are maintained in Lakeside Park, Rangeley, and the village of Oquossoc.

DOWNHILL SKIING **Saddleback Mountain** (864-5671; snow phone: 864-3380), Box 490, Rangeley 04970. This is a very big mountain with a very

Photo courtesy of Saddleback Mountain

Panoramic views from Saddleback's 4116' summit

small, fiercely loyal following. Saddleback itself, 4,116-feet-high and webbed with 40 trails, forms the centerpiece in a semicircle of mountains rising above a small lake. Twelve thousand acres—comprising most of this natural bowl—are now under Saddleback ownership, and a major four-season resort is planned. Trails and slopes include glade skiing, a 2.5-mile beginner trail, and an above-treeline snowfield in spring. The vertical drop is 1,826 feet. Most trails are a shade narrower and twistier than today's average but most intermediate runs such as Haymaker and White Stallion are memorable cruising lanes, and experts will find plenty of challenge on Bronco Buster, Powderkeg, and the Nightmare Glades terrain. Facilities include cafeteria, lounge, ski school, shop, rentals, nursery, and mountain warming hut. Lift tickets are $32 weekends, $18 midweek.

CROSS-COUNTRY SKIING   Ski Nordic Touring Center at Saddleback (864-5671) claims to be the highest altitude (2,500 feet) touring center in New England. It offers 40 km of groomed trails, guided tours, rentals, instruction, norpining, and special events.

We have seldom skied anything as beautiful as the isolated Rock and Midway pond trails—high, sheltered, and tracked by coyote, bobcat, and snowshoe rabbits as well as machine.

SNOWMOBILING   Rangeley Lake State Park offers 3 miles of marked trails with access to the lake; also a connecting trail with 20 more miles of groomed trails in **Mount Blue State Park.** Rangeley's snowmobile club maintains more than 140 miles of trails.

INNS   **Rangeley Inn and Motor Lodge** (864-3341), Rangeley 04970. Open year-round. A blue-shingled, three-story landmark from the era of railway travel and lake steamers. There are 50 guest rooms, 15 in the motel out back. Fay and Ed Carpenter, longtime innkeepers, have remodeled all of the rooms, installing all private baths (but retaining the old claw-foot tubs). The inn is handy to everything in town and has its own small beach. Although the big, attractive dining room is bustling, there is plenty of lounging space for guests in the grand columned lobby with its formal old reception desk. Popular with bus groups but also a good spot for couples. Some new motel units overlooking Haley Pond have fireplaces or wood stoves, waterbeds, and whirlpool baths; there are also a few housekeeping units. Rates that include breakfast and dinner are available. $59–$95 double.

Country Club Inn (864-3831), PO Box 680, Rangeley 04970. Open except April and November. Surrounded by an 18-hole golf course and overlooking the lake, this is a golfer's dream. Built by a millionaire sportsman in the late 1920s, this place has the feel of a private club. Massive stone fireplaces face each other across a gracious living room walled in knotty pine and stocked with books and puzzles. You are drawn to the view of lakes and mountains from the deck and from tables in the dining room. The 20 rooms are bright, motel-style with picture windows and private baths. In winter you can cross-country ski from the door, and in summer there's an outdoor pool. $54–$73 single MAP.

RUSTIC RESORTS AND SPORTING CAMPS   The complexes easily accessible by public roads tend to cater to families while the more remote "camps" (accessible only by water and private woodland roads) are geared to serious fishermen. All offer more than basic comfort and pride themselves on meals.

Kawanhee Inn (585-2243), Weld 04285. (In winter contact Sturgis Butler and Marti Strunk, 778-3809 evenings; 7 Broadway, Farmington 04938.) Dining room open mid-June to early September; cottages available from early May to mid-October. A traditional Maine lodge set atop a slope overlooking Lake Webb. There are 10 rooms in the inn itself; also 11 cabins that accommodate two to seven people each. All three meals are served in the large pine dining room and on the screened veranda overlooking the water (also see Dining Out). The open-beamed lobby has a massive central fireplace, a pool table, and numerous corners to read and talk. While the guest rooms in the lodge itself are Spartan, the cabins are delightful, each with its own fireplace and screened porch with rockers. There is a private beach and dock; canoes are available, and the local hiking is outstanding. Rooms from

$60 double; cabins $400 (one bedroom) and up; also by the day if available. Room rates include continental breakfast.

Bald Mountain Camps (864-3671), PO Box 332, Oquossoc 04964. Open Memorial Day to Labor Day. This is the surviving part of a complex that dates from 1897. Nicely old-fashioned with fireplaces in 15 cabins and a log-style dining room, a safe sand beach, tennis courts, and lawn games. Right on Mooselookmeguntic Lake and exuding the kind of hospitality found only under long-term ownership. Hosts are Rose and Ronald Turmenne. $65 single, all meals included; less in May and June.

Bosebuck Mountain Camps (243-2945), Wilsons Mills 04293. Open May through November. Accessible by boat or by a 13-mile road (phone to check gate times before you decide to drop by), the camps are sited at the remote north end of Aziscohos Lake. The lodge houses a dining room and a sitting room filled with books; all heat is from wood stoves, and the 11 cabins have kerosene lamps. Giving access to the Parmacheneearea and to the Big and Little Magalloway rivers, this place is for serious fishermen. Three full meals are included in the rate: $65 single per night. If the moosehorn (radio phone) doesn't answer, keep trying.

Tim Pond Wilderness Camps (243-2947), Eustis 04936. Open ice-out through October. Accessible only by a private road in the remote wilderness northeast of Rangeley; in business since the 1860s. The lure is fly-fishing for native square-tailed trout. There are 10 log cabins, each with a fieldstone fireplace or wood stove; three meals are served in the lodge. Canoes and motorboats are available. $85 single per night includes three meals; half price for children under age 12; no charge under age 5.

Grant's Kennebago Camps (864-3608; 864-3754 in winter), Oquossoc 04964. Open ice-out through September. A serious fisherman's haven located far up a private road. $75 single, including all meals; less for a seven-day stay.

BED & BREAKFASTS **Mallory's B&B** (864-2121/5316), Box 9, Hyatt Road, Rangeley 04970. Open year-round. A turn-of-the-century estate on the North Shore of Rangeley Lake with four guest rooms sharing two full baths, two common rooms with a wood stove and fireplace. In summer there's the lake out front; also a floating dock, canoe, and paddleboats. Children welcome, pets possible; $59 includes a muffin breakfast.

Lake Webb House (585-2479), PO Box 127, Route 142, Weld 04285. Open year-round. A pleasant, welcoming old farmhouse near the lake and village. Cheryl England makes the quilts which grace the beds in her four guest rooms (sharing two baths). We would request one of the front rooms (choice of queen and twin beds). There's a pleasant family room with a wood stove. $40 double includes a full breakfast featuring

Maine blueberries and maple syrup.

The Horsefeather (864-5465), PO Box 381, Oquossoc 04964. Comfortable rooms, shared baths; on a snowmobile trail. $45 per room includes a full country breakfast.

Farmhouse Inn (864-3446), Box 165, Rangeley 04970. Handy to the Saddleback Mountain access road, a rambling old farmhouse with six distinctively decorated suites (each sleeping two to five people and each with kitchen); also bunks. A common room with pool table, table tennis, games, puzzles, and books; also a sitting and dining room. Inexpensive to moderate; $18 per night for a bunk.

Oquossoc's Own (864-5584), Box 27, Oquossoc 04964. A comfortable house in Oquossoc Village, a short walk to tennis, restaurants, and the lake. Homecooked meals; dinner by reservation. $50 double.

COTTAGES   **Sundown Lodge and Cottages** (864-3650; 516-485-3059 in winter), Box 40, Oquossoc 04964. Open June to September. Just three delightful cottages right on Mooselookmeguntic Lake and another four miles away. Fireplaces, lawn games, and rental bikes, boats, canoes. $320–$475.

North Camps (864-2247), Rangeley 04970 (write E. B. Gibson). Open spring through hunting season. Fourteen cottages on Rangeley Lake among birches on a spacious lawn. Cottages have fireplaces and screened porches and access to the beach, tennis, sailboats, fishing boats, and canoes. During July and August rentals are available by the week only. Nightly rates and rates that include all three meals are available in spring and fall. $265–$445.

Clearwater Sporting Camps (864-5424), Oquossoc 04964. Six cottages, all different, scattered on ledges along Mooselookmeguntic Lake. Michael and Tina Warren have renovated them; also fishing boats for rent. Guide service is available. $340–$480.

Rangeley Manor Cottage Colony and Motel (864-3340), Rangeley 04970. Open year-round. The 25-acre lakeside property includes 16 log housekeeping units (each privately owned) and 8 motel units, some with kitchenettes; also a sandy beach, tennis court, and boats. $420–$540; extra for pets.

Sunset Point Cottages (864-3712; 617-344-7511 in winter, evenings). Five old-fashioned housekeeping cottages. Two or three bedrooms, gas lights, fridges and stoves, screened porches, and sandy beach on Mooselookmeguntic Lake. $250–$600 per week.

Note: Some of the area's most famous old cottage clusters have now been subdivided but are still available through local realtors. The former Flybuck, Quimby Pond, and Saddleback Lodge properties are all now handled by **Four Seasons Rental** (864-3368). **Rangeley Lakes Region Chamber of Commerce** (864-5364) also keeps listings of available cottages.

CONDOMINIUMS   **Saddleback Ski and Summer Lake Preserve** (864-5671),

Box 490, Rangeley 04970. There are two condo complexes at the ski resort—most units are exceptionally luxurious with views of the lake. Some two dozen are usually available for rent. From three to five bedrooms, many with hot tubs, cable TV; all with access to the clubhouse with its game room. $100–$200 per night in summer, $130–$350 in winter; weekly rentals also available.

DINING OUT   See also restaurants in Stratton, described under Sugarloaf Area. **Porter House** in Eustis and **Cathy's Place** in Stratton are popular dining destinations for Rangeley visitors.

Rangeley Inn (864-3341), Main Street, Rangeley. Closed mid-April to late May; otherwise open for breakfast and dinner daily. A large hotel dining room with a high pink tin ceiling and a reputation for the best food around. Entrées range from a spinach roll to veal cordon-bleu. Specialties include filet mignon, tournedos au poivre, and shrimp scampi. Some people come just for desserts like brandied raspberry mousse cake and praline tulip cups. $10.95–$17.95.

Kawanhee Inn (585-2243), Weld. Open for dining nightly, mid-June to September. One of Maine's most picturesque, traditional-style lodges is the setting for candlelight dining in the open-beamed dining room or screened porch overlooking Lake Webb. Fresh flowers garnish the tables, and meals are thoughtfully prepared. Fresh fish and Maine lobsters, crisp salads and warm breads, great desserts. Inexpensive to moderate.

Country Club Inn (864-3831). Open every evening, summer and fall, weekends in winter, by reservation only. The inn sits on a rise above Rangeley Lake, and the dining room windows maximize the view. Entrées run from $11.50 for a chicken dish (different every evening) to $15.50 for filet mignon. Specialties include roast duckling and veal du jour.

EATING OUT   **Red Onion** (864-5022), Main Street, Rangeley. Open daily for lunch and dinner. A friendly Italian–American dining place with a sun room and *bier garten*; fresh dough pizzas and daily specials. Try the veal and pepper over spaghetti.

Doc Grant's Restaurant and Cocktail Lounge, Main Street, Rangeley. Open 7–8 seasonally. A lively lounge with light lunches available; a game room with pool tables and video games, draft beer. Seafood rolls, chicken in the basket, omelets.

Gingerbread House. Open seasonally, 6–2; Sundays 7–2. Closed Tuesdays. The marble soda fountain is the big attraction, but there are also a variety of sandwiches and daily specials, breakfast.

Trading Post Restaurant and Tackle Shop, Route 16, Magalloway Plantations (30 miles west of Rangeley). Homecooked food and homebaked pies and donuts. A large assortment of custom-tied flies.

Mike's Sports Pub & Grub (864-5616), Rangeley Village. Open daily for lunch and dinner. A pubby place with a big-screen TV featuring sports events; good for chili, sandwiches, or Yankee pot roast.

Fine Ally's (864-2955), Saddleback Mountain Road, Rangeley. Open Wednesday through Sunday year-round for dinner. Cozy, informal with Mexican specialties and standard fare like veal marsala ($10.95) and linguini with meatballs ($6.95).

People's Choice (864-5220), Rangeley. Open year-round for breakfast, lunch, dinner. Standard fare. Weekend entertainment includes live bands and the only dancing around (everyone comes).

ENTERTAINMENT   **Rangeley Friends of the Performing Arts** sponsors a July and August series of top entertainers and musicians at local churches, lodges, and the high school. For the current schedule check with the chamber of commerce (see Guidance).

SELECTIVE SHOPPING   **Accents of Rangeley** (864-5347), Main Street, Rangeley. Maine books, maps, cookbooks, children's books, stationery, and calendars.

Rodney Richard's Woodcarving (864-5072), Main Street, Rangeley. "The Mad Whittler," widely known for his chain-saw sculptures, welcomes visitors.

First Farm (864-5539), Gull Pond Road, Rangeley. Open seasonally, Monday, Tuesday, Friday, Saturday 10–5. Country foods and flowers.

Yarn Barn (864-5917), Oquossoc. A source of knitting, weaving, rug-making materials.

Note: A list of local antiques shops is available from the chamber of commerce.

SPECIAL EVENTS   January: **Rangeley Lakes New England Sled Dog Races. Rangeley Snowmobile** meet.

March: **Annual Sled Dog Race. Bronco Buster Ski Challenge** at Saddleback.

July: **Independence Day** fireworks; **"Wild Mountain Time"** logging and water festival; **Old-Time Fiddler's Contest;** and **Logging Museum Field Day**.

August: **Sidewalk Art Festival; Annual Blueberry Festival;** and **Phillips Old Home Days** (third week).

November: **Hunter's Ball** at Rangeley Inn.

December: **Christmas Fair** at Episcopal Church; and **Walk to Bethlehem Pageant,** Main Street, Rangeley. **Giving Tree Celebration.**

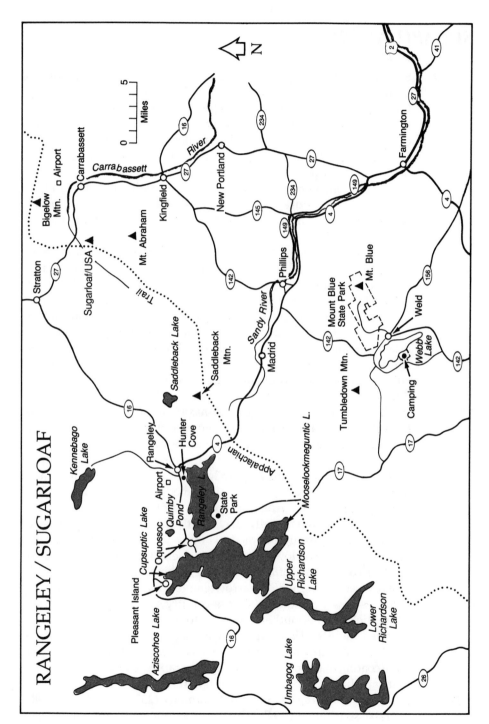

RANGELEY / SUGARLOAF

SUGARLOAF AREA

Sugarloaf/USA is Maine's biggest ski mountain. The second highest mountain in the state, it faces another 4,000-footer across the Carrabassett Valley—a narrow defile that is a 17-mile-long town.

Carrabassett Valley is a most unusual town. In 1972, when it was created from Crockertown and Jerusalem townships, voters numbered 32. The school and post office are still down in Kingfield, south of the valley; the nearest drugstore, supermarket, and hospital are still in Farmington, 36 miles away. And there are still only 300 full-time residents (plus children). But there are now more than 5,000 "beds." Instead of uptown and downtown, people say "on mountain" and "off mountain."

On mountain, at the top of Sugarloaf's access road, stands New England's largest self-contained ski village: a dozen shops and a dozen restaurants, a seven-story brick hotel, and a church. A chairlift hoists skiers up to the base lodge from lower parking lots and from hundreds of condominiums clustered around the Sugarloaf Inn and its Sugartree Health Club. More condominiums are scattered farther down the slope, all served by a chairlift. From all places you can also ski down to the Carrabassett Valley Ski Touring Center, Maine's largest cross-country trail network.

More than 800 condominiums are scattered among firs and birches. To fill them in summer, Sugarloaf has built an 18-hole golf course, fostered a lively arts program, promoted rafting and hiking, and has even seriously attempted to eliminate black flies.

Off mountain, down on Route 27, bargains are still to be found in the friendly, sometimes funky, ski lodges that predate the on-mountain bed boom. Most of the valley is still owned by paper companies and by the Penobscot Indian Nation. For a sense of the backwoods that this entire area was until recently, drive north up Route 27 to the village of Stratton and on through Cathedral Pines and Flagstaff Lake to Eustis. The 30,000-acre Bigelow Preserve, which embraces the lake and great swatches of this area, offers swimming, fishing, and camping. The old railway bed, along which narrow-gauge trains once puffed up the valley, is now a combination cross-country skiing and jogging trail.

Kingfield, at the southern entrance to the Carrabassett Valley, was founded in 1816. This stately town was the one-time home of the Stanley twins, inventors of the steamer automobile and of the dry-plate coating machine for modern photography. The town offers some first-rate dining, shopping, and lodging.

GUIDANCE   Sugarloaf Area Chamber of Commerce (235-2100), PO Box 1980, Carrabassett Valley 04947. The chamber offers an area-wide, year-round reservation service (235-2500 or 800-THE-AREA) for lodging places on and off the mountain. Sugarloaf's toll-free reservations and information number for the eastern seaboard is 800-THE-LOAF; you can also call 237-2000.

GETTING THERE   By air: **Portland International Jetport** (779-7301) (two and a half hours) offers connections to all points. **Mountain Express** (237-2747) offers ground transport year-round with regularly scheduled ground transport from Portland. **Rental cars** are available at the Portland International Jetport.

By car: **From Boston** it theoretically takes four and half hours. Take the Maine Turnpike to Exit 12 (Auburn), then Route 4 to Route 2 to Route 27; or take I-95 to Augusta, then Route 27 the rest of the way. (We swear by the latter route, but others swear by the former.)

GETTING AROUND   In ski season the **Valley Ski Shuttle Bus** runs from the base lodge to the Carrabassett Valley Ski Touring Center and Route 27 lodges. But it's only five times a day on weekends and holidays, three times on weekdays.

MEDICAL EMERGENCY   **Franklin Memorial Hospital** (778-6031), Farmington.

Sugarloaf/USA has its own emergency clinic, and the Kingfield Area Health Center (265-4555) has a full-time nurse and physician's assistant.

TO SEE AND DO   **Stanley Museum** (265-2729), School Street, Kingfield. Open year-round: July to October, Tuesday through Sunday 1–4; otherwise, office hours are Tuesday, Thursday, and Friday 9–12 and 1–5 and by appointment. Housed in the 1903 Stanley School, the collection includes varied Stanley family memorabilia, from air-brush painting and photography to violins and the steam car. A 1905 Stanley Model CX is on exhibit. Summer programs in painting and crafts are offered.

The Western Maine Children's Museum (235-2211), RR 1, Box 2153, Carrabassett Valley 04947. Open weekends, Mondays, and during school vacations in winter; otherwise hours vary. Hands-on exhibits and activities and a real plane. $2.50 per child; adults free.

Kingfield Historical Society (265-4871), Church Street. Open June to October, weekends 9–4; weekdays by appointment. Local memorabilia includes the story of Maine's first governor William King; also nineteenth-century clothes, dolls, a general store.

Dead River Historical Society (246-6901), Stratton. Open Sundays during the summer, 12–4. Displays local memorabilia.

Holmes-Crafts Homestead (645-2653 or 645-2723), Route 4, Jay. Open June to September by appointment. A striking, Federal-style house, preserved and furnished to its period.

Jay Hill Antique Auto Museum (645-4330), Jay Hill, Route 4 (across from the Historical Society). Open mid-May through mid-October, Sunday 10-6 and by appointment. $2 adults, $1 under age 15. Twenty-six antique cars ranging from a 1915 Model-T Ford touring car to a '57 hard-top Chevrolet.

BIKING   **Mainely Biking** (237-2000) at Sugarloaf Mountain offers bike rentals, guided bike trips, and biking vacation packages.

FISHING   **Thayer Pond** at the Carrabassett Valley Recreation Center, Route 27, is a catch-and-release pond open to the public with fly-fishing lessons, boat rentals, and fish for a fee.

The village of Eustis, north of Stratton, is serious fishing country with the Arnold Trail Sport Shop serving as a source of equipment, information, and canoe rentals. Check with the Sugarloaf Area Chamber of Commerce about fishing camps. The Arnold Trail Service Station (Mobil) in Stratton and Anni's Market in Kingfield also carry fishing gear.

GOLF   **Sugarloaf Golf Course** (237-2000), Sugarloaf/USA. A spectacular 18-hole course designed by Robert Trent Jones II, teaching pro. Weekend golf schools are offered in-season.

HEALTH SPAS   **Sugartree Health Club** (237-2701), Sugarloaf Inn Resort, Carrabassett Valley. Amenities include a pool, racquetball courts, saunas, outdoor hot tubs, steam rooms, Jacuzzis in the dressing rooms, and a beauty salon. Available to all guests at the Sugarloaf Inn and Sugarloaf Mountain condominiums and to the public on the basis of available space.

Herbert Hotel (265-2000), Kingfield. An attractive sauna and a Jacuzzi room—with a moose head pictured in tiles above the hot tub—can be rented by the hour.

HIKING   There are a number of 4,000-footers in the vicinity and rewarding trails up **Mount Abraham** and **Bigelow Mountain**. The Appalachian Trail signs are easy to spot on Route 27 just south of Stratton; popular treks include two hours to Cranberry Pond or four hours plus (one way) to Cranberry Peak. Pick up detailed hiking maps locally or check the AMC *Mountain Guide* or *Fifty Hikes in Northern Maine* (Backcountry Publications) by Cloe Caputo, which details several spectacular hikes in the 17-mile Bigelow Range (35,027 acres now lie within the Bigelow Preserve).

WHITE-WATER RAFTING   Numerous local ponds and the Dead and Carrabassett rivers make possible day and overnight trips.

Rolling Thunder River Company (265-2001), PO Box 291, Kingfield. April 15 to October 15. White-water rafting on the Kennebec, Dead, Penobscot, and Carrabassett rivers. Day and overnight trips, rain or shine.

New England Whitewater Center (800-766-7238) the Forks, Wyman Lake, Caratunk 04925. Trips on the Penobscot, Kennebec, and Dead rivers.

(Also see Moosehead Lake Region [White-Water Rafting/Kayaking].)

CROSS-COUNTRY SKIING   **Carrabassett Valley Ski Touring Center** (237-2205). Open in-season, 8:30 AM to dusk. This is Maine's largest touring network, with 85 km of trail loops, including race loops for timed runs.

Rentals and instruction are available. The center itself includes the Klister Kitchen, which serves soups and sandwiches; space to relax in front of the fire with a view of Sugarloaf; and a rental area.

Inquire about trails on the **golf course,** due to be developed this season with splendid views of Bigelow. Access is from the West Mountain Chair parking lot.

Holley Farm Resort (778-4869), Farmington (marked from Route 27). Trails meander across fields and into the woods; 11 km of groomed trails. This is a rustic family lodge with a dining room, an indoor pool, and a sauna.

Titcomb Mountain Ski Touring Center (778-9031), Morrison Hill Road (off Route 2/4), Farmington. A varied network of 20 km of groomed trails and unlimited ungroomed trails; used by the University of Maine at Farmington.

Troll Valley Ski Touring Center (778-3656), 16 Stewart Avenue, Farmington. Gently rolling terrain and scenic views; 30 km of groomed trails designed for the tourer rather than racer; ski school, rentals, and guided tours.

DOG SLED RIDES   T.A.D. Dog Sled Service (246-4461 or 237-2000), PO Box 147, Stratton 04982. Tim Diehl offers half-hour rides throughout the day during ski season from his base on Route 27 just north of the Sugarloaf access road. Drop by just to see his friendly, frisky Samoyeds. He owns 19 and usually uses a team of 10 to pull the light two-person toboggan sled (a child can be snuggled in too under the blanket). You glide along low to the ground (lower than the feathery tails of the white Samoyeds) through the woods on trails Diehl maintains. $20 per person; special group rates.

DOWNHILL SKIING   Sugarloaf/USA (general information: 237-2000; snow report is extension 6808. The on-mountain reservation number is 800-THE-LOAF). Sugarloaf is working hard to recapture its image as New England's "Skiers' Mountain." Sugarloaf Mountain Corporation was formed in 1955 by local skiers, and growth was steady but slow into the 1970s, with more attention to trail expansion and maintenance than to housing. Then a boom decade produced New England's largest self-contained resort, one with base buildings and a forest of condominiums and a seven-story brick hotel as the centerpiece. A bust came in the spring of 1986 after a record snow drought. The company has since been reorganized, snowmaking has been revamped and expanded to cover 80 percent of the terrain, and attention has refocused on the mountain and its services. New snowmaking insures skiing on the long, less-used trails served by the West Mountain and Bucksaw chairs, spreading the crowd around at peak periods.

Trails number 71 and add up to 45 miles. The vertical drop is a whopping 2,637 feet. Lifts include two quad chairs, a triple chair, eight double chairs, two T-bars, and a pony lift for kids. A new gondola is

Photo by Chip Carey

Sugarloaf Mountain Hotel

promised for the 91/92 season. Facilities include ski school, cub ski school, an outstanding children's ski school center in the base lodge, ski shop, rentals, base lodge, cafeteria, game room, seven restaurants, and five pubs. Services include a first-rate (day and night) nursery and children's ski school programs from three-year-olds to teens; also special women's weeks.

Two-day lift tickets cost $64 per adult and $36 per child on weekends; half-day rates are $28 adult, $17 junior. Under age 6, equipment and lifts are free.

ICE-SKATING   **Carrabassett Valley Touring Center** (237-2205) maintains a lighted rink and rents skates.

SNOWMOBILING   Snowmobile trails are outlined on many maps available locally; a favorite destination is Flagstaff Lodge (maintained as a warming hut) in the Bigelow Preserve.

ON-MOUNTAIN LODGING   **Sugarloaf/USA Inn and Condominiums** (800-THE-LOAF or 237-2000), Carrabassett Valley 04947. Some 330 ski-in, ski-out condominiums are in the rental pool. Built gradually over the last 20 years (they include the first condos in Maine), they represent a range of styles and sites; when making a reservation you might want to ask about convenience to the base complex, the Sugartree Health Club (to which all condo guests have access), or the golf club. From $108 for a studio to $380 for a five-bedroom condo during ski season; less in summer and through special packages

The 42-room **Sugarloaf Inn** offers attractive standard rooms and fourth-floor family spaces with lofts. Amenities include a comfortable living room with fireplace, a solarium restaurant (see Dining Out), a 24-hour manned front desk, access to the Sugartree Health Club and to the mountain via the Snubber Chair. $78–$189 per night, less in summer.

Sugarloaf Mountain Hotel (800-527-9879), Box 518, Carrabassett Valley, Maine 04947. So close to the base complex that it dwarfs the base lodge, this is a massive, seven-story, 120-room brick hotel with a gabled roof and a striking central tower. Built at a cost of $9 million, it is now condoed, and many of the units are "quarter shared." All rooms are large and tastefully furnished, and most have small fridges and microwaves. There are also four two-bedroom suites, each with a living room and kitchen, and two palatial tower penthouses, each with three bedrooms, three baths, and a hot tub. Amenities include a library and a health club with a large hot tub and plunge pool, sauna, and steam room. The restaurant, Arabella's, is outstanding (see Dining Out). $80–$525 per night, multi-day discounts, less in summer.

OFF-MOUNTAIN INNS AND BED & BREAKFASTS   Some Sugarloafers prefer to stay a full 17 miles south of the mountain in Kingfield because it is still a Maine village.

The Herbert (265-2000 or toll free 800-THE-HERB), PO Box 67, Kingfield 04947. Open year-round. "We're away from 'condomania,'" says Bud Dick, a longtime Sugarloaf skier who has lovingly restored this hotel, billed as a "palace in the wilderness" when it opened in 1918 in the center of Kingfield. But by 1982, when Dick purchased it, the hotel was downright derelict, with 230 broken water pipes and no electricity. The "fumed oak" walls of the lobby now gleam, and there's a fire in the hearth beneath the moose head, richly upholstered chairs from which to watch it and enjoy music from the grand piano by the big windows. The peach-colored dining room is now frequently filled for all three meals, and the fare is exceptional. The 33 rooms are simple but tasteful, with bathroom units offering a combination Jacuzzi and steambath. $60–$81 midweek specials; $49 per couple in summer, continental breakfast included.

The Inn on Winter's Hill (265-5421 or 800-233-WNTR), Box 587, Kingfield 04947. A double bow-fronted mansion designed by one of the Stanleys for Amos Winter, the man who founded the Sugarloaf ski area. An inn for many years, it has recently been reconfigured with most of the guest rooms (16) now in the former barn with minimal decor and soundproofing. Amenities include a lounge, game room, restaurant, outdoor pool, hot tub, and tennis court. $55–$135, including continental breakfast.

Three Stanley Avenue (265-5541), Kingfield 04947. Designed by a younger brother of the Stanley twins, now an attractive bed & breakfast next to the more ornate One Stanley Avenue (also owned by Dan Davis) (see Dining Out). There's a nice feel to this place but rooms vary. Number 2 has twin beds and a bath with claw-foot tub and number 1, an ornate sleigh bed with claw-foot tub. We also like number 6 (no bath), and number 4 is good for a family (three beds). Although there is no common room, guests are welcome to use the elegant sitting room with its flak wallpaper and grandfather clock next door. Breakfast is included. $55–$60, less midweek and in summer.

River Port Inn (265-2552), Route 27, Kingfield 04947. An 1840 roadside farmhouse on the edge of town with comfortable, nicely decorated guest rooms, a living room, and a big, friendly dining area in which guests tend to linger over home-baked breakfasts and bottomless cups of coffee. $40–$80 per room depending on day and season.

Widow's Walk (246-6901), PO Box 150, Stratton 04982. A Victorian home in Stratton village (closed Columbus Day through December 1 and some weeks in summer). The six twin-bedded guest rooms are very basic with shared baths, but Mary and Jerry Hopson are friendly hosts and the living room is inviting with games for children. $22 single during ski season includes a full breakfast; $15 single in summer with breakfast. No smoking.

SKI LODGES AND MOTELS **Lumberjack Lodge** (237-2141), Carrabassett Valley; off-season: RR 1, Box 2230, Kingfield 04947. Open October to May. A three-story, chalet-style complex of eight efficiency units (each sleeps up to eight people) with a sauna and a game room. As near as you can get to the slopes on 27; also the nearest lodging to the touring center. Owner Paul Schipper skis every day and may just know more about the mountain than anybody. $18–$32 per person depending on the number of guests.

Mountain View Motel (246-2033), PO Box 282, Route 27, Stratton

04982. Open year-round. A small, very clean motel with housekeeping and two-bedroom apartments, cable TV, accommodating up to six people. We enjoyed our stay in this homey place, family-run by longtime valley resident Mildred Luce. Six miles north of Sugarloaf. From $40 for a room to $120 for a two-bedroom unit with kitchen; some pleasant rooms with efficiency units for $50, less in summer.

Spillover Motel (246-6571), PO Box 427, Stratton 04982. An attractive, new two-story, 20-unit motel just south of Stratton village. Spanking clean, with two double beds to a unit, color cable TV, phone. $40–$65 plus $5 for each additional person over age six including continental breakfast.

The Valley Motel (235-2731), Route 27, Carrabassett Valley 04947. Formerly the Mountain Lodge and before that the Chateau. An old but newly renovated motel, $35–$75 depending on season; continental breakfast included and dinner served. (See Eating Out [Carrabassett Yacht Club].)

Cathy's Place (246-2922), Stratton 04982. A small, friendly motel in the village. Each unit accommodates two to five guests; cable TV, a good restaurant on the premises serves all three meals (see Eating Out). $30–$45 per room.

Sugarloafers' Ski Dorm (265-2041), Kingfield 04947. Open November to April. A unique establishment designed exclusively for groups. Dining is in the igloo-shaped Snow Dome; lodging is in the three-story Log Fort with six separate dorm rooms (each accommodating 20–40 people) and two common rooms. Inexpensive rates include breakfast and dinner.

OFF-MOUNTAIN "CAMPS" The Sugarloaf Area Chamber of Commerce (see Guidance) keeps a list of second homes, ranging from classic, old A-frames to classy condos; the average price is $100 a day in ski season for a fully equipped house sleeping at least six. Less in summer.

DINING OUT **One Stanley Avenue** (265-5541), Kingfield. Closed late October to Christmas and Easter to July 4; otherwise open from 5 PM except Mondays. Reservations are a must. Small but the number one restaurant in western Maine. Guests tend to gather for a drink in the very Victorian parlor, then proceed to one of the two intimate dining rooms. Specialties include dilled lobster on zucchini, sweetbreads with applejack and chives, maple cider chicken, and saged rabbit with raspberry sauce. We have seldom savored more tender meat or moister fish, and the herbs and combinations work well. Owner-chef Dan Davis describes his methods as classic, the results as distinctly regional. $13–$23 includes fresh bread, salad, and sherbert, but it's difficult to pass on the wines and desserts.

The Herbert (265-2000), Main Street, Kingfield. Dinner is served from 5 PM, Wednesday to Monday. Sunday brunch 12–2:30 PM. This elegant, old hotel dining room is decorated in lacy colors; tables are nicely set; service is friendly; dress is casual; and the wine list is extensive. Specialties include sesame Carrabassett Rabbit (baked with cider and apples), Grand Lake Chicken (with a guide's corn bread stuffing), Chicken Cherryfield (with blueberries and cream), and Seafood Salad (NO sea legs). All meals include a cheese tray, salad, vegetables, and homemade rolls. $5.95–$14.95, and Sunday supper is $5.

Arabella's (237-2222), Sugarloaf Mountain Hotel at the top of the Sugarloaf Mountain access road (off Route 27). Open daily for breakfast and for dinner except Tuesdays in winter, Wednesday through Sunday in summer. The best food "on mountain." Specialties include Atlantic salmon poached in a memorable lobster butter sauce and lamb roasted with a honey-mustard-herb glaze. $9.75–$14.25 includes salad and assorted vegetables; on "Country Nights," a four-course meal is $9–$14.

Hug's Italian Cuisine (237-2392), Route 27, Carrabassett Valley. A small eatery featuring northern Italian delicacies such as pesto Alfredo, carbonara, and scampi veal, prepared by Irish chef Jack Flannagan and his French-Canadian wife Huguette, for whom the restaurant is named. This is a place not to miss, if you can get in. On peak ski-season nights you have to be a member of "the club" to make a reservation.

Longfellow's Restaurant & Riverside Lounge (265-4394), Kingfield. Open year-round for lunch and dinner (from 5 PM). An attractive, informal dining place in a nineteenth-century building decorated with photos of nineteenth-century Kingfield. There's a pubby area around the bar, an open-beamed dining room, and an upstairs dining space with an outdoor deck overlooking the river. Great for lunch (homemade soups, quiche, crepes, and a wide selection of sandwiches); a find for budget-conscious families at dinner. Specialties include country-style spare ribs, chicken Longfellow, fettucini, and stir-fry dishes. Children's plates are available. $4.75–$10.75.

The Seasons (237-2000), Sugarloaf Inn, Carrabassett Valley. Dinner is served by reservation from 5 PM nightly in winter, Thursday through Sunday in summer and fall. Breakfast daily, lunch winter weekends and holidays. Request a table in the glass-walled section of the dining room, particularly pleasant in winter because it overlooks the slope below Sugarloaf's base lodge. Spacious and softly lit; weekend entertainment in the adjacent Cirque Bar. Specialties include veal piccata and sautéed shrimp scampi on fettucini. $9.95 for the pasta of the day to $16.95 for twin filet mignon.

Porter House (246-7932), Route 27, Eustis. Serving dinner except on Mondays. A country farmhouse located 12 miles north of Sugarloaf; also a pilgrimage point for Rangeley Lake visitors. There are four small dining rooms, a fire, and candlelight. Of course, there is Porter House steak. Entrées run from $6.95 for ground sirloin to $16.95 for top sirloin with shrimp in garlic butter; children's menu available. All breads, soups, and desserts are homemade. Full bar and wine list. Moderate.

The Truffle Hound (237-2355), Village West at Sugarloaf/USA, Carrabassett Valley. Open weekends in summer, for lunch and dinner in winter. Reservations are suggested for this cozy, candlelit place. Specialties include chicken Gruyère Dijon and roast duckling à l'orange. Expensive.

Tufulio's (235-2010), Valley Crossing, Carrabassett Valley. Open nightly from 4:30 PM. The menu is Italian, and the atmosphere is congenial, with Maine's only nine-piece-band player piano. Specialties include veal marsala, steak, and Amaretto cheesecake; children's menu. Moderate.

Julia's (265-5426), The Inn on Winter's Hill, Kingfield. Open for breakfast, dinner (6–10), and brunch in winter; lunch and dinner Thursday through Saturday in summer. Entrées may include beef Wellington, cornish game hen, or sole baskets with crab stuffing. Expensive.

F. L. Butler Restaurant & Lounge (778-5223), Front Street, Farmington. Steaks, broiled fish, and Italian dishes served in a restored, colonial-style tavern. Try the "Al Capone" (sweet Italian sausage, chicken, and pork simmered in homemade sauce, with spaghetti). Inexpensive.

Fiddleheads Restaurant (778-9259), 23 Pleasant Street, Farmington. Closed Sundays; otherwise serving dinner 5–9; entertainment Thursdays and Fridays. An upbeat, relaxed dining room furnished in hickory and oak, brick hearth. Specialties include fettucini with prosciutto and mushrooms. Moderate.

EATING OUT   **The Bag** (237-2451), Sugarloaf Mountain. Open for lunch and dinner. Unbeatable Bag Burgers, great pizza, homemade soups, curly french fries, entertainment, booths, and a friendly bar.

Cathy's Place (246-2922), Stratton. Open daily for breakfast, daily lunch specials, dinner and full salad bar on weekends. A find featuring homemade soups, reasonably priced entrées with local ingredients, and some of the best pies (try the peanut butter), not to mention Zebra Cheesecake, in western Maine. The sure touch belongs to co-wonder Sandy Isgrow, a former chef's assistant at One Stanley Avenue (see Dining Out). There's a nice feel to the front dining room with its flowery curtains by the bar (breakfast and lunch) and to the larger space in back where dinner is served on busier nights. Breakfast from 8 AM, $.99 and up; lunch specials from $2.25; and dinner $5.95–$13.95, with a selection of seafoods, chicken, and steaks.

Stratton Diner (246-3111), Stratton. Open year-round. An honest, old-style truck stop open for all three meals.

D'Ellies (237-2490), Village West at Sugarloaf. An on-mountain treasure: great make-your-own sandwiches on freshly made bread with your choice of condiments (like Pesto Mayo). The turkey, chicken, soups, and stews are made on the spot, all to-go, along with morning coffee and muffins.

L. C.'s Chinese Restaurant & Lounge (265-2559), marked from Route 27, just north of Kingfield. Owner/chef Ping Yuen Yu serves traditional Chinese and Szechuan dishes, some American standbys, full bar. Moderate.

Gepetto's (237-2192), Village West at Sugarloaf/USA. Casual hanging-plants atmosphere; open for lunch and dinner. Luncheon specials and homemade soups and greenhouse dining overlooking the slopes. The dinner menu ranges from pizza to lobster. Moderate.

Carrabassett Valley Yacht Club (235-2730), Route 27 at the Valley Motel. Dinner nightly, nice atmosphere. From basic pizza ($3.25) to surf and turf ($12.95).

Trail's End (246-7511), Eustis. Open for lunch and dinner daily. A full bar, hefty sandwiches, and hearty entrées like rare prime rib and charbroiled ham steak, homemade pies. Caters to skiers, snowmobilers, hunters, fishermen, and woodsmen.

SELECTIVE SHOPPING   Patricia Buck, "Emporium of the Western Mountains" (265-2101), Main Street, Kingfield and two shops in the Alpine Village at Sugarloaf/USA. Open daily except Mondays. Features Patricia Buck's own patterned sweaters, hats, and leg warmers; also carries arts and crafts supplies, books, cards, gourmet coffees, spices, clothing, antiques, and myriad stocking stuffers. Don't miss the second-floor art gallery in the Kingfield store.

Keenan Auction Company (265-2011), Kingfield. Open daily. A great family clothing store featuring brand names at discounts: Woolrich, Oshkosh, Maine Guide, and Nike are all here plus bargain baskets full of ski mittens, goggles, and the like.

The Ski Rack (237-2792), Sugarloaf Access Road, Carrabassett Valley. A beautiful building filled with beautiful gear at competitive prices; rentals were lower than at the mountain when we visited last season.

Mountain Video Inc. (265-2585), Route 27 just north of Kingfield and in Village South at Sugarloaf. Large selection of videos; also carries books.

SPECIAL EVENTS   January: **White White World Winter Carnival:** broom hockey, chili cookoff, bartenders' race, and discounts at Sugarloaf/ USA.

March: **Sugarloaf Corporate Challenge Weekend. St. Patrick's Day Leprechaun Loppet:** a 15 km citizens' cross-country race.

April: **Easter Festival:** costume parade, Easter egg hunt on slopes, and sunrise service on the summit. **White-water rafting.**

May: **Sugarloaf Marathon.**

July: **Kingfield Days Celebration:** four days with parade, art exhibits, potluck supper.

August: **Old Home Days,** Stratton-Eustis-Flagstaff. **Weekend jazz series.**

September: **Kingfield 10 km Foot Race and Sugarloaf Uphill Climb. Franklin County Fair,** Farmington.

October: **Mountain Arts Annual Auction,** Sugarloaf Mountain. **Skiers' Homecoming Weekend.**

December: **Yellow-Nosed Vole Day,** Sugarloaf Mountain. **Chester Greenwood Day** honors local inventor of the earmuff; parade and variety show in Farmington.

The North Woods and Its Gateways

Almost half of Maine's interior is privately owned. The state's official highway maps show no public roads through the 6.5 million acres bordered to the north and west by Canada. This is the largest stretch of unpeopled woodland in the East.

The ownership of this sector, technically known as the "Unorganized Townships," dates from the 1820s when Maine was securing independence from Massachusetts. The mother state, her coffers at their usual low, stipulated that an even division of all previously undeeded wilderness be part of the separation agreement. The woodlands were quickly sold by the legislature for 12.5 to 38 cents per acre, bought cooperatively by groups in order to cut individual losses.

The last inland tracts, mostly softwood, became valuable only in 1844 when the process of making paper from wood fibers was rediscovered. It seems that the method first used in 105 AD had been forgotten, and New England paper mills were using rags at the time.

By the turn of the century, however, pulp and paper mills had moved to their softwood source and assumed management responsibility and taxes for most of the unorganized townships. Mergers have since increased the size (decreased the number) of these companies. A dozen major landowners now pay the lion's share of the area's land tax and the cost of maintaining thousands of miles of private gravel roads, the ones not shown on the state highway maps but open to visitors who pay a fee and promise to abide by the rules.

The roads have multiplied since the termination of log drives in the early 1970s and have changed the look and nature of the North Woods. Many remote sporting camps, for a century accessible only by water and more recently by air, are now a bumpy ride from the nearest town.

Many of these sports camps haven't changed since the turn of the century. In fact, some have hardly altered since the 1860s, the era when wealthy "sports" first began arriving in Greenville by train from New York and Boston, to be met by American Indian guides. The genuine old camps are Maine's inland windjammers—unique holdovers from another era, but they form no "fleet." The camps are so independent that few people can agree on how many there actually are. Many simply cater to descendants of their original patrons.

For the general public, two North Woods preserves have been set

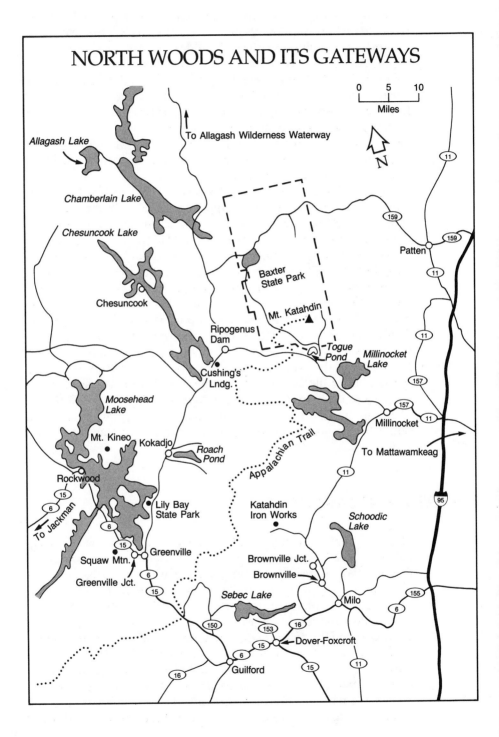

NORTH WOODS AND ITS GATEWAYS

0   5   10
Miles

N

To Allagash Wilderness Waterway

Allagash Lake

Chamberlain Lake

Chesuncook Lake

Chesuncook

Ripogenus
Dam

Cushing's
Lndg.

Moosehead
Lake

Mt. Kineo   Kokadjo

Rockwood

Roach
Pond

Lily Bay
State Park

Squaw Mtn.

Greenville

Greenville Jct.

To Jackman

Sebec Lake

Guilford

Baxter
State Park

Mt. Katahdin

Togue
Pond

Millinocket
Lake

Millinocket

To Mattawamkeag

Appalachian Trail

Katahdin
Iron Works

Schoodic
Lake

Brownville Jct.

Brownville

Milo

Dover-Foxcroft

Patten

11

159

159

11

11

157

157

11

11

95

155

6

15

6

15

6

15

6

15

150

153

16

15

6

15

11

16

aside to provide a wilderness experience. These are 200,000-acre Baxter State Park and the 92-mile ribbon of lakes, ponds, rivers, and streams designated as the Allagash Wilderness Waterway (see Canoeing the Allagash under What's Where in Maine).

Greenville, the largest seaplane base in New England and the liveliest gateway to the North Woods, sits at the toe of vast Moosehead Lake, the largest lake in New England. Rockwood, sited at a scenic narrows in the lake, also caters to sportsmen. Genuine sports camps on unpeopled lakeshores can also be found west of Moosehead in the Upper Kennebec Valley (near Bingham and Jackman) and east of the lake in the woodland around Kokadjo and beyond.

The Kennebec River flows from Moosehead Lake and has turned the tiny village of West Forks in the Upper Kennebec Valley into a white-water rafting boomtown. The West Branch of the Penobscot also draws hundreds of rafters any day from May through September.

Fishing, canoeing, rafting, horseback riding, and hiking can easily fill a North Woods summer. Downhill skiing at Moosehead Ski Area in Greenville and splendid cross-country skiing and snowmobiling throughout the area, not to mention dog-sled racing and ice-fishing, make winter equally enjoyable. For the purposes of this book, we have divided this vast region as follows: the Moosehead Lake Region, Baxter and Beyond, and Jackman and the Upper Kennebec Valley.

GUIDANCE   **North Maine Woods** (435-6213), Box 283, Ashland 04732, is a consortium of the 20 major landowners which manages the recreational use of 2.5 million acres of commercial forest in northwest Maine. It publishes a map/guide that shows logging roads and campsites, a canoe guide to the St. John River, and a listing of outfitters and camps.

MOOSEHEAD LAKE AREA

This particular 1,500-square-mile swatch of North Woods is designated by Great Pacific Paper, its principal owner, as the Moosehead Region. It is an unusually beautiful piece of woodland, distinguished by vast lakes and high mountains. Moosehead is 40 miles long with some 420 miles of shore, most of it owned by lumber companies. Greenville is the sole town.

Back around the turn of the century, one could board a Pullman car in New York City and ride straight through to Greenville, there to board a steamer for Mt. Kineo, a palatial summer hotel on a cliffy island in the lake. Greenville began as a farm town, but it soon discovered its most profitable crops to be winter lumbering and summer tourists—a group which, now that train service and grand hotels have vanished, consists largely of fishermen, canoeists, white-water rafters, and hunters, augmented in winter by skiers, snowmobilers, and ice fishermen.

But you don't have to be a sportsman to enjoy Moosehead Lake. Immense and backed by mountains (Big and Little Squaw in the foreground, the Katahdin range in the distance), it possesses unusual beauty and offers a family a wide choice of rustic, old-fashioned "camps" at reasonable prices. The town remains a lumberman's depot and jump-off point for excursions into the wooded wilderness to the north.

Greenville is New England's largest seaplane base, with five competing flying services geared to ferrying visitors to remote camps and campsites.

The community of Rockwood, a half-hour's drive north of Greenville on the west shore of the lake, is even more of an outpost: a cluster of sporting camps and stores between the lake and the Moose River, which connects with a chain of rivers and ponds that trail off to the west, all the way to Jackman.

Rockwood sits at the lake's "Narrows," across from its most dramatic landmark: the sheer cliff face of Mount Kineo, a place revered by the Indians. According to local legend, they believed it to be the petrified remains of a monster moose sent to earth by the Great Spirit as a punishment for sins. It was also their source of flint. A hotel has stood at the foot of this outcropping since 1844, and at one point the Mt. Kineo House numbered 500 rooms. The resort flourished for many years under ownership of the Maine Central Railroad (which offered service to Rockwood) and included a golf course, a yacht club, and stables.

The big hotel has long since vanished, but a three-story annex and a row of shingled Victorian "cottages" survive (one of them a B&B). Present plans are to restore the annex as a hotel. The old nine-hole golf course has also been recently revived, complete with a resident moose. Most of the island-like peninsula, including a hiking path to the top of Mt. Kineo, is now owned by the state of Maine.

At this writing the future of the Moosehead Lake region is uncertain. Three-quarters of Moosehead's 230-mile shoreline continues to be owned by lumber companies, but the value of the shorefront property now far outvalues that of the timber, and the green wall is in danger of crumbling. Beyond the town of Greenville all this land lies within "Unorganized Townships" and is under the jurisdiction of Maine's Land Use Regulation Commission (LURC), which has developed a three-volume "Comprehensive Land Use Plan for the Moosehead Lake Region." It's a complicated, controversial plan designed to preserve the lake's eastern shore as wilderness.

Most Greenville visitors explore this shore at least as far as Lily Bay

State Park, and many continue to the outpost village of Kokadjo (population 5), prime moose-watching country. It's another 40 miles northeast via Georgia Pacific's gravel Golden Road to Ripogenus Dam, from which another gravel road heads north for the western gate of Baxter State Park and on up to the foot of Chamberlain Lake, which is the put-in point for canoeists bound for Maine's last true wilderness—the Allagash Waterway.

GUIDANCE   **Moosehead Lake Region Chamber of Commerce** (695-2702), Box 581, Greenville 04441. A four-season source of information. The walk-in information center on Main Street is open year-round; Tuesday to Saturday in winter, daily in summer. This is an unusually helpful chamber, adept at finding lodging, dining, a fishing or rafting trip, or cross-country skiing expedition.

Moosehead Vacation and Sportsmen's Association (534-7300), PO Box 366, Rockwood 04478, is a source of year-round information about lodging and services in the Rockwood area.

GETTING THERE   By air: **Folsom's Air Service** (see Getting Around) offers charter service to Bangor, Augusta, and Portland.

By train: From Montreal, Halifax, and the Canadian Maritimes, you can get here year-round by **VIA Rail Service** (800-561-3949, toll-free information).

By car: **From points south** the obvious route is to take the Maine Turnpike to Exit 39 (Newport). Proceed up Route 7 to Dexter, then continue north on Route 23 to Sangerville (Guilford). From this point, proceed up Route 15 to Greenville.

GETTING AROUND   By air: **Folsom's Air Service** (695-2821), Greenville. Billed as "Maine's largest seaplane operator," founded by Dick Folsom in 1946, now headed by his son Max. Until recently his radio phone was for many camps their only link with the outside world; his fliers are adept at landing their seaplanes at most North Woods camps. Folsom's will also book you into a camp and transport you and your canoe into the Allagash or just give you a scenic flight. One-way flights, based on two passengers, run from $22–$92; $125 to Portland.

Currier's Flying Service (695-2778), Greenville Junction. An enterprising, serious outfit, generally a shade less expensive than Folsom's but not so familiar with all of the camps. Scenic flights, service to camps; will book camps and guides or set up guided backcountry, cross-country ski trips.

Jack's Flying Service (695-3020) caters to Allagash canoe trips and also offers fly-in housekeeping cottages.

Moose River Landing (534-7577), in Rockwood, offers scenic flights as well as shuttle service; also canoe, motorboat, and cottage rentals.

Paul's Flying Service at Northern Pride Lodge (695-2890), HCR 76, Box 588, Kokadjo 04441. Flights May to October.

By ferry: Service to Mt. Kineo from Rockwood is offered regularly in summer via hourly shuttles from the Kineo Landing and by the Float Boat from Moose River Landing (534-7582), both in Rockwood.

By car: If you plan to venture out on the network of private roads maintained by the lumber companies, be forewarned that it may be expensive, both in terms of gate fees and damage to your car's suspension. You need a high car, preferably four-wheel drive. (See The Road to Baxter State Park under To See and Do for details on Georgia Pacific's road user fees.)

MEDICAL EMERGENCY   Charles A. Dean Memorial Hospital and ambulance service (695-2223), Greenville.

Emergency aid is also available from **Maine State Police Headquarters** (800-452-4664).

TO SEE AND DO   Moosehead Marine Museum (695-2716 in season; for year-round information write: PO Box 1151, Greenville 04441). Home for the *S/S Katahdin,* a restored steamboat that cruises June through September (9–5). The museum's displays depict the lake's steamboat history, from 1836 until the last log drive in 1975.

Evelth-Crafts-Sheridan House (695-2992), Main Street, Greenville. Open July 4 to Labor Day, Wednesday through Friday 1–4; $1 admission. Home of the Moosehead Historical Society, a genuinely interesting nineteenth-century home.

Mt. Kineo. The State of Maine and a few local businessmen have worked together to renew access to Kineo after a hiatus of many decades. In addition to golf, lodging, dining, and camping, this island-like peninsula offers a steep but rewarding path to the lookout tower at the top of the 750-foot high cliff; a shore path also leads to Hardscrabble point. It's accessible from Rockwood by ferry (see Getting Around).

Chesuncook. One of the few surviving examples of a nineteenth-century North Woods lumbermen's village, now on the National Register of Historic Places. In summer access is by charter aircraft from Greenville or by boat from Chesuncook Dam. In winter you can come by snowmobile. In writing about the village during its heyday, Henry David Thoreau noted, "Here immigration is a tide which may ebb when it has swept away the pines." Today a church, a graveyard (relocated from the shore to a hollow in the woods when a Great Northern raised the level of the lake a few years ago), an inn, and a huddle of houses are all that remain of the village. (See Inns for lodging and boat shuttle.)

The Katahdin Iron Works and Gulf Hagas. The iron works are open May 30 to Labor Day. The Indians mined iron ore here, and a health resort later drew guests, but what remains is a mid-nineteenth-century blast furnace and iron kiln that once produced 2,000 tons of raw iron annually.Tours and books about the Katahdin Iron Works are offered by Maine author **Bill Sawtell** (965-3971) in Brownville. The iron works are 5 miles north of Brownville Junction. Take a left onto a gravel road, which follows the Pleasant River for 6 more miles.

The Gulf Hagas is a hike in behind the iron works. It's a spectacular, remote gorge with miles of hiking through steep cliffs, ledges, and waterfalls—called the "Grand Canyon of the East," 8 miles in from the Katahdin Iron Works; also accessible by the Lower Wilson Road from Greenville. For a detailed description of this hike see *Fifty Hikes in Northern Maine* by Cloe Caputo (Backcountry Publications).

The Road to Baxter State Park. Most visitors who drive as far as Greenville drive on up the eastern side of the lake. Many go all the way to Mt. Katahdin (see Baxter and Beyond [Baxter State Park]), but you need go little farther than Kokadjo to get a sense of what these timberlands are about.

Kokadjo, 18 miles north of Greenville, is a 100-acre island of independently owned land in the center of a lumber company-owned forest. Most of the buildings here were once part of a lumbering station, and they still include a general store—the northernmost year-round source of coffee and doughnuts for more than a hundred miles around, several hundred miles in some directions. Near the store stands Northern Pride Lodge (see Inns), open year-round, renting canoes and boats for use on adjacent First Roach Pond. Continuing north 20 miles this road dead ends in **the Golden Road,** a 98-mile private logging road stretching clear across Maine to Quebec on the West and Millinocket on the East. It's open to the public year-round but a user fee is charged May through November. Georgia Pacific alone maintains 3,500 miles of road through the North Woods and, while there are a number of checkpoints along this network, you need only pay once: $8 per out-of-state vehicle and $4 per Maine license plate. The first checkpoint is Sias Hill just north of Kokadjo. Motorcycles, bikes, and ATV vehicles are not permitted on Georgia Pacific roads for safety reasons. Passing through these checkpoints is like going through customs; the third degree is aimed in good part at illegal dumping.

Cushing's Landing, at the foot of Chesuncook Lake, is worth a stop. The woodsman's memorial here was created from a post in the doorway of a Bangor tavern; it is decorated with tools of the trade and an iron bean pot. This is also the logical boat launch for Chesuncook Village.

Ripogenus Dam is also at the foot of Chesuncook Lake This is the departure point for a number of white-water rafting expeditions (see White-Water Rafting/Kayaking). This is one of the two major centers for white-water rafting in Maine—the other is the Forks (see Jackman and the Upper Kennebec Valley [White-Water Rafting]). Beginning at the dam the West Branch of the Penobscot drops more than 70 feet per mile—seething and boiling through Ripogenus Gorge—and continues another 12 miles with stretches of relatively calm water punctuated by steep drops. You can get a view of the gorge by driving across the dam. Pray's Store (723-8880) sells most things and rents cottages (open year-round).

Woodlands Tours (695-2241), depart from Scott Paper Company office, Route 15 north of Greenville Junction. Wednesdays during July and August; participants must be age 12 or older. The 8 AM–4 PM tour includes a slide show and talk about how Scott harvests trees; lunch; and an afternoon visit to a harvesting site. $3 per person includes lunch.

AIR RIDES   All the flying services listed under Getting Around also offer scenic flights.

Chairlift Ride at the Moosehead Resort and Ski Area (695-2272), Route 6/15 between Greenville and Rockwood. Call for operating times. The view of lake and mountains is spectacular.

BOAT EXCURSION   *S/S Katahdin* (695-2716), Moosehead Marine Museum, Greenville. June through September, twice-daily cruises. A floating museum, built in 1914 as a member of the Coburn Steamship Co. ferry fleet, it was later used to haul log booms across the lake. This graceful, 115-foot, 150-passenger vessel was converted to diesel in 1922 and later restored as a steamer through volunteer effort, then relaunched in 1985. The two-and-a-half-hour cruises ($12) are an ideal way to see the lake. Six-hour and occasional eight-hour cruises are also offered.

CAMPING   **Lily Bay State Park** (695-2700), 8 miles north of Greenville. There are 93 sites, many spaced along the shore; boat launch; and beach. $13 for nonresidents; $10.50 per site for residents.

The state maintains some 30 campsites scattered along the lakeshore on Kineo and the islands. These are sited on maps available locally.

"Map of Scott's Maine Timberlands," available from the **Scott Paper Company** office (695-2241), in Greenville Junction, details the location and rules for camping on Scott Paper land.

Georgia Pacific's Woodlands office in Millinocket (723-5232) is also the source of a map ($3) detailing roads and campsites in that company's vast domain. Georgia Pacific charges $3 per resident and $4 per out-of-state vehicle for use of its campsites plus the checkpoint fees ($4 and $8, respectively) for use of its roads.

Fire permits must be obtained from **Western Region Forestry Headquarters** in Greenville (695-3721); the maximum stay at a site varies from 7 to 14 days. For more about free campsites throughout the area, contact the **Maine Forest Service** regional office (695-3521).

CANOE RENTALS AND TRIPS   **Allagash Canoe Trips** (695-3668), Greenville. A family business since 1953, offering professional guides and top equipment. Week-long expeditions into the Allagash Wilderness Waterway (there are also special teen trips); also a four-day trip on the Penobscot River and Chesuncook Lake.

Allagash Wilderness Outfitters (695-2821), PO Box 629, Star Route

76, Greenville 04441. Supplies gear for a canoe camping trip.

Wilderness Expeditions (534-2242 or 534-7305), PO Box 81, Rockwood 04478. A source of rental equipment and advice. Guided trips on the West Branch of the Penobscot or into the Allagash Wilderness Waterway; towing service and ground transportation. Canoe and kayak clinics are also offered.

Note: All the flying services will ferry canoes into remote backcountry (see Getting Around).

FISHING   Troll for salmon and trout in Moosehead Lake and fly-fish in the many rivers and ponds—rental boats and boat launches are so plentiful that this is one place they defy listing.

There are two prime sources of fishing information: the Inland Fisheries and Wildlife office (695-3757) in Greenville and the Maine Guide Fly Shop and Guide Service (695-2266), Main Street, Greenville. At the Fly Shop, Dan Legere sells 314 different flies and a wide assortment of gear; also he works with local guides to outfit you with a cabin cruiser and guide or to set up a river float trip or a fly-in expedition. For a list of local boat rentals check with the Moosehead Lake Area Chamber of Commerce (see Guidance).

GOLF   **Squaw Mountain Village Resort on Moosehead Lake** (695-3049). A nine-hole course with lounge, restaurant, and private beach.

Mt. Kineo Golf Course (695-2229), a spectacularly sited, newly revived course at Kineo, accessible by frequent boat service from Rockwood. Golf director Jim Devlin offers carts and club rentals.

HIKING   Easy and moderate hikes featuring great views can be found on **Mount Kineo** and on **Squaw Mountain.** The Moosehead Lake Region Chamber of Commerce (695-2702) furnishes information on climbing **Big Spencer, Elephant Mountain, Borestone Mountain,** and many other trails. (Also see Baxter and Beyond.) **Wilson Falls Picnic Area & Hiking Trails,** Willamantic (off Route 150). A majestic cascade in a forested setting.

HORSEBACK RIDING   **Pleasant River Pack Trips** (564-7781), PO Box 16, Dover-Foxcroft 04426. Judy Cross, a registered Maine guide, offers hour trail rides, day-trips, and overnight treks in the wilderness area around the Katahdin Iron Works.

Rockies Golden Acres (695-3229), Greenville. Trail rides: one-and-one-half to two-hour rides through the woods to Sawyer Pond; mountain views. $20 per person, $15 for additional riders. Call after 7 PM.

MOOSE-WATCHING   **The Maine Guide Fly Shop** (695-2266) offers guided moose photo safaris; also check with the Float Boat (534-7582) and with the Wilderness Boat (534-7305) in Rockwood.

There are two prime moose-watching spots. **Lazy Tom Bog**—a mile or so beyond Kokadjo turn left; the bog is roughly one-half mile on the right. **Smithtown and Frenchtown**—these two townships, northeast and southeast of Kokadjo, are prime moose areas. Drive around on the gravel roads, noting bogs and side roads into clearcuts.

SWIMMING   Almost all "camps" have access to water.

Lily Bay State Park, 8 miles northeast of Greenville. Open ice-out to Thanksgiving. Offers a grassy picnicking area, sandy beach, and boat launch. User fee charged.

WHITE-WATER RAFTING/KAYAKING   Two major rafting companies are headquartered in this region because Moosehead Lake is equidistant from Maine's two most popular rafting routes—Kennebec Gorge and Ripogenus Gorge.

Eastern River Expeditions (695-2411/2248 or 800-634-7238), Box 1174, Greenville 04441. May through mid-October. "There are few places from which you can get so many different rafting experiences," says Sandy Neily who, with John Connelly, runs one of Maine's most successful rafting companies. From their base at Rivers Inn they offer day-trips through the Kennebec River Gorge, through Ripogenus Gorge and Big Eddy on the Penobscot, on the Dead River and on the East Outlet (a gorge through which the Kennebec flows from Moosehead Lake; ideal for families); and overnight trips on the Penobscot and Kennebec. Their Whitewater School also offers canoeing and kayaking instruction. River and sea kayaking expeditions are also offered.

Wilderness Expeditions (534-2242 or 800-825-WILD), PO Box 41, Rockwood 04478. Based at the Birches in Rockwood (see Rustic Resorts), a family-run business specializing in half-day white-water rafting trips on the Kennebec at East Outlet (minimum age is 7); longer expeditions on the Penobscot from a base camp in The Forks where horseback riding is also offered; also canoe trips on the Moose and Dead rivers.

CROSS-COUNTRY SKIING   Note that the formal touring centers aside, this region's vast network of snowmobile trails and frozen lakes constitutes splendid opportunities for backcountry skiing. We've skied from the the cabins at Chesuncook Lake House, Pray's Cottages at Ripogenus Dam, Northern Pride Lodge in Kokadjo, and West Branch Ponds Camps (all of which remain open in winter to cater to cross-country skiers as well as snowmobilers) and can attest that this landscape is even more magnificent with snow than without.

Birches Ski Touring Center (534-7305), Rockwood. The center maintains its own network of trails leading to wilderness trails. You can also ski to Tomhegan, 10 miles up the lake, or out past the ice-fishing shanties to Kineo. Rentals and instruction; also ski mountaineering expeditions in the basin area of Mount Katahdin are offered; snowshoes are available.

Moosehead Nordic Ski Center (695-2082/2870), at the Indian Trading Post, Route 15, Greenville. Peter Sauren, who hails from

Helsinki and is a widely respected ski-touring pro in this area, maintains 25 miles of cross-country trails at the top of Indian Hill; rentals and maps are available from his center next to the Indian Hill Trading Post.

Little Lyford Pond Camps (see Rustic Resorts) also cater to cross-country skiers; you can actually ski in from Greenville.

DOWNHILL SKIING   Moosehead Resort and Ski Area (695-2272; in Maine, 800-348-6743), Greenville 04441. A ski area resort since 1963, one of New England's first base-area hotels owned by Scott Paper (1970–1974) and then sold to the state, under whose ownership it languished for 11 years.

Two owners later it is still trying to reestablish itself. The vertical drop is 1,750 feet; there are 19 trails; 30 percent snowmaking. Lifts include one double chair, one triple chair, one T-bar, and one Poma lift. Other facilities are base lodge, cafeteria, restaurant, lodging, ski school, and ski shop. Day lift tickets cost $25 per adult and $15 per junior on weekends; $15 per adult and $12 per junior midweek.

SNOWMOBILING   Some 500 miles of trails are maintained in the area. Snowmobile rentals are available from Big Lake Service & Repair (695-4487) in Greenville and from Rockwood Sales & Service (534-7387), Rockwood.

INNS   Greenville Inn (695-2206), Norris Street, Box 1194, Greenville 04441. A true lumber baron's mansion set atop a hill just off Main Street, with a sweeping view of Moosehead Lake. Rich mahogany and oak paneling, pressed tin walls, working fireplaces, and an immense leaded-glass window depicting a single spruce tree, all contribute to the sense of elegance. There are six second-floor rooms (two with fireplaces); also one room in the Carriage House and two cottages. The dining room, open to the public, is considered the best in northwestern Maine (see Dining Out). Rates run from $65 for rooms with a woodstove and deck in the cottage to $85 for the original master bedroom in the house with a working fireplace, bay window, and large, private bath; continental breakfast included.

Chesuncook Lake House (695-2821), Box 655, Route 76, Greenville 04441. Open year-round. An unpretentious 1864 farmhouse built on the site of an older log cabin that served as the center for the lumbering camp (see To See and Do [Chesuncook]). There are twelve gas-lit guest rooms and three housekeeping cabins. Maggie McBurnie, a native Parisian, serves three meals a day in summer; her husband, Bert, born and schooled in Chesuncook, meets guests at Cushing's Landing at the south end of the lake and ferries them in. Otherwise you can fly in from Greenville. Registered Maine guides and boats are available. In winter cross-country ski tours are offered. $68 per person includes three meals in the inn, which closes in winter; the year-round rate in the cabins is $20 single per day with a three-day minimum.

Northern Pride Lodge (695-2890), HCR 76, Box 588, Kokadjo 04441. Open summer, fall, and otherwise sporadically. The most elaborate house this far north of Greenville (built in the early 1900s and recently rehabbed), offers six comfortable guest rooms with shared baths. The dining room serves meals to guests only. In summer there are also 24 campsites, rental canoes, and motorboats. Snowmobiling, cross-country skiing in winter. $65 double B&B; $75 single, with all three meals as part of hunting and fishing packages. Owner Paul Wade also operates an air service and offers scenic flights, May to October.

RUSTIC RESORTS   (Classic, full-service sporting camps.)

The Birches (534-7305), Rockwood 04478. Open year-round. The Willard family, father and sons, have turned this old sporting camp into one of the most comfortable family-geared resorts in the North Woods. Sited in a birch grove on Moosehead Lake, 2 miles up a rutted road from Rockwood Village, the 17 hand-hewn log cabins are strung along the lake. Each has a porch, a Franklin stove or fireplace in a sitting room, and one to three bedrooms. Some cabins have kitchens, but three meals are available in summer. The main lodge includes a cheerful, open-timbered dining room, an inviting lobby with a trout pool, and a living room with hearth room. Upstairs are four guest rooms with decks overlooking the lake (shared bath), and back near the marina are a string of 12 "cabin tents." Amenities include an outside hot tub and sauna; windsurfers, sailboats, kayaks, canoes, and fishing boats are available as are wide-tire bikes. Canoeing, white-water rafting, and cross-country skiing expeditions are offered. Moderate in summer when rates are per person, including all meals; from $36 single or $60 double with breakfast in the lodge. Housekeeping cottages are $455–$840 per week and American Plan (all meals) runs $339 per week per person; half price for children 10 and under. Cabin tents begin at $15 single per day. A variety of rafting, canoeing, and other packages are also available, and it's possible to rent a cabin and eat meals as you wish at the inn. The dining room is open to the public.

Little Lyford Pond Camps (Folsom's radio phone: 695-2821), Box 1269, Greenville 04441. Open year-round. Best known of the remote camps among today's young, urban "sports." Sited in a sheltered, alpine-looking valley, built in the 1870s as a logging company station on a tote road into the Allagash region. Bud and Kate Fackelman share an enthusiasm for the simplicity of the place (they stress that the comfort level is high despite lack of plumbing or electricity). There are 10 shake-roofed log cabins without plumbing or electricity, sleeping from two to seven; a main lodge serving three hearty meals; a conference center (accommodating 16, electricity for audiovisuals); a sauna and a solar shower. Gulf Hagas is a short walk away, and in winter some 50 miles of cross-country trails are maintained. In winter you can ski or fly in, but in summer the pontoon planes don't like to land. The camps are 3.5 miles off the Appalachian Trail. By car it is 12 miles from Greenville via the Lower Wilson Pond Road through the Greenville gate, a private lumber company road (also accessible from the Katahdin Iron Works in Brownville Junction). $75 single includes all meals, use of canoes, and some fishing equipment. Inquire about special summer programs, like a six-day workshop in landscape painting.

West Branch Ponds Camps (695-2561), Box 35, Greenville 04441. A 10-mile drive from the main road at Kokadjo. Open ice-out through September, then after Christmas until April 1 for cross-country skiing. First opened as a moose-hunting lodge in the 1880s; the newest log cottage was built in 1938. Wonderfully weathered old cabins (each with log beds, heat, electricity, bath; three with Franklin stoves) and a square central lodge with a bell on top. Andy and Carol Stirling are third-generation owners, and they seem to enjoy it thoroughly. Motorboats and canoes are available. In winter the center of this lodge shifts from the front rooms, with their clutter of books and comfortable corners, to the big kitchen. Stirling's reputation as number one cook of the North Woods is rivaled only by Maggie McBurnie (see Chesuncook Lake House). The two have never met. In some ways West Branch Pond conveys an even greater sense of isolation than Chesuncook. Directly across the pond is the majestic bulk of Whitecap Mountain. You can ski over the lake and half way up the mountain or down the 11-mile access to the nearest plowed road. In winter the camps have plumbing and heat but no running water. $44 includes three meals and use of a canoe; children are half price.

Maynards in Maine (534-7703), Rockwood 04478. Open May through hunting season. "The only thing we change around here is the linen," says Gail Maynard, who helps run the sportsmen's camp founded by her husband's grandfather in 1907. Sited on the Moose River, a short walk from Moosehead Lake, Maynards includes a dozen tidy, moss-green frame buildings furnished with dark Edwardian furniture, much of it from the grand old Mount Kineo hotel. The lodge is filled with stuffed fish, moose heads, and Maynard family memorabilia, and it is furnished with stiff-backed leather chairs. A sign cautions, "Do Not Wear Hip Boots or Waders into the Dining Room." Two meals a day are served and one "packed." $40–$43 per adult AP (all meals); half price for children under 12; $225 single per week during hunting season.

CAMPS   (Former full-service sporting camps which no longer serve meals.) **Note:** The Moosehead Lake Region Chamber of Commerce and Greenville flying services offer easy access to almost all of the "camps" in the North Woods (see Guidance and Getting Around).

Tomhegan Wilderness Resort (534-7712), PO Box 308, Rockwood 04478. Open year-round. A 10-mile ride up a dirt road from Rockwood Village, also accessible by air; 1.5 miles of frontage on Moosehead

Mayards in Maine

Photo by Wendy Maeda

Lake. Nine hand-hewn cottages with kitchens and living rooms, rocking chairs on the porches, full baths, and woodstoves; also efficiency units in the lodge. Boats and canoes are available; cross-country skiing and snowmobiling in winter. $60 double; $17 per extra person.

Rockwood Cottages (534-7725), Box 176, Rockwood 04478. Open year-round. Ron and Bonnie Serles maintain clean, comfortable housekeeping cottages with screened-in porches overlooking the lake and Mt. Kineo just across the narrows. This is a great spot to stay if you want to explore Mt. Kineo and poke around the less-developed end of the lake. Boats, motors, and fishing licenses are available, and guests have free docking. There's also a sauna, barbecue area, and plenty of warm North Woods hospitality. $50 per couple, $10 per additional person.

Wilsons on Moosehead (695-2549), Greenville Junction 04442. Open year-round since 1865; renewed by present owners Wayne and Shan Snell. Sited right on the lake at East Outlet, there are 17 cottages, each with three to five bedrooms and screened porches, and a beach with a great view. In winter downhill and cross-country skiing, snowmobiling, and ice-fishing are all handy. No one has ever explained why General Ulysses S. Grant slept here on January 1, 1889. From $280 per week ($40 per day) for a two-people cabin to $770 per week ($110 per day) for a new four-bedroom cottage; also $945 per week ($135 per day) for a log lodge with five bedrooms.

Beaver Cove Camps (695-3171), Greenville 04441. Eight miles out of town on Lily Bay Road. Open year-round. Fully equipped housekeeping cabins with propane heater, gas range, electricity, and fridge; some with woodstoves. Boat rentals. Owner Maurice Pelletier is a registered Maine guide specializing in bear, deer, and moose hunts and fishing. $150 for three days or $300 double per week.

Spencer Pond Camps (radio service: 695-2821; winter phone: 813-922-2777), Star Route 76, Box 580, Greenville 04441. Open May to November. A long-established cluster of housekeeping camps in an unusually beautiful spot, accessible by logging road from Lily Bay Road. Boats available. $12–$18 single; two-night minimum stay for two people.

Medawisla (radio phone: 695-2821), Box 592, Second Roach Pond, Route 76, Greenville 04441. Closed December through April when the phone is 695-3082. In this remote corner of the woods, not far from Kokadjo, Mimi and Russ Whitten offer seven snug cabins with woodstoves and flush toilets (five have gas cooking stoves and fridges). Each can sleep from two to six people in varying degrees of comfort. Popular with those fishing for salmon and trout in spring; also good for moose-watching and nature photography. Boats and canoes are available. This is a lovely spot, and word has it the loon sounds from *On Golden Pond* were taped here. From $50 double, housekeeping; weekly rates.

BED & BREAKFASTS   **Sawyer House** (695-2369), PO Box 521, Lakeview Street, Greenville 04441. Open year-round. Handy to the flying services, an ideal way stop if you fly in from Portland and want to stop in Greenville en route to a remote sporting camp or inn; good for anyone who likes being in Greenville with a view of the lake. There's a first-floor suite which can accommodate up to four ($65 double, $10 per extra person) and two second-floor rooms with private bath ($55 double); rates include a full breakfast. Be sure to meet Pat Zieten's parrot.

Kineo House (534-2293), PO Box 66, Rockwood 04478. Open year-round, accessible by nominally priced boat shuttle in summer and via snowmobiles or skis in winter. Steve Prentiss and his family have turned one of the Victorian-era houses at Kineo (see To See and Do) into a B&B with eight guest rooms. Downstairs the 50-seat dining room, open to the public, is popular at lunch with golfers. Dinner is also served. $55 double, includes breakfast.

Devlin House (695-2229), PO Box 1102, Greenville 04441. A modern home high on the hill west of town with splendid views down over meadows to the lake; a ground-level suite with a sitting room and upstairs double. Ruth and Jim Devlin are longtime local residents who enjoy sharing their knowledge of the area. Moderate rates.

The Guesthouse (695-2278), PO Box 4, Pritham Avenue, Greenville Junction 04442. A spacious house on the western edge of town with an unusually pleasant feel to it: rag rugs, homemade furniture. $27 double; group rates; no meals but within walking distance of a choice of places.

Evergreen Lodge (695-3241), HCR 76, Box 58, Route 15, Greenville 04441. A comfortable cedar house offers guest rooms with private baths. $56–$64 double; no children under 10.

OTHER LODGING **The Moosehead Resort** (695-2272 or 800-347-6743), Greenville 04441. Open late June through the ski season. The 1960s complex at the base of the ski lifts includes 61 hotel rooms and a dining room. In summer there are tennis courts; private beach down on the lake; rafting packages. Pickup service at Bangor International Airport. $50 double; ask about packages.

MOTELS **Indian Hill Motel** (695-2623), Route 6/15, Greenville 04441. Sited on a hill above town, 15 units with cable TV; also housekeeping cottages, trailer hookups. Morning coffee. $50 double.

Rivers Inn (695-3737 or 800-634-7238), Box 1134, Greenville 04441. An all-efficiency motel with 16 units that sleep as many as eight; headquarters for Eastern River Expeditions. JC's Restaurant and Sports Bar, an outdoor pool and hot tubs, lighted volleyball court, trout pond, mountain bike and canoe rentals are now all part of the scene. The Moosehead Fitness Center with weight and aerobic machines, a sauna, and whirlpool are also on the premises. Most guests are here on rafting or canoeing packages. (See White-Water Rafting.)

Chalet Moosehead (695-2950 or 800-477-4386), PO Box 327, Greenville Junction 04442. Eight waterfront efficiency units accommodating three to six each. Boats and dock. $53.50 double.

Moosehead Lake Houseboat Vacations (534-7333), Old Mill Campground, Route 15, Rockwood 04478. Catamaran houseboats sleep up to six in two bunks. $135 per day; $820 per week.

DINING OUT **Greenville Inn** (695-2206), Norris Street, Greenville. Dinner served nightly by reservation from 6 PM. Thanks to Austrian-born chef Elfie Schnetzer, this former lumber baron's dining room is the present toast of northwestern Maine. The menu lists just six entrées, usually includes grilled lamb chops with garlic and herbs ($14.50), a sirloin steak, and a choice of well-dressed fish dishes like Norwegian salmon fillet with sauce verte ($16) or shrimp with mustard dill sauce ($15.25).

Cabbage Patch (695-2252), Route 6/15, Greenville Junction. Open year-round for dinner. "Early logging atmosphere." A barnboard-sided lounge with lake views; good for soup and sandwiches, salad bar, house steak, hot dogs, chicken cordon-bleu, or whatever your mood fancies; liquor; reasonably priced.

The Birches (534-2242), Rockwood. Open year-round; daily in summer and fall, vacation weeks and weekends in winter. This a popular resort (see Rustic Resorts) with one of the area's most attractive dining rooms, log-sided with a war canoe turned upside down in the open rafters and hurricane lamps on the highly polished tables. Chef Frank Bushy's Saturday night prime rib draws people from many miles around and Birches shrimp, sautéed in white wine with mushrooms and peppers, is another local favorite. Entrées run $8–$13. All three meals are served.

Cafe Catania (695-2440), Greenville Junction. Open for dinner September through June, Wednesday through Saturday; otherwise Thursday through Saturday. A bright Italian place with a big salad bar, prime rib, seafood, Italian specialties. $12.95 for mussels Catania with linguini.

Mom's Lakeside (695-3064), Pritham Avenue, Greenville. Open year-round with a seasonal lakeside deck. Touristy but with the only middle-of-town, on-lake dining. Beer, wine, and frozen alcoholic drinks; pizza and sandwiches. A wide choice of dinner entrées. Moderate.

EATING OUT **Flatlander's Pub** (695-3373), Pritham Avenue, Greenville. Open except Tuesdays for lunch and dinner. Hamburgers, chicken wings, deep-fried mushrooms, deli sandwiches; beer on tap and house wines; homemade chili, soups, and pies. Nice atmosphere, the preferred middle-of-town place to lunch.

Kelly's Landing (695-4438), Greenville Junction. Open from 7 AM to 9 PM. A breakfast bar ($5.95) and large salad bar, fried seafood platter, roast chicken ($7.95), sandwiches. A big, cheerful place with tables on the deck by the lake.

JC's Restaurant and Sports Bar (695-3737) at the River's Inn, Greenville. A large dining room with daily specials and large bar with a big TV.

Boom Chain (695-2133), Main Street, Greenville (just up from the chamber's information center). Open 6 AM to 2 PM, sometimes later. The most popular local eatery—tables, booths, a wall decoration of a deer painted on saw blades, specials.

Debbie's Restaurant (534-2212), Route 15, Moose River (Rockwood). The slogan is "something for everyone"—everything from eggs sunny-side up to a lobster dinner. This is THE place to snag breakfast, lunch, or supper (until 7 PM) in Rockwood, either at the counter or tables; beer served.

Cousin's Lodge Restaurant & Ice Cream Shop (695-2003), North Main Street, Greenville. Eat in or out from 6 AM through dinner; sandwiches and "home cooking."

Wagon Wheel Restaurant (876-3712), south of Greenville on Route 15 in Abbot. "The good food place with the big plate for a little change." Geared to sportsmen. Specializing in seafood and steaks; liquor served.

SELECTIVE SHOPPING **Indian Hill Trading Post** (695-3376). Open daily year-round, Fridays until 10 PM.

The Indian Store (695-3348) occupies Greenville's most picturesque building, the Shaw Block, at the corner of Main Street and Pritham Avenue. Since 1929 Ida Faye's store has sold baskets and feathers, candies, souvenirs, firecrackers, and knickknacks of every description. Every inch is filled.

Moosehead Crafts Co-op, Doan Street, Greenville Junction (across from the hospital). Open spring through fall 10–3 except Wednesdays and Sundays. A showcase for some beautiful work by local artisans: pottery, place mats, puzzles, maple syrup, game boards, cards, birdhouses, etc.

Cloth Creations, Greenville Junction (next to Currier's Flying Service). Susan Currier runs a colorful clothing store featuring natural fibers: skirts, blouses, and dresses. She also carries patchwork pillows and quilts; much of the stock is locally made.

The Corner Shop (695-2142), corner of Main Street and Prithern Avenue. Carol Harris operates a great little gift/bookstore.

SPECIAL EVENTS June to April: **The Ice-Out Contest** offers everyone a chance to guess the exact date. Contact the Moosehead Lake Chamber of Commerce for details (695-3702).

March: **Dog Sled Races** are held annually on Moosehead Lake the first weekend in March.

July: **Independence Day** celebrations in Greenville Junction.

September: **The International Seaplane Fly-In Weekend** is held in Greenville the second weekend in September.

BAXTER AND BEYOND

BAXTER STATE PARK This is a 201,018-acre park surrounding mile-high Katahdin, the highest peak in the state (5,267 feet). In all, there are 46 mountain peaks and 150 miles of well-marked trails. This largest of Maine's state parks was the 1931 gift of Percival Baxter, who had unsuccessfully urged creation of such a preserve during his two terms as governor.

The park accommodates 1,000 campers at a time.

GUIDANCE For information about Baxter State Park phone (723-5140) or write to Park Headquarters at 64 Balsam Drive, Millinocket 04462. For details about making reservations see Camping. The visitors information building is one mile east of Millinocket on Route 11.

Millinocket Chamber of Commerce (723-4443), PO Box 5, Millinocket 04462. The chamber maintains a seasonal information booth; serves as a year-round source of information about the motels and restaurants that are chamber members.

Georgia Pacific (723-5232), EFPMD, Box 240, Millinocket 04462. The largest landowner in this area, maintaining thousands of miles of roads and hundreds of campsites. The company's map/guide to its lands is available at checkpoints on its roads and by writing to the office.

GETTING THERE   The most direct route is I-95 to exit 56 at Medway (50 miles northeast of Bangor) and 10 miles into Millinocket. From here it's 18 miles along the Golden Road to the Togue Pond entrance of the park. Note that you must pay a user fee at Georgia Pacific's Debsconeag Checkpoint ($8 per vehicle for out-of-staters and $4 for Mainers).

The more scenic but longer access is 65 miles via the Lily Bay Road and then the gravel Golden Road from Greenville (see Moosehead Lake Region).

Yet another alternative (actually 15 miles longer than taking the interstate to Medway) is to leave I-95 at Newport and follow Routes 7, 6, and 11 through Corinna, Dexter, Dover-Foxcroft, Milo, and Brownville Junction to Millinocket.

MEDICAL EMERGENCY   Millinocket Regional Hospital (723-5161).

TO SEE AND DO IN BAXTER STATE PARK   Open daily, year-round, 6 AM–10 PM in summer, 6 AM–9 PM in winter. It takes two-and-a-half hours to drive the perimeter road around this vast park. Orchids, ferns, alpine, and dozens of other interesting plants here delight botanists. Geologists are intrigued by Baxter's rhyolite, Katahdin granite, and many fossils. Birds and wildlife, of course, also abound.

Camping. Camping is only permitted May 15 to October 15 and December to April 1. Don't come without a reservation. In all there are 10 widely scattered campgrounds among which Russell and Chimney Pond near the base of Katahdin are the most popular. Daicey Pond and Kidney Pond each offer traditional cabins with beds, gas lanterns, firewood, a table and chairs ($10 per person per night). Six more campgrounds, accessible by road, offer a mix or bunkhouses, lean-tos, and tent sites. There are two more backcountry, hike-in campgrounds and beyond that 25 more single backcountry sites (which rarely fill). In '91 tent and lean-to sites are $4 per person, minimum of $8 per reservations. Space in the bunkhouses is $5 per person.

Summer-season reservations (only accepted for the period between May 15 and October 15) must be made by mail with the fee enclosed (check or cash), posted no earlier than the first working day in January of the year you are coming. Send a stamped, self-addressed envelope if you want to receive a confirmation. Camping is also permitted December 1 to April 1 with reservations accepted after November 1, but the only payment accepted at that time of year is a money order.

For more about hiking this area see *Katahdin,* a detailed guide to Baxter State Park by Stephen Clark (Thorndike Press); also *Fifty Hikes in Northern Maine* by Cloe Caputo (Backcountry Publications).

TO SEE AND DO BEYOND BAXTER STATE PARK **Allagash Wilderness Waterway.** A 92-mile long chain of lakes, ponds, rivers, and streams through the heart of North Woods. Formally established by the Maine Legislature in 1966 to preserve, protect, and enhance the natural beauty, character, and habitat of a unique territory; further protected in 1970 as part of the National Wild and Scenic River System. There is no public transportation, and camping sites are primitive. The traditional canoe trip through the Allagash takes 10 days but 2- and 3-day trips can be worked out. Brook trout, togue, and lake whitefish are plentiful. For information about rules, regulations, permits, fees, and licenses contact the Bureau of Parks and Recreation (289-3821), State House Station 22, Augusta 04333. For information about Allagash outfitters see the Moosehead Lake Area (Canoe Rentals and Trips).

Patten Lumberman's Museum (528-2650), Shin Pond Road (Route 159), Patten. Open Memorial Day through September, Tuesday through Saturday 9–4 and Sunday 11–4; also weekends until Columbus Day. $2 per adult, $1 per child. The museum, which encompasses more than 3,000 displays housed in nine buildings, was founded in 1962 by bacteriologist Caleb Scribner and log driver Lore Rogers. Exhibits range from giant log haulers to "gum books," the lumberman's scrimshaw: intricately carved boxes to keep spruce gum, a popular gift for a sweetheart. There are replicas of logging camps from different periods, dioramas, machinery, and photos, all adding up to a fascinating picture of a vanished way of life.

Mattawamkeag Wilderness Park (947-4585), Mattawamkeag (off Route 2; a half-hour's drive off I-95). Fifty campsites, ten Adirondack shelters, a small store, a recreation building, picnic facilities, 15 miles of hiking trails, and 60 miles of canoeing on the Mattawamkeag River with patches of white water. An 8-mile gravel road leads into the park. For reservations and details write Reservation Clerk, Mattawamkeag Wilderness Park, PO Box 104, Mattawamkeag 04459.

REMOTE RUSTIC CAMPS The flying services listed under Moosehead Lake Region (see Getting Around) serve most of these camps, while **Scotty's Flying Service** (528-2528) in Patten serves those with Millinocket addresses and those east of the park.

Katahdin Lake Wilderness Camps, Box 398, Millinocket 04462. At the end of a private 3.5-mile tote trail from Roaring Brook Road in Baxter State Park; it's an hour walk. Al Cooper will meet you with pack horses or you can fly in from Millinocket Lake. Ten guest log cabins (two to seven people per cabin) and a main lodge built on a bluff overlooking the lake; firewood, linens, kerosene lamps, and outhouses go with each cabin and several also have gas stoves for housekeeping. Sandy beaches. Rates are $35 per person per night in a housekeeping cabin; $55 per person per night with all meals. Rental boats available. $20 per person for pack trip in from Baxter State Park.

The North Woods

Nugent's Chamberlain Lake Camps (695-2821), HCR 76, Box 632, Greenville 04441. Dating just from the 1930s, but built entirely by Al and Patty Nugent. This is one of the most remote camps, nicely sited and still so old-fashioned that it should be on the National Register of Historic Places. In 1987 the State awarded the lease of these camps to John Richardson and Regina Webster. Sited within the Allagash

Wilderness Waterway, 50 miles north of Millinocket between Baxter State Park and Allagash Mountain, they are best reached via Folsom's Air Service (see Getting Around under Moosehead Lake Area); otherwise it's a five-mile boat or snowmobile ride up Chamberlain Lake. The eight housekeeping cabins have the traditional front overhang and outhouses; they sleep two to ten. Boats are available. American Plan or housekeeping plans available. $20 per person per night in housekeeping cabins, $60 per person with all meals, $32 with dinner only; $20 boat shuttle (landing at the bottom of Chamberlain Lake).

Frost Pond Camps (Folsom's radio phone: 695-2821), HCR 76, Box 620, Greenville 04441 (in winter: 723-6622; 36 Minuteman Drive, Millinocket 04462). Open May to November. Located 3 miles beyond Ripogenus Dam. Eight rustic housekeeping cabins on Frost Pond (good for trout) and handy to Chesuncook Lake (landlocked salmon). Rick and Judy Givens also outfit Allagash Wilderness canoe trips (see Canoe Rentals and Trips under Moosehead Lake Area).

Nahmakanta Lake Wilderness Camps, Box 171, Millinocket 04462. Open May through November; also in winter without food for snowmobilers and cross-country skiers. Geared to serious fishermen. Housekeeping and basic cabins grouped around a traditional lodge that serves three meals each day; the specialty is trout chowder. $50 per person includes meals but not motors.

Libby Sporting Camps (435-8274), Drawer V, Ashland 04732. Open ice-out through November. One of the original sporting camps, family-operated for 100 years, featuring hearty meals and guides to take you to 40 lakes and ponds from eight outpost camps. $30 without meals, $70 per person with. Sited at the headwaters of the Aroostook and Allagash rivers. Boats and sea plane available.

Bradford Camps (radio phone: 764-6112), Box 499, Patten 04765. Open ice-out through November. Sited at the Aroostook River's headwaters, Munsungan Lake. Virtually inaccessible by land (unless you want to weather 47 miles on logging roads). This is an unusually tidy lodge with well-tended lawns, 28 firm beds in comfortable cabins lighted by propane lamps; also five cabins on outlying ponds. $85 per night includes meals, but boat and motor are extra.

Index

Lodging Index

Abbotts Mill Farm, 368
Above Tide Inn, 52
Admiral Peary House, 336
The Admirals Inn, 50
Aimhi Lodge, 323-333
Albonegon Inn, 153-154
American Youth Hostel, 298
Anchor Watch, 156
The Annex, 232
Appalachian Mountain Club's
    Echo Lake Camp, 285
Appalachian Mountain Club's
    Swan's Falls Camp, 337
Aspinquad, 48-49
Asticou Inn, 278
Atlantean Inn, 280
Atlantic Ark Inn, 157
Atlantic Oakes by-the-Sea, 284
Atlantic Seal B&B, 105
Attean Lake Resort, 356
Augustus Bove House, 335-
    336

The Bagley House Bed and
    Breakfast, 106
Bailey Island Motel, 120
Bar Harbor Motor Inn, 284
Barnswallow B&B, 176
Bass Cottage in the Field, 280
Bass Harbor Inn, 283
The Bath Bed & Breakfast,
    132-133
Bay Ledge Inn & Spa, 281
Bayview, 279
Beachcomber Motel, 264
Beachcrest Inn, 50
Beachmere, 49
Beachwood Motel, 73
Bear Mountain Inn, 334
Beaver Cove Camps, 410
Bed & Breakfast at the Red
    House, 221
Bed & Breakfast Society of
    Camden, 216
The Bell Buoy B&B, 37
The Belmont, 216-217
Ben-Loch Inn, 297-298
Bethel Inn and Country Club,
    358, 365

Bethel Opera House, 369
Bethel Point Bed and
    Breakfast, 119
Bethel Spa Motel, 369
Bingham Motor Inn, 357
The Birches, 407
The Blackberry Inn, 218
Black Lantern Inn, 50
Black Point Inn Resort, 91-92
Blueberry Mountain Inn, 368
Blueberry Patch Inn, 310
The Blue Harbor House, 218
Blue Hill Farm, 253
Blue Hill Inn, 252
Blue Shutters Inn, 50
Boothbay Harbor Inn, 158
Bosebuck Mountain Camps,
    379
Bradford Camps, 417
Bradley Inn, 173
Brannon-Bunker Inn, 174-175
The Breakwater Inn, 70
Breezemere Farm, 253
Briarwood Mountain Lodge,
    357
The Bristol Inn, 175
Broad Bay Inn & Gallery, 174
Brown Brothers Wharf, 157
Brunswick Bed & Breakfast,
    118
Buck's Harbor Inn, 253
Bufflehead Cove, 67-68

Camden Harbour Inn, 216
Cameron House, 369
Camp Knickerbocker, 158
Canterbury Cottage, 281
Canterbury House Bed &
    Breakfast, 36
Cape Arundel Inn, 68
Cape Neddick House, 36
Cap'n Am's, 195
The Capt. Butman Home-
    stead, 240
Captain Daniel Stone Inn, 118
The Captain Dodge House,
    142
Captain Drummond House,
    133-134

Cap'n Fish's Motel, 158
Cap'n Frost's, 194
Captain Green Pendleton Inn,
    239
Captain Jefferds Inn, 68
Captain Josiah A. Mitchell
    House, 105
Captain Lord Mansion, 67
Captain Sawyer's Place, 156
Captain's House, 175
Captain's Quarters Inn and
    Motel, 263
The Captain's Rest, 194
Carriage House Inn, 241
Castine Inn, 247
Cathy's Place, 390
Center Lovell Inn, 334
Chalet Moosehead, 411
Chandler River Lodge, 309
Chapman Inn, 367
The Chebeague Inn By-the-
    Sea, 92
Chesuncook Lake House, 406
Chetwynd House Inn, 66
Claremont, 278
Clark Perry House, 309
Clearwater Sporting Camps,
    380
Cliff House, 47-48
Cobb's Pierce Pond Camps,
    356
Coburn House, 155
Cod Cove Inn, 142
Colonial Sportsmen's Lodge,
    321
The Colony, 66
The Cornish Inn, 335
Cottage in the Lane Motor
    Lodge, 53
Country Club Inn, 378
Country Farm, 73
Country at Heart, 105
Cove Farm Inn, 280
Coveside Cottages, 73-74
Coveside Inn, 173
Craignair Inn, 194
Crescent Lake Cottages, 337
Crocker House Country Inn,
    283

BOOKS ABOUT NEW ENGLAND

Explorer's Guides from The Countryman Press

The alternative to mass-market guides with their homogenized listings. Explorer's Guides focus on independently owned inns, motels, and restaurants as well as on family and cultural activities reflecting the character and unique qualities of the area.

Maine: An Explorer's Guide
by Christina Tree and Mimi Steadman, $16.95
New Hampshire: An Explore's Guide
by Christina Tree and Peter Randall, $16.95
Vermont: An Explorer's Guide
by Christina Tree and Peter Jennison, $16.95

Other Books from The Countryman Press

Classic Regional Humor Books by Keith Jennison:
The Maine Idea, $7.95
Remember Maine, $7.95
Vermont is Where You Find It, $7.95
"Yup. . .Nope" & Other Vermont Dialogues, $7.95
The Humorous Mr. Lincoln, $9.95

Family Resorts of the Northeast
by Nancy Pappas Metcalf, $12.95
New England's Special Places: A Daytripper's Guide
by Michael A. Schuman, $12.95
Vermonters
photographs by Jon Gilbert Fox, text by Donald L. Tinney, $9.95
The Blue Cat of Castletown
A classic Vermont Children's Tale by Catherine Cate Coblentz, $7.95
Maine Memories
by Elizabeth Coatsworth, $10.95
The Earth Shall Blossom: Shaker Herbs and Gardening
by Galen Beale and Mary Rose Boswell, $18.95
Seasoned with Grace: My Generation of Shaker Cooking
by Eldress Bertha Lindsay, $11.95
The Story of the Shakers
by Flo Morse, $6.95

Guidebooks from Backcountry Publications

Written for people of all ages and experience, these quality softbound books feature detailed trail or tour directions, notes on points of interest, maps and photographs.

50 Hikes in Vermont
by the Green Mountain Club, $11.95
50 Hikes in the White Mountains
by Dan Doan, $12.95
50 More Hikes in New Hampshire
by Dan Doan, $12.95
50 Hikes in Northern Maine
by Cloe Caputo, $10.95
50 Hikes in Southern Maine
by John Gibson, $10.95
50 Hikes in Massachusetts
by John Brady and Brian White, $11.95
50 Hikes in Connecticut
by Gerry and Sue Hardy, $11.95
Walks and Rambles in Rhode Island
by Ken Weber, $9.95
Walks and Rambles in Westchester and Fairfield Counties: An Nature Lover's Guide to Thirty Parks and Sanctuaries
by Katherine S. Anderson, $8.95
Walks and Rambles in the Upper CT River Valley
by Mary L. Kibling, $9.95
25 Bicycle Tours in Vermont
by John Freidin, $8.95
25 Mountain Bike Tours in Massachusetts
by Robert S. Morse, $9.95
25 Mountain Bike Tours in Vermont
by William J. Busha, $9.95
30 Bicycle Tours in New Hampshire
by Adolphe Bernotas and Tom & Susan Heavey, $10.95
25 Bicycle Tours in Maine
by Howard Stone, $9.95
25 Ski Tours in New Hampshire
by Roioli Schweiker, $8.95
25 Ski Tours in Vermont
by Stan Wass, $8.95
Canoeing Massachusetts, Rhode Island, and Connecticut
by Ken Weber, $8.96
Canoe Camping Vermont and New Hampshire Rivers
by Roioli Schweiker, $7.95
Waterfalls of the White Mountains
by Bruce and Doreen Bolnick, $14.95

We also publish books about bicycling, walking, hiking, canoeing, camping, fishing, and ski touring in New Jersey, New York, Pennsylvania, Maryland, Delaware, Ohio, West Virginia and Virginia. Please write for our catalog.

Out titles are available in bookshops and in many sporting goods stores, or they may be ordered directly from the publisher. Write or call The Countryman Press, P.O. Box 175, Woodstock, Vermont 05091; (802) 457-1049. Please add $2.50 per order for shipping and handling.

READER'S SURVEY

The Countryman Press series of Explorer's Guides reflects our readers' demand for insightful, incisive reporting on the best and most exciting destinations offered in New England. To help us tailor our books even better to your needs, please take a moment to fill out this anonymous (if you wish) questionnaire, returning it to:

The Countryman Press, Inc., P.O. Box 175, Woodstock, Vermont 05091

1. How did you hear about the Countryman Press Explorer's Guides: newspaper, magazine, radio, friends, other (please specify)?

_____

_____

2. Please list in order of preference the cities or states (or areas) on which you would like to have a Countryman Press Explorer's Guide, aside from the already existing destinations.

_____

_____

3. Do you refer to the Countryman Press guides in your travels or for your own area?

a. (travels)_____b. (own area)_____c. (both)_____

4. Do you use any guide other than one by Countryman Press?

If yes, _____

5. Please list, starting with the most preferred, the three features that you like most about the Countryman Press Explorer's guides.

a._____

b._____

c._____

6. What are the features, if any, you dislike about the Countryman PressExplorer's guides?

_____

_____

7. Please list any features you would like to see added to the Countryman Press Explorer's guides.

_____

_____

8. Please list the features you like most about your favorite guidebook series if it is not Countryman Press.

a._____

b._____

c._____

9. How many trips do you make per year for business and for pleasure?

Business: International_____Domestic_____

Pleasure: International_____Domestic_____

10. Is your annual household income over (check appropriate choice)?

$20,000_____$40,000_____$60,000_____

$80,000_____$100,000_____Other (please specify)_____

11. If you have any comments on the Countryman Press Explorer's guides in general, please enclose them on a separate sheet of paper.

We thank you for your interest in the Countryman Press Explorer's guides, and we welcome your remarks and your recommendations about restaurants, hotels, shops, and services.